Routledge International Handbook of Ignorance Studies

The epistemological and political relevance of ignorance has increased in recent years and this has been mirrored in a growing but diverse body of literature concerning relevant phenomena and conceptual perspectives. This Handbook is a milestone in this course of study . . . shedding light on different approaches and offering an indispensable compass for further investigation.

Stefan Böschen, Karlsruhe Institute of Technology (KIT), Germany

Once treated as the absence of knowledge, ignorance today has become a highly influential topic in its own right, commanding growing attention across the natural and social sciences where a wide range of scholars have begun to explore the social life and political issues involved in the distribution and strategic use of not knowing. The field is growing fast and this handbook reflects this interdisciplinary field of study by drawing contributions from economics, sociology, history, philosophy, cultural studies, anthropology, feminist studies and related fields in order to serve as a seminal guide to the political, legal and social uses of ignorance in social and political life.

Matthias Gross is professor in the Institute of Sociology, University of Jena and, by joint appointment, at Helmholtz Centre for Environmental Research – UFZ, Leipzig, Germany. His research focuses on the sociology of energy, risk and ignorance, and experimental practices in science and society. His most recent monograph is *Renewable Energies* (with R. Mautz, 2014, Routledge).

Linsey McGoey is senior lecturer in sociology at the University of Essex. Recent articles appear in the *British Journal of Sociology*, *History of the Human Sciences* and *Economy and Society*. She is editor of *An Introduction to the Sociology of Ignorance: Essays on the Limits of Knowing* (Routledge, 2014).

The Routledge International Handbook Series

The Routledge International Handbook of the Arts and Education
Edited by Mike Fleming, John O'Toole and Loira Bresler

The Routledge International Handbook of English, Language and Literacy Teaching
Edited by Dominic Wyse, Richard Andrews and James Hoffman

The Routledge International Handbook of the Sociology of Education
Edited by Michael W. Apple, Stephen J. Ball and Luis Armand Gandin

The Routledge International Handbook of Higher Education
Edited by Malcolm Tight, Ka Ho Mok, Jeroen Huisman and Christopher C. Morpew

The Routledge International Companion to Multicultural Education
Edited by James A. Banks

The Routledge International Handbook of Creative Learning
Edited by Julian Sefton Green, Pat Thomson, Ken Jones and Liora Bresler

The Routledge International Handbook of Critical Education
Edited by Michael W. Apple, Wayne Au and Luis Armando Gandin

The Routledge International Handbook of Lifelong Learning
Edited by Peter Jarvis

The Routledge International Handbook of Early Childhood Education
Edited by Tony Bertram, John Bennett, Philip Gammage and Christine Pascal

The Routledge International Handbook of Lifelong Learning
Edited by Peter Jarvis

The Routledge International Handbook of Teacher and School Development
Edited by Christopher Day

The Routledge International Handbook of Education, Religion and Values
Edited by James Arthur and Terence Lovat

The Routledge International Handbook of Young Children's Thinking and Understanding
Edited by Sue Robson and Suzanne Flannery Quinn

Routledge International Handbook of Educational Effectiveness
Edited by Chris Chapman, Daniel Muijs, David Reynolds, Pam Sammons and Charles Teddlie

The Routledge International Handbook of Dyscalculia and Mathematical Learning Difficulties
Edited by Steve Chinn

International Handbook of E-learning, Volume 1: Theoretical Perspectives and Research
Edited by Badrul H. Khan and Mohamed Ally

International Handbook of E-learning, Volume 2: Implementation and Case Studies
Edited by Mohamed Ally and Badrul H. Khan

Routledge International Handbook of Ignorance Studies

Edited by Matthias Gross and Linsey McGoey

Routledge
Taylor & Francis Group
LONDON AND NEW YORK

First published 2015
by Routledge
2 Park Square, Milton Park, Abingdon, Oxon OX14 4RN

and by Routledge
711 Third Avenue, New York, NY 10017

First issued in paperback 2018

Routledge is an imprint of the Taylor & Francis Group, an informa business

British Library Cataloguing-in-Publication Data
A catalogue record for this book is available from the British Library

Library of Congress Cataloging in Publication Data
Routledge international handbook of ignorance studies / edited by
Matthias Gross, Linsey McGoey. —1 Edition.
pages cm.—(Routledge international handbooks)
1. Knowledge, Sociology of 2. Science—Social aspects. I. Gross,
Matthias, 1946- editor. II. McGoey, Linsey.
HM651.R678 2015
306.4′2—dc23
2014041477

ISBN 13: 978-1-138-59629-0 (pbk)
ISBN 13: 978-0-415-71896-7 (hbk)

Typeset in Bembo
by Swales & Willis Ltd, Exeter, Devon, UK

Contents

PART V
Ignorance in economic theory, risk management and security studies 295

Illustrations

Figures

Tables

Acknowledgements

We would like to thank Gerhard Boomgaarden for his encouragement, and Alyson Claffey for very supportive help from Routledge. Thanks to Dmitri Vinogradov and Chiara Ambrosio for assistance with refereeing two chapters, and Kathleen Cross for her assistance with translating an article. Linsey wishes to thank Darren; Matthias wishes to thank Eva, Emil, Benjamin, and Silke.

Contributors

Brian Balmer is professor of science policy studies in the Department of Science and Technology Studies, University College London. His research combines historical and sociological approaches to understanding the role of expertise in the life sciences. In particular, he has published widely on the history of the British biological weapons program. He is author of *Britain and Biological Warfare: Expert Advice and Policy-Making, 1930–65* and *Secrecy and Science: A Historical Sociology of Biological and Chemical Warfare.*

Andrew Bennett is professor of English at the University of Bristol. He is the author of *Ignorance: Literature and Agnoiology* (2009), *Wordsworth Writing* (2007), *The Author* (2005), *Katherine Mansfield* (2004), *Romantic Poets and the Culture of Posterity* (1999) and *Keats, Narrative and Audience* (1994). With Nicholas Royle, he has published *An Introduction to Literature, Criticism and Theory* (4th edition, 2009) and *Elizabeth Bowen and the Dissolution of the Novel* (1995).

Alexander Bogner is a sociologist by training and presently a senior scientist at the Institute of Technology Assessment of the Austrian Academy of Sciences and a lecturer at the University of Vienna. His main research interest is in how science and technology change when the boundaries between science, politics and the public blur. His empirical work has focused on biomedicine, agri-biotechnology and emerging technologies.

Liana Chua is lecturer in anthropology at Brunel University, London. She works on conversion to Christianity, ethnic politics, resettlement, development and conservation in Sarawak, Malaysian Borneo. She is the author of *The Christianity of Culture: Conversion, Ethnic Citizenship and the Matter of Religion in Malaysian Borneo* (2012), and has co-edited volumes on evidence in anthropology, power in Southeast Asia and Alfred Gell's seminal theory, *Art and Agency*.

François Dedieu is a research fellow in sociology at the French National Agronomic Research Institute (INRA Sens) and l'Institut Francilien recherche innovation (Ifris). His research is aimed the study the hidden dimensions of risk governance. He is the author of *Une catastrophe ordinaire: la tempête de 1999* [An Ordinary Disaster: The Storm of 1999] (2014).

Kevin C. Elliott is associate professor in Lyman Briggs College, the Department of Fisheries & Wildlife and the Department of Philosophy at Michigan State University. He is the author of the book *Is a Little Pollution Good for You? Incorporating Societal Values in Environmental Research* (2011), as well as more than 50 published or forthcoming articles and book chapters. He works on the philosophy of science, research ethics and environmental ethics, focusing especially on questions about environmental pollution, emerging technologies and the role of values in scientific research.

Shterna Friedman is the managing editor of *Critical Review: A Journal of Politics and Society* and co-editor of *The Nature of Belief Systems Reconsidered* (2012) and *Political Knowledge* (2013).

Joanne Gaudet is a former doctoral candidate in sociology (ABD) at the University of Ottawa and now co-president of a consulting firm. Her doctoral research into knowledge and ignorance mobilization and social network analysis in science contributes to helping organizations understand and sustain continual process improvement in the workplace as a scientific approach. She published on the parallel with science by bringing attention to the interplay of knowledge and ignorance mobilization in the Toyota approach to improvement and innovation.

Erinn Cunniff Gilson is assistant professor of philosophy at the University of North Florida. She is the author of *The Ethics of Vulnerability* (2014). Her current research critically analyses both the concept of vulnerability and the inequitable distribution of vulnerability as a social condition. She is also especially interested in food justice and ethics, feminist approaches to sexuality and sexual violence, racism and racial justice and critiques of neoliberal values and forms of subjectivity.

Matthias Gross is professor in the Institute of Sociology at the University of Jena, Germany, and the Helmholtz Centre for Environmental Research in Leipzig, where he is also head of the Department of Urban and Environmental Sociology. His recent research focuses on innovation and sustainability, social studies of engineering and experimental practices in science and society. His monographs include *Ignorance and Surprise: Science, Society, and Ecological Design* (2010) as well as *Renewable Energies* (2015).

Stuart Firestein is the former chair of Columbia University's Department of Biological Sciences, where his laboratory studies the vertebrate olfactory system. He serves as an advisor for the A. P. Sloan Foundation's program for the Public Understanding of Science. A recipient of the Lenfest Distinguished Columbia Faculty Award, he is a fellow of the AAAS, a Sloan fellow and a Guggenheim fellow. He is author of *Ignorance: How It Drives Science* (2012).

William Franke is professor of philosophy and religions at University of Macao and professor of comparative literature at Vanderbilt University. He is research fellow of the Alexander von Humboldt-Stiftung and has been Fulbright distinguished chair in intercultural theology at the University of Salzburg. His apophatic philosophy is articulated especially in *On What Cannot Be Said* (2007) and *A Philosophy of the Unsayable* (2014).

Scott Frickel is associate professor of sociology and environmental studies at Brown University. He is author of *Chemical Consequences: Environmental Mutagens and the Rise of Genetic Toxicology* and co-editor of *The New Political Sociology of Science* (with Kelly Moore) and *Fields of Knowledge* (with David J. Hess). Current book projects include a comparative history of urban industrial hazards (with James R. Elliott) and an edited volume on interdisciplinary research (with Mathieu Albert and Barbara Prainsack).

Jens Haas trained as a lawyer specializing in criminal appeals law, and works on agency and ignorance. He is interested in the reasons and causes that figure in crimes like murder and in the nature of life-changing actions. Haas has two law degrees from Munich, Germany, and studied poetry and 20th century American literature at Amherst. He recently began co-writing in normative epistemology and value theory with Katja Maria Vogt.

David J. Hess is professor of sociology and the James Thornton Fant chair in sustainability at Vanderbilt University, where he is also the associate director of the Vanderbilt Institute for Energy and Environment. He works on the politics of sustainability transitions in industrial systems and on science, technology and publics (including mobilized publics such as social movements and advocacy organizations). More details are available on his website at www.davidjhess.net.

Lisa W. Holstein earned her Ph.D. in mass communication at Indiana University, where she was a MacArthur Scholar. She worked briefly as a journalist at the Cincinnati Enquirer and the Columbus Dispatch, and was for 15 years a public affairs staff member at Ohio State University. Her primary research interest is the role of journalism in the public sphere, with a comparative international perspective.

Nina Janich is professor of German linguistics at Technische Universität Darmstadt, Germany, since 2004. Her research interests focus on science communication, business communication and language of advertising, language culture/politics and policy of languages, methodologically based on text linguistics and discourse analysis. Currently she is principal investigator of different projects on non-knowledge in journalistic and scientific texts, responsibility in scientific research and knowledge transfer in mass media for children.

Jean-Noël Jouzel is a research fellow at the Center for the Study of Organizations, CNRS-SciencesPo Paris. His research looks specifically at why so little is known about occupational illnesses induced by worker exposure to toxic substances such as pesticides or nanomaterials. He is the author of *Des toxiques invisibles: Sociologie d'une affaire sanitaire oubliée* [Invisible Toxics: The Sociology of a Forgotten Public Health Controversy] (2013).

Joanna Kempner is an assistant professor of sociology at Rutgers University. Her research investigates the intersection of medicine, science, politics, gender and the body. Her first book, *Not Tonight: Migraine and the Politics of Gender and Health* (2014), examines the gendered social values embedded in the way we talk about, understand and make policies for people in pain. She is currently researching the production and policing of forbidden knowledge.

Ann Kerwin was philosopher-in-residence and a co-founder of the innovative Curriculum on Medical Ignorance at the University of Arizona School of Medicine and, later, philosopher-in-residence at the Auckland University of Technology. Retired from academe, she practices Reiki and speaks on philosophy and philosophers on Radio New Zealand.

Oliver Kessler is professor for international relations at the University of Erfurt. Prior to joining Erfurt in 2012, he taught at the University of Groningen and the University of Bielefeld predominantly. He holds a doctoral degree in international relations (with economics and public international law) from the Ludwig Maxmilians University of Munich. His work focuses on problems of world society, systemic rationalities and theories of international relations. He is also international scholar at Kyung Hee University (South Korea).

Abby Kinchy is an associate professor in the Science and Technology Studies Department at Rensselaer Polytechnic Institute. She has a Ph.D. in sociology from the University of Wisconsin-Madison and is the author of *Seeds, Science, and Struggle: The Global Politics of Transgenic Crops* (2012). Her current research examines the politics of watershed monitoring in the context of the natural gas boom, focusing on how civil society organizations are challenging dominant research and regulatory practices.

Daniel Lee Kleinman is associate dean of the Graduate School at the University of Wisconsin-Madison, where he is also a professor in the Department of Community and Environmental Sociology. In addition to his collaboration with Sainath Suryanarayanan, he has written extensively about commercial pressures on academic science and the changing knowledge economy. Among his books are *Impure Cultures: University Biology and the World of Commerce* (2003) and *The Routledge Handbook of Science, Technology, and Society* (edited with Kelly Moore, 2014).

Janet A. Kourany is associate professor of philosophy and associate professor of gender studies at the University of Notre Dame, where she is also a fellow of the Reilly Center for Science, Technology, and Values. Her latest book, *Philosophy of Science after Feminism* (2010), seeks both to locate science within its wider societal context and to articulate a new, more comprehensive understanding of scientific rationality, one that integrates the ethical with the epistemic. She is currently at work on a new book, *Forbidden Knowledge: The Social Construction and Management of Ignorance*.

Christian Kuhlicke is a geographer by training and since 2004 works as senior scientist in the Department of Urban and Environmental Sociology at Helmholtz Centre for Environmental Research – UFZ, Leipzig, Germany. He has expertise in the social construction of risks in governance and everyday processes. He has been responsible for coordinating larger international projects on risk and has edited a couple of special journal issues on vulnerability and resilience.

Lev Marder is a Ph.D. candidate in political theory at the University of California-Irvine. He writes on evolving epistemological issues in a range of political theories including theories of democracy, representation, rule of law, and political resistance. His dissertation takes a genealogical approach to examine the implications of historical differences in, and conditions of emergence of, "political ignorance".

Linsey McGoey is senior lecturer in sociology at the University of Essex. Recent articles appear in the *British Journal of Sociology, Poetics, Third-World Quarterly, History of the Human Sciences* and *Economy and Society*. She is editor of *An Introduction to the Sociology of Ignorance: Essays on the Limits of Knowing* (2014).

Mike Michael is professor of sociology and social policy at the University of Sydney. Current research includes the development of speculative methodology in the relation to the study of science-society dynamics and the potentialities of everyday life. His most recent book (co-authored with Marsha Rosengarten) is *Innovation and Biomedicine: Ethics, Evidence and Expectation in HIV* (2013). He is a co-editor of *The Sociological Review*.

Charles W. Mills is John Evans professor of moral and intellectual philosophy at Northwestern University. He works in the general area of oppositional political theory, and is the author of five books: *The Racial Contract* (1997), *Blackness Visible: Essays on Philosophy and Race* (1998), *From Class to Race: Essays in White Marxism and Black Radicalism* (2003), *Contract and Domination* (with Carole Pateman, 2007) and *Radical Theory, Caribbean Reality: Race, Class and Social Domination* (2010).

Albert Ogien is research director at the CNRS, and head of the Marcel Mauss Institute at the EHESS (Paris). He has published several articles on trust, and edited *Les moments de la confiance* (with Louis Quéré, 2006). He is currently working on democracy and has published (with Sandra Laugier) *Le Principe démocratie* (2014).

Deborah A. Prentice is Alexander Stewart 1886 professor of psychology and public affairs at Princeton University. She studies social norms – the unwritten rules and conventions that govern social behaviour. She is interested in how people are guided by norms and constrained by norms; how they respond when they feel out of step with prevailing norms; how they determine what the norms of their groups and communities are; and how they react emotionally, cognitively and behaviourally to those who violate social norms. She is also interested in the use of norms in interventions designed to change behaviour. Prentice is the inaugural editor of *Motivation Science* and is currently the dean of the faculty at Princeton University.

Giovanni Prete is a lecturer in sociology at Paris 13 University. From an STS and social movement perspective, he studies the controversies surrounding the transformation of agriculture in France and in the USA. He is currently investigating the social production of knowledge regarding the health effect of pesticide use on agricultural workers and rural residents, focusing on the role of the grassroots movements that denounce those effects.

Helen Pushkarskaya is an associate research scientist at Yale Medical School. She focuses on neurobiology of individual differences in decision-making under uncertainty (risk, ambiguity, conflict and ignorance) in healthy and clinical populations. The most recent group of projects investigates abnormal patterns in value based decision-making and preferences toward uncertainty in obsessive compulsive and hoarding disorders.

Brian Rappert is a professor of science, technology and public affairs in the Department of Sociology and Philosophy at the University of Exeter. His long-term interest has been the examination of the strategic management of information; particularly in relation to armed conflict. More recently he has been interested in the social, ethical and epistemological issues associated with researching and writing about secrets, as in his book *Experimental Secrets* (2009) and *How to Look Good in a War* (2012).

Jerome Ravetz is a leading authority on the social and methodological problems of contemporary science. He wrote the seminal work *Scientific Knowledge and Its Social Problems*. With Silvio Funtowicz he created the NUSAP notational system for assessing the uncertainty and quality of scientific information, in *Uncertainty and Quality in Science for Policy*, and also the concept of Post-Normal Science, relevant when "facts are uncertain, values in dispute, stakes high and decisions urgent".

Steve Rayner is James Martin professor of science and civilization and director of the Institute for Science, Innovation and Society at Oxford University, where he also co-directs the Oxford Programme for the Future of Cities, the Oxford Geoengineering Programme, and the Oxford Martin Programme on Resource Stewardship. He has served on various US, UK and international bodies addressing science, technology and the environment, including Britain's Royal Commission on Environmental Pollution, the Intergovernmental Panel on Climate Change and the Royal Society's Working Group on Climate Geoengineering.

Joanne Roberts is professor in arts and cultural management and director of the Winchester Luxury Research Group at Winchester School of Art, University of Southampton. She is the co-founder and co-editor of *Critical Perspectives on International Business*, and an editor of *Prometheus: Critical Studies in Innovation*. She is currently co-editing *Critical Luxury Studies: Art, Design, Media* with John Armitage for Edinburgh University Press and investigating knowledge and ignorance in relation to luxury.

Devjani Roy is a research fellow at the Center for Business & Government at Harvard Kennedy School. Her research examines behavioural decision and judgment under uncertainty at the intersection of literature and culture. She holds a Ph.D. in English, and her current project studies the differences between lying and deception.

Anne Simmerling is a scientific assistant at Technische Universität Darmstadt, Germany. In 2009, she finished her degree in German literature and linguistics, sociology and economics at TU Darmstadt. Currently, she is a co-worker in a DFG-founded project within the SPP 1409 "Science and the General Public: Understanding Fragile and Conflicting Scientific Evidence". Her research interests concern internal and external scientific communication, media language and in particular the linguistic representation of uncertainty.

Michael Smithson is a professor in the Research School of Psychology at The Australian National University. His primary research interests are in how people think about and deal with unknowns, and developing statistical methods for the human sciences. His publications include eight books and over 140 refereed journal articles and book chapters.

Ilya Somin is professor of law at George Mason University. Much of his work focuses on political ignorance and its implications for constitutional democracy. He is the author of *The Grasping Hand: Kelo v. City of New London and the Limits of Eminent Domain* (2015) and *Democracy and Political Ignorance: Why Smaller Government Is Smarter* (2013), and co-author of *A Conspiracy Against Obamacare: The Volokh Conspiracy and the Health Care Case* (2013).

Allison Stewart is an associate fellow at the Saïd Business School, University of Oxford, and works in the Capital Projects Group of a major energy company. Her doctoral research at Oxford focused on the role of ignorance in planning and delivering major programs, with an empirical focus on the Olympic and Commonwealth Games. Allison has taught on undergraduate, graduate and executive education programs and has worked for a number of global companies.

S. Holly Stocking taught science writing for more than two decades at Indiana University in Bloomington, IN. Before earning a Ph.D. in mass communications, she worked as a journalist for the *Minneapolis Tribune, Los Angeles Times* and Associated Press. A fellow of the American Association for the Advancement of Science (AAAS), she has published widely on media coverage of scientific knowledge and ignorance.

Sainath Suryanarayanan is an assistant scientist in the Department of Community & Environmental Sociology at the University of Wisconsin-Madison. Suryanarayanan's recent work, in collaboration with Daniel Lee Kleinman and supported by the National Science Foundation, has appeared in a variety of periodicals, including *Social Studies of Science, Science, Technology & Human Values, Issues in Science & Technology, Insects* and *The Guardian* (UK).

Ekaterina Svetlova is a senior lecturer at the University of Leicester – School of Management. She also worked as a research fellow and a lecturer at Zeppelin University in Friedrichshafen, the University of Constance and the University of Basel. Her current research is focused on economic sociology with emphasis on social studies of finance.

Darren Thiel is senior lecturer in sociology and criminology at the University of Essex. Research interests include work, employment and economy; class and social stratification; migration; terrorism; policing and governance. He is the author of *Builders: Class, Gender and Ethnicity in the Construction Industry* (2012), and co-author of *Criminology: A Sociological Introduction* (3rd edition, 2014).

Henk van Elst is professor of applied mathematics and scientific research methods at Karlshochschule International University, Karlsruhe, Germany, since September 2005. He obtained a Ph.D. in applied mathematics from Queen Mary & Westfield College, University of London, in 1996. Subsequently he worked as a postdoc at the University of Cape Town, South Africa, and as a lecturer again at Queen Mary, University of London. His current research interests relate to decision theory under conditions of uncertainty.

Katja Maria Vogt is professor of philosophy at Columbia University. She specializes in ancient philosophy, normative epistemology, ethics and theory of action. She is interested in questions that figure both in ancient and in contemporary discussions: What are values? What kind of values are knowledge and truth? What is a good human life? What is the role of norms of thinking in ethics? She recently began to co-author articles in normative epistemology and value theory with Jens Haas.

Peter Wehling is currently senior researcher at the Institute of Sociology at Goethe-University, Frankfurt, Germany. His research interests include science and technology studies, sociology of knowledge and ignorance, sociology of biomedicine, health and illness, environmental sociology as well as sociological theory and critical sociology. Among his recent publications is *The Public Shaping of Medical Research: Patient Associations, Health Movements and Biomedicine* (2015, co-edited with Willy Viehöver and Sophia Koenen).

Richard Zeckhauser is the Frank P. Ramsey professor of political economy, Kennedy School, Harvard University. His contributions to decision theory and behavioural economics include the concepts of quality-adjusted life years (QALYs), status quo bias, betrayal aversion and ignorance (states of the world unknown) as a complement to the categories of risk and uncertainty. He is the author or co-author of 280 articles and 12 books.

Basile Zimmermann is assistant professor at the University of Geneva, Switzerland, where he teaches in Chinese studies and conducts research in the fields of sinology, science and technology studies and sociology of art. His current research projects focus on electronic music, social networking sites and methodology in China studies.

1

Introduction

Matthias Gross and Linsey McGoey

New knowledge always leads to new horizons of what is unknown. New knowledge unsettles the contours of individual and collective understanding; it perturbs more than it settles, engendering fresh debate over the appropriate way to respond to sudden or incremental awareness of earlier unknowns: *how* to respond; *when* to respond; *who* may respond; who *should* respond but is incapacitated from doing so. New knowledge is never complete knowledge. Especially in today's so-called risk, information, or knowledge societies, where sophisticated means of controlling or at least assessing the possibilities of loss or injury are developed via risk assessments, and where the acquisition of knowledge is viewed as an epoch-defining aspect of the current era, the unknown is not diminished by new discoveries. Quite the contrary: the realm of the unknown is magnified. This in turn raises questions about how to cope with growing ignorance, on new possibilities for shielding knowledge from others, and on what really needs to be known. It also illuminates how not knowing can be an important resource for successful action.

Consequently, over the last decade or so, the terrain of ignorance studies has developed into a dynamic field that has forged links across many disciplines. A wide range of scholars have begun to explore the social life and political issues involved in the distribution and strategic uses of not knowing. To note just a few examples, they have explored the potentially misleading role of risk assessments when clear knowledge about probabilities and outcomes are not available (cf. Stirling 2007) and the usefulness of feigned or willful ignorance in efforts to deny knowledge of unsettling information (cf. Cohen 2001; Stocking and Holstein 2009). Similarly, a growing number of economists and political scientists have begun to criticize the rational approach to institutions as insufficient for understanding the complexity of behavior. Sometimes the only rational decision is based on chance, which is the opposite of what Jon Elster (1989) once called hyperrationality, that is, "the failure to recognize the failure of rational choice theory to yield unique prescriptions and predictions" (Elster 1989: 17). A number of economists have started to realize and to study the importance of decision-making under situations of ignorance (cf. Caplan 2001; Faber and Proops 1990; van der Weele 2014). After all, decision-making in such circumstances requires the realization that the limits of rationality need to be acknowledged rationally. In this way, making decisions based on nonknowledge would not be irresponsible but fully justifiable as the only rational solution (cf. Bleicher 2012; Gross 2015; Heidbrink 2013). This Handbook reflects these interdisciplinary approaches by drawing contributions from economics, sociology, the neurosciences, philosophy, anthropology, and feminist studies in order to serve as a seminal guide to the uses of ignorance in social and political life.

The positive aspects of not knowing can, for instance, be illustrated with the notion of experiment in everyday life (cf. Gross 2010; Marres 2012; Overdevest et al. 2010). An experiment can be established with the explicit aim to generate unexpected events (cf. Rheinberger 1997). The surprising effects derived from this set-up can be seen as the driver behind the production of new knowledge, not least because surprises help the experimenter to become aware of her or his so far unperceived ignorance (unknown unknowns or forgotten unknowns).

Indeed, in certain experimental designs, the deliberate use of ignorance is deemed a vital step in ensuring the robustness of results. The double-blind randomized controlled trial (RCT) is the paradigmatic example of the belief that fostering "intentional ignorance" through blinding mechanisms is essential for improving experimental objectivity (Kaptchuk 1998). Given that the acknowledgement and the specification of ignorance in the form of hypothesis-building needs to be seen as a crucial element in processes of experimentation, ignorance cannot be thought of simply as a negative phenomenon.

Over recent decades, scholars have empirically studied the instrumental value of ignorance, examining its relationship with other forms of partial or limited knowledge, such as organizational ambiguity and economic uncertainty (Best 2012; Downer 2011). They have also highlighted the ways that willful ignorance can be a commendable stance in societies that place necessary brakes on their own will to knowledge. Such ignorance is an imperative, for example, within medical ethics, where physicians, patients, philosophers, and jurors argue that remaining ignorant of particular disease aetiologies and possible treatments is more morally acceptable than exploiting an individual's life or privacy through unethical means.

The moral duty to forego the possibility of obtaining new knowledge when the only way to achieve new information is through compromising human safety and the right to life was enshrined in ethical principles such as the Nuremburg Code, and reiterated since in many national legislative codes. And yet, like most ethical principles, the medical duty not to harm is breached regularly. Occasionally, this leads individuals at ethical review committees such as Institutional Review Boards (IRBs) to develop a sort of defensive ignorance, willing themselves not to see the ways that ethical guideless are politically and commercially malleable in practice (Heimer 2012; Simpson et al. 2014).

A similar tension exists in the courtroom. At least since the fifteenth century, Justitia, the Roman goddess of justice, is regularly depicted wearing a blindfold, underscoring the modern belief that impartiality and fairness are contingent to a large extent on *not* seeing and *not* judging. In the courtroom, as Robert Proctor and Londa Schiebinger (2008: 24) point out, knowledge "is interestingly attached to bias, ignorance to balance." And yet, much like the uneven and often opportunistic use and misuse of medical ethics, the principle of blind justice is something of an elusive, illusory goal. The power of its mythology diverts attention from the gulf between its ideal and its realization. In the United States, for example, as I. Bennett Capers writes, "what does it mean, connotatively and denotatively, for Justitia to be blind in a racialized society where colour is so determinative?" (Capers 2006: 4).

The belief that prejudice and exploitation can be remedied through professional ideals of legal objectivity or medical restraint might be seen as entirely commendable or simply innocuous if such principles were not themselves implicated in preventing their own self-realization. To what extent does the belief that justice *is* blind thwart recognition of the ways that legal decisions are highly subjective in practice? To what extent does adherence to "ceremonial" forms of medical compliance, such as ensuring signatures on informed consent forms, allow global structural injustices in medical exploitation to persist?

Hans-Georg Gadamer once suggested that "the fundamental prejudice of the Enlightenment is the prejudice against prejudice itself" (2004: 272). His comment points to a longstanding conceit of the Enlightenment period onwards: the idea that knowledge, when systematically produced through adherence to reliable methods of data collection or extraction, will inevitably trump superstition. That conceit dominates the social and physical sciences to this day. The belief that individuals are capable of suspending prejudice when making legal or medical decisions, or the belief that knowledge inevitably increases one's political power or leverage: these are inheritances of an Enlightenment era marked by the assumption that prejudice can and should be tamed by making knowledge more universally accessible. But what about when people do not wish to know? What about when, through the principle of *not* seeing, certain groups are rendered more vulnerable, more at risk of exploitation or punishment by legal systems that purport to function free of prejudice? What is the role of ignorance in societies that hail the importance of knowledge even as we court ignorance in a myriad of ways, at once obvious and less apparent, pernicious and commendable in turn? Contributions in this handbook address those questions. Together, they suggest that in order to understand the limits of knowledge, we must increase our awareness of the ineradicable importance of ignorance.

The promise and perils of ignorance

A number of scholars, many working in the tradition of Georg Simmel's (1906) debate on secrecies and secret societies, have explored the relationship between secrecy and the unknown. Recent empirical studies cover important terrain, such as Brian Balmer (2012) and Rebecca Lemov (2006) on secrecy in medicine and military strategies and operations; Claudia Aradau and Rens van Munster (2011) on military preparedness and the usefulness of contingency; Andrew Barry (2013) on the politics of transparency. Most recently, John Urry's work on offshoring has illuminated the economic and political sphere of secret movements, relocation and concealment of funds as well as elaborate forms of secrecy via tax havens and the like (Urry 2014). This relates to Robert Proctor's work (1995) on "agnotology," or the cultural reproduction of ignorance, where he examines the ways that different industry groups, such as big tobacco, purposefully seek to foster doubt and non-knowledge about the effects of their products.

Although studies such as Proctor's on cancer, Naomi Oreskes and Erik Conway's (2010) on the tobacco industry and global warming, Sheldon Ungar's (2008) on scientific illiteracy, Urry's (2014) on financial concealments, or Riley Dunlap's (2013) research on climate skeptics can alert us to the mongering of doubt for commercial gain, they easily tend to amplify a normative stance against commercially or politically generated forms of secrecy and uncertainty. Worse, they tend to ignore alternative ways of viewing the world by implying that an emphasis on uncertainty is somehow "anti-science" or unquestionably driven by commercial or ideological objectives. Or, as Scott Frickel and Michelle Edwards put it most succinctly: "While politically important, these studies tend to utilize a conspiratorial logic that ties the production of ignorance to the specific political, economic, or professional interests of powerful organizations and individuals intent on keeping certain research results private" (2014: 216).

Frickel and Edwards sum up these streams of studies on science as follows: "Apart from being empirically shortsighted, this narrow conceptualization is problematic because it is based on the misguided and nominally functionalist assumption that [. . .] the production of ignorance results from deviant science" (2014: 217). However indirectly, such studies also imply that increasing public transparency will inevitably help minimize the development and deployment of "deviant" science, and thereby reduce scientific ignorance. Such a notion fails to appreciate what scholars such as Michael Smithson (1989) and Stuart Firestein (2012) have long stressed:

that ignorance is an inevitable and often positive feature of scientific productivity (see also Boudia and Jas 2014; Croissant 2014; Rescher 2009; Vitek and Jackson 2008; Walton 1996; Wehling 2015).

In this handbook, we move one step further and show that ignorance needs to be understood and theorized as a regular feature of decision-making in general, in social interactions and in everyday communication. In many areas of social life, individuals often need to act in spite of (sometimes) well-defined ignorance, or what has more recently been termed nonknowledge – the possibility of becoming knowledgeable about the specifics of one's own ignorance (Gross 2010). Nor, we suggest, should ignorance be viewed as uniquely useful or profitable for the powerful. Rather, the deployment of ignorance can be an emancipatory act, skirting oppressive or demeaning demands for knowledge disclosure, such as the expectation that one should disclose one's sexual orientation (McGoey 2014; Sedgwick 1990). Feigned ignorance can also be an indispensable tool of dissimulation for overburdened workers, enabling them to carve out a space for autonomy and creativity in the workplace (Scott 1985).

Our suggestion – to view ignorance as "regular" rather than deviant – is based on the insight that human decision-making is always positioned on the boundary between knowledge and its flipside. In other words, human existence per se is a matter of constantly negotiating, calculating, or playfully experimenting with what is known and what is not known. Thus, following Simmel's classic thread, in addition to knowledge, it is important to understand the complex interweavings of what is known and what is not known if we wish to grasp the quality, the depth, and the nuances of social life in general.

The regularity of ignorance

Early work by feminist and postcolonial theorists of ignorance comes closest to exemplifying the situational and "regular" character of ignorance that we wish to emphasize. Linda Alcoff offers a useful analysis of this early work in Shannon Sullivan and Nancy Tuana's *Race and Epistemologies of Ignorance* (2007), an edited volume that has played an integral role in shaping the field of ignorance studies (cf. Townley 2011). Building on work by Lorraine Code, Sandra Harding and Charles Mills, Alcoff points out that ignorance is an inevitable consequence of the "general fact" of our situatedness as knowers. Given what Alcoff describes as the "nonfungible nature of knowers," or the bounded nature of our individual perceptual frameworks, our assumptions need to be situated within an understanding of the epistemic geography from which we speak. Alcoff and Code, like Harding, do not believe that acknowledging the situated nature of our knowledge and ignorance inevitably implies that one must possess a relativist ontology of truth. Rather, by taking into account the location of a speaker – by deliberately acknowledging their limitations as knowers – one increases, rather than decreases, the ability of others to evaluate the objectivity of their knowledge claims. In Code's phrasing, "objectivity requires taking subjectivity into account" (Code, 1995: 44, quoted in Alcoff 2007: 41).

An important stream of this research is centered on the interplay between subjectivity and objectivity that feminist scholars are at the forefront of illuminating. Will acknowledging what we do not know necessarily expose the fragile nature of our knowledge, undercutting any claims to epistemic authority? Or, as Harding, Code and Alcoff suggest, will it render our knowledge *more* robust for having its limitations and its perspectival nature exposed? Relatedly, why are certain groups taught to perceive their own knowledge as more objective than others? Why are some afforded the epistemic privilege of presuming their own beliefs are *not* beliefs, but universal truths, nurturing notions that, however misguided, receive daily reinforcement in the classroom, the media, or the courtroom?

Charles Mills' writing on the "epistemology of ignorance" has been at the forefront of philosophical inquiries into epistemic privilege. In texts such as *The Racial Contract* (1997), Charles Mills uses the term "white ignorance" to encompass the belief systems and mythologies that white colonizers, as part of the European imperialist project, actively constructed as factual reality. As Mills has stressed in earlier work, and as he reiterates in his contribution to this handbook, white ignorance *is* a type of epistemology. It is a sort of useful non-knowledge, one that consists of patterns of thought that Mills describes as local and cognitive dysfunctions. Ignorance is not a motionless state. It is an active accomplishment requiring ever-vigilant understanding of what not to know. As Alison Bailey puts it, members of a privileged racial group "must learn to see the world wrongly, but with the assurance that their mistaken ways of making sense of events count as accurate representations" (2007: 80; see also Steyn 2012; Taussig 1999). In recent years, a growing number of scholars have used the lens of willful ignorance to understand how dominant groups seek to deny, justify or simply ignore the reality of past and present atrocities against the less powerful, from Canada's subjugation and ethnocide of native groups (Samson 2013), to the Turkish denial of decades of collective violence against Armenians (Göçek 2014), to name just two examples.

Powerful groups of individuals such as white supremacists during periods of codified legal inequality are hardly alone in resisting the imposition of corrective knowledge that may force them to relinquish long-held certainties. "All religions, nearly all philosophies, and even a part of science testify to the unwearying, heroic effort of mankind desperately denying its contingency," the French biologist Jacques Monod once suggested. The political theorist John Gray quotes this passage in the opening of his *Straw Dogs,* a book decrying what he sees as the near universal tendency for politicians and philosophers to insist on the certainty of their ideological vision or scientific facts over others (Gray 2002). And yet, curiously, Monod and Gray's insight seems *less* applicable to the twenty-first century than to periods in the past. The powerful in today's century seem noticeably less enamoured of certainty than those in earlier decades. From the recent financial crisis, to the conditional wording that presaged the war on Iraq (Saddam Hussain *might* possess weapons of mass destruction, and if he does so, he *might* use them), it seems that intentionally tenuous, strategically uncertain claims are increasingly recognized for what they are: critical sources of political power.

Have attempts to harness ignorance and uncertainty for political gain always been a useful handmaiden to commercial, disciplinary and political power? If the answer is yes, then why have scholars in the social sciences taken so long to recognize the importance of ignorance in the processes of governing, creating and educating that drive daily life?

The chapters in this handbook explore these questions in detail. They do not answer them conclusively. Nor, in many ways, does a "conclusive" answer seem feasible or worth striving for. What the handbook *does* do is bring together the most diverse disciplinary perspectives on the uses of ignorance in social and economic life ever compiled in one volume to date. Never before have such disparate writings on the value and importance of ignorance from economists, philosophers, sociologists and biologists been featured together in one handbook. This collection thus serves as an indispensable guide to classical perspectives on ignorance, as well as more recent analyses in anthropology, economics, sociology, and science studies.

Part I: Historical treatments of ignorance in philosophy, literature and the human sciences

Early attention to the uses of ignorance is visible in Plato's *Republic,* where he discusses the case of the "Ring of Gyges," a magical artifact that enables one to become invisible at will. Through the story of the ring, the *Republic* explores whether crimes would be committed more freely if one's fear of being seen and punished was removed. At least since the *Republic*, scholars have explored the links between ignorance, visibility, invisibility and power – something central to renewed interest in the ways that deliberate non-knowledge serves as political resource. From ontological debates over the nature and definition of what ignorance *is* (Jens Haas and Katja Vogt; Shterna Friedman; William Franke), to the notion of literature as a diagnostic tool for things unknown (Andrew Bennett, as well as Richard Zeckhauser and Devjani Roy), this section explores the multiple ways that scholars have conceptualized ignorance throughout history.

The chapters from Haas and Vogt as well as Roy and Zeckhauser offer different categorizations of various states of ignorance. Haas and Vogt suggest that types of ignorance differ normatively, and that a useful way to delineate between different types is through attending to the relationship between ignorance and investigation: do people wish to know more or not? They suggest that it is possible to discern and to prefer states of ignorance that are oriented towards more investigation rather than states that are comfortable with a lack of understanding. In a similar vein, Roy and Zeckhauser draw on authors such as Fitzgerald, Kafka, Austen, Beckett and others to illuminate both the commonality and the plurality of different forms of ignorance in daily life, from youthful overconfidence to senile incapacity when faced with the possibility of an unpleasant surprise. Like Haas and Vogt, they conclude their pieces with a normative stipulation, suggesting that "staying alert to ignorance is an unnatural skill that has to be learned" – and *must* be learned if the social sciences want to achieve the level of realism that, quite ironically, many fictional treatments of ignorance achieve better than much empirical work to date.

An interrogation of the boundary between fiction and philosophy is at the heart of Bennett's chapter. He points out that philosophers have long defined themselves in part through a deliberate bracketing of their work from the work of poets. As early as the fourth century BC, Plato sought to contrast the ignorance of poets with the treatment of ignorance in Socratic thought. In Plato's hands, Bennett writes, Socrates emerges as the most "competitively agnoiological philosopher, the philosopher who prides himself on his knowledge of what he does not know." Poets, on the other hand, are dismissed as taking a less melioristic stance towards ignorance, ultimately seeing it not, as Socrates does, as a path to knowledge, but as an end in itself: a state that must be inculcated time and again in order to foster creative, frenzied outpourings. Such "creative ignorance" on the part of poets might produce beauty, but not truth. And thus, Bennett suggests, a normative fissure between the truth-claims of poetry and the truth-claims of philosophy emerged.

Franke's contribution points out that a centuries-long tradition of apophatic thought (sometimes referred to as "negative theology") in the humanities has long stressed the importance of the Socratic dictate that one's knowledge lies in recognizing one's ignorance. He traces this apophatic tradition through a number of adherents, in particular to Nicholas of Cusa and other classical "masters of learned ignorance" (Duclow 2006). Leaping forward to the modern era, chapters by Friedman and Ravetz explore the converse of the apophatic legacy: they each critically interrogate the limits of the rationalism that has reigned at least since the early Enlightenment. Through a somewhat iconoclastic reading of Descartes, Ravetz suggests that Descartes was acutely aware of the tenuous nature of his own claims to knowledge – but unfortunately he chose to suppress that knowledge. From Descartes onwards, we can see the founding kernel of how "ignorance-of-ignorance then became hegemonic in modern learned culture" (Ravetz, this volume).

Although Karl Popper's work on falsification is sometimes upheld as a corrective to blind "scientism," the slavish devotion to the universality of a singular scientific method, Friedman's chapter disabuses readers of a sanguine interpretation of Popper's work. As she rightly notes, falsification too often "devolves into an empty injunction to be aware of our ignorance," a stipulation that might be comforting and, for the most part, epistemologically unobjectionable but does not necessarily give us any more purchase on scientific truth.

Part II: Registering the unknown: Ignorance as methodology

Efforts to teach students the importance of ignorance has a long and sometimes tortured history in the social and medical sciences. In the 1990s, Marlys Witte, a surgery professor at the University of Arizona, sought for years for extra funding that would enable her to teach "Introduction to Medical and Other Ignorance" to first-year medical students. One director of a philanthropic foundation, in response to Witte's grant application, declared that he would rather resign before his organization funded the exploration of ignorance (Ridge 2007). With help from Ann Kerwin, a philosopher then based at Arizona, Witte convinced her colleagues of the need for a module stressing how *little* different specialists know about their various subdisciplines. "Ignorance 101," as the students nicknamed it, became a popular module for years.

Witte's experience underscores an uncomfortable reality: the registration and observation of what is *not* known is often a challenging and politically unpopular field of research and teaching. After all, how can a researcher know what an individual or an observed group of actors do not know? The section starts with Joanna Kempner's important discussion of the ways that social scientists have often lagged behind ethicists and philosophers of science in understanding and investigating the ways that political and commercial barriers can constrain scientists from investigating politically insensitive or taboo research areas. Mike Michael's chapter touches on similar terrain, but unlike Kempner he focuses less on political or commercial barriers, and more on the way that tacit assumptions can lead researchers, often unwittingly, to impose internal self-limits on the insights they can hope to glean from their research. He suggests that developing a more explicitly "speculative methodology" could help to mitigate this problem. Basile Zimmermann's contribution illuminates the value of such a speculative stance in practice. Drawing on ethnographic observations of experimental sound design in China, he elucidates how openness to one's own ignorance can generate new musical forms.

Stuart Firestein's chapter takes up the gauntlet thrown down by Witte at the University of Arizona over two decades ago: we need to embrace the teaching of ignorance, he stipulates, or else suffer the perils of imparting an overly rosy, populist notion of scientific progress to generations of students lulled into believing that they know far more than they actually do. Part of why we *think* we know more than we do can at times be attributed to the limits of an increasingly monopolistic news industry. In a related vein, one implication of the contribution from S. Holly Stocking and Lisa W. Holstein is that the news industry needs to become more attuned to ignorance, for even as most journalists embrace as their mission rooting out and dispelling ignorance, they may hew to specific roles that lead them to instead promote ignorance themselves. This can have serious ramifications, especially for the kind of strategically manufactured controversies involving science that Stocking and Holstein explore.

For three decades, Michael Smithson has carried out pioneering work on the importance of ignorance in psychological decision-making. He builds on this work in his chapter, jointly written with Helen Pushkarskaya, on how new developments in neuroscience are advancing our knowledge of the ways that the brain deals with unknowns. Advances in neurolinguistics also feature in Nina Janich and Anne Simmerling's analysis of the linguistic representation of ignorance and nonknowledge. Their piece summarizes earlier approaches to the linguistic illumination of nonknowing, such as semantics, text linguistics and discourse analysis, and considers how the field may expand in future.

Part III: Valuing and managing the unknown in science, technology and medicine

Scholars within science and technology studies have been at the forefront of literature exploring both the negative and the positive implications of the existence and exploitation of ignorance in science and medicine. Building on a rich body of literature, this section commences with an exploration by David Hess of his notion of "undone science." For this handbook, Hess develops a seminal typology, one that offers a comparison and categorization of social movements, policy and industry groups based on varying levels of epistemic conflict.

Contributions then range from a critical analysis of the ways that science has historically privileged male ways of knowing, undermining the role of women as both producers and recipients of the fruits of scientific discovery (Janet Kourany), to strategies of selective ignorance in environmental research, where individuals produce or disseminate specific sorts of information about a topic or phenomenon without disseminating other pertinent information (Kevin Elliott; Daniel Kleinman and Sainath Suryanarayanan); to an emphasis on the importance of examining the materiality of physical space and scale for understanding why certain forms of evidence become known while others remain unknowable (Scott Frickel and Abby Kinchy). Correcting the tendency to see ignorance as an inevitably detrimental phenomenon, contributions in this section point to the ways that acknowledging ignorance can lead to a productive relationship between doubt, ignorance and trust (Albert Ogien).

Medical advances in the realm of genetics and biotechnology pose new ethical and political questions surrounding the right to privacy, autonomy, ownership over bodily fluids and tissues, and the future uses and risks of genetic information and bodily materials. Chapters by Alexander Bogner and Peter Wehling offer contrasting perspectives on the ethical and epistemological implications of these changes. Bogner's piece is largely salutary. He suggests that within genetics counselling decision-making is a largely deliberative process where medical professionals embrace the knowledge of patients (Bogner favors the word client), helping to produce morally acceptable decisions. Wehling is more circumspect. He points out that although new biomedical technologies such as whole-genome sequencing and preconception carrier screening are exerting considerable pressure on the individual right not to know certain personal characteristics, there is no de facto reason why we should presume that that new knowledge must be embraced simply because it happens to be available. It is possible, Wehling insists, to resist the epistemological determinism implicit within the arrival of new technoscience options.

Part IV: Power and ignorance: oppression, emancipation, and shifting subjectivities

An explicit and implicit theme within earlier sections is the relationship between ignorance and power. This theme comes to the forefront in this section, where contributors explore the role of ignorance in fomenting and entrenching hierarchies, in marginalizing some forms of knowledge as less reliable than others, and fostering political and psychological strategies that enable states and citizens to blinker themselves against both distant and nearby tragedies. Contributors also explore how the strategic use of ignorance can be emancipatory, exposing the fragility of knowledge claims by the powerful.

In his chapter, Mills returns to some of the themes of his groundbreaking book, *The Racial Contract*. He suggests that European imperialism thrived in the nineteenth and twentieth centuries (and survives in dissipated form today) through a two-fold process: first, by the acceptance and propagation of erroneous notions of racial superiority, and then by a denial of that very history, by a steadfast non-accounting of the atrocities that accompanied imperial expansion. Erinn Cunniff Gilson's chapter offers a reminder of the ongoing reality of racial and gendered ascriptions of worth. Both Gilson and Christian Kuhlicke draw parallels between work on vulnerability and separate work on ignorance, pointing out that these distinctive fields have largely developed in isolation from each other. They suggest ways to bring the fields in better conversation with each other. Liana Chua's contribution explores the importance of loss, change and collective memory in studies of ritual and religious belief in anthropology. She suggests that recent anthropological literature on the value of ignorance helps to both extend and offer a caveat to earlier anthropological interpretations of the relationship between secrecy, ritual and identity formation (see also High et al. 2012; Caduff 2014).

To date, very little work in criminology has explored the parallels between the legal value of denial, techniques of neutralization (whereby offenders seek to rationalize and justify their offences), and "pluralistic ignorance" – defined as the tendency of groups to unwittingly reinforce one another's misunderstanding of a situation. Darren Thiel's chapter is one of the first to offer such an analysis, examining the relevance of Cohen's work on denial, Sykes and Matza on techniques of neutralization, and research over the course of the twentieth century on the role of pluralistic ignorance in fostering both street-level deviance and state crime.

Deborah Prentice – whose earlier work on binge drinking among US college students is an oft-cited example of "pluralistic ignorance" in practice – builds on her earlier research in a discussion of why and how mechanisms aimed at promoting behavioral change and knowledge adoption often fail, and how such mechanisms might be improved in future.

The strategic (and often logical) refusal to embrace new knowledge even when it is freely available is a core aspect of the influential notion of "rational ignorance," a term first coined by Anthony Downs. In his chapter, Ilya Somin offers a comprehensive overview of this notion. Contrasting the concept with irrational and inadvertent ignorance, Somin explores positive and negative aspects of rational ignorance, including its effects on voting behavior and preferences. He stresses that ignorance in nonpolitical contexts is both inevitable and in many cases beneficial, in part because it frees up time and energy for other purposes (see, additionally, Somin 2013. There is also a growing body of literature in analytical philosophy on whether the rational or irrational avoidance of knowledge is morally defensible or not, such as Smith 2011; Peels 2011; Zimmerman 1997). The relationships between the political and the non-political; individual and collective ignorance; processes of democratization and the limits and possibilities of political action is further explored in Lev Marder's provocative discussion of Jacques Rancière's work.

Part V: Ignorance in economic theory, risk management and security studies

The organizational theorist Karl Weick once suggested that in lieu of seeking more knowledge of their own functionality, organizations may be "defined by what they ignore" (Weick 1998: 74; see also Luhmann 1992; Seibel 1996; Zerubavel 2006). In some ways, the usefulness of deliberate ignorance in large bureaucratic or commercial organizations is quite obvious. Anyone who has ever worked within one knows that all large organizations are rarely as efficient as they purport to be. Examples are rife within popular television programs like *The Wire*. In the first episode of season two, news reaches the Baltimore police department that 14 unidentified female bodies were found in Baltimore's harbor. The women are all identified as Jane Does. No one appears to be looking for them. The circumstances of their deaths are unclear. The possibility of tracking their killer or killers seems slim.

The officers immediately launch into action. Loudly trying to out-argue each other, the officers stubbornly insist that the deaths fall outside each of their individual jurisdiction. In other words, they vie fiercely to *avoid* investigating the possible homicides. Why? Because having a challenging or insolvable case dropped in their laps is sure to prevent them from having respectable records of solved cases for the year. The potential reward of solving the case is not worth the safety of ignoring it altogether. Strategic ignorance becomes an indispensable tool for officers saddled with the duty to meet annual quotas (McGoey 2012).

And yet, in much literature from management, organization and regulatory studies, this reality is ignored (recent exceptions include Hodson et al. 2013; Alvesson and Spicer 2012). Too often, ignorance is treated as a liability that can and will be overcome once individuals have sufficient information about the implications of their actions. Chapters in this section mitigate this problem, from Steve Rayner's exploration of the uses of ignorance as a rhetorical resource in geoengineering debates, to Brian Rappert and Brian Balmer's consideration of the Janus-faced status of ignorance in military strategizing, to Joanne Gaudet's study of how the acknowledgement of ignorance can help to shape more robust regulatory decisions in areas such as pharmaceutical surveillance, to François Dedieu, Jean-Noël Jouzel and Giovanni Prete's rich discussion of the various organizational blind-spots and incentives that lead public authorities to willfully maintain ignorance in the field of environmental health.

Management theorists Joanne Roberts and Allison Stewart each propose avenues for admitting and embracing the role of ignorance in large organizations, suggesting that ignorance should not be derided as a liability but rather upheld as a management ideal. As they point out, this suggestion is far easier to voice than to execute, especially in the aftermath of a decades-long retreat within orthodoxy economic theory from earlier, pre-1950s recognition of the unavoidable nature of uncertainty in decision-making. Since the latter half of the twentieth-century, recognition of the importance of ignorance has largely been sidelined in favor of economic theories that assume gathering more information and formalization (translation into numbers) are primary goals (see Svetlova and van Elst; Kessler, this volume).

Building on earlier work from scholars such as Downs on rational ignorance, as well as seminal work from Thomas Schelling on the value of ignorance in bargaining strategies, a number of behavioral economists *have* very recently begun to examine the role of ignorance in experimental settings. One example is a paper by Joël van der Weele (2014) which analyzes an experimental allocation game that is staged in order to study whether people will intentionally fail to become informed of the negative outcomes of their own actions the greater there is a financial reward for doing so. His paper draws on an earlier allocation game set up by Dana et al. (2007), who investigated whether or not individuals will sacrifice personal payoffs in order to ensure that rewards are distributed fairly. Dana and colleagues found that 74 per cent of subjects *will* sacrifice personal rewards in order to increase fair distribution of pay-outs. And yet, once transparency is removed, permitting participants to behave self-interestedly while *appearing* to act fairly, the number drops to 35 per cent. A key finding of their research is that in situations where there is uncertainty over how their actions will affect others, only 56 per cent choose to resolve this uncertainty in order to make more informed choices. In other words, they deliberately choose not to know, or to act in a way that would help to clarify uncertainty (Dana et al. 2007; McGoey 2015).

These studies are important. They help to underscore the ways that strategic ignorance is not an aberration of rationality, but often a logical act in itself. They are also highly limited. One problem is that behavioral experiments which examine the role of ignorance under staged settings are *methodologically incapable* of examining the historical usefulness of ignorance in cementing the disciplinary strength of mainstream economic theories over challenges from heterodox economists. This point resonates with arguments made by Oliver Kessler in this volume. In his chapter, he revisits the ways that uncertainty and risk have been treated in much orthodox economic thought form the mid-twentieth century onward. Pointing to the influence of Bayesian decision theory, he suggests that Bayesian thought has significantly displaced mid-century recognition of the importance of ignorance in economic life – recognition that J.M. Keynes and Friedrich Hayek each shared, despite reaching their opposite policy prescriptions for how to deal with unavoidable ignorance (see also Friedman 2005).

Ekaterina Svetlova and Henk van Elst's chapter covers similar terrain as Kessler. They outline what they see as three general shifts in how mainstream economic thinkers have treated uncertainty. First, thanks in part to the influence of leading late nineteenth-century thinkers such as Francis Edgeworth, W.S. Jevons and Carl Menger, new modes of frequentist probabilistic measurement were celebrated as tools for quantifying uncertainty. This early excitement was tempered by the writing of Hayek, Keynes, G.L.S. Shackle, and Frank Knight, each of whom was skeptical about the usefulness of frequentist thinking. Their efforts influenced (and yet were in many ways misunderstood by) Leonard Savage's turn away from frequentist thought towards an axiomatic approach to decision-making under conditions of uncertainty that employs subjective probability measures within a Bayesian context. The great liability of Savage's move, Svetlova and van Elst suggest, was that the effort "to 'absorb' non-knowledge by means of probability distributions obviously precludes the consideration of 'unknown unknown'" eventualities (Svetlova and van Elst, this volume; see also Arnsperger and Varoufakis 2005).

To this day, Keynes, Shackle and Hayek's separate caveats about the limits of knowledge are largely ignored. Much orthodox, mainstream economic thought remains fettered by a willful, stubborn "ignorance-of-ignorance," to borrow an earlier phrase from Ravetz. Behavioral experiments, meanwhile, may be the *least* capable of illuminating or correcting disciplinary ignorance that has helped generate the very experimental tools for measuring psychological motivation to begin with, permitting a sort of macro-level ignorance to persist unquestioned even as micro-investigations reveal the power of ignorance at the individual level.

Some future steps

It seems fitting to conclude by considering some of the blind-spots in this handbook. We never managed to get a lawyer on board. Though Thiel, Wehling, Bogner and others each touch on legal implications of ignorance, the handbook has no systematic discussion of the uses of ignorance in jurisprudence, or any comparative discussion of the uses of the doctrine of willful blindness in different national settings. Although the right not to know in genetic testing has received some attention in public debate (cf. Andorno 2004; Knoppers 2014; Townsend et al. 2014; Weaver 1997), legal discussions on willful blindness point to larger questions on insurance, criminal culpability, human well-being, and employment relationships. Referred to alternatively as the "ostrich instruction," "willful ignorance," "conscious avoidance," "purposefully abstaining from ascertaining," and "studied ignorance," the concept of willful blindness was first used by English authorities, and today has a bearing on civil and criminal law in numerous national and legal jurisdictions. Just how great a role the notion plays in jurisprudence is still unclear.

We approached a number of legal scholars to offer a chapter summarizing the legal instruction and its implications; few replied, and those that did declined to contribute. We will not attempt to summarize existent literature on willful ignorance here (see, rather, Robbins 1990; Roiphe 2011). It will simply suffice for us to emphasize that no treatments of ignorance are robust until the importance of ignorance in judicial settings is explored in greater depth than we have yet done in this handbook. Of course, as Michael Smithson shows in his compelling afterword, the study of ignorance does not stop at disciplinary boundaries; we hope our omissions are taken up elsewhere in future. At the moment, we end up close to where we began: hovering experimentally, optimistically, at the precipice of the unknown.

References

Alcoff, L. (2007) Epistemologies of Ignorance: Three Types. In S. Sullivan and N. Tuana (eds.), *Race and Epistemologies of Ignorance* (pp. 39–57). New York: SUNY Press.

Alvesson, M., and A. Spicer (2012) A Stupidity Based Theory of Organizations. *Journal of Management Studies* 49 (7): 1194–1220.

Andorno, R. (2004) The Right Not to Know: An Autonomy Based Approach. *Journal of Medical Ethics* 30: 435–440.

Aradau, C., and R. van Munster (eds.) (2011) *Politics of Catastrophe: Genealogies of the Unknown*. London: Routledge.

Arnsperger, C., and Y. Varoufakis (2005) A Most Peculiar Failure: How Neoclassical Economics Turns Theoretical Failure into Academic and Political Power. *Erkenntnis* 59: 157–188.

Bailey, A. (2007) Strategic Ignorance. In S. Sullivan and N. Tuana (eds.), *Race and Epistemologies of Ignorance* (pp. 77–94). Albany, NY: SUNY Press.

Balmer, B. (2012) *Secrecy and Science: A Historical Sociology of Biological and Chemical Warfare*. Farnhan: Ashgate.

Barry, A. (2013) *Material Politics: Disputes along the Pipeline*. Oxford: Wiley-Blackwell.

Best, Jacqueline (2012) Bureaucratic Ambiguity. *Economy and Society* 41 (1): 84–106.

Bleicher, A. (2012) Entscheiden trotz Nichtwissen: Das Beispiel der Sanierung kontaminierter Flächen. *Soziale Welt* 63 (2): 97–115.

Boudia, S., and Jas, N. (2014) *Powerless Science? Science and Politics in a Toxic World*. New York: Berghan Books.

Caduff, C. (2014) Pandemic Prophecy, or How to Have Faith in Reason. *Current Anthropology* 55 (3): 296–315.

Capers, I.B. (2006) On Justitia, Race, Gender and Blindness. *Michigan Journal of Race & Law* 12 (203): 4.

Caplan, B. (2001) Rational Ignorance versus Rational Irrationality. *Kyklos* 54 (1): 3–26.

Cohen, S. (2001) *States of Denial*. Cambridge: Polity.

Croissant, J. L. (2014) Agnotology: Ignorance and Absence or Towards a Sociology of Things That Aren't There. *Social Epistemology* 28 (1): 4–25.

Dana, J., R.R. Weber, and J.X.J. Kuang (2007) Exploiting Moral Wiggle Room: Experiments Demonstrating an Illusory Preference for Fairness. *Economic Theory* 33 (1): 67–80.

Downer, J. (2011) "737-Cabriolet": The Limits of Knowledge and the Sociology of Inevitable Failure. *American Journal of Sociology* 117 (3): 725–762.

Duclow, D.F. (2006) *Masters of Learned Ignorance: Eriguena, Eckart, Cusanus*. Aldershot: Ashgate.

Dunlap, R.E. (2013) Climate Change Skepticism and Denial: An Introduction. *American Behavioral Scientist* 57 (6): 691–698.

Elster, J. (1989) *Solomonic Judgments: Studies in the Limitation of Rationality*. Cambridge: Cambridge University Press.

Faber, M., and J.L.R. Proops (1990) *Evolution, Time, Production and the Environment*. Dordrecht: Springer.

Firestein, S. (2012) *Ignorance: How It Drives Science*. Oxford: Oxford University Press.

Frickel, S., and M. Edwards (2014) Untangling Ignorance in Environmental Risk Assessment. In S. Boudia and N. Jas (eds.), *Powerless Science? The Making of the Toxic World in the Twentieth Century* (pp. 215–233). New York: Berghan Books.

Friedman, J. (2005) Popper, Weber, and Hayek: The Epistemology and Politics of Ignorance. *Critical Review* 17 (1–2): 1–58.

Gadamer, H.-G. (2004) *Truth and Method*. London: Continuum.

Göçek, Fatma Müge (2014) *Denial of Violence: Ottoman Past, Turkish Present, and Collective Violence against the Armenians, 1789–2009*. Oxford: Oxford University Press.

Gray, J. (2002) *Straw Gods: Thoughts on Humans and Other Animals*. London: Granta.
Gross, M. (2010) *Ignorance and Surprise: Science, Society, and Ecological Design*. Cambridge, MA: MIT Press.
Gross, M. (2015) Journeying to the Heat of the Earth: From Jules Verne to Present-Day Geothermal Adventures. *Engineering Studies* 7 (1).
Heidbrink, L. (2013) Nichtwissen und Verantwortung: Zum Umgang mit nichtintendierten Handlungsfolgen. In C. Peter and D. Funcke (eds.), *Wissen an der Grenze* (pp. 111–139). Frankfurt: Campus.
Heimer, Carol A. (2012) Inert Facts and the Illusion of Knowledge: Strategic Uses of Ignorance in HIV Clinics. *Economy and Society* 41 (1): 17–41.
High, C., A. Kelly, and J. Mair (eds.) (2012) *The Anthropology of Ignorance: An Ethnographic Approach*. Basingstoke: Palgrave Macmillan.
Hodson, R., A. Martin, S. Lopez, and V. Roscigno, (2013) Rules Don't Apply: Kafka's Insights on Bureaucracy. *Organization* 20 (2): 256–278.
Kaptchuk, T. (1998) International Ignorance: A History of Blind Assessment and Placebo Controls in Medicine. *Bulletin of the History of Medicine* 72 (3): 389–433.
Knoppers, B.M. (ed.) (2014) The Right Not to Know. *The Journal of Law, Medicine & Ethics* 42 (1): 6–114.
Lemov, R. (2006) *World as Laboratory: Experiments with Mice, Mazes, and Men*. New York: Hill and Wang.
Luhmann, N. (1992) *Beobachtungen der Moderne*. Opladen: Westdeutscher Verlag.
Mills, C. (1997) *The Racial Contract*. Ithica, NY: Cornell University Press.
Mills, C. (2007) White Ignorance. In S. Sullivan and N. Tuana (eds.), *Race and Epistemologies of Ignorance* (pp. 13–38). Albany, NY: SUNY Press.
Marres, N. (2012) Experiment: The Experiment in Living. In C. Lury and N. Wakeford (eds.), *Inventive Methods: The Happening of the Social* (pp. 76-95). London: Routledge.
McGoey, L. (2012) The Logic of Strategic Ignorance. *British Journal of Sociology* 63 (3): 553-576.
McGoey, L. (ed.) (2014) *An Introduction to the Sociology of Ignorance: Essays on the Limits of Knowing*. London: Routledge.
McGoey, L. (2015) Vom Nutzen und Nachteil strategischen Nichtwissens. In P. Wehling (ed.), *Vom Nutzen des Nichtwissens: Sozial- und kulturwissenschaftliche Perspektiven*. Bielefeld, Germany: Transcript.
Oreskes, N., and E.M. Conway (2010) *Merchants of Doubt: How a Handful of Scientists Obscured the Truth on Issues from Tobacco Smoke to Global Warming*. New York: Bloomsbury.
Overdevest, C., A. Bleicher, and M. Gross (2010) The Experimental Turn in Environmental Sociology: Pragmatism and New Forms of Governance. In M. Gross and H. Heinrichs (eds.), *Environmental Sociology: European Perspectives and Interdisciplinary Challenges* (pp. 279–294). Heidelberg: Springer.
Peels, R. (2011) Tracing Culpable Ignorance. *Logos & Episteme*, II (4): 575–582.
Proctor, R.N. (1995) *Cancer Wars: How Politics Shapes What We Know and Don't Know About Cancer*. New York: Basic Books.
Proctor, R.N., and L. Schiebinger (eds.) (2008) *Agnotology: The Making and Unmaking of Ignorance*. Palo Alto, CA: Stanford University Press.
Rescher, N. (2009) *Ignorance: On the Wider Implications of Deficient Knowledge*. Pittsburgh, PA: University of Pittsburgh Press.
Rheinberger, H.-J. (1997) *Toward a History of Epistemic Things: Synthesizing Proteins in the Test Tube*. Palo Alto, CA: Stanford University Press.
Ridge, George. (2007) The Anatomy of Medical Ignorance. *New York Times*, February 11. Available online at: www.nytimes.com/1997/02/11/news/11iht-ignore.t.html (last accessed February 7, 2015).
Samson, Colin (2013) *A World You Do Not Know: Settler Societies, Indigenous Peoples and the Attack on Cultural Diversity*. London: Human Rights Consortium.
Scott, J. (1985) *Weapons of the Weak: Everyday Forms of Peasant Resistance*. New Haven, CN: Yale University Press.
Sedgwick, E. (1990) *Epistemology of the Closet*. Berkeley, CA: University California Press.
Seibel, W. (1996) Successful Failure: An Alternative View on Organizational Coping. *American Behavioral Scientist* 39 (8): 1011–1024.
Simmel, G. (1906) The Secret and Secret Societies. *American Journal of Sociology* 11 (4): 441–498.
Simpson, B., R. Khatri, D. Ravidran, and T. Udalagama (2014) Pharmaceuticalisation and Ethical Review in South Asia: Issues of Scope and Authority for Practitioners and Policy Makers. *Social Science & Medicine* (doi: 10.1016/j.socscimed.2014.03.016).
Smith, H. (2011) Non-Tracing Cases of Culpable Ignorance. *Criminal Law and Philosophy* 5 (2): 115–146.

Smithson, M. (1989) *Ignorance and Uncertainty: Emerging Paradigms*. Dordrecht: Springer.
Somin, I. (2013) *Democracy and Political Ignorance: Why Smaller Government Is Smarter*. Stanford, CA: Stanford University Press.
Steyn, M. (2012) The Ignorance Contract: Recollections of Apartheid Childhoods and the Construction of Epistemologies of Ignorance. *Identities: Global Studies in Culture and Power* 19 (1): 8–25.
Stirling, A. (2007) Risk, Precaution and Science: Towards a More Constructive Policy Debate: Talking Point on the Precautionary Principle. *EMBO Reports* 8 (4): 309–315.
Stocking, S.H., and L.W. Holstein (2009) Manufacturing Doubt: Journalists' Roles and the Construction of Ignorance in a Scientific Controversy. *Public Understanding of Science* 18 (1): 23–42.
Sullivan, S., and N. Tuana (2007) *Race and Epistemologies of Ignorance*. New York: SUNY Press.
Robbins, I.P. (1990) The Ostrich Instruction: Deliberate Ignorance as Criminal Mens Rea. *The Journal of Criminal Law & Criminology* 81 (2): 191–209.
Roiphe, R. (2011) The Ethics of Willful Ignorance. *Georgetown Journal of Legal Ethics* 24 (1): 187–224.
Taussig, M. (1999) *Defacement: Public Secrecy and the Labor of the Negative*. Palo Alto, CA: Stanford University Press.
Townley, C. (2011) *A Defense of Ignorance: Its Value for Knowers and Roles in Feminist and Social Epistemologies*. Lanham, MD: Lexington Books.
Townsend, A., F. Rousseau, J. Friedman, S. Adam, Z. Lohn, and P. Birch (2014) Autonomy and the Patient's Right "Not to Know" in Clinical Whole-genomic Sequencing. *European Journal of Human Genetics* 22: 6–11.
Ungar, S. (2008) Ignorance as an Under-identified Social Problem. *British Journal of Sociology* 59 (2): 301–326.
Urry, J. (2014) *Offshoring*. Oxford: Polity.
van der Weele, J. (2014) Inconvenient Truths: Determinants of Strategic Ignorance in Moral Dilemmas. Available online at: http://ssrn.com/abstract=2247288 or http://dx.doi.org/10.2139/ssrn.2247288 (last accessed February 7, 2015).
Vitek, W., and L. Jackson (eds.) (2008) *The Virtues of Ignorance: Complexity, Sustainability, and the Limits of Knowledge*. Lexington, KT: The University Press of Kentucky.
Walton, D. (1996) *Arguments from Ignorance*. University Park, PA: Penn State University Press.
Weaver, K.D. (1997) Genetic Screening and the Right Not to Know. *Issues in Law and Medicine* 13 (3): 243–281.
Wehling, Peter (ed.) (2015) *Vom Nutzen des Nichtwissens: Sozial- und kulturwissenschaftliche Perspektiven*. Bielefeld, Germany: Transcript.
Weick, K. (1998) Foresights of Failure: An Appreciation of Barry Turner. *Journal of Contingencies and Crisis Management* 6 (2): 72–75.
Zerubavel, E. (2006) *The Elephant in the Room: Silence and Denial in Everyday Life*. Oxford: Oxford University Press.
Zimmerman, M. (1997) Moral Responsibility and Ignorance. *Ethics* 107 (3): 410–426.

Part I

Historical treatments of ignorance in philosophy, literature and the human sciences

2

Ignorance and investigation

Jens Haas and Katja Maria Vogt

Suppose Socrates knows nothing about fashion.[1] Indeed, he could not care less about it. Call this attitude *Preferred Ignorance*. Suppose further that he understands the concept atom, namely, smallest indivisible component of the physical universe, but he does not take himself to be in a position to assess whether such components exist. He also has some ideas about the nature of value. But as he tries to articulate what precisely it is that he takes the good to be, he must admit that he does not know. In both cases, we may speak of *Investigative Ignorance*. Socrates's ignorance motivates him to take an interest in physics, though he leaves investigation in this field to others. And his ignorance fuels his thinking about value. Other cases are such that one is unaware of one's ignorance. Suppose Socrates holds firmly that a divine being corresponds with him, though he is deluded about this; or, say, he affirms that there is a wolf approaching, though it is his neighbor's dog. Call this *Presumed Knowledge*.[2] There could also be a kind of ignorance where one does not hold any attitude to that which one is ignorant about. Perhaps Socrates has never even heard of dinosaurs, or more generally, of beings that once existed but are extinct. This is a kind of *Complete Ignorance*.[3]

Philosophers have said far less about ignorance than about knowledge.[4] As a consequence, there is not much of a discussion that could be joined—no types of theories, arguments for and against them, problems that could be re-examined, and so on. Accordingly, the objectives of this chapter must be modest. We will pursue the above examples, suggesting that typically we have reason to prefer states of ignorance that motivate inquiry over states of ignorance that do not.[5]

The chapter starts with an outline of the notion of ignorance we will employ, ignorance as absence of knowledge (see below). Next we distinguish two elements that figure in most ignorance ascriptions: a generic ascription of ignorance and a more precise description of the attitudes a cognizer holds in a given instance of ignorance (see "Ignorance and belief"). We explore kinds of ignorance where cognizers seem to hold *no* relevant attitudes (see "Complete ignorance"), and conclude with a sketch of ignorance in investigation (see "Ignorance and investigation").

Ignorance as the absence of knowledge

Arguably, the simplest answer one can give to the question "what is ignorance?" is "the absence of knowledge." This is a literal take on the word. "i-" is a negator prefix, and "-gnorance" derives from the Greek *gnôsis*, which refers to a state of mind in which the cognizer knows something or understands something.[6] These considerations suggest a minimal notion of ignorance, namely that it is the absence of knowledge in a wide sense, which may include elements of understanding and grasping.

The negator prefix "i-" could be taken in a stronger, privative sense, signaling not mere absence but lack.[7] Privation—literally, a state of being robbed of something—is a state where something is missing that *should* be there, as part of something's nature or as a feature of how things usually are. For example, blindness is a privation insofar as vision is considered the general or natural case. Is ignorance, like blindness, a privation? Some languages capture the distinction between absence and privation when it comes to ignorance. For example, Latin has *nescire* for not-knowing and *ignorare* for being ignorant in a privative sense; German has Nichtwissen for a state of not-knowing and Unwissenheit for ignorance. If ignorance were primarily or generally a privation, then ascriptions of ignorance imply that something is missing that would naturally or ordinarily be present. We reject this stronger proposal, because it has implausible implications. For every ignorance-ascription to be an ascription of a privation, one would have to consider omniscience, understood as knowing everything that anyone could possibly know, as the standard against which to measure any state of mind. This kind of omniscience is inherently implausible and it is not an ideal to strive for. Obviously, ignorance can be a lack and it often is a lack. But for someone not to know, for example, what every reader of this chapter, including you, had for breakfast today is not lack, but mere absence.

Ordinary ways of speaking about ignorance can refer to the absence of a range of cognitive achievements. Since there is no technical notion of ignorance that seems relevant for present purposes, these everyday ways of speaking are a plausible starting-point. They pull away from the idea that ignorance is standardly or primarily the absence of *propositional* knowledge. In discussions of knowledge, propositional knowledge—knowing that *p*—is considered the most straightforward case. It is also usually considered basic, insofar as other kinds of knowledge are reducible to propositional knowledge. For example, knowing *whether* Walt had cake for breakfast may be reducible to knowing *that* Walt had cake (if Walt had cake) or *that* Walt didn't have cake (if Walt didn't have cake). Now one might take a true proposition—say, that Walt had cake for breakfast today—and refer to ignorance of this proposition as propositional ignorance: Skyler does not know that Walt had cake for breakfast today.[8] But while propositional knowledge may be the standard case of knowledge, propositional ignorance seems less evidently "standard." Consider the case where Skyler does not know the answer to a fairly open-ended question, such as, "what is a good way to live for human beings?"[9] In thinking about this question, she may need to refine the terms in which she thinks about it, acquire new concepts, learn about empirical research, begin to perceive certain features of situations that are ethically relevant, and so on. Here it may just not make sense to say that what is absent is knowledge of propositions.

Perhaps one might say that what is absent is the answer to a question, leaving open how precisely to think of such answers to questions. But the idea that ignorance is typically *of* questions is not sufficiently wide. Ignorance-ascriptions often refer neither to a proposition nor to a question. Instead, we frequently say that someone is ignorant *about* X or *in* Y, for example, about fashion or in biology. In these cases, we are saying that someone is ignorant with respect to many propositions and to any number of questions in a whole field. And yet, her ignorance may not be reducible to ignorance of a set of propositions, or regarding a set of questions. It may include that a given question could not arise for her because she is unacquainted with the relevant concepts, say, in the way in which questions about dinosaurs could not arise for Socrates. This suggests that ignorance is absence of knowledge in a wide sense, where knowledge includes elements of concept-possession, grasping, understanding, as well as a range of related cognitive achievements.

What, then, is excluded by saying that ignorance is the absence of knowledge? Ignorance is the absence of *knowledge* (in the relevant wide sense), not of some other cognitive achievement, say, attention or active recollection. For example, one is not ignorant by not attending at a given moment to something one knows, or by being asleep, or in some other way not presently accessing what one knows. One can know things and yet not, right now, fully recall them, such that one would have to reconstruct an idea in one's mind in order to have it fully present again. Still, in these cases, one is not ignorant. That is, in states of ignorance knowledge is *absent*, as opposed to merely latent, dormant, unattended to, and so on.

Ignorance and belief

If ignorance is the absence of knowledge, a wide range of doxastic states—states of mind where the cognizer represents the world as being a certain way—count in a sense as ignorance. But in what sense? Suspension of judgment, hypotheses, suppositions, postulates, beliefs with greater and lesser confidence, and so on, all fall short of knowledge. And yet, cognizers who hold these doxastic attitudes are in rather different states of mind. So it is not enough to say that a cognizer is ignorant in the absence of knowledge (A). Something also needs to be said about the doxastic attitude she holds (B).

A Ignorance is the absence of knowledge. One either knows something or is ignorant of it.

B Cognizers hold a range of doxastic attitudes: suspension of judgment, beliefs with higher and lesser credence, hypotheses, suppositions, postulates, and so on.[10]

The relationship between (A) and (B), and its role in inquiry, is explored in a famous text, the so-called Meno Problem in Plato's *Meno*. How can one search for anything, when either one knows it already, in which case there is no need to search, or one does not know it, in which case one cannot know what to look for or how to recognize it? This question misconstrues what absence of knowledge amounts to: it not only describes all doxastic attitudes falling short of knowledge as ignorance, but it assumes that an ignorant cognizer lacks any doxastic attitude whatsoever to a given content. Part of the explanation that emerges in the dialogue is that cognizers are not typically bare of any doxastic attitudes regarding that which they investigate and which they do not know. Things seem a certain way to them, and they can start investigating by making hypotheses out of these seemings.

The attitudes listed in (B) fall into two categories, the attitudes of inquirers and of believers. Cognizers in the first group make an effort to attend to epistemic norms of thinking carefully, assessing evidence, or assigning a given status to some idea (as a postulate, premise that is under investigation, etc.). Cognizers in the second group fail to make this kind of effort, either because they are unaware that something could be wrong with the way they see the world or because they are epistemically lazy.

To be sure, one often holds some view, and though it may be false, one buys into it without reservation. Sometimes one may just make an honest mistake about a trivial matter, being ignorant while one takes oneself to have knowledge. Suppose one is entirely confident that one put a pen in a certain drawer and takes oneself to be in a position to assert "the pen is in *this* drawer," and yet it is not. From the inside, this kind of ignorance feels like knowledge, which is why we refer to it as *Presumed Knowledge*. This cognizer is not motivated to inquire, qualify her views as tentative, or anything of that sort. She may simply be making a mistake, one that appears inexplicable to her once she realizes that, say, the pen is *not* in the drawer where she thought she put it. Here we tend to think that mistakes are just part of life; they do not elicit any strong kind of blame. What may count as offensive, however, is insistence that reflects a delusional self-image, where a cognizer assumes that, unlike the rest of us, she is not liable to make mistakes. Other instances of *Presumed Knowledge* are the target of negative evaluations because cognizers display the vices of dogmatism, often combined with an air of superiority: they preach their views about the world, and it does not register with them that they may be wrong. Further, *Presumed Knowledge* can be related to *Preferred Ignorance*. A cognizer may pronounce her views on X, all the while not considering X worth any serious attention. *Preferred Ignorance* can thus be blameworthy in similar ways that *Presumed Knowledge* is. Those who prefer not to know can seem to dismiss domains of knowledge that to others appear valuable or even urgent.

Still, many cases of *Preferred Ignorance* seem unobjectionable. For example, suppose you prefer to remain ignorant about the chants of some new satanic cult. Similarly, you may be perfectly happy to not know anything about the contents of some TV shows. And so on. These cases are not about avoiding unpleasant, though ultimately useful, knowledge, as when one may be tempted to avoid information about the health effects of smoking because one enjoys it. These are phenomena in which, for example, a sociologist may take an interest, while others may reasonably prefer ignorance, given who they are and what else is going on in their lives.[11] Cognizers may have psychological reasons for avoiding knowledge (say, fearing trauma and nightmares, or worrying that certain knowledge may be stultifying) in cases that border on the bizarre, perverse, or trivial.[12] Relatedly, *Preferred Ignorance* can reflect an agent's considered values. Someone may decide that—though in a sense she would know something of which she is now ignorant—filling her mind with the trivia of soap operas or the details of satanic chants is not a cognitive advantage for her.

Consider next the doxastic attitudes that figure in inquiry. In an effort to avoid dogmatism, inquiring minds are committed to assessing—with significant and at times seemingly excessive effort—whether they are in a position to make claims about the world. They assign probabilities to assumptions, qualify views as preliminary, formulate hypotheses, and so on, adopting the attitudes of *Investigative Ignorance*. Given the cognizer's epistemic effort, would it not seem more plausible to refrain from ascribing ignorance to her? Arguably, the answer is "no." Both (A) and (B) contribute relevant descriptions of her states of mind. Insofar as knowledge is absent, she is ignorant (A). Inquirers *themselves*, in fact, often choose this description. They come across something they are ignorant of and that they would like to know. Hence they investigate. (B) supplies a description of where they stand in their quest for knowledge: as of now, one merely has a hypothesis, a promising model, inconclusive evidence, and so on.

In practical contexts, similar considerations apply. Suppose a car riddled with bullet holes stops right in front of you with screeching tires. A passenger is lying on the back seat with what appear to be gunshot wounds. It seems obvious that a lot hangs on your giving the driver the right directions to the hospital. You may be quite sure about the best way, but not entirely sure. If all you said was "I don't know," ascribing ignorance to yourself, you would be just as unhelpful as if you confidently asserted a view that might turn out to be false. The driver who seeks your input would be much more helped by a response like "I don't know for sure, but to the best of my knowledge, *p*." That is, if one *only* said "I don't know whether *p*" in cases where one strictly speaking lacks knowledge, one would misrepresent one's doxastic state. These considerations support that there is a place for both (A) and (B), the ascription of ignorance and the ascription of a certain doxastic attitude. On its own, each ascription is insufficient for characterizing a cognizer's state of mind.

Complete ignorance

And yet there are also cases of ignorance where (B) does not apply: the cognizer does not hold any particular doxastic attitude to content of which she is ignorant. Call this *Complete Ignorance.* It occurs in (at least) three variations. First, it is possible to be ignorant of something that one has never even heard about. Schematically, in this kind of complete ignorance, the cognizer does not have any attitude to X, and X exists.[13] Say, Socrates has never heard of dinosaurs, has no views about anything relating to dinosaurs, and also no self-assessment to the effect that he is or is not ignorant about dinosaurs. Socrates is ignorant, and he is entirely unaware of his ignorance. This kind of ignorance is widespread with respect to trivia, but also with respect to any number of facts that simply do not figure in a particular person's life. It is a kind of ignorance *without* particular doxastic states. That is, here the level of description that (B) picks out does not apply. In a case in which someone has never even heard of that which she is ignorant about, her ignorance has no specific place in the cognizer's mind. Nevertheless, it is true to say of her that she is, with a view to a given matter, ignorant.

Consider a second kind of complete ignorance. Here one does not altogether lack attitudes related to X. Instead, assume that the cognizer has a belief about something that may not exist, as when someone thought about the Form of the Good while in reality there is no such thing. Such thinking can be quite extensive: someone may have developed a detailed theory about imperceptible and unchangeable Forms.[14] He posed any number of questions about why these Forms are the highest kind of reality and how they explain everything else—and yet it could turn out that there are no Forms. Is it true to say that this cognizer was thinking about nothing? There is a sense in which he was thinking about what is not, assuming he thought about Forms although there are no Forms. And yet, there is also a sense in which he cannot have thought successfully about Forms if there are none; for his thinking was meant to refer to something, but the very objects that it was meant to refer to do not exist.

Schematically, in cases like this the cognizer has attitudes to X, but X does not exist. This kind of ignorance is complete in a peculiar fashion: much goes on in the mind of the cognizer, and yet all of it is in some basic ways misdirected. Though it gets the very existence of that which is thought about wrong, this kind of ignorance can have upsides. It can fuel theorizing, sometimes over centuries or even millennia. Consider other examples, such as the question of whether there are atoms, or whether there is void. Since the times of Pre-Socratic atomism, debates about smallest constituents of the physical world and about the void motivated major projects in physics, many results of which are important independently of whether later generations of scientists come to hold the view that there are atoms or that there is void. The second kind of complete ignorance thus differs from the first, which—given that the cognizer does not have any relevant attitudes—cannot motivate further thinking.

Third, consider cases where ignorance is almost, though not entirely, complete. Suppose a cognizer is ignorant about something that is relevant to her way of making sense of the world. This kind of ignorance can be described by the metaphor of a mental blank.[15] Assume that a cognizer who knows nothing about evolutionary biology nevertheless refers to kinds of animals and plants, and takes a certain interest in the natural world. Now suppose she is aware that she does not have a clear understanding of the ways in which kinds of living beings differ from each other, of whether there were any living beings in the past that no longer exist, and so on. There is a self-perceived gap in her web of assumptions about the world. Though the cognizer cannot pinpoint the kind of knowledge that would fill this gap, she may be able to locate it as situated, say, somewhere in the sphere of talk about kinds of living beings and their history. In such cases, ascriptions of ignorance refer to some actual mental states of the agent—not just to their absence. They refer to attitudes that delineate the domain where a reflective cognizer perceives gaps.[16] This kind of perception can be vague or well-defined; it can be at the periphery of a cognizer's attention, or it can be acutely felt; it can be extensive, as when one has never heard of evolutionary biology at all, or specific, as when one is unaware of a specialized field such as phylogenetics, or misses one particular bit of information.

These three kinds of *Complete Ignorance*, therefore, differ in how they relate to investigation. The first cannot motivate inquiry. The second motivates inquiry, even though it can be misdirected in basic ways. The third can lead a cognizer to ask questions that are, as it were, on the right track—questions that are geared toward her understanding of the world and gaps in her knowledge.

Ignorance and investigation

That knowledge is valuable has been defended in any number of ways: say, as a starting-point that one should take for granted without demonstration; because we have a natural desire to make sense of the world; because we have practical ends; or insofar as even skeptics presuppose that knowledge—if only it were available—would be good to have.

If ignorance is the absence of knowledge, and if knowledge is valuable, ignorance would seem to be bad. At least, it would seem to be comparatively bad, a state where something of value is absent.[17] This premise is not in conflict with cases where knowledge is not valuable, say, because pieces of knowledge are generated by mere iteration of the same move ("I know that I know," "I know that I know that I know," etc.), or knowledge of tautologies. There is a sense in which one plausibly speaks of knowledge here; but it is a weak sense that does not invoke all normative dimensions of knowledge. Arguably, there is *some* achievement even here, for otherwise, say, the cognizer might be confused and mix up the iteration, or make some other mistake in generating the series. It is not, however, an achievement that one ordinarily considers worthwhile. There are some confined contexts where pointless memorizing or similar achievements count as praiseworthy, say, some game show where a candidate displays an idiosyncratic cognitive skill, comparable to, on the non-epistemic side of things, a hotdog eating contest. Setting these contexts aside, for the most part knowledge is used as an honorific, a success term that describes a cognitive achievement that is considered worthwhile.

Knowledge in science, or any kind of inquiry geared toward finding out how the world (or some aspect of it) is, seems to be a straightforward case: its value is fairly uncontroversial.[18] Accordingly, ignorance is thought of as disvaluable, a condition to get rid of by attaining knowledge.[19] And yet it is precisely in science that ignorance is sometimes positively appreciated. For researchers, ignorance is embedded in a mindset geared toward discovery. The (B)-type doxastic states associated with inquiry—hypotheses, postulates, and so on—seem unobjectionable. Indeed, they seem to be informed by epistemic norms of caution, dedication to truth-finding, and so on. That is, one way in which *Investigative Ignorance* seems praiseworthy is tied to the (B)-type doxastic attitudes that researchers tend to adopt. Relatedly and in addition, inquirers tend to adopt interrogative attitudes, aiming to formulate precise questions and pursuing these questions. Arguably, to ask questions that can guide inquiry is an achievement.

But how about, as it were, the ignorance itself? To register that one is ignorant about something is presumably an achievement. This condition of registered ignorance seems good at least in a comparative sense: better than holding unfounded views or not realizing that there is something one does not know. It is a step toward discovery and knowledge. Is it thereby a good state of mind?[20] It might seem outrageous not to concede this. Otherwise, only complete and ideal knowledge of the world is good and all lesser states of mind count as bad.[21] This is arguably too tragic a view, one that gives too little weight to comparative evaluations. It may seem that the researcher is not only in an improved state of mind because she can formulate questions. More than that, by formulating and re-formulating her questions, by repeatedly revising her premises and methods, etc., her ignorance itself changes. It becomes an increasingly well-defined gap with recognizable contours, such that she can see what is at its periphery, what it relates to, and so on.

Concluding this sketch of ignorance and investigation, consider again the distinction between *Presumed Knowledge* and *Preferred Ignorance*. Both incur, often, blame; and both seem closely related. One way in which they differ, however, is that *Preferred Ignorance* can play a positive role in investigation. For example, inquirers can choose to be ignorant because they think that not availing themselves of certain information is conducive to discovery. Consider the so-called veil of ignorance that the Rawlsian tradition in political philosophy recommends for the "original position." In this hypothetical setup, agents decide about norms that should be accepted in a state. When they ask which principles would be just, they might be led astray by knowing which position in a society they inhabit. Only if they do not know whether they are rich or poor, healthy or sick, and so on, are they going to think in the right ways about justice.[22] The core intuition here resembles the image of justice with a blindfold. Not seeing certain particular features of the people involved in a given interaction, so the argument goes, can be conducive to better thinking and better outcomes. Analogues exist in empirical research in any number of contexts, as in when medical researchers conduct double-blind studies, aiming to remove expectations that bias results.

Hence blinding can have epistemic value: it can be conducive to attaining knowledge. Nevertheless, blinding involves loss of information. Researchers who employ blinding as a tool, be it in political philosophy, in clinical studies in medicine, or in other domains, tend to revise their methods in an effort to balance the good and the bad of it. For example, the veil of ignorance may be revisited, because the concern may arise that, via blinding, one tends to imagine a fairly uniform "standard person." This may lead to principles of justice that are ill fit for societies that are in fact quite diverse. Similarly, in medicine methods of testing medications undergo revision. What counts as placebo, how expectations of patients are to be seen as relevant to therapies, and so on, are matters of dispute and reevaluation. That is, in fine-tuning their methods, researchers aim to balance advantages and disadvantages of undisclosed information. Where they decide in favor of blinding, they do so with the assumption that the advantages outweigh the disadvantages, *not* with the assumption that the undisclosed information is in principle without any value.

Conclusion

Ordinary ignorance ascriptions, we have argued, do not necessarily ascribe a lack or privation. They ascribe the absence of knowledge. Cognizers are not expected to aim indiscriminately for knowledge. Their considered values, psychological considerations, or even the very method of a research project can make it plausible to selectively prefer ignorance. And yet, many kinds of ignorance seem worrisome. We distinguished between the attitudes involved in what we called *Presumed Knowledge*, *Preferred Ignorance*, *Complete Ignorance*, and *Investigative Ignorance*. Much more could be said beyond this outline. For present purposes, we have tried to establish one criterion by which to assess ignorance in normative terms: generally speaking, and in spite of exceptions, ignorance that shuts down inquiry seems more vulnerable to criticism than ignorance that motivates inquiry.

Notes

1 Avery Archer, Elizabeth Balough, Jonathan Fine, Abram Kaplan, Christiana Olfert, Nandi Theunissen, Achille Varzi, and the participants of the Fordham Ethics & Epistemology Group offered much appreciated comments.
2 See Vogt (2012: Ch. 1).
3 Yet other kinds of ignorance are related to action. One may not have how-to knowledge, knowledge of what to do, or (more controversially) knowledge of what one is doing.
4 Bernard Williams (1995) focuses on skepticism and some related questions; but he does not ask what ignorance is. This is typical of the few existing contributions on ignorance. Peter Unger (2002) is a defense of skepticism, not a book about ignorance.
5 Our discussion aims to pick out kinds of ignorance that are particularly relevant to normative practices. A different approach might stipulate that an account of ignorance ought to fall out of an account of knowledge. This approach has merits, but it does *not* lead one to think about kinds of ignorance that are salient in our practices of ignorance-ascriptions.
6 The Greek word *gnôsis* also refers to "seeking to know/inquiry". This use of the Greek term relates to a question relevant to our topic, namely whether one associates inquisitive attitudes with knowledge-states or with ignorance-states.
7 Philosophers who consider the lack-view as standard tend not to distinguish between lack and absence. See Peels (2010, 2011, 2012) and Le Morvan (2011, 2012).
8 Notice that one does not tend to say "Skyler is ignorant that . . . ," but "Skyler does not know that . . . "; "ignorant that" sounds off. When we use the term "ignorant" in an ascription of propositional ignorance, we have to use a circumlocution, something like "Skyler is ignorant of the fact that . . . "
9 The nature of questions is under-explored in philosophy. For a recent contribution, see Friedman (2013).
10 An alternative view assumes that cognizers hold beliefs with certain degrees of credence. Low credence counts as ignorance; if a certain threshold of confidence is met, cognizers count as holding beliefs; in full confidence plus X (where X is justification or something else that secures the status of knowledge), they have knowledge. This approach neglects phenomena we address, for example *Presumed Knowledge*, or that absent knowledge one is, strictly speaking, ignorant. On threshold views of belief, see Foley (1992).
11 One may also prefer *others* to be ignorant, as when one prefers a terrorist to be ignorant of bomb-making (we owe this example to Avery Archer).
12 Relatedly, they may have preferences about the mode of knowledge-acquisition, for example preferring to learn about some acts of brutality by reading about them, rather than by seeing photos or video-footage. They may be aware that knowledge acquired by sense-perception may figure differently in their psychology. Some cases that we colloquially refer to as "ignorance is bliss" may be of that sort: we recognize a need for being informed, but only up to a point, realizing that it would be debilitating, for example, to know about all health risks in a way that is supported by visual material.
13 "Exists" is used here in a sense that includes past existence, the existence of abstracta, and so on. The point of our formulation is to exclude cases where a cognizer does not know X and X does not exist, as when, say, I have never heard of planet Z and planet Z does not exist.
14 This person would be Plato.
15 We *don't* mean to refer here to the idea of not being able to recall something, and in that sense "having a mental blank."
16 When access to vital information is impeded, or when one cannot put one's finger on the missing piece of a puzzle, ignorance may be a painfully perceived deficiency. Versions of this phenomenon are pervasive—and arguably, the more you know, the more you know it: the research project is at a dead end, the directions for the road trip were wrong, the manual for the fancy oven makes no sense to you, and so forth. The agony may relate to the importance of one's project, but it can also derive from a kind of cognitive unease. One may know that one knew something, cannot remember it, and then agonize over remembering it, even though one's remembering it is not important and has no consequences; we owe this last example to Abram Kaplan.
17 Badness or disvalue is not necessarily tied to blameworthiness; a disvaluable state can be unfortunate or disadvantageous, without there being anything that the cognizer did wrong.

18 This does not mean, of course, that one finds every particular research project worthwhile, or that there would be no people who distrust science in general. For present purposes, we shall take for granted that it is valuable to gain knowledge about the natural world, human psychology, cognition, physiology, and so on.

19 It is a difficult question whether inquiry is motivated by its end, knowledge, or by its beginning (for lack of a better term), ignorance. Presumably, there are instances of ignorance that are like pain, motivating cognizers in the getting away from the bad-direction, rather than in the being attracted to the good-direction. For example, illiteracy or not knowing a language can be disorienting. A cognizer finds herself in a condition she wants to get rid of, similar to wanting to get rid of pain or distress. For present purposes, this is too large a question; versions of it arise in many contexts in the theory of motivation and agency.

20 See Firestein (2012). Not only scientists can find ignorance exciting. Similar considerations apply in other creative pursuits: "[. . .] there's almost a joy in looking at your ignorance and realizing, 'Wow, we're going to learn about this and, by the time we're done, we're going to really understand and do something great.'" Sir Jonathan Ive, Senior Vice President of Design at Apple Inc., interviewed by John Arlidge for *Time*, published March 17, 2014, http://time.com/jonathan-ive-apple-interview/.

21 Complete scientific knowledge might be understood as knowledge of the most basic laws in core fields of science, combined with mastering the methods of these disciplines.

22 See Rawls (1971).

References

Firestein, S. (2012) *Ignorance: How It Drives Science*, Oxford: Oxford University Press.

Foley, R. (1992) "The Epistemology of Belief and the Epistemology of Degrees of Belief," *American Philosophical Quarterly* XXIX: 111–124.

Friedman, J. (2013) "Question-Directed Attitudes," *Philosophical Perspectives* 27: 145–174.

Le Morvan, P. (2011) "On Ignorance: A Reply to Peels," *Philosophia* 39(2): 335–344.

— (2012) "On Ignorance: A Vindication of the Standard View," *Philosophia* 40: 379–393.

Peels, R. (2010) "What Is Ignorance?" *Philosophia* 38(1): 57–67.

— (2011) "Ignorance Is Lack of True Belief," *Philosophia* 39(2): 345–355.

— (2012) "The New View on Ignorance Undefeated," *Philosophia* 40: 741–750.

Rawls, J. (1971) *A Theory of Justice*, Cambridge, MA: Harvard University Press.

Unger, P. (2002) *Ignorance: A Case for Scepticism*, Oxford: Oxford University Press.

Vogt, K. M. (2012) *Belief and Truth: A Skeptic Reading of Plato*, New York: Oxford University Press.

Williams, B. (1995) "Philosophy and the Understanding of Ignorance," *Diogenes* 43: 23–36.

3

Learned ignorance

The apophatic tradition of cultivating the virtue of unknowing

William Franke

Although ignorance has often been considered to be merely negative and indeed the root of all vice, there is also a very long counter-tradition within Western intellectual and cultural history that reverses this valence and appreciates ignorance as the necessary ground for all genuine knowledge and even as the indispensable starting point for any meaningful and productive orientation to the world as a whole. Ignorance has been consciously cultivated as the most fecund moment in the whole process of encountering and relating to an order of beings that transcends the instrumental order of objects known only in terms of their usefulness for human purposes and projects. This valorization of ignorance is found in a particularly radical form in thinkers and writers who can be characterized as "apophatic" and as participating in an internal critique of the mainstream of Western philosophical thought based on knowledge by means of the word or *logos*. "Apophasis" means literally negation and refers etymologically to the negation specifically of speech (*phasis*, "assertion," in Greek, from *phemi*, I "assert" or "say"). What is negated thereby is *logos*, the word or reason, and therewith knowledge in the sense of discourse based on logical reasoning and verbal expression. This counter-tradition of apophasis has run parallel to the mainstream thinking of the *logos*, often intersecting and overlapping with it, all through the broader philosophical tradition of the West: it appears often in underground and subversive channels, but also as the deepest, most paradoxical and challenging stratum of thought in many of the most canonical thinkers.

A crucial source can be found in Plato and particularly in the paradoxes of his *Parmenides*, according to which it is impossible to say the ultimate principle of things, the One, without inadvertently making it into two: itself and its name. On the basis of the interpretive tradition surrounding this dialogue, especially among the Neoplatonist philosophers, ignorance in the form of apophasis or the inability to say and to think conceptually or logically became a leading theme of speculation: it passed from Plotinus, Porphyry, Proclus, and Iamblichus, to Damascius (458–538 AD), whose *Dubitationes et solutiones de primis principiis* represents its most radical treatment and in crucial ways the culmination of ancient Neoplatonism. Thereafter apophatic ignorance departed in new directions and took on some new dimensions with the direct heirs of the Neoplatonists in the monotheistic traditions. It found magisterial expositions in the Christian speculative mysticism of Pseudo-Dionysius the Areopagite (*De divinis nominibus*) and of John Scotus Eriugena (*De divisione naturae*). It continued to be crucial to medieval philosopher-theologians such as Maimonides and Meister Eckhart and remained at the source of inspiration in the Kabbalah (notably the *Zohar*) as well as influential in the Sufism of Ibn al Arabi and its poetic elaboration by Jalal al-Din Rumi. Baroque mystics like John of the Cross, Jakob Böhme, and Silesius Angelus share this same obsession for what evades speech with Romantic thinkers like Kierkegaard and the late Schelling. In different ways, in all these epoch-making apophatic writers, ignorance has been consciously cultivated as the most fertile moment in any authentic awareness of reality as a whole and in its deepest grounds.

In the midst of this history, a central and exemplary paradigm of the apophatic mode of thought and discourse is the "learned ignorance" that Nicolaus of Cusa (1401–1464) brought to focus and rendered famous in his epoch-making *De docta ignorantia* (1440). Building on certain key insights of Meister Eckhart, and carrying forward the most paradoxical and penetrating teachings of Neoplatonism culled from assiduous frequentation especially of Proclus and Pseudo-Dionysius the Areopagite, "Cusanus" consistently leads all knowledge back to its inescapable origins in unknowing. All genuine knowledge can only be from God, who is infinite and therefore unknowable. Yet the infinite bears no proportion to the finite: the latter therefore can afford no knowledge of the former. And since knowledge in its deepest sources must be based on God, it cannot but be an unknowing. Book 1 of Cusanus's treatise on learned ignorance ends in the aporias and impossibilities not only of knowing but even of the naming of God (Chapters 22–24). Book 2, however, considers God as the "maximum" contracted into the form of the universe, while Book 3 considers God's further contraction into Jesus Christ. Of these contracted forms there is a kind of knowledge, even though, more deeply considered, in relation to the absolute maximum it still remains a form of ignorance.

The huge tradition of speculation on this head both before and after Cusanus can be traced from (and aligns itself with) the Socratic wisdom which lay precisely in Socrates's knowing that he did *not* know—in his declaring that he knew nothing. Socratic ignorance serves as the obligatory point of departure for vast and varied currents comprising not only forms of skeptical and critical philosophy, but also several different types of mysticism that flourished in antiquity and the Middle Ages. To the speculative apophatic ignorance of Neaplatonists, we must add the more affective styles of mysticism in which apophasis opens a vast field for knowing-by-not-knowing in various registers of feeling that draw on the so-called "spiritual senses." This new mysticism flourishes in the fourteenth century with *The Cloud of Unknowing* and with the female mysticism of the beguines and particularly of Marguerite Porete (1250–1310). It is given programmatically apophatic accents especially by Dante in his *Paradiso*. Further techniques of exploiting emotional resources of ignorance matured through the Baroque and Romantic periods. Along the more speculative line of this historical trajectory are situated modern philosophical monuments of apophatic thought on the limits of language, including figures such as Ludwig Wittgenstein, Simone Weil, Martin Heidegger, Franz Rosenzweig, and Emmanuel Levinas, whose ethical reflection focuses on traumatic and silent "Saying" as a mode of relating wordlessly to the unknowable alterity of the Other.

For all of these epoch-making authors, an insuperable but self-conscious ignorance is in crucial ways more important and fundamental than any positive kind of knowing, for it remains in touch with the grounds of knowing *and un*knowing in the infinite and incomprehensible abyss of human understanding and intellect. Expressions of this predicament can easily be broadened to imaginative literature by including writers such as Friedrich Hölderlin, Emily Dickinson, Hugo von Hofmannstahl (specifically his "Letter of Lord Chandos"), Rainer Maria Rilke, Franz Kafka, and Samuel Beckett. Such expressions can be extended even further to the arts generally so as to include radical modern aesthetic encounters with the inexpressible, for example, in Abstract Expressionism (Barnett Newman, Ad Reinhart) or in the music and music theory of Arthur Schoenberg, John Cage, and Vladimir Jankélévitch, with their fixation on Nothing, silence, and "l'indicible."

Once this continuity from the ancient Neoplatonic matrices to the modern predicament expressed still today by avant-garde artists is discerned, it becomes possible, even if inevitably something of a provocation, to form a kind of canon of apophatic thinkers by bringing into comparison some of the most enduringly significant attempts within Western culture to probe the limits of language—and perhaps to exceed them. All tend to delineate regions of inviolable silence and therefore of ignorance, at least so far as articulated, rational knowledge is concerned. A certain core of such discourses is made up of classic expressions of "negative theology," which, most simply, is the denial of all descriptions and attributes as predicated of God. For negative theologies, it is possible to say only what God *is not*. These attempts to devise and, at the same time, to disqualify ways of talking about God as an ultimate reality, or rather ultra-reality, beyond the reach of language, can be juxtaposed to and in any case interpenetrate with philosophical meditations that exhibit infirmities endemic to language in its endeavor to comprehend and express the ultimately real. Such philosophical reflections expose necessary failures of Logos that leave it gaping open towards what it cannot say. Likewise, poetry and poetics and aesthetics of the ineffable drive language into impasses, pressing its expressive powers to their furthest limits—and sometimes even beyond those limits.

All of these discourses are in various ways languages for what cannot be said—languages that cancel, interrupt, or undo discourse, languages that operate, paradoxically, by annulling or *un*saying themselves.[1] They manage to intimate or enact, by stumbling, stuttering, and becoming dumb—sometimes with uncanny eloquence—what they cannot as such say. The traditional term for this sort of self-negating discourse—as well as for the condition of no more discourse at all, upon which it converges—is "apophasis." In fact, total privation of discourse may be considered the pure, proper meaning of the term, but in practice this state is approachable only through some deficient mode of discourse that attenuates and takes itself back or cancels itself out. Thus apophasis can actually be apprehended only in discourse (we must remember that painting and music, too, are their own kind of "discourse"), but in discourse only insofar as it negates itself and tends to disappear as discourse—sometimes being sublated into non-verbal media. The many different sorts of discourses that do this may be considered together generically as "apophatic discourse."

The exigency of bringing out what all discourse leaves unsaid—what, nevertheless, by its very elusiveness, teases or disturbs speech, and tends therefore systematically to be covered over or suppressed, so as to be rendered almost completely imperceptible—features conspicuously and more or less consciously in this loosely-defined lineage of writers (in various media) stretching across the entire history of Western intellectual tradition. All produce distinctive languages which, in various ways, withdraw and efface themselves. On this basis, it is possible to define attempts to deal with the unsayable as a sort of cross-disciplinary genre spanning a great variety of periods and regions even just within Western culture, though of course this, like all genre definitions, and perhaps more so than others, can be no more than heuristic.

Whereas Plato and Aristotle use "apophasis" simply to mean a negative proposition, a denial, Neoplatonists, followed by monotheistic writers, extend the term to mean the negation of speech vis-à-vis what exceeds all possibilities of expression whatsoever: for them, apophatic discourses consist in words that negate themselves in order to evoke what is beyond words and indeed beyond the limits of language altogether. The word "apophasis" thus eventually takes on a stronger sense of negation, not just of the content of specific propositions, but of language and expression per se. Since ancient times, therefore, and again as revived in contemporary discourse, the tag "apophasis," beyond signifying logical negation, carries also a more potent, theological sense of negation informed ultimately by the divine transcendence: it indicates an utter incapacity of language to grasp what infinitely transcends it, a predicament of being surpassed irremediably by what it cannot say. "Apophasis" in its further etymological meaning, moreover, as "away from speech" or "saying *away*" (*apo*, "from" or "away from") points in the direction of *un*saying and ultimately of silence as virtualities of language that tend to underlie and subvert any discursively articulable meaning.

The ultimate apophatic expression is silence—a silence that is stretched tensely toward . . . what cannot be said. Only this negation of saying by silence "says" . . . what cannot be said. Nevertheless, apophasis constitutes a paradoxically rich and various genre of discourse. The methods and modes of silence are legion, and numerous new forms of expression of it burst forth in every new period of cultural history. The irrepressible impulse to speak essential silence is a constant (or close to it) of human experience confronted ever anew with what surpasses saying. While what is experienced remains inaccessible to speech, there is no limit to what can be said about—or rather from within and as a testimonial to—this experience which cannot be described except as experience of . . . what cannot be said.

For apophatic thinking, before and behind anything that language is saying, there is something that it is not saying and perhaps cannot say, something that nevertheless bears decisively on any possibilities whatsoever of saying and of making sense. In fact, only linguistically is this "beyond" of language discernible at all. Language must unsay or annul itself in order to let this unsayable something, which is nothing, n*o thing* at any rate, somehow register in its very evasion of all attempts to say it. Only the *un*saying of language can say . . . what cannot be said. This predicament is commonly encountered at the limits of linguistic expression, but certain interpretations emphasize, or at least illuminate, these limits as operative in the form of enabling conditions throughout the whole range of linguistic expression. In this way, the encounter with apophasis becomes pervasive and ineluctable. We begin to perceive the ubiquitous presence of the unsayable in all our saying. All that is said, at least indirectly and implicitly, testifies to something else that is not said and perhaps *cannot* be said.

This may sometimes seem to be an exercise in emptiness and futility, but some of the newer angles of approach to the topic of apophasis are bringing out its incarnate and excessively concrete nature, which is just as essential as the Neoplatonic, Plotinian path of abstraction, the so-called *via remotionis*. Much attention is being turned today towards apophatic bodies (Boesel and Keller 2010) and to apophatic erotics (Marion 2003), as well as to apophatic aesthetics (Vega 2005). Excess is as crucial a mode as privation in communicating what escapes speech. The flesh was recognized as being in excess of logical comprehension already in ancient patristic tradition by Tertullian (160-230) in *De carne Christi*, as well as by Athanasius and Augustine. This is the orientation of the tradition in Pseudo-Dionysius, for instance, as expounded by Turner (1995), and of apophasis in the Kabbalah as read especially by Wolfson (2005). It is also at the basis of a new approach to phenomenology in the wake of the so-called "theological turn" among especially French thinkers such as Michel Henry Jean-Luc Marion, and Jean-Louis Chrétien (Janicaud 2000). This line of investigation is now being developed vigorously in relation to Christian theological tradition from patristics through medieval Scholasticism by Emmanuel Falque (2008), among others.

The discovery of unsayability and of its correlative languages of "unsaying"—leading to appreciation of gaps, glitches, and impasses as constitutive of the sense of texts—is part and parcel of a major intellectual revolution that has been underway now for several decades and, in fact, if only somewhat more diffusely, for at least a century.[2] Not only modern but especially postmodern writers have been prolific in this genre. French writers, including Georges Bataille, Emmanuel Levinas, Jacques Derrida, and Edmond Jabès Maurice Merleau-Ponty and Michel Foucault (1963 and 1966), have been particularly fertile in exploring apophatic modes.[3] Perhaps most conspicuously, Jacques Lacan's linguistic formulations constantly strain beyond their own words towards something that withdraws from articulation, as Lacan himself is well aware: "There is nowhere any last word unless in the sense in which *word* is *not a word* . . . . Meaning indicates the direction in which it fails."[4] Also powerfully expressing these currents in French thought and criticism are Luce Irigaray, Hélène Cixous, and Julia Kristeva, especially in her analysis of the unspeakably abject in *Pouvoirs de l'horreur*.

Feminist discourse has been exceptionally fecund in reflection about silence and its untold significances. Early on, these reflections tended to revolve around the silencing of female voices. Such discussions focused sharply on class, color, and sex as motives for the silencing of women writers. Tillie Olsen's *Silences*, for example, stated emphatically that it was not about the natural silences intrinsic to the creative process but rather about "the unnatural thwarting of what struggles to come into being, but cannot" (1978, 6). There was frequently a determined effort to divorce enforced silences of women from every sort of empty, abstract, metaphysical, Romantic ineffable. Recently, however, there has been growing interest among feminists in silence as more than just negative and a lack due to externally imposed interdictions. Apophasis is being discovered in its multivalent potency as gendered in complex ways. Feminine discourse has become sensitive and attentive not only to the silencing of female voices but also to the subversive strategies that cultivate and exploit silence.[5] Silence plays an ambiguous role as an imposed restriction but also an elected source of unlimited power, for example, in the creative silences of a poet like Emily Dickinson. There has of late been a plethora of creative works by and on women and the paradoxical poverty/power of their silences. M. Nourbese Philip, *Looking for Livingstone: An Odyssey of Silence* and Monica Ochtrup, *What I Cannot Say / I Will Say* have begun turning this predicament into the empowering premise of a highly potent new poetry.[6]

Although apophatic tradition is not necessarily felt as their own tradition and is rarely cited, except for Wittgenstein, it is doubtful that this literature would be possible in the state in which we find it without apophasis as an element diffusely present in postmodern culture. Clearly this literature is propelled by a sense of the crisis of language. Its denial and even defiance of *Logos*, interpreted, at least implicitly, as patriarchal authority par excellence, cannot help but resonate, whether deliberately so or not, with the apophatic in its millenary manifestations. In theology itself, particular attention is now being devoted to how women's voices in the pulpit can find the most effective registers for letting silence speak.[7]

Social sciences, too, are producing a daunting bibliography on the subject of silence. The topic is approached out of the most varied disciplines such as psychology, linguistics and pragmatics, anthropology and ethnography, discourse and narrative analysis, systems and communications theory focusing on all manner of media, as well as on "natural" human conversation and interaction.[8] While not usually interrogating the apophatic directly in its fundamental motivations, these discourses nevertheless reflect upon and illuminate it. They belong to the explosion of new, broadly or tendentially apophatic approaches in every sector throughout contemporary culture.

As a newly emerging logic, or rather a/logic, of language in the humanities, this new (though also very old) quasi-epistemic paradigm for criticism, as well as for language-based disciplines and practices in general, can help us today, as late-modern readers, learn to read in hitherto unsuspectedly limber and sensitive ways. It can sharpen our critical awareness of what we are already doing even without fully understanding how and why. For we have become increasingly attuned to unsaying and the unsayable within discourse covertly undoing its own purported purposes and programs. To this extent, we are reading differently than in the past, yet this very difference has been bequeathed by the past, if we care to know about it, and we can learn to know our own minds and their mysterious ways much better if we do. For what present generations are experiencing characterizes also a recurrent, cyclical movement of culture, spirit, and intellect from time immemorial. Most immediately and directly, certain modern and contemporary models have shaped our sensibility for deciphering in discourse these limits of language and this indication of what it cannot say.

Apophasis is not itself, after all, any traditional genre or mode or discipline. It has by its elusive nature remained hitherto marginal to all systematic rhetorics of the human sciences. Only the obsessions of our contemporary culture have produced the need—until quite recently mostly latent—to delineate apophasis as a distinct corpus of literature. Indeed apophasis has become—and is still becoming—a major topic in all the disciplines of the humanities, with philosophy, religion, literature, and criticism of various arts in the lead. The impressive range of contemporary thinkers, authors, and artists who distinguish themselves as drawing from and transforming traditional apophatic currents in remarkable new ways renders imperative the attempt to understand apophasis as some kind of genre writings drawn from widely divergent cultural and historical contexts and from different disciplines, but all bearing fundamentally upon, and originating in, the experience of the unsayable, of what resists every effort of speech to articulate it.

I endeavor to identify some seminal texts and to sketch some historical parameters, and so to give a certain contour to a topic which all too easily can become nebulous and diffuse for lack of any general map of the field such as *On What Cannot Be Said* (Franke 2007) attempts to provide. Such an attempt is made imperative by the overwhelming perennial interest of this topic and the still pioneering status of attempts to try and fathom its length, breadth, and depth. Until recently, we have had only the vaguest idea of how these various discourses of apophasis fit together and little conception of the historical parabola of this problematic as a whole, even just in the West. And of course Eastern forms of apophasis, such as the Advaita Vedanta, the Madhyamaka school of Mahayana Buddhism, Zen, Taoism, etc., afford perhaps an even vaster and richer territory to be explored for the same type of treasure. We are now in the throes of an explosive proliferation of studies in all areas based on variously apophatic paradigms of production and interpretation of texts. Although we may fail to realize it, due to the widely disparate provenance of discussions of what cannot be said, the most evasive of all topics, its ineluctable and ubiquitous presence at the heart of our creative and critical endeavors across disciplines is breaking ever more conspicuously into evidence.

Just as language is fundamental to all possibilities of experience, therewith also the limits of language, where the unsayable is encountered, are implicit in and impinge upon every utterance in its very possibility of being uttered. I privilege discourses that concentrate on the unsayable and generate discourse deliberately out of this experience rather than simply those discourses (really all discourses) that in effect are touched and structured by what cannot be said. There is in each instance of programmatically apophatic discourse some more or less explicit meditation on impasses to articulation as the generative source of the discourse itself.

Great writers or artists, in whatever genre or discipline or form, are distinguished in that at some point they push to the limits the possibilities of expression in their respective linguistic means or medium. However, an apophatic border or lining can be discerned, even if it is not rendered explicit, in perhaps any significant discourse, in any expressive language whatever. If, indeed, all discourses, at least covertly, pivot on what they cannot say, in the end no author could be absolutely excluded from such a genre. One can always find an unexpressed negation, a recursive self-questioning, lurking in every expressed affirmation, so whether any given discourse is adjudged apophatic or not depends on how it is read. Consequently, the question becomes one of which discourses most directly and provocatively avow, or illuminate, this inescapable predicament of speech and script. Widely divergent discourses all approach, from various angles, what cannot be said and demand to be viewed in a common focus and as reflecting on one another in revealing ways. Bringing them together out of their different disciplinary and cultural backgrounds is part of a design to catalyze open dialogue on "what cannot be said" lurking as an ineluctable provocation perhaps in all discourses.

As a discursive mode, apophasis arises in the face of what cannot be said. It bespeaks an experience of being left speechless. There are no words for what is experienced in this form of experience, no possibility of a positive description of it. One falls back on saying what it is not, since whatever *can* be said is *not* it. By their very failure, conspicuously faltering and foundering attempts at saying can hint at what they inevitably fail to express, at what cannot be said at all. In this way, the unsayable and discourse about it turn out to be inseparable. Indeed, according to at least one view, what cannot be said can *only* (not) be said: apart from this failure, it would be altogether nought (Certeau 1973, 153). Certainly, it has no objective content or definition, for that *could* be said. Nevertheless, it can be discerned in perhaps all that is said as what *un*says saying, as what troubles or discomfits discourse.

By reading for what cannot be said, we look past expressions themselves to their limits and even beyond, and thereby cull intimations of what they do not and cannot express. The unsayable is inaccessible to direct apprehension, but it can be read in everything that *is* said, if reading means a sort of interpretive engagement that coaxes the text to betray secrets it cannot as such say. The unsayable shows up in texts as their limit of opacity. Everything said, however clear and transparent, is said *from* somewhere which is indirectly intimated, yet cannot itself be fully divulged or exhaustively illuminated in and by its own saying. It necessarily remains opaque and off-limits. Rather than discarding this as the inevitable part of non-intelligibility that is best neglected in whatever *is* said, certain new methods of reading have been bent upon recognizing this unsayable instance within discourse as essential to the meaning of everything that is said. I have aimed here to suggest how such methods are illuminated by apophatic tradition reaching all the way back to its ancient theological matrices, for they are in an at least indirect line of descent from these sources.

Claims concerning the inadequacy of language to describe experience are, of course, encountered in all different kinds of discourse, literary, religious, artistic, and philosophical alike. But the mode of apophasis need be invoked only where precisely this struggle with language in the encounter with what it cannot say demonstrably engenders the experience in question. The experience of apophasis, as an experience of not being able to say, is quintessentially linguistic: the experience itself is intrinsically an experience of the failure of language. It is not an experience that is otherwise given and secured and perhaps even approximately conveyed—with provisos regarding the accuracy of the description and apologies for the results actually achieved. In apophasis, strictly construed, unsayability or the failure of language is itself the basic experience—and indeed the only one that admits of description or objectification at all.

And yet the experience in question is *not* fundamentally experience *of* language or of any other determinate object, for this *could* be adequately expressed. The experiencing subject is affected by "something" beyond all that it can objectively comprehend, something engendering affects that it cannot account for nor even be sure are its own.[9] This entails a sort of belief in, or an openness to, something—that is, to something *or other* that is surely no *thing*—that cannot be said and that refuses itself to every desire for articulation. There is not even any "what" to believe in, but there is passion—for nothing, perhaps, certainly for nothing that can be said: and yet that passion itself is not just nothing.[10] The apophatic allows for belief before any determinate belief, passion before any object of passion can be individuated: all definitions are only relative, approximate delimitations of what is not as such any object that can be defined. Apophatic thought thus relativizes every verbal-conceptual formulation and orients us towards the unformulated non-concept or no-word that is always already believed in with in(de)finite passion in every defined or finite confession of belief.

Thus apophaticism is not nihilism. Apophatic authors may sometimes embrace an agnosticism as to whether language has any meaning at all, but their apophaticism is not nihilistic, if that means somehow *concluding* all under Nothing rather than making the admission of the inadequacy of all our names and saying an overture opening towards . . . what cannot be said. This is typically an opening towards immeasurably *more* (and less) than can be said. I generally privilege believers in apophasis as some kind of extra-logical, supra-rational revelation or liberation—though this deliverance may be of the most minimalist, desolate sort. There is, strictly speaking, no saying what the apophatic writer believes in, but there clearly is a passion of belief—or unbelief: indeed, every formulated, *expressed* belief must be *dis*believed and abjured in order to keep the faith in what cannot be said.

Acknowledgment

This essay is adapted from the prefaces to volumes 1 and 2 of Franke (2007) by kind permission of the University of Notre Dame Press.

Notes

1 Budick and Iser (1989) effectively formulated this topic for contemporary criticism.
2 Hass's (2013) intellectual history of Nothing makes the twentieth century the site of the revolution that overthrows the sovereignty of One (1 or I) and opens into an age of Nothing (0), without unilateral hegemony.
3 For madness as a silence within the discourse of rationality, see Foucault (1971) and Bernauer (1987). Other texts are treated by Bernard P. Dauenhauer (1979), 115–126.
4 Lacan 1982, 150. Cited in Sells and Webb (1995), 199. See, further, Wyschogrod et al. (1989).
5 See Kammer (1979), 153–164, as well as essays in Keller and Miller (1994) and Hedges and Fishkin (1994).
6 On these writers, see Miller (1996) and Steiner (1996).
7 See Walter and Durber (1994). Provocative new voices of feminist theologians who are keenly alive to the apophatic include Keller (2007), McFague (2007), and Schüssler Fiorenza (1999). See, further, Johnson (1992).
8 Representatives of a much larger field can be found in Jaworski (1997). Also contributing to these directions of research are Tannen and Saville-Troike (1985), Ciani (1987), and Clair (1998).
9 This is where apophaticism clearly connects with trauma theory. See Caruth (1996).
10 See Salminen and Sjöberg (2012) and, in a more popular vein, Green (2011).

References

Bernauer, James (1987) "The Prisons of Man: An Introduction to Foucault's Negative Theology," *International Philosophical Quarterly* 27/4, 365–80.

Boesel, Chris, and Keller, Catherine (eds) (2010) *Apophatic Bodies: Negative Theology, Incarnation, and Relationality*. New York: Fordham University Press.

Budick, Sanford, and Iser, Wolfgang (eds) (1989) *Languages of the Unsayable: The Play of Negativity in Literature and Literary Theory*. New York: Columbia University Press.

Cage, John (1961) "Lecture on Nothing." In *Silence*. Middletown, CT: Wesleyan University Press.

Caputo, J., and Scanlon, M. J. (eds) (2007) *Transcendence and Beyond: A Postmodern Inquiry*. Bloomington, IN: Indiana University Press.

Caruth, Cathy (1996) *Unclaimed Experience: Trauma, Narrative and History*. Baltimore, MD: The Johns Hopkins University Press.

Certeau, Michel de. (1973) *L'absent de l'histoire*. Mame, Liège.

Ciani, Maria Grazia (ed) (1987) *The Regions of Silence: Studies on the Difficulty of Communicating*. Amsterdam: Brill.

Clair, Robin Patric (1998) Organizing Silence. A World of Possibilities. New York: SUNY Press.

Dauenhauer, Bernard P. (1979) "Merleau-Ponty's Elucidation of Silence," in *Silence: The Phenomenon and its Ontological Significance*. Bloomington, IN: Indiana University Press.

Falque, Emmanuel (2008) *Dieu, la chair et l'autre: d'Irénée à Duns Scot*. Paris: Presses Universitaires de France.

Foucault, Michel (1963) "Le langage à l'infini," *Tel Quel* 15, 44–53.

Foucault, Michel (1963) "Préface à la transgression," *Critique* 195, 751–69.

Foucault, Michel (1966) "La pensée du Dehors" *Critique* 229, 523–46.

Foucault, Michel (1971) *Folie et déraison*. Paris: Plon.

Franke, W. (2007) *On What Cannot Be Said: Apophatic Discourses in Philosophy, Religion, Literature, and the Arts* (2 vols: Volume 1: Classical Formulations; Volume 2: Modern and Contemporary Transformations). Edited with Theoretical and Critical Essays by William Franke. Notre Dame: University of Notre Dame Press.

Gilbert, Sandra, and Guber, Susan (eds) (1979) *Shakespeare's Sisters: Feminist Essays on Women Poets*. Bloomington, IN: Indiana University Press.

Green, Ronald (2011) *Nothing Matters: A Book about Nothing*. Alresford: John Hunt.

Hass, Andrew W. (2013) *Auden's O: The Loss of One's Sovereignty in the Making of Nothing*. Albany: State University of New York Press.

Hedges, Elaine, and Fishkin, Shelley Fisher (eds) (1994) *Listening to Silences: New Essays in Feminist Criticism*. Oxford: Oxford University Press.

Janicaud, Dominique (2000) *Phenomenology and the "Theological Turn": The French Debate*. New York: Fordham University Press.

Jaworski, Adam (ed) 1997) *Silence: Interdisciplinary Perspectives*, Studies in Anthropological Linguistics 10. Berlin-New York: Mouton de Gruyter.

Johnson, Elizabeth (1992) *She Who Is: The Mystery of God in Feminist Theology*. New York: Crossroad.

Kammer, Jeanne (1979) "The Art of Silence and the Forms of Women's Poetry." In S. Gilbert and S. Guber (eds) *Shakespeare's Sisters: Feminist Essays on Women Poets* (Bloomington, IN: Indiana University Press, pp. 153–64).

Keller, Catherine (2007) "Rumors of Transcendence: The Movement, State, and Sex of 'Beyond.'" In J. Caputo and M. J. Scanlon (eds) *Transcendence and Beyond: A Postmodern Inquiry* (Bloomington, IN: Indiana University Press).

Keller, Lynn, and Miller, Cristanne (eds) (1994) *Feminist Measures: Soundings in Poetry and Theory*. Ann Arbor: University of Michigan Press.

Lacan, Jacques "A love letter" (1982 [1966]). In J. Mitchell and J. Rose (eds) *Feminine Sexuality: Jacques Lacan and the École Freudienne* (New York: Norton).

Marion, Jean-Luc (2003) *Le phénomène érotique*. Paris: Grasset.

McFague, Sallie (2007) "Intimations of Transcendence: Praise and Compassion." In J. Caputo and M. J. Scanlon (eds) *Transcendence and Beyond: A Postmodern Inquiry* (Bloomington, IN: Indiana University Press).

Merleau-Ponty, Maurice (1960) "Le langage indirect et les voix du silence." *Signes*. Paris: Gallimard, pp. 49–104.

Miller, Cristanne (1996) "M. Nourbese Philip and the Poetics/Politics of Silence." In Gudren M. Grabher and Ulrike Jessner (eds) *Semantics of Silence in Linguistics and Literature* (Heidelberg: Winter, pp. 139–160).

Ochtrup, Monica (1986) *What I Cannot Say, I Will Say*. Moorhead, MN: New Rivers Press.

Olsen, Tillie (1978) *Silences*. New York: Dell.

Philip, Marlene Nourbese (1991) *Looking for Livingstone: An Odyssey of Silence*. Toronto: The Mercury Press.

Salminen, Antti, and Sjöberg, Sami (eds) (2012) *Angelaki: Journal of the Theoretical Humanities* 17/3. Special Issue: "Nothing."

Schüssler Fiorenza, Elizabeth (1999) "God the Many-Named: Without Place and Proper Name." In J. Caputo and M. J. Scanlon (eds) *Transcendence and Beyond: A Postmodern Inquiry* (Bloomington, IN: Indiana University Press).

Sells, Michael A., and Webb, Richard E. (1995) "Psychoanlysis and the Mystical Language of 'Unsaying.'" *Theory & Psychology* 5/2, 195–215.

Steiner, Dorothea (1996) "Silence Pretended, Silence Defended: A Look at Monica Ochtrup's Poetry." In Gudren M. Grabher and Ulrike Jessner (eds) *Semantics of Silence in Linguistics and Literature* (Heidelberg: Winter, pp. 309–27).

Tannen, Deborah, and Saville-Troike, Muriel (eds) (1985) *Perspectives on Silence*. Norwood, NJ: Ablex.

Turner, Denys (1995) *The Darkness of God: Negativity in Christian Mysticism*. Cambridge: Cambridge University Press.

Vega, Amador (2005) *Arte y santidad. Cuatro lecciones de estética apofática*. Pamplona: Universidad Pública de Navarra.

Walter, H., and Durber, S. (eds) (1994) *Silence in Heaven: A Book of Women's Preaching*. London: SCM.

Wolfson, Elliot (2005) *Language, Eros, Being: Kabbalistic Hermeneutics and Poetic Imagination*. New York: Fordham University Press.

Wyschogrod, Edith, Crownfield, David, and Raschke, Carl A. (eds) (1989) *Lacan and Theological Discourse*. Albany: SUNY Press.

4
Literary ignorance

Andrew Bennett

Literature confronts us with the question of what it knows and of what kind of knowledge it may be said to yield. What does it mean to say that an author or a work 'knows' something or allows us to know it? Does such a text reveal something about the world that is otherwise unknown? Is it knowledge that we gain in reading a poem or novel, in watching or reading a play? Does the overall sum of human wisdom increase when a poet pens a sonnet or a novelist completes a new work?

Paisley Livingston helpfully summarizes the three major theories of literature's engagement with knowledge in philosophical aesthetics. In the first place, there are what Livingston terms 'condemnations of literature as a source of irrationality for author and audience alike' (Livingston 2010: 497). The tradition of linking literature with irrationality – and thereby with authorial ignorance in particular – extends at least as far back as Plato in the fourth century BC, who argues that to be truly inspired the poet will be intoxicated, beside him- or herself, that poets are misleading, unreliable, mistaken, and therefore that poetry involves the negation rather than the generation of knowledge. Plato insists on the ignorance of poets, thereby setting up poetry in the Western tradition as in conflict with truth, with knowledge, and indeed with post-Socratic philosophy itself. In *Meno*, Plato explains that like soothsayers and prophets, poets 'have no knowledge of what they are saying' (*Meno* 99d), while in the *Apology* he has Socrates – the competitively agnoiological philosopher, the philosopher who prides himself on his knowledge of what he does not know – joke that he has visited the poets in order to 'catch myself being more ignorant than they'. But he can't. When he asks the poets about the meaning of their poems, he finds that they cannot tell him. 'I soon realised that poets do not compose their poems with knowledge, but by some inborn talent and by inspiration, like seers and prophets who also say many fine things without any understanding of what they say', Socrates explains (*Apology* 22b-c). If poets know anything, in other words, it is only by way of so-called 'implicit' or 'tacit' knowledge. For Plato in *Ion*, the poet is 'an airy thing, winged and holy, and he is not able to make poetry until he becomes inspired and goes out of his mind and his intellect is no longer in him' (*Ion* 534 a-b). Anyone coming to the 'gates of poetry' under the impression that they can compose 'without the Muses' madness' is mistaken, Plato declares in *Phaedrus* (245a). As this suggests, however, poetic ignorance is not just a question of cognitive dysfunction: the irrationality of the poet also has to do with what we might call *constructive ignorance*. The poet's cognitive and epistemic dysfunction is itself functional, related as it is to inspiration and to creative frenzy. It produces something, even if that something is nothing more than a poem.

The second model of the relationship between literature and knowledge in Livingston's analysis concerns the idea that knowledge is 'neither hindered nor advanced' by literature, since the two 'move on separate tracks' (Livingston 2010: 497). In other words, we can say that to ask about the knowledge that a poem or play produces is to ask the wrong question. Once again, it is Plato who expresses the point most clearly. In the *Republic*, for example, the idea is presented as a somewhat milder version of his condemnation of poets for their irrationality. For Plato, poets are cognitively or epistemically insouciant: they have 'neither knowledge nor right opinion' on the question of whether their poems are 'fine or bad' (*Republic* X 602a), and their poems produce, as music does, 'a certain harmoniousness' rather than knowledge (VII 522a). This tradition of a kind of uncritical or even defensive epistemological indifference in poetry becomes mainstream in the English tradition by the late sixteenth century, when Sir Philip Sidney influentially contends Plato's stronger claim that poets are liars by declaring that the poet is 'of all writers under the sun' the 'least liar' because he 'nothing affirms and therefore never lieth' (Sidney 2002: 103). The canonical defence of poetry from the late-sixteenth century onwards, in other words, involves the assertion that if the poet is not making any kind of epistemological claim then he cannot be said to be peddling untruths: the poet neither adds to nor detracts from the sum of human knowledge, neither informs the reader nor deceives her.

The third category in Livingston's account presents a fundamental challenge to the first two by arguing that the poet does indeed affirm something (and may thereby be said to produce or articulate knowledge), and that the kinds of statement that literary works make are not in fact irrational or misleading but are instead epistemically coherent and defensible (Livingston 2010: 497). The relatively modest version of this claim is expressed by Noël Carroll as the idea that literature, like the other arts, can be of 'cognitive or epistemic value because it can deliver knowledge' (Carroll 2007: 39). The claim became particularly prominent in the Romantic period, when in what might be seen as a counter-reaction to the cultural and political marginalization of poetry, increasingly extravagant claims were made for its epistemic power. In the 1802 Preface to the *Lyrical Ballads*, for example, William Wordsworth declares that poetry is 'the breath and finer spirit of all knowledge', that the poet 'binds together by passion and knowledge the vast empire of human society', and that poetry is 'the first and last of all knowledge' (Wordsworth 1992: 752–3). In his 1821 *Defence of Poetry*, Percy Bysshe Shelley proposes, even more tendentiously, that poetry is 'at once the centre and circumference of knowledge', that it 'comprehends all science', and that it is 'that to which all science must be referred' (Shelley 1977: 503).

Rather than attempting to adjudicate between these three positions, or indeed to provide an alternative thinking of the relationship between literature and knowledge, my aim in this essay is to point to the importance of the tradition in which literature is specifically constituted in relation to the other of knowledge, to questions of unknowing – to what James Ferrier, the nineteenth-century Scottish philosopher, who also coined the term 'epistemology', named 'agnoiology', epistemology's far less successful counterpart (Ferrier 2001). I want to highlight the significance of the tradition of literary agnoiology and to investigate the ways in which ignorance may be understood to be aroused, enacted, and explored in literature. According to this model, the literary is in principle neither knowledge-yielding nor knowledge-denying, but instead effectively avoids – and self-consciously avoids – or stands to the side of the *question* of knowledge. This alternative approach recognizes that literature is centrally concerned with knowing ignorance and, crucially, with remaining *in* ignorance, in valuing and exploring the condition or the experience of not knowing. It is not a question of the unknown as 'beneath, behind or secreted within the work', as the cultural theorist Gary Peters puts it, but instead a question of the unknown *as* the work, of an 'incomprehensibility' that is 'the very *articulation* of the work itself' (Peters 2013: 110). Although Livingston's second model – the contention according to which knowledge is 'neither hindered nor advanced' by literature – is closest to the tradition that I want to explore, my point is, I think, rather different. I want to suggest that despite the protestations to the contrary – made by Wordsworth, Shelley and others – *not knowing*, the absence of knowledge, or at least the confirmation of doubt, of uncertainty, is an important and often overlooked strain in literary theory and practice – even, indeed, and despite appearances, in the practice as well as the poetics of Wordsworth and Shelley themselves, not least in their emphasis on invention, originality, and imagination.[1] To say that knowledge is 'neither hindered nor advanced' by literature suggests that literature has no stake and no interest in knowledge. But my point is, rather, that literature embraces, explores, celebrates the condition by which we are all beset, that it confronts us with the human condition of not knowing.

There are, in fact, at least three distinct spheres in which the condition of literary ignorance may be understood to operate: authorship (the author as, at some level, not knowing what it is that he or she is doing); reading (the reader as not only beginning but as remaining in a state of ignorance); and the text itself, both thematically and with respect to more formal or technical questions of narrative perspective in particular (the narrator revealed as not fully in control, conceptually or epistemically, of the events that she records). The case of the narrator is perhaps the most striking because it is the most clearly paradoxical. The narrator is, in principle, the one who knows or, to appropriate Jacques Lacan's description of the psychoanalyst, the one who is *supposed* to know (Lacan 1981: 230–43). From a certain perspective, the narrator can in principle be nothing other than the subject who imparts knowledge, who knows something that the interlocutor or reader does not know and whose sole task is to communicate what she knows. The idea is conveyed by the word 'narrate' itself: via Latin *narrare*, with its sense of 'relating', 'telling', 'explaining', the word stems from *gnarus*, 'knowing' (from the ancient Greek γνω-, 'to know'). There is a certain logic here, of course: you can tell someone something because you know it and the other person doesn't. This may be said to be the primary condition of 'narratability', in fact: I know something that you do not. In principle, there is no other reason for me to tell you what I am telling you. And yet as far as literature is concerned, narrators can and do talk about and narrate what they don't know. From Walton in Mary Shelley's *Frankenstein*, to Lockwood and Nelly Dean in Emily Brontë's *Wuthering Heights*, to Pip in Charles Dickens's *Great Expectations*, to the governess in Henry James's *The Turn of the Screw*, to Marlow in Joseph Conrad's *Heart of Darkness* and *Lord Jim*, to Raymond Chandler's Marlowe in *The Big Sleep* and other novels, to Nathan Zuckerman in Philip Roth's novels, to the collective narrators in Jeffrey Eugenides's *The Virgin Suicides*, to Stevens in Ishiguro's *Remains of the Day*, Banks in his *When We Were Orphans*, and Kathy H. in *Never Let Me Go* (just to name a few of the more notable examples), narrators turn out to be individuals who, to a greater or lesser degree, do not really or fully or reliably or adequately know or understand the story that they tell. And this is not a marginal concern and not just an arbitrary or contingent dynamic: narrators, I want to suggest, are constitutively ignorant. Their ignorance is fundamental to the operation of the literary work. Nor is it only named and personified or characterized first-person narrators that are epistemically limited. Although it often operates in more subtle ways, even the epitome of absolute epistemic authority, the nineteenth-century 'omniscient' narrator, is ultimately and necessarily limited, conceptually and cognitively regulated: her so-called 'omniscience' is itself an ingenious fiction since it too is strictly confined by the implicit rules of the language game of realism. The perspective of the omniscient narrator is defined by what she does not know as well as by what she does. George Eliot, that most knowing, most psychologically acute, insightful, not to say intrusive, of Victorian authorial personas, understands this limitation and self-consciously refers to it, for example, at the climactic moment of *Middlemarch* when Dorothea and Will finally kiss, 750 pages into a novel in which they were destined to do so all along: 'It was never known which lips were the first to move towards the other lips', we are told (Eliot 1997: 761). Much is packed into the sentence, including of course a decorous Victorian veiling of sexual desire and no doubt a sly allusion to conventions of masculine and feminine roles. But the sentence also points to a key thematic and narrative concern in nineteenth-century fiction: our knowledge of other minds – knowing what is in them, of course, but also just knowing that they are there, that other minds as such exist. There are limits, even for George Eliot's omniscient narrators, to what can be known, particularly about other people. And the point can be discerned in what is perhaps the key invention of nineteenth-century realist fiction, the technique of free indirect discourse, in which the third-person narrator silently adopts or impersonates the consciousness and perspective of her characters, thereby placing strict epistemic limits on the work via questions of perspective, of focalization, and even of the text's linguistic resources. The radicalization of free indirect discourse and interior monologue in writers like James Joyce, Virginia Woolf and Katherine Mansfield in the early-twentieth century involves even starker restrictions: in *Dubliners*, *A Portrait of the Artist as Young Man*, and *Ulysses*, for example, Joyce's strategy of what he calls 'scrupulous meanness' (Joyce 1966: 134) variously restricts the knowledge available to an impersonated or ventriloquized evocation of the viewpoint of individual characters – characters whose primary concern in many cases is the interpretation and understanding of the intractable mystery of other people's minds. I want to suggest, then, that it is precisely in the interstices of stories, in those blanks that narrators foreground but cannot narrate and in those elisions and obscurities that characters experience, that stories exist, that they live and thrive. It is there that one looks for the meaning of a tale, for its significance, and even for its affective force, just in those epistemic or hermeneutic lacunae. It is not by chance that narrators are structurally limited in their knowledge, nor that they repeatedly affirm their own epistemic limitations. Rather, not knowing is a question or impulse that is pervasive in and central to narrative fiction.

But I also want to argue that narratorial ignorance is not just a quirk of narration, that it is constitutive of the wider question of literature itself. The limitation on what the narrator knows itself plays out the ignorance, doubt, uncertainty, and conceptual or narrative hesitation that *characterizes* the literary. This is what, in an 1817 letter, the poet John Keats calls 'Negative Capability', the condition that he wonderfully glosses as the capacity for remaining in 'uncertainties, Mysteries, doubts, without any irritable reaching after fact & reason' (Keats 1958: 1. 193). With regard to the question of whether literary texts can yield propositional knowledge, the Keatsian theorist is likely to agree with Peter Lamarque that the knowledge yielded is, from a certain perspective, trivial or beside the point (Lamarque 2007). You might learn about whales and about whaling by reading *Moby Dick*, but that is not why you read Melville's novel. Woe betide the reader that tries to use the novel as his sole guide to whaling or, by the same token, tries to use Hemingway's *The Old Man and the Sea* as a handbook on sea-fishing. Similarly, regardless of Joyce's assertion that he wanted to 'give a picture of Dublin so complete that if the city one day suddenly disappeared from the earth it could be reconstructed out of my book' (Budgen 1960: 67–8) the tourist that attempts to use *Ulysses* as a guidebook to Dublin is likely to become seriously befuddled. And the historian that takes *Hamlet* as a reliable documentary source-text on the Danish medieval court will not only have his scholarship questioned but is also likely thereby to overlook what is so much more important in Shakespeare's famous play: its linguistic, thematic and dramatic richness and ingenuity.

A crucial dimension of this question has to do with the ancient assertion of authorial ignorance. The novelist Donald Barthelme expresses the point directly when he remarks, in a 1987 essay on 'Not-Knowing', that the writer is the person who 'embarking upon a task, does not know what to do' since 'without the possibility of having the mind move in unanticipated directions, there would be no invention' (Barthelme 1997: 11–12). In *Glas*, one of his more profoundly and unsettlingly literary performances, Jacques Derrida puts a slightly different spin on the problem when he comments that 'you can take interest in what I am doing here only insofar as you would be right to believe that – *somewhere* – I do not know what I am doing' (Derrida 1986: 64R). Barthelme and Derrida point to something intrinsic in literature even if it only operates in the margins of philosophical discourse: we take an interest in a poem or novel or play just to the extent that we can conceive the author – like the author's avatar, the narrator – as not knowing, as not quite knowing, *somewhere* or *at some level*, what it is that he or she is telling us. This, I think, is an important element in what we read literature *for*: for an engagement in what Emily Dickinson calls an 'Element of Blank', in a certain obscurity, in nescience, in moments of sublime obliviousness or epistemic insouciance or indifference. But literary ignorance is not simply thematic or narratological or authorial: it is not just a question of authors and narrators expressing doubt or uncertainty, nor simply a question of understanding literature as the space in which the experience of not knowing is developed and explored. Literary ignorance is also a question of reading, as Maurice Blanchot suggests in *The Space of Literature* when he declares that what most 'threatens' reading is the person who thinks that he or she 'knows in general how to read'. For Blanchot, it is a reader's 'stubborn insistence upon remaining himself in the face of what he reads' that gets in the way (Blanchot 1982: 198). As Blanchot argues, reading a unique, singular or truly inventive work 'demands more ignorance than knowledge'; it requires 'knowledge endowed with an immense ignorance'. One of the key attributes of a good reader, for Blanchot, is 'forgetfulness' (198, 192).

A poem like Emily Dickinson's 'Pain – has an Element of Blank'[2] might help to draw out some of these points. The poem deals with an experience – the experience of pain – that goes beyond language, conception, epistemic definition or cognition:

> Pain – has an Element of Blank –
> It cannot recollect
> When it begun – or if there were
> A time when it was not –
> It has no Future – but itself –
> Its Infinite contain
> Its Past – enlightened to perceive
> New Periods – of Pain.
>
> *(Dickinson 1960: 650–51)*

The poem hesitates over the distinction between enlightenment, on the one hand, and an 'element' of epistemic blankness, on the other, a hesitation that might in fact be said more generally to characterize literary works. Thematically, we can say that Dickinson communicates the idea that for someone in pain there is no sense of time. There is no before or after for the body in pain: the world collapses into imminent corporeal experience, into the immediacy of unwanted bodily sensation. But what is more pertinent to the poem as a poem, to what we might think of as the poem's 'literariness', is the fact that it moves conceptually from pain (its first word) to pain (its last), and that it references pain unremittingly in the words 'it' and 'its: 'It cannot recollect', 'When it begun', 'when it was not', 'It has no Future', 'Its Infinite contain', 'Its Past'. Every line of the poem after its first and before its last (both of which explicitly name pain), refers to pain by the pronoun it/its. In a sense, the poem stutters on the word, says nothing else: 'Pain . . . It . . . it . . . it . . . It . . . Its . . . It . . . pain'. The only thing the poem says *about* pain is that it exists and that the experience of pain encompasses all experience, that there is no temporality within pain, no past or future outside of it, and that there is no world without pain for the subject that is in it. This, we might concede, is precisely what 'in' means in the phrase 'I am in pain'. But it is not just a question of the poem 'saying' this: what is important is that the poem performs it. There is a sense in which the poem moves claustrophobically from pain to pain and 'says' nothing else, a sense in which it does nothing other than name it. One might notice some of the formal aspects of the poem – the insistent repetition; the irregular line-breaks; the idiosyncratically punctuated, vaguely spasmodic syntax; the grammatical deformations of 'begun', 'were/A time', and 'Infinite contain'; the poem's lexical circularity and the single rhyme ('contain . . . Pain') that ends it – and note that this is really what the poem may be said to be 'about', what it has to tell us, that it tells us something about the way language can be made to work. But the 'Element of Blank' to which Dickinson refers seems to involve the idea that pain is epistemically bereft, beyond knowing. And for this reason we might speculate that it can therefore only be expressed within the agnoiological discourse of literature, can only be expressed in or as a poem even as the poem struggles rhetorically against its own epistemic limits. I want to suggest that the 'Element of Blank' *is* this inability to say anything very much or to know or tell anything that is not already known and a concomitant insistence on the foregrounding of language. It is this blank, and the hesitation between enlightenment and unknowing, that is part of what constitutes the poem's poeticality – as well as part of our experience of reading it. It is this that constitutes it as a poem rather than as, say, a sickness diary or memoir, a medical textbook on pain or a phenomenological treatise that would evoke or analyze the experience.

I want to end with a story about the origin of Western philosophy, because I want to suggest that literature may be seen as the space in which the scandalous, paradoxical and ultimately Socratic assertion that 'I know that I know nothing' can be put to work, engaged, explored, performed. The part-mythical or fictive, pre-philosophical (pre-Platonic) figure of the agnoiological Socrates wanders the streets of Athens collaring individuals (until finally the authorities lose patience and sentence him to death), in order to argue two things. In the first place, he wants to insist that the people whom he meets do not in fact know what they think they know – what 'truth' is, or how to live, or what they mean when they talk about 'virtue', 'justice' or 'the Good'. Second, Socrates paradoxically insists that the one thing that he does know is that he too does not know. It is not just his interlocutors who do not know what 'truth' is, or how to live, or what they mean when they talk about 'virtue' or 'justice' or 'the Good'. Socrates, who challenges their definitions, cannot reliably and with confidence offer his own. All he can do is assert his own ignorance and thereby convince others of their ignorance, of which they have up until now been blissfully unaware. That is why Socrates asks about virtue, truth, justice and the Good: not because he knows something that others do not but because he does not know what these words mean. But his interlocutors fail to enlighten him and he only enlightens them to the extent that, having spoken to him, they now *know* that they do not know.

So I want to suggest that literature has a distinguished pedigree in its engagement with ignorance, but that despite its centrality the question is often overlooked, forgotten, elided or denied. Like the dissident, subversive figure of the pre-Platonic Socrates, literary discourse has a strange, disconcerting, dangerous, even insurrectionary function: it asserts its own ignorance and upholds the value of not knowing, or of *knowing* at least this one thing – that it does not know. Literature is, after all, the space of imagination, dreams, and fiction, of the inadmissible and the unconscious. Ludwig Wittgenstein proposes that philosophy is a 'battle against the bewitchment of our intelligence by means of language' and that it involves a struggle against the 'fascination' imposed on us by what he calls 'forms of expression' (Wittgenstein 1967: 47[e]; Wittgenstein 1965: 27). Literature, by contrast, may be considered an engagement with that bewitchment, with that fascination: it may even be considered a form of bewitchment or fascination by and in those 'forms of expression', in language. Eileen John argues that philosophy 'pushes its speculation . . . in the direction of what can be known' while, for its part, poetry pushes 'in the sprawling directions of what can be thought' (John 2007: 230). 'Sprawling' is apposite, I think, and we should never underestimate what, in a poem of that name, the Australian poet Les Murray calls 'The Quality of Sprawl'. But we should perhaps add 'said' or 'written' to John's definition because it is just by the way it presses on the limits of language, of expression, that literature questions thought, questions 'what can be known'. Literary language is 'seized by a delirium', as Gilles Deleuze has it (Deleuze 1997: 229); literature is the kind of 'language strange' that John Keats refers to when he describes the love-talk of the mysterious, deadly woman in 'La Belle Dame sans Merci'. Both understood and not understood (the woman's 'language strange' can nevertheless be understood well enough to be rendered into English as 'I love thee true'), literary language 'teases' us 'out of thought', as Keats also puts it, ruefully, of the artwork in 'Ode on A Grecian Urn'. Literature acknowledges that language, in certain forms and in certain uses, is beguiling, bewitching – which means that literature makes you not know, not know what to think, not know what you think you know, and helps you know that you do not know.[3] Literature may finally be understood as cognitively, ethically, politically and epistemically efficacious, even as truth-generating, just in its refusal to offer a respite from doubt and hesitation, in its constitutive resistance to anything that can ultimately be relied on as certainty or wisdom or truth or knowledge.

Notes

1 On Wordsworth, see Bennett (2010: 19–35); more generally on the agnoiological tradition in literary theory and practice, see Bennett (2009). And compare Peter Lamarque's comment on the 'legacy of Plato', in which the defences of poetry by Sidney, Shelley and others have 'repeatedly attempted to assimilate the literary enterprise into something like the philosophical one . . . as if the only value is the value that knowledge gives', but that we need to recognize literary value that is not tied to the question of 'learning' (Lamarque 2007: 21).

2 Reprinted by permission of the publishers and the Trustees of Amherst College from THE POEMS OF EMILY DICKINSON, edited by Thomas H. Johnson, Cambridge, Mass.: The Belknap Press of Harvard University Press, Copyright © 1951, 1955 by the President and Fellows of Harvard College. Copyright © renewed 1979, 1983 by the President and Fellows of Harvard College. Copyright © 1914, 1918, 1919, 1924, 1929, 1930, 1932, 1935, 1937, 1942, by Martha Dickinson Bianchi. Copyright © 1952, 1957, 1958, 1963, 1965, by Mary L. Hampson.

3 See Catherine Z. Elgin's comment that if 'knowing that one does not know' is 'the first step towards knowledge', then 'in dislodging unfounded claims to knowledge, fiction can advance cognition' (Elgin 2007: 52).

References

Barthelme, D. (1997) 'Not-Knowing', in Kim Herzinger (ed.) *Not Knowing: The Essays and Interviews of Donald Barthelme*, New York: Random House.

Bennett, A. (2009) *Ignorance: Literature and Agnoiology*, Manchester: Manchester University Press.

Bennett, A. (2010) 'Wordsworth's Poetic Ignorance', in Alexander Regier and Stefan H. Uhlig (eds) *Wordsworth's Poetic Theory: Knowledge, Language, Experience*, Basingstoke: Palgrave Macmillan.

Blanchot, M. (1982) *The Space of Literature*, Ann Smock (trans.), Lincoln: University of Nebraska Press.

Budgen, F. (1960) *James Joyce and the Making of Ulysses*, Bloomington, IN: Indiana University Press.

Carroll, N. (2007) 'Literary Realism, Recognition, and the Communication of Knowledge', in John Gibson, Wolfgang Huemer, and Luca Pocci (eds) *A Sense of the World: Essays on Fiction, Narrative, and Knowledge*, London: Routledge.

Deleuze, G. (1997) 'Literature and Life', *Critical Inquiry* 23: 225–30.
Derrida, J. (1986) *Glas*, John P. Leavey and Richard Rand (trans.), Lincoln: University of Nebraska Press.
Dickinson, Emily (1960) *The Complete Poems*, Thomas H. Johnson (ed.), Boston, MA: Little, Brown.
Elgin, C. Z. (2007) 'The Laboratory of the Mind', in John Gibson, Wolfgang Huemer, and Luca Pocci (eds), *A Sense of the World: Essays on Fiction, Narrative, and Knowledge*, London: Routledge.
Eliot, G. (1997) *Middlemarch*, Oxford: Oxford University Press.
Ferrier, J. (2001) *Institutes of Metaphysic*, 3rd edn (1875), John Haldane (ed.), Bristol: Thoemes Press.
John, E. (2007) 'Poetry and Cognition', in John Gibson, Wolfgang Huemer, and Luca Pocci (eds), *A Sense of the World: Essays on Fiction, Narrative, and Knowledge*, London: Routledge.
Joyce, J. (1966) *Letters of James Joyce*, vol. 2, Richard Ellmann (ed.), New York: Viking.
Keats, J. (1958) *The Letters of John Keats, 1814–1821*, Hyder Edward Rollins (ed.), 2 vols, Cambridge, MA: Harvard University Press.
Lacan, J. (1981) *The Seminar of Jacques Lacan, Book XI: The Four Fundamental Concepts of Psychoanalysis*, Alan Sheridan (trans.), Jacques Alain-Miller (ed.), New York: Norton.
Lamarque, P. (2007) 'Learning from Literature', in John Gibson, Wolfgang Huemer, and Luca Pocci (eds) *A Sense of the World: Essays on Fiction, Narrative, and Knowledge*, London: Routledge.
Livingston, P. (2010) 'Literature and Knowledge', in Jonathan Dancy, Ernest Sosa, and Matthias Steup (eds) *A Companion to Epistemology*, Oxford: Basil Blackwell.
Murray, L. (1998) 'The Quality of Sprawl', in *Collected Poems*, Manchester: Carcanet.
Peters, G. (2013) 'Ahead of Yes and No: Heidegger on Not Knowing and Art', in Elizabeth Fisher and Rebecca Fortnum (eds) *On Not Knowing: How Artists Think*, London: Black Dog Publishing.
Plato (1997) *The Complete Works*, John M. Cooper (ed.), Indianapolis, IN: Hackett.
Pocci, L. (2007) 'The Return of the Repressed: Caring about Literature and Its Themes', in John Gibson, Wolfgang Huemer, and Luca Pocci (eds) *A Sense of the World: Essays on Fiction, Narrative, and Knowledge*, London: Routledge.
Shelley, P. B. (1977) 'A Defence of Poetry', in Donald H. Reiman and Sharon B. Powers (eds) *Shelley's Poetry and Prose*, New York: Norton.
Sidney, P. (2002) *An Apology for Poetry (or The Defence of Poetry)*, Geoffrey Shepherd (ed.), R. W. Maslen (rev.), Manchester: Manchester University Press.
Wittgenstein, L. (1965) *The Blue and Brown_Books*, New York: Harper Torch Books.
Wittgenstein, L. (1967) *Philosophical Investigations*, G. E. Anscombe (trans.), Oxford: Basil Blackwell.
Wordsworth, W. (1992) *'Lyrical Ballads' and Other Poems, 1797–1800*, James Butler and Karen Green (eds), Ithaca, NY: Cornell University Press.

5

Popper, ignorance, and the emptiness of fallibilism

Shterna Friedman

The starting point of Karl Popper's philosophy of science is epistemological humility: We are ignorant and prone to error. This much may seem trivially true, but Popper (e.g., 1963: Ch. 1)[1] thought that it had too often been neglected. Such neglect, particularly for philosophers of science, is egregious because it is our ignorance of the world that makes science itself necessary. We need science not only because the world is vast and we are not, but because our senses do not infallibly yield the truth about the parts of the world with which we come into contact.

Science is for Popper a middle way between ignorance and knowledge, an alternative to both epistemological pessimism and optimism. The pessimist is impressed with human fallibility and ignorance, as Popper was. But if we thought that it was not just difficult but impossible to gain access to the truth, there would be no point in doing science. On the other hand, if we were able to get at the truth easily, as the optimist holds, then science would be unnecessary. Common sense would do.

Popper argued that unalloyed optimism leads to the "doctrine of manifest truth." This is the idea that "truth, if put before us naked, is always recognizable as truth. Thus truth, if it does not reveal itself, has only to be unveiled, or dis-covered. . . . We have been given eyes to see the truth, and the 'natural light' of reason to see it by" (1963: 7). The doctrine of manifest truth, in turn, leads to dogmatism about what we (think we) know and to an inability to accept our ignorance. Moreover, the doctrine of manifest truth tends to go hand in hand with the "conspiracy theory of ignorance," where ignorance is seen as "the work of powers conspiring to keep us in ignorance, to poison our minds by filling them with falsehood, and to blind our eyes so that they cannot see the manifest truth" (ibid.). Those who tacitly accept the doctrine of manifest truth demonize those with whom they disagree since "only the most depraved wickedness can refuse to see the manifest truth" (ibid.: 8). Anything that contradicts the optimistic epistemology of manifest truth must be the result of deliberate efforts to mask the self-evidence of the truth.

Against the doctrine of manifest truth, Popper contrasted the "doctrine of fallibility" (1963: 16)—the presupposition, as he saw it, of science. According to the doctrine of fallibility, ignorance is our natural state, not the result of a conspiracy: "All knowledge is fallible and therefore uncertain" (1992: 4), and "we are always or almost always capable of error" (ibid.: 33). Thus, "truth is often hard to come by, and . . . once found it may easily be lost again. Erroneous beliefs may have an astonishing power to survive, for thousands of years, in defiance of experience, with or without the aid of conspiracy" (1963: 8). However, recognizing our natural ignorance does not mean pessimistically accepting it as permanent—the position taken by the skeptic of science. The proper attitude of the scientist is to acknowledge that we—even scientists—are fallible. Our beliefs may be false. But the fact that we *may* be wrong does not mean that we *must* be wrong.

Science, according to Popper, risks being co-opted by the doctrine of manifest truth because of scientists' optimism about our ability to close the gap between reality and our perceptions. Arguably, it is the task of the philosopher of science to ask whether this optimism is warranted. But Popper did not just think that science *might* progress, he assumed that it *did*. He wanted to "analyse the characteristic ability of science to advance" (1959: 49) and to explain how empirical statements "can be criticized and superseded by better ones" (ibid.). Did he, too, succumb to over-optimism? On the one hand, he thought that all knowledge was fallible. On the other hand, he defanged the skepticism to which fallibilism might lead. Thus, he tried to explain how evidence can arbitrate between competing scientific paradigms so that even the most dogmatic scientists would be forced to change their minds.

This raised serious problems in the philosophy of science, some of which I shall review.[2] My guiding question in this discussion is whether anything useful can be said to follow from fallibilism. Like the science that is supposed to follow fallibilist precepts, fallibilism itself is a middle way between skepticism and optimism. But as Popper struggles between his optimism about scientific progress and his insistence on scientific fallibility, one must wonder if the *via media* accomplishes anything.

Countering dogmatism

According to Popper, science works by giving us a way to check-mate the optimist's dogmatism by showing him the errors in his doctrine. Thus, in Popper's view, the most suitable scientific method is one that exposes hypotheses to the detection of their flaws.

This "negative" approach to knowledge was Popper's attempt to counteract the dogmatism he found among Marxists, Freudians, and followers of the once-popular psychological theorist Alfred Adler—ideologues with whom he came into contact in early twentieth-century Vienna. These ideologues unfailingly interpreted even seemingly contradictory evidence as consistent with their belief systems (1963: 35). Adler's theory, for example, used the same analysis to explain both self-interested and altruistic behavior (ibid.). Popper's explanation for ideologues' dogmatism is that they optimistically leave no room for the possibility of their own ignorance. Effectively, then, the ideologue has accepted the manifest truth of the ideology.

Popper's philosophy of science was designed to provide "freedom from dogmatism" (1959: 38) by breaking through the ideologue's closed interpretation of the world. If everything counts as evidence for an ideology, then nothing counts as evidence against it. The theory is effectively garrisoned from reality; it may as well be a theological revelation. Popper (1963: 33–35) found this imperviousness to evidence to be unscientific, where science is equated with responsiveness to evidence. On first glance it might seem as if ideologues are responsive to evidence since all evidence is grist for their mill. Nonetheless, their theoretical *conclusions* remain insensitive to evidence because nothing could prove the conclusions wrong. Popper thus proposed, in *The Logic of Scientific Discovery* (1959), that we "demarcate" science from pseudo-science by defining responsiveness to evidence as "falsifiability" (1959: sec. 6). According to this principle, a theory is scientific only if it concludes that certain phenomena cannot occur if the theory is true. For example, Newton's theory of gravitation implies that if the theory were true, then a range of phenomena is impossible: to use Popper's examples, teacups cannot dance, fallen apples cannot pick themselves up from the ground, and the moon cannot suddenly drift away from the earth (1974: 1005). "Potential falsifiers" (1959: 86) of a theory do not have to actually *occur* in order to render the theory scientific; that would mean that only false theories are scientific. But specifying what *might* falsify our theory forces us to distance ourselves from it, to look at it critically instead of taking its truth for granted. The criterion of falsifiability thus operationalizes fallibilism, and it was their own fallibility that ideologues ignored.

Answering the skeptic

The ideologue thinks he has found the truth in the form of a comprehensive theoretical interpretation of some aspect of the world. In contrast, the skeptic maintains that causal theories are never fully justified given our ignorance. If the ideologue has too much faith in the power of his theory to explain reality, the skeptic has too little faith in the power of any theory to explain anything.

Popper directed his work as much against the skeptic as the ideologue. In particular, Popper took on the ultimate skeptic, Hume, who based his doubt on the problem of induction.

Induction is the practice of inferring from past observations of some conjunction of phenomena, such as whiteness and swans, a universal law, such as "all swans are white." To infer from particular instances to a universal law is to assume that "the course of nature continues always uniformly the same" (Hume 1739: 89)—that the future will resemble the past and that the parts of the world we have not observed will resemble the parts that we have. We base this assumption on our experience, but it is circular to answer the question of whether the future will resemble the past by pointing to our past experience. However, without an assumption of universal laws based on observational verification, natural science (as opposed to history) would seem to be impossible. Evidence of a certain type of phenomenon in a given place and time would count for nothing in another place and time. Popper assumed that science seeks to discover universal laws, not mere collections of facts (1959: 106), so he felt he had to ground science in something other than induction.

The problem with induction, according to Popper, is its reliance on confirmatory or verifying instances to prove a universal law. Part of Popper's solution was to point out a basic logical asymmetry between verifiability and falsifiability (1959: 41).[3] The asymmetry is illustrated by the fact that the existence of a single black swan falsifies the universal law that all swans are white despite millions of confirmatory white swans.[4] Conversely, until a black swan appears we can rely on confirmatory sightings to "corroborate" claims about all swans being white—but only on a tentative, hypothetical, or fallibilistic basis.

As Popper saw it, by pointing out the unprovability of the uniformity of nature, Hume had "establishe[d] for good that all our universal laws or theories remain forever guesses, conjectures, hypotheses" (1974: 1021). But theories are not equally questionable, as a skeptic might hold, because all evidence is not equal. Evidence that falsifies a theory is more important than evidence that confirms a theory. Evidence that falsifies a universal law adds to our store of knowledge about *what is not true*.

Thus, Popper idiosyncratically defines scientific "progress" as consisting in the accretion of falsified theories. We attempt to solve particular scientific problems by proposing "bold conjectures" about the world, where "bold" means that a conjecture has high empirical content. The more facts it tries to explain, the bolder it is—because it is all the more exposed to falsification. Pseudo-sciences, such as Marxism and Freudianism, also have high empirical content, but the difference is that *scientific* "boldness" makes a theory more vulnerable to refutation, not less.

This may not sound very optimistic, but compared to Hume, it is. If the conjecture is (as we like to say) that "the sun will rise tomorrow," it is easily falsified if the sun does not rise tomorrow. But until the sun fails to rise, we can treat the "law" that it will rise as tentatively corroborated because, thus far, it has not been falsified. Hume's mistake was in thinking that our knowledge must consist of certitudes (1959: 42). Between the false and the unfalsifiable is the fallible.

Real-world falsification

Popper is no longer taken seriously by many philosophers of science. A criticism often leveled at Popper's criterion of falsifiability is that the compelling logical asymmetry between falsifiability and verifiability is usually inapplicable in the real world. Falsificationism should force scientists to demolish scientific theories left and right because there is no end to potentially falsifying evidence. But Thomas Kuhn (1962: 81) pointed out that scientists routinely categorize potentially falsifying facts as "anomalies" or as non-threatening "discrepancies." And if they *are* categorized as falsifying evidence, scientists tend to propose ad hoc addenda to their theories to make the theories fit the facts, instead of rejecting the theories.[5] In short, there is nothing about a piece of evidence per se that automatically falsifies a theory, at least as science is really practiced. When confronted with evidence, scientists tend to act more like verificationists, not falsificationists (ibid.: 77). Scientists' actual practices might seem to exemplify the very type of ideological shenanigans that Popper tried to prevent. In principle, therefore, Popper might have responded to Kuhn by turning against science as a sophisticated form of dogmatism.

The problem with real-world falsification is not merely that scientists can disagree about the *significance* of a fact (e.g., does a black swan falsify the theory that swans are white?), but that they can *interpret* that fact in different ways (e.g., is that a black or a muddy swan?). The interpretive problem, in turn, has two closely related aspects. The first is the fact that it is hard to know when an experimental finding should be treated as falsifying the theory under investigation or whether there might have been countervailing factors at work. This might mean that it is not the theory that is at fault; instead, the problem is that that the theory's implicit ceteris paribus clause was not upheld (Lakatos 1970: 101–2).[6] There may thus never be a compelling reason to treat a theory as having been falsified.

The problem of how to interpret evidence becomes more pressing in light of "confirmation holism." W.V.O. Quine pointed out that there is no hard and fast distinction between "empirical" and "theoretical" beliefs. Instead, empirically based theories are embedded in a web of other beliefs that may be impossible to test. It would seem, then, that we are never testing a theory in isolation, but testing, instead, the whole web of beliefs (Quine 1953: 41). Popper agreed that "in every test it is not only the theory under investigation which is involved, but also the whole system of our theories and assumptions—in fact, more or less the whole of our knowledge—so that we can never be certain which of all these assumptions is refuted" (1963: 112). However, confirmation holism not only permits, but also *requires*, that we make ad hoc adjustments to our theories when confronted with counterevidence since "reevaluation of some statements entails reevaluation of others.... The total field [of beliefs] is so underdetermined by ... experience, that there is much latitude of choice as to what statements to reevaluate in the light of any single contrary experience" (Quine 1953: 42–43).

Confirmation holism, as well as scientists' ability to use the ceteris paribus clause to dismiss counterevidence, suggest that we may not be able to distinguish between legitimate and illegitimate attempts to save a theory since we often do not know whether we are explaining or "explaining away" counterevidence. In fact, it was in part because we can interpret a potentially falsifying "fact" in several ways (1963: 192) that Popper maintained that our knowledge is always conjectural (cf. 1959: 50).

However, if counterinstances to a theory can be bracketed, how can evidence break through the ideologue's dogmatic theoretical carapace? If adopting falsifiability as one's criterion of science does not change how one responds *practically* to evidence, then falsifiability may be just an interesting but impractical ideal.

Critical rationalism as an attitude

Popper clearly did not think that the criterion of falsifiability was impractical, nor did he think that individual scientists are doomed to live in the "closed framework" of an unfalsifiable scientific paradigm (1994: 53). How then did Popper explain how evidence allows scientists to change their minds?

The answer is that the individual scientist must maintain a critical attitude towards all theories, including—and especially—his own. "In searching for the truth, it may be our best plan to start by criticizing our most cherished beliefs" (1963: 6). Popper named this version of his philosophy of science "rational criticism" (e.g., 1992: 54)—or, as it is commonly called, "critical rationalism."

Critical rationalism functions as an injunction to open-mindedness. This might make us less self-protective of, and defensive about, our hypotheses. Indeed, Popper thought that the "critical tradition" of science has tamed us by turning the potential deadly violence of disagreement into mere verbal sparring (1992: 29). This is where Popper's philosophy of science meets his liberal political philosophy. But within the field of science itself, Popper thought that a self- (and other-) critical attitude was necessary in order to further the growth of scientific knowledge. You must remain open-minded or "you will never benefit from experience, and never learn from it how wrong you are" (1959: 50). Thus, Popper thinks that the open-minded attitude embodied by a critical rationalist is necessary to weeding out error, thereby contributing to the accumulation of falsified and falsifiable theories.

This sounds very good in principle. However, if enjoining people to be self-critical or open-minded were enough to make them responsive to evidence, we would not have the problem of dogmatism to begin with. Even the most ardent ideologue *thinks* he is open-minded. Open-mindedness is a mere abstraction. It amounts to holding a fallibilistic attitude *about* one's beliefs. A belief itself, however—its content—is concrete. If one believes some particular thing about the world, what can it mean to believe it open-mindedly?

If we equate open-mindedness with fallibilism, as Popper did, then we would remember that our beliefs *may* turn out to be wrong. But if we knew that a belief was, in fact, wrong, we would already have abandoned it. To continue to hold a belief, no matter how false one thinks it might be in the abstract, is to continue to believe that it is true. Nor is it the case that changing one's mind makes one any less dogmatic. One has simply replaced one belief with another, but one's conviction about its truth value is the same.

Arguably at least, belief is involuntary. It is the result of the evidence and interpretation that have *had the effect* of persuading someone that something is true. Call the involuntary process of belief formation "the determination of beliefs" by evidence and interpretation. The fact that we think of ourselves as open-minded confirms that we understand ourselves not as *choosing* our beliefs, but as having them chosen for us by reality—as we involuntarily see reality—through the lens of evidence and interpretation. A corollary, however, would seem to be the inefficacy of injunctions to be open-minded. That is what we already think we are. By the same token, changing one's mind is determined by an interpretation that seems to *compel* a change of beliefs.

But if the evidence can be interpreted as not compelling a change of belief, it would be irrational, not critically "rational," to change one's mind because of it.

Is critical rationalism, then, simply a high-minded but impractical ideal? Popper recognized that it is difficult to maintain a critical attitude towards one's theories. And he thus tried to find a way to turn open-mindedness into more than an attitude. To this end, he developed fallibilist rules of thumb.

Critical rationalism as rules of thumb

These rules of thumb are what constitute Popper's scientific *methodology*. The collective decision to adopt a given methodology is not a rational one (1959: 37), according to Popper, but some such decision *does* have to be made, however implicitly, if a scientific community is to be able to judge evidence as falsifying a proposition or failing to do so. Popper thus suggested that we view his methodology as a "proposal for an agreement or convention" (ibid.).

The view that science works by methodological agreement is commonly called conventionalism. Some form of conventionalism becomes necessary once one rejects, as Popper did, the view that science has firm foundations in "experience" or some other source of manifest truth (1959: 51–52). However, Popper thought that a shared scientific methodology could rescue science from the temptation (as he saw it) of dogmatism. This would ground the objectivity of science, where "objective" is defined as intersubjective.

What are the rules of thumb? One is that the scientist should specify in advance what evidence would falsify his theory (1959: 86). He should also commit himself in advance to refrain from trying to save a theory by adopting ad hoc modifications that add no empirical content to it (1959: 82). In fact, a scientist can treat his theory as having been falsified if he finds himself adopting empty ad hoc changes. On the other hand, severely testing a theory requires that we do *not* give it up the moment it is attacked but try to amend it by adopting "auxiliary rules" that increase the empirical content of the theory, making it *more* susceptible to falsification (ibid.: 82–83; 1974: 986).

Popper's methodology is an attempt to institutionalize open-mindedness and yet it leads to a strange dilemma: the rules amount to a dogmatic commitment to follow them *precisely* when one interprets them as conflicting with the best interpretation of the evidence. Kuhn (1970: 15) therefore described them as amounting to an ideology. A Kuhnian normal scientist might, in fact, claim that *he* is the one being open-minded if, for example, he disregards evidence that he had initially said he would treat as falsifying his theory. For example, he may see other factors as counteracting the apparently falsifying evidence. To ignore the countervailing factors is to be insensitive to evidence of their presence, and "falsification" of one's prediction may *constitute* such evidence. If the Kuhnian normal scientist is just as open-minded as, or perhaps more so than the Popperian scientist, then at best, the rules of thumb are useless at inducing open-mindedness and, at worst, induce the dogmatism that the rules were designed to avoid.

This suggests that the emptiness of fallibilism is retained even when it is translated into concrete rules. It might seem as if we're in a bind: we need to assert fallibilism given our ignorance of the truth, but we still have to make decisions, such as which research direction to follow and which theory to discard. The need to make a choice, a decision, leads us to fall back on *some* procedure, which we treat as a rational method. Indeed, Popper recognized that while "there is no 'absolute reliance'" that a theory is true, "since we *have* to choose, it will be 'rational' to choose the best-tested theory. The one which, in the light of our *critical discussion*, appears to be the best so far" (1974: 1025). Popper maintains that what appears "best" is a theory that has withstood attempts to falsify it.

However, Popper's appeal here to what "appears" to be the best theory begs the question of what is rational.[7] Just as there is no such thing as a contentless belief, there is no such thing as a contentless procedure; belief in the procedure one decides to adopt is just as subject to determination by evidence and its interpretation as is the conclusion to which the procedure leads. After all, if one thought that a given procedure was likely to lead one into error, one would not use that procedure.

Thus, Popper smuggled into his conventionalist philosophy of science a non-conventionalist criterion of the truth, namely that the method of falsification is more likely, overall, to allow one to detect errors (in more than a conventional sense).[8] On the surface it seems as if, by proposing that scientists adopt a series of conventions, Popper provided a way for conventional-following *individual* scientists to accept or reject theories in a non-arbitrary manner. But Popper's conventionalism does not fully escape arbitrariness—it simply transfers it to the level of the scientific community that adopts conventions. Doing so provides some order to scientific endeavors, but Popper wanted more than order; he wanted to explain why that order might, overall, lead not simply to agreed-upon progress, but to progress in the sense of getting closer to the truth. Given that the criteria of what counts as science are established by convention, it might seem that what counts as scientific "progress," too, is a matter of convention—but Popper did not quite want to go that far in the relativist direction.

Strictly speaking, Popper's conventionalism, however modified it may be, does not allow him to posit the stronger view of progress. This makes it all too similar to Kuhn's historical account of the process by which one paradigm is replaced, in a scientific revolution, by an "incommensurable" paradigm. In this view, progress becomes meaningless because there is no Archimedean perch from which to judge new paradigms as closer to the truth than old ones. Similarly, if a theory is falsified not objectively but merely (inter)subjectively, how can scientific progress, in an absolute sense, be affirmed?

Some of Popper's defenders have argued that although we cannot tell when our theories are true, we can nonetheless know that they are approximating truth. Bryan Magee, for example, argues that for Popper, truth is a "regulative ideal"; just as we do not have to know the exact width of a piece of steel, down to the last molecule, to judge its thickness "within a certain degree of accuracy" (Magee 1985: 23), so too science can allow us to get nearer to the truth even if "we can never know if we have reached our goal" (ibid.: 24). However, this assumes that we know that science is heading toward truth, which is what is at issue.

Inscrutable ignorance

Where does Popper leave us—with scientific optimism or skeptical pessimism? Was Popper's philosophy of science too heavy a burden to place on the fragile foundation of ignorance? Can we do more than pay "lip-service to fallibilism" (Lakatos 1970: 114)? Are the injunctions to be aware of our ignorance, to be critical, and to be open-minded anything more than "trite slogans" (Feyerabend 1975: 177)? These questions are pressing lest a focus on "ignorance" become a byword, a mere symbol of one's epistemological sophistication, or a weapon to use only against those with whom one disagrees. Yet if our beliefs are determined by our perceptions of the truth, what would it mean to apply this weapon to ourselves?

One way out might seem to be the distinction made by Donald Rumsfeld (2002) between two types of ignorance: ignorance of known unknowns and ignorance of unknown unknowns. We might call these two types of ignorance, respectively, scrutable and inscrutable. Stuart Firestein (2012), for example, considers scrutable ignorance to be essential to driving scientific developments since scientists use their knowledge of what they don't know in order to guide future research questions. This type of ignorance might very well benefit from applying at least some of Popper's views on what counts as good science.[9]

In contrast the type of ignorance upon which the Humean skeptic bases his pessimism is inscrutable. This type of ignorance, perhaps, must remain an abstraction. Ignorance of unknown unknowns can never be operationalized. It is inescapable, it is important, and it may mean that evidence will come to light that falsifies a theory that now seems true, or that revives a "falsified" theory by pointing to a countervailing factor that explains away the "falsifying" evidence. Once we make this claim, however, we can no longer fault Popper's philosophy of science for not adequately taking this type of ignorance into account. At least on these grounds, *all* philosophies of science must fail, since inscrutable ignorance is always inescapable and important. So it is not clear that Popper's theory fares worse in this respect than do others.

For example, all philosophies of science will have to face the problem of dogmatism and to explain what counts as responsive to evidence. Likewise, all philosophies of science will have to explain how we can treat a theory as false when it is always possible that unknown factors have created the spurious appearance of failure.

The inability to take into account our inscrutable ignorance might explain why philosophers of science tend to have faith in scientific progress. Even the pessimistic skeptic has to make decisions, which requires that he believe that his interpretation of relevant evidence justifies the decision. The decision-making process is thus immune to a practical awareness of inscrutable ignorance. Not just ordinary people but scientists and philosophers of science must "decide" which theories seem to be true. Since such decisions are determined by plausible interpretations of the evidence known to the decision maker, they will be optimistically oblivious to what the decision makers do not know.

The optimism of the scientist and the philosopher of science may thus be part of the human condition, even if the occasional skeptic, such as Hume, points out the logical baselessness of optimism. It may not be, as Popper put it, "our duty to remain optimists" (1994: xiii) as much as it is the unavoidable precondition of human life. Attempting to hedge optimism by opening our ideas to falsification does not turn out to work because we would not believe ideas we thought false, and we *should* not judge as false ideas that fail to meet a prescribed test but nonetheless seem as to fit the evidence as we interpret it. Therefore Popper's magnificent discovery of the asymmetry between verifying and falsifying evidence does not get us anywhere. Perhaps the problem of dogmatism cannot be solved.

Notes

1 All citations lacking an author are to Popper.
2 For frequently raised objections to Popper's philosophy of science, see Godfrey-Smith (2003, Ch. 4). See Miller (1994, Ch. 2) for a more comprehensive and sympathetic overview of the objections to Popper's philosophy of science.
3 See (1959: sec. 79) for the other part of Popper's solution to the problem of induction. See also (1974: 1013–27).
4 As J. S. Mill (1962: 7) adroitly put it, "One single well-established fact, clearly irreconcilable with a doctrine, is sufficient to prove that it is *false*."
5 Kuhn's portrait of "normal science" has been thought to challenge Popper's account of science on a number of levels. My focus, however, is only on the difficulty with real-world falsification.
6 Popper (1974: 1186n75) thought that scientific theories should avoid using ceteris paribus clauses since it was impossible to hold all things constant (at least in the natural sciences).
7 See Salmon (1981: 120) for this question-begging aspect of Popper's theory.
8 E.g., (1974: 1021–22).
9 See, for example, Popper's discussion of the "searchlight theory" of knowledge, where one begins with a question, the answer to which one is scrutably ignorant of, and thus uses a provisional theory as a searchlight, to pick out evidence (1972: Appendix).

References

Feyerabend, P. (1975 [2010]). *Against Method*, New York: Verso.

Firestein, S. (2012). *Ignorance: How It Drives Science*, New York: Oxford University Press.

Godfrey-Smith, P. (2003). *Theory and Reality: An Introduction to the Philosophy of Science*, Chicago, IL: University of Chicago Press.

Hume, D. (1739 [1888]). *A Treatise of Human Nature*, L.A. Selby-Bigge (ed.), Oxford: Clarendon Press.

Kuhn, T.S. (1962 [1996]). *The Structure of Scientific Revolutions* (3rd edn), Chicago, IL: University of Chicago Press.

Lakatos, I. (1970). "Falsification and the Methodology of Scientific Research Programmes." In I. Lakatos and A. Musgrave (eds) *Criticism and the Growth of Knowledge*, New York: Cambridge University Press.

Magee, B. (1985). *Philosophy and the Real World: An Introduction to Karl Popper*. La Salle, Ill.: Open Court.

Mill, J.S. (1962). "The Spirit of the Age." In Gertrude Himmelfarb (ed.) *Essays on Politics and Culture*, New York: Anchor Books.

Miller, D. (1994). *Critical Rationalism: A Restatement and Defence*, Peru, Ill.: Open Court.

Popper, K.R. (1959 [1968]). *The Logic of Scientific Discovery*, New York: Harper.

—— (1963). *Conjectures and Refutations*, New York: Harper.

—— (1972). *Objective Knowledge: An Evolutionary Approach*, Oxford: Oxford University Press.

—— (1974). "Karl Popper: Replies to My Critics." In *The Philosophy of Karl Popper*, vol. II, P.A. Schilpp (ed.), La Salle, Ill.: Open Court Publishing.

—— (1992) *In Search of a Better World: Lectures and Essays from Thirty Years*, London: Routledge.

—— (1994) *The Myth of the Framework: In Defence of Science and Rationality*, London: Routledge.

Quine, Willard Van Orman. (1953). *From a Logical Point of View*. Cambridge, MA: Harvard University Press.

Rumsfeld, D. (2002). News Briefing, Department of Defense, http://www.defense.gov/transcripts/transcript.aspx?transcriptid=2636.

Salmon, Wesley C. (1981). "Rational Prediction." *British Journal for the Philosophy of Science* 32: 115–25.

6

From Descartes to Rumsfeld

The rise and decline of ignorance-of-ignorance

Jerome Ravetz

Descartes, Galileo, and Bacon

My story starts with Descartes, but not on the well-known reflections on the existence of himself and of God. Rather, I focus on the professedly autobiographical account of Part 1 of the Discourse on Method. The story he tells there is of a desperate search for certainty, which was betrayed by humanistic learning and eventually satisfied by knowledge modelled on geometry. Whereas the first part is opened with paradoxical arguments about the universality of "good sense" (providing grounds for hope in real knowledge), within half-a-dozen paragraphs he tells us right away that there is a problem. We read:

> From my childhood, I have been familiar with letters; and as I was given to believe that by their help a clear and certain knowledge of all that is useful in life might be acquired, I was ardently desirous of instruction. But as soon as I had finished the entire course of study, at the close of which it is customary to be admitted into the order of the learned, I completely changed my opinion. For I found myself involved in so many doubts and errors, that I was convinced I had advanced no further in all my attempts at learning, than the discovery at every turn of my own ignorance.
>
> *(Descartes 2008 [1638]: 12)*

Further on in the section, Descartes expands on this complaint, providing first a loving apology for humanistic learning and then a detailed assassination of the curriculum. He does not merely denounce it for its insecurity and irrelevance; worse, he purports to show that each subject refutes its claims to knowledge by the properties of its own contents. In laying the foundations for this demolition job, Descartes delivers one of his characteristic throwaway lines, whose irony would have been familiar to those of his readers with humanist education and discernment. Let me repeat it here: "I was convinced I had advanced no further in all my attempts at learning, than the discovery at every turn of my own ignorance."

Rhetorically taking this criticism at face value, he explains that this defect was neither the fault of himself nor his teachers, and the narrative flows on. Few modern readers of the text would notice anything worthy of a pause. But for Descartes' readers, this passage betrays an epochal shift in the conception of knowledge. It is one on which the Scientific Revolution and the contemporary framework of knowledge all depend.

Up until the time of Descartes and indeed beyond, anyone with a claim to familiarity with philosophy would have known of the teachings of Socrates. And key among those teachings was the awareness of one's own ignorance. Indeed, Socrates was quoted as saying that knowledge of his ignorance was the main aim of his thought. His dialogues were all about enlightening his interlocutors about the limits of their knowledge, and the inescapable presence of ignorance. From that point of view, for a student to have learned about his ignorance would have been a sign of a successful education, indeed the only meaningful education that there is, as opposed to mere training.

So when Descartes silently consigned the wisdom of Socrates to the dustbin of history, he knew exactly what he was doing. All that humanistic stuff was discredited, as surely as were its predecessors in scholastic learning, religious doctrine and popular superstitions. There was no alternative to a new conception of knowledge, one we could now call "positive," with its foundations in the rigorous study of nature conceived as mathematical. Ignorance-of-ignorance then became hegemonic in modern learned culture.

Although Descartes was a great genius and visionary, he was far from alone in this new conception of knowledge. There is a close parallel with Thomas Hobbes, another genius and a consummate classical scholar. There is a legend that he had a conversion experience in 1628, on reading a page of Euclid's *Elements*, and finding there an irrefutable progression from obvious premises to surprising conclusions. With Hobbes the intellectual background to his disillusion is clear: he saw the collapse of civilized society all around him, and needed a foundation for reconstruction of society and knowledge alike, both stripped down to essentials, atoms in the one case and the Sovereign in the other. In such a scheme there is no place for ignorance.

Galileo did not display the same broader political concerns, but he was equally emphatic about knowledge. His great manifesto is worth quoting in full; there we find the same dismissal of humanistic learning, and the proclamation of his sort of science as the only way forward.

> If what we are discussing were a point of law or of the humanities, in which neither true nor false exists, one might trust in subtlety of mind and readiness of tongue and in the greater experience of the writers, and expect him who excelled in those things to make his reasoning most plausible, and one might judge it to be the best. But in the natural sciences, whose conclusions are true and necessary and have nothing to do with human will, one must take care not to place oneself in the defense of error.
>
> *(Galileo 1953 [1632]: 57)*

It would be a perpetuation of unaware ignorance to fail to mention that this ringing declaration came in the context of a treatise which was a scientific failure as well as a political catastrophe. Galileo's project of demonstrating the motions of the earth on the analogy of water swishing around a circular bowl was doomed both empirically (he got a single daily tide) and theoretically. He lacked the theory of mechanics in which the motions might have been explained, and he proudly declared the irrelevance of the attraction of the moon to the tides, an ancient Stoic doctrine which did turn out to be the core of Newton's theory.

Even Francis Bacon, who had come earlier and did not follow the geometrical way, showed signs of the same crisis of confidence in inherited learning as a defense against error and ignorance. His critique of contemporary learning was, if anything, more devastating than that of

Descartes. Ever fond of a good turn of phrase, in the *Advancement of Learning* he refers to "vermiculate questions" in the following passage from Bacon (original 1605):

> Surely, like as many substances in nature which are solid do putrefy and corrupt into worms; so it is the property of good and sound knowledge to putrefy and dissolve into a number of subtle, idle, unwholesome, and, as I may term them, vermiculate questions, which have indeed a kind of quickness and life of spirit, but no soundness of matter or goodness of quality.
>
> *(Bacon 1859: 139)*

There he is referring to the scholastics of his time, but it is not all certain that such questions have been eliminated from scholarly and scientific inquiry. Elsewhere, he refers to a study that he had conducted in his youth, the "Colours of Good and Evil" (Bacon 1859: 72–78), where he collected aphorisms, and found that for every theme, such nuggets of wisdom could be found on both sides of the argument! There we have the disillusion with humanist learning that all the other scientific revolutionaries experienced. And along with the rejection of the learning went the loss of respect for awareness of ignorance. Whatever the particular program for the new reform of learning, ignorance had no part in it nor even a mention except in Descartes' dismissal.

St. John of the Cross, Seth Ward, and Newton

The scientific revolutionaries were far from being the first to dismiss the knowledge of the learned, but there was a new element in their consciousness which made it difficult for them to include ignorance in their perspective. Dismissals of learned inquiry and its products were quite frequent in previous generations. Scholars like Nicholas Cusanus, Erasmus, Thomas More and Heinrich Cornelius Agrippa all wrote critical tracts, some of which included ignorance in their titles. But for them, as indeed for Socrates, ignorance was not absolute. Beyond worldly learning was another realm, accessible by means other than reason. For Socrates there was the Cave and the sunlight outside. Near the end of his life St. Thomas Aquinas had a vision, compared to which (as he said) all his life's intellectual productions were dross. For the great mystics, real knowledge and ignorance were united, thus St. John of the Cross (2008: 16):

> I entered into unknowing,
>
> and there I remained unknowing
>
> transcending all knowledge.

Although mystical experience was by no means extinguished in the early seventeenth century, as an accepted way of knowing it suffered a steady and terminal decline. And all the other sorts of knowing associated with an enriched and enchanted cosmos came to be rejected, vigorously. We have a precious statement of the clash between the two sorts of consciousness, in the pamphlet debate over university education that occurred in England during the civil war period. There was a radical reformer, John Webster, who wanted the two universities to reform their curriculum in line with the aspirations of Cromwell's godly revolution. His pamphlet, *Academiarum Examen*, was countered by *Vindiciae Academiarum* by Seth Ward, later to become a founder of the Royal Society. At one point Webster had recommended that students be exposed to the new learning as exemplified by Bacon and Robert Fludd. The latter is nearly forgotten, but in his time he was a highly regarded physician and also a hermetic philosopher. Ward's denunciation (original 1654) tells it all:

> How little trust there is in villainous man! He that even now was for the way of strict and accurate induction, is fallen into the mysticall way of the *Cabala*, and numbers formall: There are not two waies in the whole World more opposite, then those of the *L. Verulam* [Bacon, JR] and D. Fludd, the one founded on experiment, the other on mysticall Ideal reason.
>
> *(Ward, as cited in Debus 1977: 405)*

This judgment has persisted to the present day; any purported phenomena that pretend to violate the atomized cosmos of Descartes and Hobbes are scrutinized with overwhelming rigor. Our knowledge is of the sensible world as aided by disenchanted mathematics, and that is all that is possible and licit.

The point of this sketch of cultural history is to show that the ignorance being denied by the new philosophers was absolute. For them there was no realm of truth beyond sense experience and reason; whereof we are ignorant, thereof we have nothing, no security nor any guide to knowledge and action. Ignorance is a menace and awareness of ignorance is a threat. Some historians have seen the seventeenth century as one of "general crisis" (see Wikipedia). This was most obvious in the wars and political convulsions that peaked around mid-century, but it was also reflected in the "secularization" of basic theories in all realms including civil society and science. In such a world, an ignorance that led to higher truths was a lost cause; what we don't know we just won't know, and we will be bereft, unless we find another source of certainty, as in Science. Of course, ignorance did not disappear altogether. We find it in Newton's classic "parable of the pebbles":

> I do not know what I may appear to the world, but to myself I seem to have been only like a boy playing on the sea-shore, and diverting myself in now and then finding a smoother pebble or a prettier shell than ordinary, whilst the great ocean of truth lay all undiscovered before me.
>
> *(Newton, as cited in Brewster 2010: 331)*

Laplace, Bois-Reymond, and Lord Kelvin

But he who had discovered so much, could afford in his semi-divine status to compare his achievements to what was remaining. In the eighteenth century, Enlightenment promised unending progress, accompanied by the banishment of false doctrines and ignorance. At its end, the great mathematician Laplace (1951 [1901]) delivered a vision that comes as close to one of perfect knowledge as is possible to state.

> We may regard the present state of the universe as the effect of its past and the cause of its future. An intellect which at a certain moment would know all forces that set nature in motion, and all positions of all items of which nature is composed, if this intellect were also vast enough to submit these data to analysis, it would embrace in a single formula the movements of the greatest bodies of the universe and those of the tiniest atom; for such an intellect nothing would be uncertain and the future just like the past would be present before its eyes.
>
> *(Laplace 1951: 4)*

Of course, the all-knowing intellect here is imaginary, but his total knowledge is definitely of the scientific sort. In his own researches Laplace pushed ignorance back to the vanishing point. Newton had found it impossible to prove the total stability of the planets' orbits as mutual gravitational attraction perturbed them, and he had speculated that God might need to intervene every now and then to keep them on track. With his mathematical methods Laplace showed to his own satisfaction that the orbits are indeed totally stable. There is a legend that when he received his presentation copy of the Mecanique Celeste, Napoleon asked where God was mentioned (doubtless referring to the stability problem), and Laplace answered, in best rationalist fashion, that he did not have need of that hypothesis. Ignorance had been banished, even from the scientific domains where Newton himself had accepted it.

As the natural sciences matured through the nineteenth century, progress was accompanied by a growing realization of what we might call obscurity at their foundations. Thermodynamics was a subject of perennial debate, electrodynamics was shaken by Maxwell's derivation of his superbly powerful equations from a bizarre physical model, and even Newtonian mechanics was shown by Ernst Mach to be deeply confused. Ignorance was thrust into public debate by the distinguished German biologist Emile du Bois-Reymond. In 1880 he gave a lecture entitled "ignoramus et ignorabimus" – we don't know and we won't know. In it he listed seven great scientific questions, of which three were "transcendent." Debate was lively, and for some scientists (as the great mathematician Hilbert), "ignorabimus" was a betrayal of everything that science stands for. It was not simply a matter of the boundary with religion. For example, Lord Kelvin, a profoundly religious person who opposed Darwin's theory of evolution on what were then solid scientific grounds, still believed that there was nothing really new for physics to discover – ignorance was off the practical agenda. It was a great irony that what he considered to be two small "clouds" of unsolved problems turned out to be the core of the new revolution in physics (cf. Zimmerman Jones 2014).

Finally: The twentieth century and beyond

In the ongoing history of ignorance, the twentieth century has a paradoxical appearance. First, the scientific discoveries in the decade around the turn of the century exposed a previous ignorance-of-ignorance that could shake anyone's faith in the perfection of their scientific knowledge. From X-rays to radioactivity on the empirical front, and then relativity (supposedly refuting Newton's doctrine on absolute space) and quantum theory, the scientific universe was transformed at its foundations. In the 1920s, the choice was offered between irreducible ignorance (Heisenberg's 'uncertainty principle') and mystification (Schrödinger's complex-probability psi) in the explanation of physical processes. The double-slit experiment with single photons defied a coherent explanation. Yet the scientists' "mobilizing myth" of a universal truth-machine remained in full force, and strongly influenced the humanities and social-sciences through the century and beyond.

In Economics, the King of the social sciences, not merely ignorance but real uncertainty has been systematically denied (cf. Ravetz 1994). Leading theoretical economists have asserted that the "decision maker" must assume that "the future is governed by an already existing unchanging ergodic stochastic process" (Davidson 2012: 3). John Maynard Keynes tried to dispense with this axiom, but the consensus among theoreticians and practitioners has been that the axiom not merely needs to hold, but actually does so. Surely, the future will be like the past. For these distinguished economists Laplace's All-knowing Intellect is still alive and well, and has been employed as a "quant" on Wall Street both before and after 2008 (Ravetz 2008).

The sharing of the economists' envy for Victorian physics has been nearly universal among the sciences dealing with complex systems. This style of work has resulted in the endemic pathology of pseudo-precise numbers in estimates and policy indicators. Ignorance of ignorance is ensured by such techniques. Major government policies are thereby sent into fantasy land as surely as are the financial markets.

Although Thomas Kuhn did not discuss ignorance, his picture of "normal" scientific research, and by extension scientific education, is one of the systematic inculcation of ignorance-of-ignorance. His "paradigms" have a function nearly like those of the Kantian constitutive principles, setting boundary structures within which thought necessarily takes place. The puzzle-solving "normal scientists" cannot conceive of ideas outside the ruling paradigm, any more than an inhabitant of Flatland (as in the novel) can conceive of "up" (Abbott 1884). Kuhn was not comfortable with this anti-humanistic aspect of science, which in retrospect can be interpreted as making scientific research, and even more, science teaching, into a Truman show, but for him it seemed necessary for the progress of science.

The taboo about discussions of scientific ignorance persists in scientific fields where its presence might seem to be hard to deny. And this continues in spite of the open recognition of salient ignorance in fundamental astrophysics, as expressed in the terms "dark matter" and "dark energy." There was an illuminating episode in the discussion of uncertainty in connection with climate change science. Two well-known scientists devised a set of expressions whereby increasing degrees of uncertainty could be expressed in a simple and standard way. This was adopted by the Intergovernmental Panel on Climate Change, but there only the notations for uncertainty were reported. Concerning the presence of the notation for ignorance, the readers were left in ignorance (Risbey and O'Kane 2011).

Self-conscious, even defiant, ignorance of ignorance by politicians became a key doctrine of the second Bush administration, as it implemented the "Project for the New American Century." Quite breathtaking in its arrogance, this nearly official pronouncement about reality amounted, in historical perspective, to being the death-knell for an empire. "The aide said that guys like me were 'in what we call the reality-based community'", an obvious reference to the "faith-based communities" of religious believers. For their members "believe that solutions emerge from your judicious study of discernible reality." But "We're an empire now, and when we act, we create our own reality." Those other, lesser beings like the author, can only study the new realities being created by these new "history's actors" (Suskind 2004). Considering that this was said in 2004, almost certainly by Karl Rove, just as the catastrophe of the occupation of Iraq was unfolding, it shows just how far intelligent people can be led into fantasy when they need it.

However, the debacle in Iraq did lead to some renewed awareness of ignorance. This was stimulated by a prior news briefing which, quite paradoxically, has made the idea nearly fashionable again. This time the speaker was Donald Rumsfeld, who had not previously been noticed as having philosophical interests. His initial statement of the position was uttered in the context of a press conference in 2002, when arguments for the invasion were being prepared. He dealt with the lack of evidence for the government's claims about Iraq's supplying terrorists with WMD. It is not entirely clear how his analysis relates to that issue; perhaps he was trying to say that even if we have no idea whatever of what is actually going on, it is correct to act as if we have the necessary evidence for our policies. Such an interpretation is quite plausible in the context of other statements made by the British and American governments in justifying their actions. He prefaced his analysis with his interest in reports that something hasn't happened, and then commented on the less controversial "known knowns." And finally came the two categories that brought Socrates back to center stage: "There are known unknowns; that is to say, there are things that we now know we don't know. But there are also unknown unknowns – there are things we do not know we don't know" (Rumsfeld 2002).

Amid the general hilarity, many authors noticed the asymmetry, and developed the missing theme of the "unknown knowns." My interpretation is to use the category to describe things that are unknown by some but not by others. In the case of Iraq, it seems that the practical problems of occupying an invaded country were well known by the U.S. State Department, but not by the Pentagon or by the relevant U.K. authorities. Generally it is the "whistleblower" who makes the unknowns known, and then those adversely affected by the knowledge will "go into denial," perhaps silencing the messenger in the process.

We now live in an age where the whistleblowers are supplemented by the leakers, as Assange and Snowden. In their revelations the public has discovered a plethora of topics on which it had been the victim of unknown unknowns, or of its ignorance-of-ignorance, resulting from systematic concealment and deception. This demonstration is profoundly subversive in its effect, for it damages the public trust on which government by consent ultimately depends. And ignorance becomes directly political: we want others, and particular central authorities, to remain in ignorance about ourselves to the greatest extent possible. Thus there was a fierce popular reaction in England to government plans for the National Health Service to take over digital patient records from primary-care physicians. The anger was only aggravated by the carefully crafted assurances that these would not be sold to private firms. In regard to the protection of citizens' privacy, or maintaining the ignorance of the authorities, the situation in England now seems to be, "Don't believe it until it's been officially denied."

I confess to ignorance about the outcomes of such developments in the political sphere. More important, in the long term, are those in the sphere of knowledge as a social product and social property. Will ignorance of ignorance again be recognized as a barrier to genuine knowledge? Are we finally working our way back to Socrates? Are we recovering from the desperate certainties of Descartes and his generation? Will the democratization of scientific knowledge resulting from the IT revolution bring us out of the Kuhnian dogmatic paradigms? It has been argued that error and failure are more easily acknowledged and remedied in the small systems of the new "creative commons" of invention, than in big sclerotic corporations (Shirky 2008). Would the same effect take place in the production and diffusion of knowledge? Do our students, particularly those in the sciences of complex systems, prepare themselves for examination questions involving deep uncertainty and ignorance? To the extent that this is beginning to happen, there is hope for our civilization.

References

Abbott, E.A. (1884) *Flatland: A Romance in Many Dimensions*. London: Seeley.

Bacon, F. (1859 [1605]) *The Works of Francis Bacon, Lord Chancellor of England*. Philadelphia: Parry & McMillan.

Brewster, D. (2010 [1855]) *Memoirs of the Life, Writings, and Discoveries of Sir Isaac Newton*, Vol. 2. Cambridge: Cambridge University Press.

Davidson, P. (2012) "Is Economics a Science? Should Economics Be Rigorous?" *Real-world Economics Review* 59: 1–9.

Debus, A. (1977) *The Chemical Philosophy*. Mineola, NY: Dover.

Descartes, R. (2008 [1638]) *Discourse on Method, Part 1*. New York: Cosimo.

Galileo, G. (1953 [1632]) *Dialogue Concerning the Two Chief World Systems*. Berkeley, CA: University of California Press.

Laplace, Pierre Simon (1951 [1901]) *A Philosophical Essay on Probabilities*. New York: Dover Publications.

Ravetz, J. (1994) Economics as an Elite Folk-Science: The Suppression of Uncertainty. *Journal of Post-Keynesian Economics* 17 (2): 165–184.

Ravetz, J. (2008) "Faith and Reason in the Mathematics of the Credit Crunch." *The Oxford Magazine* (Eighth Week, Michaelmas Term): 14–16. Available online at: http://www.pantaneto.co.uk/issue35/ravetz.htm (last accessed July 10, 2014).

Risbey, J.S., and O'Kane, T.J. (2011) "Sources of Knowledge and Ignorance in Climate Research." *Climatic Change* 108 (4): 755–773.

Rumsfeld, D. (2002) Known and Unknown: Author's Note. Available online at: http://papers.rumsfeld.com/about/page/authors-note (last accessed July 14, 2014).

Shirky, C. (2008) *Here Comes Everybody: The Power of Organizing without Organizations*. London: Penguin.

St. John of the Cross (2008) *Twenty Poems*. Radford, VA: Wilder Publications.

Suskind, R. (2004) "Faith, Certainty and the Presidency of George W. Bush." *The New York Times Magazine*. Available online at: http://www.nytimes.com/2004/10/17/magazine/17BUSH.html?_r=0 (last accessed July 11, 2014).

Zimmerman Jones, A. (2014) Kelvin's "Clouds" Speech. Available online at: http://physics.about.com/od/physicshistory/p/KelvinsDarkClouds.htm (last accessed July 10, 2014).

7

The anatomy of ignorance

Diagnoses from literature

Devjani Roy and Richard Zeckhauser

Ignorance in life and literature: An introduction

Ignorance represents a situation in which some potential outcomes are not even identified. Often they are both unknown and unknowable (Gomory, 1995; Zeckhauser, 2006). On a continuum that begins with risk and progresses through uncertainty, ignorance is the third, final, and most extreme state in the sequence. With risk and uncertainty, the possible future states of the world are known. With risk, their probabilities are known as well; with uncertainty, their probabilities are unknown. A roll of two dice involves risk; a prediction about the stock market a year hence involves uncertainty.

The well-developed discipline of decision analysis prescribes how to make decisions when confronted with either risk or uncertainty. One of its central prescriptions is to start by assigning probabilities—*objective* if risk, *subjective* if uncertainty—to the alternative future states of the world. But with ignorance, where those states are not even identified, attaching probabilities is clearly impossible. Note, these states are not extreme outliers on some understood spectrum; they are outcomes that the decision maker fails to even conjecture.

Our title, "The anatomy of ignorance," introduces a medical metaphor. Our analysis diagnoses ignorance as a malady that inflicts significant damages at the individual and societal levels. Fortunately, as with many maladies, understanding ignorance can help us recognize its presence and treat it more effectively.

Focus on consequential ignorance

We should make clear at the outset that we are not studying run-of-the-mill ignorance, such as not knowing that Germany lies east and mostly north of France. The ignorance we study is characterized by the inability to identify potentially consequential future states of the world. Such ignorance is not merely a vague lack of comprehension or indeterminate cluelessness about the future. Rather it represents the unavoidable "non-knowledge" that impacts decision outcomes in notable life domains where even low-probability unforeseen events can have immense import.

Our study of ignorance addresses situations that can lead to a *consequential amazing development*, henceforth referred to by the acronym "CAD." To qualify, a CAD must be not only amazing but also consequential to the decision maker. To amaze, a CAD must be an outlier such that even an individual who has long contemplated the future might not have envisioned such an outcome. To illustrate, applying and being hired for a long-shot job would not qualify as a CAD; such a development can be anticipated and is not amazing. In contrast, receiving a phone call out of the blue from someone offering a terrific job that you take is a CAD—it is an amazing development with significant consequence.

CADs can be *narrow*, affecting one or a few individuals, or *broad*, impacting large groups, even societies as a whole. A CAD can be good or bad, but it must be *very* good or *very* bad, something an individual would have worked hard to promote or avoid, had he known of its possibility.[1] Although they can be beneficial—an unexpected economic boom, for instance—most CADs are bad news, and bad CADs shall get most of our attention.

An individual asked to identify a broad CAD will likely name a natural disaster, such as an earthquake or a tornado that strikes without warning. However, human action is the cause of many of the most dramatic broad CADs. Think of the Holocaust and the Great Chinese Famine of 1958–61 or, more recently, the collapse of the Soviet Union and the 2008 worldwide financial meltdown. CADs caused by purposeful human agency—the Holocaust and 9/11 come to mind—were meticulously planned by their perpetrators, but simply unimagined by their victims. Even natural calamities are frequently augured by scientists, authors, and public intellectuals, but turn out to be CADs for society-at-large.

CADs are determined from the standpoint of the decision maker. Thus, he must be amazed and the outcome must be consequential to him. We argue that literature can sensitize us to understand better when CADs are more likely and when less, and to bring what is conjecturable closer to conscious attention. Literature also imparts a painful powerful lesson about CADs. In many circumstances, a CAD might be readily inferred by outside observers, but nevertheless prove unknowable to the decision maker himself because he severely restricts his own thought processes. We refer to these as *blindered* CADs.[2] Poor choices undertaken in the callowness of youth, errors in judgment made under the rosy glow of infatuation, or the painful influence of alcohol, all have the potential to lead to blindered CADs, as would simple overconfidence that we know how things will turn out. Blindered CADs eventuate in literary fiction most famously through narratives of love gone awry. Leo Tolstoy's heroine Anna Karenina's blindered infatuation prevented her from contemplating that her step into an adulterous affair was onto a path littered with severely adverse CADs. Jay Gatsby, F. Scott Fitzgerald's titular hero, suffered similarly.

Deep CADs fall at the opposite extreme: they are simply unimaginable.[3] The Malaysian airliner that reversed course and wandered over the Indian Ocean till it was lost is a good example. So too is living in a seemingly sturdy building that suddenly collapses. Deep CADs receive little attention here. Our concern is an improved understanding of conjecturable CADs, including those that are missed because of blindered choices, and our prime subject, what we might think of as textbook CADs, those where objective contemplation could alert the decision maker that there is a good chance that something consequential is lurking in the shadows. Given the high stakes for both individuals and society, the 2008 financial meltdown is a good example of a textbook CAD.

Primary ignorance denotes the failure to recognize that one is ignorant and that highly consequential potential outcomes loom that cannot be identified. If a CAD does not occur—and CAD occurrences are rare—one's ignorance is never revealed. No doubt this pattern makes people less alert to ignorance. *Recognized ignorance* is the condition of being alert to and aware that one cannot identify important future states. Such recognition may arise because changed conditions convey a signal, such as birds flying low before a storm or animals seeking safety before a tsunami. At times, an individual with much broader experience may issue a warning, such as a doctor cautioning us about a medical calamity. Occasionally, our cognitive processes may subconsciously alert us to some critical but poorly understood situation.

Challenges to prescriptive and descriptive decision analysis

Why has decision analysis failed to address ignorance? We believe the answer is that the concept challenges organized, systematic study. Economists and psychologists who investigate decision making employ two common approaches:

1. controlled laboratory experiments, the most familiar asking subjects to choose among alternatives (balls of different colors, marbles from urns) with a payoff depending on chance outcomes; and
2. tracking real-world decision making—decisions such as how much people save, how they invest, what employment they choose—to create a quantitative dataset for detailed analysis.

Neither approach yields insights into the unique character of ignorance, for four reasons:

1. Ignorance is impossible to distill or recreate in a laboratory. To keep matters under control, experimental methods generally reduce decision problems to a clean, clear-cut set of variables. However, CADs arise from situations that are unusual and often complex. Beyond that, if one were studying *unrecognized ignorance*, it would be nearly impossible to describe a relevant situation without giving away the game.
2. Ignorance and the impact of CADs play out over long stretches of time and would be difficult to accommodate in a controlled experiment.
3. CADs, which by definition have high consequences, would be prohibitively expensive to create if those consequences were positive, and unethical to create were they negative.
4. CADs are rare and often highly unusual events. Extremely extensive field data would be required to produce even a modestly homogeneous set of CADs.

In brief, the traditional methods of the social scientist translate poorly to the ill-defined chaos of ignorance.

Literature as a diagnostic tool

We shall analyze ignorance through literature, drawing on some of the world's best-known stories. This approach brings two great virtues. First, the available universe of decisions expands dramatically beyond experiments in the laboratory. Second, stories enable us to get inside the heads of literary characters—the imaginary men and women who populate the world of literary fiction—who are facing CADs, and to experience the world as these characters do, in all its degrees of amazement and consequence. Stories are the central mechanism through which the human mind encodes reality.[4]

Literature as mimesis

The term *mimesis* means the representation of the real world in art and literature. The central argument of Aristotle's *Poetics* (2013) is that *mimesis*, or the imitation of reality, is one of the central functions of art.[5] Roman poet Horace goes further, and makes the case for literature as learning for life; in *Ars Poetica*, he asserts, "My advice to one who is trained in representation is to look to life and manners for his model [. . .]. Poets aim either to confer benefit or to give pleasure, or to say things which are at once both pleasing and helpful to life. [. . .] Fictions intended to give pleasure should approximate to the truth" (2011: 114). Assessing Horace's dictum that fiction can inform reality (in contrast to the social scientist's empirical approach) we notice an overlap: economists and psychologists run controlled experiments, examine behavioral phenomena, or investigate large quantities of data—strategies seeking to distill information that, following Horace, gets as "approximate to the truth" as possible. Similarly, authors depict literary characters making decisions under the very same conditions of interest to this essay: ignorance, amazement, and consequence.

For centuries, human beings have used stories as representative models of the real world, a condensed version of life. Stories offer what psychologists Raymond Mar and Keith Oatley term "simulations of the social world" (2008: 173) via abstraction, compression, and simplification, while giving readers the pleasure of losing themselves in the lives of strangers who, in many ways, share cognitive and behavioral characteristics with them. Recent work in literary studies proposes that literary fiction helps readers understand the human mind (Turner, 1996; Oatley et al., 2012). Economist Thomas Schelling distills it best: "Novels, plays . . . and stories give the reader . . . a stake in the outcome. . . . The characteristic that interests me is the engrossment[,] the participation, the sense of being in the story or part of it, caring, and wanting to know" (1988: 345). English lexicographer Samuel Johnson remarks in *Rambler No. 4* that the writer's "task . . . arise[s] from . . . accurate observation of the living world" (1752: 28). M. H. Abrams in *The Mirror and the Lamp* (1953), a classic text on literary theory, posits that literature provides a mirror for society, a looking glass reflecting the social life and mores of the real world.

Literary fiction leads us into truly interesting territory in terms of complex decision making with idiosyncratic variables. Authors convey tremendous amounts of information involving psychological insight and probability judgment on the high side, and blind ignorance on the low, by placing literary characters in situations involving complex decisions with insufficient information to identify what might happen. CADs are low-probability events that have great impact. Literature often depicts situations where a CAD unexpectedly appears and wallops its unsuspecting victims. Our literary examples often reveal that the characters involved could not have recognized the possibility of a CAD from past experience, much less calculated its probability. Moreover, they are ordinary men and women—people who resemble us in their behavior and thinking.

In Gustave Flaubert's *Madame Bovary* (2002), Charles Bovary is a stolid rural doctor who marries the young and beautiful Emma Bovary, ignorant of her true character. Dazzled by her attractions, which seemingly confirm his opinion that she will make a suitable wife, he ends up with an adulterous partner who plunges him into debt. Emma is equally ignorant of her husband's true character. Her head filled with romantic fantasies, she yearns for a sophisticated partner and the glamour of city life, but finds herself trapped in a somnolent marriage with a rustic man. In this case, neither Charles nor Emma had the past experience or warning from others to indicate the potential for the CADs that overtook their future life.[6]

These literary characters are portrayed as cognitively and behaviorally similar to men and women in real life. Characters in mythology and fantasy have experiences that ordinary folks would never encounter, but to capture our interest, they too must face decisions as do ordinary humans. And they encounter CADs, plentifully. The *Odyssey*, Homer's epic poem, describes Greek hero Odysseus's ten-year journey home to Ithaca following the destruction of Troy. Odysseus repeatedly confronts circumstances that he could not have conceived—or, to use our label, situations of ignorance. His legendary cunning, his tenacity, and his skills as a strategist do not enable him to banish or overcome ignorance, but they do enable him to grapple with it.

Odysseus has a significant advantage over most mortals; he is frequently forewarned by the gods (who are running interference) that he will be confronted with yet another unforeseeable challenge as he wends his way home. CADs continue to occur: a debilitating lethargy in the Land of the Lotus-Eaters, the catastrophic loss of all but one of his ships to the cannibalistic Laestrygonians, the lengthy marooning on Calypso's island, the looming menace of the giant Cyclops Polyphemus who threatens to eat Odysseus after consuming his men, the perilous encounter with the enchantress Circe who turns some of his men into swine, the hypnotic lure of the Sirens, the watery hazards between Scylla and Charybdis, and finally, the challenge in clearing his house of a band of rapacious and sybaritic suitors for his wife once he is back in Ithaca disguised as a beggar (a flexible and shrewd strategy that allows him to learn the lay of the land before revealing himself). Odysseus represents the ideal of measured decision making, admittedly with a bit of divine help. Had he failed to anticipate some of the CADs he faced, had he been frozen with indecision when a CAD struck, and had he not given full flight to his creativity in overcoming each one, he would have been doomed. His forward-looking and thoughtful approach to ignorance distinguishes him from the vast swath of humanity, as we detail in the final section of this chapter.

Stories such as Homer's epics, in portraying ignorance, raise empirical questions that decision theorists will someday be able to answer. They also prompt some age-old questions: How did these literary characters end up in their current predicaments? What clues did they encounter, and ignore, along the way? What should they do now? But our immediate question as analysts of decisions is: How can readers employ literature to train themselves to anticipate and respond appropriately to CADs? Literary fiction, with its narratives that are threaded through with the unknown and the unknowable, we argue, provides material for both critical self-contemplation and the development of alternative methodologies; each is necessary for training in anticipating CADs. For our purposes, a literary narrative frequently depends on unpredictable narrative arcs and the ignorance of the literary characters involved. Plots and sub-plots stretch out over long periods of time—a sufficient horizon for examining CADs, which, by their very nature, defy the human control and agency that characterize randomized controlled experiments.

Literary lessons on ignorance

There are two critical ingredients for lessons gleaned from literature: first, they require a close reading of text and sub-text (or underlying meaning) with sharp literary analysis skills; second, any useful information patterns should be translated into testable propositions. That said, literature provides two main areas of training on ignorance:

1. *Anticipation.* Literary narratives demonstrate that ignorance is commonplace, and that CADs leap in seemingly from nowhere. Literature teaches the reader the importance of anticipating possible CADs when making decisions that affect critical life areas such as education, employment, and marriage. Our analysis deals mainly with personal CADs, since they constitute the theme of most well-known works of literature, but our hypotheses extend well to societal CADs such as revolutions and financial meltdowns.
2. *Contemplation.* Examining fiction teaches the reader the importance of the imagination in contemplating and envisioning CADs. We concede that while vigilance regarding contemplation is difficult to achieve, it is a critical ingredient for dealing effectively with ignorance. Thus, we propose reading fiction to develop one's contemplation "muscles."

Three elements must be considered for an effective decision under uncertainty: the future states of the world, the probability of each, and possible actions. When an action meets a state of the world, a payoff—also called a *utility*—is reaped. For each action, an expected utility can be computed by multiplying the respective probability times the utility the action yields. Decision analysis prescribes that the action yielding the highest expected utility is the course to be chosen.

Four discouraging themes emerge below. First, if important future states cannot be identified, people cannot perform the required utility calculations just described. Second, even when ignorance might be conjectured, individuals fail to recognize it. Third, when ignorance is recognized, individuals frequently make poor decisions. Fourth, in matters of ignorance, organizations and societies fail in much the way that individuals fail: through poor anticipation and poor decisions. We pursue these themes, drawing lessons from literature. In essence, we use literature to better understand human decision processes. This chapter shows that examination of great works of literature provides untapped learning opportunities for studying ignorance in systematic ways and at modest expense.

Learning about ignorance has important implications. Once ignorance becomes a part of the decision-theoretic discourse, decision scientists can develop methods and train decision makers to cope with it. The greater our understanding of ignorance and CADs, the more improved our recognition of and responses to these phenomena will be. Even without divine intervention, we can, like Odysseus, undertake certain actions to recognize ignorance and to prepare for potential CADs.

A systematic study of ignorance is important for a number of reasons. When contemplating the future, people frequently fail to account for their ignorance of events and their outcomes. People who do attempt to be forecasters run into grave difficulties:

1 When unpredictable events occur, such as the completely unforeseen successes of ISIS in 2014, they are usually *sui generis*. For such events, it is not possible to assemble multiple instances, much less a sufficient number of instances to apply the statistical methods that provide the backbone for effective forecasting.[7]
2 Potential CADs are many. Occurring CADs are few. Moreover, for most potential CADs, their potential existence never becomes known. Furthermore, those CADs that do arise have no schedule. The 2008 financial meltdown came after a sustained boom; the Arab Spring toppled long-standing despots. These properties would make it almost impossible for a sophisticated decision theorist, much less a mere mortal, to compute a base rate for CADs of a particular type, yet knowing base rates in various situations could give fair warning.
3 People who do contemplate CADs tend to be limited by the parameters of what they have already seen or experienced. Human beings are given to over-extrapolate likelihoods from the known past to the unknown future. This is a form of the Availability Heuristic (Tversky and Kahneman, 1973) and its cousin, the Recognition Heuristic (Goldstein and Gigerenzer, 2002)—both mental shortcuts describing people's tendencies to predict the likelihood of an event based on how easily memory brings such an event to mind.

Greek mythology's Oedipus provides one of the best examples for our theory of ignorance. His fate demonstrates the invisible but nevertheless forbidding boundary that separates the present from our knowledge of the future—knowledge that is epistemologically questionable, unreliable, and frequently chimerical. Son of Theban King Laius and his wife Jocasta, the infant Oedipus is abandoned to die on Mount Cithaeron by his father, after an oracle warns Laius that his own son will kill him. But Oedipus is ultimately saved and later adopted by Corinthian King Polybus and his wife Merope. The adult Oedipus, ignorant of the history of his parentage, eventually returns to Thebes, the land of his birth. His ignorance allows him to take two consequential actions he would never consider had he possibly contemplated their implications. First, he murders Laius in a freak, rage-fuelled incident (unaware he has committed patricide). Then he marries Jocasta not knowing she is his mother. Oedipus and Jocasta have four children: daughters Antigone and Ismene, and sons Polyneices and Eteocles. Oedipus ultimately discovers the entire truth of his personal history. Jocasta commits suicide and Oedipus blinds himself. Captured by Greek tragedian Sophocles in his play *Oedipus Rex* (1984), Oedipus depicts how ignorance can neither be "domesticated" nor controlled. Frequently we make decisions not contemplating devastating CADs. Randomness in the world—a dramatic drop in the stock market, an implausibly hot summer—is readily imagined, but unique outlier events—one's love object turns out to be one's mother—are often beyond conjecture.

Cognitive biases and heuristics: What ails us?

Ignorance represents an unknown and vast ocean of unpredicted possibilities. As our study shows, ignorance can be more consequential than the much-studied uncertainty and risk, certainly in terms of expected value lost from inadequate decision making. Yet ignorance remains virtually unexamined by decision theorists. We alluded above to the poor decisions individuals make with respect to ignorance. A major reason is that cognitive biases and heuristics severely impede appropriate responses (Kahneman and Tversky, 1979). We would further argue that as problems get murkier along the spectrum from risk to uncertainty to ignorance, the challenges to effective decision making mount, and biases and heuristics play an ever-greater role.

Why should this be? One explanation is that individuals simply choose not to think about ignorance. Thus, even when it might be readily identified, it lays hidden. Psychologists Amos Tversky and Daniel Kahneman's initial research (1973, 1974) identified three prime biases—*availability*, *anchoring*, and *representativeness*—that have since been joined by dozens of additional biases identified by an entire generation of behavioral scientists. From Samuelson and Zeckhauser's (1988) *status quo bias* to Kahneman, Knetch, and Thaler's (1991) *endowment effect*, decision theory's greatest contribution in the last forty years has been recognizing patterns of behavioral quirks, and examining such irregularities through creative, often lively, experiments. Identifying new cognitive biases that surround CADs—a modest start is made here—would be an exciting frontier for future research on ignorance. We suggest that the best way to prepare people for ignorance is to train them in an awareness of inconsistencies in their thinking. Many of these inconsistencies doubly impair decision making in the presence of ignorance.

Ignorance interacts in significant ways with biases and heuristics. Under the *availability heuristic*, people contemplate events that reside within their cognitive horizons but may occur infrequently. Examples range from earthquakes in an earthquake zone to shark attacks on a beach, even a beach where sharks have never been present.[8] In contrast, CADs are not *available* since they would then cease to be amazing. CADs also defy the *representativeness heuristic* since they are usually unique and unlikely to belong to a typical class of similar events. Given *hindsight bias* (Fischoff and Beyth, 1975) people will tend to overestimate the future likelihood of a former CAD that they have experienced. In doing so, they may let down their guard. Such a person's defective reasoning might be: "I am now aware of my error in not predicting the particular CAD that happened. Therefore, I am alert to predicting CADs in the future."

Confirmation bias (Nickerson, 1998) refers to people's tendency to form an initial hypothesis and then look for evidence that supports it. People fail to consider alternative hypotheses; they also avoid looking for evidence that contradicts their initial hypothesis since they are cognitively anchored to it, finding refuge in an inadequate psychological reference point. Even when the anchor is clearly random, people tend toward estimates close to the initial anchor, seeking the comfort of a cognitive "security blanket." In the case of CADs, or indeed of any decision making under uncertainty, anchoring severely limits our contemplation of consequences.

Early humans associated natural calamities with bad behavior and drew the conclusion that the gods were angered. The Old Testament frequently elaborates on this theme, as with the Great Flood in *Genesis*. CADs continue to throw sand in the eyes of modern people. Extreme outliers, being unique, often provide too little evidence to explain their origins. The human desire to point the finger of blame when a catastrophe happens, however, often causes people to arrive incorrectly at causal conclusions. Moreover, most CADs—the sudden collapse of the Soviet Union, one's romantic calamity, or the 2008 meltdown—have multiple contributing sources. Yet, people often apply the cause-and-effect thinking we encounter in detective fiction, seeking a single perpetrator. A complementary failing arises from the bias of *persisting with prior beliefs* as an explanation of causation (Michotte, 1963; Rips, 2011). Such beliefs may lead observers to avoid noticing informative relationships that do exist. In short, people fail to learn effectively when CADs strike. Sometimes, they conclude more than the evidence will bear; at other times, they overlook available evidence on causality.

Fortunately, unlike Odysseus, few humans encounter one CAD after another. The CADs that do arise tend to be quite disparate. The rarity of such encounters is good for one's welfare, but bad for learning. Here literature can make a contribution. An hour spent with William Shakespeare or William Faulkner will expose the reader to a vicarious CAD, and the next hour to another. As we detail in the following sections, reading great works of literature makes us aware of the nuanced, often insidious, ways in which our own cognitive biases, and the decision heuristics they engender, exacerbate the affliction of ignorance.

Biases that impede the recognition of ignorance

To cope with ignorance, we urge self-awareness, asking ourselves whether a state of consequential ignorance is likely in this situation. Essentially, we suggest continually estimating a base rate for a CAD. Such estimation is challenging, since two fundamental biases intrude.

1 Overconfidence

As Alpert and Raiffa (1982) have demonstrated, individuals are overconfident when estimating quantities. Extrapolating from the Alpert and Raiffa results, if individuals are asked to identify states of the world that they can envision for the future, they will overestimate the density for which they can account.

William Shakespeare's King Lear decides to divide his kingdom among his three daughters and then retire, but not before he tests their loyalty. He is woefully overconfident that he can discern the true feelings for him of his daughters, Goneril, Regan, and Cordelia, merely by asking—a very weak test. The two older daughters respond with profuse professions of filial affection. Cordelia, Lear's favorite, is more measured in her response. This angers her father, who disowns her and proceeds to divide his time between Goneril and Regan. Lear finds that they treat him in an autocratic, peremptory, and cruel manner. Lear never contemplated the CADs that now occur. This once all-powerful monarch ends up wandering homeless during a terrifying storm, rendered nearly mad by his daughters' hypocrisy and abuse, accompanied only by his Fool, the court jester. Goneril and Regan plot against one another. Lear and Cordelia are captured, and Cordelia is hanged by her captors. Her beloved father is unable to save her. He now realizes his folly: his extraordinary overconfidence in relying on his elder daughters' cheap talk of their filial ties. This betrayal by Goneril and Regan represents a blindered CAD for Lear. An objective observer could have told him not to make consequential reliance on words that were cheap for these daughters to utter. Such reliance would risk awful CADs.

2 Salience

Individuals tend to identify states that are salient—in other words, circumstances with which they have some experience (*recognition bias*) or those that are easily brought to mind (*accessibility)* from an active to a latent state following activation by an external stimulus (Higgins, 1996). They overestimate the likelihood of such events (*availability heuristic*) when envisioning the future.

Jonathan Swift's novel *Gulliver's Travels* (2001) vividly demonstrates the hero's attempt to frame imagination-defying CADs and successive situations of ignorance in terms of *salience*, *accessibility*, and the *availability bias*. The book describes the travels of Lemuel Gulliver, a literal-minded surgeon, to four different lands that lie beyond the bounds of human expectation: Lilliput, a kingdom of tiny people where Gulliver is considered a giant; Brobdingnag, a land of giants where Gulliver finds himself defenseless on account of his small size; the floating island of Laputa; and finally, the land of the Houyhnhnms, ruled by exceedingly rational horses who are served by Yahoos—brute, human-like creatures. While *Gulliver's Travels* was intended as a satire on contemporary religion and politics in eighteenth-century England (and not as children's literature, as is frequently assumed), the novel is also an excellent study of behavioral proclivities under ignorance. Gulliver deals with each CAD by bringing to mind salient experiences from his former life as a stolid English doctor, even though these former experiences have no relevance to his current situation. He misses some cues, miscalculates the applicability of others, and frames his situation incorrectly because he has no base-rate information.[9]

Biases once ignorance is recognized

Even if ignorance is recognized, different heuristics and biases come into play.

People are likely to draw wrong lessons from the past, a bias we call *Retrospective Recollection of Contemplation* (RRC). RRC whitewashes an individual's past ignorance. Though we did not anticipate the CAD that transpired, RRC steers us to recollect erroneously that it was among the possibilities we had considered, perhaps due to a memory of a thought that can be construed as having been vaguely close.

Love affairs gone awry often bring RRC into play. In Jane Austen's *Persuasion* (2012), the heroine Anne Elliott is, at twenty-seven, unhappy, single, and full of regret at her earlier decision to reject the marriage offer of her former suitor, Frederick Wentworth. In this decision, she was *persuaded* (the source of Austen's title) by the seemingly benevolent hand of family friend Lady Russell, who believed Wentworth's financial prospects were insufficient for Anne, a baronet's daughter. This rejection strikes as a CAD in Wentworth's life, who responds by enlisting in the Royal Navy. When the novel begins, eight years have passed and he has returned as a decorated and wealthy naval captain, a reversal of fortune in contrast to the slide of Anne's own aristocratic family, who are now living in shabby gentility.

Wentworth then falls prey to RRC under recognized ignorance. He determines that in the past, he was willfully oblivious to Anne's true character, blinded by his love. With his new maturity of age and achievement, he notices that she is easily influenced by others and much diminished in beauty, retaining none of the qualities that he once found so alluring. The first CAD that happened—the rejection of his love—now appears to him to have then been on his mental map of the world as an inevitability. Although *Persuasion* ends happily with Anne and Wentworth's wedding, for much of the novel, Wentworth falls prey to RRC in contemplating his past ignorance of her character.

Ignorance recognized is, alas, not ignorance conquered. Heuristics continue to distort thinking. We highlight two of many:

1 *Status quo bias* (SQB). SQB leads one to stay the course by "doing nothing or maintaining one's current or previous decision" (Samuelson and Zeckhauser 1988: 7). One prominent psychological explanation is that errors of commission weigh more heavily than errors of omission (Ritov and Baron 1990, 1992). Potential blame, from oneself and others, reinforces this disparity. Thus, SQB is particularly potent when the CADs that loom are likely to be unfavorable.
2 *Indecision bias* (IB). IB arises when one must choose among alternatives, the future is cloudy, and consequential outcomes are possible. When individuals recognize their ignorance, they are frequently frozen with indecision and in a state of complete inaction. IB differs strongly from SQB in that it is characterized by the evasion of a decision, perhaps while waiting for something ill-defined to happen, rather than by the choice to do nothing.

We encounter IB in its full glory in Samuel Beckett's existential drama, *Waiting for Godot* (1956). On a country road, tramps Vladimir and Estragon wait endlessly for the arrival of the mysterious Godot, who continually defers arrival while sending word that he is on his way. A rational choice would be to leave, but Vladimir and Estragon continue to wait. They pass the time in rambling conversations on mundane topics and in meaningless banter with two other characters, Lucky and Pozzo. Twice, a boy brings news that Godot will arrive tomorrow. At the end of the play, Vladimir and Estragon discuss their miserable lot in life and consider hanging themselves. And yet they continue to wait. The stage directions make their indecision clear. At the end of the final act, Estragon asks, "Well, shall we go?" to which Vladimir replies, "Yes, let's go." The stage direction reads: "They do not move."

Heal thyself: Prescriptions for a world of ignorance

Ignorance is present across a multiplicity of real-life domains—from an individual's decision whether to try a new city to improve job prospects, to a society's choice as to whether or not to legalize drugs. The theme of our analysis is that literature, by reporting broadly on human experience, may offer key insights into ignorance and prescriptions for coping with it. The first challenge with ignorance is to recognize its presence. Reading great works of literature can sensitize us to clues that CADs—amazing and consequential developments—are potential future occurrences. CADs are almost always low-probability occurrences; if not, they would not be amazing. But if extremely low, they are not worth worrying about. To co-opt George Orwell's understated account of equal animals: "All low probabilities are low, but some are less low than others." CADs with probabilities less low make ignorance important.[10]

Strategic use of System 1 and System 2

Once we understand the potential for ignorance and the CADs that can follow, what is to be done? The individual can tailor his decision-making processes in response. The *dual process theory* of decision making attributes choices to either fast and unconscious intuition or to slow and deliberate reasoning. These cognitive mechanisms are labeled as *System 1* and *System 2* (Stanovich and West, 2000; Kahneman, 2003, 2011). While System 1 demands less conscious mental attention since it is largely automatic, System 2 brings superior contemplation. It is thus better at confronting ignorance, but is expensive to employ in terms of time and effort.

The key implication of this unavoidable tradeoff between dual cognitive systems is that the mind's resources should be employed strategically and parsimoniously. Where minor decisions are involved (which shirt to buy or what to order at a restaurant), reliance on the cognitively inexpensive System 1 will suffice. However, when the product of likelihood and consequence for CADs is large, the slower and more deliberate processes involved in System 2 are merited. So, too, it is for societies responding to ignorance. For one's personal life, a sound heuristic is to employ System 2 for big decisions, such as those involving marriage, jobs, or investment for retirement. Beyond that, unfamiliar circumstances reinforce the potential for CADs, implying a tilt to System 2.

Herbert Simon (1990) argues that behavior is shaped by the two blades of a pair of scissors, one blade representing cognition and the other symbolizing the decision environment. To recognize the potential presence of ignorance, both blades should be deployed. If ignorance is unlikely, seek cognitive economy and utilize System 1. However, if ignorance appears to be a factor, careful consideration using System 2 is warranted. This strategy should push thinking persons first toward efforts to avert unfavorable CADs, then toward the adoption of flexible strategies that will be superior should a CAD strike, and finally toward struggles to overcome the behavioral biases that afflict attempts to recognize and deal with ignorance. It is simply impractical to employ System 2 every time one must order at a restaurant or answer an e-mail. It would take a person a full day to address a single hour's challenges.

People should stay alert and attempt to recognize ignorance, asking themselves, "Might something truly consequential happen in this context?" System 1 should be able to do the required scanning, much as it regularly scans for everyday dangers, such as driving accidents. Perhaps 2 percent of the time, the answer will be yes, CADs are a realistic concern, and then the deliberations of System 2 should be brought into play. In the vast majority of cases in that high-alert 2 percent, nothing consequential will happen, which makes maintaining vigilance more difficult.

Summing up

The chroniclers of everyday life, from Jane Austen and Franz Kafka to those who write soap operas, make clear that even regular folks living in ordinary times experience CADs. Broad CADs—for example, revolutions and financial collapses—are portrayed by authors from Dickens and Pasternak to tomorrow's novelists of Wall Street. Ignorance abounds, yet it often goes unrecognized. Like keeping your eye on the ball in tennis, or leaning your weight downhill in skiing, staying alert to ignorance is an unnatural skill that has to be learned. So too is the skill of responding to ignorance effectively. Literature, as we have shown in these pages, can be effective as both tocsin and teacher.

Notes

1 We admit there could be a balanced CAD, very good on some dimensions and very bad on others, but we expect that balanced CADs are extremely rare.

2 We use "blinder" as a modifier and also as a verb in this essay, which we recognize is uncommon usage. It serves to convey the idea of having one's field of cognitive vision distorted and limited, like that of a horse wearing actual blinders.

3 Joseph K., an innocuous and conscientious bank employee in Kafka's novel *The Trial*, experiences a deep CAD nightmare. He is arrested one morning; charges are never revealed; and, ultimately, he is executed.
4 See, for instance, the work of psychologist Jerome Bruner who suggests that we "cling to narrative models of reality and use them to shape our everyday experiences" (2002: 7) and literary theorist Brian Boyd who argues, "Minds exist to predict what will happen next" (2009: 134).
5 "Art" here refers broadly to creative products of the imagination, and not merely to visual art such as paintings.
6 Literary narratives also present positive CADs. In Jane Austen's *Pride and Prejudice* (2000), for instance, a famous love story begins rather unpromisingly: the hero and the heroine cannot stand each other. The arrogant Mr. Darcy claims Elizabeth Bennet is "not handsome enough to tempt *me*," while Elizabeth offers the equally withering riposte that she "may safely promise . . . *never* to dance with him." Both are ignorant of the possibility of a future romance and have no idea that their lives, as detailed in the novel, will be overtaken by an impossible-to-conceive but extremely beneficial development: they fall in love, wed, and have a seemingly compatible marriage.
7 With narrow CADs, similar events may have struck other individuals, but the person affected was amazed, implying that he did not extrapolate from a substantial sample of the experiences of others. Perhaps he was unaware of such experiences. Perhaps, like Madame Bovary and Anna Karenina, strong emotions clouded his thinking.
8 Emphasizing the role played by visceral factors in decision making under risk and uncertainty, George Loewenstein argues, "People's cognitive evaluations of risks often diverge from their emotional reactions to those risks; people fear things that they recognize, at a cognitive level, to be benign, and do not fear things that they realize are objectively threatening. These divergences occur because the determinants of fear are different from the determinants of cognitive evaluations of riskiness" (2000: 430). We posit that these cognitive evaluations are further blurred, if not entirely nullified, under conditions of ignorance.
9 For more on the phenomenon wherein the decision maker incorporates irrelevant information through a combination of salience and anchoring, see Chapman and Johnson (2002).
10 Of course, the magnitude of potential CADs also matters, but ways to estimate magnitudes of unidentifiable events is beyond the scope of this chapter.

References

Abrams, M. H. (1953) *The Mirror and the Lamp: Romantic Theory and the Critical Tradition*, New York: Oxford University Press.

Alpert, M., and Raiffa, H. (1982) "A progress report on the training of probability assessors," in D. Kahneman, P. Slovic, and A. Tversky (eds) *Judgment under Uncertainty: Heuristics and Biases*, Cambridge: Cambridge University Press.

Aristotle (2013) *Poetics*, trans. and intro. A. Kenny, Oxford: Oxford University Press.

Austen, J. (2000) *Pride and Prejudice*, New York: Norton.

— (2012) *Persuasion*, New York: Norton.

Beckett, S. (1956) *Waiting for Godot*, New York: Grove Press.

Boyd, B. (2009) *On the Origin of Stories: Evolution, Cognition and Fiction*, Cambridge, MA, and London: Harvard University Press.

Bruner, J. (2002) *Making Stories: Law, Literature, Life*, New York: Farrar, Straus and Giroux.

Chapman, G. B., and Johnson, E. J. (2002) "Incorporating the irrelevant: Anchors in judgments of belief and value," in T. Gilovich, D. Griffin, and D. Kahneman (eds), *Heuristics and Biases: The Psychology of Intuitive Judgment*, Cambridge: Cambridge University Press.

Fischhoff, B., and Beyth, R. (1975) "'I knew it would happen': Remembered probabilities of once-future things," *Organizational Behaviour and Human Performance*, 13: 1–16.

Flaubert, G. (2002) *Madame Bovary*, trans. and intro. M. Roberts, Harmondsworth: Penguin.

Goldstein, D. G. and Gigerenzer, G. (2002) "Models of ecological rationality: The recognition heuristic," *Psychological Review*, 109(1): 75–90.

Gomory, R. E. (1995) "The known, the unknown and the unknowable," *Scientific American*, 272(6): 120.

Higgins, E. T. (1996) "Knowledge activation: Accessibility, applicability, and salience," in E. T. Higgins and A. W. Kruglanski (eds) *Social Psychology: Handbook of Basic Principles*, New York: Guilford Press.

Horace (2011) *Satires and Epistles*, trans. John Davie, Oxford: Oxford University Press.

Johnson, S. (1752) *The Rambler, Vol. 1*, London: J. Payne.

Kahneman, D. (2003) "Maps of bounded rationality: Psychology for behavioral economics," *American Economic Review*, 93(5): 1449–75.
Kahneman, D., and Tversky, A. (1979) "Prospect theory: An analysis of decision under risk," *Econometrica*, 47(2): 263–91.
Kahneman, D., Knetsch, J. L., and Thaler, R. H. (1991) "Anomalies: The endowment effect, loss aversion, and status quo bias," *Journal of Economic Perspectives*, 5(1): 193–206.
— (2011) *Thinking, Fast and Slow*, New York: Farrar, Straus and Giroux.
Loewenstein, G. (2000) "Emotions in economic theory and economic behavior," *American Economic Review*, 90(2): 426–32.
Mar, R. A., and Oatley, K. (2008) "The function of fiction is the abstraction and simulation of social experience," *Perspectives on Psychological Science*, 3(3): 173–92.
Michotte, A. (1963) *The perception of causality*, trans. T. R. Miles & E. Miles, New York: Basic Books.
Nickerson, R. S. (1998) "Confirmation bias: A ubiquitous phenomenon in many guises," *Review of General Psychology*, 2(2): 175–220.
Oatley, K., Mar, R. A., and Djikic, M. (2012) "The psychology of fiction: Present and future," in I. Jaén and J. J. Simon (eds) *Cognitive Literary Studies: Current Themes and New Directions*, Austin: University of Texas Press.
Rips, L. J. (2011) "Causation from perception," *Perspectives on Psychological Science*, 6: 77–97.
Ritov, I., and Baron, J. (1990) "Reluctance to vaccinate: Omission bias and ambiguity," *Journal of Behavioral Decision making*, 3: 263–77.
— (1992) "Status-quo and omission bias," *Journal of Risk and Uncertainty*, 5: 49–61.
Samuelson, W., and Zeckhauser, R. J. (1988) "Status quo bias in decision making," *Journal of Risk and Uncertainty*, 1: 7–59.
Schelling, T. C. (1988) "The mind as a consuming organ," in D. E. Bell, H. Raiffa, and A. Tversky (eds) *Decision making: Descriptive, Normative, and Prescriptive Interactions*, Cambridge and New York: Cambridge University Press.
Simon, H. A. (1990) "Invariants of human behavior," *Annual Review of Psychology*, 41: 1–20.
Sophocles (1984) *Three Theban Plays: Antigone; Oedipus the King; Oedipus at Colonus*, trans. R. Fagles, London: Penguin.
Stanovich, K. E., and West, R. F. (2000) "Individual differences in reasoning: Implications for the rationality debate?" *Behavioral and Brain Sciences*, 23(5): 645–65.
Swift, J. (2001) *Gulliver's Travels*, New York: Norton.
Taleb, N. N. (2007) *The Black Swan: The Impact of the Highly Improbable*, New York: Random House.
Turner, M. (1996) *The Literary Mind: The Origins of Thought and Language*, New York and Oxford: Oxford University Press.
Tversky, A., and Kahneman, D. (1973) "Availability: A heuristic for judging frequency and probability," *Cognitive Psychology*, 5(2): 207–32.
— (1974) "Judgment under uncertainty: Heuristics and biases," *Science*, 185(4157): 1124–31.
Zeckhauser, R. J. (2006) "Investing in the unknown and unknowable," *Capitalism and Society*, 1(2): 1–39.

Part II

Registering the unknown

Ignorance as methodology

8

The production of forbidden knowledge

Joanna Kempner

In science, the search for knowledge is often considered an unlimited good or even a "moral calling" (Weber 1946). However, the idea that some knowledge is dangerous and ought to be forbidden is deeply entrenched in Western culture. The ancients warned about such hazards in literature and myth: the Tree of Knowledge, Prometheus, and Pandora's Box all caution about the dangers of unlimited knowledge. In the contemporary world, scientists, policymakers, advocates and the public regularly engage in debates about whether and how to place limits on potentially dangerous knowledge, from fetal tissue research to genetically modified organisms (GMOs). While philosophers of science and bioethicists have long been interested in forbidden knowledge as a category, social scientists are only just starting to investigate how these limits are formulated, imposed, administrated and, at times, breached. This chapter provides a brief overview of this research.

What is forbidden knowledge?

Forbidden knowledge is defined as knowledge that is too sensitive, dangerous or taboo to produce. Scholars of the epistemology of ignorance have not yet agreed about how to categorize forbidden knowledge within the broader (and, perhaps, infinite) phenomena of ignorance. Gross (2010), who has developed a comprehensive typology of ignorance, argues that dangerous knowledge ought to be understood as a form of what Knorr Cetina (1999: 64) called "negative knowledge," or "knowledge of the limits of knowing, of the mistakes we make in trying to know, of the things that interfere with our knowing, of what we are not interested in and do not really want to know." In this view, forbidden knowledge is what might colloquially be called a "known unknown."

But, as Kass (2009: 272) notes, forbidden knowledge (or, as he calls it "forbidding science") does not necessarily refer to ignorance. The term forbidden has two meanings: first, as a past-tense verb that refers to "proscribed" or "refused to allow"; and second, as an adjective, meaning "grim, menacing, or ominous." The term "knowledge" is also ambiguous in the sense that it can refer to the *pursuit* of knowledge through research and experimentation or it can refer to the *dissemination* or *application* of knowledge. In addition, because the boundaries of forbidden knowledge are locally produced (and, therefore, ever changing and essentially contested), it is often a category of knowledge that *heightens* the interest of researchers. Indeed, as I discuss below, many researchers report that they are attracted to topics typically considered forbidden and they have developed various mechanisms for getting such research done. Forbidden knowledge, then, blurs the boundaries between knowledge and ignorance.

The extant literature typically categorizes forbidden knowledge into one of two types. The first type is methodological: any knowledge, no matter how important, which is obtainable only through unacceptable means is forbidden. Policymakers or committees create many of these limits on inquiry. For example, the Nuremberg Code of Ethics set principles for ethical conduct in human experimentation that effectively reduced the kinds of research considered appropriate. Regulatory requirements continue to place constraints on how human experimentation is done and now extend to other areas of research conduct: animal research, studies of dangerous pathogens, and disposal of hazardous waste products, among others. More recently, local ethics boards (for example, Institutional Review Boards (IRB) in the United States) are charged with making these determinations. IRBs, consisting of faculty and lay members, promote a community discussion about what is "acceptable risk"—forbidding all research deemed "unacceptable" (Proctor 2008).

The second category, forbidden knowledge in its classical sense, is consequentialist. This is knowledge considered dangerous because it violates some sacred natural order or because of its potential to undermine the social order (Johnson 1996; Cohen 1977; Nelkin 1982; Smith 1996). Critics across the political spectrum worry about technologies that appear to threaten the "natural" order; for example, the social and environmental impact of genetically modified organisms. Of particular concern are dual-use technologies, which are capable of being used in ways both beneficial and malicious. For example, well-intentioned health research into the genetics of deadly pathogens could be used to create biological weapons for which there are no treatments. But as we will see below, banning substantive topics is contentious.

How is forbidden knowledge created?

These categories, while descriptive, do not address the important question of agency: if some knowledge is forbidden, who is doing the forbidding? This is a central concern for Johnson (1999), who argues any analysis of forbidden knowledge must recognize that knowledge can only be forbidden by some authority or powerful interest. While this is an important critique, it presumes that knowledge is only forbidden via proscription. In contrast, Kempner et al. (2005) find that most topics considered forbidden by scientists are regulated through *informal* mechanisms of social control, rather than top-down forms of regulation. While these more ambiguous mechanisms tend to obscure agency, an in-depth exploration of how forbidden knowledge is produced reveals how power relations shape what it is we think we ought not to know.

Formal social regulations designed to curtail dangerous studies are the most visible way that forbidden knowledge is produced. For example, state policymakers sometimes institute formal bans on categories of research, like research involving fetal tissue transplantation or certain categories of psychoactive drugs. Other times, policymakers might allow such research to continue, while disallowing state money for its funding, effectively making the conduct of this research difficult if not impossible. In the United States, for example, Congress placed restrictions on the federal funding of gun violence research (a ban that was lifted in 2013 by President Barack Obama). While American researchers could theoretically study gun violence, a lack of federal funding made the actual conduct of this research rare in practice.

Formal regulations can also be instituted in more local formats: for example, ethics boards can deny permission to conduct potentially sensitive research and professional research organizations can place moratoriums on research within their ranks, as did the US National Academy of Sciences in 2002 when they called for a legislative ban on human reproductive cloning. Local communities may also move to ban certain forms of research deemed too dangerous, such as when Davis, California residents successfully thwarted plans to build a biosafety lab where researchers would study deadly pathogens, like anthrax (Miller 2004). Scientific journals, where research is disseminated, can also place limits on so-called dangerous knowledge, as did a consortium of 17 top science journal editors who publicly stated "that on occasions an editor may conclude that the potential harm of publication outweighs the potential societal benefits" (Journal Editors and Authors Group 2003: 771).

Scientists, advocates and the public generally agree that there ought to be at least some restrictions on human and animal experimentation, but the scope of these restrictions are often controversial. Proscribed limits to the *substance* of inquiry are almost always contentious (Marchant and Pope 2009). Forbidding knowledge based on substance poses significant challenges. The discussion regarding what is or what should be forbidden is necessarily abstract (Rehmann-Sutter 1996). First, forbidden knowledge is a dynamic category, the contents of which shift depending on culture, political climate and the interests of researchers. Radical, paradigmatic-busting ideas – that the Earth is not the center of the universe, that apes begot humans, that time is relative – become normalized. Variations in culture and governance also make restrictions on knowledge production difficult to uphold, even when there is widespread agreement that certain areas of knowledge ought to be banned. Any single country's restrictions on certain types of research may be undermined when other countries disagree or even support said research. For example, research on human reproductive cloning may be verboten in the United States, but it is actively encouraged in other countries, like South Korea. Likewise, it is noteworthy that, within IRBs, it is local communities that define "acceptable risk". Thus, although forbidden knowledge is often thought of as a static category – the contents of which do not change across culture or time – locally produced rules help create the boundaries of what ought not be known. Second, we cannot predict the consequences of knowledge prior to obtaining that knowledge. Transgressive knowledge – knowledge that threatens the existing social order – can have a positive transformative effect. Likewise, seemingly benign research can be put to malicious use. Nor can we accurately assess the counterfactual to those developments that already changed our world. How would the world look without a Manhattan project? Unlike Adam and Eve, we lack a transcendent, omniscient moral authority to provide guidance for making such determinations.

Nevertheless, the interests behind these restrictions are relatively easy to identify, which is part of what makes the question of *who* ought to be charged with placing restrictions on science so controversial. Legislators have oversight over the use of state funds, but short-term ideological interests may drive their judgment. Republicans in the United States Congress, for example, have made repeated attempts to defund research that they find trivial or salacious. In 2013, the US House of Representatives voted to defund political science grants made by the National Science Foundation (NSF), "except for research projects that the Director of the National Science Foundation certifies as promoting national security or the economic interests of the United States" (National Science Foundation 2013). This is not a new strategy: in the 1970s, Senator William Proxmire (a Democrat from Wisconsin) gave out a monthly "Golden Fleece Award" to federally funded studies that he deemed a waste of taxpayer money.

In response, many scientists have argued that they ought to be given autonomy in these decisions so that science may be kept free from social or ideological concerns (see Leshner 2003). Others argue that this position ignores the fact that expert knowledge is also guided by political and ideological motivations that may fail to reflect the moral commitments of society writ large.

Bioethicists are often called upon as expert advisors who can help guide policymakers' decisions regarding regulations on scientific production (c.f. the US President's Commission for Bioethics), but critics worry that they share scientists' secular and moral outlook (Kass 2009). These critics tend to support more democratic means of determining limits on science (Brown and Guston 2009).

Debates that focus on proscribed rules and regulations, create the appearance that the boundaries of forbidden knowledge (and the interests behind their creation) can be easily identified. However, researchers tell a far more complicated story, arguing that they perceive many topics as "forbidden" even when there are no rules limiting its production and dissemination (Kempner et al. 2011). Instead, the idea that some knowledge is too dangerous to pursue is an issue constantly negotiated in the daily working lives of knowledge-producers – negotiations that are guided by local norms and culture. For example, many researchers consider forbidden the question of whether genetic differences across racial groups affect intelligence, despite the fact that no legal restrictions "forbid" such research (Ceci and Williams 2009; Kempner et al. 2011).[1] Drug and alcohol researchers report that certain "harm reduction" studies cannot be done, despite evidence that certain controversial interventions might be effective (Kempner et al. 2011). They worry, for example, that research on teaching alcoholics how to drink moderately or research that pays addicts to stay clean would attract too much negative press and jeopardize their funding. Animal researchers often avoid working with certain kinds of animal subjects (for example, primates), because they worry about violence from animal rights activists. Others complain about so-called political correctness in academia, which purportedly silences those who hold unconventional views (Berman 2011).

The question, then, is *how* do researchers come to understand certain topics as forbidden? Some researchers suspect that peer review plays an important gatekeeping role in suppressing controversial knowledge, particularly knowledge that threatens to undercut dominant paradigms in particular disciplines (Horrobin 1990; Martin 1999). However, this mechanism is difficult to assess. There is more evidence to suggest that the boundaries of forbidden knowledge are created through controversies, which – if damaging enough – can serve as a warning to researchers "not to go there." For example, Descartes decided not to publish *The World* and *Treatise of Man* after hearing about Galileo's persecution. (These works were only published posthumously.) This same mechanism can be seen in the contemporary world. For example, it is well-known among psychologists that researching the paranormal can have damaging, if not fatal, effects on one's career. According to Hess (1992: 222) researchers in this area learn this from "'horror stories' of academic persecution."

Kempner and her colleagues (2011) interviewed 41 researchers working across a number of disciplines in elite universities and asked them how they learned that some forms of knowledge production were "forbidden." Researchers were able to list dozens of substantive topics that they perceived to be too sensitive or controversial for study, including research on race and intelligence, weapons development, and work that might undermine the "core mission" of their discipline. When asked *how* they knew that such research was off-limits, only a few pointed to formal regulations, such as bans on human cloning research. More often, researchers indicated that the boundaries of forbidden knowledge were simultaneously "revealed, created, maintained, renegotiated, expanded, or contracted" (487–8) through various controversies. Famous controversies, like Humphreys' Tea Room Trade (1970) and Herrnstein and Murray's (1996) divisive book, *The Bell Curve*, served as vivid warnings of how "legal" research could easily veer into the realm of the forbidden. But local controversies that are much less well-known also shaped what researchers believed they could or could not do. Scholars pointed towards colleagues' mishaps with activists, funding agencies, and newspapers to explain why certain kinds of research fell outside the boundaries of acceptable inquiry. For example, one researcher spoke about a colleague whose state funding for research on controlled drinking interventions was pulled. Others told of colleagues who were viciously targeted by activists who disagreed with either the substance or methods of their research (Frickel et al. 2010). Often, these controversies acted as a sort of breaching experiment – researchers were unaware that they or their colleagues had stepped into forbidden territory until trouble brewed. And then, once they had, these controversies served to warn researchers away from particular topics or methods.

A controversy involving federally funded sex and drug researchers provides a case-in-point. In 2003, members of the US House of Representatives, along with a conservative advocacy organization called the Traditional Values Coalition, questioned the "medical benefit" of more than 250 grants funded by the US National Institutes of Health (NIH). Most of these grants investigated sexual behavior and drug use, among other stigmatized behaviors. The NIH defended this research, but not before it conducted an audit all 157 implicated principal investigators (PIs). Kempner (2008) asked a subset of these PIs to comment on how this controversy shaped their subsequent research. About half reported that they now "cleanse" titles and abstracts of NIH grant submissions to remove controversial words like "sex worker," "gay," or "AIDS." A quarter reworked or dropped studies that they believed were too sensitive to be funded by a state entity. Four of those surveyed or interviewed reported that, as a result of this controversy, they changed jobs in order to avoid potential conflict in the future. In total, this study demonstrates how controversy can deter researchers from conducting sensitive research, even when that controversy does not result in formal penalties.

Agency can be obscured when forbidden knowledge is created through informal social control mechanisms, but it is still possible to see how power relations shape researchers' perceptions of what can and cannot be studied. Activists, funding agencies, media outlets, legislators, and academic colleagues are all capable of ginning up enough controversy to make certain forms of inquiry appear to be forbidden. However, it is also useful to note that researchers can use rhetoric of "forbidden knowledge" to justify research that has otherwise been debunked.

Forbidden fruit is so delicious

Forbidden knowledge does not necessarily translate into ignorance. The very controversies that create and perpetuate forbidden knowledge may serve to tantalize, even as they discourage, inquiry. For example, Kempner (2008) finds that 47 per cent of the researchers whose federally funded grants were audited reported feeling "pride" upon learning that their studies had been called into question by people who they felt harbored racist, sexist, and heterosexist beliefs. Ten per cent argued that this controversy only served to deepen their commitment to producing knowledge in areas of public health that they believed were important, if divisive. Kempner notes, however, that self-censorship practices were inevitable even within this group – indeed, she argues that it was only through self-censorship practices, like cleansing titles and abstracts of controversial words, that these researchers were able to continue to receive funding for sensitive topics.

This case might call into question the assertion that informal mechanisms can truly "forbid" controversial knowledge. However, researchers can successfully pursue forbidden knowledge, even in the case of formal regulations. Not only can knowledge that is restricted in one country be allowed in another, but researchers may find ways to produce even the most restricted knowledge. Take, for example, the resurgence of research into the medical uses of psychoactive drugs, like LSD and psilocybin. The US government has long categorized both LSD and psilocybin as Schedule I drugs because they purportedly have a high potential for abuse and "no currently accepted use in [medical] treatment in the United States." (Drug Enforcement

Administration, accessed 2013). Medical research on these drugs is tightly regulated and rarely approved. Nevertheless, a group of researchers have been able to produce and publish knowledge about the use of psychedelics as a treatment for a rare, excruciating condition called cluster headache. They have done so through collaboration with cluster headache patient advocates who, organized as a nonprofit called Clusterbusters, have experimented and collected data on the use of these drugs on their own bodies. By collecting experiential data from online forums and surveys, these patient advocates have learned how to acquire psychedelic drugs, how much and how often people with cluster headache should dose, which drugs interact poorly with recommended psychedelics, and how to take these drugs safely. They then regularly send their data to researchers for analysis and dissemination in legitimate, peer reviewed medical journals (c.f. Sewell et al. 2006). These researchers, thus, have been able to produce knowledge on a topic that is expressly forbidden by the US and most international governments.

These examples demonstrate that forbidden knowledge is a fluid category that blurs the boundaries between knowledge and ignorance. However, much more research needs to be done to learn how and under what conditions researchers choose whether or not to pursue forbidden knowledge. Undertaking such research has its own perils and obstacles. Researchers pursing explicitly forbidden topics, like the medical use of psychedelic drugs, will invariably encounter regulatory, funding, and publication problems. Those producing knowledge that is otherwise shunned by colleagues – for example, research on extrasensory perception – will likely encounter problems in their career. Those who seek knowledge in highly stigmatized areas like sexuality and drug use may find themselves embroiled in an unwanted and distracting controversy. And yet, despite these challenges, people do conduct this research in ways that ultimately create and recreate the boundaries of what we consider to be forbidden.

Note

1 Even the question of whether this research is, in fact, forbidden is contentious. Frank (2012) suggests that scholars often argue that research on race, genetics, and intelligence is forbidden in an effort to elide real methodological critiques with this work.

References

Berman, Paul (ed.) *Debating P.C.: The Controversy over Political Correctness on College Campuses.* (New York: Dell Publishing, 2011.)

Brown, Mark B., and David Guston. "Science, Democracy and the Right to Research." *Science and Engineering Ethics* 15(2009): 351–366.

Ceci, Stephen, and Williams, Wendy M. "Darwin 200: Should Scientists Study Race and IQ? YES: The Scientific Truth must be Pursued." *Nature* 457(2009): 788–789.

Cohen, C. "When May Research Be Stopped?" *New England Journal of Medicine* 296(1977): 1203–1210.

Drug Enforcement Administration. "Scheduled Drugs." Accessed December 15, 2013, http://www.justice.gov/dea/druginfo/ds.shtml.

Frank, Reanne. "Forbidden or Forsaken: The (Misuse) of a Forbidden Knowledge Argument in Research on Race, DNA, and Disease." In *Genetics and the Unsettled Past: The Collision of DNA, Race, and History.* Edited by Keith Wailoo, Alondra Nelson, and Catherine Lee. (New Brunswick, NJ: Rutgers University Press, 2012): 315–324.

Frickel, Scott, Sahra Gibbon, Jeff Howard, Gwen Ottinger, Joanna Kempner, and David Hess. "Undone Science: Charting Social Movement and Civil Society Challenges to Research Agenda Setting." *Science, Technology and Human Values* 35(2010): 444–473.

Gross, Matthias. *Ignorance and Surprise: Science, Society and Ecological Design.* (Cambridge, MA: MIT Press, 2010).

Herrnstein, Richard J., and Charles Murray. *The Bell Curve: Intelligence and Class Structure in American Life.* (New York: Simon & Schuster, 1996).

Hess, David. "Disciplining Heterodoxy, Circumventing Discipline: Parapsychology, Anthropologically," in *Knowledge and Society Vol. 9: The Anthropology of Science and Technology*. Edited by David Hess and Linda Layne. (Greenwich, CT: JAI Press, 1992): 191–222.

Horrobin, David F. "The Philosophical Basis of Peer Review and the Suppression of Innovation." *Journal of the American Medical Association* 263(1990): 1438–1441.

Humphreys, Laud. *Tearoom Trade: Impersonal Sex in Public Places*. (Chicago, IL: Aldine Publishing Company, 1970).

Johnson, Deborah B. "Forbidden Knowledge and Science as Professional Activity." *Monist* 79(1996): 197–218.

Johnson, Deborah B. "Reframing the Question of Forbidden Knowledge for Modern Science," *Science & Engineering Ethics* 5(1999): 445–461.

Journal Editors and Authors Group. "Statement on Scientific Publication and Security." *Science* 299(2003): 1149.

Kass, Leon. "Forbidding Science: Some Beginning Reflections." *Science and Engineering Ethics* 15(2009): 271–282.

Kempner, Joanna. "The Chilling Effect: How Do Researchers React to Controversy?" *Public Library of Science Medicine* 5(2008): e222.

Kempner, Joanna, Clifford S. Perlis, and Jon F. Merz. "Forbidden Knowledge." *Science* 307(2005): 854.

Kempner, Joanna, Jon F. Merz, and Charles L. Bosk. "Forbidden Knowledge: Public Controversy and the Production of Nonknowledge." *Sociological Forum* 26(2011): 475–500.

Knorr Cetina, Karin. *Epistemic Cultures: How the Sciences Make Knowledge*. (Cambridge, MA: Harvard University Press, 1999).

Leshner, Alan I. (2003) "Don't Let Ideology Trump Science." *Science* 302: 1479.

Marchant, Gary E., and Lynda L. Pope. "The Problems with Forbidding Science." *Science and Engineering Ethics* 15(2009): 375–394.

Martin, Brian. "Suppression of Dissent in Science." *Research in Social Problems* 7(1999): 105–135.

Miller, Judith. "New Germ Labs Stir a Debate over Secrecy and Safety." *New York Times*. February 10, 2004, accessed January 15, 2014, http://www.nytimes.com/2004/02/10/science/new-biolabs-stir-a-debate-over-secrecy-and-safety.html?pagewanted=all&src=pm.

National Science Foundation. "Implementation of the 2013 Federal Continuing Appropriations Act provisions affecting the NSF Political Science Program (nsf1310)," June 7, 2013, accessed January 13, 2014, http://www.nsf.gov/pubs/2013/nsf13101/nsf13101.txt.

Nelkin, Dorothy. "Forbidden Research: Limits to Inquiry in the Social Sciences," in *Ethical Issues in Social Science Research*. Edited by T. L. Beauchamp, R. R. Faden, R. J. Wallace, and L. Walters (Baltimore, MD: Johns Hopkins University Press, 1982): 163–173.

Proctor, Robert N. "Agnotology: A Missing Term to Describe the Cultural Production of Ignorance (and Its Study)." In *Agnotology: The Making and Unmaking of Ignorance*. Edited by Robert N. Proctor and Londa Schiebinger (Stanford, CA: Stanford University Press, 2008): 1–36.

Rehmann-Sutter, Christoph. "Frankensteinian Knowledge?" *Monist* 79(1996): 263–280.

Sewell, R. Andrew, John H. Halpern, H. G. Pope. "Response of Cluster Headache to Psilocybin and LSD." *Neurology* 66(2006): 1920–1922.

Smith, Dorothy. "Scientific Knowledge and Forbidden Truths." *Hastings Center Report* 8(1996): 30–35.

Weber, Max. "Science as a Vocation," in *Weber: Essays in Sociology*. Edited by H. H. Gerth and C. Wright Mills. (New York: Oxford University Press, 1946. Orig. pub. 1918).

9

Ignorance and the epistemic choreography of method

Mike Michael

> 'we don't consider ourselves authorized to believe we possess the meaning of what we know.'
>
> *(Isabelle Stengers, 2005, p.995)*

Introduction

Ignorance in all its complexity is fast becoming a legitimate object of study that is gaining increasing traction within the social sciences. The perspectives on this topic reflect its complexity as authors attempt to clarify, delineate and typologize ignorance in dynamic relation to a series of other phenomena such as non-knowledge, uncertainty and nescience (Gross, 2007; Ungar, 2008; Abbott, 2010), or establish 'its' variegated but constitutive role in contemporary societies and its chronic involvement at different scales of sociopolitical process (e.g. McGoey, 2012a,b; Heimer, 2012). In this heady 'turn to ignorance' (or perhaps that should be 'return to ignorance' given eminent precursor treatments – see especially, Smithson, 1989), the sophistication with which ignorance can be analytically and empirically studied is becoming evident. No longer the opposite of knowledge, recent perspectives, in one way or another, insist on its topological relation to knowledge – for instance, there is strategic knowledge in knowing when to cultivate ignorance in relation to particular events or phenomena (Anderson, 2010; McGoey, 2012b).

The present chapter certainly draws inspiration from these crucial insights but explicitly situates ignorance in relation to the practicing of social scientific methods, especially those designed to elicit responses rather than observe practices (though this distinction is hardly cut and dried). So, on one level, this is an exploration of the 'complex patterning of ignorance and knowledge' (a phrase which aims to take in the nexus of relations between, minimally, knowledge, uncertainty and ignorance) and the forging of the 'social scientific research event'. Yet, on another level, this chapter aims to use such patterning to explore the parameters of such research events. That is to say, methods as the means of engagement with particular participants for the purposes of gathering social data entail the 'performance' – choreography even – of ignorance and knowledgeability on the part of both researcher and researched. However, the further argument is that such social scientific research events are performative in so far as they are generative of the 'object' or 'objects' of which they speak (most relevantly for present purposes, by enacting a series of 'otherings'). Here, we see how the enactment of that which is 'ignored' – and ignored in a variety of ways – is pivotal to the process of knowing this or that social phenomenon or event. The additional point is that that which is ignored (or Othered) can nevertheless become a medium for the interrogation of what it means to know this or that social phenomenon or event. The paper thus explores how the 're-entrance' of the ignored might be enabled, not least because such 'ignored' can serve to inventively reframe what is at stake in the research in question. In the process, we touch upon how a methodology – specifically, a 'speculative methodology' – might 'embrace' the ignored through the affective and the aesthetic, as well as the cognitive.

In what follows, then, I begin with a very preliminary sketch of how research events entail an epistemic choreography of ignorance and knowledge (I focus on these terms while acknowledging that this choreography covers a range of categories of knowing and not-knowing), before moving on to consider how in certain research events there is a systematic and layered ignoring of certain sorts of behavior that do not fit in with the 'rationales' of the research. Interpreting the research event as processual, open and unfolding, it is argued there is the potential to draw on that which is ignored in order to re-work the meaning of the particular research event (and of the parameters of the research more generally). Drawing on speculative philosophy and speculative design, the paper ends with some preliminary suggestions about how this might proceed.

An epistemic choreography . . .

In Cussins' (1996) brilliant account of ontological choreography she carefully traces the ways in which the women in her study of hospital wards, instead of buying into either the medical objectivist model or the holistic subjectivist model, moved adroitly between these. They alternately engaged in the processes of objectification (in which, for instance, responsibility was removed from them, and they were simply told the medical 'truth') and subjectification (in which they were consulted as knowledgeable participants in the diagnostic process and treatment regime). In the present paper, we can say that this is also an *epistemic* choreography in which there is delicate dance between patient and physician that moves between objectifying and subjectifying forms of knowledge and ignorance with regard to a particular body.

A similar choreography can be detected in the practice of social research (which here includes not only techniques such as interviews and focus groups, but also the participatory engagements such as those deployed in science and technology studies (see, for example, Hagendijk and Irwin, 2006; Bucchi and Neresini, 2008). Moreover, such practice also encompasses the 'setting up' of the research from the conceptual and methodological grounds of the project, through the local negotiation with potential recruits and the collection of data, to the orientation of the analysis to the 'key issues' in the field of inquiry (including policy concerns). The epistemic choreography I am proposing to be a chronic part of research practice entails a dynamic and mutual enactment of ignorance and knowledge (in their various guises). As we shall see, sometimes these mutual enactments are consonant or harmonic insofar as ignorance 'points to' or 'fits in with' particular knowledge (and vice versa) leading to 'smooth' interactions in the research process; sometimes they are dissonant or cacophonous, and interaction requires repair, or, more dramatically, invites a fundamental rethinking of the research question.

At the most obvious level of research design, the social researcher has a research question that she wishes to address, a research question of whose answer she is 'necessarily' ignorant. However, the question itself is formulated in ways which demarcate its answer, for example, through sampling strategy. Even if participants are randomly selected, random-ness itself is an indication of the quality of the ignorance – namely that it is bound to a question whose answer is generalizable to the population from which the sample is randomly drawn. In the case of 'public engagement' techniques (e.g. citizens juries, citizens panels, consensus conferences, deliberative polling, focus groups) in which members of the public 'debate' controversial issues with experts, the generic aim is to derive and document the views of the 'public-in-general' (Michael, 2009). This means that the ideal participant is one who has no prior investment in, or knowledge of, these issues – such a participant is what Lezaun and Soneryd (2007) refer to as an 'idiot' whose primary focus is their own self-interest as opposed to the more civic issues in question (however, see below). Here, the epistemic choreography entails an ignorance embodied in the research question nevertheless attached to a tacit knowledge of the idealized *model* of the research participant. The general point is that the knowledgeable framing of the research question preconfigures what can be ignored.

Epistemic choreography finds further expression in the process of participant recruitment. Of course, the lure might be monetary reward, or, minimally, the reassurance that participation won't take up too much time. However, often, and despite these lures, the researcher will need to establish that the research question is of interest (and ideally of value) to the participant. So here, epistemic choreography can center around interests and their realization. Treating interests as relational (Callon and Law, 1982), and drawing on, and simplifying from, the insights of Actor-Network Theory (e.g. Callon, 1986a, b), we might suggest that prospective participants' interests are identified, problematized, and translated so that they become consonant with those attached to the research project. This translation can work at a number of interwoven 'levels'. For instance, it can be quite abstract: 'you are interested in greater democracy'; 'this means you are interested in having lay people's voices heard in the process of governmental decision making'; 'we researchers can help realize this interest by interviewing you about your understandings of ionizing radiation which will allow us to feed back to government' (however vaguely or circuitously). Or they can be more concrete: 'you are interested in the risks you face from local nuclear installations'; 'this means you are interested in conveying your concerns to local institutions and organizations'; 'we researchers can help realize this by interviewing you about your understandings of ionizing radiation which will contribute to the process of interrogating assurances about local exposures' (however vaguely or circuitously). In terms of epistemic choreography, we have an identification of interests, followed by their problematization and translation into a realizable form (of which the participant might only vaguely be aware), followed by their further translation into practicable action, namely participating in the research (of which the participant is unlikely to have any knowledge). At the same time, there might well be interests knowledge about which can lead to dissonance. For instance, relaying to the prospective participant one's interests in how the research might address more esoteric theoretical debates (for instance, around Risk Society or Reflexive Modernization), might not be welcomed, or might potentially trigger another bout of epistemic choreography in which the participant feels undermined and used, but also (explicitly or not) regards the researcher as ignorant of 'real-world' concerns.

Epistemic choreography also plays out in the process of deriving data, of course. Questions assume that the researcher is ignorant of the answers. But often, when the researcher pursues the answer with specific follow-up questions, it is clear that on the one hand, the researcher is already aware of the sorts of incomplete answers likely to be received, but on the other that the participant is not fully cognizant of the extent or elaboration of the answer. Being enacted as knowing more than one is telling, at least, initially, can be disarming. But it can also lead to a sense that the researcher knows not only more than the participant, but indeed, more *about* the participant who does not know well enough what they know. This can lead to a negative reaction, where the enactments of the researcher are resisted. In interviewing a range of participants about their understandings of ionizing radiation (Michael, 1992, 1996), we found that they would deny knowledge of this topic – that is, they would openly admit their ignorance, despite the gentle prompting and reassurances of the researchers (this included participants who clearly had extensive knowledge of ionizing radiation). However, this ignorance was also accounted for – embedded within a structure of knowledgeability. Thus, some participants would say that they did not have a 'scientific mind' and this accounted for their ignorance of ionizing radiation. Nevertheless, they were sufficiently knowledgeable about themselves to explain this ignorance and to warrant it rationally. Others claimed not to *need* this knowledge – their expertise lay elsewhere, expert knowledge about ionizing radiation that rightly belonged to those with different sorts of expertise (and professional functions). Others still, insisted that they did not *want* to possess this knowledge because it was irrelevant to the 'real' issue at stake, which, in the present case, might concern the politics or economics of the nuclear industry. Indeed, according to this last accounting, the researchers themselves were the ignorant ones, ignorant of the 'real' issues at stake. Further, by being focused on the public understanding of ionizing radiation, the researchers were also being unknowingly used by interests intent on deflecting attention from those 'real' issues at stake. Taking these examples together, we can note that epistemic choreography grounds ignorance in a variety of knowledges – knowledge about one's own capacities or skills, or institutional setting, knowledge about the 'real' issues at stake, and knowledge about how to best warrant ignorance. In turn, these knowledges can interdigitate with the imputed ignorance of the researcher – the researcher is ignorant both of these circumstances or machinations, and the unwitting part she plays in relation to these.

The last example of intentional (perhaps even celebratory or antagonistic) ignorance, uncomfortable as it was at the time, was nevertheless readily subject to analysis. However, there are behaviors that participants engage in that are not necessarily so easily grasped by the researcher – they are, in one way or another, systemically ignored – Othered – in the processes of conducting research and producing analysis. We now turn to discuss how epistemic chorography might feature in these dynamics.

Ignoring, Othering and 'misbehaving'

In John Law's (2004) influential performative model of social methodology, he persuasively argues that any method (or method assemblage in Law's terms) will entail 'the crafting and enacting of boundaries between presence, manifest absence and Otherness' (p. 85) as certain 'data' are systematically excluded by simply being, within the parameters of the method, unregisterable, that is to say, chronically and eminently ignorable.

Michael (2012) documents a number of ways in which social research is marked by a series of 'misbehaviors' in which participants do not fully commit to the discipline of the research event. As Michael notes, it is difficult to document these misbehaviors precisely because they are routinely Othered or ignored by researchers: after all, they do not 'speak' to the research question in hand. Such misbehaviors take a variety of forms, and a tentative and non-exhaustive list might include: absence (not turning up to the research event despite making an appointment); incapacity (through, for instance, exhaustion, or drunkenness, or being unwell); 'refusal' to participate appropriately (by, deliberately or otherwise, failing to address the topics under discussion – this can include focusing on 'irrelevant' concerns, claims to ignorance, or even silence); disruption (at collective events such as focus groups this might entail heckling, or forcefully challenging, the researchers); irony (where on one level there is participation, while on another a different activity is indulged such as playing or competing with other participants).

The main point here is that these 'misbehaviors' are 'ignored' or 'Othered' by the researcher: in the epistemic choreography of the research process, in order to generate knowledge within the framing of the research question, these misbehaviors are often simply not 'seen', as they make no sense in relation to such framing. Alternatively, they can be excised from the account of the research – noted but put to one side, perhaps attributed to the researcher's own inexperience (that is, ignorance of proper empirical procedure), or explained away in terms of unusually recalcitrant or unruly participants. Now, this ignoring can take place at several stages in the research process. For instance, at the time of data gathering, 'misbehaviors' can seem so 'inappropriate' that they simply are not recorded (e.g. converted into text). Or, because they 'make no sense', they do not enter into the analytic process – though recorded, they are absent as material with which to think because they do not align with what 'counts' for the research question, or, indeed, the research program. And in some cases, these 'misbehaviors' are put to one side because they cannot be connected to broader relevances – for example, with regard to policy constituencies. I should clarify that none of this is understood to be deliberate: the researcher-analyst's handling of participants' 'misbehavior' is not a matter of deliberately ignoring data, but of not seeing it (as data *per se*), or not knowing what to do with it, when one does see it. In any case, epistemic choreography seizes up here as, under these conditions, the misbehaving participant cannot even enter the dance.

Arguably, what structures all this is the 'primacy' of the research's question, program or relevances. Of course, research questions can shift and change in the process of doing research where participants' responses come to influence what counts as the relevant, or the 'real', issue at stake. In the present discussion, I am more interested in those cases where participant 'misbehaviors' are too alien to make sense within the research's framing, too alien even to prompt a reworking of that framing. We now consider this in more detail focusing especially on the notion of a research 'event' which is given a conceptual overhaul.

Eventuation and the process of research

Throughout this chapter, the term 'event' has been used with some abandon. I now want to consider this in a little more technical detail. For process philosophers such as Whitehead (1978) and Stengers (e.g. 2005), the event (or the 'actual occasion' in Whitehead's vocabulary) is necessarily a heterogeneous affair. It is comprised of the coming together and combination (or concrescence) of numerous, disparate entities (or prehensions). Such entities span the social and material, the macro and micro, the human and nonhuman, the cognitive and affective, the conscious and unconscious. It is the coming together and combination of these multifarious entities that comprises the event. This is a process which we might call 'eventuation'. The research event thus includes not only the researcher and researched (who, as we have seen above, are themselves complexly eventuated), and the materials of research (e.g. tape recorders, interview schedules, trigger materials), but also the more or less disciplined elements of the research setting (e.g. children and companion animals removed, domestic technologies silenced, 'irrelevant' concerns put to one side).

Now, eventuation can be conceptualized in two different ways. According to Mariam Fraser's (2010) path-breaking analysis of the idea of the event in Whitehead and Deleuze, she suggests that in one version, the event is characterized by a 'being-with', where the constituents of the event 'co-habit' in the process of that event, interacting with, but not changing in relation to, one another. Alternatively, the event is marked by a 'becoming-with', where constituents themselves mutually change, or intra-act as Barad (2007) phrases it. In the former case, such 'interaction' or 'being-with' means that the constitutive elements retain their 'identity'; in the latter case, intra-action or 'becoming-with' means that the elements no longer retain their 'identity' which has changed in the process of eventuation (see also DeLanda, 2002). The implication is that if the constituents of an event are changing, then so too is the event itself: these intra-active dynamics mean that the event is unfolding, under-determined, opening out onto a range of possibilities or 'virtualities' that are not directly graspable. The further implication is that as researchers, we are placed in a dilemma. Do we engage with the becoming-with of the research event? Do we pursue the not-as-yet – the virtual – of the research project's eventuation? To do so would be to develop and exercise a sensibility that is open to the openness of the research event, and its multiple potentialities. In other words, do we indulge a 'speculative methodology' in order to access this unknown – an unknown which we have had a part in constituting? To complicate matters, we would also need to deal with the prospect that in the process of becoming-with, we open up the meanings of research, researched and researcher. Crucially, we might ask: who is this emergent researcher 'we'? To follow such a path means that we incorporate the performativity of research in the doing of research, dispensing with any aspiration toward neutrality: in the process such a 'speculative methodology', to quote Stengers (2010, p. 57), 'affirms the possible, that actively resists the plausible and the probable targeted by approaches that claim to be neutral.'

One way of addressing this virtuality of the eventuation of research is, following Stengers (2005), through the philosophical figure of the 'idiot' (though we should note there are others – e.g. the parasite, the trickster, the coyote). For Stengers, the action of the idiot – which can be classed as a variant of what has hitherto been called 'misbehavior' – 'resists the consensual way in which the situation is presented' (p. 994). The idiot is a figure that refuses to enter such events, whose responses make no sense in the context of those events as typically understood; as such, the idiot can also heuristically function to challenge the meaning of those events. Stengers writes: 'the idiot can neither reply nor discuss the issue . . . (the idiot) does not know . . . the idiot demands that we slow down' (p. 995). Accordingly, the researcher's task becomes a matter of how best to 'bestow efficacy upon the murmurings of the idiot, the 'there is something more important' that is so easy to forget because it 'cannot be taken into account,' because the idiot neither objects nor proposes anything that 'counts' (p. 1001). By attending to the idiot's nonsensicalness, and as indicated in the epigraph, we become open to the possibility of a dramatic redefinition of the meaning of the research event, and the questions we can pose about it.

Thus, in reconsidering the preceding 'misbehaviors' as 'idiotic', they are no longer ignored as mishaps, mistakes or misfortunes. Rather, they become clues to a more inventive framing of the research question that addresses the openness of the research event. For example, when a participant does not address the questions, but raises issues that make little sense within the particular framing of the research (e.g. she talks about a new career in the fast food industry rather than discussing her sense of local radiation risks), then one might ask what is the eventuation we are party to? Is it a case of a 'failed interview' (the plausible response), or are we witness to a possible new question (e.g. about the local mediation of community, corporation and university)? Translated into the terms of epistemic choreography, paradoxically the researcher deliberately focuses on that which is ignored in the researched. However, here, we butt up against the limits of the idea of epistemic choreography. Access to the ignored – attending to the idiot – is unlikely to rest primarily on a cognitive engagement: after all, it is the constraints placed by cognitive investments in a particular research question that renders the ignored and situates the idiot. Rather, a sensibility needs to be nurtured, one that is open to the affects generated by the ignored. Drawing on Massumi (2002), amongst others, 'affect' here denotes the ways in which bodies with particular situated capacities (corporeal, perceptual, reactive) are impacted upon by the objects and actions around them. These affects are mediated aesthetically – that is, through the whole sensorium – and operate at a level that is not readily accessible to consciousness. They can be 'aggravating' or 'irritating' but cannot necessarily be expressed right away. Idiotic 'misbehavior', while it might not be cognized, thus can impact affectively – in a subterranean way – that only subsequently comes to be grasped. In light of this, the task becomes one of cultivating sensibilities – those situated capacities – that both register these (idiotic) affects, and translate them, not least into 'interesting problems' about the research itself.

Concluding remarks: Engaging idiots idiotically, being knowingly ignorant

In this chapter, we have addressed the constitutive role of ignorance in the eventuation of social scientific methods – an ignorance complexly intertwined with knowledge in what has been called an epistemic choreography. In discussing the process of ignoring (or Othering) in research, we have highlighted the figure of the idiot as one means of addressing the openness – the virtualities – of research events and their associated questions, programs and relevances. We ended up with a rather too programmatic plea to cultivate sensibilities that could engage the idiotic, and thus address, to paraphrase Stengers (2005), our not knowing the meaning of what we know (as researchers).

However, there are other techniques which are more proactive in their engagement with the idiotic – and more broadly, Othering. Speculative design, for instance (Michael, 2012), develops objects and probes whose oblique functionality, nonsensicalness, playfulness – in a word, idiocy – serves, at least in principle, to encourage participants to rethink the issues at stake. So a project ostensibly investigating the interactions between community and energy demand reduction, through the idiocy of a speculative object, can enable participants to query the very parameters of 'community' or 'energy', and to begin to explore more interesting questions about 'energy demand reduction'. In the process, the researchers themselves will, ideally, be surprised at these emerging participant reformulations.

Of course, speculative design is just one possible route. There are other techniques that can be drawn from the arts, poetry, or radical politics (e.g. situationism) and which do similar work with the ignored. Here, epistemic choreography (now supplemented with the affective) becomes a matter of knowingly developing and deploying techniques which engage the necessary ignorance of the prospective and the emergent.

References

Abbott, A. (2010). Varieties of Ignorance. *American Sociologist*, 41, 174–189.

Anderson, B. (2010). Preemption, Precaution, Preparedness: Anticipatory Action and Future Geographies. *Progress in Human Geography*, 34, 777–798.

Barad, K. (2007). *Meeting the Universe Halfway*. Durham, NC: Duke University Press.

Bucchi, M., and Neresini, F. (2008). Science and Public Participation. In E.J. Hackett, O. Amsterdamska, M. Lynch, and J. Wacjman (eds.), *Handbook of Science and Technology Studies* (3rd Edition), (pp. 449–473). Cambridge, MA: MIT Press.

Callon, M., and Law, J. (1982). On Interests and Their Transformation: Enrolment and Counter-enrolment. *Social Studies of Science*, 12, 615–625.

Callon, M. (1986a). The Sociology of an Actor-network: The Case of the Electric Vehicle. In M. Callon, J. Law, and A. Rip (eds.), *Mapping the Dynamics of Science and Technology*, London: Macmillan.

Callon, M. (1986b). Some Elements in a Sociology of Translation: Domestication of the Scallops and Fishermen of St Brieuc Bay. In J. Law (ed.), *Power, Action and Belief*. London: Routledge and Kegan Paul.

Cussins, C. (1996). Ontological Choreography: Agency for Women in an Infertility Clinic. In M. Berg and A. Mol (eds.), *Differences in Medicine*. Durham, NC: Duke University Press.
DeLanda, M. (2002) *Intensive Science and Virtual Philosophy*. London: Continuum.
Fraser, M. (2010). Facts, Ethics and Event. In C. Bruun Jensen and K. Rödje (eds.), *Deleuzian Intersections in Science, Technology and Anthropology* (pp. 57–82). New York: Berghahn Books.
Gross, M. (2007). The Unknown in Process: Dynamic Connections of Ignorance, Non-knowledge and Related Concepts. *Current Sociology*, 55(5), 742–759.
Hagendijk, R., and Irwin, A. (2006) Public Deliberation and Governance: Engaging with Science and Technology in Contemporary Europe. *Minerva*, 44(2), 167–184.
Heimer, C.A. (2012). Inert Facts and the Illusion of Knowledge: Strategic Uses of Ignorance in HIV Clinics. *Economy & Society*, 41(1), 17–41.
Law, J. (2004). *After Method: Mess in Social Science Research*. London: Routledge.
Lezaun, J., and Soneryd, L. (2007). Consulting Citizens: Technologies of Elicitation and the Mobility of Publics. *Public Understanding of Science*, 16, 279–297.
McGoey, L. (ed.) (2012a). Strategic Unknowns: Towards a Sociology of Ignorance (Special Issue). *Economy & Society*, 41(1).
McGoey, L. (2012b). The Logic of Strategic Ignorance. *The British Journal of Sociology*, 63(3), 553–576.
Massumi, B. (2002). *Parables of the Virtual*. Durham, NC: Duke University Press.
Michael, M. (1992). Lay Discourses of Science: Science-in-General, Science-in-Particular and Self. *Science, Technology and Human Values*, 17 (3), 313–333.
Michael, M. (1996). Ignoring Science: Discourses of Ignorance in the Public Understanding of Science. In A. Irwin and B. Wynne (eds.), *Misunderstanding Science? The Public Reconstruction of Science and Technology* (pp. 105–125). Cambridge: Cambridge University Press.
Michael, M. (2009). Publics Performing Publics: Of PiGs, PiPs and Politics. *Public Understanding of Science*, 18, 617–631.
Michael, M. (2012). Toward an Idiotic Methodology: De-signing the Object of Sociology. *The Sociological Review*, 60, Issue Supplement S1, 166–183.
Smithson, M. (1989). *Ignorance and Uncertainty: Emerging Paradigms*. New York: Springer.
Stengers, I. (2005) The Cosmopolitical Proposal. In B. Latour and P. Webel (eds.), *Making Things Public* (pp. 994–1003). Cambridge, MA: MIT Press.
Stengers, I. (2010) *Cosmopolitics I*. Minneapolis, MN: University of Minnesota Press.
Ungar, S. (2008). Ignorance as an Under-identified Social Problem. *The British Journal of Sociology*, 59(2), 301–326.
Whitehead, A.N. (1978 [1929]). *Process and Reality: An Essay in Cosmology*. New York: The Free Press.

10

Sharing the resources of ignorance

Stuart Firestein

Science produces questions more than it generates answers. Among scientists that is a matter of such common knowledge that it is rarely stated explicitly (cf. Gomory 1995; Firestein 2012; Stocking 1998). But, like the jargon-filled language that passes as easy conversation for the trained scientist while completely excluding the non-expert and nonscientist, this failure to be explicit about the value of ignorance has the unwanted effect of excluding the citizenry from the inner workings of science. Coincidentally, it seems now also to foster a growing and easily manipulated mistrust of both scientists and science.

There is a common worry in the American (and to some extent the Western European also) educational system, especially the higher educational system, that we are failing to produce a sufficient number of graduates in the so-called STEM subjects (Drew 2011; Firestein 2011; Schwartz 2008). These are, Science, Technology, Engineering and Math. Finding a place for blame we are told that American students don't have whatever it takes to pass the tough courses in these fields. (At the same time it's equally common to read editorials in *Nature* or *Science* every other month or so about how we are producing too many PhDs and there aren't enough jobs and it is unethical and immoral to continue turning them out at the rate we are. So who are we to believe?)

Nonetheless, this is seen as a crisis of our educational system. We definitely have a crisis, but this is not it. If we need more scientists, engineers and mathematicians there is a very simple and straightforward solution. It's called the market. Well-paying jobs and sufficient grant funding to pursue research would attract plenty of smart and talented people to academic or commercial positions in science, technology and math. There's nothing wrong with American students or their skills. Those possessing mathematical and reasoning skills simply wise up when they see their fellow students in economics and business courses walking out of a four-year education with job offers of $250,000 a year plus bonuses. Or, they can choose a career in science where job prospects are grim and the median age at which one receives a first research grant is now 44. So the problem, if there is one, has little or nothing to do with education, and everything to do with societal and cultural values.

As a kind of antidote to this worry we trumpet occasional reports that tell us we nonetheless remain better at producing creative and innovative scientists. That while China, Korea, India, Japan, Finland, etc., have superior curricula and higher achieving students, they do not teach or value creativity, individuality or an innovative spirit. It's hard for me not to simply say to this, bullshit. The first graduate student in my laboratory had been trained in China. His scientific preparation was unparalleled. He was also one of the three most creative people to have ever worked in my laboratory. One of the other two was also Chinese trained. Hai Qing Zhao, now a professor at Johns Hopkins, thought up and carried out an experiment that was published in *Nature* in 1998 and got me tenure in 1999. It is still regarded as one of the cleverest and seminal experiments in my field and the results are still used as a kind of gold standard against which later research continues to compare itself. I am not alone in this experience. Indeed I think it would be difficult for anyone in the American academic scientific establishment to claim that they could hope to run a laboratory without creative, thoughtful, often brilliant students and postdocs from Asia and Europe. In my opinion this notion of hard-working but unimaginative scientists from places other than America is no more than modern form of colonialism, if not outright racism. Worse – it creates a false sense of security, of believing that the US will maintain its superior position in science and technology because of some magical formula it has for producing clever folks. Of course no one can tell you what this secret formula is.

But, this rant aside, my concern here is not with whether we produce too many or too few or better or worse scientists. As I say, this is either not a problem or is one which can be fixed by market strategies and political will.

My greater concern is with the vast public who will not become professional scientists. They will, many of them, become CEOs or business executives of some type, or elected officials, or staff members in political or commercial or academic institutions, or journalists or work in the media – or in the end just plain voters. They will have an outsized effect on directing policy and public perception.

I leave it up to my fellow contributors to develop the appropriate outrage at special interests who will manipulate science for their own commercial benefit. My fury over these actions is that they are distorting science, reducing science, making science appear untrustworthy. This is a recipe for disaster. I fear that many believe science is in the newly discovered category of "too big to fail," and can thus be abused without much worry of dong lasting damage. This is not the case.

Science is shockingly fragile. It has been attempted many times in our previous history on this planet, and come to a premature end – from the classical Greeks and Romans to Arab science and even the first early attempts at Western science. These were all stopped short for one reason or another, and often followed by a period of stagnation and intolerance. It is only since the Enlightenment that we have had 400 or so continuous years of the kind of progress and release from magical mysticism that science can produce. And there have been near misses and real misses along the way – the Italian church in the sixteenth century, the post–French revolution Reign of Terror in the eighteenth century, and more recently, in case you think we're past all that, the Nazis, the Soviets and the Maoists in the twentieth century. Were it not for the anti-science policies of these regimes we would in all likelihood be writing our science in Italian or German or Russian (at least in mathematics). And if we are not careful the Tea Party and its evangelical base will chase science out of America. In the 1930s Albert Einstein was asked why he thought science, in this case physics, developed in the West but not in China or Asia more generally. This was indeed the case in the 1930s, at least as far as physics was concerned. His response was that he was not so surprised it hadn't developed in those places, but that it had developed anywhere at all. Today most of the world's cultures do not maintain any active scientific program, although they may happily partake in and benefit from the products of science and technology. The proper care and feeding of science is the responsibility of the advanced cultures that have supported it and benefited from it.

We can editorialize over this, we can publish and hold meetings, we can attempt to influence our governments with the concerted activity of the scientific organizations like the AAAS and the Societies for Neuroscience, Chemistry, Cell Biology, etc. I am strongly in favor of all these approaches. But I think the root of the problem is the way we teach science in the US – especially from the ages of 16 to 22, which would include the final years of our standard education and the four years of undergraduate university. One could extend the argument to younger children and even to adults, but it seems to me more useful to concentrate on an age that I believe is crucial and a period where the educational policy can be changed fairly rapidly.

There are numerous efforts, many official, many almost improvised, that have sprung up with the goal of developing what is commonly called "citizen science" or "public engagement with science" or "science accessibility." These range from large municipal science festivals with headliner scientists giving talks and/or participating in discussions, to so-called science cafés with informal talks by scientists to small groups in bars or restaurants. All of these have the purpose of making science more accessible to an untrained, but very interested, public audience. They generally take the form of some working scientist, often of either international or local fame, who attempts to explain some complicated part of science in so-called layman's terms. I applaud these efforts and many of them are remarkably popular, attracting sizeable crowds to public lectures or events. They also raise considerable sums of money from foundations.

In the same vein, both the American National Science Foundation (NSF) and the National Institutes of Health (NIH) have included so-called outreach components into their training grants and many other grant mechanisms, making it a requirement that the grantee program or team offer some sort of plan for public communication of their work. At Columbia University, my institution, we currently have a major development in building and organizing something known as the Mind Brain and Behavior Institute (MBBI). More than 500 million dollars have been raised to support this effort. One of the first people hired, even before a director, was an outreach officer. (By the way, a recent gift of $200 million by publisher Mort Zuckerman induced the administration to change the name of the project to the Zuckerman Mind Brain Behavior Institute – ZMBBI or Zombie! Perhaps they should have consulted with the outreach officer before taking this step.)

Again these efforts on the part of the government to correct the perceived gulf between the science they are funding and the science that people can understand are certainly worthy – if a bit strange for many scientists to understand let alone put into effect. The intention I suppose is to tear down the priesthood of science that has grown up in a tangle of incantational mumbo jumbo (technical jargon), mystical looking recipes (equations) and frightening looking machinery (colliders and scanners). All this to help us communicate better with what is known, with no apparent irony, as the lay public.

But in the end are these multi-faceted efforts the most effective means to integrate science into the life of the average citizen, to promote a culture that is based on rationality, evidence and deduction? Are we really increasing the appreciation of the value of science by promulgating what are inevitably dumbed-down versions of the real stuff? Is it realistic to believe that metaphors will replace mathematics, that narrative will replace experiment, that testimony will replace data and that all this will provide a satisfying accessibility to difficult science for this uninitiated (again no irony intended) public? Without meaning to take the wind out of the sails of this nascent and admirable movement, I have to say that I think the answer is no. Although no harm is likely to be done and many people will be entertained by good science stories and are likely to be more disposed to think kindly towards science and scientists, I don't think it will have the hoped-for effect of bringing the non-professional a useful scientific worldview. And I am almost certain that it will not help people who think they are on the side of science and are nonetheless taken in regularly by various forms of pseudoscience.

I have to be honest and say that this cannot be reduced easily to a left versus right political argument. Yes the evangelical right and the intelligent design crowd and the climate deniers make an easy target of themselves. But what about the anti-GMO food crowd; the educated parents who failed to vaccinate their children over an irrational scare about it causing autism; the devotion to alternative health fallacies that may have killed Steve Jobs prematurely? These, and worse, are subscribed to by people on all sides of the political spectrum. And they all share one common and unpleasant feature – gullibility.

These problems do not arise from insufficient knowledge of science, but rather insufficient understanding of how science works. This is a problem with our educational system. If you are looking for a crisis in education, this is it.

There is a point in the training of every scientist in which they make the transition from textbook-oriented learning to discovery, not only of facts, but discovery of questions. This may not be a single moment, but rather a transitional period, and, indeed, not every student/scientist succeeds in this developmental process (cf. Goldstein and Goldstein 1978). It is nonetheless arguably the most critical achievement attained by the apprentice scientist, aka, graduate student. The conversion from an obsessive focus on facts in textbooks to the search for better questions is the point at which a young scientist becomes an independent actor. It is the first moment when it is understood, consciously or not, that the question trumps the answer and that the scientific life is about what we don't know, the unsettled and the uncertain, "the what remains to be done," as Marie Curie phrased it.

Unfortunately this is precisely where the nonscientist gets left behind. Having been forced by an outmoded educational system to bear the misery of overweight textbooks, testing absent understanding, and valueless memorization, they are left with this as their sole experience of science. Worse than the obvious distaste that this produces in so many, it also provides a disastrously distorted view of science as authoritarian, factual, settled and immutable. Fortunately, science is none of these things. But who besides scientists knows this?

What steps can we take to reverse the situation? To begin with we must become comfortable with teaching that science is not an accumulated pile of facts but an ongoing set of questions (cf. Stocking 1998). Of course some facts are important and we will have to decide judiciously which ones are the crucial ones. But as Henri Poincare noted, science is built of facts the way a house is built of bricks; but an accumulation of facts is no more science than a pile of bricks is a house.

The facts then must be placed in context. What is that context? I suggest that the most enlightening and engaging way of presenting facts is to recreate the historical ignorance in which they were arrived at. How do we know that, contrary to all of our sensory information, the earth rotates at a very high speed and the sun remains still in the sky? Without using photographs from the space station, how could you prove to your mother or father that this "fact" which we all accept is indeed true? Why, if it is true, are you able to stand on an earth that is moving at nearly 1,000 miles per hour and your hair is not being blown off your head? The first of these questions will lead to the pendulum as the first empirical proof of the earth's rotation. From there one can try to understand the pendulum and how it works and what units of time mean in an equation. Discussions of "time's arrow" are relevant here. If the pendulum seems old fashioned to you, it might be worth remembering that until the invention of the liquid crystal in the 1970s it was the only method for keeping time. Einstein worked out relativity using the pendulum. The harmonic movement of the pendulum leads to discussions of inertia and Newton's important discoveries about gravity. The key insight of Newton, which I have yet to hear mentioned in a discussion of his work, is that he saw that the laws that governed the falling apple in his backyard also dictated the movements of the planets in space and even of the distant stars, indeed the whole universe. For the first time humans realized that what was true here could be true everywhere. And from Newton it is not as hard as many think to get to Special Relativity. All of these must be presented as puzzles, not as known facts, because they required a kind of critical thinking that we wish to recreate in the student's own mind. I personally happen to think that the laws of motion from Galileo and Newton to Einstein are among the important things to know in science. Others may feel differently, but I provide here two simple examples of teaching this information as a foray into ignorance and not as a "fact accompli" that is just to be memorized and numbers plugged into an equation in some clerical exercise.

The very same could be done with the frightening sounding thermodynamics and the discovery that heat was not fluid but motion – not at all intuitive. Or with chemistry and the non-trivial discovery of oxygen versus phlogiston (a fun word for any kid to say). And in both of these cases there is the opportunity to show how science can also be wrong, even for a very long time, and then suddenly gets it right. Opportunities like these abound in the history of science.

There will be many who complain that there is already so much to teach in the science curriculum that adding in history for context or philosophy for meaning is not possible and will take away the focus. These science teachers have it wrong on two counts. Being a slave to "coverage" may seem to fulfill your responsibilities but you have to ask yourself how much of all that material will the student possess 20 minutes after they have passed the exam? Second, I think it is a mistake to think that students will be less interested in the history and philosophy of scientific discoveries than in the science itself. Indeed my experience in teaching and talking to young students is that they want to be challenged by ideas and that it is precisely the history and the philosophy that engages them to learn the science.

In the age of Google and Wikipedia, and whatever will be next, the facts are at our disposal as never before. The schools and in particular the universities will have to change their business model, now in effect for a thousand or so years. We can no longer traffic in facts. We must learn to teach an appreciation for what is beyond the facts, for doubt, uncertainty and above all ignorance. This is where opportunity lies.

William Butler Yeats claimed that "Education is not the filling of pails, it is the lighting of fires." The time has come to get out the matches.

References

Drew, C. (2011) Why Science Majors Change Their Minds (It's Just so Darn Hard). *New York Times*, November 4. Online at: http://www.nytimes.com/2011/11/06/education/edlife/why-science-majors-change-their-mind-its-just-so-darn-hard.html (accessed June 30, 2014).

Firestein, S. (2011) Why Do Science Majors Change Their Mind? They Wise Up. *New York Times*, November 6, Online at: http://www.nytimes.com/2011/11/08/opinion/giving-up-on-math-and-science-careers.html (accessed June 30, 2014).

Firestein, S. (2012) *Ignorance: How It Drives Science*. Oxford: Oxford University Press.

Goldstein, M. and I. F. Goldstein (1978) *How We Know: An Exploration of the Scientific Process*. New York: Plenum Press.

Gomory, R. E. (1995) The Known, the Unknown and the Unknowable. *Scientific American* 272(6): 120–122.

Schwartz, M. A. (2008) The Importance of Stupidity in Scientific Research. *Journal of Cell Science* 121: 1771.

Stocking, S. H. (1998) On Drawing Attention to Ignorance. *Science Communication* 20: 165–178.

11

Expect the unexpected

Experimental music, or the ignorance of sound design

Basile Zimmermann

During a winter evening at the end of 1990s, a friend took me to a record shop in downtown Geneva, Switzerland. It was located in a small apartment on the first floor of an old building. The shop consisted of one room, furnished with shelves, a coffee table, a sofa, and a couple of chairs next to a fireplace. Records, mostly compact discs, were arranged on the shelves, listed according to their novelty. A box provided a selection of older records, arranged alphabetically by composer and musician. It was open only on Thursday and Sunday evenings, from 9 p.m. until late.

I started to visit the shop often. I would buy records, bring friends, and attend concerts that it hosted, where one or two musicians sat on the chairs and a crowd of three to ten people listened to them. Most of the time, the owner of the shop was standing behind a desk next to the shelves, where he sold records, answered questions, and offered wine or beer, for free. One day, I remember asking him about the kind of music he specialized in – *experimental music*, as people were calling it. I asked what sort of records he sold. "Music you cannot find elsewhere", he answered.

Experimental music is a style of music that defines itself by opposition to other music styles. Many music lovers define their musical experience in opposition to other music styles,[1] but experimental music bases its own characteristics not on rythmic or melodic patterns, or specific instruments, but on the very idea of *difference*. Experimental music is music that differs. And quite often, together with this idea of difference, comes the idea of *surprise*. The audience expects that songs or performances will contain something unexpected.[2]

In this chapter, I will discuss briefly two sets of observations of the practices of experimental musicians. The first set is based on *participant comprehension*[3] (Collins, 1984) and relies on my experience as a participant in a local music community in Switzerland between 1996 and 2013. I will use elements of my *contributory expertise*[4] (Collins and Evans, 2002), together with informal interviews of people involved in these activities in Geneva, as a research field for the practice of sound art, which I discuss in detail below. The second set of data consists of observations of the activities of a Chinese musician which I collected using participant observation and in-depth qualitative field work between 2003 and 2004 in Beijing.

I will attempt to illustrate how experimental music, practiced in a developing country, is a fascinating object of study for scholars interested in the various guises of ignorance as an asset (see Gross, 2010; McGoey, 2012, for an overview). Exploratory methodologies used by experimental musicians are techniques of dealing with the (re)production of non-knowledge, where ignorance, failures and misuses play a central role as both expected and unexpected elements in the production of surprises.

Lao Li

In 2003, the experimental music scene in Beijing was intriguingly similar to the one in Geneva. There was one experimental music shop in the city, selling the same kind of music as the one I described above, with the important difference that the population size ratio between Geneva and Beijing was 1 to 60. The audience at experimental music concerts looked quite similar, with a mix of Chinese and Western attendees.

I met Lao Li[5] for the first time one November evening at a concert where he gave a live performance together with other local and international artists in a small-scale electronic music festival. In a similar way to how experimental music concerts were organized in Geneva, the audience was small (a few dozen people), who were listening while seated.

Lao Li's performance was beautiful. It surprised me in two aspects. First, he played with a multi-track recorder. He used the device as a live music instrument where normally this kind of device is used for recording and mixing sounds. I was used to seeing musicians play instruments in unusual ways – for instance, a drummer could produce rhythms by playing with bottles, tables and plates, instead of using percussion instruments – but I could not figure out how a multi-track recorder could be turned into an instrument; it was a playback machine, the interface did not allow one to play it in real-time.[6]

My second surprise was that Lao Li managed to produce changes in the sound which I had been unable to understand technically. I was rather proud of my technical skills (I had read Curtis Roads' 1,000-page *Computer Music Tutorial* twice, and I congratulated myself for being able to differentiate software instruments by listening and recognizing their sound characteristics), the feeling of incomprehension was a little humiliating.

During the months that followed, I managed to meet with Lao Li several times and he agreed to let me know more about his work. We had a deal: I worked as a sound engineer for him and, in exchange, he answered questions about his practice. Without going too much into the details of the field research (see Zimmermann, 2006, for more), I summarize here some of the observations I made of his working methods, and my understandings of them.

Lao Li was, I think, completely ignorant of the physics of sound as taught in colleges or universities in the West. This situation related to his personal background – he didn't go to college – and also to his lack of command of English. This was a time when documents that conveyed sound engineering knowledge in Mandarin were scarce (the situation has changed since then, many books that discuss sound techniques have been published recently in Chinese). As a result, Lao Li had developed his own theoretical and methodological frameworks, which allowed him both to think about his music and to perform musical operations.

He made use of a specific vocabulary that allowed him to describe the changes in the sound while he was designing it. For instance, he relied on visual metaphors, such as colors (e.g. he would say: "My music is white"), or spatial movements involving flows (one day, he proposed the idea of designing a sound that would come out of the roof, penetrate the auditor through the shoulder, and then the ramp on the floor). These descriptions were difficult for me to comprehend, because I had been trained in western music conservatoires which made use of a different vocabulary and metaphors for most of the situations Lao Li described (familiar concepts for me were terms such as "equalization", "low and high frequencies", "compression", "panoramic", and so forth). Interestingly, while some aspects of Lao Li's frameworks connected with what I had been taught and what I had read in books, some of it did not correspond to anything I knew.

For instance, I was used to the notion of "spatialization" as a word used to refer to movements of sounds in a tridimentional space. Musicians in conservatoires in Switzerland considered it conventional to refer to the sound as coming out of the loudspeakers while the perception of the listener would attribute its position in space to another location. In the situation of a listener standing at equal distance from two loudspeakers outputting the same sound at the same time and the same level, the auditor would locate the source at the middle of the space between the loudspeakers; if the sound outputted a little later from the first loudspeaker compared to the second one, or with a little less intensity, it would make listeners perceive that its source was located closer to the second loudspeaker. From this point of view, to argue as Lao Li did that the sound would really "come out" of its perceived location such as the roof or the floor (and not from the loudspeakers) was wrong.

The colours Lao Li attributed to sounds often connected with the notion of "equalization", which sound engineers use to refer to high, medium and low frequencies contents. However, I never really managed to understand what exactly he meant when using them in a conversation (sometimes I suspected he didn't know either). Other descriptive words he was using often, such as "piling up" 叠, "attract" 吸 and "press" 压 sound files, did not really fit into categories I knew.

One of the key elements of his framework was the procedure he called the "piling up" of sounds. It consisted of adding sound files one on top of the other, while at the same time applying modifications to each one, so that one instance would influence the behavior of the others. For example, Lao Li copied the same sound several times, then removed part of it on one copy, turned up the volume on one section of another copy, and then added the two files together so that the differences in editing on the various copies of the same recording would, according to him, "attract" part of the sound of one file into the other, or "press" another part of the sound content by adding it to itself.

I believe Lao Li had found himself in a similar situation as early sound engineers who, having learned from experience what works best to produce a particular result, selected specific devices based on the kind of sound they wanted (Schmidt Horning, 2004: 710). His discourse about his music was similar to that of early sound scientists who struggled to make sense of what they heard and how to describe it (see Sterne, 2003). This aspect is reinforced by the fact that the existing vocabulary for sounds is poor when compared to visuals (in English but also in Chinese).

As discussed by Jonathan Sterne:

> While visual experience has a well-developed metalanguage, sonic experience does not. We have abstract words to describe color, texture, shape, direction, shading, and so forth. Conversely, most of the languages used to describe elements of auditory phenomena is metaphoric: aside from specialized languages in musicology, sound engineering, acoustics, and general descriptors such as loud or quiet, there are very few abstract words in common English for describing the timbre, rhythm, texture, density, amplitude, or spatiality of sounds.
>
> *(Sterne, 2003: 94.* On the history of the development of vocabulary to describe sounds, *see also pp. 131–2)*

Bad surprises . . .

Although Lao Li's framework was ingenious, it did not always work well. In a situation comparable to scientists working in ecological restoration – trying out things while the knowledge available is miniscule, and based on learning by doing as well as "reciprocal tuning" between people and the natural world (Gross, 2010: 109–110) – he complained that parts of his music often disappeared. He would design some music, and later notice, to his surprise, that "this sound has disappeared!" 声音没了! For instance, once he had managed to design a song that permanently damaged the loudspeakers on which it was played – an effect he found very interesting. Unfortunately (or fortunately, for the owner of the loudspeakers), when he recorded the song on a compact disc and played it at a friend's place, the music did not sound the way he had expected and the loudspeakers did not break.

Another problem occurred during tentative attempts we made under his direction that resulted in failure. Lao Li wanted to use software on my computer that had functions similar to his multitrack recorder. Following his procedure of "piling up" flows of sound, we duplicated a one-hour recording of a song he had written and performed modifications on each copy. We removed high frequencies on one file, and bass frequencies on the second file. Then he designed variations of volumes on each copy, which we later merged together.

The result was of poor sound quality, and it ended up with another surprise. While we were working, we listened by mistake to the original recording, and we quickly became enthusiastic about the sound quality. Lao Li insisted that we kept that version of the song. A few minutes later, we realized that it was not the file we had just processed, but the original, unprocessed recording! The processed version featuring the new sound edits sounded worse than the original, with some parts of the sound far less clear.

The difficulties mentioned by Lao Li about the disappearing sounds, seen from a Western sound engineering point of view, were related to the devices he used for listening. In most cases, he was either relying on cheap headphones or standard hi-fi loudspeakers installed in his home. Loudspeakers used when composing electronic music are crucial because they shape the sound: they are part of the "instrument". For instance, if there are too many high frequencies coming out of the loudspeakers, the listener may want to turn them down and will adjust the sound. Then, the corresponding recording will have less high frequencies.

Sound engineers emphasize the use of high quality loudspeakers and headphones in order to listen to a "neutral" sound (i.e. close to the average of public hi-fi speakers). This way, loudspeakers allow listeners to make sound adjustments that will later sound more or less the same on most hi-fi systems. I did several attempts to impart this knowledge to Lao Li but to my surprise, while confronted with these difficulties, Lao Li did not use it as a basis for action but rather considered it as *negative knowledge* (i.e. not known but considered unimportant, Gross, 2010). He simply threw away the sounds he didn't like anymore, and started anew.

The second example of a recording that didn't sound as good as the original relates to the way equalization and mixing are processed when applied to a digital recording. While two copies of the same sound file may be added one to the other without any mismatch, the calculation applied to modify the frequency content, done separately on the two copies, creates "blurring" effects. In order to achieve a similar goal, people trained to use these hardware and software devices usually process a file twice, instead of using two copies.

Good surprises . . .

Intriguingly, from another point of view, Lao Li's framework worked very well. It resulted in highly original and musical results which, in the best of what experimental music has to offer, were highly surprising.

I mentioned earlier that the first time I saw him in a live performance, he used a multi-track recorder as a musical instrument. This kind of audio device is intended to be used as a recorder and a mixer but not for a live performance. It didn't seem to me there would be a way to use it to play on stage. At best, for playing an already-finished piece, but not as a musical instrument. What was even more surprising during the performance was that I could distinctly hear modifications of the sound Lao Li was making but I had no idea what they were.

Lao Li was actually "piling up" 叠, "attracting" 吸 and "pressing" 压 sound files. His performance consisted of coming up with a series of identical sound recordings, which he mixed on stage, playing them simultaneously and applying variations to each copy of the sound.

By means of observing Lao Li's work, discussing it with him, and reading books in parallel, I eventually discovered that Lao Li's "piling-up" technique was listed as a marvel effect in the specific case of sound compression. Here is an excerpt from Bob Katz's book *Mastering Audio: The Art and the Science*, where the author describes this unusual procedure:

> Let me introduce you to a venerable compression technique which has finally come of age. Imagine compression that requires just a single knob – no need to adjust attack, threshold, release or ratio. The sound quality is so transparent that careful listening is required to even know the circuit is in operation! (. . .) The principle is quite simple : Take a source, and mix the output of a compressor with it.
>
> *(Katz, 2002, 133)*

In other words, by developing his own set of concepts to work with audio materials and playing with his multi-track recorder (which included an audio effects card), Lao Li had understood something identical to what Bob Katz, an American sound engineer with a massive amount of technical knowledge on sound processing, identified as a very valid procedure. The unknown changes heard during his live performance were what Bob Katz discussed as a sound quality "so transparent that careful listening is required to even know the circuit is in operation", what Lao Li referred to as "pressing"压 sound files and which he used as a technique of sound composition. At the same time, the procedure that Lao Li had insisted on performing on my computer failed. In other words, while his framework could produce very interesting results in the case of a compression effect, it could not when it came to equalization.

First and second degree ignorance

One evening at the beginning of the 2000s in an experimental music club in Geneva, I was struck by the performance of a group of saxophonists.[7] The musicians didn't blow into their instruments, they were using the keys of the saxophones as percussive instruments, producing rhythmic structures, amplifying the sounds using microphones and amplifiers. I had never imagined one could make a full concert that way! And, as with Lao Li, the music sounded beautiful. A few years later, I was at a concert of the famous Japanese experimental music performer Otomo Yoshihide where he threw objects in a cymbal placed on a turn-table connected to an amplifier, and did this gesture each time at the *exact moment* when I would never have expected it – he was playing intentionally at the opposite of a familiar musical movement.

In these two performances, as well as in Lao Li's work, we see that the way experimental musicians deal with surprises is different than the way, say, nuclear physicists or medical researchers do. Whereas in science, surprising events are sometimes welcomed as they offer a window to new and unexpected knowledge (Gross, 2010), one can hardly imagine nuclear physicists or medical researchers making systematic rough "ignorant" choices when using their equipment in the hope of producing totally unexpected results. Such a research procedure would carry potentially dangerous consequences, risking human safety or damaging expensive equipment. But for experimental musicians, surprises are not dangerous as they are, most of the time, limited to the domain of sound.

Some experimental musicians, such as Lao Li, work on the production of surprises mostly at home. When it comes to the moment of recording their work or presenting it on stage, surprises remain surprises only for the audience; at this point, the artist is already familiar with them. For other artists, surprises and accidents are produced directly on stage. Some artists rely on specific technical configurations (for example, a feedback chain loosely arranged, with analog gears all over the stage), that enable them to provoke unexpected results during their performance, to which they have to respond live. In that case, the concert becomes a live reaction to surprises, where (sound) surprises are the musical *instrument* of their performance.[8]

Musicians who practice experimental music often complain of a concert they dislike by arguing that an artist is acting in a way they see as too conventional. For instance, one evening in November 2013, I heard during a performance two local musicians standing next to the bar, located on the other side of the concert hall in the experimental music club (the furthest away from the stage), commenting: "*No bollocks* [in English while speaking in French, with a slightly mock tone].[9] Not only are these guys doing the same as everyone else, they don't even manage to do it well."[10] This aspect could also be observed in the e-mail announcements of the manager of the club, where the unexpected ways the artists were expected to play was emphasized regularly: "unpredictable"; "bold and radical / sharp"; "in complete synchronization with the newest stuff and the self-questioning of the international experimental / improvised scene, therefore renewing itself constantly"; "disconcerting twists, grainy and rough synthetic modulations",[11] and so forth. In the words of one of the two musicians, who I asked about the role of surprises or unexpected elements in experimental music performances: "It's like going on a ghost train. You don't know what will make you feel afraid, but you expect something that will make you feel this way."

Since a prerequisite to the surprise of others is first to surprise oneself, in order to produce unexpected performances for their audience, experimental musicians often travel beyond the limits of their knowledge of sound. One well-known technique is the (re)production of failures. In a similar way to Lao Li, pushing his devices into the unknown by misusing them (for instance, ending up by breaking the membranes of the loudspeakers), sound artists constantly attempt to push the technical objects they use as instruments beyond the limits of their normal/ expected use, in the hope of finding a useful surprise. Once this task is achieved, part of their future performance or recording will consist of reproducing this surprise for the audience.

Of course, experimental music is not the only art practice which makes use of surprises and innovation as a core element. Art in general provides us with a vast domain of similar practices, and classical music, rock music, jazz or even techno are to experimental music what Renaissance paintings are to the latest exhibition in a museum of contemporary art. My argument here, illustrated mainly by Lao Li's practice, is that observations of experimental music in developing countries are interesting in that they provide a double point of view on the use of ignorance.

First, China, and developing countries in general, can be used as laboratories for live observations of outdated knowledge, as they provide a unique point of view on the interaction between ignorance and production of new knowledge. Such field research enables someone such as myself, with a technical training in a specific field, to observe colleagues working in conditions that are reminiscent of other nations' earlier technological refinements, with the advantage of knowing somehow in advance where the technical experiments may, or may not, end up after a long period of trialing and testing. As I was observing Lao Li's practice, it enabled me not only to work for him as a technical assistant but also to compare his framework with the ones I had learned years ago in music conservatoires in the West.

Second, countries such as China offer a highly different cultural, social, and economical environment which gives a rich perspective on alternative possibilities for technical development. In Lao Li's story, we saw that "bad knowledge" (such as the framework of "piling up of flows") can lead to useful surprises for the artist (loudspeakers breaking down), to useful knowledge (parallel compression), as well as to non-useful surprises (sounds disappearing). In the second case, *nescience* for Lao Li, turned into ignorance, that I saw as *non-knowledge* but which Lao Li treated as *negative knowledge* in the sense defined by Gross (2010: 68). While Lao Li worked on the (re)production of surprises in his music, ignorance was taking him in divergent directions.

What Lao Li teaches us about ignorance is the necessity for a musician like him to handle non-knowledge in a two-step procedure. At first, conscious misuses of the tools, or hazardous attempts, are helpful to offer access to the production of surprises and to new knowledge. However, in a second step, the very same ignorance becomes an obstacle for the reproduction of these surprises: to be reproduced, the ins and outs of the process that ended up in the creation of new sounds need to be figured out in detail, and mastered. For an experimental musician, ignorance is crucial during the exploratory phase, but it may become harmful during the reproduction phases, such as the production of a recording, or a live performance.

Within ignorance studies, experimental music practice can be regarded as a professional attitude toward ignorance, with specific sets of exploratory methodologies where surprises play the role of the ultimate goal. As both a laboratory for the live observation of outdated knowledge and a realm for the production of unexpected surprises – experimental music among others – China provides a unique vantage point for glimpsing the interaction between ignorance and production of new knowledge. It offers an unusual point of view on knowhow developed to create surprises, where bad knowledge, sometimes, becomes good design.

Notes

1 See the first two chapters in Thornton (1996) for a discussion on distinction and authenticity in music subcultures.

2 "Experimental music", in this chapter, refers to a generic word for a group of music practices. Besides the general argument of difference I discuss here, it also includes subcategories such as *noise music* (which relies on the evolution in time of sound materials whose contents usually do not include rhythms or melodies but variations of sound density, timbre, and volume), or jazz improvisations with acoustic instruments such as guitars or brass, with melodies and rhythms, contemporary classical music, musique concrète, and other music genres.

3 "Participant comprehension" is a term coined by the sociologist of science Harry Collins (see Collins, 1984). Collins uses it to describe an interpretative research approach (which he derives from participant observation in anthropology) where a researcher gets the closest possible to a full participant of the situation s/he observes, becoming conversant with the details of the discipline s/he is observing. Specifically, in participant comprehension, claims of objectivity are considered less valuable than a deep and personal understanding of what the participants are actually doing; "The stress is not on recording events (. . .) but on internalising a way of life." (Collins, 1984, p. 61).

4 "Contributory expertise" is used by Harry Collins and Robert Evans to describe the kind of expertise fully socialised members of a community have, including the ability to carry out the practical tasks associated with it (Collins and Evans, 2002). Collins uses the term in connexion with the one of "interactional expertise", which describes the ability to talk about the practical tasks without being able to contribute to it. For instance, a music journalist may have enough expertise in music to have a discussion with professional musicians, while at the same time not being able to play on a stage with them (hence, he would have "interactional expertise" in music). A full member of the same musicians' community will be able to have the discussion *and* to play on stage ("contributory expertise").

5 Fictitious name.

6 DJs and musicians mixing reggae tracks are used to "playing" with a mixer. But, based on my experience, this is usually not considered comparable to someone playing a musical instrument live. DJs use the mix to add a personal touch to the records they play (in particular when moving from the previous record to the next one), and reggae tracks are mixed live in the studio in order to add a personal feeling to the way the equalisation and other effects are applied.

7 The place was run by the owner of the record shop described in the introduction, who plays an important role in regard to the local music scene in Geneva. Unfortunately, I haven't been able to track down the name of this band.

8 During an interview with me, the owner of the record shop mentioned in the previous note described the deliberate creation of surprises which artists themselves can't foresee.

9 The use of English words in French in this kind of context often goes with a humorous tone. My understanding is that French speakers rely on the tone to indicate that they don't mean to impress with their knowledge of a foreign language, but to create an effect, in most cases derogatory.

10 "*No bollocks*. Non seulement ils font la même chose que tout le monde, mais ils le font mal."

11 "imprévisible"; "audacieux et radical/pointu"; "en phase complète avec l'actualité et questionnement de l'internationale expérimentale/improvisé, se renouvelant du coup lui-même sans cesse"; " torsions/modulations synthétiques granuleuses et agitées à souhait réellement déconcertantes [*sic*]".

References

Collins, Harry (1984), 'Researching spoonbending: Concepts and practice of participatory fieldwork', in Colin Bell and Helen Roberts (eds.), *Social Researching: Politics, Problems, Practice* (London: Routledge), 54–69.

Collins, Harry, and Robert Evans (2002), 'The third wave of science studies: Studies of expertise and experience', *Social Studies of Science*, 32(2), 235–96.

Gross, Matthias (2010), *Ignorance and Surprise: Science, Society, and Ecological Design* (Cambridge, MA: MIT Press).

Katz, Bob (2002), *Mastering Audio: The Art and the Science* (Burlington: Focal Press).

Roads, Curtis (1996), *The Computer Music Tutorial* (Cambridge, MA: MIT Press).

Schmidt Horning, Susan (2004), 'Engineering the performance: Recording engineers, tacit knowledge and the art of controlling sound', *Social Studies of Science*, 34(5), 703–31.

McGoey, Linsey (2012), 'Strategic unknowns: Towards a sociology of ignorance', *Economy and Society*, 41(1), 1–16.

Sterne, Jonathan (2003), *The Audible Past: Cultural Origins of Sound Reproduction* (Durham, NC: Duke University Press).

Thornton, Sarah (1996), *Club Cultures: Music, Media, and Subcultural Capital* (Middletown, CT: Wesleyan University Press).

Zimmermann, Basile (2006), 'De l'impact de la technologie occidentale sur la culture chinoise: les pratiques des musiciens électroniques à Pékin comme terrain d'observation de la relation entre objets techniques et création artistique', (Université de Genève). Available online at: http://archive-ouverte.unige.ch/unige:409.

12

Purveyors of ignorance

Journalists as agents in the social construction of scientific ignorance

S. Holly Stocking and Lisa W. Holstein

Ask any journalist about the role of news media in society, and chances are you will be assured that it is to shine a light, to raise the curtain, to reveal "the truth." What journalists do, or mean to do, is to dispel ignorance. Yet, constrained by competing interests and concerns, they can sometimes become unwitting allies of powerful actors who strategically construct ignorance to protect and advance their own interests. In so doing, journalists can themselves become purveyors of ignorance and muddle public discourse about science.

This is often seen in scientific controversies, where powerful actors are motivated to discredit and derail threatening research, and where the practices of journalism shape coverage and non-coverage in ways that can leave the public confused or in the dark about matters of public importance. So, for example, the fossil fuel industry for years made sparsely supported claims about the unknowns and uncertainties in the science of global climate change; it reaped substantial news coverage for these claims, in part because many news media – to avoid the appearance of bias – routinely balanced opposing claims without regard to the relative scientific merit of those claims. As a result of the industry's efforts, much news media coverage of climate change shifted over time from science-based reporting based on scientific consensus to stories that were more political in nature and, by implication, more skeptical of the accumulating evidence (Trumbo 1996; McComas and Shanahan 1999; Carvalho 2007; Boykoff 2008).

In the pages that follow, we offer illustrative studies that have addressed some of the ways in which powerful actors who are threatened by research engage in efforts to construct public ignorance about that work, often targeting journalists to advance their causes. We then consider how journalists respond to these efforts, and some of the factors that influence how, in violation of the ideals of journalism (but, ironically, in keeping with what we know about newswork), journalists can become agents in the social construction of scientific ignorance. In so doing, we provide a snapshot of what we have come to know about these matters and a taste for what we still don't know, in the hope of stimulating further research.

Research strands in the social construction of scientific ignorance

Over the last two decades, it has come to be accepted that scientific ignorance, like scientific knowledge, is socially constructed. In that time, our own interests have focused on two of the now-many strands of research on the social construction of scientific ignorance that have emerged — one that documents the social construction of scientific ignorance through a process of claimsmaking, and the other that documents the social construction of ignorance through efforts to suppress threatening or uncomfortable science. The following sections explain and illustrate these two strands, with particular attention paid to the role played by journalists, who – despite changes in the media landscape – remain key players in the social construction of scientific ignorance.

Studies documenting strategic use of ignorance claims

In 1993, following the lead of Smithson (1989) in viewing ignorance as a social construction, we laid out a case for attention to the importance of claimsmaking in this process. Drawing on insights and research from a variety of disciplines, we argued that scientists, driven by interests that include (but are not limited to) furthering scientific knowledge and presenting themselves as credible investigators, routinely make claims about ignorance in their communication with other scientists; they make claims that gaps in knowledge exist, issue caveats to pre-empt the criticisms of reviewers, and in other ways use ignorance claims as rhetorical resources in constructing scientific knowledge. In making our argument, we adopted Smithson's early taxonomy of ignorance (Smithson 1989), which encompassed, among other elements, uncertainty, incompleteness, omission, bias, error, inaccuracy, irrelevance, and distortion.[1]

Not only in scientific discourse, but in public discourse, too, we argued, scientists who seek to influence public policy debates routinely issue ignorance claims. Some of these claims, aimed primarily at experts, are what Aronson (1984) labeled "cognitive claims," about the specifics of research findings, while others are "interpretive claims," which use research findings to draw broader implications for non-specialist audiences. Various advocacy groups, from corporations to grassroots organizations, then appropriate such claims and amplify or attenuate them – along with claims they may generate themselves – as strategic tools in the mobilization of ignorance to protect and advance their own particular interests (Funtowicz and Ravetz 1990; Smithson 1980 and 1989). Finally, extrapolating from a large number of studies on newsmaking, we speculated that the ways in which journalist cover (or don't cover) ignorance claims are likely to reflect, protect, and advance their own interests. We went on to call for studies of the significant role that journalists play in the social construction of scientific ignorance.

Following this theoretical thread, we subsequently investigated a case in which the North Carolina Pork Council, on behalf of an industry that felt threatened by the findings of new scientific research, initiated a strategic campaign to discredit the science (Stocking and Holstein 2009).

In this case, two government-funded studies by a University of North Carolina epidemiologist cast the industry in a negative light regarding the environmental injustice of geographic distribution of large industrial hog farms (Wing and Wolf 2000) and the negative health effects suffered by neighbors of these mega-farms (Wing et al. 2000). Deliberately using methods learned from the playbook of Big Tobacco (Miller 1992; Proctor 1995), the North Carolina Pork Council, in news releases and interviews with journalists, made a variety of claims about the studies, including claims that the research was flawed, misleading, incomplete and even "pseudo-science," wide-ranging claims that were wholly consistent with Smithson's original taxonomy of ignorance. The Council also claimed that the lead researcher himself was biased, politically motivated and even incompetent. None of industry's claims was empirically based. In the absence of countervailing knowledge, the Pork Council simply claimed ignorance.

Our approach was to analyze news stories to see how the news media treated industry's ignorance claims, and to then interview the journalists with an eye toward understanding the factors that had led them to cover the claims as they did.[2]

In subsequent analyses of our interviews with journalists, we discovered that the ways in which individual journalists perceived their journalistic roles had a strong bearing on their treatment of the claims of industry. Specifically, the "attitudinal clusters" identified by Weaver and Wilhoit (1996) in their longitudinal studies of American journalists were useful in differentiating the ways journalists responded to and used scientific ignorance claims in their stories. These four types of journalists, briefly described, consist of:

- the disseminator, who reports as news the claims of all "legitimate" sources;
- the interpretive/investigative reporter, who takes responsibility for providing context for the news through independent research into sources' claims;
- the populist-mobilizer, who seeks to give voice to audiences and set public agendas; and
- the adversarial reporter, who sees special interests behind all sources and so views all claims with skepticism.

Although we didn't expect individual reporters' attitudes to necessarily fall neatly within a single category, we found these to be useful descriptors of the role perceptions exhibited in our case study.[3] For example, one journalist, a writer for the editorial pages who appeared to adopt the interpretive/investigative role, went out of his way to assess the science on his own, deeming it worthy of an editorial that backed the scientists' claims against the pork industry's claims.

Others who adopted different journalistic roles unwittingly played into the hands of the pork industry. One reporter for the Associated Press, who perceived his journalistic role as a news disseminator, simply presented one claim after the other, with the rationale that newspaper readers, presented objectively with "both" sides of a story, could make up their own minds. In this he reflected a practice of thousands of journalists who over the years have given equal weight to scientists' and industries' claims in the cases of tobacco, global climate change and many other controversies, even when the claims of science clearly are the weightier (cf. Dearing 1995; Gelbspan 1997; Zehr 2000; Boykoff and Boykoff 2004; Mooney 2005; Nestle 2013). This practice is driven by a perceived need to maintain the appearance of objectivity, an ideal of traditional U.S. journalistic practice that has received considerable attention from scholars in the field of mass communication (Tuchman 1972; Schudson 1978 and 2001; Schiller 1981; Reese 1990), and by news values that place a premium on controversy (Dunwoody 1999; Gans 2004).

Another reporter, who saw his role as adversarial, believed he was fulfilling his "watchdog" role by distrusting both industry and academic claims. In treating the scientists' claims skeptically, he unwittingly gave credence to the Pork Council's charges, undermining the trustworthiness of the scientists' findings. Whereas the disseminator journalist reproduced all claims for his audience to judge, the adversarial reporter took it upon himself to write stories that raised doubts not only about the research findings, but also about the impartiality of the scientist and his employer, the School of Public Health at the University of North Carolina at Chapel Hill.

In short, most of the journalists' interests in meeting their perceived role obligations created the circumstances in which the pork industry, even without countervailing scientific evidence, was able to gain a hearing for its ignorance claims.

The strategic construction of ignorance to fight research that threatens actors' interests is not an unusual tactic in controversial matters involving science. A manufactured scientific controversy serves to distort public agendas and "denies publics proper political debates by hiding political agendas behind invented scientific concerns" (Weinel 2012: 429). As other investigators have shown, injecting ignorance claims into scientific controversies can be a powerful weapon indeed (e.g., Stauber and Rampton 1995; Gelbspan 1997; Beder 1998; Rampton and Stauber 2001; Michaels 2008).

Studies documenting strategic suppression of research

The second strand of research that we have focused on in the social construction of ignorance attends to certain kinds of "ignorance arrangements." Such arrangements are designed to benefit actors by suppressing threatening or uncomfortable knowledge (Smithson 1989). While there are likely to be many kinds of ignorance arrangements related to many different kinds of knowledge, our own work has focused on strategic efforts to disrupt, if not replace, existing institutional arrangements that support the creation of new scientific knowledge, presumably with the intention of preventing certain areas of science from being investigated at all. An early example of actions taken to redirect, if not scuttle, the very development of science was documented in Proctor's (1995) study of private industry's extensive – and largely successful – efforts to steer the direction of federal funding for cancer research toward disease processes and the biologically based search for cures, and away from funding for research into environmental causes; industry also worked aggressively to suppress and even prevent research that might be used to regulate cancer-linked chemicals in the workplace. Such efforts can lead to what Hess (2009) has called "undone science" (Frickel et al. 2010).[4]

News media attention to orchestrated efforts to suppress controversial science has too often been neglected or treated cursorily in prior studies, a neglect that we addressed specifically in our own research. Well before the time-frame of our case study, the pork industry had succeeded in promoting a state law that prohibited the sharing of data about hog farming, including across internal governmental agencies (Stith and Warrick 1995), an action that also created an obstacle for independent scientists who might have wanted to use the data to conduct their own research. When the scientist in our study made his particular claims to knowledge, the pork industry, in addition to its strategic use of ignorance claims to discredit the research findings, undertook many behind-the-scenes efforts to disrupt the scientist's work. Among their broad-based attacks (Wing 2002), they leveled criticisms about the researcher through each level in the university bureaucracy, from his department head up to the Board of Trustees. They also threatened him with a defamation lawsuit, arranged to have him summoned to the state capitol to face hostile questioning by a legislative committee of the General Assembly, and even approached the North Carolina Congressional delegation to demand an investigation of the National Institutes of Health funding for one of the scientist's studies in an attempt to shut it down. In addition, the industry used the state Freedom of Information Act to gain access to questionnaire data of people who lived around the hog farms and who had been assured of human subjects privacy protection, an action that tied up the research for months as investigators scrambled to cleanse the data of all identifying markers.

Most of the small sample of journalists we studied failed to write about these particular industry tactics, although a news item did appear about the threatened lawsuit (Wagner 1999), and was picked up and circulated by the Associated Press; a subsequent editorial also appeared (*News & Observer* 1999), condemning such intimidation tactics. There are a number of possible explanations as to why journalists paid more attention to industry's ignorance claims in this controversy than to its efforts to disrupt existing institutional arrangements so as to shut up the researcher and shut down his research. Although pork was a huge industry, with enthusiastic support from the state legislature (Stith et al. 1995) during the time-frame of our case study, most of its tactics to derail the research were not particularly visible. Moreover, the impoverished people most threatened by massive hog production facilities, and so most likely to have an interest in news about efforts to derail research that supported their interests, were not among typical audiences for newspapers (and their advertisers). It would have been relatively easy for journalists to overlook these tactics, and almost certainly – given the comparative popularity of news stories about new research findings (Clark and Illman 2006) – a lot easier than to ignore the results of government-funded research trumpeted by a prestigious university.

One of the two journalists in our study who did write about an industry tactic to derail the science – the threatened defamation suit – was responding to the state Department of Health and Human Services release of the Pork Council's letter announcing their exploration of legal action. Another journalist, who wrote about the legal demands for back-up data from the study and the threat of a lawsuit, fit the role of the populist-mobilizer journalist. Her story reported industry's ignorance claims attacking the research, but also quoted hog farm neighbors, which bolstered the impact of the scientist's findings; in addition, it quoted the scientist himself about some of the disruptive tactics that had been used to stymie his work (Williams 1999).

We've come a long way, fellow ignorami, but ignorance remains

When we began our explorations of ignorance in the 1990s, it was considered novel, as well as illuminating, to direct the attention of scholars in science studies and mass communication to ignorance (Stocking 1998). But by now, the insight that ignorance, like knowledge, is socially constructed has lost the patina of novelty. It is clearly time for scholars to turn their attention from the fact that ignorance is socially constructed to the many ways in which it is, and to factors that influence these constructions.

Our own research has pointed to how role perceptions of individual journalists can affect the reporting of strategic ignorance moves made in scientific controversies. However, they are not the only influencing factors. Our study also implicated journalists' perceptions of their audiences and their general understanding of science and how it works, though given the small number of journalists in our case study, our conclusions are merely suggestive.

Looking back, our original theoretical article on the social construction of ignorance (Stocking and Holstein 1993) in the journal *Knowledge* (now *Science Communication*) proposed other matters worthy of study with respect to news media, among them:

- What is the nature of the ignorance claims that journalists most often cover?
- What changes take place as these claims move from scientific discourse into the public sphere, and particularly into the stories journalists produce, and what factors account for these changes?
- Are claims negotiated and, if they are, between whom (scientists and journalists? Reporters and their editors?), under what circumstances (when the ideals of journalism and economic interests conflict?), and what specific interests can be tied to the results of these negotiations?

In later work, Stocking (1999) suggested a hierarchy of likely factors that influence how journalists cover strategic efforts to construct scientific ignorance. These factors, identified through decades of research in the field of mass communication, include:

- individual characteristics of journalists, such as education, experience, and allegiance to professional standards and values (journalists' perceptions of their professional roles operate at this level);
- media routines, such as the balancing routine for controversial stories, but also including routines for defining news; and
- organizational demands, such as the need to tailor stories to particular audiences and to take into account advertiser and ownership pressures.

Culture and ideology (often intertwined with ownership patterns and political systems) also are likely to shape how journalists cover the claims of their sources (Weaver and Willnat 2012). So, for example, U.S. elite newspapers, with their traditional cultures related to objectivity and balance, have been found to emphasize "uncertainty" in science more than their counterpart newspapers in other countries (Anderson 2009). And the conservative press in the UK has been found to grant more credibility than other elite newspapers to industry's "climate skeptical" sources (Carvalho 2007). All these factors are worthy of attention from those who seek to understand the important role that journalists often play in these matters.

As much as we want to encourage work that seeks to understand journalists as key players in the social construction of scientific ignorance, we would be remiss if we did not acknowledge the many ways that powerful actors increasingly make end-runs around the news media, taking their messages directly to targeted publics. In some cases, actors may advertise directly to affected publics and even recruit ordinary citizens to do their work, as Philip Morris did in 1993 when it quietly funded the "Advancement of Sound Science Coalition" with the initial goal of discrediting a government report on secondhand smoke. This group's "local coalitions" were created to work against what the industry cynically labeled "junk science" and advocate for what it called "sound science in the public policy arena" by making ignorance claims about research findings (Mooney 2005: 67). In another more recent example, a major climate change denial organization targeted thousands of teachers across the U.S. with a direct mailing in 2013. The mailing attacked the scientific consensus on climate science and offered denialist claims as a suggested source for informing their students; it also included an offer for teachers to "win $500" by giving the packet their attention (McCaffrey 2013).

Such efforts to reach audiences directly without going through journalists are only growing with the use of the Internet and social media. Grassroots organizations of all sorts – religious, environmental, and those devoted to social justice and other issues – increasingly work to supplement, and in some instances even to replace, traditional efforts to reach a wide public through news media outlets by turning to websites, video posts and social media apps. Often such actions inspire strong pushback from powerful opponents, as happened when supporters of animal rights smuggled cameras inside factory farms, seeking video to post online, and industry followed with well-funded state-by-state lobbying for so-called "ag-gag" laws to outlaw the tactic (Oppel 2013).

Without question, the growing diversity of media platforms is an increasingly important factor in the entire "information climate" that affects public understanding of science (Hornig Priest 1999). Among other things, new media tempt mainstream journalists to use the sometimes sketchily sourced content, all too often absolving even the most traditional reporters and editors of the dedication to fact-checking that they would normally bring to their professional roles (Kang 2013; Shih 2013). Despite this, such media remain underrepresented in academic studies of science topics in the news (Anderson 2009; Schäfer 2012).

Conclusion

"All our science, measured against reality, is primitive and childlike," Einstein famously remarked, "and yet it is the most precious thing we have." As a way of knowing, science *is* precious. It is also an important public good. Yet as the discourse of science enters the public sphere, it often becomes less about specialized knowledge than about politics, perceptions and competing values.

Especially when an issue involving science becomes a locus of public controversy (think evolution, genetically modified foods, or public concerns about vaccines and autism along with climate change and so many other topics), the conflict can quickly devolve into one of competing knowledge and ignorance claims. How journalists reconstruct ignorance claims that are used as strategic assets to manufacture doubt remains deeply consequential for public issues and society as a whole (Best 2012). The same is true of how journalists respond when government agencies, corporations and others seek to suppress research and deny the public access to developing areas of science.

What we know about journalists' responses to deliberate efforts to construct ignorance is tantalizing, but hardly definitive. At least in the U.S. where we conducted our study, some journalists appear able to resist such efforts, while other journalists – out of allegiance to particular journalistic roles, adherence to the routines of daily newswork, and other factors including their own understandings of science – can all too easily become unwitting allies of such motivated actors. This is not to say that there are not some who regard themselves as journalists who, to attract niche audiences, consciously ally themselves with interest-driven purveyors of ignorance[5] and so cloud public discourse. But our findings should serve as a caution to the significantly greater number of journalists around the world who have no intention of violating traditional journalistic ideals (Weaver and Willnat 2012) – ideals that may lead them to believe they won't fall victim to sources' efforts to manipulate the news – but who do so just the same.

Notes

1 Smithson's useful categorization schedule has been amplified by Gross (2007) to incorporate distinctions in levels of analysis and philosophical positions and to attempt to account for connections among differing types of unknowns.
2 Stocking and Holstein (2009) describes the strengths and limitations of these methods.
3 These categories were also found to be useful descriptors of the role perceptions of Greek environmental reporters for three out of the four clusters in Giannoulis et al. (2010).
4 Scholars studying ignorance from different perspectives have used the term "strategic ignorance" in a less pejorative context, identifying and analyzing how such arrangements can be an unavoidable and socially useful resource in personal, political and organizational contexts (cf. McGoey 2012), and serve as social strategies that actors use to deliberately avoid gaining unsettling scientific knowledge (Wynne 1989).
5 This chapter has focused on journalists in the U.S. and similar press cultures, where news media are traditionally viewed as an essential part of the public sphere in a democratic society; we do not address the very real differences in some media cultures where journalists and certain news outlets routinely affiliate with political parties or operate under formal or assumed government constraints on press freedom, whether through official propaganda or through self-censorship. For a focus on differences among journalists in different countries and cultures, see Weaver and Willnat (2012).

References

Anderson, A. (2009) 'Media, politics and climate change: towards a new research agenda', *Sociology Compass* 3(2): 166–82.

Aronson, N. (1984) 'Science as a claims-making activity: implications for social problems research', in J. W. Schneider and J. I. Kitsuse (eds.) *Studies in the Sociology of Social Problems,* Norwood, NJ: Ablex: 1–30.

Beder, S. (1998) *Global Spin: The Corporate Assault on Environmentalism*, Devon, UK and White River Junction, VT: Green Books Ltd. and Chelsea Green Publishing Co.

Best, J. (2012) 'Constructionist social problems theory', *Communication Yearbook* 36: 236–69.

Boykoff, M. T. (2008) 'Media and scientific communication: a case of climate change', in D. G. E. Liverman, C. P. G. Pereira and B. Marker (eds.) *Communicating Environmental Geoscience*, London: Geological Society Special Publications 305: 11–18.

Boykoff, M. T. and Boykoff, J. M. (2004) 'Balance as bias: global warming and the U.S. prestige press', *Global Environmental Change* 14(2): 125–36.

Carvalho, A. (2007) 'Ideological cultures and media discourses on scientific knowledge: re-reading news on climate change', *Public Understanding of Science* 16: 223–43.

Clark, F. and Illman, D. L. (2006) 'A longitudinal study of *The New York Times* Science Times section', *Science Communication* 27(4): 496–513.

Dearing, J. W. (1995) 'Newspaper coverage of maverick science: creating controversy through balancing', *Public Understanding of Science* 4: 11–16.

Dunwoody, S. (1999) 'Scientists, journalists and the meaning of uncertainty', in S. M. Friedman, S. Dunwoody and C. L. Rogers (eds.) *Communicating Uncertainty: Media Coverage of New and Controversial Science*, Mahwah, NJ: Lawrence Erlbaum.

Frickel, S., Gibbon, S., Howard, J., Kempner, J., Ottinger, G. and Hess, D. (2010) 'Undone science: charting social movement and civil society challenges to research agenda setting', *Science, Technology and Human Values* 35(4): 444–73.

Funtowicz, S. O. and Ravetz, J. R. (1990) *Uncertainty and Quality in Science for Policy*, Theory and Decision Library, Series A(15), Dordrecht: Kluwer.

Gans, H. J. (2004) *Deciding What's News: A Study of CBS Evening News, NBC Nightly News, Newsweek, and Time*, Evanston, IL: Northwestern University Press.

Gelbspan, R. (1997) *The Heat Is On: The High Stakes Battle Over Earth's Threatened Climate*, Reading, MA: Addison-Wesley.

Giannoulis, C., Botetzagias, I. and Skanavis, C. (2010) 'Newspaper reporters' priorities and beliefs about environmental journalism', *Science Communication* 32(4): 425–66.

Gross, M. (2007) 'The unknown in process: dynamic connections of ignorance, non-knowledge and related concepts', *Current Sociology* 55(5): 742–59.

Hess, D. (2009) 'The potentials and limitations of civil society research: getting undone science done', *Sociological Inquiry* 79: 306–27.

Hornig Priest, S. (1999) 'Popular beliefs, media and biotechnology', in S. M. Friedman, S. Dunwoody and C. L. Rogers (eds.) *Communicating Uncertainty: Media Coverage of New and Controversial Science*, Mahwah, NJ: Lawrence Erlbaum.

Kang, J. C. (2013) 'Crowd-sourcing a smear: should Reddit be blamed for the spreading of a smear?' *The New York Times*, 25 July, Magazine section.

McCaffrey, M. (2013) RE: 'Denial's in the Mail', group email alert about a Heartland Institute mailing, received by S. H. Stocking from the National Center for Science Education, 11 November.

McComas, K. and Shanahan, J. (1999) 'Telling stories about global climate change: measuring the impact of narratives on issue cycles', *Communication Research* 26(1): 30–57.

McGoey, L. (2012) 'Strategic unknowns: toward a sociology of ignorance', *Economy and Society* 41(1): 1–16.

Michaels, D. (2008) *Doubt Is Their Product: How Industry's Assault on Science Threatens Your Health*, New York: Oxford University Press.

Miller, K. (1992) 'Smoking up a storm: public relations and advertising in the construction of the cigarette problem 1953–4', *Journalism Monographs* 136(December).

Mooney, C. (2005) *The Republican War on Science*, New York: BasicBooks.

Nestle, M. (2013) *Food Politics: How the Food Industry Influences Nutrition and Health*, Berkeley: University of California Press.

News & Observer, The (Raleigh, NC) (1999) 'Pork or porcupine?' editorial, 14 May: A18.

Oppel, R.A., Jr. (2013) 'On farm, taping cruelty is becoming the crime', *The New York Times*, 7 April: A1.

Proctor, R. N. (1995) *Cancer Wars: How Politics Shapes What We Know and Don't Know About Cancer*, New York: BasicBooks.

Rampton, S. and Stauber, J. (2001) *Trust Us! We're Experts! How Industry Manipulates Science and Gambles With Your Future*, New York: Jeremy P. Tarcher/Putnam.

Reese, S. D. (1990) 'The news paradigm and the ideology of objectivity: a socialist at the *Wall Street Journal*', *Critical Studies in Mass Communication* 7(4): 390–409.

Schäfer, M. S. (2012) 'Taking stock: a meta-analysis of studies on the media's coverage of science', *Public Understanding of Science* 21(6): 650–63.

Schiller, D. (1981) *Objectivity and the News: The Public and the Rise of Commercial Journalism*, Philadelphia: University of Pennsylvania Press.

Schudson, M. (1978) *Discovering the News: A Social History of Newspapers*, New York: BasicBooks.

Schudson, M. (2001) 'The objectivity norm in American journalism', *Journalism* 2(2): 149–70.

Shih, G. (2013) 'Truth and consequences: a dilemma for Twitter and its users', Reuters, 25 April. Available online at: www.reuters.com/article/2013/04/25/net-us-twitter-credibility-idUSBRE93N10920130425.

Smithson, M. (1980) 'Interests and the growth of uncertainty', *Journal for the Theory of Social Behaviour* 10: 157–68.

Smithson, M. (1989) *Ignorance and Uncertainty: Emerging Paradigms*, New York: Springer-Verlag.

Stauber, J. C. and Rampton, S. (1995) *Toxic Sludge Is Good for You! Lies, Damn Lies and the Public Relations Industry*, Monroe, ME: Common Courage Press.

Stith, P. and Warrick, J. (1995) 'Law restricts hog information, even from N.C. officials: disclosure bill used instead for secrecy', *The (Raleigh, NC) News & Observer*, 19 February.

Stith, P., Warrick, J. and Sill, M. (1995) 'Boss Hog', *The (Raleigh, NC) News & Observer*, 19, 21, 22, 24, 26, 28 February; Pulitzer Prize Winning Newspaper Articles Online Archive. Available online at: www.pulitzer.org.

Stocking, S. H. (1998) 'On drawing attention to ignorance', *Science Communication* 20(1): 165–78.

Stocking, S. H. (1999) 'How journalists deal with scientific uncertainty', in S. M. Friedman, S. Dunwoody and C. L. Rogers (eds.) *Communicating Uncertainty: Media Coverage of New and Controversial Science*, Mahwah, NJ: Lawrence Erlbaum.

Stocking, S. H. and Holstein, L. W. (1993) 'Constructing and reconstructing scientific ignorance: ignorance claims in science and journalism', *Knowledge: Creation, Diffusion, Utilization* 15(2): 186–210.

Stocking, S. H. and Holstein, L. W. (2009) 'Manufacturing doubt: journalists' roles and the construction of ignorance in a scientific controversy', *Public Understanding of Science* 18: 23–42.

Trumbo, C. (1996) 'Constructing climate change: claims and frames in U.S. news coverage of an environmental issue', *Public Understanding of Science* 5(3): 1–15.

Tuchman, G. (1972) 'Objectivity as strategic ritual: an examination of newsmen's notions of objectivity', *American Journal of Sociology* 77(4): 660–80.

Wagner, J. (1999) 'Under the dome: hog study raises legal hackles', *The (Raleigh, NC) News & Observer*, 11 May: A3.

Weaver, D. H. and Wilhoit, G. C. (1996) *The American Journalist in the 1990s: U.S. News People at the End of an Era*, Mahwah, NJ: Earlbaum (see also 5th edn 2006: Weaver, D. H., Beam, R. A., Brownlee, B. J., Voakes, P. S. and Wilhoit, G. C. *The American Journalist in the 21st Century: U.S. News People at the Dawn of a New Millennium*, Mahwah, NJ: Earlbaum).

Weaver, D. W. and Willnat, L. (eds.) (2012) *The Global Journalist in the 21st Century*, New York, NY: Routledge.

Weinel, M. (2012) 'Expertise and inauthentic scientific controversies: what you need to know to judge the authenticity of policy-relevant scientific controversies', in J. Goodwin (ed.) *Between Scientists and Citizens*, Ames, IA: Great Plains Society for the Study of Argumentation.

Williams, L. (1999) 'Health links inconclusive', *The Fayetteville (NC) Observer*, 1 August, local/state section.

Wing, S. (2002) 'Social responsibility and research ethics in community-driven studies of industrialized hog production', *Environmental Health Perspectives* 110(5): 437–44.

Wing, S. and Wolf, S. (2000) 'Intensive livestock operations, health and quality of life among Eastern North Carolina residents', *Environmental Health Perspectives* 108(3): 233–8.

Wing, S., Cole, D. and Grant, G. (2000) 'Environmental injustice in North Carolina's hog industry', *Environmental Health Perspectives* 108(3): 225–31.

Wynne, B. (1989) 'Sheepfarming after Chernobyl: a case study in communicating scientific information', *Environment* 31(2): 10–39.

Zehr, S. C. (2000) 'Public representations of scientific uncertainty about global climate change', *Public Understanding of Science* 9: 85–103.

13

Ignorance and the brain

Are there distinct kinds of unknowns?

Michael Smithson and Helen Pushkarskaya

Setting the scene: What can brain imaging tell us about how the brain processes ignorance?

The brain is a human organ responsible for processing external and internal information and deciding how to respond to new information. One of many fascinating capabilities of the brain is an ability to make decisions even when not all objectively necessary information is available (this arguably distinguishes the brain from the computer). There is a fast-growing brain-imaging research literature on how the brain deals with unknowns (i.e., uncertainty). One branch of this literature focuses primarily on low-level processing (e.g., visual perception) and another mainly on high-level processing (e.g., executive functions). This chapter will present a brief review of selected findings from both literatures.

Functional magnetic resonance imaging (fMRI) studies of judgment and decision making under uncertainty have provided some insights into how the brain processes incomplete information when making decisions (e.g., Platt and Huettel 2008), although more questions remain unanswered than answered. Neuroeconomists have focused on the impacts of what behavioral economists and psychologists refer to as "risk" and "ambiguity" on brain activation patterns. "Risk" here refers to uncertain settings with known outcomes of choices and known probabilities of these outcomes (von Neumann and Morgenstern 1944), and "ambiguity" refers to uncertain settings with known outcomes but unknown or partially known probabilities (Ellsberg 1961). An older, roughly synonymous, term is "uncertainty" (Knight 1921).

Somewhat confusingly, perhaps, another line of neurological research has entailed investigating "ambiguity" in a sense that is closer to the traditional philosophical notion, i.e., multiple plausible states or meanings. For instance, Zeki (2004: 175) presents a neurobiological definition of ambiguity as involving "many, equally plausible interpretations, each one of which is sovereign when it occupies the conscious stage". Optical illusions such as the Necker or Kanisza cube or the Rubin vase-face figure exemplify this kind of ambiguity, and it should be no surprise that much of the research into this kind of ambiguity has been conducted by neuroscientists interested in visual perception.

Before moving on to survey both literatures, however, we require some attention to what studies of the brain can tell us about how humans deal with, construct, and interpret unknowns. For instance, the integration of behavioral and neural evidence and a convergence on a single general theory of human decision making are explicit goals in programmatic reviews such as Glimcher and Rustichini (2004). They begin by claiming that economic, psychological, and neurobiological explanations of decision making operate at three different levels. The economists' approach encompasses choice behavior in a "single logically consistent formalism" (p. 448). The psychologists posit motivational forces and cognitive heuristics that may account for choice behavior. Neuroscientists attempt to explain behavior by positing neural circuitry that could produce it. Glimcher and Rustichini claim that early work in neuroeconomics already had succeeded in initiating the synthesis of these three approaches. The key proposition (Glimcher and Rustichini 2004: 450) behind their claim is that "neural circuits may compute and represent the desirability of making a response."

Claims such as this one raise the question of whether and when fMRI studies can adjudicate among rival accounts of how people think about and deal with unknowns. Consider, for example, the issue of whether people think and act as if there are distinct kinds of unknowns or uncertainties. Smithson (2008: 211–212) nominated four criteria for evidence of such distinctions at the social level. Here, we incorporate them and add criteria at the level of the individual.

1 Neurobiological (e.g., are different networks in the brain involved in processing different kinds of uncertainty?)
2 Consequentialist (e.g., does one kind influence behavior independently of another kind on the basis of perceived consequences?)
3 Doxastic (e.g., are different kinds accorded different moral statuses?)
4 Correlational (e.g., do different variables predict orientations toward different kinds, or are orientations towards all kinds predicted by the same variables?)
5 Functional (e.g., are different kinds used for distinct purposes, or do they play different social or psychological roles?)
6 Cultural (e.g., are kinds consistently distinguished from one another when referred to by members of the same linguistic community?)

A key concern is whether these criteria may be related to or constrain one another. We will focus just on the neurobiological criterion and its relationship to the other five. To begin, it seems unlikely that we could claim anything about selective or preferential involvement of particular neural networks in processing of various kinds of unknowns solely on the basis of even a strong finding for the satisfaction of any of criteria 2 through 6. At most, these criteria may be used to generate hypotheses for brain imaging research, as indeed has been the case with ambiguity in the judgment and decision literature.

Conversely, a finding that different neural networks are selectively or preferentially activated by different kinds of unknowns (i.e. criterion 1) may not permit strong inferences about the other criteria. While it is possible that completely separate neural networks could entail criteria 2–6, there is no guarantee of these entailments. Moreover, partially shared networks make such entailments less clear-cut. It is also possible that humans may not be aware of these differentiated activation patterns, so there is no guarantee that people would label them with different terms (i.e., as in criterion 6).

A self-described "ultra" skeptical viewpoint on whether brain imaging tells us anything about what the mind does is Coltheart's position. His major claim (Coltheart 2004: 22) is that "facts about the brain do not constrain the possible natures of mental information-processing systems. No amount of knowledge about the hardware of a computer will tell you anything serious about the nature of the software that the computer runs. In the same way, no facts about the activity of the brain could be used to confirm or refute some information-processing model of cognition." Nor is Coltheart alone; see for instance an earlier work by Uttal (2001) whose book title (*The New Phrenology*) squarely indicates where he stands on these matters.

The inference of specific mental states from neural activation data is referred to as "reverse inference" by Poldrack (2006), who argued that its validity is constrained by the selectivity of the activation region (i.e., when a region is activated exclusively during the specified cognitive process). When involvement of a particular neural network in a particular process is investigated, the first step is to identify the network nodes involved in this process. Unfortunately, many relevant brain regions do not exhibit strong selectivity. Not only are the same brain regions recruited by multiple processes, they also serve as nodes for multiple networks. For instance, in the neuroeconomics literature, ventral striatal activation is considered to imply the experience of a reward, but this region has also been found to be activated by novel non-rewarding stimuli (Berns et al. 1997). Furthermore, the low resolution of the fMRI technique does not allow speculation about involvement of micro networks in the decision making under uncertainty, whereas these networks have been shown to play a crucial role in other cognitive processes such as working memory (Lim and Goldman 2013). Mapping a specific process onto a specific network is a non-trivial aim. Poldrack (2006) therefore urges a cautionary stance regarding reverse inference.

Nevertheless, the question we have raised here really is just the first step in the process of linking a cognitive process to particular neural networks: When presented with different "kinds" of uncertain stimuli, are they processed by neural networks that rely on different nodes (i.e., areas in the brain)? Neuroimaging seems to be well-suited to answering this question at least in some cases; nor do we regard the question as unimportant. Nevertheless, even if we are not as skeptical as Coltheart, the implications of these considerations are twofold. First, a reliance on behavioral, socio-cultural, or attitudinal evidence for distinct kinds of unknowns provides no guarantee of correctly and exhaustively identifying neurological kinds. Second, neuroimaging investigations cannot obviate the need for behavioral scientific, psychological, sociological, or anthropological investigations research and, importantly, theory development on this topic. Evidence at each level only weakly constrains conclusions about the others, and therefore the question of whether ignorance is unitary is, itself, not unitary.

Ambiguity type 1: Multistability (ambiguity) in visual perception

Multistability occurs when a stimulus produces alternations among different interpretations (or percepts) of the stimulus. For over two centuries, multistability has inspired entire research programs on visual perception. As Kleinschmidt et al. (2012: 988) put it, "Few phenomena are as suitable as perceptual multistability to demonstrate that the brain constructively interprets sensory input." Most of the work on it (including brain imaging) has focused exclusively on the visual system, but there have been recent forays into other sensory modalities (Schwarz et al. 2012), primarily the auditory system.

The phenomenology of multistability raises two chief observations: The apparent stability of the temporarily dominant percept, and the instability of that dominance. Early imaging experiments (Kleinschmidt et al. 1998; Lumer et al. 1998) indicated that the switch from one interpretation (or percept) to another when viewing bistable images (i.e., where the stimulus is static but the percept oscillates between two states) is accompanied by a shift in the activated areas of the brain. The notion that distinct percepts might occupy different locations in the brain has been discussed as a possible explanation for their apparent stability when one of them dominates. Moreover, as might be expected, visual perceptual dominance is identified with activity levels in regions that are functionally tailored for dealing with the properties of the percept involved.

However, studies of perceptual switching have not yet resolved at which stage in the hierarchy of visual cortical areas the activity corresponds to the perceptual state. According to Coltheart's (2004: 22) view this should not surprise us, because hardly any attempts to use neuroimaging data for localizing cognitive system modules have succeeded. Apparently the difficulties regarding multistability are at least partly due to issues in disentangling simultaneous processes. Most of the evidence regarding cortical activity in bistable perception is based on binocular rivalry, i.e., the spontaneously oscillating dominance of one eye over the other when the eyes receive separate incongruent images. However, this approach presents interpretive difficulties because they involve both competition between the two eyes and the two perceptual contents. An alternative method is to present an ambiguous figure identically to both eyes, similar to naturally occurring perceptual ambiguity. Unfortunately, in this approach the link between perceptual and neural states has been difficult to establish.

What about explanations of switching? Some researchers (e.g., Parkkonen et al. 2008) found evidence that the parietal cortex and/or lateral prefrontal cortex are active whenever a percept switches from one condition to another, suggesting that they may be involved in dictating the percept so that we only become conscious of the dominant percept through their intervention. This claim is supported by evidence that patients with focal damage to the prefrontal and parietal cortex exhibit slower perceptual alternations than health controls (Windmann et al. 2006). The guiding of perceptual processing in one area by "top-down" directives from another has been attributed to neural networks involved in planning and goal-directed behavior regulation (Windmann et al. 2006). A similar line of reasoning suggests that spontaneous perceptual switching when a new stimulus is initially viewed may serve to prevent the visual system from being trapped by an early interpretation that is later invalidated. Nonetheless, some scholars in this area urge caution about such inferences, noting, for instance, that being able to establish activity in the prefrontal and parietal cortex prior to percept switching does not establish a causal link between the two.

Recent developments in this area include a growing appreciation of individual differences in perceptual fluctuation rates. This line of investigation was motivated by findings that these rates are consistent for a particular individual but vary considerably among individuals, by up to an order of magnitude (Aafjes et al. 1966). A recent study comparing monozygotic and dizygotic twins found that close to half of the variance in spontaneous switch rate can be accounted for by genetic factors (Miller et al. 2010). Additional work on this topic has suggested that individual variability in switching rates is correlated with variability in the grey matter density of specific regions of the bilateral superior parietal cortex and the microstructure of the white matter underlying those regions (Kanai et al. 2011). However, the mechanism underpinning this association is not yet known (Kleinschmidt, et al. 2012: 996). In any case, the brain seems to be well-equipped to deal with a possibility of multiple interpretations of the same visual stimuli (in contrast to a computer), although this ability seems to vary greatly among individuals.

Ambiguity type 2: Decision making under imprecisely known probabilities

Before moving directly to the topic of how the brain deals with unknown or partially known probabilities (that is, "ambiguity" in the neuroeconomic sense), we briefly review research on how probabilities and values of potential outcomes are processed and combined to make decisions under risk when both are known. Neuroimaging researchers have found that several neural networks might be sensitive to expected reward (or "value"). The most well-established candidates for a "reward center" are dopaminergic regions such as the striatum and midbrain structures (Knutson et al. 2001; Abler et al. 2006; Tobler et al. 2007; Bartra et al. 2013). Bartra et al. (2013) conducted a coordinate-based meta-analysis of 206 publications, and found two general patterns of reward-correlated brain responses. In the anterior insula, dorsomedial prefrontal cortex, dorsal and posterior striatum, and thalamus, both positive and negative effects of reward are reported in the fMRI literature. This may reflect an underlying U-shaped function, indicative of a signal related to arousal or salience. In the ventromedial prefrontal cortex and anterior ventral striatum positive effects are seen both when a decision is confronted and when an outcome is delivered, for monetary and primary rewards. Bartra et al. suggest that these regions constitute a unified "valuation system," carrying a domain-general reward signal and potentially contributing to value-based decision making. Schultz et al. (2008) present results indicating that blood oxygen level-dependent response measured by fMRI in the ventral striatum, the anterior insula, and orbitofrontal cortex is proportional to risk, defined as the variance of the reward outcomes.

An alternative view is that the brain has more than one evaluative mechanism (network) for decision making. For instance, early attempts to explain violations of expected utility theory such as the Allais paradox or the Ellsberg paradox posited they arose from the selective involvement of competing neural networks. In support of this hypothesis, Dickhaut et al. (2003) present evidence that the processes involved when a sure outcome is one of the alternatives in a choice set differ from those when all alternatives involve risk, potentially accounting for the Allais paradox. However, this and other similar findings do not exclude a possibility that different systems might be involved at the earlier stages of valuation, but projecting to the same network in later stages.

Several recent studies have explored the neurological basis for the behavioral findings that have been accounted for by prospect theory (Kahneman and Tversky 1979; Tversky and Kahneman 1992; see Fox and Poldrack 2014 for a review). The neural correlates of loss aversion and framing effects have been investigated with fMRI studies (e.g., Rangel et al. 2008), suggesting that there is the neural equivalent of a nonlinear value function analogous to that proposed by prospect theory. Tom et al. (2007) identify activation in the striatum in response to gambling monetary values, linking neural loss-aversion (relative to equal-sized gain) to behavioral loss-aversion. De Martino et al. (2006) correlate regional activation patterns with the gain-loss framing effects predicted by prospect theory. Finally, Hsu et al. (2009) report fMRI results suggesting that striatum activity in evaluation of risks is nonlinear in probabilities in ways that are consistent with probability weighting functions derived from empirical behavioral studies. Although there is some debate about how solid the evidence is for prospect theory versus a mean-variance approach (e.g., Boorman and Sallet 2009), there seems to be supporting evidence that central aspects of prospect theory have been established as having a neural basis.

Now let us turn to the issue of whether brain imaging studies shed light on whether the human brain distinguishes among different kinds of unknowns (such as risk or ambiguity). To begin, we consider two sources of unknowns to which human (and other animal) responses appear to be analogous: Temporal and probabilistic discounting. Humans and other animals respond similarly to inverse delay and probability. Immediacies are treated as if they are certainties; more delayed events are treated as if they are less certain. Delayed outcomes are discounted relative to immediacies in an analogous fashion to probabilistic discounting relative to certainties (see Rachlin, 1989, for a systematic exploration of and experimental evidence for this analog). Thus, many of the predictions of prospect theory hold for delay as well as for probability.

Consequently, it seems plausible that the structures in the brain dealing with decisions involving delayed consequences also handle decisions under probabilistic uncertainty. However, decisions under probabilistic and delayed outcomes appear to entrain different neural networks.

Comparisons between immediate and delayed rewards involve an interaction between the ventral striatum, the medial and ventral pre-frontal cortex, and lateral prefrontal cortex (Kable and Glimcher 2007; Purves et al. 2008: 617), whereas decisions under probabilistic uncertainty also entrain areas in the fronto-median cortex. So, although they invoke analogous behaviors and some theorists have argued that they are functionally equivalent, probability and inverse delay may not be the same kind of unknown after all.

Now we turn to another research program along these lines, namely neuroimaging experiments that compare activation patterns under probabilistic uncertainty with activation when the probabilities themselves are uncertain (i.e., "ambiguity" in the sense used in the psychology of judgment and decision making and in behavioral economics). Comparing brain activation regions in risk trials versus ambiguity trials, Hsu et al. (2005) found that ambiguity trials resulted in stronger activation in the lateral orbitofrontal cortex and amygdala, whereas risk trials produced stronger activation in the striatum and precuneus, which suggest differential involvement of neural networks that rely on these nodes in processing risk and ambiguity.

Almost contemporaneously, Huettel et al. (2006) reported neural responses to ambiguity in the posterior parietal cortex, posterior dorsolateral prefrontal cortex and anterior insula, suggesting a representation distinct from that for first-order uncertainty in gambles. Activation within the lateral prefrontal cortex was predicted by ambiguity preference and also correlated negatively with a measure of behavioral impulsiveness. By contrast, activation of the posterior parietal cortex was predicted by risk preference. Both the Hsu et al. (2005) and Huettel et al. (2006) papers concluded that decision making under ambiguity is not a special case of risky decision making, but instead a form of uncertainty that entrains distinct mechanisms in the brain.

Beyond ambiguity: Second-order uncertainty, state space ignorance, and conflict

Although some subsequent investigations (e.g., Bach et al. 2009) have supported the portrayal by Huettel, Hsu, and their colleagues of brain activation in decisions under ambiguity, there have also been extensions of and even dissent from their view. For example, Pushskarskaya et al. (2010) reported selective activation in the left anterior insular cortex under ambiguity, which was not reported in Hsu et al. (2005) as distinguishing between ambiguity and risk. They attributed the discrepancy to differences between the experimental designs in the Hsu et al. and Pushskarskaya et al. studies. They argued that their design ensured that the type of gamble was not confounded with the probability splits, whereas in Hsu et al. all ambiguous gambles had the same split (50%) while their splits for risky gambles were varied. In effect, Hsu et al. contrasted a variety of risky gambles with the same ambiguous gamble.

Bach et al. (2011) addressed the question of whether ambiguity itself is processed by the brain differently from imprecise probabilities. They did so by designing a new experimental setup where participants are given scenarios in which one or another precise probability will be implemented in the course of a gamble, but the participant is not told which probability that will be. Instead, they are provided with a second-order probability that one or the other first-order probability will be selected.

When Bach et al. (2011) compared activation patterns in the ambiguous and nonambiguous trials, they found enhanced activation in regions overlapping with those reported by Huettel et al. (2006) and Bach et al. (2009). However, the effect of second-order probability within ambiguous trials yielded an association between the Shannon entropy of the ambiguous probabilities and activation in bilateral posterior areas including the posterior cingulate and cuneus, extending laterally into adjacent parts of the parietal, occipital, and temporal cortices. On the other hand, regions associated with subjective valuation such as the striatum and prefrontal/orbitofrontal regions did not track second-order entropy. Bach et al. (2011) concluded that behavioral and neural responses to ambiguity may not be driven by second-order uncertainty, thus proposing that second-order uncertainty and ambiguity are distinct kinds of unknowns.

Other kinds of unknowns, such as uncertainty arising from conflicting information (Smithson 1999; Cabantous 2007), or uncertainty stemming from an incomplete knowledge of possible outcomes (i.e., sample space ignorance, as in Smithson et al. 2000), remain largely unexamined by neuroimaging researchers in the judgment and decision making area. Exceptions to this are Pushkarskaya et al. (2010) and Pushkarskaya et al. (2013). The impetus for these studies came from experimental evidence regarding responses to conflict and sample space ignorance of a similar kind to the classic Ellsberg (1961) demonstrations regarding ambiguity. Briefly, Smithson (1999) demonstrated that people act as if they are conflict averse (this effect was replicated with professional insurers by Cabantous, 2007), and Smithson et al. (2000) showed that people also act as though they are averse to sample space ignorance; both experimental results suggesting that these may be kinds of unknowns that humans treat as distinct from probability and ambiguity.

The Pushkarskaya et al. (2010) article reports findings regarding sample space ignorance (SSI). Their experiment also investigated conflict but those results have not yet been reported in the literature. The experiment was designed to test a "full hierarchy reductive" model of the relations between SSI, ambiguity and risk against three alternatives. The full hierarchy reductive model hypothesized that during decision making SSI is reduced to subjectively formed ambiguity, and in turn, ambiguity is reduced to subjectively formed risk. This model implies that neural networks for SSI would include those for ambiguity, which in turn would include those for risk. The alternatives allowed for SSI and ambiguity to rely on unique, possibly overlapping, neural networks that in turn possibly overlap with but not fully subsume the risk network.

Pushkarskaya et al. (2010) reported that SSI most strongly activated regions in the bilateral inferior parietal lobe, the left anterior cingulate cortex, and the left lateral orbitofrontal cortex; while ambiguity most strongly activated the left anterior insula (this latter finding replicated Huettel et al. 2006). These findings rule out a full hierarchy reductive model, and suggest existence of neural networks that, at the very least, are differentially involved in processing of SSI and ambiguity. They speculated that the SSI-specific network is associated with higher level cognitive control and higher demands on deliberative evaluative processing, whereas the ambiguity network is more strongly associated with intuitive processing.

They also found that activation patterns in response to SSI depended on individuals' attitudes towards ambiguity. Ambiguity-averse individuals yielded evidence supporting the full hierarchy model, whereas ambiguity-tolerant individuals produced evidence against this model and in favor of unique activation regions for SSI. The ambiguity–SSI-conjoined nodes whose activation levels were modulated by ambiguity tolerance reside chiefly in the bilateral middle frontal gyrus. It has been suggested that they are involved in networks entrained by the selection of information relevant for a decision and understanding the context in which information is to be evaluated (Brass and von Cramon 2004). These regions have also been associated with deliberative rather than intuitive decision making (Kuo et al. 2009) and with working memory (Wager and Smith 2003). Thus, Pushskarskaya et al. speculated that ambiguity-averse individuals may prefer deliberative processing, therefore activating these regions more under SSI than under ambiguity (consistent with the reductive viewpoint). Ambiguity-tolerant individuals, on the other hand, may engage in less deliberative processing, activating these regions only for storing information about the environment, thereby activating the regions more under ambiguity than under SSI.

Pushkarskaya et al. (2013) investigated the neural responses to conflicting information about probabilities (conflict), compared with ambiguity and risk. They tested a null hypothesis that conflict is a special case of ambiguity. Behaviorally, this hypothesis implies that attitudes toward ambiguity covary with attitudes toward conflict. Neurally, it implies that ambiguity and conflict are processed by largely overlapping neural networks, and that behavioral attitudes toward ambiguity and conflict are predicted by the activation in those networks. This hypothesis was tested in an fMRI experiment requiring participants to make choices in gambles involving conflict, ambiguity, or risk, with equivalent expected payoffs.

Models of participants' choices in the gambles showed that in this specific design they avoided conflict more than ambiguity, and attitudes toward ambiguity and conflict did not correlate across subjects. The results replicated findings and claims in the behavioral experimental literature on conflict versus ambiguity (Smithson 1999; Cabantous 2007; Baillon et al. 2012). Activation in the ventromedial prefrontal cortex correlated exclusively with ambiguity level (negatively) and individual ambiguity aversion (positively), whereas activation in the striatum correlated exclusively with conflict level (positively) and individual conflict aversion (negatively). These findings agree with Hsu and colleagues' (2005) report of higher activation under ambiguity than under risk in ventromedial prefrontal cortex, and lower activation in the striatum. They also contradict the hypothesis that conflict is a special case of ambiguity, suggesting that conflict and ambiguity have distinct neurobiological signatures.

These studies suggest the existence of multiple, possibly interacting and overlapping, neural networks that selectively or differentially are involved in the processing of different types of unknowns during decision making under uncertainty. Thus, these findings suggest that the brain has evolved to deal with incomplete information not only at the low cognition, sensory level, but also at the high cognition, decision making level.

So, what can brain imaging tell us about ignorance?

A crucial test of the value of neuroimaging research and theory is, in effect, the "Coltheart test" of whether they can provide insights into how people perceive, think, and act in the face of unknowns. Thus far, the neuroimaging body of work has been subjected only to highly constrained versions of this test. The most common version is ascertaining associations between individual differences in brain activation patterns and differences in risk preferences in healthy subjects or between clinical cases and healthy controls (e.g., Tobler et al. 2007; Ernst and Paulus 2005), or differences in perceptual switching-rates (Kleinschmidt et al. 1998; Kleinschmidt et al. 2012). Another version involves exciting or suppressing activity in key brain regions (via transcranial magnetic or direct current stimulation) and determining effects on risk-taking behavior (e.g., Fecteau et al. 2007). In the decision making realm, both of these versions have had some success, at least in terms of linking brain activation with risk-attitude parameters in monetary choice models. However, to date there have been few fully fledged attempts to connect brain imaging studies with naturalistic or real-world decision making under uncertainty or ignorance.

An obvious obstacle to studying what the brain does in naturalistic decision making or perception is simply that the requisite technology for measuring or manipulating brain activity in a controlled fashion makes it impossible to do brain imaging while the subject is engaged in everyday life. A second obstacle is that several crucial influences on risk-taking behavior are typically absent from laboratory tasks, such as emotional engagement, motivational factors, and domain-specific risk attitudes. A third somewhat less obvious, but important, impediment to decision making experiments is limitations on the external validity of laboratory-based measures of risk preferences and on the decomposability of risk preference measures that have greater external validity. This point is nicely elaborated in the review by Schonberg et al. (2011). They observe that while the Iowa Gambling Task and Balloon Analogue Risk Task have met with considerably greater success in predicting real-world risk-taking behaviors than the laboratory-based measures based on choices in monetary gambles, neither task is readily decomposable. In both tasks, increased riskiness (in terms of increased variance in outcomes) is confounded with changes in expected value and the requirement to learn the long-term expected value of the tasks.

Schonberg et al. (2011: 17) propose three criteria for laboratory experimental paradigms with the potential to close the gap between neuroeconomic experiments and/or models, and naturalistic risk-taking. These are decomposability, external validity (i.e., correlating appropriately with risk-taking behaviors in healthy and relevant clinical populations), and emotional engagement. They conclude that no task or measure in the literature satisfies all three criteria.

To sum up, our understanding of what the brain does when humans cope with unknowns is primarily limited to knowledge about some aspects of localization. We have a sketchy comprehension of what neural networks might be involved in processing probabilistic uncertainty and ambiguity, and some evidence that the brain operates as if these are distinct kinds of unknowns. We have tentative, suggestive evidence for the possibility that there may be other kinds of unknowns such as conflict and sample space ignorance that entrain other neural networks than those entrained by ambiguity or probability. Progress certainly has been made, but we still are far from understanding much about the neural processes involved in any of this, and from connecting brain imaging findings with naturalistic risk-taking behavior.

References

Aafjes, M., Hueting, J.E., and Visser, P. (1966) 'Individual and interindividual differences in binocular retinal rivalry in man', *Psychophysiology*, 3: 18–22.

Abler, B., Walter, H., Erk, S., Kammerer, H., and Spitzer, M. (2006) 'Prediction error as a linear function of reward probability is coded in human nucleus accumbens', *Neuroimage*, 31: 790–795.

Bach, D.R., Hulme, O., Penny, W.D., and Dolan, R.J. (2011) 'The known unknowns: Neural representation of second-order uncertainty, and ambiguity', *The Journal of Neuroscience*, 31: 4811–4820.

Bach, D.R., Seymour, B., and Dolan, R.J. (2009) 'Neural activity associated with the passive prediction of ambiguity and risk for aversive events', *The Journal of Neuroscience*, 29: 1648–1656.

Baillon, A., Cabantous, L., and Wakker, P. (2012) 'Aggregating imprecise or conflicting beliefs: An experimental investigation using modern ambiguity theories', *Journal of Risk and Uncertainty*, 44: 115–147.

Bartra, O., McGuire, J.T., and Kable, J.W. (2013) 'The valuation system: A coordinate-based meta-analysis of BOLD fMRI experiments examining neural correlates of subjective value', *NeuroImage*, 76: 412–427.

Berns, G.S., Cohen, J.D., and Mintun, M.A. (1997) 'Brain regions responsive to novelty in the absence of awareness', *Science*, 276: 1272–1275.

Boorman, E.D., and Sallet, J. (2009) 'Mean-variance or prospect theory? The nature of value representations in the human brain', *Journal of Neuroscience*, 29: 7945–7947.

Brass, M., and von Cramon, D.Y. (2004) 'Selection for cognitive control: A functional magnetic resonance imaging study on the selection of task-relevant information', *Journal of Neuroscience*, 24: 8847–8852.

Cabantous, L. (2007) 'Ambiguity aversion in the field of insurance: Insurers' attitude to imprecise and conflicting probability estimates', *Theory and Decision*, 62: 219–240.

Coltheart, M. (2004) 'Brain imaging, connectionism, and cognitive neuropsychology,' *Cognitive Neuropsychology*, 21: 21–25.

De Martino, B., Kumaran, D., Seymour, B., and Dolan, R.J. (2006) 'Frames, biases, and rational decision-making in the human brain', *Science*, 313: 684–687.

Dickhaut, J., McCabe, K., Nagode, J.C., Rustichini, A., Smith, K., and Pardo, J.V. (2003) 'The impact of the certainty context on the process of choice', *Proceedings of the National Academy of Sciences of the United States of America*, 100: 3536–3541.

Ellsberg, D. (1961) 'Risk, ambiguity, and the Savage axioms', *Quarterly Journal of Economics*: 75, 643–669.
Ernst, M., and Paulus, M.P. (2005) 'Neurobiology of decision making: A selective review from a neurocognitive and clinical perspective', *Biological Psychiatry* 58: 597–604.
Fecteau, S., Knoch, D., Fregni, F., Sultani, N., Boggio, P., and Pascual-Leone, A. (2007) 'Diminishing risk-taking behavior by modulating activity in the prefrontal cortex: A direct current stimulation study', *Journal of Neuroscience*, 27: 12500–12505.
Fox, C.F., and Poldrack, R. (2014) 'Prospect theory and the brain'. In P. Glimcher, C.F. Camerer, E. Fehr, and R.A. Poldrack (Eds.), *Neuroeconomics: Decision making and the brain*, 2nd edn. New York: Elsevier, pp. 145–174.
Glimcher, P.W., and Rustichini, A. (2004) 'Neuroeconomics: The consilience of brain and decision', *Science*, 306: 447–452.
Hsu, M., Bhatt, M., Adolphs, R., Tranel, D., and Camerer, C.F. (2005) 'Neural systems responding to degrees of uncertainty in human decision-making', *Science*, 310: 1680–1683.
Hsu, M., Krajbich, I., Zhao, C., and Camerer, C.F. (2009) 'Neural response to reward anticipation under risk is nonlinear in probabilities', *Journal of Neuroscience*, 29: 2231–2237.
Huettel, S., Stowe, C., Gordon, E., Warner, B., and Platt, M. (2006) 'Neural signatures of economic preferences for risk and ambiguity', *Neuron*, 49: 765–775.
Kable, J.W., and Glimcher, P.W. (2007) 'The neural correlates of subjective value during intertemporal choice', *Nature Neuroscience*, 10: 1625–1633.
Kahneman, D., and Tversky, A. (1979) 'Prospect theory—analysis of decision under risk', *Econometrica*, 47: 263–291.
Kanai, R., Carmel, D., Bahrami, B., and Rees, G. (2011) 'Structural and functional fractionation of right superior parietal cortex in bistable perception', *Current Biology*, 21: 106–107.
Kleinschmidt, A., Büchel, C., Zeki, S., and Frackowiak, R.S. (1998) 'Human brain activity during spontaneously reversing perception of ambiguous figures', *Proceedings of the Royal Society: Biological Science*, 265: 2427–2433.
Kleinschmidt, A., Sterzer, P., and Rees, G. (2012) 'Variability of perceptual multistability: From brain state to individual trait,' *Philosophical Transactions of the Royal Society B*, 367: 988–1000.
Knight, F. (1921) *Risk, uncertainty and profit*, Boston, MA: Houghton-Mifflin.
Knutson, B., Adams, C.M., Fong, G.W., and Hommer, D. (2001) 'Anticipation of increasing monetary reward selectively recruits nucleus accumbens', *Journal of Neuroscience*, 21: RC159(1–5).
Kuo, W.-J., Sjöström, T., Chen, Y.-P., Wang, Y.-H., and Huang, C.-Y. (2009) 'Intuition and deliberation: Two systems for strategizing in the brain', *Science*, 324: 519–522.
Lim, S., and Goldman, M.S. (2013) 'Balanced cortical microcircuitry for maintaining information in working memory', *Nature Neuroscience*, 16: 1306–1314.
Lumer, E.D., Friston, K.J., and Rees, G. (1998) 'Neural correlates of perceptual rivalry in the human brain', *Science*, 280: 1930–1934.
Miller, S.M., Hansell, N.K., Ngo, T.T., Liu, G.B., Pettigrew, J.D., Martin, N.G., and Wright, M.J. (2010) 'Genetic contribution to individual variation in binocular rivalry rate', *Proceedings of the National Academy of Sciences of the United States of America*, 107: 2664–2668.
Parkkonen, L., Andersson, J., Hamaiainen, M., and Hari, R. (2008) 'Early visual brain areas reflect the percept of an ambiguous scene', *Proceedings of the National Academy of Sciences of the United States of America*, 105: 20500–20504.
Platt, M.L., and Huettel, S.A. (2008) 'Risky business: The neuroeconomics of decision making under uncertainty', *Nature Neuroscience*, 11: 398–403.
Poldrack, R.A. (2006) 'Can cognitive processes be inferred from neuroimaging data?' *Trends in Cognitive Science*, 10: 59–63.
Purves, D., Brannon, E.M., Cabeza, R., Huettel, S.A., LaBar, K.S., Platt, M.L., and Woldorff, M.G. (2008) *Principles of cognitive neuroscience*. Sunderland, MA: Sinauer Associates.
Pushkarskaya, H., Liu, X., Smithson, M., and Joseph, J.E. (2010) 'Beyond risk and ambiguity: Deciding under ignorance', *Cognitive, Affective, and Behavioral Neuroscience*, 10: 382–391.
Pushkarskaya, H., Smithson, M., Joseph, J.E., Corbly, C., and Levy, I. (2013) *The neurobiology of decision making in the presence of imprecise and conflicting information about probabilities*. Unpublished manuscript.
Rachlin, H. (1989) *Judgment, decision, and choice: A cognitive/behavioral synthesis*. New York: Freeman.
Rangel, A., Camerer, C., and Montague, P.R. (2008) 'A framework for studying the neurobiology of value-based decision making', *Nature Reviews Neuroscience*, 9: 545–556.

Schonberg, T., Fox, C.R., and Poldrack, R.A. (2011) 'Mind the gap: Bridging economic and naturalistic risk-taking with cognitive neuroscience', *Trends in Cognitive Sciences*, 15: 11–19.

Schultz, W., Preuschoff, K., Camerer, C., Hsu, M., Fiorillo, C.D., Tobler, P.N., and Bossaerts, P. (2008) 'Explicit neural signals reflecting reward uncertainty', *Philosophical Transactions of the Royal Society B*, 363: 3801–3811.

Schwartz, J.-L., Grimault, N., Je Hupé, J.-M., Moore, B.C.J., and Pressnitzer, D. (2012) 'Multistability in perception: Binding sensory modalities, an overview', *Philosophical Transactions of the Royal Society B*, 367: 896–905.

Smithson, M. (1999) 'Conflict aversion: Preference for ambiguity vs. conflict in sources and evidence', *Organizational Behavior and Human Decision Processes*, 79: 179–198.

Smithson, M. (2008) 'Social theories of ignorance'. In R. Proctor and L. Schiebinger (Eds.), *Agnotology: The making and unmaking of ignorance*. Stanford, CA: Stanford University Press, pp. 209–229.

Smithson, M., Bartos, T., and Takemura, K. (2000) 'Human judgment under sample space ignorance', *Risk, Decision and Policy*, 5: 135–150.

Tobler, P.N., O'Doherty, J.P., Dolan, R.J., and Schultz, W. (2007) 'Reward value coding distinct from risk attitude-related uncertainty coding in human reward systems', *Journal of Neurophysiology*, 97: 1621–1632.

Tom, S.M., Fox, C.R., Trepel, C., and Poldrack, R.A. (2007) 'The neural basis of loss aversion in decision-making under risk', *Science*, 315: 515–518.

Tversky, A., and Kaheman, D. (1992) 'Advances in prospect theory: Cumulative representation of uncertainty', *Journal of Risk and Uncertainty*, 5: 297–323.

Uttal, W.R. (2001) *The new phrenology: The limits of localizing cognitive processes*. Cambridge, MA: MIT Press.

Von Neumann, J., and Morgenstern, O. (1944) *Theory of games and economic behavior*. Princeton, NJ: Princeton University Press.

Wager, T.D., and Smith, E.E. (2003) 'Neuroimaging studies of working memory: A meta-analysis', *Cognitive, Affective, and Behavioral Neuroscience*, 3: 255–274.

Windmann, S., Wehrmann, M., Calabrese, P., and Güntürkün, O. (2006) 'Role of the prefrontal cortex in attentional control over bistable vision', *Journal of Cognitive Neuroscience*, 18: 456–471.

Zeki, S. (2004) 'The neurology of ambiguity', *Consciousness and Cognition*, 13: 173–196.

14

Linguistics and ignorance

Nina Janich and Anne Simmerling

State of the art

Research on the concept of "ignorance" and its societal and epistemic status has been going on for some years now in philosophy, sociology and psychology as well as in communication and media studies (cf. the present Handbook with nearly all the major contributors to this research to date).[1] Somewhat surprisingly, linguistics scholars have not been among the front-runners in this field, despite the fact that it lends itself to a linguistic approach: "It is difficult to communicate clearly about uncertainty, and even more difficult to find out very much about it. However, it is not so difficult to find out how people talk about uncertainty, what they think it is, and how they deal with it" (Smithson 2008: 13).

In fact, speaking (and writing) about uncertainty and ignorance – that is, how people name, describe and express judgments about ignorance and uncertainty, in what kinds of situations and texts they do so, and what significance this has regarding the subject matter and arguments put forward in their conversations, texts and discourses – is a linguistic issue through and through. Although linguistics scholars in many sub-disciplines have indeed dealt with various aspects of communicating *knowledge* and thus necessarily with asymmetries of knowledge,[2] there are still only few truly relevant studies in this discipline that directly address the way ignorance is rendered in language and communication. The articles by Janich et al. (2010) and Simmerling et al. (2013) discuss this gap in the research along with potential linguistic approaches to eliminating it by specifically looking at ignorance in science and popular science media. Prior to this, German studies scholar Erben (1994) had looked at the linguistic "Problem of markers of uncertainty and fuzziness" (*Problem der Unsicherheits- und Unschärfemarkierung*), examining relevant linguistic markers in Theodor Fontane's theatre reviews. Taking a rather different route, work by Schlosser (2003) on the etymology of German-language verbs and nouns from the lexical field of *wissen* (to know) forms more of an historical framework: this kind of approach makes it possible to detect a variety of epistemic concepts of *wissen* and *begreifen* (to grasp (conceptually)) and to shed renewed light on possibly "extinct" metaphors. Since knowledge and ignorance *qua* non-knowledge can be understood as opposites (at least in linguistic terms), such etymological studies offer insight into cognitive concepts of ignorance (for corresponding metaphorical pairings, see below). Although a few studies from computational linguistics have analyzed the quantitative distribution of linguistic markers of ambiguity and uncertainty in scientific texts (Vincze et al. 2008; Szarvas et al. 2012), they are ultimately faced with the problem – given the complexity of the phenomenon of "uncertainty" – of justifying their keyword selection. There have been no such studies to date whatsoever on markers of ignorance. German language scholars Warnke (2012) and Janich and Simmerling (2013) are the first to adopt discourse analysis perspectives. Warnke's foundation laying theoretical analysis is concerned with communicative factors and linguistic functions in the communication of knowledge and ignorance and the regulating factors that emerge from this in relation to discourse. Meanwhile, Janich and Simmerling use a case study on the public debate about climate research to look at specific language users' semantic conceptualizations of ignorance and the linguistic forms taken by the latter. As yet, however, there has been no systematic linguistics-based research on linguistic marking, stylistic-rhetorical emphasis or the discursive relevance of ignorance in texts and conversations. Research of this kind would initially have to be conducted within a specific language and culture in order to establish a sound basis for generating broader insights for comparative linguistics and cross-cultural contexts.

Given this situation the present chapter seeks to explore ways of addressing ignorance from a systematic linguistics perspective. A number of instructive studies from other disciplines do exist: despite having a completely different methodological emphasis they are nonetheless related to such a linguistic approach in that they complement and extend it. Some of these studies will be used and cited but not described in any detail here, however, due to the limited space available as well as the fact that many of their authors have written pieces for this Handbook. These include studies on metaphors and the rhetorical functions of ignorance (e.g. Smithson 1989, 2008), on ignorance claims in science and the media, the functions they perform and the associated interests of the discourse participants (e.g. Stocking & Holstein 1993; Heidmann & Milde 2013), on shifting conceptualizations of ignorance and their impacts on (public) discourse (e.g. Wehling 2010, 2012) and on scientists' responsibility for the way they deal linguistically and communicatively with ignorance (e.g. Elliott 2012). In addition, social scientists have shed empirical light on the recipient perspective, for example, on the impact of descriptions of uncertainty and risk on experts as opposed to lay people (e.g. Wiedemann et al. 2008). What all these studies have in common, however, is that they do not "describe (as a discourse analyst [or, more specifically, a linguist N.J. and A.S.] might) the specific rhetorical forms that ignorance claims may take" (Stocking & Holstein 1993: 195, 206f.).

In the following then, we seek to establish a few prototypical linguistic research questions and to explore the levels at which potential methodological approaches can be implemented. On this basis we then present some initial findings with regard to the ways ignorance is named, described and linguistically attributed a positive or negative value, on the one hand, and the way it is dealt with discursively in texts and discourses, on the other.

Given the rather desperate research situation – with regard to linguistics, that is – the present chapter cannot offer a review of research results from an already elaborated field; instead, it should be regarded as setting out a program for future research on the communication of ignorance (for greater detail cf. Janich & Simmerling, 2016/forthcoming). As regards what linguists mean when they refer to ignorance, this question will be addressed (albeit superficially for now) in the course of the following discussion, since the answer to it is an outcome rather than a pregiven assumption of linguistic analyses of the communication of ignorance.

Linguistics research questions and methodological approaches

Given that the discipline of linguistics is concerned with linguistic signs, their rules of use, their history and the function they perform (i.e. their role in specific texts and conversations), what is it about ignorance that is of interest to linguistics scholars? If we set about developing a systematic set of prototypical linguistic research questions, the first one we encounter is how ignorance is identified and marked linguistically and what range of options arises for articulating it. However, since language is always used in specific interactions and contexts, this kind of systematic, descriptive approach is quickly followed by pragmatic and discourse analytic questions regarding the discursive functions and consequences of ignorance. The questions outlined in the following can and must be addressed using different methods appropriate to each. Thus any linguistics research program set up to explore the communication of ignorance will consist not only of a range of questions to be addressed but also suggestions for a potential set of methods to do so.

Ways of naming, describing and interpreting ignorance

Practices of speaking or writing about ignorance can be examined from at least three perspectives with a special focus on vocabulary and grammar:

- *Naming and describing ignorance:* What words are used to name and describe – or circumscribe – ignorance? That is, which nouns, verbs, adjectives and adverbs would we consider to be semantically relevant, to what extent and why (e.g. *knowledge gap, error, doubt, uncertainty; research, close gaps; contested, doubtful, not known*)? Can these expressions be arranged taxonomically according to their lexical origins, the history of their meaning or their current meaning, independently of specific contexts, in such a way that the structure of a given lexical field may offer insights into possible types of ignorance? These questions cannot be answered in general terms, they can only be explored in the context of a specific language: the important semantic differences between the German word *Nichtwissen* (which corresponds semantically to the English word *ignorance*) and the German word *Ignoranz*, which conveys a deliberate wish to not know, are a case in point. These linguistic analyses can be done either synchronically (in relation to a specific historical stage of a language) or diachronically (by comparing different historical stages with one another), revealing whether or not there have been any changes in meaning.
- *Linguistic conceptualizations of ignorance:* Which terminological and semantic concepts can be reconstructed from the ways ignorance is named and described? The ways of naming ignorance mentioned above generally do not occur in isolation but are embedded within sentences; as such they collocate with, among other things, modal expressions (e.g. *probably, it seems, we may suggest*) and temporal expressions (e.g. *not yet, not so far, in the future*) which in turn give rise to other, more subtle differentiations of concepts of ignorance. Here it may be possible to identify generally valid concepts of ignorance by comparing different languages.
- *Positive/negative attributions of ignorance:* What positive or negative attributions of ignorance (or different types of ignorance) can be reconstructed from textual and syntactical structures? Are there, for example, types of ignorance that generally have a positive connotation or ones that generally have a negative connotation? This question demands, for example, examination of the attributions attached to different namings of ignorance as well as the metaphors, personifications and other rhetorical forms (such as irony) used in association with them. At this point there is a degree of overlap with issues concerning textual linguistics, i.e. ones related not merely to the linguistic form of individual expressions (however complex they may be) but also to textual structures and patterns (for further details see below).

Initial studies (especially Janich & Simmerling 2013; see also below) show that nearly every linguistic expression that can be used to address ignorance, whether explicitly or implicitly, is highly context sensitive: even supposedly unambiguous expressions referring to a lack of knowledge – such as *ignorance, knowledge gap* and *error* – may also be used in contexts in which ignorance has been transformed into knowledge, a knowledge gap closed or an error recognized and eliminated. Thus from a linguistic point of view there are hardly any unambiguous or universally valid linguistic markers of ignorance in texts. In other words, it is extremely difficult to identify words which in any given instance would definitely mean a person is really speaking or writing about ignorance. What we can assume, however, is that certain linguistic patterns and metaphors are "prototypical" when it comes to addressing ignorance and attributing a positive or negative connotation to it (this is the assumption, for example, on which the above-mentioned computational linguistics analyses by Vincze et al. 2008 and Szarvas et al. 2012 are based). However, these linguistic patterns need to be studied more closely with regard to their grammatical, lexical and rhetorical form using qualitative hermeneutical methods (cf. Simmerling & Janich 2016/forthcoming) before they can then be confirmed quantitatively using larger corpora.

A number of linguistic sub-disciplines in particular offer suitable methodological ways of addressing this first set of issues. First and foremost, *semantics* (with an emphasis on pragmatic and cognitive aspects) makes it possible both to establish the presence of "ignorance" and "uncertainty" as an explicit semantic component of specific linguistic expressions and to study more complex utterances in terms of their underlying conceptualizations and framings of ignorance. This semantic approach should be rounded out using *grammatical and phraseological perspectives* to facilitate insights into the function of negation, the use of tense (past, present, future) and modality (possibility, impossibility, necessity, etc.), as well as fixed phrases and patterns.

When it comes to exploring the point of overlap between individual linguistic expressions and texts as genres and modes of communication, *stylistics* (with an emphasis on pragmatic and semiotic aspects) is suited to the task. Stylistics can be used to examine potentially divergent "styles of ignorance" in the context of specific domains (e.g. science, journalism or politics), genres (e.g. a scientific project proposal, journalistic editorial or parliamentary speech) and media (e.g. newspaper, television or press conference). The key point here is that style is not an outcome of a (supposedly) straightforward selection from a set of linguistic resources but rather is geared towards textual routines and idiomatic influence (Feilke 1994). At the same time, style always also indicates the speaker's or writer's attitude towards his or her subject matter, communication partners or the communicative situation (Fix 2007). As such, stylistics is suited to analyze positive/negative interpretations of ignorance as well as their relevance in the context of social relationships.

Another specifically linguistic approach is of course the focus on a given text and its linguistic form, i.e. *textual linguistics*. Although texts are produced and received largely in the context of discourses, there are also good reasons to study them in their own right: they can be looked at as specific linguistic products in order to examine the extent to which they follow certain patterns or are genuinely original compared to the underlying genre, the ways they relate to other individual texts or textual genres and – from a critical linguistics perspective – their rhetorical appropriateness.

Discursive functions and consequences of ignorance

In linguistics the term "discourse" generally refers to the sum of utterances (in written *and* spoken texts) that are connected to one another by virtue of their subject matter. The reasons why discourse is an important point of reference for analyzing the communication of ignorance is that not only many social scientists but also linguists assume knowledge – and therefore also ignorance – to be an outcome of social construction. Accordingly, the assumption is that speakers or writers are pursuing quite specific interests with their knowledge and their ignorance claims (e.g. Smithson 1989 and 2008; Stocking & Holstein 1993, 2009). According to this view, the knowledge that has established itself in discourse counts as societally recognized (i.e. accepted) knowledge. The process of becoming established in this way involves the construction of knowledge through truth claims, its justification through argumentation and its dissemination through successful validity claims (Warnke 2009: 116–122).

When it comes to the discursive relevance of ignorance, it is important from the perspective of linguistic discourse analysis to look at a number of levels (Warnke & Spitzmüller 2008): (a) the level of *discourse participants* ("*Akteure*") who, by means of utterances, come into contact with one another, adopt certain positions and pursue certain interests; (b) the *transtextual level*, i.e. the ways these utterances are interwoven in discourse, the ways they reference one another, their linguistic-rhetorical commonalities and differences; and (c) the *intratextual level*, i.e. the individual text, its internal structure and its style (also see above).

We can formulate the following linguistic questions in relation to these different levels (note: this list should not be considered exhaustive):

(a) Discourse participants

- *Who does not know something?* Of interest here are, for example, definitions or attributions of expertness in spoken and written texts, their role in discourse and their (historical, situational) transformations.
- *Who knows more/less than whom?* This kind of question focuses on situational or institutional asymmetries of knowledge between discourse participants, how they are characterized by certain interactive links prototypically or in relation to a given situation (e.g. between teachers and pupils, doctors and patients, advisors and decision makers, etc.), their diachronic transformations and the way they occur in texts and conversations.
- *Who is pursuing what interests and purposes?* Here the objects of study for textual and conversational linguistics are the different textual functions and behavior patterns associated with attributions of ignorance (such as teach/instruct, question, negotiate a shared knowledge base, legitimize research, justify decisions, caution against decisions made under uncertainty, trigger a controversy, etc.). Here we might ask what behavior patterns can be identified prototypically in which communication genres (e.g. in various kinds of scientific text and, within these, in functionally different sections such as status of research, research question, discussion, etc.). It is also interesting to note whether and at what points ignorance is claimed as a right and responsibility is attributed, demanded or rejected (Wehling 2012).

(b) Transtextual level

- *What are the issues being addressed – what is not known and why?* The focus here is on what kind of ignorance (e.g. propositional or instrumental ignorance) is considered to be relevant in relation to what issue, by whom and to what extent; and in terms of argumentation, what consequences are associated with this for one's own or someone else's actions. It can be assumed that different conceptualizations of ignorance take on different "trajectories" in different discourses – in part due to different combinations of discourse participants, different decision-making options or the way a third party is affected (in relation, say, to climate change, prenatal diagnostics, debates about the impact of mobile phone radiation or the effectiveness of homeopathy), but perhaps also due to highly varied complex situations (Wehling 2012).

- *In which communicative genres and media is what kind of ignorance talked about?* By way of expanding on the previous set of questions, it is important to note in the context of which media and communicative genres (and therefore also in which domains) communication occurs and about what type of ignorance (from "not yet knowing" through to "not wanting to know"). In this respect, for example, original scientific articles differ fundamentally from investigative newspaper articles or interviews. This is where the level of discourse participants comes into play again, as it is important to clarify for the transtextual level of discourse which participants have access to which media and genres and thus are able to gain a public hearing for their positions or to receive others' positions (one might think, for instance, of the differences in terms of public access between scientific reports, on the one hand, and online commentaries, blogs or newspaper texts, on the other). Media provide varied opportunities for engagement based on the external form and the size of texts; communicative genres have varied functions and patterns; and discourse communities such as science or politics follow different discursive rules. All this has consequences for writing and talking about ignorance, which in turn may reflect back on the patterning of a communication context or the options available for articulation.

(c) Intratextual level

- *What form do rhetorical and argumentational attributions of ignorance take?* Here we return full circle to the first set of questions outlined above: the questions that are of a genuinely linguistic nature are those regarding positive/negative attributions and semantic conceptualizations of ignorance as they are manifested in linguistic form, the extent to which these concepts are dependent on textual style and structure, and the rhetorical form and pragmatic function of attributions of ignorance.
- *What kind of linguistic imagery supports the perception of ignorance claims?* Images have a more powerful emotional impact than language, meaning that they can be used in texts about conflict-laden issues such as climate change to either trivializing effect or in a way that highlights a sense of danger. In so doing they are capable of influencing public perceptions in terms of what is considered to be certain or uncertain knowledge. Accordingly, any research on the communication of ignorance should include corresponding text-image analyses (e.g. based on an image analysis grid such as that devised by Kress & van Leeuwen 2001 or Bateman 2008).

If applied linguistics is to contribute not only towards understanding communication of ignorance in its discursive dimension but also to derive recommendations from textual and discourse analyses for an enlightened communicative approach to uncertainty and ignorance, then linguistics should focus its attention in the short term on the following issues (among others):

- A comparison of communicative genres on the one hand and of entire discursive orders and communicative economies/textual worlds in different domains (e.g. science vs. journalism vs. politics) on the other;
- Analysis of communication conflicts arising from uncertainty and ignorance and exploration of the extent to which these can be explained on the basis of a divergence between such competing orders;

- Comparison of the rhetorical significance, argumentational inclusion and transparency of attributions of ignorance in various single text events, communicative genres and discourses;
- Analysis of possible discursive risks for those who attribute ignorance to themselves or someone else or to whom ignorance is attributed.

The methodological framework for addressing questions of this kind is given largely by *linguistic discourse analysis*, which consists of a wide range of methods (from purely descriptive through to critical) and is based not least on textual linguistics, conversational linguistics, pragmatics, rhetorical studies and stylistics. *Textual and conversational linguistics* offer analytical approaches suited to a variety of types of texts and conversations along with their respective prototypical patterns and functions. They are therefore useful as a bridge between the two research approaches, that is, the grammatical/systematic and the discursive one. *Linguistic pragmatics*, stemming from Ordinary Language Philosophy, is the discipline of reference for all those approaches that see speaking and writing as a form of social/communicative action. Stylistics was introduced above.

Initial (linguistic or linguistically relevant) findings

Ignorance claims: how they function in discourse . . .

Taking as their starting point Smithson's (1989) theory of the social constructedness not only of scientific knowledge but also of scientific ignorance, Stocking and Holstein (1993, 2009) look at specific functions of ignorance claims in scientific and journalistic texts, based on a wide ranging overview of relevant research literature (cf. also their chapter in this Handbook).

In *scientific discourse* they identify (1) references to "knowledge gaps" in the context of research policy interests, (2) "caveats" for the purpose of backing up and legitimizing research results and (3) attributions of ignorance to others that are deployed in order to demarcate one's own areas of expertise in debate with advocates of other positions or representatives of other disciplines (Stocking & Holstein 1993: 191–193). The study of textual content by Heidmann and Milde (2013: 8) illustrates clearly that there are vast differences in types of text here and that "[s]cientific uncertainties, sources, and consequences were most widely discussed in review papers, whereas research papers and mass media tend to emphasize more the certainty of their results or topics" (similar findings are presented by Szarvas et al. 2012: 349–351; see also below).

In the *context of popular science*, by contrast, scientists seek above all, according to Stocking and Holstein, to bolster their "cognitive authority" vis-à-vis the general public by claiming ignorance. Ignorance claims are uttered here, then, in order to legitimize one's own research and to render oneself indispensable as an expert; this is done by referring to other people's knowledge gaps or knowledge gaps in general – especially those that are significant in social and political terms (Stocking & Holstein 1993: 194f.). These functions of ignorance claims are abundantly confirmed in the linguistic case study conducted by Janich and Simmerling (2013) on German climate research and public perceptions of it. This study illustrates the fact that ignorance claims are frequently used in close combination with knowledge claims. An author's own reputation and their expertise in transforming the postulated lack of knowledge into knowledge are thus explicitly mentioned and emphasized. Given the different discourse participants involved (in the sense of "interest groups"), these discursive mechanisms lead, according to Stocking and Holstein (1993: 197), to a "politicization of ignorance", something that plays a significant role not only in the policy arena but also in the domain of business practice.

Interestingly, there is far less mention of scientific ignorance in *journalistic texts* as compared to the scientific source texts (Stocking & Holstein 1993: 199 speak of a "loss of uncertainty in the popularized accounts", an observation confirmed in the recent study by Heidmann and Milde 2013). But even in journalistic texts there are also references to gaps in scientific knowledge, caveats and controversies among experts (Stocking & Holstein 1993: 199f.) – it is just that these ignorance claims usually serve quite different interests than those of the scientists themselves, depending of different journalists' roles (Stocking & Holstein 2009). The linguistic case studies by Janich and Simmerling (2013) and Simmerling and Janich (2016/forthcoming), for example, show that ignorance claims in discourses marked by conflict are often used to polarize or dramatize an issue (and thus to generate publicity) or else to warn people with regard to upcoming (research) policy decisions, as is done in investigative journalism. Heidmann and Milde (2013: 8) confirm this finding and conclude on this basis that there is a lack of dialogue between science and the mass media. What appears important in this connection is the finding by Stocking and Holstein (1993: 205) that the interests pursued by scientists with their ignorance claims are not revealed (and in some cases, we might conjecture, are obviously not reflected upon) by journalists; it is hardly surprising, then, that the journalists' own interests in relation to picking up on and perhaps reinforcing scientific ignorance claims themselves remain concealed.

Like the non-linguistic literature mentioned above, the overview offered by Stocking and Holstein (1993) appears fruitful because it draws attention to various aspects of communication as well as to the varied interests of discourse participants. Such findings are therefore directly relevant and can be developed further in the context of pragmatics and discourse analytic studies of the communication of ignorance. Understandably enough, what these studies do not focus on sufficiently is the linguistic-rhetorical form of discourses, something referred to often by Stocking and Holstein as a much neglected area of research (Stocking & Holstein 1993: 205–207). They mention only in very broad brush terms "echoic speech and contingent language to suggest uncertainty, ironic reversals to suggest error" (Stocking & Holstein 1993: 206, 193), focusing just cursorily on different linguistic patterns relating to different types of ignorance and uncertainty. Linguistic approaches to ignorance at the level of discourse thus encounter a closely studied, interdisciplinary field of research in which above all genuinely linguistic expertise is required with regard to the linguistic-rhetorical form of ignorance claims in specific written and spoken texts. This would make it possible to systematize discourse analytic findings more clearly according to the specific characteristics of the domain, discourse participants, media and text types concerned and to shed new light on issues such as the public image of science or discursive processes of negotiation in the knowledge society.

. . . and the linguistic form they take

The ways ignorance is named and described – and sometimes also judged in positive or negative terms – do not occur in isolation but rather in situations and in texts. This means that, in addition to the relevant lexical field surrounding knowledge/non-knowledge, the immediate context – set phrases, sentences, textual environments – also needs to be investigated.

Computational linguistics studies seek to analyze quantitatively linguistic markers of uncertainty in various domains and genres (Vincze et al. 2008; Szarvas et al. 2012 – see the latter for further references). In doing so, Szarvas et al. (2012: 340f.) distinguish between different semantic types of uncertainty: epistemic uncertainty vs. hypothetical uncertainty (and – as subtypes of hypothetical uncertainty – investigation uncertainty, condition uncertainty, doxastic modality, and a dynamic modality, not further expanded upon, that encompasses deontic, dispositional, circumstantial and bouletic modality). Various key words are allocated to these types, including adjectives and adverbs such as *probably, possibly, unsure, perhaps*, auxiliary and modal verbs such as *may, could, would, will*, conjunctions such as *if, whether, or* and various verbs and nouns, e.g. *suggest, seem, question* (= epistemic); *think, believe, rumor* (= doxastic); *investigate, analyze, examine* (= investigative) (Szarvas et al.

2012: 342). Using corpora from three domains (biomedical scientific papers and abstracts, encyclopedic texts, newswire) as their source, Szarvas et al. (2012: 349–351) conclude that there is a basic set of expressions that act as markers of uncertainty which vary widely in terms of their frequency depending on domain and genre and which may accordingly be extended by further lexical cues: *may*, *if*, *possible*, *might* and *suggest* (the latter being highly frequent) occur most frequently in all three domains equally; *charge*, *accuse*, *allege*, *fear*, *worry* and *rumor* for doxastic uncertainty barely occur at all in scientific texts (most prominent here instead is investigation uncertainty, marked by words such as *investigate*, *examine* and *study*: it is more present percentage-wise in abstracts than in scientific papers, in which, conversely, markers for condition uncertainty occur six times more often than in abstracts). The grammatical forms of these key words (mentioned only in passing in the study) also vary: whereas "uncertain" verbs found in encyclopedia and mass-media texts are used more in the third person singular, in scientific texts they are used mainly in impersonal forms (e.g. in the passive voice). Although the problem of lexical polysemy and of disambiguation is recognized as one of the biggest challenges (Szarvas et al. 2012: 345f., 362f.), the selection of lexical cues in such analyses is subject to too little reflection. Indeed, the approach chosen by Szarvas et al., namely, to analyze semantic uncertainty by means of lexical markers alone (Szarvas et al. 2012: 336) seems problematic: expressions such as *would* and *will*, for example, as well as the frequency of modal verbs and *if* constructions are not seen then as variations of modality and temporality evoked predominantly through syntax. And yet modality and temporality serve to achieve a further differentiation of epistemic uncertainty such as is lacking in the study concerned. At the same time, lexically more complex and semantically indirect modes of expressions (such as phraseologisms and tropes) are also neglected because they are more difficult (or even impossible as yet) to detect automatically (cf. Vincze et al. 2008, who raise and discuss this issue).

It therefore appears more useful to proceed from the start in a qualitative and hermeneutical manner in order to come up with reliable search commands. These would then have to be implemented in quantitative studies using extensive corpora. Erben (1994) undertook just such a hermeneutical attempt using theater reviews written by Theodor Fontane. He concludes that, alongside some highly variable syntactic phenomena, it is patterns of word formation that are also responsible for marking uncertainty and fuzziness. Erben's findings are supported and considerably extended by the studies done by Janich et al. (2010), Janich and Simmerling (2013) and Simmerling and Janich (2016/forthcoming). According to these studies, the following elements are at least relevant with regard to speaking/writing about ignorance:

1. Morpho-syntactic phenomena

a *Tense* (references to the past, present and future resulting in temporal conceptualizations such as "do not yet know", "have not known up to now", "will never know", etc.).

b *Mode* (use of the conditional, of modal verbs such as *can*, *should*, *must* and verbs of modality such as *seem,* of modal words/hedging terms such as *perhaps*, *probably*, *possibly*, of question constructions, etc.).

c *Negation* (negation of certainty and knowledge using adverbs and articles of negation such as *not, no ("not one"), never*, frequently in combination with temporal constructions).

2. Word formations

Identified as an intermediate phenomenon between grammatical and lexical features, including affixes of negation (such as *un-*, *in-*, *-less*, e.g. in *unsure*, *insecure* and *helpless*) and modality (such as *-able*, e.g. in *questionable*).

3. *Lexical phenomena*

a *Words* that refer prototypically to ignorance and uncertainty (including e.g. *error, ignorance, doubt, controversy, risk, uncertain*).
b *Expressions* that, on account of shared semantic features relating to context, may point to ignorance and uncertainty (such as *lack of data, unresolved issues, contested*).
c *Rhetorical figures* such as metaphors (including e.g. *unmapped terrain, knowledge gaps, stepping into new territory*), personifications (*poor cousin of [health] research*) and comparative constructions (*a kind of [x]*). Such figures also include hyperbole and irony, even if they are less easy to identify by pointing to a specific word.

Smithson (2008: 17f.) has produced an overview of metaphoric fields in the English language (similarly applicable in essence to the German language) relating to the relationship between knowledge and uncertainty or ignorance. This overview includes information about prototypical spheres that provide plenty of imagery as well as traditions of positive/negative interpretation (Smithson shows that there are more metaphors that interpret ignorance in negative than in positive terms!). Metaphors of this kind reveal, among other things, the way we deal with ignorance cognitively: it seems we either compare it with something that exists in reality or else we interpret as socially constructed. There are ten metaphoric fields in English language cultures "that stem from commonsense realism" (Smithson 2008: 17): unknown as obstructed vision and blindness; unknown can be felt; discovery as a journey; unknown as ocean; unknown as wilderness; seeking knowledge as hunting and gathering/unknown as prey; ideas as food/ bad ideas as raw and half-cooked; uncertainty as gaps or holes; theories as buildings/uncertainty and error as shaky and unfounded; uncertainty as variability; and there are ten metaphoric fields in English language cultures "stemming from commonsense sociality" (Smithson 2008: 17f.): inquiry as invasion/uncertainty as to be conquered; knowledge as resource/uncertainty as poverty; argument as war; knowledge as power/uncertainty as impotence and helplessness; uncertainty as enslavement/knowledge as freedom; ignorance, error and uncertainty as chastity and sign of innocence; knowledge as fertility/uncertainty as sterile or barren; ignorance as inequality; unknown as secret and locked away; uncertainty as insecurity and fear.

As we can see, then, ignorance can be referred to in texts in varying gradations and can be judged in either positive or negative terms in linguistically explicit or implicit ways. These initial findings thus point to at least two important insights: one is that the existence of various possibilities for expressing varying degrees of ignorance and uncertainty visually and linguistically means that the text *producer*, by communicating knowledge, is constantly making decisions about how to formulate meaning concerning the different degrees of certainty of his or her knowledge and that these decisions are by no means trivial. On the other hand, they also point to the fact that a broad scope for interpretation can arise in the course of text *reception*, something that may be highly significant for a given discourse and cannot be avoided even by more fine-grained semantic analyses. Empirical studies have shown that, when lay people wish to assess the degree to which they are at risk of contracting cancer, they do not benefit much at all from the carefully worded or terminologically standardized differentiations drawn in descriptions of this risk for different groups – an example being the description provided by the International Agency for Research on Cancer (IARC), formulated precisely in order to make it accessible to non-scientists (declining risk: *is* > *probably* > *possibly* > *not classifiable* > *probably not*) (Wiedemann et al. 2008: 171f.). In fact, even scientists themselves do not necessarily agree regarding which modal expressions in scientific texts refer to greater uncertainty or greater certainty in sentences containing such modifiers. In surveys, medical scientists were asked to rate 20 sentences containing variations on the theme "Therapy A is more effective than Therapy B" that had been modified using different modal constructions (e.g. using *probably*, *evidently*, *beyond any doubt*, *it seems that*, *it can be speculated*) on a scale between 'statement indicates certainty' and 'statement indicates uncertainty' (Beck-Bornholdt & Dubben 1997: 142–149). The survey did reveal a degree of consensus around modal expressions of certainty or uncertainty (in this experiment the straightforward indicative (*is*), verbs such as *to prove* and phrases such as *beyond any doubt* were all identified as indicating certainty, while formulations such as *it is not inconceivable that*, *it has become popular to assume that*, and *others have suggested that it could be* were all identified as indicative of uncertainty). However, what it also showed was that there are clearly formulations which are ranked in completely different ways across all gradations of the scale (e.g. *Evidently therapy A is/was more effective than therapy B*, *We have the strong feeling that therapy A is more effective than therapy B*, or *The present results are not in contradiction to the hypothesis that therapy A is more effective than therapy B*). Thus 'certain' or 'uncertain' are not semantic features of individual words that can be attributed fixed definitions but are rather the outcome of a highly context-dependent process of interpretation. Linguistically speaking, then, it may be that uncertainty cannot even be described exhaustively in intersubjective terms.

Summary: discursive relevance of concepts of ignorance from a linguistics perspective

In his monograph on "emerging paradigms" of ignorance and uncertainty, Smithson (1989: 9) uses a taxonomy he considers to be a "viable framework" for describing the way society deals with ignorance and uncertainty (see also his coda chapter in this volume). Taking *ignorance* as an overarching rubric he initially distinguishes only between *error* and *irrelevance*. He includes within the latter phenomena that are of marginal interest to us here such as *untopicality*, *taboo* and *undecidability*. In contrast to this, he differentiates *error* into *distortion* and *incompleteness*: *distortion* includes *confusion* and *inaccuracy*, while *incompleteness* contains both *uncertainty* and *absence*. According to Smithson, *uncertainty* can be sub-divided again into *vagueness* (= *fuzziness* or *nonspecificity*), *probability* and *ambiguity*. This taxonomy – not so much semantic as phenomenological in nature – highlights three things. First, Smithson proposes a very broad concept of ignorance, one that goes beyond epistemic interpretation; second, despite this he seems to not consider an *unknown unknown* as described by Kerwin (1993: 178) (such a concept would fit neither under *error* nor under *irrelevance*); and, third, he advocates a purely synchronous – almost isolational – take on ignorance that initially leaves no room, in conceptual terms, for temporal descriptions (e.g. differences between *not yet*, *no longer* and *never*) or modal descriptions of ignorance (e.g. not *being able to* know vs. not *wanting* vs. not *being allowed to*) – although such perspectives certainly do play a role in his discussion (cf. the term *taboo* in the taxonomy).

In contrast to this, however, the linguistics studies by Janich and Simmerling (2013) and Simmerling and Janich (2016/forthcoming) shows that it is precisely specific modal and temporal renderings of ignorance that are highly relevant in discourse in relation to attributions of ignorance to oneself or to others: the linguistic resources mentioned in above are used to construct a range of semantic concepts in texts. To some extent these have already been postulated in the sociology of knowledge (e.g. Gross 2007; Wehling 2010, 2012) but they can perhaps be examined in a more subtle and differentiated way by means of linguistic-rhetorical analysis. In climate change discourse, for example, there is a very wide range of discourse participant-specific attributions of ignorance. These include variations on "do not yet know" (implying a desire to know, e.g. among scientists), "do not yet know with enough certainty/accuracy" (e.g. among scientists seeking to legitimize their research, in newspaper articles expressing warnings, and among politicians delaying or forcing decisions through), "will not (ever) be able to know" (*unknown unknown*) or "will never be able to know with enough certainty/accuracy" (as an expression of concern in blog pieces written by private individuals and hobby scientists), a mistaken or negligent lack of knowledge – and even "do not want to know" (in German: *Ignoranz*, *unknown known*) (e.g. mutually attributed by politicians to one another). Another prominent phenomenon in discourses among scientists in particular, but also in non-scientific discourses, is that of calling existing knowledge into question in terms of being not (no longer) reliable knowledge.

Thus it is clear that both the intentions and interests of speakers/writers of ignorance claims as well as the temporality and modality inherent to the concepts of ignorance they use (and possibly even their chronological order) play a considerable role in discourse (cf. also Wehling 2010: 265; Gross 2007: 751). And so we come full circle from linguistics back to the other disciplines. An applied and critical linguistics would also have to confront issues – preferably in interdisciplinary debate – to do with communicative ethics when dealing with ignorance (cf. e.g. Elliot 2012 and in this volume).

Acknowledgements

We would like to express our gratitude to the German Research Foundation (DFG) for providing funding for this project. Our thanks also go to our colleagues in Priority Programme 1409 "Science and the public" (http://wissenschaftundoeffentlichkeit.de/en/) for discussions on the issues addressed here and to Kathleen Cross for her translation of the paper.

Notes

1 Cf. also the DFG (*Deutsche Forschungsgemeinschaft*) Priority Program "Science and the General Public: Understanding Fragile and Conflicting Scientific Evidence" (2009–2015). Available online at: http://wissenschaftundoeffentlichkeit.de/en/; as at 28.02.2014.

2 This has been done in German-speaking countries, for example, in relation to expert communication and different gradations of expert/terminological knowledge (cf. e.g. Wichter 1994 on the asymmetries in experts' and lay people's vocabularies), to lay-expert discourses in medicine, politics and the media (cf. e.g. the book series "Sprache und Wissen" published by de Gruyter), to forms and media of knowledge dissemination and knowledge transformation (cf. e.g. Liebert 2002 as well as the book series "Transferwissenschaften" published by Peter Lang) and to scientific controversies (cf. e.g. the essays contained in Liebert & Weitze 2006).

References

Bateman, John A. (2008): *Multimodality and Genre: A Foundational for the Systematic Analysis of Multimodal Documents*. New York: Palgrave.

Beck-Bornholdt, Hans-Peter & Hans-Hermann Dubben (1997): *Der Hund, der Eier legt: Erkennen von Fehlinformation durch Querdenken*. Reinbek bei Hamburg: Rowohlt.

Elliott, Kevin C. (2012): *Ignorance, Uncertainty, and the Development of Scientific Language*. In: Janich, Nordmann & Schebek, 295–315.

Erben, Johannes (1994): *Sprachliche Signale zur Markierung der Unsicherheit oder Unschärfe von Aussagen im Neuhochdeutschen*. Berlin: Akademie Verlag.

Feilke, Helmuth (1994): *Common sense-Kompetenz: Überlegungen zu einer Theorie "sympathischen" und "natürlichen" Meinens und Verstehens*. Frankfurt am Main: Suhrkamp.

Fix, Ulla (2007): "Stil als komplexes Zeichen im Wandel: Überlegungen zu einem erweiterten Stilbegriff". In: Irmhild Barz et al. (Eds.) *Stil – ein sprachliches und soziales Phänomen*. Berlin: Frank & Timme, 61–79.

Gross, Matthias (2007): "The unknown in process: dynamic connections of ignorance, non-knowledge and related concepts." *Current Sociology* 55(5), 742–759.

Heidmann, Ilona & Jutta Milde (2013): "Communication about scientific uncertainty: how scientists and science journalists deal with uncertainties in nanoparticle research." *Environmental Sciences Europe* 25(1), 25.

Janich, Nina, Alfred Nordmann & Liselotte Schebek (Eds.) (2012): *Nichtwissenskommunikation in den Wissenschaften.* Frankfurt am Main: Peter Lang.

Janich, Nina, Lisa Rhein & Anne Simmerling (2010): "'Do I know what I don't know?' The communication of non-knowledge and uncertain knowledge in science." *Fachsprache. International Journal of Specialized Communication* 32(3–4), 86–99.

Janich, Nina & Anne Simmerling (2013): "'Nüchterne Forscher träumen . . . ' – Nichtwissen im Klimadiskurs unter deskriptiver und kritischer diskursanalytischer Betrachtung." In: Meinhof, Ulrike, Martin Reisigl & Ingo H. Warnke (Eds.): *Diskurslinguistik im Spannungsfeld von Deskription und Kritik.* Berlin, 65–99.

Janich, Nina & Anne Simmerling (2016/forthcoming): "Nichtwissen in Text und Gespräch." In: Birkner, Karin & Nina Janich (Eds.): *Text und Gespräch.* Berlin/New York.

Kerwin, Ann (1993): "None too solid: medical ignorance." *Science Communication* 15(2), 166–185.

Kress, Gunther & Theo van Leeuwen (2001): *Multimodal Discourse: The Modes and Media of Contemporary Communication.* Oxford: Oxford University Press.

Liebert, Wolf-Andreas (2002): *Wissenstransformationen: Handlungssemantische Analysen von Wissenschafts- und Vermittlungstexten.* Berlin: de Gruyter.

Liebert, Wolf-Andreas & Marc-Denis Weitze (Eds.) (2006): *Kontroversen als Schlüssel zur Wissenschaft. Wissenskulturen in sprachlicher Interaktion.* Bielefeld: Transcript.

Schlosser, Horst Dieter (2003): "Changing metaphors for intellectual activities in German." In: Siefken, Hinrich & Anthony Bushell (Eds.): *Experiencing Tradition: Essays of Discovery. In Memory of Keith Spalding (1913–2002).* York: Sessions Books, 55–62.

Simmerling, Anne & Nina Janich (2016/forthcoming): "Rhetorical functions of a 'language of uncertainty' in the mass media." *Public Understanding of Science.*

Simmerling, Anne, Lisa Rhein & Nina Janich (2013): "Nichtwissen, Wissenschaft und Fundamentalismen – ein Werkstattbericht." In: Ballod, Matthias & Tilo Weber (Eds.): *Autarke Kommunikation. Wissenstransfer in Zeiten von Fundamentalismen.* Frankfurt am Main: Peter Lang, 129–155.

Smithson, Michael (1989): *Ignorance and Uncertainty: Emerging Paradigms.* New York: Springer.

Smithson, Michael (2008): "The many faces and masks of uncertainty." In: Smithson, Michael & Gabriele Bammer (Eds.): *Uncertainty and Risk: Multidisciplinary Perspectives.* London: Earthscan, 13–26.

Stocking, Holly S. & Lisa W. Holstein (1993): "Constructing and reconstructing scientific ignorance: ignorance claims in science and journalism." *Science Communication* 15(2), 186–210.

Stocking, Holly & Lisa W. Holstein (2009): "Manufacturing doubt: journalists' roles and the construction of ignorance in a scientific controversy." *Public Understanding of Science* 18, 23–42.

Szarvas, György, Veronika Vincze, Richárd Farkas, György Móra & Iryna Gurevych (2012): "Cross-genre and cross-domain detection of semantic uncertainty." *Computational Linguistics* 38(2), 335–367.

Vincze, Veronika, György Szarvas, Richárd Richard, György Móra & János Csirik (2008): "The BioScope corpus: biomedical texts annotated for uncertainty, negation and their scopes." *BMC bioinformatics* 9/ Suppl. 11, S9.

Warnke, Ingo H. (2009): "Die sprachliche Konstituierung von geteiltem Wissen in Diskursen." In: Felder, Ekkehard & Marcus Müller (Eds.): *Wissen durch Sprache. Theorie, Praxis und Erkenntnisinteresse des Forschungsnetzwerkes "Sprache und Wissen".* Berlin: de Gruyter, 113–140.

Warnke, Ingo H. (2012): "Diskursive Grenzen des Wissens – Sprachwissenschaftliche Bemerkungen zum Nichtwissen als Erfahrungslosigkeit und Unkenntnis." In: Janich, Nordmann & Schebek, 51–69.

Warnke, Ingo H. & Jürgen Spitzmüller (2008): "Methoden und Methodologie der Diskurslinguistik – Grundlagen und Verfahren einer Sprachwissenschaft jenseits textueller Grenzen." In: Warnke, Ingo H. & Jürgen Spitzmüller (Eds.): *Methoden der Diskurslinguistik: Sprachwissenschaftliche Zugänge zur transtextuellen Ebene.* Berlin: de Gruyter, 3–45.

Wehling, Peter (2010): "Nichtwissen: Entstehungskontexte, Pluralisierung Politisierung." In: Engelhardt, Anina & Laura Kajetzke (Eds.): *Handbuch Wissensgesellschaft. Theorien, Themen und Probleme.* Bielefeld: Transcript, 259–270.

Wehling, Peter (2012): "Nichtwissenskulturen und Nichtwissenskommunikation in den Wissenschaften." In: Janich, Nordmann & Schebek, 73–91.

Wichter, Sigurd (1994): *Experten- und Laienwortschätze. Umriß einer Lexikologie der Vertikalität.* Berlin: de Gruyter.

Wiedemann, Peter, Holger Schütz & Andrea Thalmann (2008): "Perception of uncertainty and communication about unclear risks." In: Wiedemann, Peter & Holger Schütz (Eds.): *The Role of Evidence in Risk Characterization.* Weinheim: Wiley-Blackwell, 163–183.

Part III

Valuing and managing the unknown in science, technology and medicine

15

Undone science and social movements

A review and typology

David J. Hess

As modern societies have become increasingly technological, science has become both more important and more politicized. Funding shifts into new research fields and out of old ones, and the changes in priorities among research fields also reorder the contours of what is known and unknown. The humanities, institutional approaches in economics, and natural science research fields that are not directly linked to industrial applications face declining prospects, whereas the support for emergent new research fields linked to industrial innovation (e.g., biotechnology, information technology, nanotechnology) raises questions about how little is known about their environmental, health, safety, and societal implications. Thus, ignorance in this historical sense is socially produced through underlying changes in the political economy of the scientific field.

Although the dominant actors in the political and economic fields exert a strong influence on the funding flows that affect the priorities of research agendas, there is a countervailing trend of epistemic modernization; that is, the opening of the scientific field to the knowledge needs of extrafield agents in less privileged and dominant positions (Hess 2007). One vector of epistemic modernization is the globalization of science and the diversification of workforces, which have altered the social composition of research fields and opened them up to new perspectives. Feminist, multicultural science studies have documented the important role of historically excluded groups who, once allowed into the scientific field and granted the training necessary to practice as peers, often bring perspectives conditioned by the habitus of their general social position. These changes are often generative for research fields, because they challenge underlying assumptions, develop new methods, and, to use Harding's phrase, strengthen rather than weaken the objectivity of scientific research by pointing to previously unrecognized biases (Harding 1998; Hess 1995).

Another vector of epistemic modernization is the more direct interaction of scientists with their publics. Scientists sometimes join social movements or provide research support for movements that have identified environmental, health, and other risks but have not been able to convince policymakers to respond with better regulation (Hess 2011b; Kinchy 2012; Moore 2008). In some cases, scientists also engage citizens and communities to develop partnerships that lead to new research questions and new methods (Brown 2007). The result can be new research fields, such as environmental toxicology (Frickel 2004), that respond to the new problems that scientists and their publics have identified. The opening up of the scientific field to the perspectives of social movements and communities also has implications for technology policy, which has undergone its own transitions to include, albeit often in highly controlled ways, greater levels of public engagement in the policy process through various mechanisms of public consultation.

Thus, a paradox emerges in the relations between the scientific and other social fields. Scientific knowledge becomes more politicized, more caught in the cross-fire of social conflicts, but as a result of the politicization, new research programs and even new research fields emerge, and scientific research can, at least in some cases, become more strongly objective in Harding's sense. One reason is that the politicization of the scientific field also makes possible the identification of and amelioration of the problem of undone science.

Undone science

The epistemic modernization of the scientific field, as a countervailing process to its industrialization and neoliberalization, involves the identification of a specific type of ignorance. The term "undone science" refers to a situation of unequal power that is associated with absent knowledge and that involves a conflict between reformers, such as social movement leaders, and industrial and political elites. It is based on a situation in which reformers look to "science" for answers to questions but find a lack of research, whereas their better funded adversaries often have much more research available to support their claims (Hess 2007: 22). Thus, the concept of undone science does not refer to all research that is recognized as not having been completed, nor does it refer simply to the idea of a research agenda of identifiable but incomplete research. Rather, the idea of undone science draws attention to a kind of non-knowledge that is systematically produced through the unequal distribution of power in society, where reformers who advocate for a broad public interest find that the research that would support their views, or at least illuminate the epistemic claims that they wish to evaluate, is simply not there.

Situated within the broad interdisciplinary study of ignorance, undone science can be categorized as a known unknown rather than an unknown unknown. The potential for nescience, what Gross defines as knowledge that we only know later in the form of a surprise, is also possible (Gross 2010; Hoffmann-Riem and Wynne 2002), but mostly what scientists and their publics seek in the identification of undone science is a kind of knowable unknown that they see as positive or desirable to study. For example, undone science takes the form of the following lament: if we only had more research on X, then we would be in a better position to known how much risk is involved in a laissez-faire approach to the regulation of X. Of course, the view of undone science as positive non-knowledge in the sense of illuminating policies that could generate a potentially broad public benefit is often contested, because industrial elites that shape the contours of research agendas through their funding preferences may not be as eager to have more evaluation of X, and they may view additional research that addresses undone science as negative non-knowledge. In other words, the distinction between positive and negative non-knowledge is perspectival. Large industrial corporations and large governmental units such as the military often have a strong influence on the political opportunity structure of research funding, either directly through their own funding processes or indirectly through influence on broader government research policy. Whereas social movements and public interest organizations may view an area of future research as positive non-knowledge, the firms and other organizations that face potential regulation may view it as negative non-knowledge.

A corollary of the concept of undone science is that it involves the systematic underfunding of a specific research agenda, and the underfunding occurs through a continuum of mechanisms. At one end, there is a well-documented literature on the active suppression of scientists who produce evidence that demonstrates risk and dangers associated with new technologies or technologies for which there is a broad public dispute (Delborne 2008; Martin 1996, 2007). At the other end, there is the more subtle process by which a government response to undone science leads to the selection of problems that create new pockets of undone science even as the first-order undone science is addressed. For example, the U.S. government created the Office of Alternative Medicine and later the National Center for Complementary and Alternative Medicine within the National Institutes of Health in response to claims of undone science from patient advocacy leaders, clinicians, nutritional and mind-body researchers, and allies in Congress who argued for public funding of the evaluation of complementary-and-alternative medicine (CAM) approaches to the treatment of cancer. However, the research funded through these organizations tended to emphasize complementary over alternative modalities, prevention over treatment, and other chronic diseases over cancer. Thus, a response to first-order undone science created second-order undone science. As I have shown (Hess 2015), it is possible to map these gradations of second-order undone science with a degree of quantitative precision; nevertheless, although quantitative analysis is possible, the ability to see what kinds of studies are unfunded requires a fairly deep ethnographic knowledge of the history and political context.

Research on undone science has revealed several areas of complexity that have moved the analysis beyond the first-level binary of movements versus industrial and political elites. First, the articulation of a known unknown does not always mean that it is technically possible to get the undone science done. As Howard points out in our extended discussion of undone science, some knowledge, such as the interaction of a suite of chemicals with complex biological processes, may be undone but also undoable (Frickel et al. 2010). Of course, the barrier of "undoable" science may be partly technical and financial, and consequently it is potentially surmountable over the long run. Recognition of not only undone but undoable science has policy implications for the deployment of precautionary rationales in the regulatory field, because it transforms a precautionary policy from a temporary status (a moratorium until more research is done) into a permanent status. Second, as Kempner has noted, social movements can also play a role in creating undone science, because they may argue for the broad social benefits associated with not pursuing a line of research (Frickel et al. 2010; Kempner et al. 2005). In addition to the example of animal rights research, there is also work on the role of scientists in attempting to halt various types of weapons research (Gusterson 1996, 2004; Moore 2008; Oreskes and Conway 2011). Third, social movements and reformers themselves are often divided, and consequently there may be different articulations of undone science (Gibbon in Frickel et al. 2010). Large civil society organizations have the financial capacity to fund some kinds of scientific research, thus generating "civil society research" as one mechanism of getting undone science done, but the research of large civil society organizations tends to be more moderate politically than the kind advocated by the less well-funded, often more radical organizations in a social movement field (Hess 2009b). Insider organizations may also lobby governments to get funding released—such as occurred for the increase in funding for environmental, health, and safety research for nanotechnology (Hess 2010)—but the more radical social movement organizations in the field, which in this case advocated for a broad moratorium, view such research as limited and coopted.

Another area of complexity in the study of undone science is the relationship between social movements and scientists. Activists and advocates are sometimes able to recruit scientists to work with them, either by providing them with funding or by gaining their support on a pro-bono basis. In the environmental health field, this work often involves challenges to what Brown (2007) calls the "dominant epidemiological paradigm." The relationships can involve quid-pro-quo negotiations between scientists and reformers (Clarke 1998), and they can also create tensions and ambiguities, because scientists do not often produce the results that reformers want to see (Yearley 1992). Scientists also make choices about the strategies they use to draw attention to the need for new research. As Allen (2003, 2004) has shown, they may adopt a highly public and media-oriented strategy that produces the political will for more research, or they may shun the public limelight and try to produce robust, peer-reviewed knowledge.

When forming alliances with social movements and community groups, scientists sometimes step out of their role as actors within a research field, in which there is generally a struggle among networks of researchers to define the dominant research programs, to a more public role in which they address the broad policy issue of a blockage of one area of research that is of potentially broad public benefit. When scientists "go public" with their criticisms of research funding priorities and the public benefits of changes in those priorities, they form an alternative scientific counterpublic that contests the linkage that official publics draw between broad public benefit and the status quo of research funding patterns (Hess 2011b). In some cases, scientists also form alliances with social movements and alternative industrial groups to develop political support for alternative research agendas. These scientific counterpublics are often linked to the more traditional counterpublics associated with advocacy groups and social movements connected to persons in subordinate positions in the social structure—by race, ethnicity, class, gender, sexuality, etc.—and to the sciences from below that emerge from those differences in perspective (Fraser 1997; Harding 1998, 2008). However, the scientific counterpublics need not have that connection; they can be composed of relatively privileged persons, such as credentialed research scientists and well-educated leaders of social movements and professional reform organizations. Thus, the scientific counterpublics are distinguished by their subordinate positions in the political field, and sometimes also in the scientific field, rather than their subordinate position in the broader social structure.

A typology of undone science, industrial change, and social movements

The concept of undone science is best understood when embedded in a theory of scientific field dynamics and industrial change. Theory in the social sciences can be based on models in the tradition of economics, where the theory relates agents such as advocacy organizations and firms to each other via a set of decision rules and optimization dynamics, but it can also be based on the Weberian tradition of the construction of ideal types that involve sequences and processes in the interactions among types of agents. The ideal types are intended less as the basis for formal models that can be tested and more as the basis for empirical research on specific historical and ethnographic cases that are often an amalgam of types. This latter, Weberian concept of theory is utilized here, and within that broad approach to theory this analysis draws on the theory of social fields.

Table 15.1 provides a typology of undone science with respect to the relationship between social movements and industrial-technological change. The term "social movement" is used here as an umbrella concept that includes both extra-institutional action (e.g., disruptive protest) and institutionalized action (reform) that includes technological and market innovation as well as policy change. Social movements are understood as broad mobilizations of persons and/or organizations that oppose the dominant patterns of society and politics, whereas interest groups are configurations of persons and organizations that attempt to garner more resources for a social

Table 15.1 A typology of undone science, industrial innovation, and social movements

	High Epistemic Conflict: Scientific Counterpublics	*Low Epistemic Conflict*
Technology/ Technique Targeted for Sunrise	Alternative industrial movements (undone science as research on alternative technologies, products, and production techniques)	Industrial restructuring movements (undone science as research into the new organizational forms)
Routinization Phase	• Funding granted for research but often limited • Countervailing industrial power • Complementarization through incorporation & transformation • OR industrial regime transition through transformation and/or certification schemes	• Diffusion of new organizational forms • Radical restructuring of firms or organizations in an industry • OR organizational forms remain in niche position, and large firms coopt some aspects of organizational innovation
Technology/ Technique Targeted for Sunset	Industrial opposition movements (undone science as research on research on risk, safety, uncertainty)	Industrial access movements (undone science as support for research on access issues)
Routinization Phase	• Funding granted for risk evaluation and partial moratorium with precautionary politics • Governments respond with public participation mechanisms and softening of technocratic governance • Industry may block change with contrarian science strategies	• Funding granted for access research • Advocacy organizations partner with industry to develop research agendas • Advocacy organizations shift into service provisioning • Contrapublic dynamics emerge more from neoliberal ideology

segment or sector. There are gradations between the two categories, and the access movements can be very close to traditional interest groups.

The typology is based on case studies developed mainly in the STS literature, and the discussion that follows is a modified and more elaborate version of the one originally developed in Hess (2007). The first organizing axis is the level of epistemic conflict engendered by the identification of undone science. Although epistemic conflict is endemic to all scientific research fields, this typology assumes that a distinction can be drawn between relatively higher and lower levels of epistemic conflict in a research field and its extrafield relations. The second organizing axis is the relationship to industrial and technical change, that is, reforms that support the creation of alternative technologies, techniques (practices), and/or organizational structures (sunrising) or those opposed to existing or emergent ones (sunsetting). Again, the level of conflict is variable, based on the degree of opposition to an existing industrial order. These typological categories can be thought of as representing a continuum when applied to concrete cases.

In the first type (upper left quadrant), alternative industrial movements (AIMs) focus on the sunrising of new technologies. There are two basic types of AIMs, technology- and product-oriented movements (TPMs) and certification movements, and the latter may develop out of the former. Thus, consistent with the literature on social movements, the issue of phases is very important (e.g., Soule and King 2006). Both types of AIMs may be anchored in formal nonprofit organizations and informal movement networks, but the TPMs are also frequently located in small, entrepreneurial business enterprises that occupy a potentially disruptive niche in a broader industry. Examples include, during the early phases, the movements for sustainable and local food, rooftop solar, alternative medicine, recycling and reuse, open-source software, community media, and alternative-fuel vehicles. What may begin as a TPM (e.g., off-grid rooftop solar in a home power movement) may later become the basis of certification campaigns directed at the state and/or corporations that have the aim of shifting the existing industrial regime to adopt standards that are compatible with the new product (e.g., solar carve-outs of renewable portfolio standards). However, the certification campaigns may be developed by a different set of organizations, such as environmental organizations, in contrast with the networks of inventors and entrepreneurs that characterize the TPMs. Often large industrial organizations ignore both the TPMs, which are seen as fringe niches, and the certification efforts, but later they may adopt modifications in their production technologies and products in response to perceived market opportunities from the TPMs and market pressures from the certification movements. In turn, the large organizations may even adopt certification schemes. However, it is also widely recognized that when large firms adopt certification schemes, they tend to attempt to dilute them through various mechanisms, such as by creating industry controlled certification labels (Jaffee 2012).

Within AIMs the TPMs frequently draw attention to the problem of undone science (Hess 2005, 2011b). Scientists who support the development of new technologies in these industrial fields may do so quietly, for example by devoting a portion of their research portfolio to pro-bono works in this area, or they may decide to leave the research field to become entrepreneurs or advocates. But they may also join with the networks of advocates and entrepreneurs as scientist-researchers to form an alternative scientific counterpublic that advocates for higher levels of research funding in support of the new technologies. When they do so, they raise the level of epistemic controversy by politicizing the funding agendas for a research field. Examples include the movements and associated scientists that draw attention to the relative imbalances of public funding in areas such as food and agriculture toward small, sustainable forms of agriculture or in medicine toward nutritional therapeutics for cancer (Hess 2007). The challenger knowledge can include networks of local and alternative professional knowledge (farmers, CAM practitioners) that are linked to credentialed researchers who occupy subordinate positions in their research fields (e.g., organic agriculture researchers in schools of agriculture and alternative medicine researchers in schools of nutrition or naturopathy). Conflicts can become intense scientific controversies, as in the case of the claim that enzyme-based nutritional therapies can be effective in the treatment of pancreatic cancer (Gonzalez 2012; Hess 2015).

If the TPMs were to scale up successfully from industrial niches to new industrial regimes, and/or if the certification movements were to enforce a significant change in industrial production processes and products, they would bring about a disruptive transformation of an existing industry. One might think of this outcome, in the terminology of innovation studies, as an industrial transformation in which the fundamental basis of the sociotechnical regime changes (Geels and Schot 2007), and in the terminology of institutional analysis, as a new settlement after a period of deinstitutionalization (Rao and Kenny 2008). However, the tendency is for the movements to undergo an incorporation and transformation process that results in much more modest forms of technological and industrial change. For example, the challenger technology embedded in entrepreneurial firms can be acquired by large corporations (e.g., by buying up small solar or organic food companies), or the corporations can set up their own divisions to colonize the niche (e.g., organic food divisions in large food companies). In the process, the alternative technologies are often redesigned to make them more compatible with the existing industrial regime (the "complementarization" process). For example, large food processing companies now offer frozen and packaged variants of organic food, and off-grid solar energy has been transformed from local to non-local ownership as a result of the shift to financing based on power-purchase agreements (Hess 2005, 2013). Often a countervailing industry plays a significant role in the transformation process by providing financing to the alternative research programs and to the scale shift (escape from industrial niche status) of the new technologies and products, such as the nutraceutical industry for the alternative medicine field and the finance and technology industries for the solar energy field (Hess 2013, 2014).

The second type of relationship among undone science, industrial change, and social movements, industrial restructuring movements, also involves a "sunrise" dynamic, but it is less focused on material technologies and products and more on the ownership dimensions of industrial organization (what one might think of, in the science and technology studies context, as organizational technologies or techniques). Historically, social movements representative of this type of industrial change called for government ownership of the major means of production, and these movements can still be found, especially in less developed countries where there can be intense struggles over privatization and public ownership, such as for water in Bolivia and petroleum in Mexico. At the other extreme, in the U.S. today, there are few socialists who occupy positions of power (e.g., Senator Bernie Sanders of Vermont), and movements to support increased public ownership are not influential at the state or federal government levels, with a few exceptions at the local level, such as mobilizations to support the municipalization of electricity in some cities and to protect public ownership of drinking water. In general, in developed countries other kinds of restructuring movements are more prominent, such as reform movements that attempt to shift policies and consumer loyalties toward locally owned, independent businesses (Hess 2009a). There are also movements in support of alternative forms of economic ownership, such as cooperatives, B corporations, social enterprise, and employee ownership (Williamson et al. 2002). In some cases, such as municipal electricity utilities and various cooperatives, the organizational forms are legacy outcomes of previous eras of social movement mobilization that have undergone subsequent reinvigoration, such as cooperative and small-business movements that became invigorated in the wake of the 1960s social movements (Hess 2009a; Schneiberg et al. 2008). Certification movements can also support alternative industrial forms, such as agrarian cooperatives and modified labor regimes found in fair trade and supply-chain certification schemes.

Industrial restructuring movements are similar to the alternative industrial movements in the sense that they also attempt to create alternatives to the existing industrial order, and in this way both are about sunrising new industrial forms. However, the level of epistemic conflict is generally lower than for the AIMs, because the relevant research fields are in the social sciences that study the alternative organizational forms. These research fields tend to appear in the lower-status social science disciplines such as sociology and in the humanistic social studies fields such as cultural anthropology and history. Within these relatively marginalized fields, researchers who study alternative economic organizations are not necessarily marginalized, but those who adopt explicitly socialist perspectives may be or at least may be located outside the elite universities (e.g., Foster et al. 2010). Again, the marginalized position of related research programs can be studied with quantitative precision, including reflexively for the position of certain types of research agendas in the STS field (Hess 2011a). Conversely, the elite networks of the social sciences that connect the business schools with the departments of economics tend to shun such work as "normative," "political," or "not rigorous." Thus, the research is not necessarily intensely controversial within its reference research field, but studies of the topic are also undone science within the dominant networks of the dominant social science disciplines.

The routinization phase for these movements can involve industrial transformation, such as would occur with the nationalization of an industry or the municipalization of an electricity or water system. However, the more common form of routinization is the widespread diffusion of the new organizational models and the incorporation and transformation of those models into the large industrial corporations. Thus, in the U.S. today there is a proliferation of local first movements, bank local and local currency movements, cooperatives, credit unions, B corporations, worker ownership, and, to a lesser degree, the municipalization or remunicipalization of services, but these innovations tend to remain in a niche position with respect to the model of the publicly traded, large corporation. Instead, large corporations have selectively adopted some of the elements of the movements while simultaneously rejecting the fundamental challenge that they had aimed to propose. Thus, large corporations have incorporated fair trade and local products in their retail offerings, and "buy local" movements encounter the use of local loss leaders in the large chains (a few locally made products strategically positioned at the entrance to stores) or even the creation of stealth independent coffee shops owned by large chains. Likewise, cities such as San Francisco may turn to community choice aggregation when their efforts at municipalization are rebuffed by the investor-owned utility (Hess 2009a).

The third type of movement and undone science involves industrial opposition movements, which advocate the sunsetting of specific technologies and products (e.g., especially toxic chemicals) or even of whole industries (e.g., nuclear power). This is the more well-traversed terrain of social movement studies with respect to industry (e.g., King and Soule 2007; Weber et al. 2009). Examples include mobilizations against genetically modified food, specific chemicals or classes of chemicals (e.g., chlorinated chemicals) that pose environmental and/or health threats, electromagnetic radiation risk (both ionizing and non-ionizing), and nuclear and fossil-fuel energy. Epistemic conflicts emerge between social movements and the government and/or industry over the level of risk associated with existing or emerging technologies, products, and production techniques; the potential unknowns and the credibility of existing research on risks; and the degree to which there is undone science on risks and potential harm. As in the AIM type, there is a high level of epistemic conflict, because scientists who produce studies that document risk for the technologies of established industrial regimes often find that their work is attacked or at least rebutted by industry-funded scientists. Epistemic conflict can also increase when communities affected by toxic exposure develop their own methodologies to document their exposure, as in the case of "lay epidemiology" and "bucket brigades" (e.g., Brown and Mikkelson 1990; Kroll-Smith and Floyd 2000; Ottinger 2013).

In addition to conflict over the credibility of research that documents risks and other potential problems of industrial technologies and products, there is broader epistemic conflict over how to translate knowledge or the lack of knowledge into policy. Strategies range from hyper-precautionism, which urges a temporary or partial moratorium until more knowledge is available, to free-market liberalism, which urges release of products onto markets because they have not been proven to be unsafe. When governments do not accept demands from movements for a precautionary approach, street protests in favor of a moratorium may occur, and they may exert a radical flank effect that opens the political opportunity structure for moderate reformers who call for greater funding for risk assessment (as occurred for genetically modified foods in Europe, with spillover effects to nanotechnology). In most cases we find a modest regulatory response, such as the labeling of genetically modified food or a moratorium on a small number of nanomaterials. Industry may also redesign some products in order to mitigate public concerns but also to keep the products on the market (e.g., removing the most allergenic genes from GM food). Where there is an absence of a social movement mobilization, regulatory policy will tend to follow the directions established by industry, even if civil society organizations have institutionalized access to the policy process, as we have shown in the case of nanotechnology policy in Europe (Lamprou and Hess 2014).

In some cases, industry shifts its strategy from merely criticizing research that suggests risk and safety issues to full-blown disinformation campaigns by industry-funded researchers. The paradigmatic cases are smoking and climate research in the U.S., but Oreskes and Conway (2011) discuss other cases. Analogous to the alternative scientific counterpublic discussed above, we can think of these networks of researchers as a scientific contrapublic. Contrapublic scientists have general scientific capital but generally lack standing within the relevant research field, such as the climate contrarian scientists who do not have standing in the field of climate science but who may be otherwise respected in their home fields. On this point, an editorial in the *Wall Street Journal* by climate scientist Kevin Trenberth (2012), and cosigned by 37 other climate scientists, compared skeptical statements by a group of prominent scientists to consulting a dentist for a condition that requires heart surgery. Credentialed in their own fields but not in the relevant field, the contrapublic scientists develop a claim that there is undone science, when in fact there is a relatively high level of consensus among credentialed experts in the research field. Although science is never done, there is enough consensus within the research field to make policy recommendations, such as the need to eliminate airborne emissions that cause acid rain, ozone depletion, and global warming.

Although in the case of climate science there is low epistemic conflict within the relevant research community, the contrapublic makes epistemic claims in the political field (e.g., climate science denialism) that in turn lead to the corralling or sequestering of the legitimately credentialed scientists from their role in the policy process. Thus, rather than playing a neutral role in the political field, in which scientists inform policymakers of problems that need to be addressed and therefore create the doxa upon which diverse policy responses can be debated, their knowledge itself becomes framed in a politically polarized field as associated with one side of a policy dispute. An epistemic rift occurs in which the traditional advisory relationship between a research field and policymakers breaks down, because the polarized policy field utilizes the contrarian science to make the claim that the scientific research is equally divided by ideological currents. In this situation, the mainstream of scientific researchers acts as a countervailing counterpublic in policy debates that are dominated by industry-oriented official publics and their contrapublic scientist allies (for more on these relationships, see Hess 2014).

Social movements that wish to develop a stronger political opportunity structure for precautionary policy may also draw attention to scientistic or technocratic aspects of the decision-making process (Kinchy et al. 2008). In response, governance processes can undergo epistemic modernization, at least in a limited form, by integrating mechanisms of public engagement such as open-commentary periods, lay consultations, focus groups, and consensus conferences. One result of increased public engagement can be the identification of undone science in the form of risk assessment; however, a fully democratic process could generate a situation in which risk assessment shows that a new technology is not very risky, but the public could reject it on other grounds, such as simply wanting to preserve the sociotechnical system dynamics of an existing regime. An example is the rise of grassroots opposition to smart meters. Although scientific risk assessment of the health concerns of household level microwave radiation has not reached a consensus, if the consensus were to emerge in favor of the claim that there is minimal or no health risk, public rejection of the technology could be on other grounds, such as desiring analog systems that are less amenable to terrorist attacks and privacy invasion (Hess and Coley 2013). Winner (1986) has argued that social movements should avoid getting stuck in the frameworks of technocratic decision-making by instead asking questions about the general social desirability or lack of desirability of new technologies and products.

Because of this risk to industrial elites and sympathetic policymakers that is embedded in a fully democratic process of public engagement, the mechanisms of public deliberation are often tightly controlled so that they end up with outcomes that are consistent with decisions that have already been made (Wynne 2005). One form of control is to restrict the definition of the "public" to the individual layperson who is relatively ignorant of the regulatory issues at stake, and although the lay public can be transformed into an opinion-generating public, these mechanisms of participation tend to exclude social movement organizations along with industrial firms and associations on the assumption that all are interested "stakeholders" (Hess 2011b). The result is the construction of participatory mechanisms that enables a continuation of scientistic politics but with the legitimating mantle of public consultation that also displaces the capacity of movements to claim legitimacy as representatives of broad public interest. Furthermore, often a condition of participation is a restriction of the terms of debate to issues of safety and risk. When participatory processes include public-interest and social movement organizations, a dilemma emerges for those organizations: either refuse to become involved in technical decision-making by remaining on the outside of the political process, or become caught up in the restricted risk frames and attempt to gain incremental changes in policy outcomes that lead to more research and some regulation (Kleinman and Kinchy 2007; Kinchy 2012). These strategic decisions produce divisions among civil society and social movement organizations that can then weaken their capacity to mobilize broadly and effectively.

The final category involves movements that advocate the end or sunsetting of specific kinds of inferior products, such as substandard housing, transportation, health care, and inferior food options for low-income communities. Access movements can include conventional poor people's movements that advocate for affordable access to basic material goods such as shelter, transportation, quality health care, and food. However, class, race, and traditional social inequalities are not the only source of mobilization. In the health field, these movements can include groups that mobilize against the existing lack of therapeutic choice for identified diseases, such as advocacy work by patient organizations that view their diseases as under-represented in public funding portfolios (Epstein 1996; Klawiter 2008). Diseases may be relatively rare and therefore orphaned, not rare but at one point relatively underfunded (e.g., AIDS and breast cancer before the patient advocacy movements), or not rare but with little incentive from the private sector to invest due to poor profitability (e.g., diseases prominent in low-income countries). Access movements thus span the range from disruptive anti-poverty movements to organizations that operate as interest groups in the sense of seeking greater resources from the government and from corporations for research about a specific disease.

In the politics of access, there is low epistemic conflict because the goal is gaining access to a higher quantity and/or quality of conventional technologies and products rather than challenging the dominant knowledges and technological designs. In contrast, in the AIMs such as the movement for complementary and alternative cancer therapies, the goal is to redefine the horizon of therapeutic choices by challenging dominant epistemic assumptions. The difference in perspective is crystallized by a comment once made to me by a CAM advocate about the AIDS movement, who said that AIDS patients were a model of "success," but they should be careful what they ask for when they say they want "drugs into bodies" (i.e., drugs that at the time had low efficacy and high side effects). Likewise, when talking about green affordable housing with a low-income housing advocate, the reply I once received from an affordable housing advocate was that he would love to have green housing, too, but he did not want to ask for too much. So this typological distinction aims at capturing these practical cognitive categories that divide the field of advocacy and activism (see also Brown et al. 2004, who make a similar distinction in their discussion of health social movements).

Because the access movements, as a type, do not challenge the dominant epistemic paradigms and technological regimes, they are easy to incorporate into existing industrial regimes. Once funding is available to support the access (from financial institutions as loans or from the nonprofit or public sectors as grants or aid), it is merely a question of increasing the quantity of goods provided. A confluence of interests emerges among the movement organizations, the funding sources, and the supplying firms. To the extent that a contrapublic is identifiable in this field, it is the general contrapublic of neoliberal ideologues who reject non-market approaches to solving problems of societal inequality. They frame access movements as asking for hand-outs and transfers from the hard-working citizens to their lazy counterparts, and successful disease advocacy organizations may also be portrayed as having gained a level of research and therapeutic support that is not calibrated to the disease population (e.g., an oversupply of funding to AIDS and breast cancer research). Political compromises that emerge from such disputes tend to use market mechanisms, public-private partnerships, governmental devolution, and other strategies to accomplish access goals while also moderating neoliberal framing.

In response to the growth of access funding and its privatized forms, movement organizations that may have once mobilized to demand access may find new opportunities as service provisioning organizations that have new revenue streams and organizational missions based on funds flowing from their government, nonprofit, and corporate sponsors. Corporate sponsors may even provide the organizations with training to lobby governments for more funding, including research funding to support the expansion of access. For example, in the case of breast cancer organizations, there has been a strong trend toward increased funding to the organizations that support conventional drug research (and marginalization of the original, more epistemically "radical" organizations that had connections to the TPM of CAM cancer therapies). Likewise, patient advocates in the larger and more well-funded organizations learn to lobby for changes in the allocation of research funding that is consistent with industry's goals of developing new, patentable, and profitable products (Batt 2012; O'Donovan and Glavanis-Granthan 2005).

Conclusion

In summary, the problem of undone science is approached from a political sociological perspective that includes the extrafield relations with governments, industries, and social movements and civil society (Moore et al. 2011; Frickel and Hess 2014). Although the conflict between the more and less powerful is fundamental for understanding undone science, it is also necessary to move beyond a simple "vertical" model of conflicts between disempowered movements and elites; hence, the analysis shifts into a typology of relationships among science, the state, industry, and civil society.

A typological approach to the analysis of movements, industrial change, and undone science can provide a valuable framework for research on the complex dynamics of the interfield relations and the politics of scientific knowledge and non-knowledge. Although some dimensions of the types could be formulated as testable hypotheses amenable to quantitative analysis, it is likely that the primary benefit is more in the Weberian tradition of providing a source of sensitizing categories and sequences for historical and ethnographic case studies and their comparative analysis. Furthermore, there is also a second-order benefit from the project of constructing the ideal types and their sequences in the manner suggested here: it suggests the value of bringing together the fields of science and technology studies, social movement studies, industrial innovation studies, and institutional analysis.

References

Allen, Barbara. 2003. *Uneasy Alchemy: Citizens and Experts in Louisiana's Chemical Corridor Disputes.* Cambridge, MA: MIT Press.

Allen, Barbara. 2004. "Shifting Boundary Work: Issues and Tensions in Environmental Health Science in the Case of Grand Bois, Louisiana." *Science as Culture* 13(4): 429–448.

Batt, Sharon. 2012. From Grassroots to Pharma Partnerships: Breast Cancer Advocacy in Canada. In Wilhelm Viehover and Peter Wehling, eds. *The Public Shaping of Medical Research: Patient Associations, Health Movements, and Biomedicine.* New York: Routledge.

Brown, Phil. 2007. *Toxic Exposures: Contested Illnesses and the Environmental Health Movement.* New York: Columbia University Press.

Brown, Phil, and Edwin Mikkelsen. 1990. *No Safe Place: Toxic Waste, Leukemia, and Community Action.* Berkeley, CA: University of California Press.

Brown, Phil, Stephen Zavestoski, Sabrina McCormick, Brian Mayer, Rachel Morello-Frosch, and Rebecca Altmann. 2004. "Embodied Health Movements: New Approaches to Social Movements and Health." *Sociology of Health and Illness* 26(1): 56–80.

Clarke, Adele. 1998. *Disciplining Reproduction: Modernity, American Life Sciences, and "the Problems of Sex,"* Berkeley, CA: University of California Press.

Delborne, Jason. 2008. "Transgenes and Transgressions: Scientific Dissent as Heterogeneous Practice." *Social Studies of Science* 38(4): 509–541.

Epstein, Steven. 1996. *Impure Science: AIDS, Activism, and the Politics of Knowledge.* Berkeley, CA: University of California Press.

Foster, John Bellamy, Brett Clark, and Richard York. 2010. *The Ecological Rift: Capitalism's War on the Earth.* New York: Monthly Review Press.

Fraser, Nancy. 1997. *Justice Interruptus: Critical Reflections on the "Postsocialist" Condition.* New York: Routledge.

Frickel, Scott. 2004. *Chemical Consequences: Environmental Mutagens, Scientist Activism and the Rise of Genetic Toxicology.* New Brunswick, NJ: Rutgers University Press.

Frickel, Scott, and David J. Hess. 2014. "Fields of Knowledge: Science, Politics, and Publics in the Neoliberal Age." *Political Power and Social Theory* 27: 1–30.

Frickel, Scott, Sahra Gibbon, Jeff Howard, Joana Kempner, Gwen Ottinger, and David Hess. 2010. "Undone Science: Social Movement Challenges to Dominant Scientific Practice." *Science, Technology, and Human Values* 35(4): 444–473.

Geels, Frank, and Johan Schot. 2007. "Typology of Sociotechnical Transition Pathways." *Research Policy* 36: 399–417.

Gonzalez, Nicholas. 2012. *What Went Wrong: The Truth Behind the Clinical Trial of the Enzyme Treatment of Cancer.* New York: New Spring Press.

Gross, Matthias. 2010. *Ignorance and Surprise: Science, Society, and Ecological Design.* Cambridge, MA: MIT Press.

Gusterson, Hugh. 1996. *Nuclear Rites: A Weapons Laboratory at the End of the Cold War.* Berkeley, CA: University of California Press.

Gusterson, Hugh. 2004. *People of the Bomb: Portraits of America's Nuclear Complex.* Minneapolis, MN: University of Minnesota Press.

Harding, Sandra. 1998. *Is Science Multicultural? Postcolonialisms, Feminisms, and Epistemologies.* Bloomington, IN: Indiana University Press.

Harding, Sandra. 2008. *Sciences from Below: Feminisms, Postcolonialities, and Modernities.* Durham, NC: Duke University Press.

Hess, David J. 1995. *Science and Technology in a Multicultural World.* New York: Columbia University Press.

Hess, David J. 2005. "Technology- and Product-Oriented Movements: Approximating Social Movement Studies and STS." *Science, Technology, and Human Values* 30(4): 515–535.

Hess, David J. 2007. *Alternative Pathways in Science and Industry.* Cambridge, MA: MIT Press.

Hess, David J. 2009a. *Localist Movements in a Global Economy.* Cambridge, MA: MIT Press.

Hess, David J. 2009b. "The Potentials and Limitations of Civil Society Research: Getting Undone Science Done." *Sociological Inquiry* 79(3): 306–327.

Hess, David J. 2010. "Environmental Reform Organizations and Undone Science in the United States: Exploring the Environmental, Health, and Safety Implications of Nanotechnology." *Science as Culture* 19(2): 181–214.

Hess, David J. 2011a. "Bourdieu and Science and Technology Studies: Toward a Reflexive Sociology." *Minerva* 49(3): 333–348.

Hess, David J. 2011b. "To Tell the Truth: On Scientific Counterpublics." *Public Understanding of Science* 20(5): 627–641.

Hess, David J. 2013. "Industrial Fields and Countervailing Power: The Transformation of Distributed Solar Energy in the United States." *Global Environmental Change* 23(5): 847–855.

Hess, David J. 2014. "When Green Became Blue: Epistemic Rift and the Corralling of Climate Science." *Political Power and Social Theory* 27: 123–153.

Hess, David J. 2015. "Beyond Scientific Consensus: Scientific Counterpublics, Countervailing Industries, and Competing Research Agendas." In Peter Wehling, Willy Viehöver, and Sophia Koenen, eds. *The Public Shaping of Medical Research: Patient Associations, Health Movements, and Biomedicine*. New York: Routledge, pp. 151–171.

Hess, David, and Jonathan Coley. 2013. "Wireless Smart Meters and Public Acceptance: The Environment, Limited Choices, and Precautionary Politics." *Public Understanding of Science*, in press.

Hoffmann-Riem, Holger, and Brian Wynne. 2002. "In Risk Assessment, One Has to Admit Ignorance." *Nature* 416 (March 14): 123.

Jaffee, Daniel. 2012. "Weak Coffee: Certification and Co-Optation in the Fair Trade Movement." *Social Problems* 59(1): 94–106.

Kempner, Joanna, C. S. Perlis, and J. F. Merz. 2005. "Forbidden Knowledge." *Science* 307: 854.

Kinchy, Abby. 2012. *Seeds, Science, and Struggle: The Global Politics of Transgenic Crops*. Cambridge, MA: MIT Press.

Kinchy, Abby, Daniel Kleinman, and Roby Autry. 2008. "Against Free Markets, Against Science? Regulating the Socio-Economic Effects of Biotechnology." *Rural Sociology* 73(2): 147–179.

King, Brayden, and Sarah Soule. 2007. "Social Movements as Extra-Institutional Entrepreneurs: The Effects of Protests on Stock Price Returns." *Administrative Science Quarterly* 52(3): 412–443.

Klawiter, Maren. 2008. *The Biopolitics of Breast Cancer: Changing Cultures of Disease and Activism*. Minneapolis, MN: University of Minnesota.

Kleinman, Daniel, and Abby Kinchy. 2007. "Against the Neoliberal Steamroller? The Biosafety Protocol and the Regulation of Agricultural Technologies." *Agriculture, Food, and Human Values* 24(2): 195–206.

Kroll-Smith, Stephen, and Hugh Floyd. 2000. *Bodies in Protest: Environmental Illness and the Struggle over Medical Knowledge*. New York: NYU Press.

Lamprou, Anna, and David Hess. 2014. "Between Collaboration and Advocacy: Non-State Actors and the Governance of Nanotechnology in the European Union." Under review.

Martin, Brian. 1996. "Sticking a Needle into Science: The Case of Polio Vaccines and the Origin of AIDS." *Social Studies of Science* 26(2): 245–276.

Martin, Brian. 2007. *Justice Ignited: The Dynamics of Backfire*. Lanham, MD: Rowman & Littlefield.

Moore, Kelly. 2008. *Disrupting Science: Social Movements, American Scientists, and the Politics of the Military, 1945–1975*. Princeton, NJ: Princeton University Press.

Moore, Kelly, Daniel Kleinman, David J. Hess, and Scot Frickel. 2011. "Science and Neoliberal Globalization: A Political Sociological Approach." *Theory and Society* 40(5): 505–532.

O'Donovan, Orla, and Glavanis-Granthan, Kathy. 2005. "Patients' Organizations in Ireland: Challenging Capitalist Biomedicine? Final Report to the Royal Irish Academy." Online. Available at: http://www.ria.ie/getmedia/87b7f804-c1ba-4c66-8a46-00c57300b491/ODonovan.pdf.aspx (accessed 30 March 2013).

Oreskes, Naomi, and Erik Conway. 2011. *Merchants of Doubt: How a Handful of Scientists Obscured the Truth on Issues from Tobacco Smoke to Global Warming*. London: Bloomsbury.

Ottinger, Gwen. 2013. *Refining Expertise: How Responsible Engineers Subvert Environmental Justice Challenges*. New York: NYU Press.

Rao, Hayagreeva, and Martin Kenny. 2008. "New Forms as Settlements." In Royston Greenwood, Christine Oliver, Roy Suddaby and Kerstin Sahlin-Andersson, eds., *Handbook of Organizational Institutionalism*. Thousand Oaks, CA: Sage.

Schneiberg, Marc, Marissa King, and Thomas Smith. 2008. "Social Movements and Organizational Form: Cooperative Alternatives to Corporations in the American Insurance, Dairy and Grain Industries." *American Sociological Review* 73(4): 635–667.

Soule, Sarah, and Brayden King. 2006. "The Stages of the Policy Process and the Equal Rights Amendment, 1972–1982." *American Journal of Sociology* 11(6): 1871–1909.

Trenberth, Kevin. 2012. "Check with Climate Scientists for Views on Climate." *Wall Street Journal*, Feb. 1. http://online.wsj.com/article/SB10001424052970204740904577193270727472662.html.

Weber, Klaus, Hayagreeva Rao, and L.G. Thomas. 2009. "From Streets to Suites: How the Anti-Biotech Movement Affected German Pharmaceutical Firms." *American Sociological Review* 74(1): 106–127.

Williamson, Thad, David Imbroscio, and Gar Alperovitz. 2002. *Making a Place for Community: Local Democracy in a Global Era.* New York: Routledge.

Winner, Langdon. 1986. *The Whale and the Reactor: A Search for Limits in an Age of High Technology.* Chicago, IL: University of Chicago Press.

Wynne, Brian. 2005. "Risk as Globalizing 'Democratic' Discourse? Framing Subjects and Citizens." In Melissa Leach, Ian Scoones, and Brian Wynne, eds., *Science and Citizens: Globalization and the Challenge of Engagement.* London: Zed, pp. 66–82.

Yearley, Steven. 1992. "Green Ambivalence about Science." *British Journal of Sociology* 43(4): 511–532.

16

Science

For better or worse, a source of ignorance as well as knowledge

Janet A. Kourany

Science has traditionally been billed as our foremost producer of knowledge. It has rarely been billed, as well, as an important producer of ignorance. Yet, the production of ignorance by science may well be inevitable, at least as inevitable as the production of knowledge. In fact, the two may go hand in hand. Consider, for example, how ignorance as well as knowledge typically results from pursuing certain lines of research rather than others—research regarding cancer detection and treatment, for instance, rather than research regarding cancer causation and prevention. Or consider how ignorance as well as knowledge frequently results from organizing scientific communities in particular ways. Think, for example, of the knowledge that was lost to anthropology from such traditional contributors as travellers, merchants, soldiers, missionaries, and local intelligentsia when these "amateurs" were excluded from anthropology in the process of its professionalization, but think also of the knowledge that was then made available to anthropology by that same process of professionalization.

Ignorance as well as knowledge is produced by science in many other ways, such as by framing research problems to foreground certain issues rather than others or by choosing certain technologies rather than others to carry out the research. What is most salient in all these cases is the relative importance of the knowledge and ignorance thus produced and their effects on particular groups or society at large. Here and there, however, another factor is also salient: the overall pattern of knowledge and ignorance thereby produced and the possibly distorted picture of the world or some part of the world that it supports. In what follows I shall consider features of our present pattern of knowledge and ignorance regarding one subject in particular—women. I shall also consider what is being done and still needs to be done to change that pattern.

Manly science: knowledge of men/ignorance of women

Toward the end of her essay *Three Guineas*, Virginia Woolf makes a curious remark: "Science, it would seem, is not sexless; she is a man, a father, and infected too." When Woolf made this remark back in 1938, science *was* like a man in a variety of ways. To begin with, science was dominated by men—by both the large numbers of men in science and the status and power they enjoyed. By the 1930s, after all, the possibilities for scientific training and accomplishment had been largely closed to women for centuries. Second, the qualities thought to characterize the successful scientist were overwhelmingly associated with men. At a time when women were expected to be nurturing and emotional and dependent, scientists were expected to be detached and unemotional and independent. And third, and most important, the knowledge that science produced catered to men—to men's interests and needs and accomplishments. In many ways, in fact, that knowledge was all about men. Regarding women, by contrast, science, for the most part, produced ignorance—or worse, a kind of "knowledge" that served the interests of men. And, of course, all this was damaging to women.

Much has changed since Woolf's time, but also much has remained the same. Though women in recent years have been pursuing science in ever-increasing numbers, science is still dominated by men. What's more, despite the achievements of all these women, science is still associated with men's characteristics and modes of behavior. Finally, even with the sometime dramatic changes in science brought about by these women and their male supporters, the balance of knowledge and ignorance produced by science still tilts unnaturally in men's favor. And all this is still damaging to women. In short, nearly a century after Woolf wrote, science is still much like a man, a father, and infected too.

Consider, to begin with, the way much of science still focuses on men and ignores women. The historical sciences—the *his-story* sciences—form particularly compelling examples. Take archaeology, a field in which, traditionally, the search for origins and pivotal developments in human evolution defines the "big" questions. It is this search, in fact, that allows archaeologists to structure their discipline and make their sometime-stirring pronouncements about human nature and human society when presenting the results of their research. Until very recently, however, what archaeologists have recognized as the "hallmarks" of human evolution—tools, fire, hunting, food storage, language, agriculture, metallurgy—have all been associated with men.

Take agriculture. Although women have been firmly associated by archaeologists with plants, both with gathering them (before the emergence of agriculture) and with cultivating them (after), when archaeologists have turned to the profoundly culture-transforming shift in subsistence practice represented by the invention of agriculture women have disappeared from discussion. Until the 1990s, for example, dominant explanations of the emergence of agriculture in the eastern woodlands of North America posited either male shamans and their ceremonial use of gourd rattles as the catalysts for this transition or plants' "automatic" processes of adaptation to the environmentally disturbed areas of human living sites (in which case, the plants essentially domesticated themselves). According to these explanations, in short, either men invented agriculture, or no one did (Watson and Kennedy 1991).

Archaeologist Margaret Conkey of the University of California, Berkeley, concludes:

> We have had, it seems, little problem in attributing a great deal of the archaeological record to men (the more salient stone tools, the hunting of big game, the making of "art," the development of power politics, the building of pyramids and mounds, the invention of writing by priests or temple accountants, domesticating gourds in order to have them available for shamans' rattles, etc.).
>
> *(Conkey 2008, 49)*

At the same time, Conkey adds, archaeologists have had little problem leaving out of the archaeological record what might easily, even stereotypically, have involved the experiences and contributions of women, such as midwifery and mothering practices, the socialization and gendering of children, sexual activities and relationships, and the social negotiations surrounding death, burial, and inheritance, topics that also hold enormous importance for the evolution of humans (see, for the beginnings of change on such topics, Meskell 1998; Joyce 2000; Schmidt and Voss 2000; Wilkie 2003; Baxter 2005).

As a result of this mode of representation of the past, this persistent association of men with the great turning points of human evolution, man as active, instrumental (as in man the toolmaker), man as provider, man as innovator, man as quintessentially human, has been made to seem natural, inevitable. At the same time, woman as outside the domain of innovation and control, woman as not active (that is, passive) and less than quintessentially human, has been made to seem natural and inevitable as well, and thus capable of explaining (and justifying) the gender inequalities we still find today (Conkey and Williams 1991; and cf. Conkey 2008).

Medical research forms another telling example of the way much of science still focuses on men and ignores women (see, for what follows, Rosser 1994; Weisman and Cassard 1994; Gura 1995; Mann 1995; Meinert 1995; Sherman, Temple, and Merkatz 1995; Schiebinger 1999, 2014; Women's Heart Foundation 2014). Until 1993—when Congress passed the National Institutes of Health Revitalization Act that mandated the inclusion of women and minority men in NIH-funded, U.S. medical research—females tended to be neglected in both basic and clinical research. Three of the more egregious areas of neglect were heart disease, AIDS, and breast cancer research—despite the fact that heart disease is the leading cause of death among women, AIDS is increasing more rapidly among women than among the members of any other group, and breast cancer has for years been the most frequently occurring cancer in women. The result was that these diseases were often not detected in women—often not even suspected—and not properly managed when they were detected.

Consider just heart disease. Slightly more than one out of every two women in the United States will die from cardiovascular illnesses. In fact, since 1984 more women than men have died each year from heart disease, and the gap between men's and women's survival continues to widen. Yet until the 1990s, heart disease was defined as a men's disease and studied primarily in white, middle-aged, middle-class men. The large, well-publicized, well-funded studies of the past are illustrative: the Physicians' Health Study, whose results were published in 1989, examined the effect of low-dose aspirin therapy on the risk of heart attack in 22,071 male physicians; the Multiple Risk Factor Intervention Trial (MR. FIT), whose results were published in 1990, examined the impact of losing weight, giving up smoking, and lowering cholesterol levels on the risk of heart attack in 12,866 men; the Health Professionals Follow-Up Study, whose results were also published in 1990, examined the relationship between coffee consumption and heart disease in 45,589 men. And these studies were no exceptions: in a 1992 *Journal of the American Medical Association* analysis of all clinical trials of medications used to treat acute heart attack published in English-language journals between 1960 and 1991, for example, it was found that fewer than 20 percent of the subjects were women.

The consequences of that neglect of women were profound. Since women were not researched along with the men, it was not discovered for years that women differed from men in symptoms, patterns of disease development, and reactions to treatment. As a result, heart disease in women was often not detected, and it was often not even suspected. What's more, it was not properly managed when it was detected. Drug treatments were a particularly glaring example. Drugs that were beneficial to many men caused problems in many women. For example, some clot-dissolving drugs used to treat heart attacks in men caused bleeding problems in women, and some standard drugs used to treat high blood pressure tended to lower men's mortality from heart attack while they raised women's mortality. What's more, the dosage of drugs commonly prescribed for men was often not suitable for women. Some drugs (such as antidepressants) varied in their effects over the course of the menstrual cycle, while others (such as acetaminophen, an ingredient in many pain relievers) were eliminated in women at slower rates than in men. Studying only, or primarily, men resulted in failures to prescribe appropriate kinds and doses of drugs for women as well as, of course, failures to offer other treatments (cardiac catheterization, coronary angioplasty, angiography, artery bypass surgery) at appropriate times. And it resulted in women's limited access to experimental therapies.

Of course, all this was to be rectified in 1993 with the N.I.H. Revitalization Act. But as it turns out, the Revitalization Act had serious limitations. For one thing, it does not apply to early-phase medical studies. In consequence, most basic research with animal models continues to focus on male animals and exclude females, most studies at the tissue and cellular levels either fail to report the donor sexes of the materials studied or report that they are male, and early phase clinical trials (that is, Phase I and II trials) don't always include women. Even in the case of the medical studies to which the Revitalization Act does apply (that is, Phase III clinical trials), women remain under-enrolled relative to their representation in the patient population. In fact, women still comprise only 24 percent of the participants in all heart-related studies. As a result of these limitations, medicine may still be failing to develop drugs and other therapies that work only in women, and medicine may still be failing to gain other important information about women.

Meanwhile, the effects of the pre-1993 exclusions still linger. For example, women consume roughly 80 percent of the pharmaceuticals used in the United States, but they are still frequently prescribed drugs and dosages devised for men's conditions and average weights and metabolisms. As a result, adverse reactions to drugs occur twice as often in women as in men.

> The net effect of gender bias in medical research and education is that women suffer unnecessarily and die. . . . Not only are drugs developed for men potentially dangerous for women; drugs potentially beneficial to women may [have been] eliminated in early testing because the test group [did] not include women.
>
> *(Schiebinger 1999, 115)*

Manly science: "knowledge" of women

Of course, women are not always cast in the shadows by the particular topics and approaches scientists adopt in their research. Often, in fact, women share the spotlight along with the men. But too often, in these cases, men function as the standard against which the women are judged, and the women are found wanting. So the knowledge of women that results, like the ignorance of women in other cases, still serves the interests of men. Consider the situation in psychology and biology, for example. One of psychology's central messages, historically, has been that women are inferior to men—intellectually, socially, sexually, and even morally (Marecek 1995; Wilkinson 1997). And biology historically has set for itself the task of explaining the basis and origin of that inferiority in terms of what is largely unchangeable—biology. This has had the effect of justifying—and, thus, helping to perpetuate—women's inferior educational and employment opportunities, as well as women's inferior positions in the family, government, and other social institutions.

Consider women's intellectual capacity, for example. For centuries it was claimed that women are intellectually inferior to men, and for centuries the basis for such inferiority was sought in biology. In the seventeenth century, women's brains were claimed to be too "cold" and "soft" to sustain rigorous thought. In the late eighteenth century, the female cranial cavity was claimed to be too small to hold a powerful brain. In the late nineteenth century, the exercise of women's brains was claimed to be damaging to women's reproductive health—was claimed, in fact, to shrivel women's ovaries. In the twentieth century, the lesser "lateralization" (hemispheric specialization) of women's brains compared with men's was claimed to make women inferior in visuospatial skills (including mathematical skills) (Schiebinger 1989; Fausto-Sterling 1992, 2000).

And now, at the beginning of the twenty-first century, the claims continue: that women's brains are smaller than men's brains, even correcting for differences of body mass; that women's brains have less white matter (axonal material); that women's brains have less focused cortical activity (lower "neural efficiency"); that women's brains have lower cortical processing speed (lower conduction velocity in their white matter's axons); and so on. And once again, these differences are being linked to differences in intellectual capacity: that people with smaller brains have lower IQ test scores; that less focused cortical activity is associated with lower intellectual performance; that lower cortical processing speed is associated with lower working-memory performance, which is correlated with lower "fluid intelligence" scores; and so on (see Hamilton 2008 for a recent account). At the same time, much attention now focuses on the mappings of brain activity produced by brain imaging, particularly fMRIs (functional magnetic resonance imaging), and the differences in "emotional intelligence" these disclose. But once again, the "male brain," the "systemizer" brain, comes out on top—is the more scientific brain, the more innovative brain, the more leadership-oriented brain, the more potentially "elite" brain, than the "female brain," the "empathizer" brain (Karafyllis and Ulshofer 2008).

And, this is just a peek at the history of biological and psychological claims about women's intellectual inferiority. The claims include not only these about the structure and functioning of women's brains, but also claims about women's hormones, and women's psychological propensities, and women's genetic endowment, and women's evolutionary past—how all these are connected to intellectual inferiority—and the claims go back in history at least to Aristotle and his observation that women are literally misbegotten men, barely rational at all. Of course, there are problems with many of the studies used to support these claims: they fail to report findings of no sex differences ("nonsignificant" findings); they fail to report the effect size of sex differences they do find; they fail to include replication samples to back up their initial findings; they assume a biological basis in the absence of biological data or cross-cultural data; and so on (Halpern 2012). No matter. Sweeping conclusions regarding female deficits are drawn nonetheless. And although the claims of intellectual inferiority continue to be contested and corrected, they also continue to be made, and the endless succession of claims and counterclaims both feeds on and helps to sustain the centuries-old stereotype of intellectual inferiority associated with women.

Meanwhile, the effects are profound. For example, studies have documented the harm done to women and girls by the publication of scientific claims suggesting an innate female deficit in mathematics (see, e.g., Steele 1997; Spencer, Steele, and Quinn 1999; and Dar-Nimrod and Heine 2006). One of the researchers involved in these studies, social/personality psychologist Steven Heine of the University of British Columbia, reports: "As our research demonstrates, just hearing about that sort of idea"—that female under-achievement in mathematics is due to genetic factors rather than social factors—"is enough to negatively affect women's performance, and reproduce the stereotype that is out there" (quoted in Ceci and Williams 2010, 221). But that harm has been recognized for years. Virginia Woolf described it almost a century ago:

> There was an enormous body of masculine opinion to the effect that nothing could be expected of women intellectually. Even if her father did not read out loud these opinions, any girl could read them for herself; and the reading, even in the nineteenth century,

> must have lowered her vitality, and told profoundly upon her work. There would always have been that assertion—you cannot do this, you are incapable of doing that—to protest against, to overcome.
>
> *(Woolf 1929, quoted in Spencer, Steele, and Quinn 1999, 5)*

Nevertheless, the research investigating women's intellectual capacity still continues.

An alternative to manly science

The gendered science Virginia Woolf drew attention to nearly a century ago lives on, and it is still producing harm for women—in fact, multiple interlocking harms. To be sure, scientific accounts that celebrate the past achievements of men while they make invisible—that is, promote ignorance of—the past achievements of women support, and are in turn supported by, scientific accounts that portray women as intellectually (emotionally, physically, . . .) inferior to men, and all this undermines women's self-esteem and the esteem of men. What's more, these accounts, because they suggest that women are worth less than men, also support a science that privileges the medical (economic, sexual, . . .) needs of men while it underserves and even promotes ignorance of the needs of women, and this further harms women. In short, the knowledge and ignorance produced by science work together to form a multiply distorted and multiply harmful picture of women. The few examples given above are just the tip of the iceberg.

Fortunately there is an alternative to Woolf's manly science already being developed. Premised on equality—equality of research opportunities for women and men regarding issues of interest to women and men that promise to promote equality between women and men—this new research enterprise frequently goes by the name of *feminist science*. And women scientists, both those calling themselves feminists and those resisting that epithet, have done much of this new research.

Women archaeologists, for example, have challenged the old origins stories—such as the "man the toolmaker" story—as resting on assumptions about the division of labor between the sexes applicable only quite recently and only in European and American cultures. At the same time they have worked to include women in these stories as active participants—for example, as active developers of pottery, an invention of major historic significance, and as active domesticators whose agricultural feats provided the staples of ancient diets. Most important, women archaeologists have opened up new questions for research such as how tools were used in activities other than big-game hunting (the traditional tool question in archaeology): they have asked how tools were used in food preparation and leatherworking and grain harvesting and woodworking; they have asked what early people usually ate, and what the economic and cultural goals of tool-making were; and they have asked other new questions as well, questions that equally explore men's activities as well as women's (see, e.g., Conkey 2003 and 2008 for descriptions of some of this work).

Women medical researchers have not only worked to bring about equal attention to women's and men's needs in medical research, but they have also begun the difficult but necessary reconceptualization of what such equality of attention requires. Indeed, medical researchers such as NIH reproductive endocrinologist Florence Haseltine have presided over a shift in women's health research from merely reproductive research (involving attention to childbirth, contraception, abortion, premenstrual syndrome, breast and uterine cancers, and the like) to more general health research (involving attention to women's distinctive physiology), and this has been critical to improving health care for women. Other medical researchers, in turn—such as Adele Clarke, Elizabeth Fee, Vanessa Gamble, and Nancy Krieger—have moved the understanding of health research toward a broader social model that does more than focus on disease management and biochemical processes. This broader model takes into account how health and disease are produced by people's daily lives, access to medical care, economic standing, and relations to their community. It thereby takes into account the differing health needs of women and men of different races and ethnic origins and classes and sexual orientations (see, e.g., Moss 1996; Schiebinger 1999; and for some of the latest work, Schiebinger 2014).

Women archaeologists and medical researchers, then, are producing knowledge of women to replace the ignorance that manly science promoted, knowledge that can help women achieve equality, and they are matched by women scientists in many other fields engaged in the same sort of activity. What's more, these women are producing path-breaking knowledge of men as well. But what about the *knowledge* of women that manly science provided—the "knowledge" of women's intellectual incapacity, for example? Women biologists, psychologists, and medical researchers have been doing a heroic job of damage control—emphasizing that, with few exceptions (such as the ability to do three-dimensional mental rotation), the cognitive differences between men and women that have actually been established are exceedingly slight (this includes mathematics performance and verbal skills); that none of these differences prevent women from successfully engaging in all the scientific and other activities that men successfully engage in; that the environmental context of women's intellectual labors, with its socialization pressures and biases and stereotypes and still-limited opportunities and mentoring, has far more to do with any gender gap in achievement than women's biology; that child care and other family responsibilities not equally shared by men also get in the way of women's achievement; and so on (see, for example, among the biologists and medical researchers, Anne Fausto-Sterling 1992, Cordelia Fine 2010, and Rebecca Jordan-Young 2010; and, among the psychologists, Virginia Valian 1998, Melissa Hines 2004, and Diane Halpern 2012; for an up-to-date review of the literature, see Hyde 2014).

Some scientists, men as well as women, are moving beyond damage control, however. They are asking why cognitive differences between women and men continue to command so much attention when much larger, more significant cognitive differences between other groups command relatively little attention and when ways to effectively deal with all these differences also command relatively little attention. "For instance," Cambridge University psychologist Melissa Hines explains,

> math and science achievement in students in the United States lags far behind that in many other countries that are generally viewed as less developed, and these differences are far larger than sex differences in performance. This deficiency among U.S. students extends even to those considered to be the best in the country. In regard to these students, the American author of a recent multinational report notes "our best students in mathematics and science are simply not 'world class.'"
>
> *(Hines 2004, 223)*

So, why aren't these cognitive group differences, or a myriad of other cognitive group differences at least as pressing, occupying center stage instead of cognitive gender differences? In fact, why are cognitive differences related to gender still being researched even after centuries of such research have turned up so little in the way of practically significant, verifiable differences? Open University, London, neuroscientist Steven Rose has an answer: sexism. "In a society in which racism and sexism were absent, the questions of whether whites or men are more or less intelligent than blacks or women would not merely be meaningless—they would not even be asked" (Rose 2009, 788).

Accordingly, in a two-month-long debate in the journal *Nature* in 2009, Rose and a number of other scientists from a variety of disciplines argued that race- as well as gender-related cognitive differences research should be abandoned. Said one of these scientists, University of North Carolina anthropologist Jonathan Marks:

> Decisions about what kinds of scholarly research questions and methods are considered worthy of attention and funding are fundamental to modern science. Stupid science and evil science . . . should not be permitted to coexist casually alongside the normative intellectual activities we admire.
>
> *(Marks 2009, 145)*

In fact, a science's very "standing as a scholarly enterprise" depends on selecting such activities out (Marks 2009, 145). But others strongly disagreed. Cornell University developmental psychologists Stephen Ceci and Wendy Williams, for example, complained that,

> when scientists are silenced by colleagues, administrators, editors and funders who think that simply asking certain questions is inappropriate, the process begins to resemble religion rather than science. Under such a regime, we risk losing a generation of desperately needed research.
>
> *(Ceci and Williams 2009, 789)*

New Zealand University of Otago psychologist James Flynn agreed:

> As the philosopher John Stuart Mill points out, when you assert that a topic is not to be debated, you are foreclosing not some narrow statement of opinion on that topic, but the whole spiraling universe of discourse that it may inspire.
>
> *(Flynn 2009, 146)*

And he added that "I invite everyone to search the social-science literature of the past 34 years and ask whether or not they really wish that everything on the subject [of biologically based cognitive group differences], pro or con, was missing" (Flynn 2009, 146).

In short, Rose, Marks, and other scientists are advocating ignorance regarding cognitive differences between men and women, and they are doing this in order to help bring about a more adequate picture of women. Indeed, such ignorance would work together with the knowledge currently produced by feminist science in much the same way as the ignorance and knowledge produced by manly science worked together, but this time the result would be empowering for women rather than disempowering. The result this time would also be free of distortion. On the other hand, Ceci, Williams, Flynn, and other scientists are arguing against this approach. And the debate continues.

Taking stock

We noted at the outset that science produces ignorance as well as knowledge and that the two may go hand in hand—inevitably rather than by choice. So, ignorance is not something automatically to be criticized when it results from science. In the case of the male-dominated/male-focused/male-privileging science that Virginia Woolf drew attention to, however, ignorance *was* something to be criticized. It was far from inevitable; it empowered men at the expense of women; and it closed off important avenues of enquiry that could have been helpful to both men and women. What's more, it contributed to a highly distorted and damaging picture of women. Unfortunately, it and the manly science that produces it still flourish today.

But there is an alternative: feminist science. Premised on equality—equality of research opportunities for women and men regarding issues of interest to women and men that promise to promote equality between women and men—feminist science also aims to empower both women and men. Still, although great strides have been made to bring about such a feminist science, many throwbacks to manly science remain. One example is gender-related cognitive differences research. Although there is much evidence in support of the "gender *similarities* hypothesis" now that "mountains of research" on "gender *differences*" have been completed, the quest for difference continues (Hyde 2014). Abandoning that quest would deliberately produce ignorance. But this time the ignorance would disempower no one. Nor would it close off important avenues of enquiry that could be helpful to both men and women. On the contrary, it would make room for more important questions, such as how to train men and women or intervene in some other way to maximize the cognitive competences they do have. Finally, it would contribute to no distortion in our picture of either men or women. Instead, it would encourage us to respond to the needs, abilities, and potential of *individuals* with no reinforcement of group stereotypes to get in the way. A truly worthwhile sort of ignorance!

References

Baxter, Jane Eva (2005), *The Archaeology of Childhood: Children, Gender, and Material Culture.* Walnut Creek, CA: AltaMira Press.

Ceci, Stephen and Wendy M. Williams (2009), "Should Scientists Study Race and IQ? Yes: The Scientific Truth Must Be Pursued," *Nature* 457(7231), 12 February: 788–789.

Ceci, Stephen and Wendy M. Williams (2010), *The Mathematics of Sex: How Biology and Society Conspire to Limit Talented Women and Girls.* New York: Oxford University Press.

Conkey, Margaret W. (2003), "Has Feminism Changed Archaeology?" *Signs* 28(3): 867–880.

Conkey, Margaret W. (2008), "One Thing Leads to Another: Gendering Research in Archaeology." In Londa Schiebinger (ed.), *Gendered Innovations in Science and Engineering.* Stanford, CA: Stanford University Press, 43–64.

Conkey, Margaret W. and Sarah H. Williams (1991), "Original Narratives: The Political Economy of Gender in Archaeology." In Micaela di Leonardo (ed.), *Gender at the Crossroads of Knowledge: Feminist Anthropology in the Postmodern Era.* Berkeley and Los Angeles: University of California Press. 102–139.

Dar-Nimrod, Ilan and Steven J. Heine (2006), "Exposure to Scientific Theories Affects Women's Math Performance," *Science* 314(5798), 20 October: 435.

Dar-Nimrod, Ilan and Steven J. Heine (2006), "Exposure to Scientific Theories Affects Women's Math Performance," *Science* 314(5798), 20 October: 435.

Fausto-Sterling, Anne (1992), *Myths of Gender,* 2nd ed. New York: Basic Books.

Fausto-Sterling, Anne (2000), *Sexing the Body: Gender Politics and the Construction of Sexuality.* New York: Basic Books.

Fine, Cordelia (2010), *Delusions of Gender: How Our Minds, Society, and Neurosexism Create Difference.* New York: W.W. Norton.

Flynn, James (2009), "Would You Wish the Research Undone?" *Nature* 458(7235), 12 March: 146.

Gura, Trisha (1995), "Estrogen: Key Player in Heart Disease among Women," *Science* 269(5225), 11 August: 771–773.

Halpern, Diane (2012), *Sex Differences in Cognitive Abilities,* 4th ed. New York: Taylor and Francis.

Hamilton, Colin (2008), *Cognition and Sex Differences.* New York: Palgrave Macmillan.

Hines, Melissa (2004), *Brain Gender.* New York: Oxford University Press.

Hyde, Janet Shibley (2014), "Gender Similarities and Differences," *The Annual Review of Psychology* 65: 373–398.

Jordan-Young, Rebecca M. (2010), *Brain Storm: The Flaws in the Science of Sex Differences.*Cambridge, MA: Harvard University Press.

Joyce, Rosemary (2000), "Girling the Girl and Boying the Boy: The Production of Adulthood in Ancient Mesoamerica," *World Archaeology* 31(3): 473–483.

Karafyllis, Nicole C., and Gotlind Ulshofer (2008), *Sexualized Brains: Scientific Modeling of Emotional Intelligence from a Cultural Perspective.* Cambridge, MA: MIT Press.

Mann, Charles (1995), "Women's Health Research Blossoms," *Science* 269(5225), 11 August: 766–770.

Marecek, Jeanne (1995), "Psychology and Feminism: Can This Relationship Be Saved?" In Domna C. Stanton and Abigail J. Stewart (eds.), *Feminisms in the Academy.* Ann Arbor, MI: University of Michigan Press, 101–132.

Marks, Jonathan (2009), "Is Poverty Better Explained by History of Colonialism?" *Nature* 458(7235), 12 March: 145–146.

Meinert, Curtis L. (1995), "The Inclusion of Women in Clinical Trials," *Science* 269(5225), 11 August: 795–796.

Meskell, Lynn (1998), "Intimate Archaeologies: The Case of Kha and Merit," *World Archaeology* 29(3): 363–379.

Moss, Kary L. (ed.) (1996), *Man-Made Medicine: Women's Health, Public Policy, and Reform*. Durham, NC, and London: Duke University Press.

Rose, Steven (2009), "Darwin 200: Should Scientists Study Race and IQ? No: Science and Society Do Not Benefit," *Nature* 457(7231), 12 February: 786–788.

Rosser, Sue (1994), *Women's Health-Missing from U.S. Medicine*. Bloomington and Indianapolis: Indiana University Press.

Schiebinger, Londa (1989), *The Mind Has No Sex?* Cambridge, MA: Harvard University Press.

Schiebinger, Londa (1999), *Has Feminism Changed Science?* Cambridge, MA: Harvard University Press.

Schiebinger, Londa et al. (2014), "Designing Health and Biomedical Research," *Gendered Innovations in Science, Medicine, and Engineering* Project. Available online at: http://genderedinnovations.stanford.edu/methods/health.html.

Schmidt, Robert and Barbara Voss (eds.) (2000), *Archaeologies of Sexuality*. London: Routledge.

Sherman, Linda Ann, Robert Temple, and Ruth B. Merkatz (1995), "Women in Clinical Trials: An FDA Perspective," *Science* 269(5225), 11 August: 793–795.

Spencer, Steven J., Claude M. Steele and Diane M. Quinn (1999), "Stereotype Threat and Women's Math Performance," *Journal of Experimental Social Psychology* 35: 4–28.

Steele, Claude M. (1997), "A Threat in the Air: How Stereotypes Shape Intellectual Identity and Performance," *American Psychologist* 52(6), June: 613–629.

Valian, Virginia (1998), *Why So Slow? The Advancement of Women*. Cambridge, MA: MIT Press.

Watson, Patty Jo and Mary C. Kennedy (1991), "The Development of Horticulture in the Eastern Woodlands of North America: Women's Role." In Joan M. Gero and Margaret W. Conkey (eds.), *Engendering Archaeology: Women and Prehistory*. Oxford and Cambridge, MA: Basil Blackwell, 255–275.

Weisman, Carol S. and Sandra D. Cassard (1994), "Health Consequences of Exclusion or Underrepresentation of Women in Clinical Studies (I)." In Anna C. Mastroianni, Ruth Faden, and Daniel Federman (eds.), *Women and Health Research*, vol. 2. Washington, DC: National Academy Press, 35–40.

Wilkie, Laurie (2003), *The Archaeology of Mothering: An African-American Midwife's Tale*. London: Routledge.

Wilkinson, Sue (1997), "Still Seeking Transformation: Feminist Challenges to Psychology." In Liz Stanley (ed.), *Knowing Feminisms: On Academic Borders, Territories and Tribes*. London: Sage Publications, 97–108.

Women's Heart Foundation (2014), "Women and Heart Disease Facts." Available online at: http://www.womensheart.org/content/heartdisease/heart_disease_facts.asp.

Woolf, Virginia (1929), *A Room of One's Own*. London: Hogarth Press.

Woolf, Virginia (1938), *Three Guineas*. London: Hogarth Press.

17

Selective ignorance in environmental research

Kevin C. Elliott

Introduction

Scholars from a number of different academic disciplines have recently drawn attention to the ways in which ignorance about socially significant topics can be generated and maintained (Frickel et al. 2010; Mills 1997; Proctor and Schiebinger 2008; Tuana 2006). This chapter focuses on a particular form or type of ignorance—namely, selective ignorance. It occurs when people produce or disseminate specific sorts of information about a topic or entity while failing to produce or emphasize other information about it. Defined in this way, selective ignorance is unavoidable; investigators do not have the time or energy to study every aspect of every topic. Nevertheless, in some cases this selective emphasis on particular sorts of information about a topic can be highly socially significant, because it can influence major public policy decisions or cultural forces. Thus, powerful interest groups often have a great deal of incentive to promote selective ignorance about socially relevant topics, which means that it is important for society to recognize this phenomenon and develop strategies for responding to it.

The next section of the chapter clarifies the concept of selective ignorance and its relationship to other literature on the topic of ignorance. It shows that this concept can be helpful both from a practical perspective (i.e., recognizing how interest groups can marshal knowledge to advance their goals) and from a theoretical perspective (namely, understanding how information is produced and distributed). The following two sections illustrate the significance of selective ignorance in case studies involving agriculture and pollution. The last section gleans some strategies from these case studies for responding to socially significant forms of selective ignorance.

Selective ignorance

The concept of selective ignorance discussed in this chapter is inspired by Robert Proctor's introductory essay in the volume on *Agnotology* that he edited with Londa Schiebinger (Proctor and Schiebinger 2008). In his introduction, he suggested a taxonomy of ignorance organized around three categories: (1) ignorance as a starting point or native state; (2) ignorance as a lost realm or selective choice; and (3) ignorance as a strategic ploy or active construct (Proctor 2008, 3). The second category—ignorance generated by selective choices to focus on some pieces of knowledge rather than others—is the focus of this chapter. Nevertheless, it is important to emphasize that Proctor's second category is not entirely distinct from the third. Interest groups can employ a variety of strategies in order to construct ignorance as a strategic ploy, and some of these strategies involve selectively collecting or disseminating some pieces of information rather than others (Elliott forthcoming-a).

In his own discussion of selective ignorance, Proctor uses Londa Schiebinger's (2008) contribution to their volume as his primary example. Schiebinger points out that when sixteenth-century European explorers returned from the New World, they brought back some bodies of information (e.g., about potatoes and quinine) but not other sorts of information (e.g., about abortifacients and contraceptives). Based on this example, one might suppose that selective ignorance arises primarily as a result of obvious social decisions to put more money into studying some topics (e.g., cancer research) rather than others (e.g., high-energy particle physics). But the situation is arguably much more complex, for at least three reasons.

First, selective ignorance often stems from subtle decisions to study a single complex topic in some ways rather than others (Elliott 2013b). For example, agricultural companies have significant financial incentives to perform research on agricultural strategies that involve potentially lucrative inputs like pesticides and fertilizers rather than more environmentally friendly agroecological strategies that are likely to generate fewer profits for the companies (Elliott 2013b; Lacey 1999). Second, selective ignorance can stem from efforts to collect specific sorts of information about a product (e.g., its benefits) rather than others (e.g., its potentially harmful side-effects). Third, selective ignorance stems not only from choices about what sorts of information to collect but also from choices about how to disseminate and mobilize the available information. For example, the pharmaceutical industry engages in massive "publication planning" efforts to control the flow of information about their products so that important decision makers receive a carefully crafted message (Sismondo 2007). These examples highlight the fact that there is often a great deal of money and power and social influence at stake in decisions about what information to collect and how to disseminate it.

In addition to being an important concept for understanding social and political conflicts over science, the concept of selective ignorance plays a valuable theoretical role in science studies. As early as the 1920s, Alfred North Whitehead argued that scientists and philosophers suffer from a tendency to assume that their abstractions of a phenomenon adequately capture all its nuances (Whitehead 1925). The concept of selective ignorance provides one way of highlighting this error, which Whitehead called the "Fallacy of Misplaced Concreteness." More recently, philosophers of science have been emphasizing that scientists often develop multiple explanations and models of complex phenomena (Kellert et al. 2006; Kitcher 2001; Mitchell 2009). The concept of selective ignorance provides one way of thinking about how these different explanatory accounts fit together—each one highlights some features of the phenomena under investigation while failing to do justice to others (Elliott 2013b). The concept of selective ignorance is also closely related to work in feminist epistemology and science studies that discusses how some scientific methods (e.g., expert analyses based on "impersonal" data and statistical analyses) are often given primacy over other methods (e.g., community-based approaches that incorporate extensive testimonial evidence and qualitative data) (Code 2012; Elliott 2013a). Finally, science and technology studies (STS) scholars have introduced the concepts of "technoscientific imaginaries" (Marcus 1995) and "undone science" (Frickel et al. 2010), which are similar to the concept of selective ignorance insofar as they highlight the ways in which scientists' attention can be funneled down particular paths, thereby encouraging some research trajectories and inhibiting others.

Selective ignorance in agricultural research

In a previous paper (Elliott 2013b), I highlighted some of the ways in which contemporary agricultural research illustrates the phenomenon of selective ignorance. By analyzing a recent report created by the International Assessment of Agricultural Knowledge, Science, and Technology for Development (IAASTD), I argued that selective ignorance can arise from a wide variety of subtle research choices. These include decisions about what questions to ask, what metrics or standards to employ, what research strategies to pursue, what information to disseminate, what terminology or categories to employ, and what technological applications to pursue.

For example, the IAASTD report notes that recent agricultural research has tended to focus on the question of how to maximize the production of individual agricultural products (IAASTD 2009a, 16). In contrast, the report focuses on a much broader question: "How can AKST [agricultural knowledge, science, and technology] be used to reduce hunger and poverty, improve rural livelihoods, and promote equitable environmentally, socially, and economically sustainable development" (IAASTD 2009a, 3)? When agricultural funders and researchers focus only on the narrower question of how to maximize the yield of specific products, they are likely to remain ignorant of many ways that agricultural practices affect rural communities and their environments. This is significant, because Hugh Lacey has argued that environmentally friendly agroecological approaches often have significant advantages over more intensive "industrial" approaches once one considers the wider environmental and social context in which agricultural production occurs (Lacey 1999). Even the decision to address agricultural problems with scientific and technological solutions rather than social or political changes such as land reform can reflect and perpetuate ignorance of the ways that social structures contribute to current problems (Elliott 2013b; Patel 2007, 121–124).

The IAASTD report also highlights the way attention to particular metrics and even terminology can promote knowledge about some features of a problem while hiding other facets of it. For example, the report emphasizes that a measure like gross domestic product (GDP) can effectively track some impacts of agricultural production while failing to track impacts on equity and the environment (IAASTD 2009a, 7). When it comes to terminology, the authors of the report note that they prefer the term 'multifunctional' when referring to agriculture, because it draws attention to the fact that it ideally performs a number of other social functions besides supplying food. To ignore these other functions risks creating crucial blind spots in our understanding of this phenomenon.

Finally, it is crucial to recognize that selective ignorance can be promoted not just by choices about what information to collect but also by decisions about what to disseminate and how to do so. After all, various small farmers and activist groups are often acutely aware of problems with contemporary agriculture, such as the high prices of fertilizers and pesticides and their detrimental effects on the surrounding environment. The problem is that it is often difficult to transmit this information to crucial policy makers and researchers. Contemporary research on genetically modified organisms (GMOs) provides an example of selective information dissemination that runs in the opposite direction (i.e., from scientists to the public). As the IAASTD report notes, it is difficult to promote public trust in GMOs while the agricultural biotechnology industry maintains tight proprietary control over all research on them (IAASTD 2009b, 394). The public understandably believes that the industry is likely to overemphasize information about their potential benefits while failing to discuss their weaknesses and potential harmful effects (Elliott 2013b, 339). Even when non-industry-funded studies on GMOs are performed, Fern Wickson and Brian Wynne (2012) have shown that industry groups and government regulatory agencies can block these studies from receiving serious consideration by arguing that they do not follow the standardized protocols created by agencies such as the Organization for Economic Cooperation and Development (OECD). This is an excellent example of how the creation of standardized guidelines can promote important forms of selective ignorance, insofar as the study designs that are dismissed can sometimes be preferable to the standardized protocols for bringing specific sorts of hazards to light (Elliott forthcoming-b); Ottinger 2010).

Another problem related to the dissemination of information about agricultural practices is that the entities with the power to inform farmers about new and more environmentally friendly techniques often have significant financial conflicts of interest. In particular, agricultural biotechnology companies have a major financial stake in encouraging farmers to employ expensive genetically modified seeds and chemicals. Even universities, which could play an important public-interest role as sources of information about socially beneficial but less commercially lucrative agricultural techniques, are often heavily influenced by the agricultural biotechnology industry. In response to evidence that he collected regarding the harmful effects of neonicotinoid insecticides, Dave Goulson of the University of Sussex aptly summarizes the selective ignorance about alternative techniques that is perpetuated among farmers:

> To me, it seems pretty clear that these [neonicotinoid] insecticides do a lot of harm but offer little, if any, genuine benefit . . . Unfortunately, we have a situation whereby the agronomic advice that farmers receive is almost entirely provided by people who sell pesticides . . . [S]o it should come as no surprise to hear that these people are advising them to buy pesticides. It seems to me that we have a system that is fundamentally flawed. It has been set up to oversubscribe agricultural chemicals, and this is terrible for our environment.
> *(Morgan 2013)*

Selective ignorance in pollution research

Research on the environmental effects of pollution also vividly illustrates the phenomenon of selective ignorance. First, as Carl Cranor (1999) has emphasized, we face a situation of asymmetric knowledge. We often know a great deal about the beneficial effects of pollutants but relatively little about their harmful effects. This selective ignorance is exacerbated by the manufacturers of these products, because they have an interest in actively constructing the contours of our knowledge. Recent books such as *Merchants of Doubt* (Oreskes and Conway 2010), *Bending Science* (McGarity and Wagner 2008), *Is a Little Pollution Good for You?* (Elliott 2011), and *Doubt Is Their Product* (Michaels 2008) highlight the way industry groups fund strategic research projects and employ public relations firms and front groups to disseminate their preferred messages widely among the public.

But even entities that put a high priority on protecting public health often suffer from assumptions and biases that result in collecting and disseminating information about pollutants in selective ways that can disadvantage already marginalized social groups. Maria Powell and Jim Powell (2011) provide a particularly vivid illustration of this phenomenon in their discussion of the Madison Environmental Justice Organization (MEJO). MEJO is a small, non-profit, multicultural community organization in Madison, Wisconsin, that focuses on alleviating environmental injustices. One of the organization's central goals has been to address the exposure of subsistence anglers to toxic substances in the fish that they catch and eat. Even though state and federal regulatory agencies collect information about toxicants in fish and inform citizens about hazards via advisories, MEJO has highlighted at least three ways in which the available information provided by these agencies is selective: (1) it includes very little information about toxicity in Madison lakes as compared to other waterways in Wisconsin; (2) it includes relatively little information about fish consumption levels, especially by subsistence anglers; and (3) the communication of information about fish advisories to local citizens is seriously limited, especially to those who do not speak English (Powell and Powell 2011).

The Powells point out that government agencies and university researchers have justified their lack of effort to collect data about the toxic chemicals in fish from Madison lakes based on the assumption that those lakes are not contaminated enough to be of concern compared to Superfund sites in places like Green Bay and Milwaukee (2011, 158). But this lack of concern appears to stem from social and cultural "blinders" that prevent these researchers from paying attention to the risks faced by minority groups that consume a great deal of fish from Madison lakes. As the Powells put it: "The choices that actors at local and state levels—including individual scientists—make about what environmental health issues to study and act on, given political and funding constraints, are not deliberately ill-intentioned. Rather, they are rooted in long-standing political and socio-cultural values that shape institutional priorities" (2011, 165). Unfortunately, as is common in situations of ignorance, a chicken-and-egg scenario ensues, in which the lack of official data ends up creating the impression that there is nothing to worry about, which in turn prevents researchers from collecting additional data: "High deference to institutional scientists' data on fish risks—perceived as more 'valid' than other data—along with reluctance to recognize data gaps in institutional science, play pivotal roles in this chicken-egg feedback cycle" (2011, 169). Lorraine Code has described the same vicious cycle in occupational health research, where researchers do not think about looking for occupational causes and therefore pursue explanations and forms of evidence that minimize the chance of identifying these sorts of causes (2012, 123).

In addition to this selective ignorance about pollutants in Madison lakes, it is also enlightening to consider the selective ignorance about fish consumption and about the communication of risks in this case. As mentioned earlier, part of the reason for failing to collect data about toxic substances in Madison lakes is the assumption by regulators that people do not eat large quantities of fish from these sources. But efforts by MEJO to collect data among a wide range of Madison citizens revealed that, while the regulators' assumptions about fish consumption may be accurate for some citizen groups, a number of subsistence anglers eat fish (including large, more polluted fish) every day or several times a week. Moreover, some immigrant groups eat the entire fish (sometimes with organs), which runs counter to assumptions in standard risk assessments. Unfortunately, these immigrant groups are also among the least likely to be able to understand fish advisory signs and messages given in English. Thus, another major effort of MEJO has been to address this source of ignorance by convincing local regulatory agencies to post advisory signs in Spanish and in Hmong (one of the languages of the local immigrant communities).

The MEJO case illustrates many of the ways in which risk assessments of polluting chemicals can reflect selective ignorance. First, local communities' qualitative experiences with pollution are often discounted by experts, who prefer to rely on quantitative, standardized data that may not bear out the concerns of citizens (Barrett and Raffensperger 1999; Code 2012; Ottinger 2010). Second, the experts' data sometimes suffer from crucial gaps that go unrecognized. Third, these data gaps can be caused by mistaken assumptions that are exacerbated by experts' ignorance of the ways that specific groups of people are actually exposed to polluting substances. In the MEJO case, experts didn't understand the fish consumption patterns of particular minority groups; in other cases, experts have failed to recognize the ways pesticides are actually applied on agricultural fields or the ways in which crops are actually planted (Irwin 1995). Of course, this is not to say that citizens are always correct or that they cannot benefit from the input of experts. Rather, the point is that citizens can sometimes contribute to "street science" (Powell and Powell 2011, 154) or "popular epidemiology" (Brown and Mikkelsen 1990) or "precautionary science" (Barrett and Raffensperger 1999; Elliott 2013a) that fills selective gaps in the knowledge provided by typical regulatory science.

Solutions

Looking at these two areas of research, we can glean several insights about the nature and significance of selective ignorance. First, it often stems from subtle methodological choices about how to study a particular topic. Decisions about which facets of a problem to study, or what metrics to employ, or what statistical analyses to use, or what terminology to adopt, can all promote ignorance about some pieces of information and knowledge about others. Second, traditional scientific practices that appear to be value-free can actually promote selective ignorance by failing to consider the unique experiences of marginalized groups or by failing to explore alternatives to current technologies (Code 2012). Third, selective ignorance is often promoted and maintained by failing to *disseminate* particular sorts of information, not just by failing to *produce* the information in the first place. Fourth, selective ignorance can have significant impacts on society. In agriculture, for example, choices to engage in some forms of research rather than others (and to disseminate some kinds of information rather than others) can have major impacts on the environment and the well-being of farming communities. And in the case of pollution, these selective choices can determine whether people's exposure to toxic chemicals is ignored or whether it is brought to the attention of key decision makers.

These lessons suggest that selective ignorance is an important phenomenon but that it can be difficult to recognize and to challenge. Even when researchers appear to be studying a particular topic, they can still be promoting socially significant forms of selective ignorance. Therefore, one of the most important strategies for addressing selective ignorance is to promote social activism about scientific and technological issues. Activist groups are often acutely sensitive to the ways in which existing science fails to address their concerns. This is obvious in the MEJO case, and it is important in the agricultural context as well. Peasant movements and NGOs such as La Via Campesina, the Landless Rural Workers Movement, the Rodale Institute, Greenpeace, and Navdanya International have all drawn attention to the ways in which current agricultural research fails to meet the needs of poor farmers and the environment, especially in developing countries (Elliott 2013b).

Another important strategy for addressing selective ignorance is to encourage the proposal of new paradigms that can shake up existing research strategies. Activist groups can be an important source of ideas for new paradigms, especially when their members have specific, local knowledge about the problems under investigation. But new ideas can also develop out of interdisciplinary efforts to bring natural scientists, social scientists, and humanists together with various stakeholders to deliberate about future avenues for research (see e.g., Elliott 2013a). In the case of agriculture, many scholars have suggested that the field of agroecology could represent an innovative new paradigm for research. It attempts to find creative, ecologically friendly ways to increase agricultural production without depending on expensive inputs (see e.g., Elliott 2013b; Lacey 1999; Patel 2007). In the case of research on pollution, an intriguing new paradigm is the "cradle-to-cradle" design strategy promoted by William McDonough and Michael Braungart (2002). They argue that instead of trying to minimize waste from industrial practices, designers should aim to eliminate waste completely; they should imitate the way natural processes recycle the output from one process so that it becomes the input of another process. The effort to engineer "safety by design" into new industrial chemicals is another promising approach for alleviating pollution risks (see e.g., Maynard et al. 2006).

A final strategy for addressing selective ignorance is to provide significant funding for socially relevant research projects from government sources. About two-thirds of U.S. funding for research and development comes from industry (Elliott 2011), and this research is significantly constrained by the need to obtain short-term profits. Therefore, if scientists are to alter their research methodologies in order to better address long-term environmental problems or issues that afflict the poor, they need other sources of funding. Moreover, when products have harmful effects on the environment or on human health, it is often in the best interests of their producers to avoid obtaining or disseminating that sort of information (McGarity and Wagner 2008; Michaels 2008). Thus, research from independent sources is crucial in order to bring those public-health issues to light. Unfortunately, as the IAASTD report discussed earlier in this chapter emphasizes, research on socially relevant topics like agriculture is increasingly coming from the private sector (IAASTD 2009b, 224). Therefore, in addition to trying to slow or reverse the loss of funding from the public sector, it may also be valuable to explore whether collaborative research projects between industry, government, and NGO representatives can also generate research projects that alleviate socially significant forms of selective ignorance (see e.g., Busenberg 1999; Pew Initiative on Food and Biotechnology 2002).

Conclusions

This chapter introduced the notion of selective ignorance as a valuable concept both for understanding how scientific information is produced and disseminated as well as for recognizing how interest groups manage the flow of information to serve their interests. The chapter analyzed research on agriculture and environmental pollution as case studies. These cases illustrate that selective ignorance often stems from subtle methodological choices that uncover some information about a complex topic or entity while leaving other sorts of information uncollected. Sometimes these methodological choices are enshrined in standardized protocols or the accepted practices of scientific disciplines and regulatory agencies, which makes them even more difficult to recognize and criticize. These case studies also illustrate that the aggressive dissemination of some sorts of information (e.g., about agricultural techniques based on expensive inputs), along with efforts to suppress other sorts of information (e.g., about the hazards of polluting chemicals), can generate socially significant forms of selective ignorance. In order to alleviate the social problems caused by selective ignorance, the chapter proposed three strategies: (1) encouraging activist groups and NGOs to critique policy-relevant science; (2) promoting broadly based deliberation about new paradigms for scientific research and development; and (3) investing in significant government and/or collaborative funding for policy-relevant research.

References

Barrett, K., and C. Raffensperger (1999), "Precautionary Science," in C. Raffensperger and J. Tickner (eds.), *Protecting Public Health and the Environment: Implementing the Precautionary Principle*. Washington, DC: Island Press, pp. 106–122.

Brown, P., and E. Mikkelsen (1990), *No Safe Place: Toxic Waste, Leukemia, and Community Action*. Berkeley, CA: University of California Press.

Busenberg, G. (1999), "Collaborative and Adversarial Analysis in Environmental Policy," *Policy Studies* 32: 1–11.

Code, L. (2012), "Thinking Ecologically: The Legacy of Rachel Carson," in B. Kabesenche, M. O'Rourke, and M. Slater (eds.), *Environment: Philosophy, Science, and Ethics*. Cambridge, MA: MIT Press.

Cranor, C. (1999), "Asymmetric Information, the Precautionary Principle, and Burdens of Proof in Environmental Health Protections," in C. Raffensperger and J. Tickner (eds.), *Protecting Public Health and the Environment: Implementing the Precautionary Principle*. Washington, DC: Island Press, pp. 74–99.

Elliott, K. (2011), *Is a Little Pollution Good for You? Incorporating Societal Values in Environmental Research*. New York: Oxford University Press.

Elliott, K. (2013a), "Ethical and Societal Values in Nanotoxicology," in B. Gordijn and A. M. Cutter (eds.), *In Pursuit of Nanoethics*. Dordrecht: Springer, pp. 147–166.

Elliott, K. (2013b), "Selective Ignorance and Agricultural Research," *Science, Technology, & Human Values* 38: 328–350.

Elliott, K. (forthcoming-a), "Environment," in A. J. Angulo (ed.), *Miseducation: A History of Ignorance Making in America and Beyond*.

Elliott, K. (forthcoming-b), "Standardized Study Designs, Value Judgments, and Financial Conflicts of Interest in Research," *Perspectives on Science*.

Frickel, S., S. Gibbon, J. Howard, J. Kempner, G. Ottinger, and D. Hess (2010), "Undone Science: Charting Social Movement and Civil Society Challenges to Research Agenda Setting," *Science, Technology, and Human Values* 35: 444–473.

IAASTD (International Assessment of Agricultural Knowledge, Science, and Technology for Development) (2009a), *Agriculture at a Crossroads: Executive Summary of the Synthesis Report*. Washington, DC: Island Press.

IAASTD (2009b), *Agriculture at a Crossroads: Global Report*. Washington, DC: Island Press.

Irwin, S. (1995), *Citizen Science: A Study of People, Expertise, and Sustainable Development*. New York: Routledge.

Kellert, S., H. Longino, and K. Waters (eds.) (2006), *Scientific Pluralism*. Minneapolis, MN: University of Minnesota Press.

Kitcher, P. (2001), *Science, Truth, and Democracy*. Oxford: Oxford University Press.

Lacey, H. (1999), *Is Science Value Free?* London: Routledge.

Marcus, G. (ed.) (1995), *Technoscientific Imaginaries: Conversations, Profiles, and Memoirs*. Chicago, IL: University of Chicago Press.

Maynard, A., et al. (2006), "Safe Handling of Nanotechnology," *Nature* 444: 267–269.

McDonough and Braungart (2002), *Cradle to Cradle: Remaking the Way We Make Things*. New York: North Point Press.

McGarity, T., and W. Wagner (2008), *Bending Science: How Special Interests Corrupt Public Health Research*. Cambridge, MA: Harvard University Press.

Michaels, D. (2008), *Doubt Is Their Product: How Industry's Assault on Science Threatens Your Health*. New York: Oxford University Press.

Mills, C. (1997), *The Racial Contract*. Ithaca, NY: Cornell University Press.

Mitchell, S. (2009), *Unsimple Truths: Science, Complexity, and Policy*. Chicago, IL: University of Chicago Press.

Morgan, J. (2013), "Do Neonicotinoids Harm Organisms Other than Insects?" *ScienceΩ* (June 14). Available online at: http://www.scienceomega.com/article/1142/do-neonicotinoids-harm-organisms-other-than-insects (accessed July 2, 2013).

Oreskes, N., and E. Conway (2010), *Merchants of Doubt*. New York: Bloomsbury Press.

Ottinger, G. (2010), "Buckets of Resistance: Standards and the Effectiveness of Citizen Science," *Science, Technology, and Human Values* 35: 244–270.

Patel, R. (2007), *Stuffed and Starved: The Hidden Battle for the World's Food System*. Brooklyn, NY: Melville House.

Pew Initiative on Food and Biotechnology (2002), *Three Years Later: Genetically Engineered Corn and the Monarch Butterfly Controversy*. Available at: http://www.pewtrusts.org/uploadedFiles/wwwpewtrustsorg/Reports/Food_and_Biotechnology/vf_biotech_monarch.pdf (accessed July 26, 2013).

Powell, M., and J. Powell (2011), "Invisible People, Invisible Risks: How Scientific Assessments of Environmental Health Risks Overlook Minorities—and How Community Participation Can Make Them Visible," in G. Ottinger and B. Cohen (eds.), *Technoscience and Environmental Justice: Expert Cultures in a Grassroots Movement*. Cambridge, MA: MIT Press.

Proctor, R. (2008), "Agnotology: A Missing Term to Describe the Cultural Production of Ignorance (and Its Study)," in R. Proctor and L. Schiebinger, eds., *Agnotology: The Making and Unmaking of Ignorance*. Stanford: Stanford University Press, 1–36.

Proctor, R., and L. Schiebinger (2008), *Agnotology: The Making and Unmaking of Ignorance*. Stanford, CA: Stanford University Press.

Schiebinger, L. (2008), "West Indian Abortifacients and the Making of Ignorance," in R. Proctor and L. Schiebinger, eds., *Agnotology: The Making and Unmaking of Ignorance*. Stanford, CA: Stanford University Press, pp. 149–162.

Sismondo, S. (2007), "Ghost Management: How Much of the Medical Literature Is Shaped Behind the Scenes by the Pharmaceutical Industry?" *PLoS Medicine* 4: e286.

Tuana, N. (2006), "The Speculum of Ignorance: The Women's Health Movement and Epistemologies of Ignorance," *Hypatia* 21: 1–19.

Whitehead, A. N. (1925), *Science and the Modern World*. New York: Macmillan.

Wickson, F., and B. Wynne (2012), "Ethics of Science for Policy in the Environmental Governance of Biotechnology: MON810 Maize in Europe," *Ethics, Policy & Environment* 15: 321–340.

18

Lost in space

Geographies of ignorance in science and technology studies

Scott Frickel and Abby Kinchy

Ignorance is an idea whose description is curiously tethered to the spatial. Scientists who write about ignorance seem to prefer metaphors with dimensionality, perhaps as a way to give their topic some conceptual heft. Thus, a mathematician:

> Likening the growth of knowledge to the progressive construction of an atlas of our world, imagine two cartographers setting out to map the Pacific, one starting from the West and the other from the East, each one ignorant of latitude and longitude but using his [sic] own empirical coordinate system centered on his homeland. The initial gulf of ignorance between them would dwindle away until, finally, the maps overlap.
>
> *(Clarke 1977: 112)*

A physicist:

> The catalogue of our ignorance has *two*, not one, gates: there is the obvious exit gate, through which questions answered and settled by experimental and theoretical developments march out and disappear into the textbooks and applications; but there is also a more important, albeit less perspicuous, *entrance gate*, through which *new* riddles come to life in the scientific world.
>
> *(Bertotti 1977: 92)*

A geologist:

> Knowledge advances like the concentric ripples that spread outward from a pebble tossed into a mill pond. Its expanding front is in contact with an ever-widening periphery of ignorance as growing comprehension generates new and more subtle questions.
>
> *(Cloud 1977: 388)*

These descriptions invoke spatial concepts: coordinate position, boundary, and distance. They appear in *The Encyclopedia of Ignorance* (Duncan and Weston-Smith 1977), a compendium of

51 short essays penned by experts representing a range of physical, biological, earth, and social sciences.[1] Curiously, given the book's disciplinary breadth and the peppering of spatial metaphors throughout it, none of the essays derive from the science that claims space as its core concept. Thoughtful readers will learn what cosmologists do not know about "curved" space, but they will learn nothing of a geographer's view of absences in knowledge about the regions of the Earth.

This chapter takes up the problem of ignorance and geographical space from the vantage point of Science and Technology Studies (STS). This field's long-held focus on the social production of expert knowledge has begun to yield in recent years to a wave of exciting new studies of ignorance production as a related, yet distinct problem of epistemology (e.g. Proctor and Schiebinger 2008; Rappert and Bauchspeis 2014; Sullivan and Tuana 2007). Unlike the scientists quoted above, who treat ignorance as a background condition of scientific work generally unrelated to epistemology, we follow fellow STSers in viewing ignorance as a cultural artifact whose production is deeply intertwined with epistemic, social, *and spatial* processes. Here, two contemporary streams of STS research guide our thinking. One is the "turn" toward geography, a move that has focused primarily on the role of place in the production of expert knowledge (Shapin 1998). Another is studies of epistemic inequality that seek social explanations for what Nancy Tuana (2008: 111) has called "knowledge/ignorance" to signal the imbrication of knowledge and non-knowledge through the "active production" of power (see also Harding 2006). We see great potential in bringing these two streams of research into closer dialogue. Accordingly, we attend to three geographical concepts that we believe have relevance for studies of the social production of ignorance. After briefly exploring the relevance of "place" and "space", we train our focus on "scale" and present some observations from our own and others' studies of regulatory environmental science.

Place- and space-based ignorance

The "geographical turn" (or turns; Henke and Gieryn 2006) in STS has primarily been concerned with the concept of place, and with the "local" character of expert knowledge. Gieryn (2002, 2006) contends that certain geographical locations become "truth-spots" that lend credibility to claims about the world. "Truth-spots are 'places' in that they are not just a point in the universe, but also and irreducibly: (1) the material stuff agglomerated there, both natural and human-built; and (2) cultural interpretations and narrations (more or less explicit) that give meaning to the spot" (Gieryn 2006: 29n3). For contemporary science, two kinds of places have come to be associated with this sort of credibility: laboratories (Latour and Woolgar 1979; Kleinman 2003) and field-sites (Henke 2008; Kohler 2002). As "centers of calculation" (Latour 1987), the knowledge produced in laboratories and field-sites can also be spatially variegated and delimited. As Henke (2000: 485) observes of agricultural extension research, "if science is not crafted to address the local character of farming places and practices, then growers are unlikely to accept the research-based advice of advisors." In other words, far from being "here and everywhere" (Shapin 1995), some kinds of scientific knowledge only work in local, place-based contexts.

Place- and space-based findings from lab and field studies have important implications for our understanding of ignorance. If knowledge claims are produced and certified in certain places, then we are compelled to consider the ways in which ignorance, irreducibly intertwined with knowledge, also "takes place" in ways that mark it as local too. Scholars find evidence of this in the women's health movement of the 1970s and 80s when women identified and challenged medical sciences' lack of knowledge about female sexuality and reproduction from the local spaces of "their own kitchens or . . . borrowed rooms in schools, churches, and community centers" (Sandra Morgen, quoted in Tuana 2006: 1). By implication, the research hospitals and laboratories of post-war medical science concentrated male power and scientific authority in ways that produced knowledge, to be sure, but also certain types of gendered ignorance, suggesting that Gieryn's "truth-spots" can also operate simultaneously as "ignorance-spots." In a study of sick building syndrome, Michelle Murphy (2006: 9; emphasis added) conceptualizes the place-ness of ignorance as "domains of imperceptibility" where the objects (and subjects) of scientific inquiry are rendered "measurable, quantifiable, assessable, and knowable in some ways *and not others*." She finds that the racialized location of the US Environmental Protection Agency's Washington DC office building contributed to those predominantly white scientists' imperceptions of chemical exposures, even in their own workplace. In *Being Nuclear*, Gabrielle Hecht (2012) shows how globalization reproduces domains of imperceptibility in the laboring bodies of African miners and other invisible "others" implicated in the global production and international trade in uranium. In all three studies, ignorance is produced *in situ* as a specific function of scientific and technological work occurring in particular kinds of places.

Another way that ignorance attaches to place is through spatial processes of geographical exclusion: some places do not attract the attention of science, resulting in the non-production of knowledge about those places. We see this most clearly in the way that racist segregation policies have historically conditioned expert constructions of race and indigenous or non-white cultures (Mills 2007). Ignorance-by-exclusion gains spatial dimensions that can encompass entire regions or nations. Historical studies of colonialist science show how indigenous knowledge practices have been lost (e.g. Schiebinger 2008). In other examples, local knowledge is ignored by science, as in Wynne's (1996) classic study of Cumbrian (UK) sheep irradiated by nuclear fallout from Chernobyl. In the latter case, scientists' unwillingness to consider the nature of local grazing customs (place) or the variegated topography of the grazing lands (space) resulted in inaccurate risk assessments that compounded local environmental and economic risk and led to the rapid erosion of scientists' epistemic authority in the region.

Urban spaces that similarly mark the absence of knowledge production are described by Frickel and Vincent (2011) as "spatial knowledge gaps." In their efforts to map the US Environmental Protection Agency's hazard assessment research in New Orleans following Hurricane Katrina, they discovered large contiguous areas within the floodprint where no soil and sediment sampling occurred. Ignorance about contaminated soils, therefore, is spatially distributed in ways that intensify and complicate other forms of urban inequality. The flood itself created a new form of environmental inequality between flooded and not-flooded neighborhoods while, at the same time, "regulatory agencies' efforts to assess risk within the flood zone created a new form of epistemic inequality (sampled vs. not sampled)" (Frickel 2014a).

Efforts to map spatial knowledge gaps are extended in Kinchy and colleagues' (2013) study of stream monitoring across Pennsylvania, a state whose water resources are threatened by shale gas development involving hydraulic fracturing, or "fracking." Investments in water quality monitoring by public agencies vary widely across watersheds in Pennsylvania. Historical decisions not to invest in water quality monitoring in parts of southwest Pennsylvania, for example, have left areas that are heavily impacted by gas development with sparse baseline data and minimal public infrastructure to detect changes. This is likely to obscure the impacts of gas development. While volunteer groups and environmental organizations have sought to fill these knowledge gaps by monitoring streams themselves, these civil society efforts are also unevenly distributed across the gas drilling region (Jalbert et al. 2014; Kinchy, Parks, and Jalbert 2015). The causes of spatial knowledge gaps, therefore, are complex, involving both policy decisions that predate the gas boom and the uneven distribution of organizational resources that facilitate volunteer monitoring.

Efforts to locate ignorance on a map bring the concept into sharper empirical focus, but also reveal under-explored questions about another spatial property of ignorance: "scale." In the remainder of this short chapter, we begin to develop an understanding of ignorance as a scaled phenomenon, drawing widely on studies of environmental science that help us to conceptualize ignorance and scale and the links between them.

Ignorance and the problem of scale

First we address scale in the context of problem definition, making the case that differently scaled questions lead individuals and organizations to pursue certain kinds of knowledge but also channel attention away from other questions/kinds of knowledge (McGoey 2012). Then we turn to the scales at which data are organized, arguing that strategies of aggregation and disaggregation also hide information while making other information visible in particular ways (Croissant 2014).

Scale frames and counter-scale frames

In common parlance, scale refers to the "level" at which particular processes operate, in comparison to other, nested levels of different territorial sizes (e.g. neighborhood versus city, local versus global). In the field of geography, "scale" can mean different things, including the depicted size of a feature on a map relative to its actual size in the world, the size of the unit at which some problem is analyzed, such as at the county or state level, or the size at which human or physical earth structures or processes operate (Montello 2001). For our purposes, it is useful to conceptualize scale as socially constructed and contested. This approach has been widely adopted by human geographers, whose research focus is often on how a particular scale came into being or how political actors, such as social movements, seek to shift decision-making processes from one scale to another. As Jones (1998: 27) sums up, "participants in political disputes deploy arguments about scale discursively, alternately representing their position as global or local to enhance their standing"; in other words, scale is a "representational trope." Kurtz (2003: 894) further advances this notion with the concept of "scale frames," discursive practices in social movement struggles "that construct meaningful (and actionable) linkages between the scale at which a social problem is experienced and the scale(s) at which it could be politically addressed or solved." Counter-scale frames, in turn, are deployed to undermine the scale frames deployed by a social movement.

Scale framing processes are related to ignorance when they affect the kinds of scientific questions that are asked and answered, and what topics or ideas are treated as uninteresting, irrelevant, or remain invisible and thus unacknowledged. Here we build on a line of analysis in human geography that examines "the ways in which scalar narratives, classifications and cognitive schemas constrain or enable certain ways of seeing, thinking and acting" (Moore 2008: 214). Jones (1998: 28) argues that a shift in scale does "not merely shift politics from one level to another. Rather, it recast[s] what [is] true or knowable . . . Certain questions . . . simply become un-askable." A key example in the social sciences, as Moore (2008) notes, is the way that the political project of building a national identity has affected research. Moore (2008: 214) writes,

> national-scale epistemologies do not merely underpin territorially bounded states; they also contribute to the widespread tendency – among both academics and laypeople – to think of "national societies" as homogenous and discrete container-like units . . . which in turn generates static and reductive subjects of study such as "German" or "Thai" society.

This suggests the production of various kinds of ignorance, including unknowns about diversity within a "national society" and the existence of cultural patterns and social groupings that transcend or transect national boundaries.

Social movements and civil society groups often challenge prevailing research approaches and research agenda-setting practices, using counter-scale frames to highlight areas of ignorance or "undone science" (Frickel et al. 2010). For example, the dominant epidemiological paradigm for breast cancer is "characterized by an outlook on disease that emphasizes individual behavioral factors rather than environmental and social factors in disease causation and health promotion" (Brown et al. 2006: 500). Critics of the dominant model have argued that progress toward cancer prevention has been stymied by an overemphasis on processes that occur at the scale of the individual body, at the expense of studies at the various environmental scales at which cancer-causing pollution is produced, as well as the social scales at which "lifestyles" are shaped (Brown et al. 2006). In another example, Phadke (2014) indicates that the national conversation about the benefits of wind power has suffered from the absence of attention to how wind farms affect livelihoods in "geographically concentrated" ways. Protest against wind farms, however, has drawn attention "down" to the local scale, where these industrial installations change landscapes and, in some cases, disrupt everyday life. Thus, social protest can reveal and redress areas of ignorance by pushing the scale of investigation both "up" (as in the environmental breast cancer movement) and "down" (as in the case of wind farms).

The conflict over "fracking" for shale gas also illustrates how scale framing produces knowledge/ignorance. Among energy policy experts, natural gas has typically been considered in relation to national and global debates about climate change and greenhouse gas emissions. For instance, a multidisciplinary report published by MIT in 2011 indicated that natural gas could offer a carbon-reducing substitute for coal in many applications and that it would help support wind power generation.[2] Even prominent environmental activists failed, for some time, to ask questions about gas development at anything but the national and climate scales. Bill McKibben (2010: 59), for example, included shale gas development on a list of good news about the climate in his 2010 book, *Eaarth*, since the "new discoveries of natural gas in the United States . . . could help wean us off dirtier coal." A growing anti-fracking movement, however, has reframed shale gas as a localized problem with consequences that are visible at the scale of everyday rural life: drinking water wells, farms, roads, streams, and landscapes. In one notable example, a local chapter of the Sierra Club set about the "long, arduous task of educating" the national organization about why it should abandon its favorable position on gas development.[3] Ultimately, the Sierra Club, like many other environmental organizations, did change position on shale gas, acknowledging that its former support for it had been based, at least in part, on ignorance about its implications at the regional or local scale. The shift in the Sierra Club's position mirrors a broader shift in the public debate about fracking, which now centers on the need for more stringent regulations and better understanding of the ecological and public health impacts of gas development. While there remain many unknowns about those impacts, there is now compelling pressure, largely as a result of increasing grassroots opposition, to reconcile the framing of natural gas as a national and global good with localized framings of fracking as socially and ecologically disruptive (Kinchy 2014).

The dynamics of environmental debates such as those involving fracking, wind power generation or the etiology of breast cancer ultimately center on an ontological question: what is the nature of the matter? The dynamics of scale/counter-scale framing help us understand how scale can render socio-ecological processes politically meaningful, irrelevant, or altogether invisible, and how those meanings can change shift over time. This sort of ontological scaling also has implications for epistemological practice – how scientists collect and organize their evidence.

Organizing ignorance with spatial data

All of the recent hype for "big data" would seem to suggest that more data is better than less. Having more data enhances our ability to produce more knowledge, while having less data creates conditions of ignorance. But ignorance is not only generated from the absence of evidence; it can also emerge from conditions of evidentiary wealth. We can see this most clearly by considering the ways in which ignorance can be produced by aggregating or disaggregating data in ways that mask evidence of existing patterns.

In the Pennsylvania hydraulic fracturing case described earlier, ignorance about the effects of gas development on groundwater can be attributed, in part, to a failure to aggregate well water quality data. Researchers have found it difficult to establish whether polluted groundwater is a consequence of shale gas development (Jackson et al. 2013), in part because there is no centralized repository of well water data for Pennsylvania that would provide a baseline. The US Geological Survey collects groundwater quality data from a few monitoring locations, and state agencies monitor municipal water supplies, but private drinking water wells in rural areas where gas drilling is most intensive are on the whole unregulated and unmonitored. Landowners with private water supplies may pay to have their wells tested, but this remains private knowledge. Gas companies in Pennsylvania routinely take pre-drilling well water samples; however, they maintain that this is private information that cannot be released to the public (or even to research scientists). Furthermore, when groundwater pollution does occur, gas companies typically negotiate legal agreements that provide payments, drinking water deliveries, or water filtration systems to affected well owners but the agreements also come with gag orders that buy well owners' silence. This strategy "keeps data from regulators, policymakers, the news media and health researchers, and makes it difficult to challenge the industry's claim that fracking has never tainted anyone's water" (Efstathiou and Drajem 2013). In sum, while measurements of water quality are being made, the failure to aggregate that data obscures patterns that might appear at a neighborhood or regional scale.

In this context, environmental groups have sought to aggregate data in order to interrogate industry assertions of safety. One organization in Ithaca, NY, has created a database to map results of private well water tests, in anticipation of future drilling in that area. In another example, one website compiles individual reports of harm caused by gas development (not only well water pollution, but also illness, property damage, etc.) into a national database.[4] By aggregating such reports, experiences of harm at the individual scale are connected to the rapid expansion of shale gas production that is occurring at much larger scales above shale gas deposits across the US. In this case, aggregating data about places that are spatially dispersed is tactically used to illustrate the need for deeper investigation and to identify patterns not apparent when problems are treated as isolated, local incidents.

Ignorance about environmental problems can be produced not only by the failure to aggregate observations, but also by aggregating data at an inappropriately large scale. Barbara Allen (2005) shows that data aggregation can mask environmental illness by analyzing data at a scale that obscures fine-grained detail. Allen's analysis focuses on a series of court cases brought against the Louisiana Tumor Registry (LTR) by state medical scientists and environmental activists. Expanded in the late 1980s to document cancer incidence among Louisiana residents across the state, the LTR is charged with organizing medical data in ways that may occlude possible connections between industrial contaminants and public health. While LTR collects detailed cancer data, the data are aggregated by disease etiology into ambiguous categories such as "childhood cancer"; aggregated over time, condensing annual data summarized for public consumption into 5-year blocks; and aggregated geographically by organizing site-specific patient data into eight large multi-parish regions. Because Louisiana's petrochemical industry is concentrated for historical reasons along the Mississippi River (see Allen 2003), lumping different parishes together has meant that the cancer incidence data for "industrial parishes are 'diluted' by non-industrial parishes, making the determination of elevated cancer rates near chemical plants impossible to decide" (Allen 2005: 469). Yet, as Allen reports, scientists' and citizens groups' repeated requests that the data be made publicly available at the zip code level – a scale more meaningful for understanding public health impacts – were repeatedly denied by the LTR, citing difficulties with data retrieval and privacy concerns.

The consequences of this data aggregation strategy are simultaneously tragic and absurd. Aggregation by multi-parish regions makes it impossible for medical researchers and public health officials to study cancer incidence in relation to patients' residential proximity to petrochemical facilities. Yet the same strategy also allows the LTR and chemical industry representatives to over-interpret the absence of a positive relationship between cancer and geography. For example, the LTR's website offers viewers a comparison of state and national data to suggest that living near petrochemical facilities in Louisiana is *less* risky for most cancers nationwide, and is the basis for rejecting environmental activists' "assertion that Louisiana's Industrial Corridor is a 'Cancer Alley'" (Stevens 2004; cited in Allen 2005: 473). More troubling still, the vinyl industry has used the LTR's non-findings to challenge proposed LEED standards that would reward builders who avoided the use of polyvinyl chloride, a common building material manufactured in Louisiana. While a Louisiana appellate judge ruled in 2004 that LTR reorganize its data by cancer type and year, it was not – and still is not – required to disaggregate the data at the zip code level.

Conclusion

Ignorance is an unusually difficult topic to study empirically since, by definition, it exists in a negative sense as an absence or near-absence (Frickel 2014b). Against this challenge, geographical concepts can help render those absences more visible. Like knowledge, ignorance too is tied to places in complex ways that give it local forms and histories; such place-ness can generate epistemic inequalities – domains of imperceptibility or knowledge gaps, for example – that can be mapped across space and measured against areas or regions where knowledge investments are more uniform. And scale also matters – for the rhetorical frames that constitute ignorance as an object of analysis and for the aggregations of data that pattern our understanding of those same objects. In short, there are many ways that geography's conceptual concern with spatial processes can inform studies of ignorance, just as there are many ways that STS scholars can "scale" studies of ignorance by thinking through it at different levels of analysis (Fortun 2009). Here, we have barely scratched the surface. Best get moving. And bring a compass.

Acknowledgment

We thank the editors for helpful suggestions.

Notes

1 Alison Wiley (2008) provides a more studied description of this volume.
2 MIT Energy Initiative (2011) "The Future of Natural Gas: An Interdisciplinary MIT Study," Cambridge: Massachusetts Institute of Technology. Available online at: http://web.mit.edu/mitei/research/studies/natural-gas-2011.shtml. Accessed September 12, 2012.
3 "Fracking: Is National Catching up with the Grassroots?" Available online at: http://newyork2.sierraclub.org/content/fracking-national-catching-grassroots. Accessed July 8, 2013.
4 The "List of the Harmed" contains many reports of well water pollution, among other harms reportedly caused by gas drilling. Available online at: http://www.fractracker.org/2013/03/pacwas-list-of-the-harmed-now-mapped-by-fractracker/.

References

Allen, B. (2003) *Uneasy Alchemy: Citizens and Experts in Louisiana's Chemical Corridor Disputes*, Cambridge, MA: MIT Press.

Allen, B. (2005) "The Problem With Epidemiology Data in Assessing Environmental Health Impacts of Toxic Sites," in M. M. Aral, C. Brebia, M. L. Maslia, and T. Sinks (eds.), *Environmental Exposure and Health*, Billercia, MA: Computational Mechanics Inc., 467–475.

Bertotti, B. (1977) "The Riddles of Gravitation," in R. Duncan and M. Weston-Smith (eds.), *The Encyclopaedia of Ignorance*, New York: Pocket Books, 91–98.

Brown, P., S. McCormick, B. Mayer, S. Zavestoski, R. Morello-Frosch, and L. Senier (2006) "'A Lab of Our Own': Environmental Causation of Breast Cancer and Challenges to the Dominant Epidemiological Paradigm," *Science Technology & Human Values* 31(5): 499–536.

Clarke, C. J. S. (1977) "The Hinterland Between Large and Small," in R. Duncan and M. Weston-Smith (eds.), *The Encyclopaedia of Ignorance*, New York: Pocket Books, 111–118.

Cloud, P. (1977) "The Veils of Gaia," in R. Duncan and M. Weston-Smith (eds), *The Encyclopaedia of Ignorance*, New York: Pocket Books, 387–390.

Croissant, J. L. (2014) "Agnotology: Ignorance and Absence or Towards a Sociology of Things That Aren't There," *Social Epistemology* 28(1): 4–25.

Duncan, R., and M. Weston-Smith (eds.) (1977) *The Encyclopaedia of Ignorance*, New York: Pocket Books.

Efstathiou, J., and M. Drajem (2013) "Drillers Silence U.S. Water Complaints With Sealed Settlements," *The Washington Post*, June 6. Online at: http://washpost.bloomberg.com/Story?docId=1376-MLINWB6JTSEH01-6U0MH3P8FBUDIRILT8R969070D.

Fortun, K. (2009) "Scaling and Visualizing Multi-Sited Ethnography," in M.-A. Falzon (ed.), *Multi-sited Ethnography: Theory, Praxis and Locality in Contemporary Social Research*, Farnham, UK: Ashgate, 73–85.

Frickel, S. (2014a) "Not Here and Everywhere: The Non-Production of Knowledge," in D. L. Kleinman, and K. Moore (eds.), *Routledge Handbook of Science, Technology and Society*, London: Routledge, 263–276.

Frickel, S. (2014b) "Absences: Methodological Note on Nothing, In Particular," *Social Epistemology* 28(1): 86–95.

Frickel, S., S. Gibbon, J. Howard, J. Kempner, G. Ottinger, and D. Hess (2010) "Undone Science: Charting Social Movement and Civil Society Challenges to Research Agenda Setting," *Science, Technology & Human Values* 35(4): 444–473.

Frickel, S., and M. B. Vincent (2011) "Katrina's Contamination: Regulatory Knowledge Gaps in the Making and Unmaking of Environmental Contention," in R. A. Dowty and B. L. Allen (eds.), *Dynamics of Disaster: Lessons in Risk, Response, and Recovery*, London: Earthscan, 11–28.

Gieryn, T. F. (2002) "Three truth-spots," *Journal of the History of the Behavioral Sciences*, 38(2): 113–132.

Gieryn, T. F. (2006) "City as Truth-Spot: Laboratories and Field-Sites in Urban Studies," *Social Studies of Science* 36(1): 5–38.

Goldman, M. J., P. Nadasdy and M. D. Turner (2011) *Knowing Nature: Conversations at the Intersection of Political Ecology and Science Studies*, Chicago: University of Chicago Press.

Harding, S. (2006) "Two Influential Theories of Ignorance and Philosophers' Interests in Ignoring Them," *Hypatia* 21(3): 20–36.

Hecht, G. (2012) *Being Nuclear: Africans and the Global Uranium Trade*, Cambridge, MA: MIT Press.

Henke, C. R. (2000) "Making a Place for Science: The Field Trial," *Social Studies of Science* 30(4): 483–511.

Henke, C. R. (2008) *Cultivating Science, Harvesting Power: Science and Industrial Agriculture in California*, Cambridge, MA: MIT Press.

Henke, C., and T. Gieryn (2008) "Sites of Scientific Practice: The Enduring Importance of Place," in E. J. Hackett, O. Amsterdamska, M. E. Lynch and J. Wajcman (eds.), *The Handbook of Science and Technology Studies*, 3rd edn, Cambridge, MA: The MIT Press, 353–376.

Jackson, R. B., A. Vengosh, T. H. Darrah, N. R. Warner, A. Down, R. J. Poreda, S. G. Osborn, K. Zhao, and J. D. Karr (2013) "Increased Stray Gas Abundance in a Subset of Drinking Water Wells Near Marcellus Shale Gas Extraction," *Proceedings of the National Academy of Sciences of the United States of America* 110(28): 11250–11255.

Jalbert, K., A. J. Kinchy, and S. L. Perry (2014) "Civil Society Research and Marcellus Shale Natural Gas Development: Results of a Survey of Volunteer Water Monitoring Organizations," *Journal of Environmental Studies and Sciences* 4(1): 78–86.

Jones, K. (1998) "Scale as Epistemology," *Political Geography* 17(1): 25–28.

Kinchy, A. (2014) "Political Scale and Conflicts over Knowledge Production: The Case of Unconventional Natural Gas Development," in D. L. Kleinman and K. Moore (eds.), *Routledge Handbook of Science, Technology and Society*, London: Routledge, 246–262.

Kinchy, A., K. Jalbert, and S. Parks (2013) "The Production of Ignorance about the Impacts of Shale Gas Development: A Study of Spatial Knowledge Gaps," Paper presented at the annual meetings of the American Sociological Association, New York, NY, August.

Kinchy, Abby, Sarah Parks, and Kirk Jalbert (2015) "Fractured Knowledge: Mapping the Gaps in Public and Private Water Monitoring Efforts in Areas Affected by Shale Gas Development." *Environment and Planning C: Government & Policy*. Accepted for publication.

Kleinman, D. L. (2003) *Impure Cultures: University Biology and the World of Commerce*, Madison, WI: University of Wisconsin Press.

Kohler, R. E. (2002) *Landscapes and Labscapes: Exploring the Lab-Field Border in Biology*, Chicago: University of Chicago Press.

Kurtz, H. E. (2003) "Scale Frames and Counter-Scale Frames: Constructing the Problem of Environmental Injustice," *Political Geography* 22(8) (November): 887–916.

Latour, B., and S. Woolgar (1979) *Laboratory Life: The Social Construction of Scientific Facts*, Cambridge, MA: Harvard University Press.

Latour, B. (1987) *Science in Action*, Cambridge, MA: Harvard University Press.

Marston, S. A., J. P. Jones and K. Woodward (2005) "Human Geography Without Scale," *Transactions of the Institute of British Geographers* 30(4): 416–432.

McGoey, L. (2012) "The Logic of Strategic Ignorance," *The British Journal of Sociology* 63(3): 553–576.

McKibben, B. (2010) *Eaarth: Making a Life on a Tough New Planet*, New York: Henry Holt and Co.

Mills, C. (2007) "White Ignorance," in S. Sullivan and N. Tuana (eds.), *Race and Epistemologies of Ignorance*, Albany, NY: SUNY Press, 11–38.

Moore, A. (2008) "Rethinking Scale as a Geographical Category: From Analysis to Practice," *Progress in Human Geography* 32(2): 203–225.

Montello, D. R. (2001) "Scale in Geography," in N. J. Smelser and P. D. Baltes (eds.), *International Encyclopedia of the Social and Behavioral Sciences*, Oxford: Pergamon Press, 13501–13504.

Murphy, M. (2006) *Sick Building Syndrome and the Problem of Uncertainty*, Durham, NC: Duke University Press.

Phadke, R. (2014) "Green Energy, Public Engagement and the Politics of Scale," in D. L. Kleinman and K. Moore (eds.), *Routledge Handbook of Science, Technology and Society*, London: Routledge.

Proctor, R. N., and L. Schiebinger (eds.) (2008) *Agnotology: The Making and Unmaking of Ignorance*, Stanford, CA: Stanford University Press.

Rappert, B., and W. K. Bauchspeis (eds.) (2014) "Special Issue: Absences," *Social Epistemology* 28(1).

Schiebinger, L. (2008) "West Indian Abortifacients and the Making of Ignorance," in R. N. Proctor and L. Schiebinger (eds.), *Agnotology: The Making and Unmaking of Ignorance*, Stanford, CA: Stanford University Press, 149–162.

Shapin, S. (1995) "Here and Everywhere: Sociology of Scientific Knowledge," *Annual Review of Sociology* 21: 289–321.

Shapin, S. (1998) "Placing the View from Nowhere: Historical and Sociological Problems in the Location of Science," *Transactions of the Institute of British Geographers* 23(1): 5–12.

Sullivan, S., and N. Tuana (eds.) (2007) *Race and Epistemologies of Ignorance*, Albany, NY: SUNY Press.

Tuana, N. (2006) "The Speculum of Ignorance: The Women's Health Movement and Epistemologies of Ignorance," *Hypatia* 21(3): 1–19.

Tuana, N. (2008) "Coming to Understand: Orgasm and the Epistemology of Ignorance," in R. N. Proctor and L. Schiebinger (eds.), *Agnotology: The Making and Unmaking of Ignorance*, Stanford, CA: Stanford University Press, 108–145.

Wylie, A. (2008) "Mapping Ignorance in Archaeology: The Advantages of Historical Hindsight," in R. N. Proctor and L. Schiebinger (eds.), *Agnotology: The Making and Unmaking of Ignorance*, Stanford, CA: Stanford University Press, 183–205.

Wynne, B. (1996) "May the Sheep Safely Graze? A Reflexive View of the Expert-Lay Knowledge Divide," in S. Lash, B. Szerszynski and B. Wynne (eds.), *Risk, Environment and Modernity*, Thousand Oaks, CA: Sage Publications, 44–83.

19

Ignorance and industry

Agrichemicals and honey bee deaths

Daniel Lee Kleinman and Sainath Suryanarayanan

The manufacture of uncertainty is a central strategy of corporations seeking to advance their interests. Companies may bolster uncertainty in an effort to keep a profitable product on the market or to protect themselves from liability in the case of an ostensibly dangerous good. The stories of companies hiding data, falsifying evidence, or selectively using findings to advance their interests are legend. Tobacco is the classic case of an industry that engaged in an active strategy to generate uncertainty, doubt, and ignorance through advertising, misleading press releases, support for "decoy" research, establishment of research institutes, and funding of supportive research (Proctor 2008).

The story we tell provides a different perspective on the ways in which companies can shape scientific knowledge and, simultaneously, evidence. It is neither a case of corporate manipulation nor of unfunded science (see Frickel et al. 2010; Frickel and Vincent 2007, 2011; Frickel and Edwards 2014; Hess 2007; Oreskes and Conway 2010). We focus on the case of Bayer Corporation, and the role that company has played in shaping the regulation and use of chemicals at the center of the controversy over the spike in honey bee deaths in the United States and elsewhere. In the pages that follow, we focus on three areas where Bayer's actions or positions have had the effect of maintaining uncertainty about the role of their profitable insecticides in contributing to honey bee deaths. Most centrally, Bayer has pointed to established and widely accepted research norms of toxicology to discredit evidence from beekeepers and others that merely *suggests* that neonicotinoids—a relatively new variety of systemic[1] insecticide—*could* contribute to surprisingly large numbers of honey bee deaths. This practice raises the question of what knowledge counts and what it means if some knowledge does not matter. Second, Bayer stresses alternative explanations for the evidence that beekeepers and scientists provide to explain honey bee deaths. This behavior is consistent with the widely accepted norms of science. Finally, Bayer has bolstered uncertainty about the role of its insecticides in threatening honey bees through research collaboration with beekeepers.

In terms of understanding the production of ignorance, the Bayer-honey bee case complicates our thinking about companies and the production of ignorance. When corporations are in the news for their role in ruthlessly defending their products, they are often accused of malfeasance. The companies at issue may have hidden data or falsified it, thereby keeping the public and regulators ignorant of relevant "facts" and the "truth" in the matter at issue.

They flex their corporate muscles, sometimes threatening people and other companies economically, buying people and firms off, and occasionally physically threatening and sometimes harming their opponents. The actions of companies in such cases provide excellent material for popular films and books. Sometimes the companies' actions border on the illegal or are, in fact, criminal, and citizens seeing such cases unfold in the media have little question that the companies at stake have acted immorally. In *Erin Brockovitch* (2000), a company hid evidence that specific chemicals had adverse health effects on community residents. In *The Insider* (1999), a chemist is hounded and threatened by a tobacco company when he makes clear he intends to expose the industry's misrepresentation of the science on the health dangers of smoking.

What makes the Bayer-honey bee saga interesting is not likely to provide grist for popular film. The company's behavior is less likely to prompt moral outrage among consumers than did the behavior of so-called Big Tobacco or the array of chemical companies who engaged in callous disregard for the health of consumers and community residents. Bayer has simply played by the existing rules, stressing the evidentiary norms historically established and widely accepted by academic scientists and the US federal government. This approach has allowed the company to rest its case for keeping its product under question on the market in the absence of evidence and to, thereby, advance its interests (see Hess 2007). There is "evidence" that could justify taking the product under question off the market but that evidence has largely been produced in the form of field data by practicing beekeepers and as laboratory data by bee scientists. Consistent with widely established evidentiary norms of insect toxicology in the United States, Bayer simply argues that the observational and 'anecdotal' data produced by beekeepers is not official, recognized or legitimate knowledge and that the laboratory data produced by scientists is not sufficiently realistic and, therefore, cannot be used as the basis for additional regulation.

While to a certain extent Bayer's power—its capacity—reflects its resources (it would not be able to make its case without money), fundamentally it is the social organization of science that advantages Bayer and allows the company to contribute to the production of ignorance. In describing this organization, we utilize the term *epistemic form*, which we define as the suite of concepts, methods, measures, and interpretations that shape the ways in which actors produce knowledge and ignorance in their professional/intellectual fields of practice (Kleinman and Suryanarayanan 2013; Suryanarayanan and Kleinman 2013). Relying on the established epistemic form allows Bayer to contribute to the production of ignorance by excluding beekeeper-collected data from serious consideration in the debate over honey bee health.

An epidemic of honey bee deaths

Our story begins in the winter of 2004–5, when professional beekeepers from across the United States first noticed that thousands of the honey bee colonies they maintained were inexplicably collapsing. The beekeepers were not finding their bees' bodies near the hives, as is usual when bees are afflicted by common maladies, including viruses, parasitic mites and direct accidental pesticide exposure. Scientists who learned of this epidemic dubbed it Colony Collapse Disorder (CCD).

Commercial honey bees don't just produce the honey we spread on our toast. Honey bees pollinate many of the nut, fruit and vegetable crops that are central to the US agricultural economy. And these crops—including almonds, apples, asparagus, blueberries, broccoli, carrots, cauliflower, celery, cherries, cotton, cranberries, cucumbers, onions, pumpkins, squash, and sunflowers—are pollinated by bees trucked from state to state to do their work. As of 2000, honey bees were estimated to have been responsible for increases in crop yield and quality to the US agricultural market valued at close to $15 billion (Morse and Calderone 2000).

Based on systematic observation of their honey bee colonies, many seasoned professional beekeepers in the US believe that a new generation of systemic insecticides called neonicotinoids play a major role in CCD and other recent incidents of accelerated honey bee losses. Their conclusions are not based on tightly controlled laboratory or field experiments. Instead, they are undertaken in *real time* and *in situ* and reflect actual field conditions. While *informal*—in contrast to the research undertaken by scientists—beekeeper data collection and analysis brings together valuable information about multiple, complex aspects of colony health. One might characterize the epistemic form of beekeepers as non-reductive, attentive to the dynamic, complex, local, and variable environmental conditions that affect honey bee health. But from the perspective of traditional academic entomology, beekeeper research is imprecise. Based on beekeeper research, it is well-nigh impossible to make definitive causal claims. Beekeepers' findings would likely not pass academic peer review, and they are not viewed as adequate justification for taking these systemic pesticides off the market.

One of the academic disciplines at the center of the CCD controversy is toxicology. The epistemic form reflected in the work of insect toxicologists demands that experimental practices be structured to highlight not only plausible connections between neonicotinoids and CCD, but definitive causal relations. This, in turn, requires highly controlled, repeatable experiments, where data can be analyzed using formal quantitative, statistical techniques. Using this approach and investigating chronic exposure to low levels of systemic insecticide in the field (similar to what honey bees might be exposed to), in contrast to the findings of beekeepers, scientists have found little measurable effect (but see Pettis et al. 2012).

The research norms of toxicologists—indeed, their epistemic form—are reflected in the standards required by regulators. Put in place in 1983, so-called Good Laboratory Practice (GLP) specifies standards for how experiments to be used as the basis for federal regulation should be designed, conducted, monitored, and reported (*Nature* 2010). GLP requires tightly controlled experimental designs that precisely isolate factors that may directly contribute to a specific outcome. As a result, adhering to GLP may lead to ignorance about the subtler, long-term and interactive effects of synthetic chemicals on honey bees.

Beyond the commitment to GLP, an historical goal of US agricultural entomologists to kill insects to protect crops means that historically, the EPA has not been seriously interested in the issue that most concerns beekeepers: the cumulative, sub-lethal and interactive effects of pesticides across the honey bee life cycle. Agency tests mandated in the Federal Insecticide, Fungicide and Rodenticide Act rely primarily on "acute toxicity," and adhere to the so-called LD_{50} standard. LD_{50} is the dose that causes death to 50 percent of exposed organisms within 48–96 hours as a result of a single exposure to the individual chemical of interest. LD_{50} is clearly not a reliable measure for assessing sub-lethal and longer-term effects on various stages of a honey bee's life cycle.[2]

Bayer and the production of uncertainty

Big money is at stake in the outcome of the controversy over CCD. Bayer CropScience is the seventh largest pesticide manufacturer and seed company worldwide, controlling approximately 17 percent of the global agrichemical market. The systemic insecticides at the center of the CCD controversy are widely used globally and are some of the company's largest sellers. To date, to preserve its market position Bayer has consistently called for adherence to the research norms common to insect toxicology and has advocated GLP.

Bayer used data from a 2007 field study by Chris Cutler and Cynthia Scott-Dupree—bee scientists at the University of Guelph in Ontario, Canada—as a basis for the company's request for full registration status for its latest neonicotinoid, clothianidin. When some beekeepers, academic scientists and EPA officials questioned the data from this study, Bayer pushed back, indicating that the research at issue was published in the *Journal of Economic Entomology*—"a major peer-reviewed scientific journal"—and undertaken "in accordance with Good Laboratory Practices (GLP) by independent experts", the EPA's own standard (Bayer 2010).

Importantly, given its commitment to consistency with existing established research norms, Bayer could justifiably ignore the concerns of many beekeepers: that the epistemic form Bayer was supporting fails to consider the possible indirect and sub-lethal effects of Bayer's systemic insecticides. What if low levels of newer systemic insecticides by themselves do not cause beehives to collapse, but may do so in interaction with other prevalent pesticides and pathogenic factors progressively across a beehive's lifecycle? We wouldn't know, and there would be little way to find out given established research norms: with academic scientists and the EPA, Bayer gives pride of place to 'control-oriented' (Böschen et al. 2010) field toxicological studies.

In addition to being able to draw on established research norms to support the findings of research that advances the company's interest and dismiss research that does not, established toxicological research norms have guided both the company's own research and the research it supports. In response to concerns about honey bee deaths raised by French beekeepers in the mid-1990s, Bayer scientists undertook a number of laboratory and field studies (reviewed in Maus et al. 2003). Company scientists explored the 'acute' and 'chronic' oral toxicity of the systemic insecticide imidacloprid (a neonicotinoid first commercialized by Bayer) to lethal and sub-lethal dose levels. Scientists fed honey bees sugar solutions spiked with varying levels of the chemical for a period of two to three days (acute) or five to ten days (chronic). This research allowed the company to identify the dosage levels at which half of the exposed group of honey bees died within 2 to 3 days (the LD_{50}) and the level below which 'no observed adverse effects' were discernible in exposed individual bees. This in turn permitted Bayer to set appropriate exposure levels for their chemicals, but did not move discussion closer to understanding the complex causal pathways some beekeepers believe contribute to accelerated honey bee deaths such as the 'mad bee disease' in France and CCD in the US.

Outside the laboratory, Bayer supported a set of semi-field and field studies. Here, Bayer-funded scientists simulated more natural conditions by placing beehives next to crops treated with Gaucho® (an imidacloprid 'seed-coating') under enclosed tents of several meters in length, which ensured that honey bees were only exposed to the experimental treatment. Using this approach, Bayer researchers found no measurable ill effects from exposure to Gaucho®. What is more, scientists found the insecticide level in treated sunflowers far below the no observed adverse effects level. This, in turn, suggested that the levels at which honey bees were exposed to Gaucho® in the field should not prompt worry. Bayer's conclusion: there is no *definitive* evidence of the company's systemic insecticides contributing to elevated levels of honey bee deaths. Effectively, the company had taken a false negative orientation and so could overlook the field studies of beekeepers and multiple laboratory studies of academic scientists, which suggested a different hypothesis: low levels of neonicotinoids cause damage to honey bees through progressive interactions with other ambient pesticides and pathogens. That is, Bayer, following the epistemic form privileged among US academic scientists and the EPA—'control-oriented' field toxicological experiments—decided that they would prefer to incorrectly conclude that their systemic insecticides do not contribute to CCD than to erroneously determine that they do.

In addition to dismissing research by beekeepers and others that is not consistent with the institutionalized epistemic form that guides toxicological research and undertaking its own research and supporting the research of scientists who work within the epistemic form Bayer prefers, the company has used other strategies to discredit the claims of beekeepers and others who disagree with Bayer. Bayer has argued that there are many possible factors that contribute to CCD and that there is no good quality research pointing to the role of systemic insecticides (e.g., Bayer 2014). Indeed, Bayer proposes an alternative to beekeepers' explanation for CCD. The company has argued the primary contributors to CCD are "*Varroa* mites, pathogens, nutritional deficiencies, and beekeeper use of unapproved miticides" (Fischer 2009). The company has noted that "imidacloprid had been in widespread use in US agriculture for more than a decade before" the first reports of CCD began to emerge (Fischer 2009: 3). This, the company suggests, points away from systemic insecticides as contributing to CCD and toward other factors.

Bayer has also argued that honey bee deaths reflect not EPA approved uses of systemic insecticides, but their misuse. The company has asserted that deaths rise when farmers misuse sowing equipment, releasing clouds of Bayer seed coating neonicotinoids into the air and into the paths of flying honey bees. When correctly applied, Bayer's chemicals do not play a role in the incidences of honey bee deaths, the company asserts (Bayer 2014).

A final mechanism that Bayer has used to define the terrain of knowledge and ignorance about CCD has effectively been to coopt beekeepers by recruiting them to participate in collaborative research. A central problem for beekeepers throughout the controversy is that they have lacked the time and resources to undertake independent research that meets Good Laboratory Practice and the array of institutionalized research norms viewed as essential by the EPA. In theory, a collaboration with Bayer could allow beekeepers to meet these standards and examine the hunches their field evidence has pointed to. Unfortunately, but not surprisingly, the collaboration did not work out that way.

Since the patent for imidacloprid, one of Bayer's top-selling neonicotinoid products, had expired, Bayer has promoted a new set of systemic insecticides called the ketoenols, exemplified by spirotetramat (Movento®). The EPA approved Movento® for the US market in 2008, conditional on, among other things, the company collecting data about the toxicity of this chemical to honey bees in the field. In March 2009, Bayer researchers approached a central beekeeper organization to seek the organization's assistance in a field experiment intended to assess the toxic effects of Movento® on honey bee colonies.

Bayer sought to answer two main questions: (1) what are the residues levels of Movento® in the pollen and nectar that honey bees bring back to their hives?; and (2) are brood development and colony survival adversely affected over a "long term" by Movento® exposure? To address these questions, beehives were placed for two weeks in citrus groves that had or had not been sprayed with Movento® during bloom, at the maximum dose application rate allowed for citrus by its label. The experimental beehives, which had been exposed to Movento® in citrus for two weeks, were then trucked out and managed by a beekeeper (who was part of the national beekeepers' trade group) as part of his commercial operation for pollinating various crops across the US. Bayer researchers (not beekeepers) evaluated the study hives monthly for three months, and then did a final assessment about seven months after the study started. Organization beekeepers did not believe that the time period of pesticide exposure or of evaluation was sufficient to address the systemic effects of Movento®.

Beekeepers were centrally concerned about the systemic properties of these 'new' insecticides. That is, they wanted to understand the movement and accumulation of these new insecticides in pollen and nectar over a period of several weeks to several months after application. To address these concerns, they believed Movento® should have been sprayed several weeks *prior* to bloom. However, Bayer determined the methodological boundaries of this study. The experimental design was not, in fact, a product of genuine collaboration. According to one of the beekeepers who participated in the initial discussion with Bayer, the beekeepers' role was limited to one teleconference phone call where they "went over some details of the design", moving and managing bee colonies, and monitoring health.[3] Bayer defined the terrain on which knowledge about Movento® was produced. They sprayed citrus groves *during* bloom for a period of two weeks, which is also when they exposed the study hives. This meant that any residue levels that were found in pollen and nectar were probably from the non-systemic, immediate spray of Movento®, rather than from its longer-term (systemic) effects. Seen in this light, it came as no surprise to beekeepers when Bayer scientists reported that over the 14 days of exposure, sampled nectar, pollen and blossoms had relatively safe levels of Movento® residues.

Bayer researchers and beekeepers participating in the study disagreed about the effects of Movento® on the "long-term survival" of hives. During an initial discussion about research design, Bayer had proposed a 2-month study, while organization beekeepers insisted that hives be assessed for at least a whole year. Bayer ended its assessment of hives after 7 months, at which point they observed no difference in the "long-term" survival of Movento®-treated vs. untreated hives. However, when a participating beekeeper inspected hives at later 9- and 10-month time points, there were many fewer of the Movento®-treated hives alive compared to the control untreated hives. Bayer rejected the beekeepers' interpretations, claiming they were based on spurious control hives that were a result of differential management practices of the beekeepers. Hence, from Bayer's standpoint, a legitimate comparison did not include all the healthy untreated hives managed by participating beekeepers. Excluding these hives, Bayer concluded that Movento®-treated hives were no different than untreated hives. Beekeepers and allied scientists, in turn, pointed out that if, indeed, the healthy untreated colonies were removed, the total number of assessed hives (sample size) would become so low that it would put into doubt the validity of the entire study.

The conflict between Bayer and the beekeepers who assisted with the study reflects their divergent stakes and interests, which shaped their different epistemological orientations, and ultimately the inequality of their epistemic status. The beekeepers were obliged to enter into an asymmetric exchange with Bayer's researchers in a context where the EPA and other dominant actors made it clear that the knowledge the beekeepers constructed on their own—their expertise—was not credible. The dominant epistemic form, upon which the Bayer researchers relied, ignored issues that beekeepers drew attention to, including questions of bio-accumulation and interactions with other environmental factors. At the same time, these GLP toxicological epistemic forms that Bayer researchers constructed were compatible with Movento®'s market expansion. The beekeepers' experientially grounded understanding of what "long-term" (chronic) exposure connoted for a honey bee colony did not conform to Bayer's 2-week-long framing. Bayer researchers questioned the alternative understanding of the beekeepers, arguing that the beekeepers' results were an artifact of their approach to managing hives. In the process, Bayer researchers concluded that not only were the *chronic* effects of Movento® benign for honey bee brood and colony survival, they were so benign that Movento® could be applied on blooming crops, at a time when bees were foraging on treated plants.

Conclusion

What does it mean for corporations to be implicated in the production of ignorance? We know from many high-profile cases that it can involve cover-up, harassment, illegal activity and malfeasance. Companies engage in strategic action. At some level, cases like these, instances that are unambiguously immoral, are easy. As political matters, we can turn to state authorities to right the wrong perpetrated. While sometimes challenging given the close connections between states and corporations and the substantial resources available to large corporations, the law need only be enforced. As researchers, again while not simple, we need only connect hidden dots, working like investigative journalists.

Cases like the one we describe in this chapter are more complicated. Here, Bayer may be acting strategically, but since the virtues of the epistemic form on which it relies is largely taken for granted by academic scientists and government regulators, for the most part, the company need only assert that these norms and practices be adhered to. In this context, Bayer has contributed to the production of ignorance by repeatedly asserting that the knowledge produced by beekeepers is not knowledge at all. Beekeepers have not utilized established epistemic forms in their research and so Bayer need only point to beekeepers' failure to use standardized techniques and measures as reason to dismiss the data collected by beekeepers. Following this logic, we are not really ignorant, since beekeepers have not produced knowledge. Effectively, however, Bayer has heightened uncertainty in this case. Using the tools of the established epistemic form, we do not know that neonicotinoid pesticides *are* contributing to CCD, but equally we do not know that they *are not* involved.

In the United States, this uncertainty has serious regulatory implications for honey bees, beekeepers, and the public. While beekeeper data might justify taking Bayer's chemicals off the market in the interest of protecting honey bees, formally, the data collected by beekeepers in the course of their everyday observations of their colonies is not considered data at all. The Environmental Protection Agency's "sound science" approach to regulation does not permit the use of informal observational data in federal rulemaking (Edwards 2008; EPA official 2009). Beekeepers face a further challenge. Federal regulatory policy is premised on a preference for type II (false negative) over type I (false positive) errors. Consistent with the epistemic form on which Bayer relies to bolster its position in this controversy, this amounts to a willingness to fail to take a product off the market that might be doing harm, rather than restricting the use of a chemical that further research could determine is perfectly safe.

It is common wisdom that knowledge and power are related. By the same token, ignorance and power are also linked. Bayer is empowered in its effort to produce ignorance (or minimally, uncertainty) by the fact that it has the established norms and practices of toxicological science—the institutionalized epistemic form—on its side. But this tool alone would not suffice. The company must have the resources to collect its own data and to hire others to do so, and the resources to impress its position upon other powerful stakeholder-actors in the CCD controversy. Framing questions consistent with the reductionistic underpinnings of the established epistemic form in this case means that the answers that will result from the research undertaken are unlikely to capture the indirect and sub-lethal effects of Bayer's systemic insecticides on honey bees. Ignorance reigns.

Relying on established research norms and practices might very well have been sufficient for Bayer to keep its chemicals on the market. But public relations matter too. And this likely explains the company's inclination to engage in a research collaboration with beekeepers. Confident that the results of these field studies would bolster its position, the company could build good will (and perhaps put some beekeepers at ease). But perhaps Bayer did not expect the beekeepers' response to the results of this collaboration: the experiment was not done correctly, beekeepers contended. If it had been, the results might very well have been different. Interestingly, this position is commonly taken by competing scientists in the midst of research controversy. But while opposing scientists might undertake a retest using different parameters, beekeepers lack the resources to do so. In this context, the research collaboration may not have satisfied all beekeepers, but may have placated some, and, in any case, put in the context of other accepted data, the results of this collaboration serve to bolster Bayer's position.

While Bayer has complied with the law in this case and not violated widely agreed-upon norms of corporate behavior, it is not clear that the actions and policies springing from adherence to established research norms and practices serve the public interest. The demand for certainty of harm prior to regulatory action may not only place beekeepers' livelihoods at risk, but also the honey bees on which we depend for substantial crop pollination. In this context, it may make sense to rethink the dominant epistemic form and the sound science regulatory orientation. Given the environmental risk, erring on the side of caution may be the prudent thing to do (see Magnus 2008; Suryanarayanan and Kleinman 2011).

Acknowledgements

This work is supported by the National Science Foundation (Award numbers 0924346 and 1257175). Daniel Lee Kleinman's work is also supported by the National Research Foundation of Korea (NRF-2010-330-B00169).

Notes

1 Systemic insecticides penetrate, persist and move through plant tissue to provide treated plants an extended duration of protection from 'pest' insects.
2 In the aftermath of the CCD controversy, agency officials are beginning to acknowledge the limitations of the LD_{50} standard, arguably due to pressure from beekeepers and environmental advocacy groups. In collaboration with Bayer CropScience and other agrochemical firms, university scientists, governmental agencies, and non-governmental groups, the EPA is seeking to devise new test protocols that better address the multifactorial effects of various pesticides on honey bees *and* other insect pollinators (e.g., Fischer and Moriarty 2011).
3 Ethnographic field notes of meeting with beekeepers and scientists, December 1, 2009.

References

Bayer (2010) 'Bayer CropScience Responds to Honey Bee Concerns'. Available at: http://westernfarmpress.com/management/honey-bee-concerns-addressed-bayer-cropscience (accessed March 10, 2015).

Bayer (2014) 'Our Commitment to Bee Health'. Available at: https://www.bayercropscience.us/~/media/Bayer%20CropScience/Country-United-States-Internet/Documents/Our%20Commitment/Bee/Our%20Commitment%20to%20Bee%20Health_Ag%20Solutions.ashx (accessed March 10, 2015).

Böschen, S., Kastenhofer, K., Rust, I., Soentgen, J., and Wehling, P. (2010) 'The Political Dynamics of Scientific Non-Knowledge', *Science, Technology, & Human Values* 35 (6): 783–811.

Cutler, C.G., and Scott-Dupree, C.D. (2007) 'Exposure to Clothianidin Seed-Treated Canola Has No Long-Term Impact on Honey Bees', *Journal of Economic Entomology* 100 (3): 765–772.

Edwards, Debra (2008) Director, Office of Pesticide Programs, US Environmental Protection Agency. Letter to the Sierra Club Genetic Engineering Committee, October 10.

EPA Official (2009) Interview with EPA official. October 29.

Fischer, David (2009) 'Response to National Honey Bee Advisory Board Letter on Imidacloprid Registration Review', 5 June. Available at: http://www.regulations.gov/#!documentDetail;D=EPA-HQ-OPP-2008-0844-0115 (accessed February 13, 2014).

Fischer, D., and Moriarty, T. (2011) *Pesticide Risk Assessment for Pollinators: Summary of a SETAC Pellston Workshop* (Pensacola, FL: Society of Environmental Toxicology and Chemistry (SETAC) Press).

Frickel, S., and Edwards, M. (2014) 'Untangling Ignorance in Environmental Risk Assessment', in Soraya Boudia and Nathalie Jas (eds.), *Powerless Science? The Making of the Toxic World in the Twentieth Century* (Oxford and New York: Berghahn Books): 1–29.

Frickel, S., and Vincent, M.B. (2007) 'Katrina, Contamination, and the Unintended Organization of Ignorance', *Technology in Society* 29: 181–188.

Frickel, S., and Vincent, M.B. (2011) 'Katrina's Contamination: Regulatory Knowledge Gaps in the Making and Unmaking of Environmental Contention', in Rachel A. Dowty and Barbara Allen (eds.), *Dynamics of Disaster: Lessons on Risk, Response and Recovery* (Washington, DC: Earthscan): 11–28.

Frickel, S., Gibbon, S., Howard, J., Kempner, J., Ottinger, G., and Hess, D. (2010) 'Undone Science: Charting Social Movement and Civil Society Challenges to Research Agenda Setting', *Science, Technology, & Human Values* 35 (4): 444–473.

Hess, D. (2007) *Alternative Pathways in Science and Industry: Activism, Innovation, and the Environment in an Era of Globalization* (Cambridge, MA: MIT Press).

Kleinman, D.L., and Suryanarayanan, S. (2013) 'Dying Bees and the Social Production of Ignorance', *Science, Technology, and Human Values* 38 (4): 492–517.

Maus, C., Curé, G., and Schmuck, R. (2003) 'Safety of Imidacloprid Seed Dressings to Honey Bees: A Comprehensive Review and Compilation of the Current State of Knowledge', *Bulletin of Insectology* 56 (1): 51–57.

Magnus, D. (2008) 'Risk Management versus the Precautionary Principle: Agnotology as a Strategy in the Debate over Genetically Engineered Organinsms', in Robert N. Proctor and Londa Schiebinger (eds.), *Agnotology: The Making & Unmaking of Ignorance* (Stanford, CA: Stanford University Press): 250–65.

Morse, R.A., and Calderone, N.W. (2000) 'The Value of Honey Bees as Pollinators of U.S. crops in 2000', *Bee Culture* 128: 1–15.

Nature (2010) 'The Weight of Evidence', *Nature* 464 (7292): 1103–1104.

Oreskes, N., and Conway, E.M. (2010) *Merchants of Doubt: How a Handful of Scientists Obscured the Truth on Issues from Tobacco Smoke to Global Warming* (New York: Bloomsbury).

Pettis, J.S., VanEngelsdorp, D., Johnson, J., and Dively, G. (2012) 'Pesticide Exposure in Honey Bees Results in Increased Levels of the Gut Pathogen *Nosema*', *Naturwissenschaften* 99 (2): 153–158.

Proctor, R.N. (2008) 'A Missing Term to Describe the Cultural Production of Ignorance (and Its Study)', in Robert N. Proctor and Londa Schiebinger (eds.), *Agnotology: The Making & Unmaking of Ignorance* (Stanford, CA: Stanford University Press): 1–33.

Suryanarayanan, S., and Kleinman, D.L. (2011) 'Disappearing Bees and Reluctant Regulators', *Issues in Science and Technology* 27 (4): 31–36.

Suryanarayanan, S., and Kleinman, D.L. (2013) 'Be(e)coming Experts: The Controversy of Insecticides in the Honey Bee Colony Collapse Disorder', *Social Studies of Science* 43 (2): 215–240.

20

Doubt, ignorance and trust

On the unwarranted fears raised by the doubt-mongers

Albert Ogien

Introduction

About ignorance *in itself*, there is little to say, as the word only states a matter of fact: knowing something or not knowing something. But ignorance is a concept each use of which implies a particular value judgment. One form of such a judgment derives from the mere existence of rationalized and literate modern societies. In such a context, ignorance can be contrasted with scientific knowledge to elicit a discrediting effect. This is what happens in the current debate about "doubt-mongers" who challenge the reality of the facts established by science concerning, for example, climate change, GMOs or the health effects caused by tobacco or bisphenol A (BPA). This defiance has been dubbed "agnotology," that is the social construction of ignorance through the strategic and systematic expression of suspicion about scientific truths. This debate raises two questions: (1) *does doubt in science foster ignorance*; (2) *does dispelling doubt in science require a proper command of scientific knowledge?* These are the questions I will deal with in this chapter, first by analysing the relationship between doubt and ignorance as understood in relation to science, then by considering whether trust may serve, as often professed, as an antidote to doubt in science and with respect to scientists.

Does doubt foster ignorance?

Let us start from a somewhat rough distinction between the practice of doubt and the strategy of doubt. One can easily assume that the former is a constitutive component of the scientist's ethos. Common sense usually attaches an attitude of rigor and humility to the concept of science. Accordingly, this attitude rests on two principles: (1) results must be constantly subjected to experimental verification; (2) any explanation depends on the present state of scientific knowledge and is always temporary (Chalmers 1987; Granger 1993). In short, epistemological scepticism is held to be an essential feature of scientific activity.[1] Moreover, every scientist knows that the professional environment in which he or she works strives to continuously track and deal with issues of error, fraud, plagiarism or conflict of interests – sometimes resorting to legal avenues to resolve the most difficult cases. In brief, the practice of doubt is an institutional fact since it operates as a golden rule that scientists can decide to infringe upon while knowing that this will not be without risk.

The strategy of doubt is something else. It is an enterprise led by people who intend to contest, out of sheer interest or, sometimes, true despair, the results of a scientific research that jeopardizes economic or ideological interests or disproves an entrenched element of knowledge. Scientists who are associated with such a strategy are relatively few, a fact that must be emphasized, since failure to gather a large number of scientists to deny the validity of scientific data appears to be, in itself, sufficient proof that doubt is exploited to serve a cause which is alien to the work of science. Another proof is semantical in nature. When a strategy of doubt is a real strategy – that is, when it does not amount to a pathological resistance to new data invalidating old habits of thought – it makes use of unfamiliar rhetorical means: inconsistent arguments, all-out disputes centered on ancillary or peripheral matters, plain denigration, focus on any avowed uncertainty, or *ad hominen* accusations (Wilholt 2013). An easy way to discriminate between a strategy of doubt and a scientific controversy is that the former regularly displays a deliberate intention to spurn any potential agreement on controversial issues.

Scientists who are engaged in counteracting such a strategy by using the means of epistemological critique are wasting their time. Other tools need to be used – in particular those devised to nip in the bud the innuendo spread by rumor (Kapferer 2010). Which is what some scientists are already doing when they refuse to debate in the media with those colleagues who object to the results produced by, for example, the Intergovernmental Panel on Climate Change (IPCC). This attitude has even led the more fatigued among them to disregard the charge of dogmatism and censorship that their opponents formulate on behalf of the necessary practice of doubt in science. Another effective method of defusing such rumors is to openly endorse the supposedly discrediting information which they circulate. Thus some scientists loudly and ostensibly proclaim the value of doubt, stating that true science never produces 100 percent accurate results – implying that those who ask for such a degree of certainty are incompetent scientists. A third way to combat a rumor is to sue those who disseminate false news for defamation or intellectual fraud. Taking such steps would certainly invalidate one of the tenets of the strategy of doubt: exploiting the scientific ethos to join in the scientific debate and pervert it from within by systematically refusing to abide by its common rules.

Everyone will agree, I hope, that the practice of doubt differs from the strategy of doubt. Yet some scientists continue to sustain a confusion between them. There are three ways to do so. The first is to fight tooth and nail against claims which are deemed to be absurd. The second is adopted by those scientists engaged in the defence of rationalist thought who are prone to struggle against what they anticipate as a threat: turning citizens into easy prey for obscurantism. The third way of confusing the practice with the strategy of doubt is to assert that only science offers the solutions able to secure a viable future for the human species. This stance is adopted by those scientists who refute a lay person's right to criticize science – even when the disastrous technical developments science has brought about are pointed out. These three attitudes rest on the same category mistake: presenting doubt as a feature which is external to scientific activity – though most scientists know that it is one of its key pillars.

Is trust the antidote to doubt?

One cannot tell whether doubt breeds ignorance or not unless ignorance has been clearly defined. But definitions are context-dependent (Pettit 1991). Hence, in the debate on the validity of scientific knowledge, ignorance mainly refers to the candid adherence of ordinary people to the false truths promoted by the detractors of scientific explanations. Such a definition is confusing, for no one would admit that blind assent to scientific facts is the opposite of ignorance. We unreflectively tend to believe that knowledge is the only remedy to ignorance. But this is not necessarily true. A common conviction asserts that to counteract a strategy of doubt, and win over the public to science, restoring trust in it might suffice. This is dubious, however, since trust is not something one can secure at will.[2] To understand why this is so, let us turn to the ordinary grammar of trust. I will restrict my analysis to two major kinds of usage: trust as a state and trust as an action (Ogien 2006).

Trust as a state

The key property of a state is that it has a certain degree of stability. Accordingly, one can produce a description of its components, explain the conditions of its emergence and predict its ensuing conduct. Such a knowledge enables one to devise methods which pretend to elicit trust or restore it when it is held to be missing or failing, or to sell opinion polls that measure the level of citizens' trust in the political and social institutions or of consumers' trust in firms, products or brands. Though trust is often presented as a statistical reality, its definition remains notably wanting since it can be thought of either as an independent variable (trust is explained by external factors such as beliefs or legitimacy), or as a dependent variable (beliefs or legitimacy are explained by trust). For some researchers (Carlisle et al. 2010), both approaches are erroneous because trust must be seen as an endogenous variable since beliefs and opinions vary together according to the level of "expressed" trust (Blackburn 1998).

Statistical data on trust in science can be dismissed on another ground. One has just to recall that commissioning and publishing a survey on this topic occurs chiefly when a scandal arises (contaminated blood, HIV, asbestos, avian flu, the Chernobyl or Fukushima accidents, large-scale pollution, etc.) or when a question of general interest in which scientific knowledge is involved hits the headlines and gives rise to a political dispute. There is every reason to believe that the emotions raised and staged on these occasions significantly affect the answers given to pollsters. Hence, noticing that the level of trust in science is low when an affair, a fraud or a conflict of interest are disclosed and high in periods when nothing like that occurs cannot be considered as surprising. But in no case do these results measure the relation between ignorance and trust.

Trust as action

Let us turn now to the uses of the word "trust" as action. It generally refers to a commitment, which can be personal or impersonal. Let us start with the former. For Annette Baier (1986), trust is a social relationship in which one party agrees to rely on the willingness (or unwillingness) of the person he or she entrusts to achieve something he or she cares for. Personal trust can therefore be summed up by this formula: A entrusts B to perform a subset of X, and B receives a discretionary power to do so (or not). Engaging in a dynamic relationship of this sort implies solving a number of practical problems: how can one allow certain individuals to take care of things one finds important and why does one avoid doing so with some others; how can one concede to someone else the power to encroach on one's life and possibly cause harm (while being confident that this will not be the case); and how can one exert control over what the entrusted will do to fulfil his or her commitment in one's absence?

As verification procedures about the moral attributes of the person to whom a discretionary power is given cannot last too long in real life, one has to rapidly give up any further inquiry (Williamson 1993; Hardin 2000; Quéré 2006). Hence the idea that entrusting is an action which requires taking two rapid and simultaneous decisions: (1) granting to the entrusted person a limited discretionary power; and (2) suspending the search of any additional information that would reduce uncertainty about the successful completion of the transaction. In this way, trust entails a positive practice of ignorance, as one has to voluntarily accept being vulnerable to others while renouncing control to the person to whom delegation has been given. In other words, to trust is deliberately accepting epistemic asymmetry and its possible consequences (Harré 1999). It is this kind of asymmetry that Russell Hardin explores – but from a different perspective than Baier's.

For Hardin, trust is a rational decision resulting from a calculation that combines two elements: the advantage obtained by an individual relying on someone else and the knowledge that the individual has about the interest the entrusted one has in taking his or her interests to heart. Hence Hardin's instruction: "Trust should not be conceived of from the standpoint of ego's interests but from the standpoint of alter's interests. It is encapsulated into ego's judgment about the interests the entrusted might have to honor that trust" (Hardin 1993: 505). This is the meaning of his "encapsulated interest theory of trust."

How should one apply this theory to science and scientists? In Hardin's thesis, trust necessarily involves direct contact between two human beings. So if a relationship of trust is to be established, two conditions must be met: the reliability of the person to whom the task of doing something is delegated and the certainty one has about the entrusted's reliability. However, these two conditions can never be met in the case of such a remote relationship as the one laymen may entertain with scientists, let alone with science. According to Hardin, there is no reason to think that an ordinary citizen should know whether socially distant people like civil servants or members of any institution do really have his or her interests at heart. It is quite the opposite, for practical as well as for personal reasons. First, the tasks that these agents are ordered to enact are defined by the institution which employs them and are implemented only at the service of its goals; second, these tasks are performed in order to gain an advantage in terms of advancement or promotion. Hardin concludes that the interests these agents abide by are first and foremost their own.

Hardin goes even further and claims that the many "arrangements of trust" (Karpik 1996) set up to control the work of an institution's agents (evaluations, publications, regulations, controversies, etc.) fail to ensure the impartiality and honesty of these professionals or to establish the rationality of their decisions. Ordinary citizens are at best able to assume that these arrangements – when they are aware of them, which is seldom the case – actually do enforce the control function assigned to them. Hardin's conclusion is quite straightforward: those who assert they "trust" institutions – as they do in surveys – pronounce a judgment which only reports a conviction that everything is done to guarantee that science and scientists fulfil their missions appropriately. Thus, social distance ensures that ignorance does not generate doubt.

As Hardin contends, applying the word trust to the impersonal type of relationship that links an individual to a social institution is controversial. This is so because a necessary condition for the establishment of a trust relationship is missing: the party to whom delegation is made must either have full freedom to do what it is committed to do or not. This condition is not met by institutions or artifacts. Any man-made object is created to achieve an end. Only writers of children stories, science fiction and horror novels are able to make believe that these creations can suddenly come to life and decide to act the way they fancy. In the ordinary world, we generally do not attribute such a freedom to a car, a computer, an equation, software, a train or a plane. We simply expect institutions and artifacts to enact the task for which they have been designed and when they fail to do so, we think they are broken or that they no longer function properly. It is only in a metaphorical way that we allow ourselves to attribute to artifacts and institutions a property that we usually reserve for humans: intentionality. And where intentionality is absent, it is simply impossible to speak of trust.

Is it reasonable to ascribe intentionality to science? This is only possible when science is viewed as an institution pursuing a single ambition served by agents who systematically behave according to its prescriptive rules. I wonder whether anyone would defend such a totalitarian view of institutions today. Another difference between personal and impersonal trust is that people are now caught in a society which is by and large structured by scientific activity. They live in a legal and material world defined in many mays by what science and technique impose as useful or mandatory. In short, science is an institution and a power (Barber 1987), and one cannot speak of trust between two parties when one of them stands in a subordinate position to the other. Hence I surmise that confusing epistemic asymmetry with ignorance is another category mistake. To clarify this point, let us turn once again to ordinary language.

The grammatical limits of the criticism of science

The concept of science, as it is generally used in ordinary language, is directly associated to the notion of truth. Therefore, "scientific facts" are antinomian to superstition and obscurantism and oppose the dogmas of religion. This ordinary use is sometimes reinforced by invoking quarrels dating back to the Enlightenment: reason against ignorance as it breeds subservience and alienation. In short, the concept of science contains within itself the permanent reminder of an ideal of rationality and emancipation.

Ordinary uses show that these attributes of science are firmly established in the common lexicon. Few – apart from the militants of organizations that have turned the thwarting of science's authority into a useful rhetorical weapon – contest science's worth and usefulness. On the one hand, because the progress associated with science is entirely obvious to the majority of the inhabitants of the planet; on the other hand, because scientific data are essential to the workings of a multitude of realms of activity in modern societies. And yet, it is also true that science is intricately entangled in the implementation of bio-political decisions or in the pursuit of major economic interests (Habermas 1978). This interweaving may, at times, lead to social protest. But one can contend that these disputes are not an indictment of the ability to use scientific methods to discover and present "scientific truths."

The criticism levelled against certain forms of scientific activity that are clearly serving questionable purposes is far from being an obscurantist or irrational endeavor. A primary aim of such criticism is to question the ways that appeals to scientific authority are used to legitimate often hazardous decisions taken by commercial entities. In this sense, rebuffing these criticisms in the name of science is an overreaction. One should admit instead that the rightful objections people raise against what they see as scientific misuses do not question science or the usefulness of the advances it offers to humanity. In other words, depicting occasioned and justified doubts as an attack against truth and reason amounts to committing a category mistake (Wynne 1992). Wouldn't it be simpler to accept that these criticisms only challenge the appropriateness of a political decision which many informed citizens see as contemptuous of ethical principles or commonly accepted obligations and expectations of democratic life (Wagner 2007)?

Another element of agnotology consists in contending that the dismissal of science is supported by public opinion because people have a poor level of education and training.[3] Many surveys have clearly demonstrated though that the only factor explaining denigration and rejection of science is commitment to a conservative party (Gauchat 2012; Hmielowski et al. 2013). This can hardly come as a surprise. We are aware of what these conservative groups fiercely advocate (creationism, free exploitation of natural resources). Sometimes, a third type of criticism is also heard: it condemns the ravages of progress and champions a halt to economic growth. But even if this third voice denounces the trappings of science, it seldom questions the rigor and utility of science itself since, most of the time, its criticisms are based on scientific data. Thus, claiming that public opinion is largely formatted by reactionary movements' propaganda amounts to committing another category mistake, for ordinary citizens in modern societies do not necessarily share all the prejudices frightened scientists suppose they have about science.

Common sense tends to associate scientific activity with this obscure, repetitive and constantly peer-reviewed work in which self-sacrifice, selflessness and spirit of discovery determine the conduct of those who perform it. And 'science' still refers to an institution which brings together people (who usually wear white coats) working to improve knowledge and technology for the benefit of humankind. The institution and its agents may experience slippages (atomic bomb, pollution, chemical waste, genetic mutations, climate change), but it is accustomed to regularly digest and correct them without its vocation being truly affected.

I contend that no one can seriously believe that doubts distilled by some scientists or industry groups could be a real threat to science. Or that questioning partial results produced in a specific area of research could lead people to think that science and scientists are useless or dangerous. A last category mistake consists in publicly contending that such opportunistic challenges to scientific activity are attacks which may potentially jeopardize the principles of rationality attached to science, the benefits of knowledge and the ideal of emancipation and progress it bears.

Trust in science is not just a matter of opinion that can be cleared up by showing that 63 percent of the population is confident in what scientists do. When conceived of in terms of a relationship between ordinary citizens and the institutions that govern them, trust sums up under a single word a situation in which an expedient balance of power is actually observed. As far as science is concerned, preserving this relationship would require enhancing citizen's control over the technical implementation of scientific research or developing the legal means available to voice their criticisms. It would also depend on their capability to negotiate the limits of the discretionary power granted to scientists to set the pace of progress or to decide the level of impunity to be afforded to those of them who knowingly disseminate false information.

Conclusion

Doubt should not be mistaken for the outcome of propaganda as it is a constitutive feature of scientific activity. Ignorance should not be seen as necessarily inducing irrational outcomes since one may act rationally without knowing that one does so. Trust should not be taken as an antidote to doubt in science simply because our ordinary conception of science cannot be jeopardized by casual (and legitimate) criticisms of some of its spurious or endangering developments.

There is an entrenched belief that people's ignorance cannot but bear fatal consequences – in political, moral or scientific terms. I have given some reasons why these fears are mostly unwarranted. Such a claim should not be brushed aside as naïve. It is founded on an analysis demonstrating that it is useless to think that citizens' opposition to powers and institutions can be fought against simply by campaigns designed to restore trust (in either the government or science). In fact, in a democratic regime the best way to take into consideration people's defiance would be to renounce the temptation to keep citizens away from decisions that concern them. An efficient antidote to the putative effects attributed to people's ignorance would then consist in reducing as much as possible "epistemic injustice."[4] This is a task that could easily be dealt with through handing over exhaustive information to the citizens and organizing as much public debate as possible to allow a larger sharing of responsibility for any decision taken in the name of society's common good.

Notes

1 This epistemological skepticism must be distinguished from Peirce's conception of doubt as starting point for inquiry. See Chauviré (1995) and Meyers (1967).
2 O'Neill (2002) recalls that the more one endeavors to be trusted, the more one elicits defiance.
3 An historical analysis is offered by Bensaude-Vincent (2013). See also Roberts & Reid, 2011.
4 To use the notion introduced by Fricker (2006).

References

Baier, A. (1986) "Trust and Anti-trust", *Ethics*, 96(2): 231–260.

Barber, B. (1987) "Trust in Science", *Minerva*, 25(1/2): 123–134.

Bensaude-Vincent, B. (2013) *L'opinion publique et la science*, Paris, La Découverte.

Blackburn, S. (1998) "Trust, Cooperation and Human Psychology", in V. Braithwaite & M. Levi (eds.), *Trust and Governance*, New York, Russell Sage Foundation.

Carlisle, J. E., Feezell, J. T., Michaud, K., Smith, E. R. & Smith, L. (2010) "The Public's Trust in Scientific Claims Regarding Offshore Oil Drilling", *Public Understanding of Science*, 19(5): 514–527.

Chalmers, A. (1987) *Qu'est-ce que la Science?* Paris, La Découverte.

Chauviré, C. (1995) *Peirce et la signification*, Paris, PUF.

Fricker, M. (2006) *Epistemic Injustice*, Oxford, Oxford University Press.

Gauchat, G. (2012) "Politicization of Science: A Study of Public Trust in the United States 1974 to 2010, *American Sociological Review*, 77(2): 167–187.

Granger, G. G. (1993) *La Science et les sciences*, Paris, PUF (Que sais-je?).

Habermas, J. (1978) *La technique et la science comme idéologie*, Paris, Denoel-Gonthier.

Hmielowski, J., Feldman, L., Myers, T., Leiserowitz, A. & Maibach, E. (2013) "An Attack on Science? Media Use, Trust in Scientists and Perceptions of Global Warming", *Public Understanding of Science* [DOI: 10.1177/0963662513480091].

Hardin, R. (1993) "The Street-Level Epistemology of Trust", *Politics and Society*, 21(4): 505–529.

Hardin, R. (2000) "Conceptions and Explanations of Trust", in D. Gambetta (ed.), *Trust in Society*, New York, Russel Sage Foundation.

Harré, R. (1999) "Trust and Its Surrogates: Psychological Foundations of Political Process", in M. E. Warren (ed.), *Democracy and Trust*, Cambridge, Cambridge University Press.

Kapferer, J. N. (2010) *Rumeurs: le plus vieux média du monde*, Paris, Le Seuil (Points).

Karpik, L. (1996) "Dispositifs de confiance et engagements crédibles", *Sociologie du travail*, 38(4): 527–550.

Meyers, R. G. (1967) "Peirce on Cartesian Doubt", *Transactions of the Charles S. Peirce Society*, 3: 13–23.

Ogien, A. (2006) "Eléments pour une grammaire de la confiance ", in A. Ogien & L. Quéré (éds.), *La confiance et ses moments*, Paris, Economica.

O'Neill, O. (2002) *A Question of Trust*, Cambridge, Cambridge University Press.

Pettit, P. (1991) "Realism and Response-dependence", *Mind*, 100: 587–626.

Quéré, L. (2006) "La confiance comme engagement", in L. Quéré & A. Ogien (éds.),*La confiance et ses moments*, Paris, Economica.

Roberts, M. R. & Reid, G. (2011) "Causal or Spurious? The Relationships of Knowledge and Attitudes to Trust in Science and Technology", *Public Understanding of Science*, 22(5): 624-641.

Wagner, W. (2007) "Vernacular Science Knowledge: Its Role in Everyday Life Communication", *Public Understanding of Science*, 16: 7–22.

Wilholt, T. (2013) "Epistemic Trust in Science", *British Journal for the Philosophy of Science*, 64(2): 233–253.

Williamson, O. E. (1993) "Calculativeness, Trust and Economic Organization", *Journal of Law and Economics*, 36: 453–486.

Wittgenstein, L. (1969) *On Certainty*, Oxford, Blackwell.

Wynne, B. (1992) "Misunderstood Misunderstanding: Social Identities and Public Uptake of Science", *Public Understanding of Science*, 1(3): 281–304.

21

Decision-making under the condition of uncertainty and non-knowledge

The deliberative turn in genetic counselling

Alexander Bogner

For the social sciences, non-knowledge has only recently become a subject of systematic reflection and conceptual work (see Gross 2010; Wehling 2006). Sociologists got interested in the issue when controversies over risk and ecological crises indicated particular limits of scientific knowledge. Consequently, an early debate on non-knowledge developed with close reference to the categories of risk and uncertainty (Collingridge 1980; Funtowicz and Ravetz 1993; Smithson 1985; Wynne 1992).

This aspect is still relevant. To date, conflicts over risk of technologies associated with serious ecological and/or health impacts have been the main subjects stimulating empirical analyses with a focus on non-knowledge. Prominent cases have been agri-biotechnology and mobile phones (Böschen et al. 2010), the BSE crisis (Dressel 2002), or the impairment of ozone layer by CFC (Gareau 2013). Such empirical studies clearly indicated that science and technology cause a number of problems and non-knowledge constitutes a serious challenge for science and society: the classical Enlightenment idea that non-knowledge would, inevitably, give way to new knowledge and therefore contribute to rational problem-solving, to innovation and a better life, is now contested. In the era of technological risk and ecological disaster, non-knowledge is not only seen as a precondition for problem solving – a perspective advanced by Robert Merton (1987) with his notion of 'specified ignorance' – but also as subject to political dispute.

The long-lasting debate about genetically modified organisms (GMOs), particularly, centres on the question of non-knowledge and risk. The argument is not primarily what is morally acceptable but what we know and what we do not know. The central question is: What ecological dangers, as well as dangers to human health, result from the attempt to use genetic engineering to make plants resistant to pests? Are there unforeseeable long-term consequences for the environment arising from an intervention in nature? Is there an unknown risk for protected animals?

The GM conflict is still the paradigmatic case for political conflicts where the question of knowledge and non-knowledge becomes highly influential. In other words, who holds the relevant knowledge and how much non-knowledge can be tolerated in taking a decision. In such conflicts, the reason for and the context of non-knowledge, its extent as well as its consequences, is subject to political and public debate. This is what Wehling (2013, 64) calls the 'politicisation' of non-knowledge.

With a view to genetic diagnosis and prenatal testing, non-knowledge becomes political for other reasons. In this context, the disputes do not focus on how insufficient the knowledge at stake is (like in the struggle over the carcinogenicity of mobile phoning) or who could have had the relevant knowledge to avoid a real or potential disaster (as in the CFC case). Rather, the controversies in the context of predictive genetic diagnosis challenge the basic idea that gaining knowledge always entails an increase in autonomy and a more rational way of decision-making. The case of hereditary breast cancer illustrates this as only few women with a genetically higher risk are taken ill. That means: the knowledge provided by genetic diagnosis often results in new uncertainties, as there is no therapy at present (Lemke 2011), and it establishes new standards of rationality by favouring precautionary action (e.g. mastectomy). In order to avoid unresolvable dilemmas, the emerging international biomedical law tends to emphasise the *right not to know* one's genetic status (Andorno 2004). This mirrors the belief meanwhile widely held that, under certain circumstances, non-knowledge may have a positive function.

In the following I will show, with a view to prenatal diagnosis, that providing scientific information and science-based diagnostics not only results in more rational decisions and a better care, but previously clear-cut boundaries between sick and healthy become blurred, leading to new uncertainties (1). In order to reflexively deal with non-knowledge and uncertainty, the knowledge and the experiences of the women affected supplement expert knowledge (2). Decision-making turns out to be a deliberative process, where the voice and the values of patients tend to gain a constitutive role (3).

Always being 'at risk': From an aged-based to a science-based indication

Obviously, prenatal testing is inspired by the project of Enlightenment taking for granted that an increase of knowledge always leads to an increase of autonomy, control and safety. Essentially, prenatal testing includes examinations and tests relating to the development of the foetus over the course of pregnancy. Ultrasound is the most common form of non-invasive prenatal testing. In addition there are invasive diagnostics, that is, surgical interventions which sample cells from the unborn child and test them, mostly for Down's syndrome (amniocentesis, chorionic villus sampling).

According to this Enlightenment project women should not suffer pregnancy and birth as an inescapable fate; rather, this sensitive phase of life should be better planned and designed with the help of various techniques and prenatal tests. Non-knowledge is considered to keep women from autonomously shaping this phase of life and, therefore, from having a safe and happy pregnancy. However, this project of Enlightenment triggers new uncertainties professionals as well as patients must learn to cope with. This can be illustrated with respect to the new, science-based way of answering the key question to which women undergoing prenatal diagnosis should be offered.

Until a short time ago, the age of the women was the relevant indication for invasive diagnostics. Mostly, these diagnostics aim at detecting trisomies (mostly Down's syndrome). This age-based indication was established following the widely held belief that the risk for giving birth to a disabled child significantly increases from the age of 35 onwards. Today, the age-based indication is considered to be a pragmatic and – with a view to the restricted resources – partly legitimate threshold, but in no case a science-based one. From a human geneticists' point of view, the pragmatic way of selecting women for prenatal testing is simply wrong, because it means defining women under the age of 35 as being 'healthy' and prevents the detection of any genetically impaired foetus. The aged-based indication, in other words, creates the illusion of healthiness for younger women while discriminating older women as being the main source of genetically caused birth defects. The professionals' critique of the aged-based indication is mirrored in the following quote, taken from an in-depth interview I carried out with an eminent gynaecologist at the university hospital in Vienna:[1]

> Until recently, the medical community made it in a very banal way saying: Women older than 35 years are affected by an increased risk of a chromosomal aberration. At stake is not exclusively but predominantly the trisomy 21 (. . .) In this case it has been made relatively simple, but probably featherbrained as it has been said: We make an arbitrary cut off at the age of 35, and all women who are 35 and older are offered a diagnostic method, namely the amniocentesis. The screening simply consisted of the question: How old are you? If you are under 35, you will be screened out as being healthy and if you are older, you will be part of the risk collective. If you are older than 35 years, I will offer you an amniocentesis. This is probably an extremely featherbrained screening insofar as the incidence minimally increases from the age of 35 on, but the number of children affected by trisomy 21 is much higher in the crowd of women under the age of 35 than in the crowd of women older than 35.

Currently, the "featherbrained" prenatal screening based on women's age is gradually replaced by a science-based indication. By scanning the foetus' nuchal translucency by an early ultrasound investigation (around week 10) the risk of the baby having Down's syndrome is identified on an individual level. Indeed, the woman's age is still taken into account, but the risk assessment is informed by the result of the ultrasound detection. More concretely, the nuchal scan revised the statistically determined risk for women of giving birth to an infant with Down's syndrome (about 1 in 350 for 35-year-old women). Possibly, the 35-year-old woman turns out to have a much lower (or higher) risk than determined by statistics alone. By enriching the risk assessment with additional, technoscientific knowledge the character of risk changes: from an abstract key number referring to a sector of the population to an individualised item. However, the risk assessment maintains the form of statistical information. In order to get a definite conclusion over potential birth defects of the foetus the woman has to undergo an invasive diagnostics.

Obviously, overcoming the pragmatic, aged-based indication by a science-based one has serious consequences for the 'medical code' (Luhmann 1990), that is, the professionals' way of differentiating between healthy and sick. Establishing a clear-cut boundary between healthy and sick is an important prerequisite for the medical system as it provides a general 'goal of action' and helps to legitimise the professionals' activities. This boundary becomes blurred with the enforcement of a science-based indication. In the past, all women under the age of 35 were screened out due to their statistically determined risk; they were considered to be 'healthy'. Today, all women are suspected of being at risk. There is no way to be classified as being healthy prior to undergoing the respective tests. By reformulating the differentiation of healthy and sick in scientific-medical terms the suspicion of illness spreads out. Relieving oneself from this suspicion means accepting the offers provided by medicine. In the era of a science-based risk regime there are no definitely ill, but also no really healthy pregnant women – regardless of what their personal feeling really is. There are only low- and high-risk patients, which are equally called to check their personal risk in a scientifically sound way.

To avoid any misunderstandings: By critically analysing the consequences of a science-based indication for the individual experiences of pregnancy, I do not plea to retain the old custom. To maintain the aged-based indication is no alternative. With regard to the issue of this handbook we just have to recognise that prenatal diagnosis is another example of the close interrelation between knowledge and risk. In this case, the scientific progress characterised by new and individualised diagnostics options results in a proliferation of risk.

Lay participation as a way of dealing with non-knowledge and uncertainty

In the context of prenatal diagnosis several questions associated with uncertainty and non-knowledge arise. As we have seen, new methods like the nuchal scan in the first trimester of pregnancy lead to new options and new pressures to make decisions (Wieser 2006). On the basis of a risk assessment providing an underdetermined prognosis of being at risk, women are asked to decide whether they want to have an invasive prenatal test in order to get definite information about the genetic status of their child. As the diagnosis relates to the question of what chromosomal anomalies the child will be affected with, new questions arise such as: How severely will the child be disabled? Will suitable therapies be developed in the future? Will there be a reasonable chance for the child of having a life worth living?

Apparently, disabilities (such as Down's syndrome) discovered by prenatal testing transcend a purely biomedical interpretation. Referring to phenomena usually subsumed under the term 'disability' implies certain challenges for medicine. With regard to 'disabilities', and in contrast to 'diseases', medicine obviously can no longer refer to the kind of objective meaning that would normally result from the close link between expert knowledge (diagnosis) and decision (treatment), and which finds expression in the stable character of the distinctions between healthy and sick or normal and abnormal. In other words, prenatal diagnostics aimed at providing precise knowledge by using invasive methods is burdened with non-knowledge.

How to constructively deal with such non-knowledge in medical practice? From the point of view of sociology of knowledge, I would say that the modern, deliberative ideal of non-directive genetic counselling provides an answer. This new model aims at supporting people in reaching their own decisions, based on their own unique medical and social circumstances. Going beyond the paternalistic model of the 1970s and 80s, the deliberative, non-directive model claims to adequately recognise (as far as possible) patient autonomy and value-neutrality in the counselling process. The counsellor is reduced to a supportive role. He or she provides medical or statistical information to enable well-informed decision-making but refrains from giving recommendations and advice with regard to the experts' value preference or maybe to certain bio-political visions. Even though there is ongoing confusion over what 'non-directive' means, the new model offers a clear vision that contrasts with the old-fashioned, expert-centred model of counselling, departing from the assumption that there is a very close connection or some sort of automatism between expert knowledge and decision-making. The new model implies a communication process primarily shaped by the patients' values and preferences, even if there is a gap between this ambitious ideal and the daily routines, as ethnographic studies have revealed (Bosk 1992).

The deliberative model can be seen as an institutionalised form of giving patients a say in issues of life and death; it mirrors the increased significance attached to value aspects and active peoples' involvement in decision-making. During the deliberation process, professionals and patients implicitly deal with how to draw boundaries between sick and healthy, boundaries which have become blurred in the course of scientific progress. Obviously, drawing these boundaries by referring to expert knowledge alone is not deemed legitimate any more. Even though expert knowledge is considered to provide necessary information, the value preferences of the counselees heavily influence the outcome of this boundary work. The issue at stake, in other words, is considered to be a value issue, which requires actively involving the people concerned as value issues cannot be resolved by expert knowledge alone.

The trend towards a deliberative model indicates that the issue at stake, previously considered to basically be a subject to expert knowledge, is now considered to be a value issue. Otherwise it would not be adequate to assign an active role to the counselees within the counselling process. By the way, this means that the framing of an issue and the way to legitimately deal with it relate to each other: framing issues as value issues reinforce lay participation and vice versa (Bogner 2012). This framing process results from the fact that phenomena taken into account by medicine ('disabilities') are not considered legitimately to be dealt with on the basis of expert knowledge alone. The most common example is Down's syndrome. Even if it is possible to provide a precise diagnosis, there is no well-defined way or legitimate routine of how to deal with this diagnosis *ex ante*.

From the point of view of sociology of knowledge, the rise of the deliberative model of genetic counselling – associated with a sustainable revision of the old-fashioned hierarchy between experts and lay people – is related to new ambiguities and uncertainties resulting from the medical code becoming blurred. Of course, this does not mean that the deliberative model was introduced on the basis of sociological reflection. But whatever has contributed to the implementation of this model: with a view to sociology, it implies a fundamental change of how the boundaries between sick and healthy are drawn in practice; it indicates that value preferences fundamentally shaping decision-making are explicitly recognised; and it shows that lay participation is a way of dealing with uncertainty and non-knowledge in medical practice.

Rethinking the "deliberative turn"

On various occasions, critical scholars have pointed out that in the era of prenatal diagnosis, the cultural meaning and individual experience of pregnancy change fundamentally (Katz Rothman 1993; Lippman 1994). The increasingly technological nature of prenatal care implies the development of new, technoscientific identities (Clarke et al. 2003) shaped for example by risk assessment techniques (Fosket 2004). With a view to the science-based indication and other constructions of risk factors, it becomes obvious that it is impossible not to be at risk. Today, individuals who are aware of their own genetic risk factors may be required to take precautions in managing their lives. This underlines the importance attached to (bio)medical numbers and predictions for the interpretation and management of our self. Instead of (compulsory) state measures to improve the biological quality of the population, the individual is now expected to constantly make efforts to shape his or her genetic 'fate' by means of checks and precautionary measures (Rose 2001).

Obviously, the ongoing technicalisation or biomedicalisation of pregnancy does not result in a regime of risk and surveillance primarily controlled and exercised by experts. Rather, it rests on the Foucauldian 'techniques of the self' (Foucault 1988), in other words, on our preparedness to actively participate in precautionary activities aimed at achieving and maintaining health. This turn towards a new, individualised kind of governing life is mirrored, on the level of concrete decision-making processes, in the 'deliberative turn' as outlined above.

The deliberative turn indicates that in prenatal diagnosis there are a variety of possible decisions and standpoints deemed legitimate. With the medical doctors' role reduced to that of a kind of ally in the decision-making process, the activated patient bears the brunt. Even though expert knowledge still has a constitutive role for the perception and interpretation of the issues at stake, this knowledge is no longer the primary source of legitimising decisions; rather, it serves as a resource for rendering the counselees' decisions reliable. While the paternalistic model of genetic counselling implies that 'one best way' of dealing with the issues of genetic disorder and disability exists, the new model explicitly abstains from that. It presumes that the value preferences of the patients do not have to match those of the professionals. This means in practice that there will be reasons for various conflicts focusing on where the boundaries of the patients' autonomy lie.

With respect to the ongoing debate on non-knowledge, prenatal diagnosis has some implications to be further reflected upon. It shows that assigning a more active role to patients in decision-making may be a way of constructively dealing with uncertainty and non-knowledge. Possibly, this thesis could be generalised with a view to technology policy. Indeed, there is a deliberative turn in technology governance first announced in the context of nanotechnology (Kearnes 2009). As soon as nanotechnology appeared on the agenda, scholars, such as Wilsdon and Willis (2004), argued for upstream engagement. The central idea was to intensify public involvement through a stimulated dialogue much earlier than before. From 2000 on, a series of public engagement events on nanotechnology took place in several countries (Kurath and Gisler 2009).

Many issues regarding innovation, technology and the environment are associated with uncertainty, non-knowledge and long-lasting disagreement. This, among others, will contribute to an increasing tendency towards lay participation and public dialogue events in the years to come. Of course, lay participation is not always welcomed since expert knowledge is sometimes considered to be necessary and sufficient for decision-making. But the current intense efforts to involve lay people, concerned citizens and stakeholders in technology and environmental governance point at the appraisal of knowledge and worldviews shared by a wider audience. Obviously, non-knowledge and uncertainty are considered fundamental issues not to be tackled by increased expert knowledge but by including lay people in decision-making processes. Whether this kind of involvement is more than symbolism remains to be analysed.

Note

1 From 2002 to 2004 I carried out 25 interviews with human geneticists and gynaecologists from university hospitals and research institutes in Austria engaged in prenatal diagnosis. This work was done as part of the research project "Life Science in European Society" supported by the European Commission, DG Research; the Austrian case study was conducted at the Institute of Technology Assessment of the Austrian Academy of Sciences, Vienna.

References

Andorno, Roberto. 2004. The Right Not to Know: An Autonomy Based Approach. *Journal of Medical Ethics* 30: 435–39.

Bogner, Alexander. 2012. The Paradox of Participation Experiments. *Science, Technology, & Human Values* 37: 506–27.

Böschen, Stefan, Karen Kastenhofer, Ina Rust, Jens Soentgen, and Peter Wehling. 2010. Scientific Nonknowledge and Its Political Dynamics: The Cases of Agri-biotechnology and Mobile Phoning. *Science, Technology, & Human Values* 35: 783–811.

Bosk, Charles L. 1992. *All God's Mistakes. Genetic Counseling in a Pediatric Hospital.* Chicago/London: The University of Chicago Press.

Clarke, Adele, Janet K. Shim, Laura Mamo, Jennifer Ruth Fosket, and Jennifer R. Fishman. 2003. Biomedicalization: Technoscientific Transformations of Health, Illness, and U.S. Biomedicine. *American Sociological Review* 68: 161–94.

Collingridge, David. 1980. *The Social Control of Technology*. Milton Keynes: The Open University Press.

Dressel, Kerstin. 2002. *BSE – The New Dimension of Uncertainty: The Cultural Politics of Science and Decision-Making*. Berlin: Sigma.

Fosket, Jennifer. 2004. Constructing "High-Risk Women": The Development and Standardization of a Breast Cancer Risk Assessment Tool. *Science, Technology & Human Values* 29: 291–313.

Foucault, Michel. 1988. Technologies of the Self. In Luther H. Martin, Huck Gutman, and Patrick H. Hutton (Eds.), *Technologies of the Self: A Seminar with Michel Foucault*. Amherst: The University of Massachusetts Press, pp. 16–49.

Funtowicz, Silvio, and Jerome Ravetz. 1993. Science for the Post-Normal Age. *Futures* 25: 739–55.

Gareau, Brian J. 2013. *From Precaution to Profit: Contemporary Challenges to Environmental Protection in the Montreal Protocol*. New Haven and London: Yale University Press.

Gross, Matthias. 2010. *Ignorance and Surprise: Science, Society and Ecological Design*. Cambridge, MA: MIT Press.

Katz-Rothman, Barbara. 1993. *Tentative Pregnancy: How Amniocentesis Changes the Experience of Motherhood*. New York: Norton.

Kearnes, Matthew. 2009. The Time of Science: Deliberation and the "New Governance" of Nanotechnology. In Mario Kaiser, Monika Kurath, Sabine Maasen, and Christoph Rehmann-Sutter (Eds.), *Governing Future Technologies – Nanotechnology and the Rise of an Assessment Regime: Sociology of the Sciences Yearbook, ,Vol. 27*. Dordrecht: Springer, pp. 279–301.

Kurath, Monika, and Priska Gisler. 2009. Informing, Involving or Engaging? Science Communication, in the Ages of Atom-, Bio- and Nanotechnology. *Public Understanding of Science* 18: 559–73.

Lemke, Thomas. 2011. *Biopolitics: An Advanced Introduction*. New York/London: New York University Press.

Lippman, Abby. 1994. Prenatal Genetic Testing and Screening: Constructing Needs and Reinforcing Inequalities. In Angus Clarkec (Ed.), *Genetic Counselling: Practice and Principles*. London: Routledge, pp. 142–86.

Luhmann, Niklas. 1990. Der medizinische Code. In *Soziologische Aufklärung 5: Konstruktivistische Perspektiven*. Opladen: Westdeutscher Verlag, pp. 183–96.

Merton, Robert K. 1987. Three Fragments from a Sociologist's Notebook: Establishing the Phenomenon, Specified Ignorance, and Strategic Research Materials. *Annual Review of Sociology* 13: 1–28.

Rose, Nikolas. 2001. The Politics of Life Itself. *Theory, Culture & Society* 18: 1–30.

Smithson, Michael. 1985. Toward a Social Theory of Ignorance. *Journal for the Theory of Social Behaviour* 15: 151–72.

Wehling, Peter. 2006. *Im Schatten des Wissens? Perspektiven der Soziologie des Nichtwissens*. Konstanz: UVK.

Wehling, Peter. 2013. Die Vielfalt und Ambivalenz des Nicht-Gewussten: Fragestellungen und theoretische Konturen der Soziologie des Nichtwissens. In Dorett Funcke and Claudia Peter (Eds.), *Wissen an der Grenze. Zum Umgang mit Ungewissheit und Unsicherheit in der modernen Medizin*. Frankfurt: Campus, pp. 43–79.

Wieser, Bernhard. 2006. Inescapable Decisions. Implications of New Developments in Prenatal Testing. *Science, Technology & Innovation Studies* 2: 41–56.

Wilsdon, James, and Rebecca Willis. 2004. See-Through Science: Why Public Engagement Needs to Move Upstream. London: Demos.

Wynne, Brian. 1992. Uncertainty and Environmental Learning. Reconceiving Science and Policy in the Preventive Paradigm. *Global Environmental Change* 2: 111–27.

22

Fighting a losing battle?

The right not to know and the dynamics of biomedical knowledge production

Peter Wehling

Introduction

If we follow Michel Foucault's assumption that Western modern societies are pervaded by a "will to knowledge", and given the fact that in recent years these societies have come to increasingly conceive of themselves as "knowledge societies", then a "right not to know", or a "right to ignorance", must appear (at least at first glance) as a strange and vexing thing. Indeed, since this right has gradually emerged during the 1980s in the context of biomedicine, and in particular of genetic medicine, it has never ceased to be questioned in medical, ethical and legal discourse, mainly with regard to its reach and its argumentative foundations (see for an early critique Ost 1984).[1] In addition, the right not to know one's genetic make-up as well as the corresponding social practices are continuously challenged by new scientific and technological developments which promise better health, more autonomy and rationality of choices by providing ever more supposedly useful genetic information. On the other hand, however, this rather fragile and endangered right (some dispute whether it is a "right" at all) is explicitly recognized, protected and rather firmly established in many countries' legislation, as well as supranational agreements regarding genetic medicine and testing (see "Not-knowing as a legal right and social practice" below). Thus, the right not to know can be seen as one of the most important and illuminating cases for studying both social practices of not-knowing and discursive controversies on the respective pros and cons of knowledge and ignorance. Although this right basically refers to the medical field, the debates revolving around it cut across this sphere and constitute one of the most significant arenas in which the wider cultural meanings and political or ethical understandings of knowledge and ignorance, as well as their respective interrelations with autonomy, rationality, responsibility and solidarity, are negotiated.

In what follows, I will briefly summarize how the right not to know emerged during the 1980s and 1990s. Then I will illustrate how this right has been politically and legally recognized and how it corresponds with actual social practices of not wanting to know one's genetic traits. Subsequently, I will exemplarily discuss the discursive and argumentative contestation of the right not to know, mainly referring to an often-cited paper written by British ethicists John Harris and Kirsty Keywood in 2001. Their article is remarkable in that it maintains that a right to ignorance can by no means be justified by appealing to individual (or parental) autonomy since in the authors' view autonomy is essentially based on continously acquiring knowledge in order to be able to make informed choices. Using the example of novel technologies for preconception genetic carrier screening of (potentially all) couples planning to have children, I will then point to the ongoing dynamics of biomedical knowledge production which exerts considerable pressure on the right to ignorance as well as on social practices of not-knowing one's genetic dispositions. In this context, the right to ignorance is frequently countered by claims of a "duty to know" in the name of genetic solidarity and responsibility. Nevertheless, although these are serious challenges to not-knowing, even, and perhaps especially with regard to such new biomedical options and related debates, remaining ignorant continues to be a both legitimate and adequate way of acting.

The peculiarities of genetic knowledge and the emergence of the right not to know

Since the 1980s, and in particular since the 1990s when the Human Genome Project was launched, genetic knowledge became increasingly available and was introduced into medical research and health care. A growing number of widespread diseases such as breast cancer were linked to specific genetic variations (although only a rather small proportion of about 5 to 10 percent of all cases of breast cancer can currently be linked to genetic mutations); at the same time, for many monogenetic diseases such as Huntington's disease (HD) or cystic fibrosis (CF) the responsible genes and mutations were discovered during the 1980s and 90s. This new knowledge created (or seemed to create) a number of new medical options. The most important of these are as follows: *first*, confirming, correcting or refining symptoms-based diagnosis of an illness that has already become manifest, thus possibly improving the success of treatments; *second*, developing new and effective causal therapies based on knowledge of the relevant genes and their "activities"; *third*, testing for disease-related genetic variations in order to identify genetic risks and make predictions about the probability of future diseases affecting the tested persons themselves or their children. Such *predictive testing* can be done preconceptionally in individuals or couples, that is prior to conception and pregnancy, or prenatally in fetuses, or postnatally, mainly in adults.

While the development of effective therapies based on genetic knowledge turned out to be extremely difficult, and up to now has been successful in only a rather small number of cases, it was the first, and even more the third option that advanced the application of genetic knowledge and genetic testing to medicine (Wailoo and Pemberton 2006; Wehling 2011). However, it was also these uses that revealed the peculiarities and ambiguities of genetic knowledge and thus helped establish a seemingly strange and unusual idea: the *right not to know* one's genetic traits and dispositions for certain (future) diseases. Very briefly, the peculiarities of genetic knowledge can be described by the following aspects (see also Vossenkuhl 2013: 93-97).

First, genetic knowledge frequently offers a "medical look into the future" (Kollek and Lemke 2008) by making predictions about future diseases or disease risks of persons who, at the time of being tested, are healthy and "asymptomatic"; thus a new category of people, the so-called "healthy ill" or "presymptomatic ill", are created. Predictions based on genetic knowledge can either be close to deterministic, which means that the respective illness will appear with almost complete certainty (the case of HD), or probabilistic, that is, indicating "merely" a more or less increased risk of developing the disease (as is the case with inherited breast cancer and other multifactorial illnesses). This latter case implies that some "carriers" of the respective gene will become ill whereas others will never do so. In both cases, however, the point in time when symptoms will become manifest is at best only roughly predictable, with the result that affected people may live for years or (in case of late-onset conditions) even decades in fear of a severe illness.

Second, while these uncertainties of genetic knowledge might already suffice to produce anxiety and unsettledness in affected people, the situation is exacerbated by the fact that in many instances there exists no effective prevention or therapy of the predicted disease. This is the case with HD or Alzheimer's (Lock 2009), but in a way also with breast cancer, since one might question that prophylactic mastectomy is an appropriate means of prevention.

Third, generally speaking, there is no linear and deterministic relation of the genotype to the individual phenotype. This fundamental uncertainty not only includes the above-mentioned question of whether or not a positively tested person will become ill at all, but also leaves open when this will occur and how severe the disease will be. In fact, in quite a few instances the natural course of disease can vary from very mild symptoms to severe or even fatal impairments, although there seems to be no difference in the genetic dispositions.

Fourth, genetic information is transpersonal, which means that genetic knowledge about a person A (for instance, the information that A carries the gene for a severe illness) is relevant also to A's relatives, above all siblings, children and parents. Thus, if A's test results are disclosed to her or his siblings, these might be faced with an information about their own health risks which they did not want to have.[2]

Fifth, genetic knowledge is potentially linked with new forms of discrimination and stigmatization (Lemke 2013); this may include, for instance, discrimination of people with increased risk of future illness (the "healthy ill") on the labor or insurance markets or reservations against carriers of recessively inherited diseases as marriage partners.

Whereas none of these features as such is unique to genetic information, their close connection and interrelation is indeed specific for genetic knowledge.[3] This might be the reason why a "right not to know," although previously discussed also with regard to other kinds of medical information (such as the disclosure that a patient suffers from a lethal disease), has gained particular momentum since the mid-1980s as a reaction to the uncertainties of genetic knowledge. More precisely, the claim for a "right to ignorance" was simultaneously pushed on by emerging debates about the benefits and harms of presymptomatic testing for Huntington's disease and inspired by the philosopher Hans Jonas (1980: 160ff.), who, as early as in the 1970s, was perhaps the first to assert that not-knowing one's genetic "fate" might be a virtue in certain situations and that each individual should have a right to such ignorance. This right is intended to protect individuals (or sometimes also groups) from unwillingly obtaining informations about their genetic constitution. The principle also usually stipulates that people should not be forced or subtly exhorted to acquire such informations, for instance by employers or insurance companies demanding genetic testing prior to offering contracts of labor or insurance agreements.

Not-knowing as a legal right and social practice

As mentioned earlier, the right not to know one's genetic make-up has been acknowledged and legally established in international agreements and conventions as well as in almost all industrialized states' national legislation, albeit with varying scope and intensity in different countries. Despite considerable variation, the general principle – that individuals have a right not to be informed – is widely accepted. The UNESCO Universal Declaration on the Human Genome and Human Rights from 1997, for instance, says, in Article 5(c): "The right of each individual to decide whether or not to be informed of the results of genetic examination and the resulting consequences should be respected." The European Convention on Human Rights and Biomedicine (also adopted in 1997) as well as a number of national laws emphasize quite similarly every person's right to remain ignorant of genetic information about herself or himself. By confirming this right, it is recognized that knowledge about genetic risks can be harmful and therefore threatens to undermine people's control of their lives, in particular when there is no prevention or treatment available.

The right not to know is, however, not merely a somewhat artificial legal construction without any social resonance. Rather, the right reflects a social tendency to avoid health information and, in particular, knowledge about one's genetic dispositions that might impair a sense of individual autonomy. One example is predictive testing for Huntington's disease for persons at familial risk. HD is an autosomal dominant and late-onset fatal disease (with the mean age of onset being 40 years) for which there exists no cure; a person who carries the genetic mutation will develop the disease with almost complete certainty. Predictive testing for HD has been available since the 1980s, yet, as various studies show, the uptake of the test is very low in a number of countries such as Sweden, Canada, England and the USA: in fact, no more than "around 3–21% of at risk persons enter predictive testing programs now that DNA-testing is available worldwide" (Robins-Wahlin 2007: 282). Among the reasons for this reluctance, as expressed by those who declined being tested, are fear of depression, inability to cope with the tests results, and fear of discrimination. Similarly, even for diseases such as breast cancer, where a positive test result typically indicates an increased risk of about 40 to 80 percent of developing the disease, not all women at risk undergo testing.

With regard to these social practices, in a *normative* perspective it is important not to depreciate such reluctance to acquiring genetic knowledge as a sign of irrationality or individual timidity and weakness of character, thus suggesting that "strong" individuals are able to face and live with the "truth". Instead, it is indispensable to recognize that living with persistent uncertainty (for instance, about whether or not one carries the "gene for Huntington") is no less demanding and no less legitimate than being tested in order to have certainty, for good or bad. What is most important from an *analytical* perspective is to adopt a strict "symmetry principle" when it comes to examining people's reasons and motivations for being or not being tested. Similarly to David Bloor's (1976) well-known symmetry principle in the sociology of scientific knowledge, one must explain the will to know by the same class of reasons as the will not to know. To put it differently, it would be deeply flawed to tacitly assume that seeking knowledge is the normal and natural case which does not require further examination, while refusing to know is conceived as an anomaly, a deviation from the norm that must be explained by specific, additional factors such as lack of psychic strength or irrationality on the part of those who refuse to be tested.[4]

Discursive contestations: ignorance and autonomy

Given the deeply rooted institutional and cultural commitment of Western societies to the production and implementation of (scientific) knowledge, it is hardly surprising that the proclaimed right not to know has been subject to criticism right from the outset. However, even most opponents do not entirely deny that there might be situations where it seems to be better not to know than to know. Yet many critics claim that not-knowing cannot be conceived of as a "right", as well as that the will to remain ignorant cannot be justified by appealing to autonomy. In this section, I will argue against these objections, although I do not think that not wanting to know one's genetic make-up must necessarily be based on individual autonomy, since autonomy of the supposedly free, independent and rational individual is itself anything but an unambiguous concept. However, as long as opponents maintain that exclusively the "right to know" is rooted in autonomy, it is important to make clear that (in the field of genetic medicine and elsewhere) not-knowing is not an inferior phenomenon, but instead an in principle equally legitimate and autonomous social practice as is striving for knowledge. In addition, as I will illustrate in the following paragraphs, those who hold ignorance to be entirely incompatible with autonomy tacitly presuppose a prescriptive and biased understanding of individual autonomy.[5]

In their above-mentioned paper "Ignorance, information and autonomy", Harris and Keywood argue that there is no such thing as "a moral right to remain in ignorance" (2001: 432) and they substantiate this statement by claiming that "(i)gnorance of crucial information is inimical to autonomy" in a very fundamental way. In their words, "where the individual is ignorant of information that bears upon rational life choices, she is not in a position to be self-governing" (ibid.: 421). According to these authors, wishing to *not* be informed about certain facts necessarily undermines autonomy and cannot be justified in the name of autonomy.[6] Moreover, in a way that is almost cynical to those who are at genetic risk of HD and struggle with the question of whether or not they should undergo predictive testing, Harris and Keywood extend their argument to acquiring knowledge about the point in time of one's own death: "If I lack information, for example about how long my life is likely to continue I cannot make rational plans for the rest of my life" (ibid.: 421). According to such a curious argument, almost nobody could make any rational plans in their lives since, except for cases of severe and fatal illness, no one knows in advance when they will die. Apart from this, quite the opposite of Harris and Keywood's claim seems to be true. That is to say, a person who knows that her life will end in one or two years will hardly be able to make rational, let alone autonomous decisions, but is possibly more inclined to feel incapacitated. The tacitly normative model of autonomy which is underlying Harris and Keywood's considerations is that of the idealized consumer who ostensibly is able to act more rationally and autonomously in markets the more information she has about prices, varieties and qualities of products and options.

However, at one point in their paper (when they try to explain why suicide is consistent with their idea of autonomy) Harris and Keywood (2001: 420) themselves admit that "Autonomy is not simply the exercise of choice but of control – literally self-government". More precisely one could say, following Bortolotti (2013), that autonomy is about "self-authorship" of one's life (within the social relations one lives in as well as within the given external restrictions of self-authorship) rather than about an obligation to be perfectly informed. Seen from this perpective, a person who feels compelled to acquire ever more knowledge and to continously make informed choices can swiftly lose control of her life and thus appears to be far less autonomous than another person who follows her own life plans and decides on her own how much and which genetic information she wants to have. In addition, given the above-mentioned uncertainties and ambiguities of genetic knowledge, it is undisputable that in many cases such knowledge does not at all enable people to make informed, and therefore supposedly rational, choices. If a woman has been told to have a genetic risk of, say, 40 percent of developing breast cancer up to the age of 70, is it then rational or not for her to undergo prophylactic mastectomy at an early stage of her life? Obviously, both decisions can turn out to be "wrong", which highlights that genetic information is far from providing unambiguous grounds for making rational decisions. There is, therefore, no reason to deny that not wanting to have such information may be a rational and autonomous choice as well.

A duty to know? The case of preconception carrier screening

While attempts at fundamentally denying the legitimacy of a right to ignorance have not been fully successful, given the legal confirmation of that right in many countries and international conventions, more serious challenges to practices of not-knowing seem to emerge from new scientific and technological developments in the field of genetic diagnostics and genome sequencing. To the extent that technologies such as "next generation sequencing" or "whole genome sequencing" make it possible to produce huge quantities of seemingly useful information, the right not to know increasingly appears untenable in practice. Simultaneously, since much of this knowledge is held to be relevant for informed reproductive choices (or is even produced with this aim), one can observe in recent years that the right to ignorance is increasingly challenged by appeals to responsibility and solidarity both with one's offspring and with society as a whole (see Chadwick 2009). Frequently, such appeals even result in claiming a "duty to know". While these developments doubtlessly exert enormous pressure on the right to ignorance, choosing not to know continues to be an adeaquate and legitimate way of acting, as I will show in this section. I will draw in particular on the example of preconception screening for carriers of rare, recessively inherited genetic mutations related to diseases such as cystic fibrosis, Tay-Sachs disease, sickle-cell anemia or muscular dystrophies.[7]

In a recently published opinion on the "future of genetic diagnosis", the German national ethics council (Deutscher Ethikrat, DER) raises doubts about the unequivocal legitimacy of the right not to know in biomedicine. The council asks:

> Does the right not to know apply without exceptions, or is there a duty in certain circumstances to inform family members? Even if one conceded to the right not to know a high rank as an individual defensive right, it may possibly reach its limits where serious injuries to the health of others are to be feared. Then, exceptionally, a moral "duty to know" may even arise, that is to say, a duty to have oneself tested and to make it possible for information to be passed on to third parties.
>
> *(Deutscher Ethikrat 2013: 115)*[8]

It remains unclear whether the council extends this ostensible duty to know to preconception carrier testing for rare recessively inherited diseases. However, following the logic of the DER's argument, and given the fact that every human carries on average about three genetic mutations for such diseases, one might come to the conclusion that "serious injuries to the health of others" are to be feared if would-be parents *do not know* whether or not both of them are carriers of the mutation for the same disease. In case they happen to be carriers, each child of the couple would have a 25 percent chance of carrying two disease-related mutations; thus, in the line of the council's argument a "duty to have oneself tested" for carriership might indeed be proclaimed even if there is no indication of specific risk prior to testing. From this point of view, insisting on one's right to remain ignorant of one's genetic dispositions would appear to be simply irrational and irresponsible.

Nevertheless, there are several good reasons to contradict such claims for a moral or even legal duty to know and to point to the virtues of ignorance, even with regard to novel diagnostic tools such as preconception carrier screening. Since I cannot discuss this issue in detail here, I will focus on two important aspects.

First, it is certainly not too far-fetched to assume that a duty to know is likely to turn into a subtle and tacit moral "duty to prevent", not least since having the option to prevent the birth of an affected child is doubtless the ultimate rationale of preconception testing. Against this background, a couple's decision to *not* take preventive measures in spite of a positive test result (or to have a child without using the test) might easily be labelled "irresponsible". However, couples who refuse to be tested or to use preventive technologies must not necessarily act irresponsibly but may follow a different understanding of responsibility such as fully accepting and caring for any child they may have, whether healthy or not (see Raspberry and Skinner 2011). In addition, while the conditions which are tested for are comparable with respect to their "rarity" and recessive inheritance, they differ considerably regarding severity, age of onset, and availability of treatment. Those preconception carrier tests that are currently offered, or announced for the near future, not only include severe diseases which are fatal in early childhood, such as Tay-Sachs disease, but also conditions for which effective treatment is available, like phenylketonuria (PKU) or hemochromatosis, as well as contested illnesses such as certain kinds of deafness. Given this heterogeneity, future parents are likely to have contrasting opinions on which of these diseases should be "prevented" or not. Therefore, an unspoken duty to prevent, which would presumably emerge, turns out to be one-sided and highly questionable. However, one can reasonably assume that conditions such as deafness or PKU will appear to be "worth being prevented" to many couples simply due to the fact that they have been included in the list of conditions which are tested for. In addition, the principles of informed consent and informed choice are seriously challenged and ultimately undermined by the fact that comprehensive genetic counselling prior to testing for hundreds of conditions with often highly variable natural courses will prove to be unrealizable.

Second, even if couples adhere to the idea of prevention, it remains an open question in what way they would react to a positive test result. In this case, apart from ignoring the result, they have several "reproductive options", ranging from adoption or not having children at all to the use of biomedical technologies such as prenatal diagnosis with possible termination of pregnancy, preimplantation genetic diagnosis (PGD), and sperm or egg donation. However, one can easily imagine that for many couples (or at least one part of the couple) none of these technological options is truly attractive, with the likely consequence that they will abstain from having children, as several social science studies have demonstrated (see for instance Kelly 2009; Raspberry and Skinner 2011). From a statistical point of view, this means that three of four couples who will not have children would have had (at least) a first unaffected child in case they had *not known* about their genetic risk as a couple. To put it differently: while genetic knowledge may prevent the birth of one affected child, it may simultaneously "prevent" the birth of three healthy children.

Shifting to a more general societal context, two further ambiguous implications of preconception carrier screening can be anticipated. First, the concept of genetic risk will be generalized and expanded to cases where there is no known risk for a specific disease but only the "risk of having a genetic risk". Thus, while on the one hand preconception carrier screening would certainly ensure that most couples are not carriers of the same disease-related genetic dispositions, it will, on the other hand, result in the extension of "genetic responsibility" to all couples wishing to have children. Second, one should reckon with the fact that genetic responsibility and solidarity will not only be conceived of in terms of preventing children's suffering but also with regard to economic arguments. Again, the German national ethics council may serve as an example when it mentions a social interest in "the reduction of the costs of the treatment of illnesses by avoiding the conception of affected individuals" (DER 2013: 135). Thus, one can reasonably ask whether preconception genetic screening undermines, rather than fosters, social solidarity in that it tends to draw attention to the "avoidable" costs of treatment of those suffering from "preventable" diseases.

Conclusion

The "right to ignorance" in biomedicine is one of the first and most important areas where the idea and experience that knowledge can be harmful and not-knowing, by contrast, may support individual autonomy, has been institutionally and legally acknowledged. Nevertheless, as I have illustrated in the previous two sections, social practices of not wanting to know one's genetic make-up as well as the moral or legal status of the right to ignorance continue to be contested, not least by appealing to a duty to know. However, apart from the fact that such a duty obviously contradicts the otherwise glorified reproductive autonomy of individuals or couples, genetic knowledge often does not deliver what it seems to promise, as the example of preconception carrier testing underscores. Not only does testing for hundreds of conditions undermine the idea of informed consent, it may also end in the undesirable situation that a positive result might make many couples decide to remain childless because the residual "reproductive options" (termination of pregnancy, PGD, etc.) may appear unattractive to them. In addition, they may be discouraged from taking the chance of having an affected child even if effective treatment may be available for the respective disease. This is, of course, not to say that the wish to know one's genetic dispositions is illegitimate or misleading. It is, rather, to emphasize that not-knowing is an equally legitimate and appropriate response.

Notes

1 By arguing against a *right* to refuse information and in favor of a patient's *duty* to be informed in order to act autonomously, David Ost anticipated in the mid-1980s much of the later criticism of the right not to know (see "Discursive contestations: ignorance and autonomy" above).

2 This transpersonal character of genetic knowledge is not only a rationale for establishing an individual right to reject unwanted information, but also one of the most prominent argumentative resources for demands to restrict the reach of the right not to know or even to completely abandon it in favor of a "duty to know" (see "A duty to know? The case of preconception carrier screening" above).

3 Saying this is, however, far from any genetic exceptionalism or essentialism, in the sense that "the genes" determine people's lives or tell the "truth" about them. By contrast, in many instances genetic knowledge is a source of uncertainty rather than certainty, and it differs from other kinds of medical information gradually rather than substantially.

4 High et al. (2012) convincingly criticize this biased view from an anthropological perspective.

5 However, such a concept of autonomy has been continously contested in the "right not to know" debate, see for instance Husted (1997), Häyry and Takala (2001), Andorno (2004), Bortolotti (2013).

6 Remarkably, this alliance of autonomy and knowledge appears to be so strong that even some defenders of genetic ignorance such as Graeme Laurie (1999) are reluctant to justify it by appealing to autonomy, but instead attempt to ground it on a right to privacy. This does not mean, however, that privacy is necessarily a "weaker" argumentative foundation of not-knowing. To the contrary, referring to genetic privacy one may reasonably ask whether there is even a "duty to remain in ignorance" (Brassington 2011) about one's own genetic make-up because, otherwise, knowledge would allow to draw conclusions regarding the genetic dispositions of related persons such as siblings, parents or children, thus violating their genetic privacy.

7 Preconception carrier testing means that future parents are tested before conception and pregnancy in order to determine whether both of them are carriers of the genetic mutation for the same recessively inherited rare condition. While commercial direct-to-consumer testing for about one hundred conditions is already available, in future up to 600 such conditions might be tested in a single and rather inexpensive run (Kingsmore 2012).

8 Similar arguments with regard to preconception genetic testing and screening are made by the British government's former Human Genetics Commission (2011).

References

Andorno, Roberto (2004) The right not to know: an autonomy based approach. *Journal of Medical Ethics* 29: 435–439.

Bloor, David (1976) *Knowledge and Social Imagery*. Chicago/London: University of Chicago Press.

Bortolotti, Lisa (2013) The relative importance of undesirable truths. *Medicine, Health Care and Philosophy* 16: 683–690.

Brassington, Iain (2011) Is there a duty to remain in ignorance? *Theoretical Medicine and Bioethics* 32: 101–115.

Chadwick, Ruth (2009) The right to know and the right not to know – ten years on. In Christoph Rehmann-Sutter/Hansjakob Müller (eds.) *Disclosure Dilemmas: Ethics of Genetic Prognosis after the "Right to Know/Not to Know", Debate.* Farnham, UK/Burlington, VT: Ashgate, 9–19.

Deutscher Ethikrat (DER) (2013) *The Future of Genetic Diagnosis: From Research to Clinical Practice—Opinion.* Berlin: Deutscher Ethikrat.

Harris, John and Keywood, Kirsty (2001) Ignorance, information and autonomy. *Theoretical Medicine* 22: 415–436.

Häyry, Matti and Takala, Tuija (2001) Genetic information, rights, and autonomy. *Theoretical Medicine* 22: 403–414.

High, Casey, Kelly, Ann H. and Mair, Jonathan (eds.) (2012) *The Anthropology of Ignorance: An Ethnographic Approach.* Basingstoke: UK/New York: Palgrave Macmillan.

Human Genetics Commission (2011) Increasing options, informing choice: A report on preconception genetic testing and screening. Available online at: http://f.hypotheses.org/wp-content/blogs.dir/257/files/2011/04/2011.HGC_.-Increasing-options-informing-choice-final1.pdf.

Husted, Jørgen (1997) Autonomy and the right not to know. In Ruth Chadwick, Mairi Levitt and Darren Shickle (eds.) *The Right to Know and the Right Not to Know.* Aldershot, UK: Avebury, 55–68.

Jonas, Hans (1980) Biological engineering – a preview. In Hans Jonas: *Philosophical Essays: From Ancient Creed to Technological Man.* Chicago/London: University of Chicago Press, 141–167 (first published in 1974).

Kelly, Susan (2009) Choosing not to choose: reproductive responses of parents of children with genetic conditions or impairments. *Sociology of Health & Illness* 31: 81–97.

Kingsmore, Stephen (2012) Comprehensive carrier screening and molecular diagnostic testing for recessive childhood diseases. *PLOS Currents, Evidence on Genomic Tests,* 2012 May 2. Edition 1. doi: 10.1371/4f9877ab8ffa9.

Kollek, Regine and Lemke, Thomas (2008) *Der medizinische Blick in die Zukunft: Gesellschaftliche Implikationen prädiktiver Gentests.* Frankfurt/New York: Campus.

Laurie, Graeme T. (1999) In defense of ignorance: genetic information and the right not to know. *European Journal of Health Law* 6: 119–132.

Lemke, Thomas (2013) *Perspectives on Genetic Discrimination.* New York/London: Routledge 2013.

Lock, Margaret (2009) Testing for susceptibility genes: a cautionary tale. In Christoph Rehmann-Sutter/Hansjakob Müller (eds.) *Disclosure Dilemmas: Ethics of Genetic Prognosis after the "Right to Know/Not to Know" Debate.* Farnham, UK/Burlington, VT: Ashgate, 65–83.

Ost, David E. (1984) The "right" not to know. *The Journal of Medicine and Philosophy* 9: 301–312.

Raspberry, Kelly and Skinner, Debra (2011) Enacting genetic responsibility: experiences of mothers who carry the fragile X gene. *Sociology of Health & Illness* 33: 420–433.

Robins-Wahlin, Tarja-Brita (2007) To know or not to know: a review of behaviour and suicidal ideation in preclinical Huntington's disease. *Patient Education and Counseling* 65: 279–287.

Vossenkuhl, Cosima (2013) *Der Schutz genetischer Daten.* Dordrecht: Springer.

Wailoo, Keith and Pemberton, Stephen (2006) *The Troubled Dream of Genetic Medicine.* Baltimore, MD: Johns Hopkins University Press.

Wehling, Peter (2011) The "technoscientization" of medicine and its limits. Technoscientific identities, biosocialities, and rare disease patient organizations. *Poiesis & Praxis: International Journal of Technology Assessment and Ethics of Science* 8: 67–82.

Part IV

Power and ignorance

Oppression, emancipation and shifting subjectivities

23
Global white ignorance

Charles W. Mills

In a 2007 essay, "White Ignorance" (Mills 2007), I set out to map a non-knowing grounded specifically in white racial privilege. I was trying to contribute to the new "social epistemology" in philosophy by introducing the issues of race, white racism, and white racial domination into the debate. These factors have been crucial to the distortion of social cognition over the past few hundred years (i.e., modernity), but have been little discussed in philosophy in general and in epistemology in particular.[1] "White ignorance" was meant to denote an ignorance among whites—an absence of belief, a false belief, a set of false beliefs, a pervasively deforming outlook—that was not contingent but causally linked to their whiteness. "Whiteness" here, of course, has no biological connotations, but is being used in the sense that has become standard within critical whiteness studies, to refer to *people socially categorized as white* within a racialized social system (Painter 2010; Allen 2012). So I am presupposing throughout a social constructionist analysis, for which race is real but a social rather than natural kind (Haslanger 2012).

My discussion in the essay was focused mainly on the United States, but I intended the application of the concept to be much broader. Insofar as the modern world has been created by European colonialism and imperialism, and insofar as racist assumptions/frameworks/norms were central to the theories justifying white Western conquest and domination of that world, we would expect white ignorance to be global (Mills 1997). Modernity is supposed to be illuminated by the Enlightenment, but as numerous books on the Enlightenment have pointed out in recent decades, it was an enterprise cognitively compromised from the start. In the judgment of Dorinda Outram (2005, p. 135): "[The] contradiction between support for supposedly universal rights, and the actual exclusion of large numbers of human beings from the enjoyment of those rights, is central to, and characteristic of Enlightenment thought." The political economy of racial domination required a corresponding cognitive economy that would systematically darken the light of factual and normative inquiry. This chapter sets out—necessarily very schematically, considering our limited space, but as a possible stimulus for further research on the usefulness of the concept—some of the key features of a white ignorance conceived of as global.

Global white ignorance: Space, time, content

First, some clarificatory points. Obviously white ignorance is not best theorized as an aggregate of individual mistaken white beliefs (though a sampling of such beliefs can be dramatically enlightening for bringing home the extent of white miscognition). Rather, it should be seen as a particular optic, a prism of perception and interpretation, a worldview—in the phrase of American sociologist Joe Feagin (2010, p. ix), a "white racial frame" which incorporates multiple elements into a "holistic and gestalt . . . racial construction of reality."

Depending on one's theoretical sympathies, this framing could be conceptualized in the old-fashioned language of Marxism's claims about "ideology," more recent Foucauldian "discourses," Bourdieu's "habitus," or Anglo-American analytic philosophy's apparatus (some of it derived from cognitive psychology) of motivated irrationality, self-deception, implicit bias, hot and cold cognitive distortion, and so forth. But whatever the overarching theoretical scaffold, "whiteness" needs to be playing an appropriate causal role in explaining the generation of mistaken cognitions; it cannot be merely a matter of ignorance among people who are white. The possible causal factors are multiple (and not at all necessarily mutually exclusive): socialization into a racist belief-set or a Eurocentric normative starting-point, inherited culture and tradition, inculcated social amnesia, typically skewed inferential pattern, deficient conceptual apparatus, material group interest, or epistemically disadvantaged social-structural location. But "whiteness" must be operative in the right way in producing, at least tendentially, a particular cognitive orientation to the world, an aprioristic inclination to get certain kinds of things wrong. So the claim is that, absent "whiteness" in one or more of the foregoing senses, or (for subordinated populations of color) absent the socialization into a white worldview,[2] the attainment of veridical cognitions on the particular matter at hand would be, if not certain, at least far more likely.

However, to speak of a "global" white ignorance should not be taken to imply that it is uniform either in space or over time. The European population spreads all over the world as a result of colonialism and conquest, but their social categorization as white is not coextensive with this process. Controversy exists as to when race enters the world as a concept and a social reality,[3] and also indeterminacy about when "whiteness" emerges as a generally accepted racial social identity. In addition, the boundaries of whiteness will not always be drawn in the same way in different countries, nor does the designation of whiteness rule out internal "racial" heterogeneities and hierarchies within the white population itself. At one time, different European races would have been taken to exist—Teutons/Nordics, Alpines, Mediterraneans—which are no longer recognized as such today (Painter 2010, Chapter 15). Some literature has suggested that "inferior" Europeans were not really "white" at all, whether in their home European country or in emigrant destinations like the United States, while other theorists have replied that a hierarchy of "superior" and "inferior" white races is being mistaken for a hierarchy of whites and nonwhites (Ignatiev 1995; Guglielmo 2004).

So various issues are contested and unresolved. Scholarship in the field so far has been dominated by the U.S. experience, with Australia a respectable second (Carey and McLisky 2009). But as (one hopes) critical whiteness studies becomes globally established, presumably more detailed and country-specific accounts will become available that will track the geographical divergences in the boundaries both between whiteness and nonwhiteness and within local whitenesses. Steve Garner's (2007) introduction to the subject, for example, looks at whiteness in the Caribbean and Latin America as well as the United Kingdom. Nonetheless, these uncertainties and lacunae should not be taken to threaten the central claim that over the past few hundred years whites were (and are) in general privileged across the planet, originally saw themselves as the superior race, and that this foundational miscognition necessarily ramified throughout their other perceptions, conceptions, and theorizations, both descriptive and normative, scholarly and popular. Hence the justification for the affirmation of a global white ignorance.

But if there is a periodization and spatialization of whiteness, there also needs to be a periodization and spatialization of ignorance. The nature of white ignorance—what whites characteristically get wrong—changes over time and place. A macro-periodization roughly accurate for the planet as a whole would distinguish the period of several hundred years when racist beliefs (and their implications) were generally taken for granted among the white population from the more recent period (with the classic dividing-line being World War II, the Holocaust, and postwar decolonization) when such beliefs became generally less permissible, at least in Western nations. (This cautionary note is necessary because in many other white-dominated nations today, e.g., in Latin America, unreformed racism among the majority of whites is still alive and well.[4]) In the heyday of white racism and formal European domination of the planet, global white ignorance took the form of the acceptance of the inferiority (whether grounded in theological, cultural, or biological causes, or some combination thereof) of people of color, the normative legitimacy of white rule (colonialism and imperialism; indigenous expropriation, displacement, and killing; racial slavery), and the corollary racialized assumptions and frameworks, blindnesses and indifferences, necessary to render such domination consistent with both asserted fact and proclaimed moral principle. Today by contrast global white ignorance is more likely to take the form of at least a nominal, and sometimes even genuine, acceptance of nonwhite equality (conceived of in biological terms), coupled with prejudicial views along other axes, such as cultural ones, and broadly deracialized conceptions of social causality.

It is not, of course, that old-fashioned racism has ever gone away. Barack Obama's 2008 election, hailed at the time and for some time afterwards as definitive proof of the new "postracial" United States, has instead brought out from the underground a level of oppositional viciousness that has forced even mainstream commentators to concede its racial character. (In February 2014, the mixed-race President of the United States was referred to as a "subhuman mongrel" by Ted Nugent, former rock star, while campaigning for a Republican candidate for governor of Texas.) And even apart from individual blog rantings and the publications of unreconstructed racist fringe groups in Western nations (white-supremacist, Klan, Nazi, skinhead), "scientific" racism continues to have its defenders in respectable quarters. Consider, for example, the bestseller success of *The Bell Curve* (Herrnstein and Murray 1994), or Nobel Laureate James Watson's matter-of-fact 2007 statement that Africans are indeed intellectually inferior to whites (CNN.com/technology 2007).

But such outbursts and declarations are not the norm. In general whites expressing racial sentiments today use a facially neutral language which has to be semantically "decoded," "cultural" racism taking the place of old-fashioned biological racism.[5] Focusing on the United States, but I suggest with broader applicability, Eduardo Bonilla-Silva (2014) describes what he calls "color-blind racism," "racism without racists," in which whites deny any racism, declare their support of non-discriminatory liberal norms and ideals, but simultaneously decry the unwillingness to work, preference for living on welfare, culture of poverty, and/or refusal to assimilate of particular nonwhite groups. The real heart of white ignorance today, whether accompanied by such prejudicial characterizations or not, is the refusal to recognize how the legacy of the past, as well as ongoing practices in the present, continues to handicap people of color now granted nominal juridical and social equality. If classic white ignorance justified white advantage as the legitimate entitlements of the superior race, contemporary white ignorance generally either denies such advantage altogether or attributes it to differential white effort. That a system of illicit racial empowerment and disablement inherited from the past may still be at work, reproducing unfair privilege and handicap at different racial poles through a wide variety of interlocking societal mechanisms, is what is refused credence. To the (limited) extent that racism is still recognized as a social factor, it is individualized and personalized. Thus structural changes to achieve racial justice by correcting this legacy are not required.

Racial erasure

The common element, then, is what could be called racial erasure: the retrospective whiting-out, the whitewashing, of the racial past in order to construct an alternative narrative that severs the present from any legacy of racial domination. Racism as idea and ideology, racism as national and global system, racial atrocity and racial exploitation, are collectively denied or at least causally minimized. Not merely in terms of factual account, but conceptual framework, a fanciful history is constructed whose upshot is the denial or downplaying of the extent of the violence and subordination of the previous epoch of formal Euro-domination, its structural and long-term shaping of systemic white advantage, and an accompanying white "innocence" about the role of racial exploitation in making the world what it is today, particularly its transcontinental distribution of "Northern" wealth and "Southern" poverty, but also its national racial patterns of white-over-nonwhite privileging. If the past few hundred years have been marked by the hegemony of white racist ideology and by global white domination with enduring effects, then the shape of the world needs reconsideration and remaking. A radical rethinking of inherited narratives and frameworks, and the prescription of corresponding measures of corrective racial justice—whether milder measures like affirmative action or more drastic policies like reparations—would seem to be called for. But if they have not, then the current shape of the world can be otherwise explained, and no such dramatic reconceptualization, no such policies of social reconstruction and moral rectification, are necessary.

Erasing white racism as the central modern ideology

To begin with, the centrality to Western thought of racism as an ideology—a system of thought itself—is denied. This erasure of the intellectual past was not the work of uninformed laypersons with a hazy sense of history; it was spearheaded by intellectual elites (just as racist theory had been). Writing two decades ago, Saul Dubow (1995, pp. 1–2) begins his book on scientific racism by observing that:

> A curious form of collective amnesia has, until quite recently, obscured the centrality of intellectual racism in Western thought during the early part of the twentieth century. . . . There were, of course, always people who questioned the truth of [white] race superiority, but these critics were compelled to argue within the established terms of what amounted to a dominant racial consensus. . . . [T]he horrors perpetrated by Nazism have also had the effect of disguising the extent to which similar racial ideas were current in European and American thought in the pre-war generation.

Similarly, Frank Füredi (1998, pp. 1, 9) points out that "Assumptions about the superiority of the white races were rarely contested in Europe or the United States. The domination of the world by the West was seen as proof of white racial superiority. . . . [As late as the 1930s] the principle of racial equality had few intellectual defenders." Only after World War II would this change.

What accounts for what Füredi calls this "volte-face"? The answer is Nazism, the Holocaust, and the postwar emergence as global players of independent nations of color, the (then) Third World caught up in the Cold War struggle between First and Second Worlds for their allegiance. In such a world, racism as official Western norm was no longer politic. Thus, in Léon Poliakov's (1974, p. 5) judgment, the "collective amnesia" cited by Dubow was not at all contingent, but engineered. Poliakov argues that in the postwar period, embarrassed by the death camps, Western intellectuals undertook a sanitization of the record in order to mask the simple truth that Hitler's ideas were built on a long tradition of racial thinking central to Western theory: "A vast chapter of western thought is thus made to disappear by sleight of hand, and this conjuring trick corresponds, on the psychological or psycho-historical level, to the collective suppression of troubling memories and embarrassing truths." The framing of racism as a deviation from the Western norm, the depiction of Nazism as an unprecedented break with Western morality and humanism, inverted the historical reality. Racism *had been* the norm. Racism was the white "common sense" of the age.

Moreover—a further crucial postwar misrepresentation—racism was not to be conceptualized and psychologized as individual "prejudice." Rather, as George Mosse (1985, pp. ix, 231) insisted in his *Toward the Final Solution*, "[racism] was, rather, a fully blown system of thought, an ideology like Conservatism, Liberalism, or Socialism, with its own peculiar structure and mode of discourse," indeed "the most widespread ideology of the time." A case could be made that racism was the meta-ideology that framed other ideologies, in the sense that its assumptions were in broad outline shared among political theorists with seemingly starkly divergent views (conservative, liberal, socialist).

In recent decades, a wave of revisionist scholarship has begun to reconstruct this occluded and denied past of white racial ideology and global domination. Oddly, postcolonial theory itself has not been as central to this undertaking as one would have expected. Alfred López (2005, p. 3) points out that—whether because of its "affinity for linguistic and literary, as opposed to sociological, critique"—"postcolonial studies has generally shied away from explicit discussion of race." More fruitful resources have been political theory, "critical" IR (international relations), the new imperial history, and that small body of scholars in philosophy working on race. From different disciplinary angles, they have sought to expose the complicity of most of the leading Western thinkers, political theorists, and philosophers of the age with racism and Euro-domination.

In political theory, what has come to be called the "imperial turn" has, for the last two decades or so, been charting the relationship between domestic and international political theory. A reconceptualization is under way that locates liberalism as the ideology not merely of (western) Europe but of Empire, with a corresponding shaping of its key terms (Mehta 1999; Pitts 2005; Levy and Young 2011; Losurdo 2011; Hobson 2012). It is no longer as shocking and heretical as it once would have been to declare that most of the leading thinkers of Western modernity—Locke, Hume, Voltaire, Kant, Jefferson, Hegel, Mill, de Tocqueville, and others—had racist views about people of color (Eze 1997; Valls 2005). Yet in mainstream white philosophy there is still resistance to the case that, for example, its leading ethicist, Immanuel Kant, has a far better claim to being the "father of modern racism" than the Comte de Gobineau (Bernasconi 2001).

But these intramural battles aside, the really interesting question now becomes what the implications are for the received view of liberalism. If liberalism—the most important ideology of Western modernity—has, in its dominant incarnations,[6] been a *racist* ideology—a *Herrenvolk* ideology of white rule—then orthodox narratives of its evolution and its "principled" opposition to ascriptive social hierarchy (as in John Locke's famous critique of Sir Robert Filmer) are fundamentally misleading. Hegemonic liberalism was only ever opposed to intra-white *class* ascriptive hierarchy, not *racial* ascriptive hierarchy (nor, of course, intra-white hierarchies of gender). Thus the overcoming of past and present white ignorance would require a systematic excavation of the shaping by racial ideology and racial liberalism of both past theory (the social sciences and humanities; the relevant natural sciences, such as biology and physical anthropology) and practice (law, public policy, government), and an uncompromising investigation of what the purging of its legacy in the contemporary world would require of us, both nationally and internationally.

Denying white supremacy as a global system

Correspondingly white racism needs to be seen not merely in ideational terms, but as a system of domination—white supremacy—which, by the early twentieth century, after the partitioning of Africa, becomes global. Domenico Losurdo (2011, p. 227) emphasizes that "master-race democracy . . . . characterized the overall relations between the West and the colonial world, whether internal or external." That the European empires controlled most of the planet cannot itself, of course, be denied. But in keeping with the postwar sanitization of the past, an acknowledgment that this domination was *racial* and itself constitutive of a transnational *political* system became impermissible. What had once been taken for granted became a tabooed subject.

In a recent important contribution toward a social epistemology more sensitive than the mainstream literature to the realities of social oppression, Miranda Fricker (2007, p. 1) demarcates "testimonial" and "hermeneutical" injustice as two "distinctively epistemic" forms of injustice. Testimonial injustice involves the prejudicial derogation of an epistemic agent's credibility, hermeneutical injustice the absence (because of social domination) of collective interpretive resources to make sense of some section of the world. Applying these concepts to racial domination, we could say that white ignorance is achieved and perpetuated through both varieties working in tandem: a general skepticism about nonwhite cognition and an exclusion from accepted discourse of nonwhite categories and frameworks of analysis. Thus a double handicap will result—people of color will be denied credibility and the alternative viewpoints that could be developed from taking their perspective seriously will be rejected as a priori wrong.

More than a century ago, W. E. B. Du Bois (1996, p. 13) famously indicted the global "color-line" separating "lighter" and "darker" races of men, a demarcation simultaneously normative, political, and economic. But it is only in the last few years that a new body of "critical" perspectives on empire and "critical" IR has begun to catch up with this insight—the perspective of a person of color involved in the transnational anti-racist movements of his time. Historians Marilyn Lake and Henry Reynolds pay tribute to Du Bois in their book title, *Drawing the Global Colour Line: White Men's Countries and the International Challenge of Racial Equality* (2008), as do IR theorists Alexander Anievas, Nivi Manchanda, and Robbie Shilliam in their edited collection, *Race and Racism in International Relations: Confronting the Global Color Line* (2014).

From the perspective of mainstream IR, however, these categories are heretical. The official story of IR recounts a raceless post-World War I "virgin birth at Versailles" narrative, and race makes virtually no appearance in journal articles and books in the field. Yet it was at that same conference that the six "Anglo-Saxon" nations (Britain, Canada, the United States, South Africa, Australia, New Zealand) vetoed the Japanese proposal to introduce a racial equality clause into the League of Nations' Covenant, thereby, so to speak, formally ratifying the normative racial dichotomization in the planet's population already evident in the fact of imperial and colonial rule (Lake and Reynolds 2008, Chapter 12). And in any case, as various critical IR theorists have pointed out, international relations theory in the modern period clearly dates back much earlier, in effect to the bloody birth of Empire.

Indeed, the successful whitewashing of this past is manifest, as emphasized at the start, not merely in particular proscribed belief-sets but in the way competing conceptual frameworks and their related categories now appear odd, perhaps even bizarre, to us. It is hard for us even to grasp them because of the deep cognitive naturalization of Eurocentrism and whiteness in our outlook. The very space and time of the polity—what could be more fundamental?—are being challenged insofar as the nation-state seems the "natural" political unit, located in a sequential temporality of antiquity/medievalism/modernity, with modernity marking the advent of moral egalitarianism in the West. Thus anthropologist Jack Goody (2006) speaks of the "theft of history," and the imposition of a Eurocentric periodization of world events that has become so foundational to our perceptions that we can no longer see its contingency and arbitrariness. But alternative categorizations of both space and time are possible that would bring to cognitive salience the existence of larger supra-national political entities of domination and subordination, which are normatively characterized by the *inequality* of most of the world's population under "modern" Western racial rule.

For white supremacy was global, not merely in the aggregative sense of an assembly of white-dominated polities, but to a significant extent in transnational patterns of cooperation, international legislation, common circulating racist ideologies, and norms of public policy (slave codes, indigenous expropriation, colonial governance) in which white rulers in different nations learned from each other. White popular consciousness was likewise shaped by everyday cultures of imperialism, such as national literatures underwritten by unquestioned white entitlement, whether the American Western that pits courageous white settlers against hostile red fauna, or the imperial adventure novel in which intrepid British and French explorers risk their lives in darkest Africa and Asia. So even when there was inter-white conflict, it took place within a framework of the assumed legitimacy of white rule, and a related conviction that nonwhite rebellion in any of the discrete white systems was a threat to *all* of them. David Brion Davis (2007, pp. 7, 168) points out that the 1791–1804 Haitian Revolution "hovered like a weapon of mass destruction in the minds of slaveholders as late as the American Civil War": "The blacks turned the entire white cosmos upside down when they forced the French to evacuate Saint-Domingue in late 1803." Similarly, a century later, the 1905 Japanese defeat of Russia would send tremors through the transcontinental racial system. Thomas Borstelmann (2001) suggests that one could think of the decolonial movement (and, arguably, the earlier abolitionist movement) as a global civil rights struggle to establish the nonwhite equality denied—contra the orthodox narrative—with the advent of modernity.

Whitewashing white atrocity, eliminating nonwhite contribution

Finally, a reconstructed and racially sanitized past is crucial for the pre-emptive blocking of the question of the dependence of current white wealth and privilege, both nationally and globally, on the historic racial exploitation of the labor, land, and techno-cultural contributions of people of color.

The unquestioning adherence to Feagin's "white racial frame" has been so complete until the last few decades that as recently as 1975, American historian Francis Jennings's book title *The Invasion of America* could still carry an electric shock. Not a science fiction "parallel worlds" scenario (where, say, the Nazis win World War II), it performs the "simple"—but actually cognitively revolutionary—feat of telling the U.S. narrative from the Native American perspective, for whom, of course, invasion is precisely what European settlement actually was. Similarly, Australian historian Henry Reynolds cites a rare 1831 white "correspondent" who observes of Native Australians that "they look upon us as enemies—as invaders—as their oppressors and persecutors—they resist our invasion. . . . What we call their crime is what in a white man we should call patriotism" (Reynolds 2013, p. 12).

But such cognitive inversions were too thoroughly incompatible with the national white Australian story to be admissible; instead, bloodshed was either justified or obfuscated in Social Darwinist fantasies of "dying races": "The iron laws of evolution had predetermined their

[Native Australians'] fate and there was little anyone could do about it." By the early twentieth century, with aboriginal resistance over, the Aborigines were simply written out of official histories: "The national narrative became one of a hard and heroic fight against nature itself rather than one of ruthless spoliation and dispossession" (Reynolds 2013, p. 16). Only in the 1960s did critics begin to indict the "great Australian silence" on this issue, initiating a revisionist historiography (still resisted today by many white Australians) which began to face up to the ubiquitous violence and massacres of the frontier wars against native peoples. Likewise, Argentinians, citizens of the "whitest" country in Latin America, are not educated about the explanation for this whiteness, which is the genocide of the Amerindian population in a series of brutal wars, and the deliberate sending of Afro-Argentines to the frontline as cannon fodder in the country's various late-nineteenth-century conflicts with its neighbors.

In the case of the European powers—as against the white settler states—it is the violence of extra-continental colonial conquest and colonial rule that is disavowed. So pervasive is this phenomenon that it has now actually been given a name: "postcolonial forgetting" (Aldrich 2011, p. 334). Schoolchildren in Belgium do not learn that in the late nineteenth/early twentieth centuries King Leopold II presided over the deaths of ten million people in the Belgian Congo (Hochschild 1999). Italians are largely ignorant of their country's colonial record, especially its atrocities in Libya, Eritrea, and Ethiopia, and its use of mustard gas in the 1920s–1930s wars, in violation of the Geneva Protocol to the Hague Conventions (Ben-Ghiat and Fuller 2005). Far from admitting the tortures and massacres of the Algerian War (Lazreg 2008), the French Government actually passed legislation in 2005 to make it mandatory for teachers to emphasize the "positive role" of French colonial rule, especially in North Africa, though this was later repealed in response to protest. Germans know about the Holocaust, of course, given the importance of postwar de-Nazification (however incomplete in practice), but far fewer are aware of the earlier 1904 *Vernichtungsbefehl* of General von Trotha in German Southwest Africa (now Namibia), and the connections some have drawn between genocidal colonial policy against the Herero and Nama peoples and later Nazi exterminism (Langbehn and Salama 2011).

In his book on the European conquest of what he (somewhat unfortunately) calls "tribal" societies, Mark Cocker (1998, p. 23) observes that in doing his research, nowhere "could [he] locate the raw data to assemble the statistics of mass death inflicted by European invasion upon its tribal subjects." These are numbers that whites simply do not want to know, because unlike the six million Jewish deaths of a defeated and discredited Third Reich that only lasted twelve years, they constitute the unacknowledged necropolis of the Euro-Reich still in existence today, hundreds of years later. Whether through indigenous land expropriation, African slavery, or colonial pillage, "tribal society made a contribution to the wealth of European nations which is of incalculable magnitude" (Cocker 1998, p. 19).

Moreover, it is not merely the centrality of racial exploitation and genocide to the making of the modern world and its racialized configurations of wealth and poverty that is denied, but the intellectual achievements of people of color in general. Dick Teresi (2002, p. 15) starts his book on non-Western science with the admirably frank, but still remarkable, declaration: "I began to write with the purpose of showing that the pursuit of evidence of nonwhite science is a futile endeavor." He was chastened to discover how wrong he was, but the interesting question is why a major American science writer should have had such presuppositions in the first place, and what it says about his education and the broader culture. The pre-Columbian Americas were inhabited by many technologically sophisticated urban civilizations, yet so thoroughly extinguished were they by conquest, disease—and apologist colonial history—that their accomplishments are only now, hundreds of years later, being belatedly recognized and acknowledged by their European conquerors (Mann 2006). Jennings (1976) and Reynolds (2013) both describe how the landscapes of their respective nations, the United States and Australia, were characterized by white settler ideology (and innumerable movies, at least in the U.S.) as "virgin" territories, unhumanized, when in fact they were the result of generations of careful land use and management, so that the Anglo "settlers" were actually walking (literally) in the footsteps of indigenous trail-blazers. Nor is there any general recognition of the contribution that Amerindian agriculture has made to the world supply of staples, such as the globally disseminated potato.

In his *The Eastern Origins of Western Civilisation*, John M. Hobson (2004, pp. 5, 11), great-grandson of the famous J. A. Hobson, makes a case for the crucial role of Islamic, African, and Chinese resources ("technologies, institutions and ideas") for a British Industrial Revolution standardly represented as autarkically generated, in keeping with the general picture of a Europe falsely "seen as autonomous or self-constituting." In sum, by the official story Europe and the Euro-implanted states have created themselves, owing nothing to others. Hobson (2004, p. 322) ends his book with a call, in the name of "global humanity," "[to rediscover] our global-collective past," thereby "[making] possible a better future for all." Achieving a new world will require an admission of the white lies that have been central to the making of our current unjust and unhappy planet. Global justice demands, as a necessary prerequisite, the ending of global white ignorance.

Notes

1 See, for example, the complete non-discussion of race in Goldman and Whitcomb (2011).

2 To the extent that, in particular time periods and societies, whites have cognitive hegemony over people of color, at least some aspects of white ignorance will be shared by nonwhites, so that one would need to distinguish the generative from ascriptive senses of the "whiteness" in white ignorance—how it came about as against who actually has the beliefs.

3 Contrast for example the periodization of Fredrickson (2002) (race and racism as modern) with the periodization of Isaac (2004) (race and racism as going back to the ancient world).

4 See Andrews (2004, pp. 178–80): "The survival into present-day Latin America of anti-black stereotypes and prejudices dating from the colonial period and slavery has been amply documented in survey research throughout the region ... In dealing with employment agencies, many Latin American firms explicitly indicate that they will not accept nonwhite applicants for white-collar positions ... [R]acial barriers, if not actively worsening in the postwar period, at the very least remained very much in place."

5 However, the growing psychological literature on implicit bias has raised the possibility that biological racism may simply have descended to the subconscious level, and that large numbers of whites who sincerely proclaim and believe themselves to be free of old-fashioned biologistic assumptions continue, unawares, to be affected by them.

6 I phrase it this way because some theorists, like Pitts (2005), argue that a racist "imperial liberalism" only becomes the norm after the start of the nineteenth century.

References

Aldrich, R. (2011) The Colonial Past and the Colonial Present. In: Thomas, M. (ed.) *The French Colonial Mind*, Vol. 2, *Violence, Military Encounters, and Colonialism*. Lincoln, NE: University of Nebraska Press.

Allen, T.W. (2012) *The Invention of the White Race* (2 vols.). 2nd ed. New York: Verso.

Andrews, G.R. (2004) *Afro-Latin America, 1800–2000*. New York: Oxford University Press.

Anievas, A., Manchanda, N., and Shilliam, R. (eds.) (2014) *Race and Racism in International Relations: Confronting the Global Color Line*. New York: Routledge.

Ben-Ghiat, R., and Fuller, M. (eds.) (2005) *Italian Colonialism*. New York: Palgrave Macmillan.

Bernasconi, R. (2001) Who Invented the Concept of Race? Kant's Role in the Enlightenment Construction of Race. In: Bernasconi, R. (ed.) *Race*. Malden, MA: Blackwell, pp. 11–36.

Bonilla-Silva, E. (2014) *Racism without Racists: Color-Blind Racism and the Persistence of Racial Inequality in America.* 4th ed. Lanham, MD: Rowman & Littlefield.
Borstelmann, T. (2001) *The Cold War and the Color Line: American Race Relations in the Global Arena.* Cambridge, MA: Harvard University Press.
Carey, J., and McLisky, C. (eds.) (2009) *Creating White Australia.* Sydney: Sydney University Press.
CNN.com/technology (Oct. 18, 2007) Nobel winner in "racist" claim row. (Accessed June 7, 2014).
Cocker, M. (1998) *Rivers of Blood, Rivers of Gold: Europe's Conflict with Tribal Peoples.* London: Jonathan Cape.
Davis, D.B. (2006) *Inhuman Bondage: The Rise and Fall of Slavery in the New World.* New York: Oxford University Press.
Du Bois, W.E.B. (1996) *The Souls of Black Folk.* New York: Penguin.
Dubow, S. (1995) *Scientific Racism in Modern South Africa.* New York: Cambridge University Press.
Eze, E.C. (ed.) (1997) *Race and the Enlightenment: A Reader.* Cambridge, MA: Blackwell.
Feagin, J.R. (2010) *The White Racial Frame: Centuries of Racial Framing and Counter-Framing.* New York: Routledge.
Fredrickson, George M. (2002) *Racism: A Short History.* Princeton, NJ: Princeton University Press.
Fricker, M. (2007) *Epistemic Injustice: Power and the Ethics of Knowing.* New York: Oxford University Press.
Füredi, F. (1998) *The Silent War: Imperialism and the Changing Perception of Race.* New Brunswick, NJ: Rutgers University Press.
Garner, S. (2007) *Whiteness: An Introduction.* New York: Routledge.
Goldman, A.I., and Whitcomb, D. (eds.) (2011) *Social Epistemology: Essential Readings.* New York: Oxford University Press.
Goody, J. (2006) *The Theft of History.* New York: Cambridge University Press.
Guglielmo, T.A. (2004) *White on Arrival: Italians, Race, Color, and Power in Chicago, 1890–1945.* New York: Oxford University Press.
Haslanger, S. (2012) *Resisting Reality: Social Construction and Social Critique.* New York: Oxford University Press.
Herrnstein, R.J., and Murray, C. (1994) *The Bell Curve: Intelligence and Class Structure in American Life.* New York: The Free Press.
Hobson, J.M. (2004) *The Eastern Origins of Western Civilization.* New York: Cambridge University Press.
Hobson, J.M. (2012) *The Eurocentric Conception of World Politics: Western International Theory, 1760–2010.* New York: Cambridge University Press.
Hochschild, A. (1999) *King Leopold's Ghost: A Story of Greed, Terror, and Heroism in Colonial Africa.* New York: Houghton Mifflin.
Ignatiev, N. (1995) *How the Irish Became White.* New York: Routledge.
Isaac, B. (2004) *The Invention of Racism in Classical Antiquity.* Princeton, NJ: Princeton University Press.
Jennings, F. (1976) *The Invasion of America: Indians, Colonialism, and the Cant of Conquest.* New York: W.W. Norton.
Lake, M., and Reynolds, H. (2008) *Drawing the Global Colour Line: White Men's Countries and the International Challenge of Racial Equality.* New York: Cambridge University Press.
Langbehn, V., and Salama, M. (eds.) (2011) *German Colonialism: Race, the Holocaust, and Postwar Germany.* New York: Columbia University Press.
Lazreg, M. (2008) *Torture and the Twilight of Empire: From Algiers to Baghdad.* Princeton, NJ: Princeton University Press.
Levy, J.T., and Young, I.M. (eds.) (2011) *Colonialism and Its Legacies.* Lanham, MD: Lexington Books.
López, A.L. (2005) Introduction: Whiteness after Empire. In: López, A.L. (ed.) *Postcolonial Whiteness: A Critical Reader on Race and Empire.* Albany, NY: State University of New York Press, pp. 1–30.
Losurdo, D. (2011) *Liberalism: A Counter-History.* Trans. Elliott, G. New York: Verso.
Mann, C.C. (2006) *1491: New Revelations of the Americas before Columbus.* New York: Vintage.
Mehta, U.S. (1999) *Liberalism and Empire: A Study of Nineteenth-Century British Liberal Thought.* Chicago, IL: University of Chicago Press.
Mills, C.W. (1997) *The Racial Contract.* Ithaca, NY: Cornell University Press.
Mills, C.W. (2007) White Ignorance. In: Sullivan, S., and Tuana, N. (eds.). *Race and Epistemologies of Ignorance.* Albany, NY: State University of New York Press, pp. 13–38.
Mosse, G.L. (1985) *Toward the Final Solution: A History of European Racism.* Madison, WI: University of Wisconsin Press.

Outram, D. (2005) *The Enlightenment*. 2nd ed. New York: Cambridge University Press.
Painter, N.I. (2010) *The History of White People*. New York: W.W. Norton.
Pitts, J. (2005) *A Turn to Empire: The Rise of Imperial Liberalism in Britain and France*. Princeton, NJ: Princeton University Press.
Poliakov, L. (1974) *The Aryan Myth: A History of Racist and Nationalist Ideas in Europe*. Trans. Howard, E. New York: Basic Books.
Reynolds, H. (2013) *Forgotten War*. Sydney: NewSouth Publishing.
Teresi, D. (2002) *Lost Discoveries: The Ancient Roots of Modern Science—from the Babylonians to the Maya*. New York: Simon & Schuster.
Valls, A. (ed.) (2005) *Race and Racism in Modern Philosophy*. Ithaca, NY: Cornell University Press.

24

Intersubjective vulnerability, ignorance, and sexual violence

Erinn Cunniff Gilson

Around three o'clock in the morning, while stranded during a snowstorm, Olivia was violently attacked and raped by a supervisor who had continually harassed her and others in the Iowa meatpacking plant where she worked. In fields in California, Genoveva, who works picking produce, dealt with constant harassment and sexual propositions from her supervisor, who also happened to be her only means of transportation to work. Immigrant women working in the fields and slaughterhouses of the US food industry face dramatically high rates of sexual harassment and assault. Some reports estimate that 80 percent of women face harassment, and rape is so common that in California the women refer to the fields as "fils de calzón," fields of panties (see Bauer and Ramírez 2010, 41-52). Yet, their stories often go unvoiced and unheard; their attempts to speak out are discouraged, their stories dismissed and silenced. Ignorant of the working conditions of those who produce their food, most of the US public is likewise ignorant of the sexual violence endemic to those working conditions. When rape and sexual assault do receive public attention, women like Olivia and Genoveva are not those whose stories are heard. Yet they are among the most vulnerable because of their immigration status (they are often undocumented), race and ethnicity, and socio-economic status. They are also made more vulnerable because of the ignorance surrounding their experiences. Throughout this chapter, I seek to explain this kind of ignorance, that of a particular pattern of susceptibility, in terms of a deeper ignorance, that which concerns the phenomenon of vulnerability in general.

In the first two sections I present the methodological background for this inquiry, considering first how ignorance is schematized by philosophers engaged in social criticism, and then how vulnerability has been conceptualized in relationship to ethical and political concerns. The third section sketches the forms taken by ignorance of vulnerability, focusing on the particular case of ignorance concerning rape and sexual assault. I propose that many types of ignorance are undergirded by one particular type: willful ignorance. Moreover, in relation to rape and rape culture, this kind of ignorance takes the form of denials of the fundamental nature of vulnerability as a social and corporeal condition.

Critical philosophical perspectives on ignorance

Within particular corners of philosophy, epistemologies of ignorance have sought to develop "theories of knowledge of ignorance" (Tuana 2004, 227). Contra much mainstream philosophical doctrine, critical race, feminist, and science studies theorists propose that ignorance is more than the mere absence of knowledge. If ignorance is not a simple lack of knowledge, which could easily be remedied through knowledge acquisition, then ignorance is actively produced and perpetuated, and warrants far more investigation than it has been given in traditional epistemology. In particular, as Nancy Tuana maintains, ignorance has a complex relation to power. Thus, epistemologies of ignorance focus on "the intersections of power/knowledge-ignorance" (Tuana 2004, 196). They explore the practices through which ignorance is produced and maintained, the norms that govern these practices, the relationships between identities, social position, and ignorance, and the way these are "linked to issues of cognitive authority, doubt, trust, silencing, and uncertainty" (ibid., 195). In this way, epistemologies of ignorance theorize the social and political dimensions of knowing and not knowing, focusing on the actual – rather than ideal – conditions in and practices through which knowledge is acquired and ignorance is cultivated. As a consequence, they involve "work that explores the range of epistemically unreliable but socially functional belief-forming practices" (Alcoff 2007, 39). Accordingly, the main concerns of epistemologists of ignorance are the "power/knowledge-ignorance" practices pertaining to issues of social and political relevance: race, gender, socio-economic inequality, health and illness, and so on.

To facilitate an inquiry into the relationship between ignorance and intersubjective vulnerability, I briefly outline a few different types of ignorance, and sketch a picture of some ways ignorance is produced and maintained. Since forms of ignorance manifest as complex phenomena, different types serve different interests, have different purposes and roles, and vary in both significance and value. In an attempt to elucidate these diverse phenomena of ignorance, Tuana offers a helpful taxonomy in a 2006 article, "The Speculum of Ignorance." She demarcates at least four distinct types of ignorance: (1) knowing that one does not know, but not caring to know because knowing is not in one's immediate interest; (2) not even knowing that one does not know because one's current interests and existing knowledge prevent knowing; (3) ignorance on the part of some that is systematically cultivated by powerful others; (4) willful ignorance wherein one does not know, does not know that one does not know, and yet also does not want to know. This last form of ignorance – willful ignorance – is the most complex. It entails a subconscious refusal to know as well as an active and repeated cultivation of ignorance. One's developed ignorance protects one from knowing something that one implicitly does not want to know. Willful ignorance is often a product of privilege in systems of injustice; one remains willfully ignorant of the disadvantage or oppression of others, as well as of one's own privilege, because at a subconscious level one does not want to recognize these features of one's social world and one's implication in them.

What are the sources of such ignorance? How does it arise, develop, and continue? In another typology of ignorance, Linda Martín Alcoff identifies three distinct but interrelated sources of ignorance. First, ignorance can be the product of the situatedness of the knower – including her social position, individual experiences, and background knowledge – as it relates to the topic of inquiry. The knower's epistemic location "renders ignorance contextually dependent on the particular configuration – that is, the fit – between knower and known"; because of a variety of factors, some knowers are not well equipped to understand some topics of inquiry (Alcoff 2007, 49). Second, building on this understanding of the roots of ignorance, another perspective proposes that features of group identity obscure or make unknowable some types of knowledge; the situatedness of knowers is understood in terms of social group identity, to which "epistemic advantages and disadvantages accrue" (ibid., 47). These advantages and disadvantages facilitate or hinder knowledge attainment – for instance, making it less likely that those with dominant group identities will question power structures that privilege them – and affect epistemic credibility. By extension, the third source of ignorance is oppressive social structures that foster systematic distortion of social reality; such structures are the basis for willful ignorance. Ignorance is not just a matter of misguided belief, but has a structural basis in the creation of "cognitive norms of assessment" that are the consequence of the inculcation of "a pattern of belief-forming practices" common to a dominant group (ibid., 48). As Charles Mills argues, the racial contract, which comprises a tacit agreement among whites to establish and perpetuate a racial polity (i.e., white supremacy) with the aim of economic exploitation, is "an agreement to *mis*interpret the world" with the result that "*white misunderstanding, misrepresentation, evasion, and self-deception on matters related to race* are among the most pervasive mental phenomena of the past few hundred years" (1997, 18-19). This structural argument about the sources of ignorance highlights the process through which ignorance is legitimized via the creation of cognitive norms. In other words, ignorance is produced in tandem with standards for knowledge, which have the effect of prescribing ignorance of a whole range of phenomena and topics. For instance, norms of impartiality and neutrality are conceived as the basis for colorblindness, which perpetuates white evasion of issues pertaining to race. Thus, Lucius Outlaw concludes, "lack of knowledge and understanding would be a consequence of the certainties produced by the sanctioned and legitimated knowledge" (2007, 198).[1]

Intersubjective vulnerability

Vulnerability has become a central concept in a diverse array of fields, including philosophy, sociology, feminist theory, international relations, social work, bioethics, and legal theory, among others.[2] Vulnerability has been afforded increasing attention for a variety of reasons. The concept is taken to highlight a core feature of common human social, corporeal life that has been relatively neglected given the way normative theories have traditionally presumed an (implicitly adult white male) autonomous, rational, independent, and self-sufficient agent. In contrast, the concept of vulnerability foregrounds our frailty, dependence, susceptibility, interrelatedness, and the contingency of our development. Further, in a globalizing world with a seemingly ever-increasing pace of change, it appears as if uncertainty and instability are likewise increasing. Accordingly, there is greater awareness of extensive vulnerability (or at least the perception thereof) to disease, violence, climate destabilization, natural disasters, food insecurity, political upheaval and suppression, among other hazards. Lastly, vulnerability is regarded as having special ethical and political salience, that is, as constituting the basis for ethical, political, and legal prescription and policy.

In the various recent treatments of the topic, vulnerability is understood in at least two different ways: on the one hand, as a condition of impairment and heightened susceptibility to harm, and, on the other hand, as a fundamental condition that characterizes the corporeal and social nature of humanity. The first approach to vulnerability defines it simply as "susceptibility to harmful wrongs, exploitation, or threats to one's interests or autonomy" whereas the second approach conceives it more broadly as "an ontological condition of corporeal humanity" (Rogers, MacKenzie, Dodds 2012, 2-3). Both approaches perceive a significant link between vulnerability and ethical responsibility. When vulnerability is recognized as a condition of impairment, more extensive responsibility for others who are especially vulnerable is warranted. This approach is dominant among bioethicists and political and ethical philosophers, such as Robert Goodin (1985) and Alasdair MacIntyre (1999), as well as many feminist ethicists (e.g., Kittay 1999). When vulnerability is recognized as a fundamental condition, one shared by all living beings, a different connection to ethical responsibility appears: ethical responsiveness is perceived as depending on the ability to experience and avow vulnerability rather than willfully ignore it in favor of fantasies of mastery and control. If vulnerability is, as Judith Butler defines it, "an unwilled susceptibility" that "one cannot will away without ceasing to be human[,]" then it is a condition that binds us to one another unavoidably (2005, 91; 2004, xiv). Vulnerability both makes it possible for us to be undone, often by one another, and be harmed or violated, and makes it possible for us to take care, be empathetic, and forge relationships. Seeking mastery and invulnerability is a way of attempting to repudiate a condition that cannot be willed away, and such projects of mastery inevitably entail the exploitation of the vulnerability of others. Thus, the possibility of choosing ethical responses, ones that attend to vulnerability rather than deny, willfully ignore, and then exploit it, lies in recognizing the extent of vulnerability and its shared nature.

From this perspective vulnerability is an intersubjective condition. To call vulnerability intersubjective indicates how we are vulnerable both as corporeal beings and as social beings, as well as the way these dimensions of our existence are intertwined. The corporeal dimension of vulnerability is quite clear: as embodied beings, we are open to morphological changes ranging from pernicious physical injury to benign sensations and alterations to valorized and desired transformations. Corporeal vulnerability is most manifest in injury, the immediate pain it involves, and its potentially more enduring harm. Yet, it is also a matter of processes of change such as aging and other willed or unwilled bodily transformations (such as pregnancy, changes in perceptual abilities, changes in physical abilities such as strength, endurance, and flexibility, weight gain and loss, and so on). The social dimension of vulnerability is multifaceted. Fundamentally, sociality itself is a form of exposure; we are open and vulnerable to others as well as to the norms that circulate throughout, and constitute, the social milieu. We are vulnerable to appraisal by others, to the impact of their actions and perceptions, and our perceptions of their appraisal. Only as corporeal beings, though, are we affected by others in this way: open to affection and disdain, ill-treatment and concern, indifference and passion that is experienced through and in terms of embodiment. Butler's account in particular evinces this understanding of vulnerability:

> The body has its invariably public dimension. Constituted as a social phenomenon in the public sphere, my body is and is not mine. Given over from the start to the world of others, it bears their imprint, is formed within the crucible of social life.
>
> *(2004, 26)*

Thus, most fundamentally, the idea of intersubjective vulnerability indicates that vulnerability is our ability to be open to others, to be shaped by them, to become a self only through relation to them; it is the condition that makes it possible for us to become who we are and will make it possible for us to become otherwise. Given vulnerability's intersubjective nature, conceiving vulnerability as a fundamental condition also entails recognizing how that condition is actualized and experienced differently given the varying ways people are situated in the social milieu. A notion of intersubjective vulnerability therefore encompasses the view that vulnerabilities are particular patterns of "susceptibility to harmful wrongs, exploitation, or threats to one's interests or autonomy." Accordingly, vulnerability has a particular kind of reality as a fundamental condition – an openness to being affected and affecting that none of us can avoid – however, it also manifests in widely divergent ways and, as a condition of susceptibility to wrongs, is differentially distributed in inequitable ways.

Ignorance of vulnerability and sexual violence

Given vulnerability's significance, ignorance of vulnerability has considerable implications for social justice. Ignoring vulnerability can comprise a serious ethical, political, and social failure. My main concern is willful ignorance surrounding rape and rape culture and related forms of vulnerability, which is an example of such failure, one of compromised cognition and "epistemically unreliable but socially functional belief-forming practices." Before turning to this analysis, I elaborate some different ways one can be ignorant of vulnerability, especially as it pertains to sexual violence. Generally, ignorance involves the misapprehension and absence of apprehension of vulnerability in two central ways: we can misapprehend or fail to perceive particular patterns of vulnerability, especially those affecting others but also those affecting ourselves, and we can fail to perceive the way intersubjective vulnerability constitutes a common condition. These two general forms of ignorance are intimately related. Ignorance of intersubjective vulnerability as a shared condition is a central form of willful ignorance. It can operate as a basis for ignorance of particular patterns of vulnerability, but, additionally, the other forms of ignorance can shore up willful ignorance.[3]

Ignorance about particular patterns of vulnerability can take the form of the types in Tuana's taxonomy: (1) One may consciously choose not to know about the specific vulnerabilities of others because it is not in one's interest to know. (2) One may be unknowingly ignorant about these specific vulnerabilities simply because the knowledge and interests one does have preclude knowing. Such beliefs can be the result of the social position and/or group identity of the knower (one's gender, race, or socio-economic class status, for instance).[4] (3) Ignorance of particular patterns of vulnerability can be instilled by powerful others. These types of ignorance overlap and mutually reinforce one another within systems of ignorance.

Like ignorance of sexual harassment and assault in farms and meatpacking plants, the mishandling of reports of rape and sexual assault by the US military is another particularly egregious example of these forms of ignorance and their interlocking nature. Reports have been systematically dismissed as higher ranking officers have chosen not to know about the pervasive problem of rape and sexual assault: incidents are covered up, victims are intimidated to prevent them from making reports, and some female victims are even charged with adultery in military courts when their assailants were married men, which is classified as conduct unbecoming an officer (see Dick *The Invisible War*, 2012). Many of those higher up in the chain of command actively attempt to suppress reports of rape in order to keep the number of allegations low and maintain the appearance of a well-run unit. A variety of powerful parties attempt to prevent knowledge about sexual assault – accurate statistics about its prevalence, its effect on victims, the way victims are treated within the military, the way the climate in branches of the military is conducive to sexual violence, and so on – from being disseminated.[5] The public, those in the military, and those who may consider enlisting are prevented from knowing about rape and sexual assault, as well as their own vulnerability to it. Ignorance is also cultivated by depicting rape in the military as a minor rather than pervasive problem, a belief that prevents recognition that one does not know. One's social position (e.g., masculine gender identity, middle-class socio-economic status) can shore up ignorance since the particular beliefs that accompany that social location (e.g., patriotism and automatic esteem for military personnel) also prevent one from perceiving other's vulnerabilities. Thus, the vulnerabilities of those who have been assaulted remain obscured.[6]

Underneath these ways of being ignorant is willful ignorance, that is, an unconscious but active interest in denying the pervasiveness of rape, its causes, and the nature of the vulnerabilities at play. Oppressive social structures, not just particular powerful parties, foster ignorance and, for that reason, generate a deeper form of ignorance. In the following analysis, I propose that we can understand systemic ignorance surrounding rape and rape culture better by considering it in terms of ignorance about vulnerability. Ignorance about rape requires willful ignorance about vulnerability and, in particular, about what it means to be vulnerable, who can be vulnerable, how, and when. Specifically, our present beliefs and interests concerning vulnerability include a limited understanding of what it means to be vulnerable, which defines vulnerability solely in terms of particular conditions of impairment, and thus as being powerless, passive, and weak;

such beliefs about vulnerability lead to patterns of behavior (avoidance of vulnerability) that prevent full understanding of it.[7] Such ignorance of vulnerability promotes ignorance of rape.

A key feature of this understanding of vulnerability is its link with gender, with femininity and femaleness. Vulnerability is conceived both as uniquely female, and as a susceptibility to harm that arises in virtue of weakness and deficiency. In relation to sexual violence, a specifically feminine and/or female form of vulnerability is assumed; that is, feminine/female vulnerability is not just susceptibility to any kind of harm but rather is viewed as particularly *sexual* vulnerability. This form of vulnerability is a synecdoche for the vulnerability of women in general. Women are regarded as vulnerable because feminine and female bodies are sexualized, perceived as especially sexually stimulating and available for use, but also perceived as weaker and thus unable to avert the unwanted sexual attention they attract. Given this understanding of vulnerability, it is believed that it is women, not men, who are vulnerable and almost inherently so; female vulnerability, coded as especially sexual, and male aggression are naturalized. As Rachel Hall notes, when perceived this way, women's bodies and "sexual anatomy" are treated as "one risk factor among others" (2004, 2).

This view of vulnerability, however, relies on racist and classist assumptions in addition to sexist ones. Hall argues that through the reiteration of this particular construction of female vulnerability "[rape] prevention discourses reinvest white and middle-class women with a sense of preciosity[,]" and obstruct recognition of the risk non-white and working class women face (2004, 4). This view of vulnerability actually renders an array of people more vulnerable because it buttresses rigid norms for victims (i.e., female, feminine, heterosexual, sexually pure, non-agential, invested with social worth). It precludes understanding and recognition of the victimization of those who do not fit this description, including transgender people, gay men, straight men, as well as nonwhite, working class, cis-gender women and those who cannot or refuse to assume the role of "culturally approved victim" (Lamb 1999, 117). Vulnerability is divvied up along gender lines, construed as a burden women bear and an impairment men avoid,[8] but also a quality that indicates one's value, one's worthiness of protection. Thus, although Black men are historically vulnerable to racist allegations of rape and violent reprisals that serve to maintain the white supremacist racial order, perceiving vulnerability in terms of sexual violability and a generalizable weakness works with racist stereotypes (Black men as sexually aggressive) to render vulnerability antithetical to Black masculinity. Overall, these beliefs about vulnerability work in conjunction with willful ignorance of intersubjective vulnerability as a shared condition.

Pervasive myths about rape, such as the belief that most rapists are strangers to those they attack or that victims usually have done something to cause the rape or should have done more to prevent it, block the formation of more sound beliefs (Fanflik 2007, 17).[9] Social position and group identity can facilitate ignorance.[10] For instance, Lisa Campo-Engelstein argues that because there are no dominant and pervasive cultural representations of men as victims of rape, their ability to empathize is curtailed: "men's knowledge of rape . . . constitutes only facts and information, not other's experiences that they relate to in such a deep way that they may (subconsciously) incorporate them into their self-understanding and their own memories" (2009, 33).[11] Moreover, existing frameworks for understanding the wrong of rape – such as a legal model that can only comprehend rape as either theft (because one owns one's body) or simple physical violence – preclude knowledge of the way rape affects embodied subjectivity.[12] Other common assumptions about rapists and victims include the dichotomous belief that rapists are invulnerable moral monsters, and rape victims are vulnerable, innocent, and pure. These paired beliefs perpetuate the misguided, sexist criteria for who can 'count' as a 'true' victim, sever the connection between the perpetrator and the broader society, and obstruct awareness of the potential complexity of events of rape and victims' experiences.

Additionally, the belief that rape is an exceptional occurrence, both in its incidence and in the nature of the crime, results in various instances of ignorance: of the pervasiveness of rape and the number of people it affects, who it affects and where, the continuum between rape and other forms of sexual violence, and thus how norms of everyday life can sanction sexual violence. Thus, victims are met with incredulity or cannot be heard. Their presence and experiences challenge the dominant worldview and so they are reinterpreted as making false claims, "asking for it," or, more benignly, failing to take the necessary precautions (see Code 2009, 333). These normal beliefs orient prevention measures around managing the behavior of potential victims. When prevention is a woman's responsibility, other members of the broader culture are excused: "current prevention techniques privatize the woman's body in order to refuse the responsibility for safeguarding her freedom to live, move, and socialize unharmed" (Hall 2004, 6–7). By appealing to entrenched ideas about gender roles, "rape myths" also constitute norms for cognition and behavior for the women deemed potential victims. In particular, they delimit female agency as exercised via avoidance and define "responsible citizenship" for women in terms of fear (ibid., 6, 10).

These all too common instances of ignorance concerning rape rest upon a foundation of willful ignorance about the nature of vulnerability. The aforementioned beliefs and frameworks for understanding rape maintain the socio-politico-economic status quo, that is, the inequitable distribution of the benefits and burdens that accompany vulnerability. Willful ignorance preserves this status quo. One who is willfully ignorant is so because of what one's social location and group identity precludes one from understanding, but also because of what one's position in oppressive social structures precludes one from *wanting* to understand. As Mills elucidates the concept, willful ignorance entails "moral cognitive dysfunction" that "take[s] for granted the appropriateness of concepts *legitimizing*" the status quo, and limited "patterns of affect and empathy" (1997, 95).[13] One's very understanding of right and wrong, the fundamental ethical concepts with which one operates are distorted. Thus, one's identity as an ethically good person inhabiting a basically just social world hinges on willful ignorance, which is sustained to prevent the loss of that identity (see McIntosh 1989). A middle-class white woman may develop a willful ignorance so as to maintain her status – as good, responsible, vigilante about danger, possessing self-control – over and against those who fail on this metric (e.g., those stereotyped as promiscuous "sluts," who lack self-control, drink too much, dress inappropriately, and so on). This ignorance protects her from the awareness that her safety, social value, and success is a matter of advantages secured through social structures that systemically disadvantage others, enabling her to inhabit relatively safe spaces while consigning others to marginalized positions in fields and factories. Recognizing the role these structures, and the systems of social meaning woven through them, play in making some people's lives more precarious than others (and affording those like her the privilege of having their vulnerability recognized and valorized if only in a disempowering way) would require challenging the accepted socio-politico-ethical norms of the dominant culture.

Thus, common beliefs regarding vulnerability and rape promote interrelated interests. They preserve (1) normative gender and sexuality (e.g., retaining norms for female purity and innocence, male roles as protector, a gendered division of vulnerability qua susceptibility to harm), (2) the status quo articulation of these normative roles in terms of race and class, and (3) a sense of security and invulnerability within a society in general. Taken together these beliefs obstruct knowledge about the complexity, ambiguity, frequency, and ordinariness of rape.

Thus, the frameworks through which rape is understood, which in their more overtly problematic forms constitute "rape myths," prevent the entrance of intersubjective vulnerability into dialogue about rape.[14] They do so by sustaining a fantasy of invulnerability that involves clear gendered roles and a gendered division of vulnerability: (cis-gender heterosexual) men as protectors or, in cases construed as exceptional and deviant, aggressors; women as agents only via avoidance of risk, which they cannot entirely avoid since it inheres in their sexualized bodies, and thus as responsible for what befalls them. Mapping the moral domain of who is responsible for what, and who absolved of responsibility, in this way renders the social world predictable and ostensibly confines danger to those who transgress these norms. The inequity of this orientation – this inverted image – is clear: it produces non-recognition and mis-recognition of those who do not fit into this paradigm.

All these particular ways of being ignorant of vulnerabilities related to rape are premised on willful ignorance of intersubjective vulnerability as a shared condition, one that transcends gender, race, and class, and pertains to all. Willful ignorance operates as a protective mechanism; it is oriented toward preserving the status quo for cognition and social organization. As such, it is a way of seeking invulnerability. More specifically, to be willfully ignorant is to seek to absent oneself from the shared condition of intersubjective vulnerability: to abstain from being affected by others' situations and experiences, to eschew alterations in one's beliefs and interests, and to refrain from locating oneself in a network of relations with others and acknowledging oneself as participating in such social structures. It is to strive to exempt oneself from the very public-ness that defines our corporeal and social being by maintaining ignorance of it. Ignorance of one's self as sharing in intersubjective vulnerability is willful ignorance since one does not choose it but rather continuously comports oneself in disavowal of this fact of one's existence. One does not consciously choose *not* to believe that one's bodily and social existence renders one vulnerable in a way that all others are also vulnerable, but rather the social structures in which one is immersed disincentivize recognition of this basic condition. Given one's position within inequitable social structures and the beliefs about what vulnerability is and means (weakness, female sexual violability), one's interest lies in denying this fact by seeking an invulnerable existence. By willfully ignoring intersubjective vulnerability as a shared condition, one necessarily ignores how others are unavoidably vulnerable in this way. Not only are the specific features of their vulnerability – vulnerability to physical harm, psychological distress, and social stigma, among other things, in the case of rape – ignored but the way others are situated in relation to one's self is ignored: one's impact on them, the way one inhabits a shared social world with them, and the way one participates with them in forging this world.

Conclusion

A core problem for social justice is the failure of many to understand fully and accurately the particular patterns of vulnerability to sexual violence experienced by those situated in diverse ways. Yet this problem has deeper roots in the repudiation of intersubjective vulnerability: a pervasive unwillingness to be vulnerable in this most fundamental of ways preempts understanding of the complexity and depth of vulnerability. One cannot understand others' experiences, one's responsibility in relation to others, and the limits of one's beliefs if one cannot acknowledge that one too shares in a basic openness to the corporeal and social world. Denying intersubjective vulnerability goes hand in hand with more limited, social functional beliefs about vulnerability. Thus, ignorance of intersubjective vulnerability as a common condition means that one cannot understand how rape often affirms and exploits the socially sanctioned gendered image of what vulnerability is and how it is distributed. Rape and sexual violence in general are violations of our shared condition of intersubjective vulnerability and constitute attempts to disavow it by reducing vulnerability to a gendered susceptibility to harm. In this way, willful ignorance of how intersubjective vulnerability is a basic, shared facet of human existence is one of the most deeply rooted sources of common forms of ignorance about rape. At the most basic level, it prevents the kind of openness to altering one's views, interests, and dispositions that are required for altering rape culture and dispelling rape myths. Accordingly, the kinds of ignorance that crop up around rape and sexual violence must, I think, be understood in relation to the kinds of ignorance that surround vulnerability in general. If sexual violence is always a matter of vulnerability, then undoing ignorance about sexual violence will entail knowing more about and challenging ignorance about vulnerability.

Notes

1 Most epistemologies of ignorance focus on harmful types of ignorance, but some articulate the value of strategic ignorance in circumstances of inequality and oppression where it is a tool of resistance rather than a means of upholding them. See Alison Bailey (2007) "Strategic Ignorance" and Sarah Lucia Hoagland (2007) "Denying Relationality."

2 See, e.g., Amanda Russell Beattie and Kate Schick, ed. (2013) *The Vulnerable Subject*; Debra Bergoffen (2013) *Contesting the Politics of Genocidal Rape*; Estelle Ferrarese (2009) ""Gabba-Gabba, We Accept You, One of Us": Vulnerability and Power in the Relationship of Recognition"; Martha Albertson Fineman and Anna Grear, ed. (2013) *Vulnerability: Reflections on a New Ethical Foundation for Law and Politics*; Erinn Gilson (2014) *The Ethics of Vulnerability*; Samia Hurst (2008) "Vulnerability in Research and Health Care: Describing the Elephant in the Room?"; Florencia Luna (2009) "Elucidating the Concept of Vulnerability: Layers Not Labels"; Catriona Mackenzie, Wendy Rogers, and Susan Dodds (2014) *Vulnerability: New Essays in Ethics and Feminist Philosophy*; as well as the *International Journal of Feminist Approaches to Bioethics* volume 5, no. 3 and *SubStance* volume 42, no. 3.

3 For a more extended argument to this effect, see my "Vulnerability, Ignorance, and Oppression" (2011).

4 This kind of ignorance is also often experienced by those who are marginalized and/or exploited in ways that increase their vulnerability. For example, immigrant women farmworkers may not know what constitutes sexual harassment, that it and other types of sexual exploitation are illegal in the US, or that they have legal recourse despite their undocumented status (see Bauer and Ramirez 2010). This form of ignorance is an example of what Miranda Fricker (2007) describes as hermeneutic injustice.

5 Communities and powerful members therein also cover up instances of rape and sexual assault; consider the recent cases in Maryville, Missouri, US, Steubenville, Ohio, US, Cleveland, Texas, US, and Halifax, Nova Scotia, Canada.

6 Other examples include the pervasive failure of law enforcement and crime labs to test rape kits and the mishandling of evidence collected from such kits, and frequent dismissal of reports of rape and sexual assault by college and university police, counselors, administrators, and others. Over the past year in the US there have been increasing numbers of lawsuits filed by and on behalf of college students reporting that their cases of sexual assault were dismissed or mismanaged by campus authorities, constituting a violation of the Title IX policy that ensures gender equity in access to education.

7 For an extended critique of a "reductively negative" view of vulnerability see my *The Ethics of Vulnerability* (2014).

8 For a consideration of the gendered distribution of vulnerability, see Debra Bergoffen (2013) *Contesting the Politics of Genocidal Rape.*

9 For a discussion of rape myths in media coverage, see Shannon O'Hara (2012) "Monsters, Playboys, Virgins and Whores: Rape Myths in the News Media's Coverage of Sexual Violence." On how these myths affect victims, see Patricia L. Fanflik (2007) *Victim Responses to Sexual Assault: Counterintuitive or Simply Adaptive?*

10 For instance, "male athletes were significantly more likely than females to demonstrate a greater acceptance of rape myths[,]" and, in one study, reported that they believed that fifty percent of rapes were fabricated by women (Fanflik 2007, 18).

11 Limited empathy is also conducive to further ignorance, such as ignorance of the impact that publicly reporting rape has on the person who has been victimized. Failure to consider or understand the way reporting may subject a victim to further victimization means that one cannot recognize what is at stake in reporting rape and is more inclined to believe that most or many reports are fabricated. One cannot, therefore, take stock of how those very responses – disbelief, resistance, antipathy – impact and stigmatize the victim, compounding her vulnerability.

12 See Ann J. Cahill (2001) *Rethinking Rape* for a discussion of the limitations of conventional models for understanding the wrongs and harms of rape, and Louise du Toit (2009) *A Philosophical Investigation of*

Rape: The Making and Unmaking of the Feminine Self, and Susan Brison (2002) *Aftermath: Violence and the Remaking of a Self*, for feminist analyses of the experience and wrongs of rape.

13 Rape myths encompass certain moral cognitive norms that sustain said myths. Norms, such as those of neutrality and rationality, impact epistemic standards for credibility, preventing victims from being believed or requiring them to comport themselves deliberately in line with such standards so as to be found "convincing" by those who would judge the validity of their claims (Lamb 1999, 116–118). For an account of the challenges of getting law enforcement officers to believe rape victims and a strategy for improving their disposition toward them, see Rebecca Ruiz (2013) "Why Don't Cops Believe Rape Victims?"

14 Lorraine Code proposes that a new epistemology surrounding rape would entail "narrating vulnerability into being" (2009, 343).

References

Alcoff, Linda Martin. (2007) "Epistemologies of Ignorance: Three Types." In *Race and Epistemologies of Ignorance*, by Shannon Sullivan and Nancy Tuana, 39–57. Albany, NY: SUNY Press.

Bailey, Alison. (2007) "Strategic Ignorance." In *Race and Epistemologies of Ignorance*, by Shannon Sullivan and Nancy Tuana, 77–94. Albany, NY: SUNY Press.

Bauer, Mary, and Monica Ramirez. (2010) *Injustice on Our Plates: Immigrant Women in the U.S. Food Industry*. Montgomery, AL: Southern Poverty Law Center.

Beattie, Amanda Russell and Kate Schick, ed. (2013) *The Vulnerable Subject*. London: Palgrave Macmillan.

Bergoffen, Debra. (2013) *Contesting the Politics of Genocidal Rape*. New York: Routledge.

Brison, Susan. (2002) *Aftermath*. Princeton, NJ: Princeton University Press.

Butler, Judith. (2005) *Giving an Account of Oneself*. New York: Fordham University Press.

Butler, Judith. (2004) *Precarious Life*. New York: Verso.

Cahill, Ann J. (2001) *Rethinking Rape*. Ithaca, NY: Cornell University Press.

Campo-Engelstein, Lisa. (2009) "Cultural Memory, Empathy, and Rape." *Philosophy in the Contemporary World* 16 (1): 25–41.

Code, Lorraine. (2009) "A New Epistemology of Rape?" *Philosophical Papers* 38 (3): 327–345.

Dick, Kirby. (2012) *The Invisible War* (DVD), New Video.

du Toit, Louise. (2009) *A Philosophical Investigation of Rape: The Making and Unmaking of the Feminine Self*. London: Routledge.

Fanflik, Patricia L. (2007) *Victim Responses to Sexual Assault: Counterintuitive or Simply Adaptive?* American Prosecutors Research Institute, Alexandria, VA: National District Attorneys Association.

Ferrarese, Estelle. (2009) "'Gabba-Gabba, We Accept You, One of Us': Vulnerability and Power in the Relationship of Recognition." *Constellations* 16 (4): 604–614.

Fineman, Martha Albertson and Anna Grear, ed. (2013) *Vulnerability: Reflections on a New Ethical Foundation for Law and Politics*. Farnham, UK: Ashgate.

Fricker, Miranda. (2007) *Epistemic Injustice*. Oxford: Oxford University Press.

Gilson, Erinn. (2014) *The Ethics of Vulnerability*. London: Routledge.

Gilson, Erinn. (2011) "Vulnerability, Ignorance, and Oppression." *Hypatia* 26 (2): 308–332.

Goodin, Robert. (1985) *Protecting the Vulnerable*. Chicago: University of Chicago Press.

Hall, Rachel. (2004) "'It Can Happen to You': Rape Prevention in the Age of Risk Management." *Hypatia* 19 (3): 1–19.

Hoagland, Sarah Lucia. (2007) "Denying Relationality: Ethics and Epistemology and Ignorance." In *Race and Epistemologies of Ignorance*, by Shannon Sullivan and Nancy Tuana, 95–118. Albany, NY: SUNY Press.

Hurst, Samia. (2008) "Vulnerability in Research and Health Care; Describing the Elephant in the Room?" *Bioethics* 22 (4): 191–202.

Kittay, Eva Feder. (1999) *Love's Labor*. New York: Routledge.

Lamb, Sharon. (1999) "Constructing the Victim: Popular Images and Lasting Labels." In *New Versions of Victims: Feminists Struggle With the Concept*, by Sharon Lamb, 108–138. New York: New York University Press.

Luna, Florencia. (2009) "Elucidating the Concept of Vulnerability: Layers Not Labels." *The International Journal of Feminist Approaches to Bioethics* 2 (1): 121–139

Mackenzie, Catriona, Wendy Rogers, and Susan Dodds, ed. (2014) *Vulnerability: New Essays in Ethics and Feminist Philosophy*. New York: Oxford University Press.

McIntosh, Peggy. (1989) "White Privilege: Unpacking the Invisible Knapsack." *Peace and Freedom* (July/August): 10–12.

MacIntyre, Alasdair. (1999) *Dependent Rational Animals*. Chicago: Open Court Press.

Mills, Charles W. (1997) *The Racial Contract*. Ithaca, NY: Cornell University Press.

O'Hara, Shannon. (2012) "Monsters, Playboys, Virgins and Whores." *Language and Literature* 21 (3): 247–259.

Outlaw, Lucius T. (2007) "Social Ordering and the Systematic Production of Ignorance." In *Race and Epistemologies of Ignorance*, by Shannon Sullivan and Nancy Tuana, 197–211. Albany, NY: SUNY Press.

Rogers, Wendy, Catriona Mackenzie, and Susan Dodds. (2012) "Why Bioethics Needs a Concept of Vulnerability." *International Journal of Feminist Approaches to Bioethics* 5 (2): 11–38.

Ruiz, Rebecca. (2013) "Why Don't Cops Believe Rape Victims?" *Slate*, June 19, 2013. Available from http://www.slate.com/articles/news_and_politics/jurisprudence/2013/06/why_cops_don_t_believe_rape_victims_and_how_brain_science_can_solve_the.html (accessed February 19, 2014).

Tuana, Nancy. (2004) "Coming to Understand: Orgasm and the Epistemology of Ignorance." *Hypatia* 19 (1): 194–232.

Tuana, Nancy. (2006) "The Speculum of Ignorance: The Women's Health Movement and Epistemologies of Ignorance." *Hypatia* 21 (3): 1–19.

25

Vulnerability, ignorance and the experience of radical surprises

Christian Kuhlicke

Introduction

Some events take us quite radically by surprise; they hit us unprepared and unveil our vulnerability. The reasons for this are manifold: some events are beyond any type of anticipation; for others, while warning signals existed, they were misinterpreted or not effectively communicated, defense structures were miscalculated and poorly designed or the possibility of low-probability/high-consequence events was systematically underestimated in management practices and strategies.

When the unexpected materializes into unforeseeable destruction, trauma and death, public scrutiny about failures and negligence is usually a consequence: someone or something needs to be made responsible and accountable. Were the drastic consequences not anticipatable or even knowledgeable in foresight? Why were warnings not made public, or steps taken to prevent the most severe impacts? Who is actually responsible for this mess?

Although it goes without saying that one is always wiser in hindsight, the retrospective engagement with foresight knowledge quite often unveils that not only weak signals existed (Weick and Sutcliffe, 2007), which pointed to possibly calamitous developments, but that vulnerable conditions were systematically overlooked and ignored by responsible authorities, resulting in public accusation and blame. As a consequence, responsible organizations often try to shift responsibility to the institutional regulatory context ("we acted according to the rules"), to individual operators or simply deflect from previous misconducts and wrong decision-making (Hood, 2002; Rothstein et al., 2006). In other cases a constructive engagement with the underlying reasons may be the consequence having quite positive effects: calamities and subsequent "public account giving may [. . .] have an important ritual, purifying function—they can help to provide public catharsis" (Bovens, 2007, 464). They have the potential to provide victims a forum to express their views and sorrows and to give responsible authorities the possibility to account for their own action and to justify or even excuse their previous decisions (Bovens, 2007). On a more operational level, individual, organizational or institutional learning processes might be initiated aiming at a greater sensitivity towards underlying vulnerabilities (O'Keefe et al., 1976) or organizational procedures (Weick and Sutcliffe, 2007).

This chapter argues that engaging with ignorance and radical surprises is central for the analysis of vulnerability, for both its practical efforts to reduce it as well as for better understanding and engaging in public and political contestations about its root causes. This is done by specifying, first, how, through the experience of radical surprises, vulnerabilities can be discovered. In this vein, ignorance signifies the moment when an actor, be it an individual or an organization, becomes aware of his/her/its limits of knowledge and hence becomes vulnerable. Second, this chapter turns towards underlying causes that need to be addressed in order to unveil the root causes of vulnerability. Therefore, the interrelation of "willful ignorance" and the idea of "invulnerability" (Gilson, 2011) are further specified. Throughout this chapter, empirical examples are introduced to support the argumentation.

Vulnerability and ignorance—an ignored relation

The strength of vulnerability studies lies in understanding the expectable: A person, a group or an entire region that is marginalized or oppressed in everyday life is also more often exposed to the risk of hunger, violence, illness, diseases or disaster and thus also more vulnerable during times of crisis and stress—at least this is the central assumption of most vulnerability studies (Watts and Bohle, 1993). During the 1970s a group of researchers became increasingly dissatisfied with how hazard research was conducted until then (Waddell, 1977; Watts, 1983) and started to criticize the "prevailing scientific view" (Hewitt, 1983, 3) and its focus on perception and individual decision-making processes (Burton et al., 1993; White, 1974). As a result, scholars introduced the notion of vulnerability and aimed at better understanding and explaining the social reasons for the occurrence of disasters by focusing on societal causes for conditions that result in an increased exposure to as well as lacking capacities or resources of individuals to anticipate, cope with, resist and recover from the impact of a hazard (Blaikie et al., 1994). The focus is usually on limiting societal structures and processes (e.g., political economy) that places some groups of people at greater risk than others (Watts and Bohle, 1993). In recent years, the concept became quite fashionable in climate impact studies (Adger, 2006) as well as sustainability science (Turner II et al., 2003).

Surprisingly, most vulnerability studies do not engage with ignorance; they hardly touch upon structurally produced lack of knowledge experienced by specific groups of actors, the systematic oppression of knowledge or the ignorance of ignorance and how these processes translate into vulnerable conditions. Vulnerability is predominantly understood as a result of lacking capabilities, of lacking access to resources, power or entitlements. The role of knowledge in vulnerability studies is limited to being romanticized as a relevant resource of people (i.e., local knowledge) that is systematically overlooked in official management efforts (Berkes et al., 2000). Despite this apparent oblivion in vulnerability studies towards ignorance, a more thorough engagement with how ignorance and vulnerability are interrelated appears a quite necessary task, as the following paragraphs argue.

Both the concept of vulnerability and ignorance share a similar challenge. How to observe it? Or more specifically, on what ground is an observer able to state that someone or something is ignorant or vulnerable? The term "ignorance" is mostly associated with a negative connotation (cf. also Bishop and Phillips, 2006). A person might either be ignorant of a specific fact or, even more reprehensibly, he might generally be ignorant. Talking or writing about ignorance is hence a risky endeavor, since one quickly takes a "judgmental stance" (or is blamed for taking such a stance) (Reason, 1990, 214). Vulnerability studies face a similar risk: They have the tendency for oversimplifying a quite complex relational construct (Green, 2004) by emphasizing a strong positive correlation between socio-economic-political status of a person, group or an entire region and their vulnerability. Statements such as "the poor suffer more from hazards than the rich" (Blaikie, et al., 1994, 9) meanwhile made operational within uncountable vulnerability assessments (Fekete, 2009) underline the tendency of many vulnerability studies to understand the vulnerability of specific actors, groups and entire regions as a pathological condition that is shaped by "poverty, underdevelopment and overpopulation" (Hewitt, 1997, 167).

As a consequence, both vulnerability as well as ignorance studies have paid more attention in recent years to underlying epistemological assumptions. Smithson, for instance, underlines that ignorance is not an absolute concept that implies a superior standpoint from which one is easily able to define what is distorted, faulty or even absent knowledge. Rather, Smithson understands ignorance as a "relational configuration that depends largely on disparate awareness of ideas and knowledge between actors" (Smithson, 1990). Gross adds that ignorance itself is a dynamic construct that alters recursively over time: Only if unknown unknowns (nescience) are discovered (ignorance), can one take this into account in further actions and either consider it as important and try to gather more knowledge about it (non-knowledge) or regard it as unimportant, problematic, dangerous or neglectable (negative knowledge) (Gross, 2007). For others, ignorance is a strategic resource utilized, consciously or unconsciously, "in ways that perpetuate privilege and domination" (Schaefli and Godlewska, 2014, 111). It is thus a more or less intentional process of refusing to know something which is already or at least potentially knowledgeable (Tuana, 2006).

Similarly, in vulnerability studies, it is increasingly acknowledged that people held to be vulnerable might perceive or experience their own "vulnerability" differently than an external observer. Therefore, actor-oriented approaches, such as the "sustainable livelihood security approach" were developed (Carney et al., 1999) putting greater attention on people's activities and assets (van Dillen, 2002, 64). In this vein, it is argued, it is more promising to depart from "local people's perception of vulnerability" or "vulnerable people's view of their vulnerability" (Delica-Willison and Willison, 2004; Heijmans, 2004) and hence not consider vulnerability simply as function of increased weakness, poverty, exposition or defenselessness (Gilson, 2011).

Radical surprises and vulnerability

Generally, surprises constantly happen to us and most of them are by no means radical, some are even welcome as they enrich our daily lives; they make living more livable, at least for some of us. At the same time, they allow us to question certain phenomena; they confuse us and hence set the precondition for learning. Yet, some surprises are quite painful, if they are survived at all.

An examination of the findings of Weick's study of the Mann Gulch Disaster, in Montana, USA, which is itself drawn from Maclean's award-winning book *Young men and fire,* (Maclean, 1992) helps to illustrate how radical surprises relate to the idea of vulnerability. Weick reconstructs how smokejumpers had specific expectations when they were landing at Mann Gulch and approaching a fire they were supposed to extinguish. These expectations were by no means met by the fire. The fire was triggered by a lightning storm on August 4, 1949. Sixteen firefighters were flown to the Mann Gulch area to fight the fire. The smokejumpers expected a 10:00 fire; that is a fire that "can be surrounded completely and isolated by 10:00 the next morning" (Weick, 1993, 635). However, the fire turned out to be anything but a 10:00 fire. Thirteen out of the 16 smokejumpers lost their lives.

The moment the smokejumpers discovered that the fire was not a 10:00 fire, is, according to Weick, "the most chilling sentence in the entire book" (1993, 629). It describes how the fire had crossed the gulch and was moving towards the firefighters. At this moment they discovered that something radically unexpected had occurred. They realized, in other words, something what was previously entirely unknown to them; that is their nescience (Gross, 2007). Nescience belongs to a different epistemic class than other forms of the unknown, since it is not part of any conscious reflections. Its central characteristic is that it can "only be used by a god-like sociological observer who already knows about the nescience of his or her object of study" (2007, 750). It is hence impossible for actors to refer to their current nescience, "at most, people can refer to someone else's or their own earlier nescience" (Gross, 2007, 746). Before the firefighters approached the fire, they had not anticipated that the fire might turn out to be considerably more violent than a 10:00 fire; only in retrospect, at least those who survived the fire, could reflect that the fire was not a 10:00 fire.

It is the discovery of nescience, which is the precondition for a radical surprise (Gross, 2007, 750). Such surprises "exceed and detonate" typical reference schemes and "radically question their validity and adequateness" (Wehling, 2006, 139–140; translation C.K.). Expectations based upon previous experiences and considered so far as valid turn out to be problematic and no longer as helpful. According to Weick, the moment the firefighters discovered their nescience they faced a fundamental, quite shattering experience: "their old labels were no longer working" (Weick, 1993, 633) and Weick proceeds "as Mann Gulch loses its resemblance to a 10:00 fire, it does so in ways that make it increasingly hard to socially construct reality" (1993, 636). While knowledge is systematically connected with sense-making, the discovery of nescience is, in this case, systematically connected with the collapse of sense-making.

In this vein, actors are vulnerable if they discover their previous nescience since by definition they cannot prepare for this. This moment exceeds their established routines, capacities and stocks of knowledge that they usually rely on. From this perspective, the moment of ignorance recognition is central, since it is impossible for actors to refer to their nescience before they discover it, since it is not part of any conscious reflections. Only if they discover it (ignorance) can they take it into account in their further actions and either consider it as important or regard it as unimportant, problematic or neglectable.

Epistemologically, vulnerability is here not understood as something negative. It's neither framed as the simple exposure or susceptibility to a physical process (e.g., an earthquake), to pandemics, violence or illness nor as actors' lacking capacities or assets to deal with cries and stress. Vulnerability is a rather ambivalent concept in the sense that it is "a condition of potential that makes possible other conditions" (Gilson, 2011, 310). Being vulnerable opens up the possibility to suffer, to be harmed (physically, financially, emotionally, bodily, etc.), at the same time it set the precondition for change, for learning or transformation. As Erinn Gilson states: "Vulnerability is not just a condition that limits us but one that can enable us. As potential, vulnerability is a condition of openness, openness to being affected and affecting in turn" (2011, 310).

From this perspective the primary "root causes" of vulnerability can no longer be understood as a result of socio-political-ecological macro-structures that translate into some kind of dynamic pressures and finally result in unsafe conditions (Wisner et al., 2005). A vulnerability analysis would rather need to develop an understanding of why actors do not consider themselves as vulnerable, it should thus scrutinize the "practices and habits that propagate invulnerability" (Gilson, 2011, 312). The smokejumpers, for instance, considered themselves for a long time as not being vulnerable. They relied on their previous routines, their practical knowledge, which they gained through a multiplicity of exercises, and their resources at hand (e.g., equipment). "People rationalized this image [they would extinguish the fire until 10 am the next morning] until it was too late" (Weick, 1993, 635). The smokejumpers believed in their own ability to control and master the fire and hence intersubjectively reproduced a fallacious sense of security (cf. also Gilson, 2011, 312 ff.) until it was too late and they could not flee the fire anymore.

Was the occurrence of such a radical surprise simply beyond any type of anticipation for the firefighters? Did some of the smokejumpers not implicitly assume that something like this could happen? What about such vaguely known anticipations? Empirically, the answer is quite straightforward: The (sociological) observer can only refer to the moment actors refer to the moment of detection of previous nescience in some kind of narrative (be it spoken, written or in another) form in order to unveil their vulnerability. In Maclean's story this is the moment when the firefighters recognized that the fire was crossing the gulch and heading towards them. Only when Maclean writes about this moment is the observer (Weick and hence the reader) able to identify their vulnerability. Apparently, the reconstruction of ignorance and hence vulnerability therefore requires great care for identifying how the unknown enters reality by referring to actors' narratives or acting.

More troubling, however, is the question why did the firefighters consider themselves as invulnerable at all? Was this an intentional process necessary for the firefighters to be able to act and fulfill their duties? Or, to put it differently, shouldn't the firefighters have been prepared for such a surprise, shouldn't they have anticipated this possibility? Was it not within the responsibility of the Forest Service or the regulatory framework to better prepare firefighters for such event? The subsequent inquiry was pretty clear on this and concluded: "There is no evidence of disregard by those responsible for the jumper crew of the elements at risk which they are expected to take into account in placing jumper crews on fire" (Maclean, 1992, 151; quoted in: Weick, 1993, 629). Law suits against the Forest Service were also dismissed by the Ninth Circuit U.S. Court of Appeals. However, Weick points to doubts about the legitimacy of these judgments: the inquiry was "judged by many to be inadequate" (1993, 629) opening up the possibility that ignorance to existing vulnerability was more or less willfully maintained by the Fire Service and the Court did not hold the Service accountable for this.

Willfully ignoring vulnerabilities?

Ignoring vulnerabilities is not just an individual or group-related process; it rather constitutes a "substantive epistemic practice" that is systematically grounded in everyday practices and institutions (Gilson, 2011, 312). This requires a more institutionally and politically inspired mode of inquiry that puts structural modes of not further engaging with the limits of knowledge and/or the systematic ignorance of others actors' knowledge or ignorance at the forefront. This is what Tuana defines as "wilful ignorance" (Tuana, 2006). This form of ignorance comprises both the subconscious refusal to know as well as a more active and conscious form of ignorance (Gilson, Chapter 24, this volume). In its active interpretation ignorance becomes quite a strategic resource:

> Yet, socially approved acceptance of what counts as valuable knowledge silences exactly those with that essential insight because their knowledge and identity are often assumed to be intellectually, morally, politically, and socially suspect [. . .]. The difficulty of challenging ignorance arises in large part from the fact that ignorance allows strategic denial of its existence.
>
> *(Schaefli and Godlewska, 2014, 111)*

In this sense, it is the intentional process of maintaining and reproducing an advantageous and privileged position at the cost of someone else's position that is decisive for utilizing ignorance strategically (Gilson, Chapter 24, this volume).

Jasanoff's analysis of the fatal gas leak at a Union Carbide plant in Bhopal, India, in 1984 is a good example for strategically utilizing ignorance: "For Bhopal's tragedy was as much about the capacity of powerful institutions to selectively highlight and screen out knowledge as it was about maimed lives and justice denied or delayed" (Jasanoff, 2007, 344). This screening out of knowledge related to the denial of medical knowledge about the toxicity of chemical substance tragically released in Bhopal, to the elucidation of what happened on the site as well as to the legal responsibility of actors and even national regulatory frameworks were decisive for unravelling the responsibility for both the explosion as well as its consequences (Jasanoff, 2007, 347).

However, in other cases, the ignorance to vulnerability might be willful, but less strategic; it might be based on implicit assumption about how certain things should be co-produced in everyday life. The residents of many communities along the Mulde River and its tributaries, for instance, were entirely surprised by the 2002 flood causing major devastations not only in Germany but in large parts of Central Europe. As an external observer one wondered how it occurred that residents and responsible organizations alike were so radically surprised by such a flood? Why are communities that have resided in the middle of a flood plain, admittedly quite well protected by dikes and draining systems since the 1950s, so radically surprised by something that could be expected, at least from an ecological point of view: the inundation of the flood plain? More troubling, the flood did not come out of the blue—there were indications by relatives and friends living upstream and most citizens received an official warning that the area could eventually be flooded, allowing residents and organizations alike to take preventive actions, at least in principle. Why, then, was it so difficult to understand both weak and strong signals pointing to this flood event?

To blame responsible authorities for intentionally keeping residents in a state of ignorance with regard to the possibility of being flooded would fall too short in providing an understanding of the processes resulting in this surprise. In this case, it is more helpful to relate the experience of a surprise or the discovery of something unknown to different societal expectations about the instability and/or stability of nature. These expectations again are shaped and influenced, as Kates states, by underlying "metaphors, models and belief systems that rarely receive critical scrutiny" (Kates and Clark, 1996, 8). The Mulde case demonstrates a society systematically producing an ecological blind spot; that is, knowledge about the environment that has been forgotten, neglected or even suppressed, and exists only in realms that lie outside of a societal imagination and which are no longer or have never been part of a collective memory.

Prior to the flood, many citizens did not consider that the "stability" of the river was artificially created by engineering work that reduced its naturally given variability quite drastically since the 1950s (see for more details: Kuhlicke, 2013). Since the 1950s many cities along the Mulde River were systematically protected by dikes, drainage systems and large retention basins in the upper part of the catchment. As a consequence, the practice of individual adaptation played virtually no role in flood protection practice. Previously, households attempted to prevent water from penetrating the ground floor by installing iron splints enabling them to fix boards, filled with sand in case of heavy rainfall. This form of household adaptation survived for centuries and only became obsolete during the 1950s when a levee was constructed surrounding the city and electric pumps were installed to drain water from the city towards the Mulde River. Timmermann's modification of the organic-functional model captures this loss of knowledge pointedly (1981), representing a historical change from a high-frequency/low amplitude event scenario towards a low-frequency/high-amplitude environment whereas technological interventions like dikes are the main reasons for this alteration. This prepared the ground for a major perturbation like the 2002 flood, since the river seemed to be controlled and therefore the problem of flooding appeared to be adequately solved. Only the aftermath of the 2002 flood revealed that this reliance on state-based technical measures was an inadequate solution because it promoted certainty and stability where uncertainty and instability are still possible.

To be sure, that this interpretation of the river has become powerful is closely related to the everyday experience of people. The river—apart from a few exceptions—appeared to be mostly under control and the levees and other technical devices protecting the city also offered an unquestioned sense of security. The established belief about the river is hence deeply interwoven with the reality of everyday life. It has been produced and reproduced in the daily interaction with the social and physical environment and was part of a collective memory. It was thus, paradoxically, the effective control of the river that co-produced the ground for experiencing the 2002 flood as a radical surprise.

Conclusion

Ignorance is a topic hardly considered in vulnerability studies. However, to better understand the interrelation of ignorance and vulnerability appears a promising undertaking, at least this was the argument pursued in this essay and this in a twofold sense. First, making sense of the radically surprising discovery of nescience (ignorance) helps raise awareness of previously unrecognized vulnerabilities. Only if such vulnerabilities are openly acknowledged does the possibility arise to prevent further harm by gathering more knowledge or by rethinking established practices. Making sense of ignorance is hence vital for efforts to identify vulnerabilities and how this relates to the establishment of the idea of invulnerability. Second, vulnerabilities can also be willfully ignored. In its conscious and more or less strategic interpretation it aims at oppressing other people's knowledge or ignorance in order to maintain or manifest a position of superiority. Ex-ante, this might mean that a group of actors intentionally does not consider other people's knowledge or ignorance about existing vulnerability. Ex-post, responsible organizations may have a vivid interest in not being held accountable and shift blame by strategically using ignorance in public scrutiny about underlying root causes resulting in calamitous developments. In its less explicit and more co-productive interpretation, ignorance is deeply interwoven with everyday processes that result in the systematic production of blind-spots; that is, in the forgetting of knowledge, in its negligence or collective oppression. As has been shown here, ignorance and vulnerability intersect in numerous ways. This chapter has outlined some of these connections, helping to build bridges between vulnerability studies on the one hand and ignorance studies on the other, two fields of enquiry that hardly take notice of each other.

References

Adger, N. W. (2006). Vulnerability. *Global Environmental Change*, 16, 268–281.

Berkes, F., Colding, J., and Folke, C. (2000). Rediscovery of traditional ecological knowledge as adaptive management. *Ecological Applications*, 10(5), 1251–1262.

Bishop, R., and Phillips, J. (2006). Ignorance. *Theory, Culture & Society*, 23(2–3), 180–182.

Blaikie, P., Cannon, T., Davis, I., and Wisner, B. (1994). *At risk: Natural hazards, people's vulnerability, and disaster.* London: Routledge.

Bovens, M. (2007). Analysing and assessing accountability: A conceptual framework. *European Law Journal*, 13(4), 447–468.

Burton, I., Kates, R. W., and White, G. F. (1993). *The environment as hazard.* New York: Guilford Press.

Carney, D., Drinkwater, M., Rusinow, T., Neefjes, K., Wanmali, S., and Singh, N. (1999). Livelihood approaches compared. A brief comparison of the livelihood approaches of the UK Department of International Development (DFID), CARE, Oxfam and the United Nations Development Programme (UNDP). *Institute of Development Studies (IDS) Bulletin*, 20(2), 1–7.

Delica-Willison, Z., and Willison, R. (2004). Vulnerability reduction: A task of the vulnerable people themselves. In G. Bankoff, G. Frerks and D. Hilhorst (Eds.), *Mapping vulnerability: Disasters, development and people* (pp. 145–158). London: Earthscan.

Fekete, A. (2009). Validation of a social vulnerability index in context to river-floods in Germany. *Natural Hazards and Earth System Sciences*, 9(2), 393–403.

Gilson, E. C. (2011). Vulnerability, ignorance and oppression. *Hypatia*, 26(2), 309–332.
Green, C. (2004). The evaluation of vulnerability to flooding. *Disaster Prevention and Management*, 13(4), 323–329.
Gross, M. (2007). The unknown in process: Dynamic connections of ignorance, non-knowledge and related concepts. *Current Sociology*, 55(5), 742–759.
Heijmans, A. (2004). From vulnerability to empowerment. In G. Bankoff, G. Frerks and D. Hilhorst (Eds.), *Mapping vulnerability: Disasters, development and people* (pp. 115–127). London: Earthscan.
Hewitt, K. (1983). The idea of calamity in a technocratic age. In K. Hewitt (Ed.), *Interpretation of calamity: From the viewpoint of human ecology* (pp. 3–32). Boston, MA: Allen & Unwin.
Hewitt, K. (1997). *Regions of risk: A geographical introduction to disasters*. Essex: Longman.
Hood, C. (2002). The risk game and the blame game. *Government and Opposition*, 37(1), 15–37.
Jasanoff, S. (2007). Bhopal's trials of knowledge and ignorance. *ISIS*, 98(2), 344–350.
Kates, R. W., and Clark, W. C. (1996). Environmental surprise: Expecting the unexpected. *Environment*, 28(2), 6–11; 28–34.
Kuhlicke, C. (2013). The institutionalisation of vulnerable conditions and a case study from Germany. In S. Linda, K. O'Brien and J. Wolf (Eds.), *A changing environment for human security: Transformative approaches to research, policy and action* (pp. 248–256). New York: Routledge.
Maclean, N. (1992). *Young men and fire*. Chicago, IL: University of Chicago Press.
O'Keefe, P., Westgate, K., and Wisner, B. (1976). Taking the naturalness out of natural disasters. *Nature*, 260(April), 566–567.
Reason, J. (1990). *Human error*. Cambridge: Cambridge University Press.
Rothstein, H., Irving, P., Walden, T., and Yearsley, R. (2006). The risks of risk-based regulation: Insights from the environmental policy domain. *Environment International*, 32(8), 1056–1065.
Schaefli, L. M., and Godlewska, A. M. C. (2014). Ignorance and historical geographies of Aboriginal exclusion: Evidence from the 2007 Bouchard-Taylor Commission on Reasonable Accommodation. *The Canadian Geographer / Le Géographe canadien*, 58(1), 110–122.
Smithson, M. (1990). Ignorance and disasters. *International Journal of Mass Emergencies and Disaster*, 8(3), 207–235.
Timmerman, P. (1981). *Vulnerability, resilience and the collapse of society*. Toronto: Institute for Environmental Studies, University of Toronto.
Tuana, N. (2006). The speculum of ignorance: The women's health movement and epistemologies of ignorance. *Hypatia*, 21(3), 1–19.
Turner II, B. L., Kasperson, R. E., Matson, P. A., McCarthy, J., Corell, R. W., Christensen, L., and Schiller, A. (2003). A Framework for Vulnerability Analysis in Sustainability Science. *PNAS*, 100(14), 8074–8079.
van Dillen, S. (2002). A measure of vulnerability. *Geographica Helvetica*, 57(1), 64–77.
Waddell, E. (1977). The hazards of scientism: A review article. *Human Ecology*, 5(1), 69–76.
Watts, M. (1983). On the poverty of theory: Natural hazards research in context. In K. Hewitt (Ed.), *Interpretation of calamity: From the viewpoint of human ecology* (pp. 231–262). Boston: Allen & Unwin.
Watts, M., and Bohle, H.-G. (1993). The space of vulnerability: The causal structure of hunger and famine. *Progress in Human Geography*, 17(1), 43–67.
Wehling, P. (2006). *Im Schatten des Wissens: Perspektiven der Soziologie des Nichtwissens*. Konstanz: UVK.
Weick, K. E. (1993). The collapse of sensemaking in organizations: The Mann Gulch disaster. *Administrative Science Quarterly*, 28, 628–652.
Weick, K. E., and Sutcliffe, K. M. (2007). *Managing the unexpected: Resilient performance in an age of uncertainty* (2nd Edn). San Francisco, CA: John Wiley & Sons.
White, G. F. (1974). Natural hazards research: Concepts, methods, and policy implications. In G. F. White (Ed.), *Natural hazards: Local, national, global* (pp. 3–16). New York: Oxford University Press.
Wisner, B., Blaikie, P., and Cannon, T. (2005). *At risk: Natural hazards, people's vulnerability, and disasters*: London: Routledge.

26

Anthropological perspectives on ritual and religious ignorance

Liana Chua

Although ignorance has long played a critical off-stage role in anthropological discussions, controversies and theories about ritual and religion, it has only recently been cast under the analytical spotlight as an ethnographic topic in itself. Following a brief overview of the long-standing but largely implicit presence of ignorance in the anthropology of religion over the last century, this chapter will explore three broad themes in the current literature on ritual and religious ignorance: (1) loss, change and collective memory; (2) the politics of ignorance; and (3) ignorance as a strategic or ethical project. I suggest that these recent contributions can be seen as both extensions of and rejoinders to earlier debates on ritual and religion—notably those revolving around the distinction between praxis and propositional knowledge and the relationship between individuals and society. At the same time, they lay bare the many overlaps and slippages between ignorance and other cognate phenomena such as secrecy, ambiguity, loss and indifference. Rather than attempting to delineate a clear-cut category of 'ignorance', then, this chapter will take seriously its definitional 'fuzziness' as central to the real-world complexities with which anthropologists inevitably have to grapple.

An implicit presence: Ignorance in the anthropology of religion

For most of the last century, anthropologists tended to treat propositional knowledge—beliefs, symbols and discourse, for example—as constituting the core of ritual and religion. This proclivity is traceable to the late-nineteenth and early-twentieth centuries, when the foundations of the anthropology of religion were being laid. Disputing the then-widespread image of 'primitive [i.e. many small-scale, non-Western] religions' as 'grotesque and . . . unintelligible' (Morgan 1877: 5), scholars such as E.B. Tylor and Emile Durkheim sought to emphasize their internal logic and coherence—the former by depicting them as a rational 'primitive philosophy' (1871) and the latter by defining them as systems of beliefs and practices that expressed and reproduced social realities (1915). In this way, they set the parameters for future anthropological engagements with religion, effectively characterizing it as a body of (mainly propositional) knowledge that was enacted and expressed through ritual.[1]

This knowledge-centred view of ritual and religion has continued to hold sway in much of anthropology, long after its original proponents' evolutionist precepts were discarded.

The notion that ritual and religion serve as systems of 'explanation-prediction-control' (Horton 1971: 97), for example, was taken up by various twentieth-century anthropologists, including E.E. Evans-Pritchard (1976: 18), who portrayed Azande witchcraft as a 'natural philosophy by which the relations between men and unfortunate events are explained', and Robin Horton (1971, 1975a, b), who adopted Tylor's 'intellectualist' model to account for processes of conversion in Africa. Meanwhile, echoes of Durkheim's socio-symbolic approach can be heard across the theoretical spectrum, from Mary Douglas's (1966) celebrated analysis of the symbolic classification of dirt, to Victor Turner's (1967) discussion of Ndembu symbols and ritual. Like Clifford Geertz (1993), whose essay on religion as a cultural system popularized a different interpretivist branch of symbolic anthropology, these scholars treated symbols, beliefs and myths as central to the collective experience of ritual and religion.

The works cited above are merely some of the best-known contributions to an extensive anthropological tradition of apprehending religion in propositional terms—that is, in terms of what it means, represents or symbolises to its adherents. From this perspective, ritual and religious knowledge is an intrinsically worthwhile end: a key to power, belonging or spiritual fulfilment to be acquired and amassed. Accordingly, ignorance can only be its obverse: a lack of knowledge, a gap, an index of flawed or incomplete religiosity. Yet even this observation would have been a moot point in much of the literature of the twentieth century, in which ignorance was quite simply a non-issue. Even when appearing in more noteworthy ethnographic guises—as cultivated secrecy, practices of exclusion or ambiguity, for instance—it was generally taken for granted as a failure of knowledge rather than a phenomenon to be analysed and theorized on its own terms.[2] From this analytical perspective, it was fidelity to or command of religious *content* that mattered.

The 1960s, however, saw the growing prominence of an alternative approach to religion: one that underscored action, praxis and effect, as well as the *contexts* in which knowledge was created, acquired and manipulated. Rather than investigating how religion could mean or represent things in public, collective ways, anthropologists became increasingly interested in how ritual acted on individuals and the world, such as through 'symbolic action' (Lienhardt 1961), initiation ceremonies (Barth 1975), performances (Schieffelin 1985) and rites of passage (Turner 1969). This trend was further extended from the 1980s when a number of scholars began to deconstruct the hitherto unquestioned link between the ideological, symbolic or aesthetic substance of ritual and its capacity to act on reality. Although none of them dealt directly with the theme of ignorance, they presaged much of the current literature by showing how ritual and religion could be apprehended in terms that were not purely semantic or discursive.

Two particularly significant contributions to this arena were the work of Maurice Bloch (1989) on ritual and power and Caroline Humphrey and James Laidlaw's (1994) theory of 'ritual action'. Bloch consistently decried the widespread anthropological treatment of ritual and religion as primarily communicative and explanatory phenomena, arguing instead that ritual *forms*—physical conventions, linguistic formulae and repetitious performance, for example—were often more critical than their semantic content. He argued that among the Merina of Madagascar, ritual served as a potent 'form of social control' (1989: 29) by drawing participants into heavily circumscribed interactive regimes that manifested and reproduced existing power hierarchies (28–29). For him, ritual was 'the last place to find anything "explained"' (37); indeed, its very opacity and lack of semantic creativity enabled it to mask and sanctify those power relations.

This explicit decoupling of content from praxiological effect in the study of ritual was taken further, albeit in a different direction, by Humphrey and Laidlaw (1994) in their ethnography of the Jain *puja*. While also refuting prevalent depictions of ritual as 'essentially communicative and expressive' (73), they put forward a model of ritual—or rather, ritualized action—as a prescribed, rule-bound entity containing no intention or intrinsic meaning. Unlike Bloch's Merina ceremonies, ritual was thus not a 'mask for something else' (263), but an empty, open-ended mode of action that individual actors could infuse with their own meanings. Crucially, this approach to ritual proffered a solution to a methodological problem that continues to haunt anthropologies of both religion and ignorance: how to deal with situations in which 'actors simply do not have an interpretation to offer' (cf. Lewis 1980). Rather than seeing this as 'an embarrassment,' they argued, such instances showed that 'variety, discordance, and even absence of interpretation are all integral to ritual' (1994: 264).

In their own ways, Bloch's and Humphrey and Laidlaw's work emblematized a diffuse but noticeable trend in the anthropology of religion towards privileging ritual action, practice and effect over propositional knowledge. By knocking propositional knowledge off its traditional analytical perch and showing how it was not the only standard against which ritual and religious phenomena could be assessed, these praxis-oriented contributions cleared the space for the emergence of alternative models, conceptualizations and concerns. Among them was ignorance.

Anthropologizing ritual and religious ignorance

Since the early-2000s, ignorance has become the subject of mounting interest across anthropology.[3] Thanks in part to the debates discussed earlier, the anthropology of religion has provided particularly fertile ground for such explorations. Recent publications on this theme have clustered around a number of overlapping ethnographic contexts: the productive role of ignorance in ritual and religious reformulations following periods of momentous change (Abrams-Kavunenko 2013; Buyandelgeriyn 2007; Højer 2009); politics or economies of ignorance (Berliner 2005; Scott 2000; see also Mair et al. 2012: 4–7); and ignorance as an individually cultivated ethical, strategic or self-protective project (Chua 2009; High 2012; Mair forthcoming; Vitebsky 2008).

Despite having mostly emerged independently, these ethnographies are underpinned by two broad objectives: first, to think through and theorize ignorance as both an analytical category and a feature of 'native' discourses and practices; and second, to reflexively challenge anthropologists' own proclivity to define their craft—and often, their informants' lives—in terms of knowledge acquisition and management (Mair et al. 2012: 1; see also Chua 2009: 344–45; Højer 2009: 575). Taken together, they show how ritual and religious ignorance—like knowledge—can be apprehended in different ways: as actual states or conditions, practices of not-knowing or forgetting, imaginative and moral projects, relational configurations, and *senses* of loss or absence, among others. The rest of this chapter explores some of these topics through the three main contexts mentioned earlier.

Change, loss and collective memory

Although societies are never static, some changes—such as those wrought by war, genocide and natural disaster—are so stark or momentous that they become tropes and frameworks through which people make sense of their new realities. Several recent ethnographies revolve around one such instance: the fate of religious traditions in the contemporary Republic of Mongolia. The period of socialist rule in Mongolia (c. 1921–1990) saw a concerted state-led drive to obliterate the pre-socialist past, resulting in purges of thousands of Buddhist lamas, the demolition of monasteries and the suppression and destruction of shamanist practices and paraphernalia. While causing the indubitable and extensive loss of religious knowledge, places, objects and experts, such processes also fostered an overwhelming *sense* of loss that is today played out in discourses of ignorance, absence and uncertainty.

A number of anthropologists have examined the implications of such discourses for contemporary Mongolian Buddhism and shamanism (Buyandelgeriyn 2007; Højer 2009; Abrams-Kavunenko 2013). Their ethnographies tease out the relationship between ignorance arising from actual losses and absences on the one hand and *perceptions* of (present) ignorance and (past) knowledge on the other, showing how their intersection produces new objects, interactions and realities. In his article on the 'creative aspects of absent knowledge' (2009: 575), for example, Lars Højer argues that the socialist regime's suppression of religious traditions throughout the twentieth century paradoxically increased their potency in the eyes and memories of ordinary Mongolians. Today, religious artefacts and practices are viewed as indecipherable, dangerous fragments from a suppressed past which mediate 'powerful and precarious agencies' about which people feel they know very little (583). Rather than treating their ignorance (both real and professed) as a loss or failure, however, Højer shows how this deeply-felt 'absence' of the past serves as 'a potent space for magical possibilities and magical agency' (579) that gives Mongolians a technology through which to imagine and create new religious realities.

The agency of absence and loss is also explored in Buyandelgeriyn's (2007) discussion of contemporary Buryat shamanism. Although many of her informants use shamanic diagnoses and rituals to cope with the challenges posed by Mongolia's transition to a market economy, they nevertheless remain dubious about the power and legitimacy of the shamans whom they consult. Their uncertainty—forged by an awareness of the widespread loss of shamanic knowledge, paraphernalia and personnel during the twentieth century as well as their own ignorance of shamanic traditions—is compounded by the suspicion that many contemporary shamans are driven by avarice in a profitable climate (133). During consultations, moreover, this 'knowledge vacuum' is often expanded by the appearance of spirits from distant, pre-socialist pasts about whom clients know little and with whom they are thus unwilling to enter into full-blown ritual relations (134). The result of these overlapping levels of ignorance and uncertainty is that clients often consult more than one shaman and sponsor several rituals '"just in case it helps"' (135): a trend that has led to a proliferation of shamans and the ongoing excavation and reassessment of distant pasts through shamanic ceremonies. In this way, both actual and perceived ignorance and loss merge with uncertainty, scepticism and the willing suspension of disbelief (134) to create a multiply productive space: one that creates new shamans and (old) spirits, forges new relations with Mongolia's 'incipient capitalism' (142), and reshapes Buryats' collective and individual memories (142–43).

Højer and Buyandelgeriyn's ethnographies highlight the often close entanglement between history, collective memory (or forgetting), loss and ignorance. They show how ignorance is not simply a cognitive state confined to individual persons, but often dispersed across an entire socio-cultural, political and temporal field, with effects at different scales and levels. Viewed from this angle, ignorance does not have to be defined as a lack of knowledge; rather, it is the *sense* of ignorance—the knowledge of what is unknown or partially known—that lends these Buddhist and shamanist interactions their creativity and agency. Rather like the praxis-oriented scholarship examined earlier, these articles underscore the fact that semantic or propositional knowledge is not necessarily central to the operation of ritual and religion. But rather than displacing knowledge from the study of ritual or focusing primarily on form and action (cf. Bloch 1989; Humphrey and Laidlaw 1994), Højer and Buyandelgeriyn show how its apparent obverse—ignorance, loss and uncertainty—can spark off creativity and improvisation, such that in ritual, 'everything becomes possible' (Højer 2009: 582). In the process, they foreground the agency but also predicaments of individuals as they navigate changing ritual and religious configurations and morally freighted processes of remembering and forgetting—a theme to which we shall shortly return.

The politics of ignorance

More than being a productive space, ignorance can have powerful restrictive and detrimental effects. Focusing less on ritual per se and more on its broader political context, a number of anthropologists have explored the highly charged role of ignorance in constituting difference and, at times, perpetuating inequalities. Their analyses both draw on a long genealogy of anthropological studies of religious politics, of which Bloch's work is part, and feed into recent discussions of the strategic deployment of ignorance by groups and individuals across the power spectrum (e.g. Gershon and Raj 2000; Hobart 1993; Mathews 2005; McGoey 2007; Proctor and Schiebinger 2008; Scott 2000). In the process, they reveal how states of ignorance are not neutral absences of knowledge but can be actively enforced, ascribed and manipulated at structural and relational levels.

This is demonstrated with particular clarity in David Berliner's (2005) ethnography of youth religious memories in Guinea-Conakry. Advocating the need to trace 'the concrete social and cultural contexts through which memories are passed down' (577), he shows how the contributions of Bulongic youth to 'preserving religious culture must be understood in a highly specific intergenerational configuration of interactions' (579). Bulongic society underwent a period of Islamization from the 1920s to 1950s, during which time their indigenous rituals were progressively abandoned and denigrated by the urban elite who spearheaded conversion. Consequently, the only people in today's wholly Muslim communities with direct experience of pre-Islamic rituals are members of the older generation.

Berliner reveals how these Bulongic elders shape the younger generation's knowledge of the old ways by 'overload[ing]' them with 'a [vicarious] memory shaped by fear and fascination' (2005: 582), and portraying the pre-Islamic period as 'a real golden age' (583). These processes, however, are shrewd and selective, with the elders deliberately and publicly withholding ritual secrets from the youth as a means of maintaining a moral and hierarchical advantage over them (583). Here, younger people's first-hand ignorance of the old ways—which they keenly aim to overcome—and the elders' calculated enforcement of their ignorance become mutually reinforcing, culminating in a profound nostalgia for an illusory unspoiled past. Interestingly, however, young Bulongic have responded to their situation by creating their own secret language from which older people are excluded. These efforts, he suggests, reflect how they have 'internalized . . . [their fathers'] epistemology of secrecy' (584) even while being complicit in it.

Berliner's article shows how ignorance is always relational—how it can mediate relations and serve as a relation in itself. What matters here is not propositional content or its lack thereof, but the mechanisms through which ignorance is admitted to or attributed by different parties and the effects that these have on social-structural relations. Unlike the Arosi elders of the Solomon Islands, discussed by Michael Scott (2000), who withhold their knowledge of genealogy-based lineages in order to forestall potential land conflicts and keep the peace, Bulongic elders use ignorance as an exclusionary tactic: one that continually (re)inscribes an older distinction between initiates and noninitiates (Berliner 2005: 582). As Berliner demonstrates, however, this strategy is only partially successful, for the young people with whom he works have found ways to exercise their own agency in the face of what they perceive as a lamentable loss.

This brings us to the third main theme of this chapter: the ways in which the cultivation of ritual or religious ignorance can become an individual project in itself. By eschewing the determinism of many earlier anthropological approaches to religion—such as Durkheim's thesis on social solidarity and reproduction, Geertz's depiction of religion as a model of and for reality, and Bloch's pessimistic take on the convergence of ritual and political authority—ethnographies such as Berliner's invite us to consider the subtleties of specific (socially inflected but often deeply individual) relationships to knowledge and ignorance. Doing so pushes us to apprehend ignorance not only as a state or condition but also, as the next section reveals, as comprising practices and 'form[s] of culturally elaborated unknowing' (Abrams-Kavunenko 2013: 6).

The individual cultivation of ignorance

The ethnographies featured in this chapter have, thus far, revolved around various modalities of ignorance—lost or forgotten memories, uncertainty, withheld knowledge, secrecy. While reflective of local discourses, these are mainly analytical devices through which anthropological observers describe their subjects' lived realities. In this section, we turn to another body of work that focuses less on ignorance as a condition and more on people's own exegeses and practices of ignorance. These ethnographies demonstrate that ignorance is not only a scholarly concern, but can also be the object of local theories and philosophies or the basis of purposeful projects of unknown/not-knowing.

I explore one such project in my work on ignorance among young Christian Bidayuhs in Malaysian Borneo (Chua 2009). While broadly sympathetic to the old rituals, *adat gawai*, these Christians prefer not to learn anything about their substantive content, often asserting that 'we are all Christian now'. But such pronouncements are not merely displays of apathy or distaste for this lingering pre-Christian remnant; rather, they reflect the seriousness with which such young people take the potency of the old rituals. My article examines the intimate connection between knowing and relationality in *adat gawai*, showing how knowledge of the old ways inevitably enmeshes the knower in a relationship of reciprocity with its spirits (2009: 336–41): one that, if not maintained and cultivated, could bring misfortune to the knower. In contrast to common anthropological depictions of knowledge-acquisition as agentive and empowering, then, knowing *adat gawai* is seen by Bidayuhs as *dis*empowering, 'generat[ing] relational consequences well beyond knowers' intentional reach' (341).[4] Whereas many older Christians try to accommodate the fragments of *gawai* knowledge that they still possess (e.g. how to read omens), most young Christians simply aim not to learn about them in the first place. Their protestations that they 'don't know' thus encompass 'passive ignorance (never having learned anything), partial but innocuous knowledge (the fact that omen birds exist, but not how to identify them), wilful ignorance (the active rejection of knowledge), and strategic attempts to "forget" what is already known' (343)—all of which, I suggest, engender a concerted discourse of ignorance that enables them to get on with life in a world in religious transition.

If young Christian Bidayuhs use not-knowing as a strategy of self-protection, some Buddhists have turned ignorance itself into an 'ethical project' (Mair forthcoming). In his work in Inner Mongolia in China, Jonathan Mair has explored the features of a particular over-determined 'discourse of ignorance' among followers of Tibetan Buddhism, for whom 'talking about ignorance is part of a culture of faith' (ibid.). He points out that for his Inner Mongolian acquaintances, 'ignorance of Buddhism arises from its mysterious "deep meaning", not so much as an unnoticed blind spot as a conspicuously mysterious Bermuda Triangle' (ibid.). By constantly reiterating and analysing their ignorance of Buddhist teachings, they distinguish themselves from genuinely enlightened beings such as buddhas and lamas from the past who are deemed to have genuinely understood Buddhism's 'deep meaning'. Such narratives, Mair argues, constitute an ethical project of self-cultivation: 'a principled detachment from Buddhist teachings' that 'produces an awareness of ignorance that . . . must be acquired, can spread and can be studied, though it makes itself felt as a lack'. In this regard, their discourse of ignorance belongs to a wider set of practices that seek to cultivate humility and faithfulness among Buddhists; indeed, Mair suggests that ignorance may be seen as 'a kind of knowledge, since the more elaborate an awareness of ignorance the believer develops, the more he or she knows about what is unknown' (ibid.).

Like Berliner's ethnography, the Bidayuh and Inner Mongolian case studies lay bare the inherent relationality of ignorance as well as its role in creating religious subjects. Indeed, the two often go hand-in-hand: young Bidayuhs' invocations of ignorance are both ways of denying relations with *gawai* spirits and efforts to stabilize their Christian personhood, while Inner Mongolian Buddhists adopt a specific relationship of detachment to Buddhist knowledge as a means of religious self-formation. However, the links between ignorance, relations and personhood are not always straightforward, as Casey High's (2012) exploration of Waorani shamanism reveals. For Waorani, shamanism is not an immutable subject position based on accumulated knowledge, but 'a particular state of being or perspective that enables relations with nonhuman entities' (127). In this capacity, shamans can adopt the predatory perspectives of animals or spirits and use witchcraft to attack humans, whom they momentarily see as animal prey (127). High argues that to deny knowledge about shamanism (thus protecting oneself from witchcraft accusations) is to make an agentive claim to *personhood*—that is, to possessing a peaceable human perspective (131) that must be consistently asserted and stabilized through various mechanisms. Like my work and Mair's, High's ethnography highlights the complex relationship between individual and collective discourses of ignorance—discourses that may converge and overlap but that can also be filled with contradictions and contestations.

Conclusion

Like the other contributions to this Handbook, the ethnographies discussed in this chapter reveal how ignorance can be construed as more than a lack of knowledge and apprehended instead as a constructive, agentive space that engenders new social, religious and other realities. Fundamental to this realization is the simultaneous recognition of its inherent 'slipperiness': ignorance may be a state or condition, an active position (unknowing/not-knowing), a relation or a feature of local exegesis, to name but a few of its manifestations. Moreover, the boundaries between ignorance and other cognate phenomena, such as secrecy, loss and uncertainty are vague and porous in practice; consequently, anthropological categories of 'ignorance' are often better seen as heuristic devices than indexes of reality. At the same time, however, it is crucial not to overlook the ways in which the subjects of anthropological analysis—Mongolians, Bulongic, Waorani and so on—engage in their own efforts to define, think through and articulate ignorance; indeed, the challenge that faces many anthropologists is how to hold analytical and 'native' categories in a productive balance.

All these insights both derive from and contribute to current discussions in the field of ignorance studies. But they must also be seen as part of several ongoing conversations in the anthropology of religion. Much of the current work on ritual and religious ignorance extends the trend, discussed earlier, towards moving beyond the conventional anthropological focus on propositional content and opening new analytical spaces for understanding religion in terms of praxis, effect and context. In their own diverse ways, the above ethnographies demonstrate how knowledge and knowing are not always necessary components of ritual and religious realities—and can even be hindrances in certain circumstances. Yet it is important to note that their discussions do not simply sideline knowledge but also point to new ways of apprehending it: as an awareness of what has been lost or forgotten, a sense of exclusion or inclusion, a particular relation, an individual project (knowing not to know). In this way, they also point to the inseparability of knowledge and ignorance—not as clear-cut opposites, but as distinctive phenomena that very often imply each other. In this respect, the anthropology of ignorance can also be seen as a vital and long-overdue reworking of the anthropology of knowledge.

Acknowledgement

I am grateful to the editors for inviting me to revisit this topic, to Jonathan Mair for his comments on an earlier draft, and to various contributors to a Facebook thread on ignorance in religion for their helpful reading suggestions.

Notes

1 Such writings were, of course, premised on a more fundamental attribution of ignorance to 'the natives', assumed to be unaware of larger ontological realities such as natural phenomena (Tylor 1871) or the social nature of religion (Durkheim 1915).
2 For an illustration of this problem, see Mair, Kelly and High's re-reading of Fredrik Barth's classic ethnography, *Ritual and Knowledge among the Baktaman of New Guinea* (1975), which argues that 'the experience of ignorance and exclusion of knowledge' (2012: 5) is as important to the functioning of Baktaman society as the knowledge-acquiring rites on which Barth focuses.
3 See Mair et al. (2012) for a discussion of the emergence of an anthropology of ignorance more broadly.
4 See also High (2012) for a parallel exploration of the relational consequences of knowing/not-knowing in Waorani shamanism.

References

Abrams-Kavunenko, Saskia. (2013) The blossoming of ignorance: Uncertainty, power and syncretism amongst Mongolian Buddhists. *Ethnos*. Online. DOI: 10.1080/00141844.2013.844193 (accessed 16 January 2014).

Barth, Fredrik. (1975) *Ritual and Knowledge among the Baktaman of New Guinea*. Oslo: Universitetsforlaget.

Berliner, David. (2005) 'An "impossible" transmission: Youth religious memories in Guinea-Conakry'. *American Ethnologist* 32 (4): 576–92.

Bloch, Maurice. (1989) [1974] 'Symbols, song, dance and features of articulation', in *Ritual, History and Power: Selected Papers in Anthropology*. London: The Athlone Press, 46–88.

Buyandelgeriyn, Manduhai. (2007) 'Dealing with uncertainty: Shamans, marginal capitalism, and the remaking of history in postsocialist Mongolia'. *American Ethnologist* 34 (1): 127–47.

Chua, Liana. (2009) 'To know or not to know? Practices of knowledge and ignorance among Bidayuhs in an "impurely" Christian world'. *Journal of the Royal Anthropological Institute* 15 (2): 332–48.

Douglas, Mary. (1966) *Purity and Danger: An Analysis of Concepts of Pollution and Taboo*. London: Routledge and Kegan Paul.

Durkheim, Emile. (1915) [1912] *The Elementary Forms of the Religious Life*, trans. Joseph Ward Swain. London: Allen and Unwin.

Evans-Pritchard, E.E. (1976) [1937] *Witchcraft, Oracles and Magic among the Azande*. Oxford: Clarendon Press.

Geertz, Clifford. (1993) [1973] 'Religion as a cultural system', in *The Interpretation of Cultures*. London: Fontana Press, 87–125.

Gershon, Ilana, and Dhooleka Sarhadi Raj. (2000) 'Introduction: The symbolic capital of ignorance'. *Social Analysis* 44 (2): 3–13.

High, Casey. (2012) 'Between knowing and being: Ignorance in anthropology and Amazonian shamanism', in *The Anthropology of Ignorance: An Ethnographic Approach*, ed. Casey High, Ann Kelly and Jonathan Mair. New York: Palgrave Macmillan, 119–36.

Hobart, Mark. (ed) (1993) *An Anthropological Critique of Development: The Growth of Ignorance*. London: Routledge.

Højer, Lars. (2009) 'Absent powers: Magic and loss in post-socialist Mongolia'. *Journal of the Royal Anthropological Institute* 15: 575–91.

Horton, Robin. (1971) 'African conversion'. *Africa* 41: 85–108.

Horton, Robin. (1975a) 'On the rationality of conversion: Part one'. *Africa* 45: 219–35.

Horton, Robin. (1975b) 'On the rationality of conversion: Part two'. *Africa* 45: 373–99.

Humphrey, Caroline, and James Laidlaw. (1994) *The Archetypal Actions of Ritual: A Theory of Ritual Illustrated by the Jain Rite of Worship*. Oxford: Clarendon Press.

Lewis, Gilbert. (1980) *Day of Shining Red: An Essay on Understanding Ritual*. Cambridge: Cambridge University Press.

Lienhardt, Godfrey. (1961) *Divinity and Experience: The Religion of the Dinka*. Oxford: Oxford University Press.

Mair, Jonathan. (Forthcoming) 'The "Buddhist knowledge gap": Ignorance and the ethics of detachment in Inner Mongolian Buddhism', in *Detachment: Essays on the Limits of Relational Thinking*, ed. Matei Candea, Joanna Cook, Catherine Trundle and Thomas Yarrow. Manchester: Manchester University Press.

Mair, Jonathan, Ann Kelly, and Casey High. (2012) 'Introduction: Making ignorance an ethnographic object', in *The Anthropology of Ignorance: An Ethnographic Approach*, ed. Casey High, Ann Kelly and Jonathan Mair. New York: Palgrave Macmillan, 1–32.

Mathews, Andrew S. (2005) 'Power/knowledge, power/ignorance: Forest fires and the state in New Mexico'. *Human Ecology* 33 (6): 795–820.

McGoey, Linsey. (2007) 'On the will to ignorance in bureaucracy'. *Economy and Society* 36 (2): 212–35.

Morgan, Lewis H. (1877) *Ancient Society*. New York: H. Holt.

Proctor, Robert N. and Londa Schiebinger. (2008) *Agnotology: the Making and Unmaking of Ignorance*. Stanford: Stanford University Press.

Schieffelin, Edward. (1985) 'Performance and the cultural construction of reality'. *American Ethnologist* 12: 707–24.

Scott, Michael W. (2000) 'Ignorance is cosmos; knowledge is chaos: articulating a cosmological polarity in the Solomon Islands'. *Social Analysis* 44 (2): 56–83.

Turner, Victor. (1967) *The Forest of Symbols: Aspects of Ndembu Ritual*. Ithaca, NY: Cornell University Press.

Turner, Victor. (1969) *The Ritual Process: Structure and Anti-Structure*. Chicago: Aldine Press.

Tylor, E.B. (1871) *Primitive Culture*. London: J. Murray.

Vitebsky, Piers. (2008) 'Loving and forgetting: moments of inarticulacy in tribal India'. *Journal of the Royal Anthropological Institute* 14 (2): 243–61.

27
Criminal ignorance

Darren Thiel

Ignorance and denial of the intentions and outcomes of transgressive activities are central to understanding how individuals and organizations bend, break, create and manipulate moral and legal rules. Indeed, the concept of denial has a distinguished pedigree in criminology. This chapter describes how it has been used to understand crimes ranging from minor youthful delinquencies to major genocides. Drawing on the work of Sykes and Matza (1957) and Matza (1964), I begin by describing how 'techniques of neutralization' – the accounts and stories that structure various denials – are said to operate to release people from moral binds and enable transgression. I then turn to the concept of 'pluralistic ignorance' – where members of groups inadvertently reinforce one another's misunderstanding of a situation – showing how it facilitates the commission of crimes, and illustrating its pivotal role in patterning public reaction to crime and injury.

Next, drawing on Stanley Cohen (2001), I examine how large and powerful organizations, in particular, modern states, also manufacture ignorance and use neutralization techniques in order to break and manipulate moral and legal rules. Here, unlike individual transgressions, techniques of neutralization have the effect of shaping organizational members' behaviour and the broader public understanding of crime and injury, facilitating state ability to commit serious crimes and atrocities with often relatively little social reaction and legal sanction. Last, I describe how ceremonial acknowledgment processes, which signify public agreement about what constitutes immoral activity, are a necessary condition for the creation and clarification of moral knowledge. I examine how such ceremonies act to suppress denials and neutralizations, reshaping what is known about injurious activity and realigning moral boundaries.

Moral ambiguity and neutralization

While much early positivist criminology drew distinctions between the normal and the deviant, framing those labelled criminal as somehow holding different norms and values to mainstream conformists, Sykes and Matza's (1957) ground-breaking work drew attention to how 'delinquents',[1] when asked, commonly expressed guilt and shame about their actions. 'Delinquents' also spent most of their time not being delinquent, valorised 'certain conforming figures' and distinguished 'between appropriate and inappropriate targets' (1957: 666) of their transgression. This, Sykes and

Matza suggested, indicated a likelihood that most youthful offenders were subsumed by the same broad morality as everyone else. They were not Al Capone figures who held alternative values to the mainstream and which drove them to break rules and laws, but they used various narrative 'techniques of neutralisation' to temporarily release themselves from the binds of their own morality. These techniques have the effect of neutralizing inter-subjective and external disapproval of the deviation through linguistic strategies that deny, ignore or transform knowledge of the morally transgressive nature of an action or of one's ability to have been able to avoid it.

To convict someone of criminal behaviour, the law should establish both that the action occurred and that it was intended. Intention implies that the offender held some knowledge about what they doing, while, for instance, mistake, madness or accident – the unknowing commission of a crime – should not be held fully criminal but only negligent or reckless (see, for example, Haque and Cumming, 2003).[2] Delinquent subcultures draw on and develop the cultural recipes and forms of moral knowledge that underlay these laws pertaining to mitigating circumstances and intent. The neutralisation techniques that result are not only excuses and justifications offered *post-facto* but they are 'vocabularies of motive' (Mills, 1940) said to pre-figure deviation[3] – operating as narrative commands that act to absolve or deny personal responsibility and the potentially injurious outcomes of delinquent behaviour.

Sykes and Matza identify five types of neutralization. First, 'denial of responsibility', which claims an inability to prevent the transgression. Delinquents suggest they were somehow pushed into it by accident, through being drunk or high, or by forces outside of their control. They may draw on broader positivist constructions of human behaviour by saying that they 'went crazy', were led-on by a 'bad crowd', or that they 'knew no different' because of their impoverished neighbourhood and upbringing. Here, some forms of knowledge are utilised to deny others in order to create a form of ignorance of intention to one's own and others potential moral reactions to the deviation – a denial of one's ability to choose. The second neutralisation, 'denial of injury', denies the hurt occasioned by the transgression, reasoning, for example, that the car stolen and smashed up was actually insured, or that the boy attacked was a seasoned fighter and so not affected. Third, 'denial of the victim' represents the construction of a victim as actually a perpetrator or, at least, of no moral worth, implying that there was no real victim of the deviation and, thereby, no injury caused. The most frequent form of denial of the victim is the claim that 'they started it', and thus the ensuing transgressive act was a rightful one of self-defence – another common legal and cultural precept that can and does morally allow for certain behaviours that would otherwise be deemed immoral or illegal. I would add, following Cohen (2001), that another frequent account for delinquency is 'I don't know' – implying a literal ignorance of one's motivations or actions and, thus, again, linguistically evading moral precepts.

The final two techniques: 'condemnation of condemners' – implications made that those condemning the delinquent's behaviour are themselves transgressive and thus have no moral right to pass judgement ('who are they to say I'm wrong?'); and 'appeals to higher loyalty' – implying that the delinquent did not act out of personal desire but rather as a result of loyalty to others, like, for instance, their family, religion or gang. These later neutralization types do not imply denial of moral responsibility but, rather, the elevation of some forms of morality over others – although both forms do serve to minimize potential knowledge of the wrongfulness of deviant behaviour. Nonetheless, what the theory of neutralization suggests is that to engage in transgression, people need not reject mainstream norms or learn new ones but, rather, the seeds of deviation and criminality are embedded in the necessary flexibility of law and custom themselves and in the accompanying narratives pertaining to that. Through that flexibility, offenders are able to rationalize and deny the immoral nature of their activities by selectively ignoring or embracing forms of non- and novel knowledge that morally enable and justify transgression. Indeed, we all learn techniques of neutralization from an early age in order to temporarily ignore, adjust or reframe the rules and norms that we otherwise claim to agree to (cf. Goffman, 1971).

Neutralization theory has been used to understand all manner of criminal behaviour from fiddling and pilfering at work (Mars, 1982), to youth violence (Agnew, 1994), domestic violence (Cavanagh et al., 2001), war crimes and genocide (Alvarez, 1997; Cohen, 2001). It can be used to reflect on and understand the 'banality of evil' (Arendt, 2006 [1963]) – that good people can and do engage in horrific acts – not necessarily because they are different from the rest of 'us', but, in particular situations and circumstances, people use the inherent flexibility of common cultural guidelines to deny – to themselves and others – the intentions and outcomes of their actions. I return to techniques of neutralizations and the meaning and process of denial below.

Pluralistic ignorance

David Matza (1964) develops his earlier ideas about the normative processes involved in delinquency by drawing on the concept of 'pluralistic ignorance' (from Schanck, 1932) – the belief of individual members that the group hold particular norms and values which, in actuality, no individual member holds to, or, alternatively, individuals wrongly believe that they hold beliefs that no one else subscribes to when, in fact, others do share them (see Dollard, 1937). Matza suggests that because the rules and norms of a delinquent subculture are largely tacit and non-verbal, and thus ambiguous, members experience considerable anxiety about their roles and status. That anxiety, however, is not discussed as it would likely be seen as weakness and become the object of ridicule. Rather, it is expressed through 'sounding' – a form of mockery that members use to attack one another's status (a process known in the UK as 'piss-taking' – see Willis, 1977).

Sounding is 'both a source of anxiety and a vehicle by which it may be temporarily alleviated' (Matza, 1964: 45). It is a means through which members attempt to overcome their own anxieties but it simultaneously reinforces the normative framework that the members are anxious that they do not want to live up to and secretly disbelieve. This makes it appear that the group is committed to delinquent displays of, usually, machismo, when, in fact, through sounding, group members are merely trying to dissipate their own anxiety. In the delinquent group, members thus misperceive the group norms and come to accept the messages entwined in mockery. They may, then, via neutralization techniques, drift into acting out the imagined norms despite those norms being counter to their own personal morality. Pluralistic ignorance of this kind is self-reinforcing because, by acting out, the illusory norms are further reinforced to other group members.

Matza suggests that this form of masculine-bound pluralistic ignorance can also account for why most young men appear to 'grow out' of delinquency as they age – when boys become men by virtue of work, physique or marriage, they no longer suffer masculine status anxiety. Although, of course, men sometimes do continue to experience such anxiety, and there have been a number of criticisms of this later view (see, for example, Foster, 1990). Nonetheless, pluralistic ignorance has been shown to facilitate the conditions conducive to adolescent (male) transgression, and it illuminates how ignorance frames and reinforces some forms of macho-bound activity more generally (see, for example, Anderson, 1999; Haas, 1977; Thiel, 2012: 106–130; Willis, 1977). As considerable data confirm, men and boys commit the majority of both 'street' and 'suite' crime, and pluralistic ignorance of masculine-bound norms may be seen to play a part in this. Pluralistic ignorance is not, of course, a sole property of men and male delinquents but it can be seen to affect all manner of groups. In studies of student alcohol consumption at Princeton University, for instance, Prentice and Miller (1993) found that pluralistic ignorance of drinking norms was widespread amongst male and female students. Yet, they also found that males, more than females, were likely to adjust their behaviour towards the imagined norm and express more support for high alcohol consumption than they privately believed.

Bystander ignorance and social reaction

It is a truism in criminology, and it stands to reason, that crime and deviance only become so when they are reacted to and named as criminal or deviant – nothing is inherently criminal or deviant (Becker, 1963; Plummer, 2011). It follows, then, that crime and the reaction to crime are bound up with one another in a simultaneous process and, to understand crime, one must understand the social reaction to it. Ignorance and denial play major parts in the social reaction to crime, and this, therefore, can have deleterious consequences. Pluralistic ignorance is, for instance, a fundamental ingredient of 'bystander apathy' (cf. Latané and Darley, 1970) where crime or suffering is not reacted to or intervened in when those witnessing it are members of large groups. The most infamous case was the violent assault and murder of Kitty Genovese in New York in 1964 near to her apartment block where up to 38 people living nearby reported (afterwards to journalists) hearing her screams or seeing the assault but few, or none, tried to assist or even call the police. Essentially, those hearing her screams for help simply assumed that everyone else would also hear and, that if the situation was serious, someone else would do something about it – resulting in no one doing anything. Although the exact details of the event have since been contested (Manning et al., 2007), many residents did hear, some saw, but none did very much, if anything, to prevent the murder. Here, individual bystanders were ignorant of the ignorance of one another, and this provided ready neutralizations for their inactivity.

Social psychologists have since carried out numerous experiments to explore the conditions of bystander apathy (see Cohen, 2001: 140–168). They indicate that bystander intervention is less likely when, first, there are many bystanders rather than few, resulting in pluralistic ignorance which diffuses responsibility and thus enables its neutralization. Second, when people are unable to identify with the victim because they are seen as outside of the bystander's symbolic community. This is effectively a kind of moral ignorance – strategic, partial or otherwise – of a victim's humanity whereby identification and empathy are limited by notions of the moral worth of various out-groups, most notably by stark racial and ethnic categorizations. Last, bystander apathy occurs when audiences are unable to conceive of an effective intervention to the situation – implying ignorance or denial about what can be done. Bystander processes are thus underpinned by various forms of ignorance which facilitate non-intervention and muted-reaction to criminality and injury. This consequently feeds back onto the commission of crimes and other injurious activity, providing anomic spaces for particular forms of transgression to occur and sometimes flourish.

For the types of street crimes that so much haunt the public imagination like the attack on Kitty Genovese, when the bystander ignorance was made public knowledge, its occurrence was met with subsequent shock, guilt, and investigation. Yet, in the case of many highly injurious crimes initiated or facilitated (cf. Kramer et al., 2002) by complex and powerful organizations, particularly modern states, the manipulation and creation of pluralistic and strategic ignorance has the effect of motivating perpetrators, pacifying bystanders, and shielding the organization from public and legal reaction often long after the event has occurred.

Power and denial

Juvenile offenders brought before the courts tend to be drawn from relatively powerless positions, and, their neutralization techniques, when offered as *post-facto* explanations or excuses, tend to be judged as lies and excuses. Indeed, the criminal justice system commonly views neutralizations negatively and, in many circumstances, applies increased sanctions as a result (see Maruna and Copes, 2005). Of course, as suggested above, modern legal systems do also take into account mitigating circumstances (although in many Western nations this is increasingly less so – see Garland, 2001). The very existence of specific juvenile justice systems are testament to this, whereby being a juvenile is seen as mitigating in itself.[4] For powerful organizations, on the other hand, neutralizations too serve to evade legal and moral conjunctions but, as a result of their elevated power and influence, they can also shape the actions of incumbent perpetrators, influence the form of social reaction to the injurious event, evade censure, and, by fostering ignorance of harm and criminality, may temporarily reframe morality itself.

The way in which modern states construct and manage knowledge about their involvement genocides, illegal wars, terrorism, torture and widespread abrogation of human rights are the subject of Cohen's (2001) work on state crime and denial. Cohen follows other state crime scholars in wondering why illegal and highly injurious state crimes often receive less attention than much less injurious street crimes – especially within criminology itself. To comprehend this, he adopts denial as a 'master category' for understanding the normalization of state-influenced suffering, and he uses techniques of neutralization as a fundamental part of his conceptual armoury. In Sykes and Matza's original work, however, the meaning of denial is taken-for-granted and un-examined but, Cohen digs into this, highlighting how denial implies not simply non-knowledge of something wrong, injurious or upsetting, but that it is a simultaneous condition of both knowing and not knowing. This is what Cohen calls the 'denial paradox' – in order to evade the knowledge of something, we must have some knowledge of what to evade. For denial to occur, then, at least a partial knowledge must exist but this is somehow not attended to or fully acknowledged.

Processes of denial are likely to be influenced by a psychological inability to live life with full knowledge of disturbing or deleterious events – as in Freudian understandings of the term. This occurs, for instance, where family members are unable to comprehend the ugly knowledge of intra-familial child abuse (see Russell, 1986; Turton, 2008) or where European Jews in the 1940s and 50s did not accept the scale and nature of the holocaust (Cohen, 2001: 140–142). Yet, Cohen suggests, collective and individual denial is also constructed, shaped and enabled by the various vocabularies, neutralizations and justifications constructed by powerful organizational perpetrators.

Crimes of obedience

As Max Weber (1970 [1919]) maintained, modern states legitimately monopolize violence to enforce their order, and, presently, those monopolies constitute vast armies and killing technologies. The bureaucratic organization of modern states and their military capacity have been refined over history to enable the effective manipulation of soldiers and other personnel (Collins, 2008), and bureaucratic organization itself provides ideal conditions for the 'will to ignorance' (McGoey, 2007) and subsequent 'cover up' (Katz, 1979). Complex divisions of labour, the compartmentalization of specialist knowledge, and the organization of 'dirty work' specialists allow organizational members to deny their role in injurious activity: those at the top of a hierarchy claim they did not know what those at the bottom were doing; and those at the bottom claim they were unable to know the consequences of their actions and were only following the orders of those at the top. The most abhorrent examples of this are state-sponsored genocides where ignorance is spun and utilized throughout the state organization of killing. In Zygmunt Bauman's (1989) analysis of the holocaust, for example, he describes how the modern division of labour enabled German soldiers and civilians to divorce themselves from the outcomes of their own and their neighbours' actions, facilitating denial of personal responsibility and a largely unquestioning obedience to bureaucratic aims and authority.

Kelman and Hamilton (1989) identify three main conditions of 'crimes of obedience', which can be seen as organizational conditions that enable perpetrators of various state crimes to deny the moral intentions and outcomes of their actions. First, 'authorization' enables the denial of personal responsibility by allowing individuals to pass and defer responsibility to the authority issuing orders, claiming they had little choice other than to comply. Second, 'routinization' functions to normalize morally dubious activity and thus inhibits moral reflection on it, enabling the denial of injury. Indeed, stopping and questioning one's previous murderous routine would involve acknowledgement of the morally dubious nature of previous behaviour and it is thus psychologically simpler to remain in denial and carry on (Bauman, 1989). The final condition is 'dehumanization' of the enemy – commonly through reframing people as lowly and unwanted animals. This excludes people from the moral human universe, denies their humanity and moral worth, and thus permits their ill-treatment. I would add that pluralistic ignorance is also likely to play a part in 'crimes of obedience', as, if perpetrators do not discuss with one another moral concerns about organizational aims and activities, situational norms will be developed and confirmed through interpretations of the behaviour of others within the organization, further routinizing and thus normalizing murderous behaviour (cf. Kelman and Hamilton, 1989: 18).

Each of these conditions of crimes of obedience enable otherwise good people to neutralize, deny and ignore the morality that they would usually adhere to (cf. Alvarez, 1997; Arendt, 2006 [1963]). Just like Sykes and Matza's delinquents, however, this does not mean that all such perpetrators are able to totally suppress their own morality – rather, denial is partial. As Milgram's (1963) studies into 'behavioural obedience' illustrate, many of those following orders to administer (unknowingly bogus) electric shocks to a human subject, demonstrated all manner of concern, anxiety and worry about their actions. Yet, they (or 98 per cent of them) nonetheless continued until 300 volts when the subject had fallen silent, apparently collapsed or dead (and 65 per cent continued long after that until they reached the capacity 450 volts). Moreover, many frontline soldiers involved in the holocaust had psychological breakdowns, were issued medication for stress, and some committed suicide but they nonetheless engaged in murderous activity (Alvarez, 1997; Browning, 2001).

Spirals of denial

Outside of the back regions of state bureaucracy, the 'front stages', or public faces, of states manage impressions of themselves through what Cohen (1993) calls 'spirals of denial' that aim to hide, reframe and refract public and outsider knowledge of illegal and injurious events. States may claim complete ignorance of an injurious event through 'literal denial' – suggesting that it simply did not happen. The Turkish state's total denial of the genocide of at least one million Armenians in 1915–1917 is a clear example. If literal denials come under continued scrutiny, states may turn to 'interpretative denial' where it is admitted that something happened that seems bad but they claim that it is actually not what it seems. A contemporary example is the 'Allied forces' reframing of civilian deaths in the war in Iraq with euphemisms such as 'collateral damage', denying and, at the same time, justifying, injury. Under the pressure of critique of their interpretative denial, or simultaneously, states also engage in 'implicatory denial' where the facts of an event are acknowledged but not their implications, which are denied, rationalized and neutralized. Here, states reframe knowledge about an injurious event in order to construct a form of moral ignorance in the eyes of their own public and outside observers, and, akin to individual offenders; they employ denials of injury, responsibility, and victims. In the contemporary 'war on terror', for example, the USA defined the use of hooding, stress positions, deprivations and 'water boarding' not as injurious physical and psychological torture but as mere stress, and they framed the death and injury of some of the victims of 'torture lite' as a non-intended negligence of troops on the ground resulting from the stressful conditions of war. Moreover, torture victims were not deemed victims at all but 'unlawful combatants', which denies and evades both moral and legal culpability (Cohen, 2006; Gourevitch and Morris, 2008; Kramer and Michalowski, 2005). States also regularly engage in 'condemnation of their condemners' and they 'appeal to higher loyalties' in order to justify and neutralize their transgressions. These are commonly constructed through claims to exceptional mitigating circumstances (cf. Agamben, 2005) and the constriction of defensive Manichean frameworks that obliterate the moral character of the enemy, denying their humanity. Yet, as Cohen (2001: 61) suggests, 'Denial of the responsibility is the master account' – states most frequently claim they did not intend the injurious activity.

In the contemporary world with increased democratization and pressure for transparency, Cohen (1993, 2001) suggests that states are less able to engage in total denial but, as a result, more interpretative and implicatory denials are spun. These can serve to evade and inhibit legal censure but they also reframe public knowledge, forming smokescreen-like frameworks that enable state operatives, bystanders, and future populations to deny deleterious events. Indeed, this leads into Cohen's main question – why it is that in a multi-mediated global world where all of us know at least something about the everyday suffering that is initiated or facilitated by state action or inaction, people, even humanists, somehow stand by and largely go on with their lives in denial of the suffering of others? For Cohen, the entire affluent world is a passive bystander to suffering.

In order to answer this question, Cohen turns to theories of denial and bystander apathy, and the research and practice of rights organizations and 'moral entrepreneurs' that aim to forge public acknowledgment of suffering. He suggests that public denial of suffering is perhaps partly subconscious and un-strategic, the result of psychoanalytic processes that split the self and shut out traumatic information, or through our becoming caught up in pluralistic ignorance processes – 'knowing' that someone else will do something, that nothing can be done, or simply being unable to identify with the victims. Yet, denials may also occur in 'bad faith' (Sartre, 1956) but, Cohen maintains, as a result of the denial paradox, they are largely an unknowable combination of the two – and that ambiguity is, of course, part of the power of denial. Nonetheless, state manipulation of knowledge, the human ability to deny, and readily available techniques of neutralization have, at least to some degree, normalized barbarism and suffering in the contemporary world.

Knowing and acknowledging

As denial is a peculiar form of both knowing and not-knowing, Cohen argues that awakening people from its suppressive capabilities is not simply a case of replacing bad knowledge with good, or false with correct knowledge. Rather, the neutralizations, normalizations, and routines of knowledge surrounding abhorrent actions and events require collective and ceremonial rejection and renouncement. Here, agreement and the ensuing negation of epistemological ambiguity, turns partial or non-knowledge into actual knowledge – or 'acknowledgement' – that 'closes the space in which vocabularies of denial can occur' (2001: 75). Indeed, it may be said that all knowledge requires public agreement and ceremony to become recognized as such (cf. Berger and Luckman, 1991 [1966]), which is partly why state denial is so powerful in suppressing full knowledge – the state or, at least democratic states, masquerades as the ultimate representative of moral agreement (see Garland, 1991).

Private knowledge, rumour, or open secrets without official confirmation or broader agreement are, then, effectively ambiguous forms of belief or speculation rather than actual knowledge. Yet, once transformed into 'official truth', they enter into public discourse, lowering the tolerance threshold for such crimes and opening the space for victim narratives. As an example, Cohen examines the changing meanings of domestic abuse in the West, describing how until the quite recent campaigns to publicly raise the issue, victims were often silenced by spirals of denial in families and institutions. Of course, denials and cover-ups by those in powerful positions continue to hide instances of abuse and silence their victims. It was only in 2011, for instance, when the spirals of denial about sexual abuse of teenage girls at the BBC in the 1970s and 80s were unravelled, transforming previously open secrets into 'activated knowledge', which was followed by new accusations against other British TV and radio presenters and a rise in reported offences of child sex abuse in Britain more generally (Greer and McLaughlin, 2013). This 'trail by media' had led to official court proceedings, and, indeed, it is the courts themselves that constitute the major ceremonial representatives of moral agreement and, therefore, the primary creators of moral acknowledgement.

The theatres of acknowledgement for state crimes are international courts, tribunals, and various transitional justice systems and forms of memorialization. They include, for example, the Nuremburg trials of Nazi war criminals, the International Criminal Courts for Rwanda and the former Yugoslavia, the South African Truth and Reconciliation Commissions (TRCs), the Rwandan Gacaca, and various public commemorations of past atrocity such as those memorializing the holocaust, slavery or colonial violence. While the notions of truth and redress differ for each kind of theatre (see Parmentier et al., 2008; Teitel, 2003), each has the effect of producing official narratives and knowledge about abhorrent state-sponsored events. TRCs, for instance, were set up specifically to banish various denials about the apartheid system of South Africa by encouraging, through amnesty, perpetrators to truth-tell and victims to air their narratives. This acknowledged the perspectives held by victims and their families, and, thereby, their status as victims that had previously been denied to them. More punitive systems like Nuremburg work to uncover different types of truth and knowledge but they nonetheless serve to reject offender denials as lies. What the different mechanisms share, however, is the production of a knowledge stripped of denial and moral ignorance. While more restorative forms like TRCs produce admittances, apologies and victim narratives to replace previous denials, more punitive systems produce counter-arguments to rule that offender denials are false. Once established, the punitive mechanisms engage in 'status degradation ceremonies' (Garfinkel, 1956) in which the perpetrator's moral character is ceremonially besmirched. This may be said to signify that any claimed ignorance or ambiguity about offender responsibility and injury must have been made in 'bad faith'. Stripped of their moral status, offenders' neutralizations, denials and justifications can only be wilful ignorance. Previous official denial is acknowledged as false, opening an agreed space for alternative narratives and knowledge to move into.

Of course, it tends to be the losers of wars or revolutions, or relatively weak states, which are bought before truth commissions or international courts (see Teitel, 2003; Kramer, 2010). States that win the battle are left ceremonially immune from challenges to their denials and, consequently, their methods of war or of suppressing revolutions thereby remain speculative non-knowledge. There are many contemporary examples. The various denials made about torture in the 'war on terror' described above, for instance, have received little ceremonial challenge. Their perpetrators' moral status thus remains officially intact and their denials accepted, paving the way for what Cohen (2006) calls a new paradigm of twenty-first-century torture.

Similarly, Ronald Kramer (2010) describes how, as a result of the USA being on the winning side of World War II, their large-scale terrorist atrocities against civilians through area bombing during World War II and later atomic bombing of Hiroshima and Nagasaki, went largely unacknowledged. This, Kramer argues, opened the way for the normalization of the mass murder of civilians in US conflicts since, killing between two and three million Koreans in the 1950s, up to four million Vietnamese in the 1970s, and an as yet unknown number in contemporary Iraq, Afghanistan, and Pakistan. The denials and neutralizations of today's winner states pattern our social reaction to their atrocities, and this opens up an ambiguous moral space in which they can flourish.

Notes

1 'Delinquents' would today be called 'offenders' or 'transgressors'. Also, almost all early criminology refers largely to the criminality men and boys only (see Smart, 1977).
2 The law on 'wilful blindness', however, rules that ignorance of one's crimes cannot be mitigating if the perpetrators 'should' and 'could' have known. The 'ostrich principle' is thus not defensible in law and wilful ignorance is viewed as equivalent to knowledge (see Robbins, 1990).
3 Although very problematic to conclusively test, there have been criticisms of this aspect of neutralization theory but, nonetheless, neutralizations certainly allow the repeated occurrence of transgressive behaviour (see Maruna and Copes, 2005).
4 Paradoxically, as Matza (1964) suggests, legal mitigation is regularly viewed by delinquents as inconsistent and thus unjust, thereby further weakening legal and moral constraints on their behaviour (cf. Tyler, 1990).

References

Agamben, G. (2005) *State of Exception*. Chicago, IL: University of Chicago Press.
Agnew, R. (1994) 'The techniques of neutralization and violence', *Criminology* 32: 555–579.
Alverez, A. (1997) 'Adjusting to genocide: The techniques of neutralization and the holocaust', *Social Science History* 21(2): 139–178.
Anderson, E. (1999) *Code of the Street*. New York: Norton.
Arendt, H. (2006 [1963]) *Eichmann in Jerusalem*. New York: Penguin.
Bauman, Z. (1989) *Modernity and the Holocaust*. Cambridge: Polity.
Becker, H. (1963) *Outsiders*. Glencoe: Free Press.
Berger, P., and Luckman, T. (1991 [1966]) *The Social Construction of Reality*. London: Penguin.
Browning, C. (2001) *Ordinary Men*. London: Penguin.
Cavanagh, K., Dobash, R., Dobash, R., and Lewis, R. (2001) 'Remedial work: Men's strategic responses to their violence against intimate female partners', *Sociology* 35(1): 695–714.
Cohen, S. (1993) 'Human rights and crimes of the state: The culture of denial', *Australian and New Zealand Journal of Criminology* 26(2): 97–115.
Cohen, S. (2001) *States of Denial*. Cambridge: Polity.
Cohen, S. (2006) 'Neither honesty nor hypocrisy: The legal reconstruction of torture', in T. Newburn and P. Rock (eds.) *The Politics of Crime Control*. Oxford: Oxford University Press.
Collins, R. (2008) *Violence: A Micro-sociological Theory*. Princeton, NJ: Princeton University Press.
Dollard, J. (1937) *Caste and Class in a Southern Town*. Newhaven, CT: Yale University press.
Foster, J. (1990) *Villains*. London: Routledge.
Garfinkel, H. (1956) 'Conditions of successful degradation ceremonies', *American Journal of Sociology* 6: 420–424.
Garland, D. (1991) *Punishment and Modern Society*. New York: Clarendon Press.
Garland, D. (2001) *The Culture of Control*. Oxford: Clarendon Press.
Goffman, E. (1971) *Relations in Public*. New York: Basic Books.
Gourevitch, P., and Morris, E. (2008) *Standard Operating Procedure*. London: Picador.
Greer, C., and McLaughlin, E. (2013) 'The Sir Jimmy Savile scandal: Child sexual abuse and institutional denial at the BBC', *Crime, Media, Culture* 9(3): 243–263.

Haas, J. (1977) 'Learning real feelings: A study of high steel ironworkers' reactions to fear and danger' *Sociology of Work and Occupations* 4(2): 147–170.
Haque, Q., and Cumming, I. (2003) 'Intoxication and legal defences', *Advances in Psychiatric Treatment* 9: 144–151.
Katz, J. (1979) 'Concerted ignorance: The social construction of cover-up', *Urban Life* 8(3): 295–316.
Kelman, Herbert C., and Hamilton, V. Lee (1989) *Crimes of Obedience: Toward a Social Psychology of Authority and Responsibility*. New Haven, CT: Yale University Press.
Kramer, R. (2010) 'From Guernica to Hiroshima to Baghdad: The Normalization of the Terror bombing of Civilians', in W. Chambliss, R. Michalowshi, and R. Kramer (eds) *State Crime in a Global Age*. Cullompton: Willan.
Kramer, R., and Michalowski, R. (2005) 'War, aggression and state crime: A criminological analysis of the invasion and occupation of Iraq', *British Journal of Criminology* 45: 446–449.
Kramer, R., Michalowshi, R., and Kauzlarich, D. (2002) 'The origins and development of the concept and theory of state-corporate crime', *Crime and Delinquency* 48(2): 263–282.
Latané, B., and Darley, J. (1970) *The Unresponsive Bystander*. New York: Appleton-Century-Crofts.
Manning, R., Levine, M., and Collins, A. (2007) 'The Kitty Genovese murder and the social psychology of helping', *American Psychologist* 62(6): 555–562.
Mars, G. (1982) *Cheats at Work*. London: Allen and Unwin.
Maruna, S., and Copes, H. (2005) 'What have we learned from five decades of neutralization research?', *Crime and Justice* 32: 221–320.
Matza (1964) *Delinquency and Drift*. New York: Wiley.
McGoey, L. (2007) 'On the will to ignorance in bureaucracy', *Economy and Society* 36(2): 212–235.
Milgram, S. (1963) 'Behavioural study of obedience', *Journal of Abnormal Social Psychology* 67: 371–378.
Mills, C.W. (1940) 'Situated actions and vocabularies of motive', *American Sociological Review* 5: 904–913.
Parentier, S., Vanspauwen, K., and Weitekamp, E. (2008) 'Dealing with the legacy of mass violence: Changing lenses to restorative justice', in A. Smeulers and R. Haveman (eds) *Supranational Criminology*. Oxford: Intersentia.
Plummer, K. (2011) 'Labelling theory revisited: Forty years on', in H. Peters and M. Dellwing (eds) *Langweiliges Verbrechen* [Boring Crimes]. Weisbaden: VS Verlag.
Prentice, D., and Miller, D. (1993) 'Pluralistic ignorance and alcohol use on campus: Some consequences of misperceiving the social norm', *Journal of Personality and Social Psychology* 64: 243–256.
Robbins, I. (1990) 'The ostrich instruction: Deliberate ignorance as a criminal mens rea', *The Journal of Criminal Law and Criminology* 81(2): 191–234.
Russell, D. (1986) *The Secret Trauma*. New York: Basic Books.
Sartre, J.P. (1956) *Being and Nothingness*. New York: Philosophical Library.
Schanck, R. (1932) 'A study of community and its groups and institutions conceived of as behaviours of individuals', *Psychiatry Monographs* 43(2): 1–33.
Smart, C. (1977) *Women, Crime, and Criminology*. London: Routledge and Kegan-Paul.
Sykes, G., and Matza, D. (1957) 'Techniques of neutralisation: A theory of delinquency', *American Sociological Review* 22(6): 664–670.
Teitel, R. (2003) 'Transitional justice genealogy', *Harvard Human Rights Journal* 16: 69–94.
Thiel, D. (2012) *Builders: Class, Gender and Ethnicity in the Construction Industry*. London: Routledge.
Turton, J. (2008) *Child Abuse, Gender, and Society*. Abingdon: Routledge.
Tyler, T. (1990) *Why People Obey the Law*. New Haven: Yale University Press.
Weber, M. (1970 [1919]) *From Max Weber: Essays in Sociology*. Translated by H. Gerth and C. W. Mills. London: Routledge and Kegan and Paul.
Willis, P. (1977) *Learning to Labour*. Farnborough: Saxon House.

28
Targeting ignorance to change behavior

Deborah A. Prentice

Ignorance is a popular explanation for dysfunctional behavior. For example, it is widely held that if people knew the dangers of sun exposure, they would lather on the sunscreen. If they knew the damage they were doing to the planet, they would turn down their thermostats and leave their SUVs at home. If they knew how much food and alcohol they were consuming, they would cut back. If they knew that people were in trouble, they would help. If they knew how to donate blood or save for retirement, they would do so. If they knew how things looked from another person's perspective, they would interact more harmoniously. In short, ignorance—of the cumulative and aggregate effects of behavior, of how to behave differently, and of other points of view—is what keeps people from leading healthier, happier, and more sustainable lives.

This perspective on human dysfunction has given rise to a family of behavior-change strategies that target ignorance. Some of these strategies seek to alleviate ignorance by providing relevant information; others circumvent ignorance and constrain behavior directly; and still others seek to override ignorance of one kind with knowledge of something else—typically, of how other people feel or act in the same situation. Research on the effectiveness of these strategies has yielded a good deal of practical information about how to design information campaigns, institutional contexts, and public policies to facilitate human flourishing. It has also yielded vivid illustrations of and insights into the links between ignorance, knowledge, and behavior. This chapter focuses on the latter set of contributions. It begins with an overview of the facts and assumptions about human psychology that have guided the development of this approach to behavior change and then proceeds to an examination of the strategies themselves and their effectiveness.

Facts and assumptions about human psychology

One of the most influential insights about human psychology to emerge in the last 30 years concerns the dual nature of information processing and storage (Chaiken & Trope, 1999; Kahneman, 2003, 2011). According to this view, the mind has two separate systems (insightfully termed System 1 and System 2) for processing incoming information and making judgments about it. System 1 is quick and intuitive, driven largely by perceptual inputs and operating with simple heuristics. For System 1, things are as they appear; judgments are dominated by the information that is immediately available in the environment and the inferences it brings to mind.

System 2, by contrast, is slow, deliberate, and effortful. Incoming information is integrated with relevant information stored in memory and processed according to principles of logic and inference. System 2 thinking requires ability and motivation; it is the system one uses to calculate the answers to complex math problems, for example. System 1 is the system one uses to guess the answers in advance.

This dual-process model of human thought has a number of important implications for understanding ignorance and knowledge. One, just as the two information-processing systems are separate, their knowledge is also separate. In particular, even if System 2 knows something—that sun exposure causes skin cancer, for example, or that the location of the nearest blood-donation clinic is probably available online—System 1 may not. Thus, an individual can have knowledge in a domain and yet be ignorant of it in any particular moment. Two, the systems have different ways of knowing. System 2 knows through logic and reason: It scrutinizes incoming information in light of other knowledge and principles and commits that information to memory, as knowledge, if it passes the veracity test. System 1 knows intuitively, perceptually, based on the information immediately available. It does not scrutinize or evaluate; it takes incoming information at face-value and uses it to make inferences and judgments (Gilbert, 1991). Knowledge comes easily, naturally to System 1—so naturally, in fact, that it is an open question whether System 1 can experience ignorance. I return to this question later in the chapter. Three, because its operation is comparatively easy and undemanding, System 1 serves as a kind of information-processing default. Its judgments come to mind unbidden, whereas the judgments of System 2 require effort. As a consequence, System 1 is a more common and reliable guide to behavior than System 2.

These implications have obvious significance for the science and practice of behavior change. Traditionally, behavioral interventions have focused primarily on educating System 2: Programs provide people with information and experiences designed to change their beliefs about the desirability and feasibility of target behaviors, with the goal of increasing their intentions to enact those behaviors (see Fishbein & Ajzen, 2009, for a review). The theories that underpin these programs—the Theory of Reasoned Action and later the Theory of Planned Behavior—are grounded entirely in System-2 psychology. Increasing evidence for the existence, workings, and significance of System 1 has had two effects on this field: It has provided a compelling explanation for the modest success of the System-2-based programs and has opened up an entirely new approach to behavior change grounded in System-1 psychology. This new approach replaces educational campaigns with minor structural modifications and simple messaging designed to "nudge" behavior in the right direction (Shafir, 2012; Sunstein, 2013, Thaler & Sunstein, 2008). It replaces System-2 reasoning with System-1 intuition, guided by a "libertarian-paternalist" hand that points intuition toward the desired behavior. Interventions using this approach have had some marked successes in changing behavior, as I detail in the next sections.

At the same time, the shift in focus from System 2 to System 1 places considerable weight on an assumption of shared values. System-2-based approaches to behavior change are grounded in an expectancy-value framework, whereby behavior is a function of its expected consequences multiplied by the value of those consequences (McGuire, 1985). Programs in this tradition typically balance information about expectancies (e.g., smoking increases one's chance of contracting lung cancer) with information about values (e.g., lung cancer is a highly negative outcome). System-1-based programs, by contrast, either collapse the distinction between expectancy and value (e.g., by presenting horrific images of diseased lungs on a cigarette package) or assume shared values and focus entirely on the expectancy side of the equation. When these programs fail, it is more often because their assumptions about shared values are wrong than because their grasp of human psychology is wrong.

Behavior-change strategies

Programs designed to change behavior target ignorance in three ways: by alleviating it, circumventing it, and overriding it. I consider each of these strategies in turn.

Alleviating ignorance

If ignorance is what stands in the way of people exhibiting desirable behavior, then the most obvious strategy for changing behavior is to alleviate their ignorance—help them to know better so they will behave better. The allure of this logic has produced generations of information campaigns designed to cure the ignorance that leads people to engage in short-sighted, self-centered behaviors and to fail to act in their own and others' long-term interests. The uneven success of these programs has provided considerable insight into how to alleviate ignorance and when this strategy is likely to be effective for changing behavior. Among the insights are the following:

How to confer knowledge

Early efforts to alleviate ignorance took the form of information-dense communications that varied in their source, recipient, style, goal, and medium of delivery (McGuire, 1985). These communications focused entirely on System 2, seeking to change people's enduring beliefs and attitudes about everything from socio-political issues and health-related behaviors to new products and everyday practices. The Yale Communication and Attitude Change Program got this line of research off to a strong start in the 1950s, and the tradition is still prominently represented in the fields of communications, marketing, and consumer behavior (Hovland, Janis, & Kelley, 1953; McGuire, 1996).

One of the primary insights to emerge from this tradition is how many distinct psychological processes are required to gain new knowledge. Consider, for example, what must happen for a communication about the importance of energy conservation, the dangers of smoking, or the benefits of exercise to become part of a recipient's knowledge base. The recipient must attend to the communication, understand the information it contains, remember that information, believe it to be true, and integrate it with his or her existing knowledge. Each of these processes requires motivation and mental capacity to carry out; the processes must occur in sequence, and with no missed steps. Ignorance, in short, is not easy to vanquish, at least not with a predefined body of knowledge supposed to replace it. That said, systematic efforts to identify the processes through which information becomes knowledge has created a rigorous science of how to deliver communications in a way that maximizes change in beliefs and attitudes (see McGuire, 1985 for a review).

Which knowledge to confer

Of course, changing minds is one thing; changing behavior is another. A common outcome of studies that seek to confer knowledge in order to change behavior is that beliefs and attitudes change but behavior does not. Confronted with this outcome across many, many studies, researchers turned their attention to the identification of other sources of ignorance that might explain it. Their efforts yielded two additional targets for intervention. One, beliefs and attitudes may remain disconnected from behavior. For example, people may develop an understanding of why it is important to conserve energy or adopt a healthier lifestyle and yet not translate that understanding into specific behaviors through which they could realize those goals. Interventions are more successful to the extent that they build knowledge of and support for specific behaviors as well as broader aims. Two, people may understand what they need to do but not know how to do it. They may know that they need to invest their money for retirement, for example, but not know how to go about it. They may know that they need to drive less but not know how else to get around. They may know they need to get regular exercise but not know how to work trips to the gym into their daily routines. Interventions are more successful to the extent that they include concrete and specific information about how to enact desirable behaviors (Fishbein & Ajzen, 2009; McGuire, 1985).

Compartmentalization of knowledge

If the human mind functioned through System 2 alone, then the foregoing insights might exhaust what psychologists have to contribute to the illumination and elimination of dysfunctional behavior. However, the mind does not function through System 2 alone, and the existence of System 1 adds a number of complexities to the task of conferring knowledge. One source of complexity is the ignorance System 1 has of knowledge developed in System 2. Even after being exposed to strong arguments in favor of getting more exercise, attending to, remembering, accepting, and incorporating those arguments into long-term knowledge stores, developing intentions to exercise daily, and joining a local gym, people often fail to follow through because nothing in their immediate environment cues the need to exercise. The beliefs, attitudes, and intentions contained in System 2 are inaccessible to System 1. Anyone who has ever failed to follow through on a diet, an exercise regime, or a plan to quit smoking has experienced this disjunction.

Solutions to the compartmentalization of knowledge include social, structural, and psychological strategies for making System 2 knowledge available to System 1. In the exercise domain, for example, social strategies include running clubs, exercise dates, and appointments with a personal trainer; structural solutions include in-home and in-office gyms and treadmill desks; psychological strategies include mindfulness training and the development of heuristics that promote physical activity (e.g., "Always take the stairs"). These and similar strategies have been implemented in interventions across a wide variety of behavioral domains (e.g., Thaler & Sunstein, 2008; Wansink, Just, & Payne, 2009; Zelazo & Lyons, 2011).

Ignorance and misknowledge

An additional complexity comes from System 1's way of knowing and not knowing. Because System 1 constructs knowledge out of any potentially relevant information that is readily at hand, it almost always knows something, albeit something shallow, partial, and biased. This misknowledge can mask ignorance in System 2, or alternatively, can interfere with the ability of System 2 to translate its knowledge into action.

These dynamics underlie a phenomenon known as pluralistic ignorance. Pluralistic ignorance is a behavioral phenomenon in which people act in accordance with norms that belie what they truly feel (Prentice & Miller, 1996). The observation of many others doing the same gives rise to the mistaken belief that these others are acting authentically and that their own misgivings are not shared. Pluralistic ignorance is typically driven by misknowledge in System 1 masking ignorance in System 2. Consider, for example, the famous case of the unresponsive bystander. Bystanders to emergencies are notorious for their failure to intervene, a failure whose likelihood increases with the number of bystanders present. Early research on bystander behavior highlighted how pluralistic ignorance inhibits action (Latané & Darley, 1970): Bystanders are typically caught off-guard by an unfolding emergency. They hesitate, unsure of what is happening, whether the situation is an actual emergency, and what they should do to help. They look to the behavior of others to help them answer these questions, and what they see is inaction. Of course, this inaction is driven by the same uncertainty and confusion that they themselves are experiencing, but that is not how System 1 interprets it. System 1 is conditioned to take other people's behavior at face value, as evidence of what they truly think and feel (Gilbert & Malone, 1995). Confronted with the inaction of other bystanders, therefore, System 1 interprets this behavior as a lack of concern, a signal that intervention is not an appropriate response. In this way, a behavior originally rooted in ignorance is perpetuated by the misknowledge generated by System 1.

A second case of pluralistic ignorance highlights its imperviousness to efforts to educate System 2. Public concern over the dangers of excessive drinking by college students has led to a multitude of interventions designed to teach students to drink more responsibly. These interventions have foundered on two erroneous beliefs, widely held on college campuses: That *everyone* drinks heavily and that *everyone* is comfortable with heavy drinking (Prentice & Miller, 1993). These erroneous beliefs are rooted in students' observations of campus social life, observations that give System 1 ample evidence of the prevalence and pleasures of heavy drinking. Contrary evidence—the negative outcomes students experience when they drink too much, the misgivings most students feel about heavy drinking and its consequences, and the sizable fraction of students who abstain from alcohol use—is hidden from view. Thus, when students are in drinking situations, the knowledge they have gained from well-intentioned educational programs about the dangers of excessive alcohol use and strategies for drinking responsibly remains lodged in System 2, disconnected from the immediate reality of a situation in which heavy drinking is seemingly experienced by all as a source of pleasure and camaraderie. Interventions that seek to correct their erroneous beliefs about drinking attitudes and behaviors run up against this same reality and are therefore often met with disbelief (Prentice, 2008).

In cases of pluralistic ignorance, the most effective behavioral interventions are those that address both the ignorance of System 2 and the misknowledge of System 1. For example, interventions to promote bystander action address both the question of how to behave in an emergency ("ask the victim if she is OK; call 911") and how to overcome other people's inaction ("be an upstander, not a bystander"). Interventions to reduce college-student drinking reveal pluralistic ignorance in a group setting and engage students in a discussion of how people's behavior in social situations gives rise to erroneous beliefs (Schroeder & Prentice, 1998). These and similar interventions seek to educate System 2 and, at the same time, give people insight into the psychological dynamics that lead them to misinterpret the causes of others' behavior. The ultimate goal of these programs is to give people a new lens through which to view social situations in the moment, so that System 1 gains more valid knowledge of what others are feeling and doing (Prentice, 2008).

Circumventing ignorance

The many challenges involved in alleviating ignorance have led researchers to explore strategies for changing behavior that do not rely on imparting knowledge. One set of strategies channels behavior in a desirable direction by structuring the environment in ways that capitalize on the proclivities of System 1. These approaches are both libertarian and paternalist—libertarian because they preserve freedom of choice and paternalist because they use psychological insights to put a strong thumb down on the scale in favor of socially desirable behaviors. Consider the following examples (all taken from Thaler & Sunstein, 2008).

Efforts to encourage healthy eating often founder at the cafeteria line, where the unlimited and simultaneous availability of healthy and unhealthy alternatives encourages people to indulge their cravings at the expense of their waistlines. Observations of behavior in cafeteria lines, however, suggests that people do not experience all foods as simultaneously available: They start loading up their plates at the beginning of the line, and tend to take more of the early foods, often running out of room on their plate by the time they reach the later foods. This primacy effect suggests an effective strategy for encouraging healthy eating: Place the healthy salads at the beginning of the line, where people will load up their empty plates, and the unhealthy desserts at the end, where the finite capacity of a plate will become most apparent. Note that the effectiveness of this strategy does not rest on any change in people's thoughts, feelings, or behavioral proclivities; on the contrary, it rests on the extent to which the environment is restructured so that their existing thoughts, feelings, and behavioral proclivities yield the desired behavior.

Modifying the environment to fit the psychology has also proven to be a highly effective strategy for raising levels of participation in voluntary programs. The insight here came, in part, from the failure of more traditional, ignorance-alleviating approaches. For example, despite numerous campaigns designed to raise awareness of the importance of organ donation, the rate of people registering as organ donors remains below 15 percent in the U.S. The same is true in all countries in which people must actively choose to be an organ donor (so-called opt-in countries). However, in many countries, people are automatically registered as organ donors and must actively choose to remove themselves from the registry (opt-out countries). There, the rate of organ donation is uniformly over 85 percent (Johnson & Goldstein, 2003). Encouraged by this correlational evidence for the power of defaults, researchers have experimented with opt-out procedures to increase participation in a wide variety of voluntary programs, including employee-benefit programs, retirement-savings programs, child-vaccination programs, and also opinion surveys. In all cases, opt-out procedures produce much higher levels of uptake than opt-in procedures.

One important question about this family of strategies is whether it requires ignorance to be effective. The strategies are tailored specifically to System 1 thinking; they require no input from System 2 to be effective. The question is whether they remain effective when the domain is subject to System 2 reasoning and analysis. Does the arrangement of food in a cafeteria line still influence food consumption, for example, when people are monitoring carefully their food choices and portion sizes? Do default options still affect program participation when people have the capacity and motivation to make deliberate choices? Absent direct, empirical evidence on these points, dual-process theory predicts that System 2 deliberation would override the effects of these modest behavioral nudges. That said, it is important to note how rare System 2 thinking is in these domains. Indeed, even if nudge strategies are effective only when people are ignorant, they will still be effective most of the time.

Overriding ignorance

A final set of strategies rests on the same logic as the preceding set, but rather than a modest nudge, intended to direct System 1, it uses a more substantial shove, capable of motivating System 2 as well. Specifically, these interventions employ information or structured activities to trigger a psychological process whose effect on behavior is strong and reliable enough to overcome other influences (e.g., Schultz, Nolan, Cialdini, Goldstein, & Griskevicius, 2007; Sherman & Cohen, 2006; Walton & Dweck, 2009). One of the best-developed examples of this strategy is social norms marketing, which seeks to trigger people's reliable proclivity to conform by providing them with information about what others like them think, feel, or do.

Social norms marketing works because (and when) information about similar others is compelling enough to command the attention of System 1 and conformity's motivating effects are strong enough to mobilize the necessary resources in System 2.

One behavioral domain in which social norms marketing has proven highly effective is household energy consumption. Field experiments have shown that brief reports of how one's own energy consumption compares with the consumption of one's neighbors (along with tips for how to conserve) have a reliable influence on consumption at the next meter reading: People who learn they consume more than their neighbors reduce their consumption, whereas people who learn they consume less than their neighbors increase their consumption (Schultz et al., 2007). This is a classic example of conformity at work. Of course, the goal of most interventions is to encourage conservation, without any offsetting increase in consumption by those already well-behaved. To produce this asymmetry, interventions introduce injunctive information that signals the desirability of low consumption: They deliver smiley faces or other signs of approbation to low-consumers to override their inclination to conform and frowny faces or other signs of reprobation to high-consumers to enhance their inclination to conform. This injunctive information is highly effective, though reprobations generate such strong negative affect in recipients that they are rarely used (Allcott, 2009; Schultz et al., 2007).

This set of intervention strategies incorporates the strengths of the previous two approaches: It uses the gentle touch of the nudge programs to trigger a psychological process powerful enough to motivate System 2 and mobilize behavior. Combined with relevant procedural information, this approach has the potential to lead to the development of new habits and therefore to long-term behavior change. The main challenge is how to control the direction of change. The psychological processes triggered in these interventions do not privilege functional over dysfunctional behavior; they do not insure that people will conform only to the right people, affirm only the right values, or defend self-esteem in a socially beneficial way. To achieve this outcome, programs must include a normative component (e.g., the injunctive information in the energy conservation program), and this is often where they founder.

Concluding remarks

Ignorance is an appealing explanation for dysfunctional behavior. Ignorance is endemic and therefore leaves individual actors blameless; as an explanation, it preserves the generally benevolent view of human nature that is part of the current zeitgeist (e.g., Rand, Greene, & Nowak, 2012; Pinker, 2011; Sachs, 2008). Ignorance is also a condition that can be alleviated, circumvented, or override with a family of increasingly well-understood intervention strategies. Finding the right application of these strategies for any particular behavior-change project is a challenge, but a manageable challenge that small-scale experimentation can usually meet.

Ignorance is neither a complete nor an adequate explanation for dysfunctional behavior, however, for it ignores the critical role that values play in shaping behavioral choices. People drink, spend, consume, and otherwise indulge themselves while failing to attend to the basic needs of others not solely, or even mainly, because they are ignorant of the downstream and collective consequences of their actions. They do these things because they do not care about the downstream and collective consequences of their actions, or at least do not care as much as some think they should. Behavioral scientists, drawing on insights from psychological research, have made great strides in developing effective means for mobilizing and channeling behavior, but they have done much less to tackle the thorny question of how to build agreement on desirable ends. Until they address this question, the full potential of these interventions will remain unrealized.

References

Allcott, H. (2009). *Social norms and energy conservation.* MIT Center for Energy and Environmental Policy Working Paper 2009-014 (October).

Chaiken, S., & Trope, Y. (Eds.). (1999). *Dual-process theories in social psychology.* New York: Guilford Press.

Fishbein, M., & Ajzen, I. (2009). *Predicting and changing behavior: The reasoned action approach.* New York: Psychology Press (Taylor & Francis).

Gilbert, D. T. (1991). How mental systems believe. *American Psychologist, 46,* 107–119.

Gilbert, D. T., & Malone, P. S. (1995). The correspondence bias. *Psychological Bulletin, 117,* 21–38.

Hovland, C. I., Janis, I. L., & Kelley, H. H. (1953). *Communication and persuasion.* New Haven, CT: Yale University Press.

Johnson, E. J., & Goldstein, D. (2003). Do defaults save lives? *Science, 302,* 1338–1339.

Kahneman, D. (2003). A perspective on judgment and choice: Mapping bounded rationality. *American Psychologist, 58,* 697–720.

Kahneman, D. (2011). *Thinking fast and slow.* New York: Straus & Giroux.

Latané, B., & Darley, J. M. (1970). *The unresponsive bystander: Why doesn't he help?* Englewood Cliffs, NJ: Prentice-Hall.

McGuire, W. J. (1985). Attitudes and attitude change. In G. Lindzey & E. Aronson (Eds.), *The handbook of social psychology* (3rd ed., Vol. 2, pp. 233–346). New York: Random House.

McGuire, W. J. (1996). The Yale communication and attitude-change program in the 1950s. In E. E. Dennis & E. Wartella (Eds.), *American communication research: The remembered history. LEA's communication series* (pp. 39–59). Hillsdale, NJ: Lawrence Erlbaum.

Pinker, S. (2011). *Better angels of our nature: Why violence has declined.* New York: Viking Press.

Prentice, D. A. (2008). Mobilizing and weakening peer influence as mechanisms for changing behavior: Implications for alcohol intervention programs. In M. J. Prinstein & K. A. Dodge (Eds.), *Understanding peer influence in children and adolescents* (pp. 161–180). New York: Guilford Press.

Prentice, D. A., & Miller, D. T. (1993). Pluralistic ignorance and alcohol use on campus: Some consequences of misperceiving the social norm. *Journal of Personality and Social Psychology, 64*(2), 243–256.

Prentice, D. A., & Miller, D. T. (1996). Pluralistic ignorance and the perpetuation of social norms by unwitting actors. In M. Zanna (Ed.), *Advances in experimental social psychology* (Vol. 28, pp. 161–209). San Diego, CA: Academic Press.

Rand, D. G., Greene, J. D., & Nowak, M. A. (2012). Spontaneous giving and calculated greed. *Nature, 489,* 427–430.

Sachs, J. (2008). *Common wealth: Economics for a crowded planet.* New York: Penguin.

Schroeder, C. M., & Prentice, D. A. (1998). Exposing pluralistic ignorance to reduce alcohol use among college students. *Journal of Applied Social Psychology, 28*(23), 2150–2180.

Schultz, P. W., Nolan, J. M., Cialdini, R. B., Goldstein, N. J., & Griskevicius, V. (2007). The constructive, destructive, and reconstructive power of social norms. *Psychological Science, 18*(5), 429–434.

Shafir, E. (Ed.) (2012). *The behavioral foundations of public policy.* Princeton, NJ: Princeton University Press.

Sherman, D. K., & Cohen, G. L. (2006). The psychology of self-defense: Self-affirmation theory. In M. P. Zanna (Ed.), *Advances in experimental social psychology* (Vol. 38, pp. 183–242). San Diego, CA: Academic Press.

Sunstein, C. R. (2013). *Simpler.* New York: Simon & Schuster.

Thaler, R. H., & Sunstein, C. R. (2008). *Nudge: Improving decisions about health, wealth, and happiness.* New Haven, CT: Yale University Press.

Walton, G. M., & Dweck, C. S. (2009). Solving social problems like a psychologist. *Perspectives on Psychological Science, 4*(1), 101–102.

Wansink, B., Just, D. R., & Payne, C. R. (2009). Mindless eating and healthy heuristics for the irrational. *American Economic Review, 99*(2), 165–169.

Zelazo, P. D., & Lyons, K. E. (2011). Mindfulness training in childhood. *Human Development, 54*(2), 61–65.

29
Rational ignorance

Ilya Somin

The idea that ignorance can be rational may at first seem paradoxical. How can it ever be rational to avoid acquiring knowledge? In reality, however, rational ignorance is a ubiquitous aspect of our lives. Because there are severe constraints on our time, energy, and cognitive capacity, it often makes sense to devote our limited resources to activities other than acquiring additional information. Much of the time, such rational ignorance is actually beneficial. But there are situations where individual rationally decisions to forego acquiring knowledge can lead to harmful collective outcomes.

In the first section, I consider what it means to be rationally ignorant, contrasting rational ignorance with irrational or inadvertent ignorance. The next section explains why such ignorance is both widespread and often desirable. The final section strikes a cautionary note, focusing on situations where individually rational ignorance could lead to harmful results for society as a whole. By far the most significant such case is the rational ignorance of voters about politics. Because effective democratic government requires an informed electorate, the rational ignorance of voters could be a serious problem for democracy. Rational ignorance is an enormously important social phenomenon that scholars are only beginning to properly understand. The conclusion suggests a few possible avenues for additional research.

The meaning of rational ignorance

For social scientists, the idea of rational ignorance has a specific meaning that is distinct from the way the term "rational" is sometimes used in ordinary language. A person is rationally ignorant whenever he or she has decided not to learn some body of knowledge because the costs of doing so exceed the benefits, based on the decision-maker's own objectives. Finding, studying, and assimilating information is a costly activity, not just in terms of money, but in terms of time and effort as well. The time we spend studying philosophy or seeking out information about the best possible deal on a new car could instead be used on other activities. The rational decision-maker therefore will try to expend resources on searching for it only up to the point where expected returns exceed expenditures (Stigler 1961). While the idea of rational ignorance was not formalized by scholars until the twentieth century,[1] it is based on a simple intuition that many people implicitly acted on long before: because information-seeking is costly, it often makes good sense to forego additional learning in order to concentrate on other, more useful activities.

Rational behavior in this sense need not be precisely calculated behavior. Often, it would actually be *irrational* to precisely calculate the potential costs and benefits of learning a particular piece of information, because calculation itself requires more time and effort than it is worth. A person who knows he has little interest in the lives of celebrities can rationally decide not to give careful consideration to the question of whether he should try to read every new article in *People* magazine. He can simply make what Herbert Simon (1959) called a "satisficing" decision to avoid *People* altogether, without scrutinizing each new issue in detail. While that decision may lead him to miss out on the occasional *People* article that might actually be interesting, it is still rational because it enables him to focus his limited time and effort on information sources that are more likely to prove useful overall.

Rational ignorance and other rational decision-making is also distinct from morally praiseworthy behavior. Rationality is defined in terms of maximizing the decision-maker's own objectives (Becker 1976), regardless of whether those goals are morally good, bad, or indifferent. A Mafia boss focused on increasing his wealth and power acts rationally when he devotes time and effort to learning information that enables him to operate a more successful protection racket, rather than to studying ethical philosophy which might make him a better person.

Rational ignorance may also be usefully distinguished from two other types of ignorance: *inadvertent* ignorance and *irrational* ignorance. Inadvertent ignorance occurs when an individual simply has no idea that a particular body of information exists, or that it might be useful for her purposes (Friedman 2005). An emotionally troubled person who has never heard of psychotherapy might not even consider the possibility that her troubles could be alleviated by therapeutic treatment. She may never have made a rational decision to avoid seeking out information about therapy, because it simply never occurred to her to even consider it.

The line between rational and inadvertent ignorance is not always completely clear. For example, a person who has never heard of psychotherapy might still be aware of the possibility that there might be some experts out there who help people deal with psychological trauma. That knowledge might lead her to make a rational decision to search for information about those experts, which in turn might lead her to find out about psychotherapy. Yet she might still make a rational decision to forego searching for information about relevant experts if the cost of the search in time, money, and effort seems likely to exceed the benefits. Despite such complications, the distinction between rational and inadvertent ignorance is still analytically useful, even if it is not always easy to tell the difference between real-world cases of the two.

Rational ignorance is also distinct from irrational ignorance. The latter occurs in situations where an individual avoids learning information that would be useful to him because of cognitive biases that lead him to take actions that run counter to his own goals. For example, "motivated skepticism" might lead an individual to avoid information that cuts against his preexisting beliefs (Taber and Lodge 2006), even though the new information might be very useful in achieving his goals. A variety of other psychological biases might similarly lead people to avoid, or deny, the validity of new information.[2]

The key distinction between rational and irrational ignorance is not that the irrational decision-maker makes mistakes, while a rational one does not. Even the most rational individual might choose not to seek out information that in retrospect turns out to have been worth the cost of acquiring it. The real difference is that the irrational person makes poor decisions from the standpoint of his own objectives, based on the information available at the time the decision was made.

The frequency of irrational decision-making relative to rational is an important point of contention between rival scholars.[3] It is likely that both factors are often at play in causing the ignorance that we observe in the real world. As discussed below, some seemingly irrational ignorance may actually be the result of rational behavior.

The ubiquity of rational ignorance

Rational ignorance is extremely common, particularly in the modern world. The stock of human knowledge has grown so vast that not even the greatest genius can hope to learn more than a small fraction of it. We all necessarily pick and choose which information to seek out and which to ignore. And the latter category is inevitably far larger than the former. Almost every day, we make decisions to forego pursuing additional knowledge on some subjects in order to spend that time on other activities, including acquiring other knowledge that is likely to be more useful for our purposes. While few of these decisions are precisely calculated, a great many are likely to be rational.

Because the amount of information available has grown exponentially faster than individuals' capacity to learn it, we are rationally ignorant about far more things than our ancestors were. This is so despite the fact that modern technology, particularly computers and the internet, have made information more easily accessible than ever before. Although information may be easier to find, there are still tight constraints on our learning as a result of limited time, effort, and cognitive capacity.

In Athens in the fourth century BC, Aristotle was a leading scholar in almost every major field of inquiry known to the ancient Greeks. As late as the seventeenth century, John Locke was simultaneously a great epistemologist, political theorist, and physician (Woolhouse 2009). Such success in widely disparate fields is nearly impossible today, given the vastly greater amount of knowledge available and the resulting increase in specialization. In the twenty-first century, even the world's greatest minds could not excel in as many different fields as Aristotle and Locke did in their time. The time and effort needed to learn enough to become an expert in one or two fields would preclude them from studying the others to a more than superficial degree.

It is possible that future technological developments will transcend current constraints on knowledge, and allow individuals to learn vastly more information than they can at present (e.g., Kurzweil 2006; McGinnis 2012). But any such changes would have to enable us to not only access more information but process and learn it more quickly and easily than before. The technological advances of the last century made far more progress on the former front than the latter. Unless and until that changes, the stock of available knowledge is likely to continue to increase much faster than individuals' capacity to absorb it. If so, we will continue to be rationally ignorant about more and more information.

The pervasiveness of rational ignorance may seem dangerous. But much of the time it is actually beneficial. After all, rational ignorance has become so pervasive in large part because the stock of knowledge has increased so much. If instead of being rationally ignorant about many subjects, people always tried to learn as much knowledge as they possibly can, society would likely be worse off. Large amounts of time and energy would be consumed by information-seeking that might better be devoted to more productive tasks. One of the benefits of increasing specialization and division of labor is the ability to economize on information-gathering about subjects that we can choose to leave to experts. In an earlier age, many people had to rely on home remedies for medical care; today much of that task can be delegated to doctors and other specialists, so the average person need not have as much medical knowledge as in previous eras. In addition, the price system allows consumers and producers to economize on information-gathering by providing powerful signals about the relative value of different goods and services (Hayek 1945).

Sometimes, public ignorance of basic facts seems truly staggering. Survey research finds that some 20 percent of Americans and Europeans do not realize that the earth revolves around the sun, only 39 percent of Americans accept the theory of evolution, and many are ignorant of very basic scientific and geographic facts (Somin 2013, 77). But even this degree of ignorance can be rational for many people, in so far as most can go about their daily lives perfectly well without having an accurate understanding of astronomy, geography, or evolution.

Rational ignorance and democracy

Although rational ignorance is often beneficial, it can also cause harm. This is most likely to occur when rational ignorance on the part of individuals leads to harmful collective outcomes. The most significant potential example is the problem of voter ignorance in democratic political systems. Although it may well be rational for individual voters to pay little or no attention to political issues, a collectively ignorant electorate might find it difficult or impossible to make well-informed decisions at the ballot box.

A voter whose only purpose in acquiring political knowledge is to be a better voter has little reason to devote more than minimal time and effort to the task. The likelihood that his vote will make a difference to the outcome of an election is infinitesimally small – about 1 in 60 million in an American presidential election, for example (Gelman, et al., 2012).[4] While few voters know these exact odds, it is likely that most have at least an intuitive sense that there is little point to spending substantial amounts of time following politics in order to be a better voter (Somin 2013, Ch. 3).

It is more rational to devote one's time to acquiring information that is relevant to decisions that are actually likely to make a difference. As former British Prime Minister Tony Blair puts it, "most people, most of the time, don't give politics a first thought all day long. Or if they do, it is with a sigh . . . before going back to worrying about the kids, the parents, the mortgage, the boss, their friends, their weight, their health, sex and rock 'n' roll" (Blair 2010, 70–71).

Decades of survey data bear out Blair's conjecture that most voters prioritize other activities over learning about politics. Since the beginning of modern survey research in the 1930s, voter knowledge levels in the United States have been fairly stable, and consistently low (e.g., Delli Carpini and Keeter 1996; Althaus 2003; Somin 2013, Ch. 1). Political knowledge levels have stagnated despite major increases in educational attainment and increased availability of information thanks to modern technology, such as the internet and cable television news.

Majorities are often ignorant of such basic facts as the distribution of spending in the government budget, the nature of opposing liberal and conservative ideologies, and which government officials are responsible for which issues (Somin 2013, Ch. 1).

It is important to recognize that political ignorance is rational even for highly altruistic voters whose main purpose in life is to help others. For such altruists, it is more rational to spend time and effort on activities that are actually likely to effectively help others than to devote the time to studying political information in order to be a better voter – an activity which only has a tiny chance of effectively advancing altruistic purposes (ibid., 65–66).

Some voters, of course, acquire political information for reasons other than improving their ballot box decisions. Just as sports fans enjoy learning about their favorite teams and cheering them on against the opposition irrespective of whether they can influence the outcome of games, so "political fans" enjoy learning about their preferred ideologies, candidates, and parties regardless of whether they can influence electoral results (ibid., 78–79). Unfortunately, people who acquire political information for the purpose of enhancing their fan experience often process new data in a highly biased away, overvaluing any evidence that supports their preexisting views and undervaluing or ignoring anything that cuts the other way (ibid., 79–81). Those most interested in politics also have a strong tendency to discuss political issues only with those who hold similar views, and follow political news only in like-minded media (Mutz 2006, 29–41).

Such behavior is probably irrational if the goal were to find the truth. As John Stuart Mill famously pointed out, a rational truth-seeker should make a special effort to consult information sources with viewpoints different from his or her own (Mill, 1975 [1859], 36). But it makes perfect sense if the goal is not truth-seeking, but entertainment, validation of one's preexisting views, or a sense of camraderie with fellow political fans. Economist Bryan Caplan calls this phenomenon "rational irrationality." When the goal of acquiring information is something other than truth-seeking, it may be rational to be biased in the selection of information sources, and in the evaluation of new information that is learned.

The extent to which rational ignorance is a serious problem for democracy is much-debated among social scientists and political theorists. Some scholars argue that rational political ignorance can be overcome by "information shortcuts," small bits of information that can be used as stand-ins for larger bodies of knowledge that voters are not familiar with (e.g. Popkin 1991; Fiorina 1981). For example, "retrospective voting" might enable voters to make good choices at the ballot box without knowing much about the details of policy (Fiorina 1981). The retrospective voter can simply look to see whether things have gotten better or worse under incumbent political leaders, and then reward or punish them at the polls accordingly. Knowing that they will be held accountable for results in turn gives elected officials strong incentives to choose good policies.

Other possible information shortcuts include relying on cues from trusted opinion leaders (Lupia and McCubbins 1998; Lupia 1994) such as pundits and interest group leaders, and utilizing politically relevant knowledge acquired from everyday life (Popkin 1991). Each of these shortcuts can potentially enable rationally ignorant voters to vote "as if" they were much more knowledgeable than they actually are.

Critics of the shortcut literature argue that effective use of shortcuts often requires preexisting knowledge that the majority of voters do not possess. For example, retrospective voters may not be able to use this shortcut effectively if they do not know which policy outcomes incumbents can actually affect (Somin 2013, 101–2). They also contend that shortcuts fail to effectively overcome rational irrationality (ibid., Ch. 4; Caplan 2007).

A different rebuttal to the rational ignorance critique of democracy is advanced by advocates of the "miracle of aggregation," which holds that the electorate collectively makes better decisions than individual voters can (e.g. Landemore 2012; Converse 1990; Surowiecki 2004; Wittman 1995). Even if most individual voters know very little and are prone to error, this need not lead to poor collective decision-making if ignorance-induced errors in one direction are offset by errors that cut the other way. For example, if 40 percent of the electorate votes for the Democrats out of ignorance, and another 40 percent has ignorant reasons for voting for the Republicans, these errors will offset each other, and the outcome will actually be determined by the knowledgeable minority. Advocates have developed several different variants of the idea. An important recent innovation contends that cognitive diversity within the electorate may increase its collective knowledge above that possessed by a smaller, more expert group (Landemore 2012). Miracle of aggregation theories have been criticized as overoptimistic on several grounds,[5] most notably because they depend on the assumption that ignorance-induced errors are relatively uncorrelated, and will tend to cancel each other out. Critics claim that nonrandom, intercorrelated errors are extremely common (e.g. Caplan 2007; Althaus 2003; Caplan, et al. 2013).

Finally, some critics of rational ignorance theory contend that it may be rational for voters to acquire substantial political information after all. For example, even voters who know they are unlikely to cast a decisive ballot may want to acquire political knowledge in order to increase or decrease the size of the winner's "mandate" (Mackie 2012).[6]

The extent to which rational ignorance undermines democracy depends in part on one's normative theory of democratic participation. Some standards for evaluating the democratic process demand greater knowledge and sophistication on the part of voters than others.[7] "Pure proceduralist" theories of democracy could potentially dispense with the need for knowledge altogether, insofar as they justify democracy purely based on fair procedures rather than the production of good policy outcomes (Kelly 2012, 47–48). On the other hand, John Stuart Mill (1958 [1861]), and some modern political theorists (e.g. Brennan 2011) argue that voters have a moral duty to be well-informed, because electoral decisions influence the rights and interests of all of society, not just those who vote for the winning candidate. Mill argued that voting is the exercise of "power over others" and is therefore not a "right" but a "trust" that must be exercised responsibly (1958, 155).

Occasionally, rational political ignorance might actually lead to beneficial political outcomes rather than harmful ones. For example, an electorate with "bad" values might cause less harm if it is also factually ignorant about the effects of different government policies and thereby less able to incentivize elected officials to implement its preferences effectively (Somin 2013, 54–56).

If rational ignorance does turn out to be a serious problem for democracy, there are many possible potential solutions, including using public education or the media to increase political knowledge, transferring greater political power to knowledgeable experts (Breyer 1993; Sunstein 2002), and limiting and decentralizing government (Somin 2013; Caplan 2007).

The debate on rational ignorance and its implications for democracy is ongoing. It cuts across multiple academic disciplines, including economics, law, political science, and philosophy. Because of the immense importance of the issue in a world where democracy has become the most widely accepted form of government, it is safe to say that the argument is likely to continue for some time to come.

Conclusion

Public ignorance about political issues may not be the only area where individually rational ignorance contributes to dangerous collective outcomes. Survey data also shows extensive public ignorance about such subjects as science and religion. A 2010 Pew Research Center survey found that most Americans are ignorant of basic facts about major religions (Pew Research Center 2010; see also Prothero 2007). Ignorance about science might negatively influence public opinion on policy issues where science is relevant. Ignorance about religion might potentially exacerbate religious conflict and intolerance. But it is also possible that scientific and religious ignorance has few or no harmful effects. More research is needed on the extent and possible effects of rational ignorance in fields other than politics.

Rational ignorance is omnipresent in modern society. In many cases, it is unavoidable and even beneficial. In some situations, however, individually rational ignorance could lead to harmful collective outcomes. Whether and to what extent this occurs is one of the most important disputed questions in modern social science.

Notes

1 For an important early statement, see Downs (1957), Ch. 13.
2 For discussion of various cognitive biases, see, e.g., Ariely (2008) and Sunstein and Thaler (2008).
3 For arguments that irrationality is very common, see, e.g., Ariely (2008); Sunstein and Thaler (2008); Kahneman (2011). For opposing views, see, for example, McKenzie (2010) and Wright and Ginsburg (2012).

4 The theory of rational ignorance was first formally applied to voting decisions by Anthony Downs (1957), Ch. 13.
5 For a review of several potential weaknesses, see Somin (2013), 110–17.
6 For an argument that the probability of decisively influencing the size of a "mandate" is even lower than that of casting a decisive vote, see Somin (2013), 73–74.
7 For recent reviews of the different theories and their knowledge prerequisites see Kelly (2012), Ch. 4, and Somin (2013), Ch. 2.

References

Althaus, Scott L. 2003. "When News Norms Collide, Follow the Lead: New Evidence for Press Independence." *Political Communication* 20 (4): 381–414.

Ariely, Dan. 2008. *Predictably Irrational: The Hidden Forces that Shape Our Decisions*. New York: Harper Collins.

Becker, Gary S. 1976. *The Economic Approach to Human Behavior*. Chicago, IL: University of Chicago Press.

Blair, Tony. 2010. *A Journey: My Political Life*. New York: Alfred A. Knopf.

Brennan, Jason. 2011. *The Ethics of Voting*. Princeton, NJ: Princeton University Press.

Breyer, Stephen. 1993. *Breaking the Vicious Circle: Toward Effective Risk Regulation*. Cambridge, MA: Harvard University Press.

Caplan, Bryan. 2001. "Rational Ignorance vs. Rational Irrationality." *Kyklos* 53: 3–21.

Caplan, Bryan. 2007. *The Myth of the Rational Voter: Why Democracies Choose Bad Policies*. Princeton, NJ: Princeton University Press.

Caplan, Bryan, Eric Crampton, Wayne Grove, and Ilya Somin. 2013. "Systematically Biased Beliefs about Political Influence: Evidence from the Perceptions of Political Influence on Policy Outcomes Survey." *PS* 46: 760–67.

Converse, Philip. 1990. "Popular Representation and the Distribution of Information." In *Information and Democratic Processes*, eds. John Ferejohn and James Kuklinski. Urbana, IL: University of Illinois Press.

Delli Carpini, Michael X., and Scott Keeter. 1996. *What Americans Know about Politics and Why It Matters*. New Haven, CT: Yale University Press.

Downs, Anthony. 1957. *An Economic Theory of Democracy*. New York: Harper.

Fiorina, Morris. 1981. *Retrospective Voting in American National Elections*. New Haven, CT: Yale University Press.

Friedman, Jeffrey 2005. "Popper, Weber, and Hayek: The Epistemology and Politics of Ignorance." *Critical Review* 17 (1–2): 1–58.

Gelman, Andrew, Nate Silver, and Aaron Edlin. 2012. "What Is the Probability that Your Vote Will Make a Difference?" *Economic Inquiry* 50: 321–26.

Hayek, F.A. 1945. "The Use of Knowledge in Society." *American Economic Review* 4: 519–30.

Kahneman, Daniel. 2011. *Thinking Fast and Slow*. New York: Farrar, Straus & Giroux.

Kelly, Jamie Terence. 2012. *Framing Democracy: A Behavioral Approach to Democratic Theory*. Princeton, NJ: Princeton University Press.

Kurzweil, Ray. 2006. *The Singularity Is Near: When Humans Transcend Biology*. New York: Penguin.

Landemore, Hélène. 2012. *Democratic Reason: Politics, Collective Intelligence, and the Rule of the Many*. Princeton, NJ: Princeton University Press.

Lupia, Arthur. 1994. "Shortcuts vs. Encyclopedias: Information and Voting Behavior in California's Insurance Reform Elections." *American Political Science Review* 88: 63–76.

Lupia, Arthur, and Matthew McCubbins. 1998. *The Democratic Dilemma: Can Citizens Learn What They Need to Know?* New York: Cambridge University Press.

Mackie, Gerry. 2012. "Rational Ignorance and Beyond." in *Collective Wisdom: Principles and Mechanisms*, eds. Jon Elster and Helene Landemore. Cambridge: Cambridge University Press.

McGinnis, John O. 2012. *Accelerating Democracy: Transforming Governance through Technology*. Princeton, NJ: Princeton University Press.

McKenzie, Richard B. 2010. *Predictably Rational? In Search of Defenses for Rational Behavior in Economics*. Heidelberg, Germany: Springer.

Mill, John Stuart. 1958 [1861]. *Considerations on Representative Government*. Indianapolis, IN: Bobbs-Merrill.

Mill, John Stuart. 1975 [1859]. *On Liberty*, ed. David Spitz. New York: Norton.

Mutz, Diana. 2006. *Hearing the Other Side: Deliberative versus Participatory Democracy*. New York: Cambridge University Press.

Pew Research Center. 2010. "US Religious Knowledge Survey." Sept. 28. Available at: http://www.pewforum.org/files/2010/09/religious-knowledge-full-report.pdf.

Popkin, Samuel. 1991. *The Reasoning Voter.* Chicago, IL: University of Chicago Press.

Prothero, Stephen. 2007. *Religious Literacy: What Every American Ought to Know, but Doesn't.* New York: Harper.

Simon, Herbert A. 1959. "Theories of Decision-Making in Economics and Behavioral Science." *American Economic Review* 49: 253–283.

Somin, Ilya. 2013. *Democracy and Political Ignorance: Why Smaller Government Is Smarter.* Stanford, CA: Stanford University Press.

Stigler, George J. 1961. "The Economics of Information." *Journal of Political Economy* 69: 213–25.

Sunstein, Cass R. 2002. *Risk and Reason: Safety, Law and the Environment.* New York: Oxford University Press.

Sunstein, Cass R., and Richard H. Thaler. 2008. *Nudge.* Princeton, NJ: Princeton University Press.

Surowiecki, James. 2004. *The Wisdom of Crowds: Why the Many Are Smarter than the Few.* New York: Doubleday.

Taber, Charles S., and Milton R. Lodge. 2006. "Motivated Skepticism in the Evaluation of Political Beliefs." *American Journal of Political Science* 50: 755–769.

Wittman, Donald. 1995. *The Myth of Democratic Failure.* Chicago, IL: University of Chicago Press.

Woolhouse, Roger. 2009. *Locke: A Biography.* Cambridge: Cambridge University Press.

Wright, Joshua D., and Douglas H. Ginsburg. 2012. "Behavioral Law and Economics: Its Origins Fatal Flaws, and Implications for Liberty." *Northwestern University Law Review* 106: 1–58.

30

Democracy and practices of ignorance

Lev Marder

Introduction

The near consensus among political theorists is that a healthy democracy in no small part depends on the participation of citizens with necessary knowledge. However, attaching knowledge requirements to democracy that by nature presupposes equality is paradoxical. In fact, if participation in political decision-making is based on required knowledge, applying the term epistemocracy instead of democracy is more fitting.[1]

Jacques Rancière's dissociation of democracy and qualifications for ruling other than the "paradox of a qualification that is absence of qualification" (Rancière, 2001: par. 10) in such influential texts as *Disagreements* and *Hatred of Democracy* obliges political theorists to rethink the conditions of democracy. His intervention both denaturalizes the association between democracy and knowledge, and compels to differentiate between practices of ignorance, their effects, and their relations to democracy.

Rancière distinguishes between three practices of ignorance, of which two operate in accordance with police logic and one in accordance with democratic logic. After attending to the distinction between the two logics and discussing the practices of ignorance aligned with each, I draw on Étienne Balibar's critique of Rancière to propose that an additional, fourth, practice of ignorance associated with democracy deserves attention. If nothing else, this investigation refuses the theorization of ignorance as a state and even less necessarily a debilitating one. Rather, it reinforces ignorance as a practice—an activity with its own rules of what is and is not allowed—subject to change, and highlights the contested nature of ignorance and its relation to democracy. The identification of four practices of ignorance suggests expanding the study of ignorance in political theory, calling for further inquiry into the implications of these practices, the tensions between them, and their effects.

Police and democracy in perspective

For Rancière, heterogeneous logics underlie different practices. In his terms, police logic presupposes inequality, *as if* an identity necessarily qualifies for a particular way of life and disqualifies from another way of life (Rancière, 2006a: 305; 2006b: 3).[2] It is *as if* an order of hierarchy, this form of a partition [*partage*] of the sensible, is natural because some are simply more qualified and equipped for certain occupations. Presupposing inequality, the police form of the partition of the sensible enforces rigid distinctions between what can be said, seen, and done by some and not others (Rancière, 2012: 210). Women, workers, and people of colour among others in different historical contexts are deemed sensibly equipped for bare life, but incapable of participating in political life (Rancière and Liang, 2009b; Rancière, 2011b: 3). Yet by being allocated particular places and roles in the hierarchy, those not in positions of ruling share in the hierarchical order. The police partition seeks to leave no part unaccounted for, no part without its proper name and no position without strict correspondence to an exclusive form of seeing, saying and doing.

The police order is put into question by a democratic logic presupposing equality, *as if* no qualifications must determine aptitude for some positions (Rancière, 2006b: 5). For Rancière,

> democracy is not a regime or a social way of life. It is the institution of politics itself. The system of forms of subjectification through which any order of distribution of bodies into functions corresponding to their "nature" and places corresponding to their functions is undermined, thrown back on its contingency.
>
> *(Rancière, 1999: 101)*

Democracy refers to the disruptive constitution of political space through an absence of entitlement to rule that itself is the entitlement to rule by anyone or in Rancière's influential terminology, "the part that has no part" (cf. Rancière, 2001; 2004a; 2008). It blurs both the oppositions that the hierarchical order intends to preserve and the boundaries between what is political and social, by supplementing the existing partition with the "part of the uncounted", or "part that has no part" (Rancière, 2001, 2011b: 4). This equality presupposing disruption declassifies and disidentifies roles from positions, thereby undoing the naturalness of the police order and its hierarchy. The structural void—the absence of ground (*arche*) that is the ground (*arche*) to rule—challenges the exclusivity and necessity of the police logic (Rancière, 2001: par. 10). It thus exposes police logic's contingency and renders possible reconfiguration of the particular police order.[3]

Police and ethical ignorance

On the epistemic front, the clash between the logics exposes the existence of more than one practice of ignorance. Practices of ignorance can cohere with, on the one hand, the police logic or, on the other hand, the democratic logic and facilitate either the preservation of the existing configuration or a democratic moment. Rancière's discussions of practices of ignorance in "Thinking between Disciplines" and "The Aesthetic Dimension: Aesthetics, Politics, Knowledge" crystallize the distinction. The two practices of ignorance associated with the police logic mirror the two forms of knowledge (*savoir*): the first is knowledge (*savoir*) qua an ensemble of knowledges (*connaissances*) and the second is knowledge (*savoir*) qua a certain distribution of positions (Rancière, 2006b: 3). Given that the essence of police logic is inequality, each of the above senses of *savoir* divides knowledge and ignorance presupposing inequality. *As if* competence in some field of knowledge necessarily excluded from competence in another field, ignorance towards the latter field appears necessary. *As if* knowledge qua position in the distribution of positions strictly circumscribes what can be known, and prevents from knowing the whole distribution or other distributions, the wrongness of the whole distribution of positions must be ignored (Rancière, 2006b: 3).

The two practices of ignorance associated with the police logic reinforce each other in ethical circular fashion, congruent with "a relationship of reciprocal confirmation between a condition and a thought" (Rancière, 2009a: 17). I take the liberty to refer to these practices as "ethical ignorance", even though Rancière does not give them a proper name. They form and reproduce what Rancière calls the "Platonic circle, the ethical circle according to which those who have the sensible equipment suitable for the work that does not wait are unable to gain the knowledge of the social machine" (Rancière, 2009a: 8). Rancière's Plato would have us believe that in an ethical social order work does not wait, requires the workers' absolute dedication (Rancière 2009c: 24),[4] and they must ignore what they are in no position to know.

Ethical ignorance appears as a necessity within the ethical circle. It is *as if* someone knowing how to lay the floor of a palace, and thus doing one's part in a much larger whole, cannot possibly know how to see the beauty of the final result and has no time to gain such competence (Rancière, 2006b: 5; 2009a: 7–8).[5] The worker toiling on the floor is in no position qua knowledge to see beauty. So far the logic is linear, but this is not the end of the story. Presuming that the worker ignores beauty—that she practices ignorance towards knowledge she has no time for—she must maintain the division of knowledge (of working with hands) and ignorance (of seeing beauty). In other words, because she is ignorant of beauty, she must keep working and because she must keep working, she must ignore beauty. The two mutually reinforcing practices of ethical ignorance are critical for the completeness of the ethical circle.

These two practices bind the *ethos*—the position or condition—to the knowledge, perceptions, sensations, and thoughts corresponding to the *ethos* (Rancière, 2009a: 8). The fastening of each *ethos* to an occupation, this ethical imperative, demands ignorance—ethical ignorance—of what is incompatible with *ethos*. Ethical ignorance, in turn, is supposed to leave no excess of any sort, no time to be involved in community affairs aside from doing one's job (Hallward, 2005: 32; Dasgupta, 2008; Rancière, 2009b). In fact, considering that it would be unethical to meddle in affairs one is unsuited for, this disqualifies the populace from taking part in ruling. The inequality presupposing the ethical imperative dictates that those who know should rule the ignorant, and those who are ignorant should obey those who know (Rancière, 2010b: 1; Rancière, 2009a: 15; Rancière, J., 1991). Ethical practices of ignorance support the police order and try to prevent the democratic moment, or the disruption of the existing police partition of the sensible. In epistemic terms, this presupposes *as if* epistemic qualifications are necessary for ruling.

Much of empirical political science research on political ignorance and democracy operates within the police logic and reaffirms ethical ignorance. Such survey research presupposes that the surveyed must meet minimal knowledge requirements to be competent for so-called democratic participation. In the United States, finding that, for example, only 18 percent of those surveyed know "what proportion of the population lived below the poverty line" (Weinshall, 2003: 42), or 22 percent know that "it was U.S. policy to use nuclear weapons in the event of a Soviet attack on Western Europe" (Somin, 1998: 417) confirms public incompetence regarding requisite political knowledge and constitutes failure to meet minimal requirements necessary for a functioning "democracy".

This ethical ignorance is commonly referred to in political science as "rational ignorance"—a term Anthony Downs coined in *An Economic Theory of Democracy*. It explain that people naturally lack the time and motivation to acquaint themselves with political knowledge and it would be irrational for them to invest in such knowledge as opposed to investments that yield more immediate and substantial benefits (cf. Downs, 1957: 207–254). Taking into account their own relatively powerless position, given that each citizen's vote usually has so little effect in determining favourable political outcomes, citizens must ignore political knowledge and because they ignore political knowledge they must remain in their relatively powerless position.

From within the ethical circle, an entire body of literature focuses on institutional frameworks compatible with rational ignorance. Central concerns range from understanding the role of the public, experts, and government officials in political institutions (Dalton, 1977; Delli Carpini and Keeter, 1996; Salam, 2003; Murakami, 2008) to the viability and appropriate form of "democracy" (Somin, 2010; Weinshall, 2003; Talisse, 2004), and compatible economic mechanisms (Downs, 1960; Friedman, 2005; Kirzner, 2006; Somin, 2013).

Research in political science overlaps with work in other disciplines, including the sociological study of the effects and operation of ethical ignorance in corporate and institutional settings. What I call ethical ignorance restricts governmental ability to regulate financial institutions (Best, 2014; Davies and McGoey, 2012; Taleb, 2010), standards of drug safety testing (McGoey, 2009), and environmental policy enforcement (Wagner, 2004; Rayner, 2012) among other aspects of the police order. Rancière himself takes particular issue with Pierre Bourdieu's extensive empirical research into the institutional and class-based maintenance of ethical ignorance. He charges Bourdieu and sociology with reproducing the police order through the implication that the inevitably ignorant masses need the sociologist who is in a privileged position to lead them to true knowledge (Rancière, 2004b: 165–202; 2006b; 2007; Pelletier, 2009).

In spite of Rancière's objections, however, Bourdieu's findings—co-extensive with some studies in political science—should not be so quickly devalued and dismissed for lacking democratic thrust. Bourdieu's project in particular is attentive to the ways in which institutions are critical in both facilitating and impeding resistance to domination (Sonderegger, 2012). His work contributes to understanding the borders and limits of the police distribution and ethical practice from the inside.[6]

Democracy and aesthetic ignorance

The ethical practices of ignorance enforcing the police distribution are opposed to what Rancière calls "aesthetic ignorance" aligned with democratic logic. The practice of aesthetic ignorance refuses and thereby disturbs the conflation of the two forms of *savoir*, the position in a distribution of positions (*savoir*) with knowledge as collection of knowledges (*savoir*) (Rancière, 2009a: 8; 2006b: 5). Presupposing *as if* the conjunction between the two forms of *savoir* is unnecessary, this ignorance rejects the ethical circle in favour of the aesthetic circle. It re-opens a gap in sensibility, when knowledge, thoughts, and senses do not have to correspond to a particular *ethos*—a hierarchical positioning in the distribution of positions. If ethical ignorance stresses its own *necessity*—the imperative to preserve the existing epistemic partitions by conflating the two forms of *savoir*—aesthetic ignorance emphasizes the *ability* to ignore the conflation of the two forms of *savoir* and thus the ability to reconfigure the epistemic partitions (Dasgupta, 2008: 71). In effect, it exposes the contingency of the police configuration, that it is just one way of world-making, and that there are other "ways of world-making" (Rancière, 2011a: 244).

In re-opening the space of possibilities that challenges police configuration's exclusive claim to world-making, aesthetic ignorance constitutes a form of supplementation "that allow[s] us to redistribute the configuration of the *topoi*, the places of the same and the different, the balance of knowledge and ignorance" (Rancière, 2009a: 15). Unlike inequality presupposing ethical ignorance, it operates with the presupposition of equality and enacts democracy by blurring the binary distinctions between those who can and cannot rule, what constitutes knowledge and ignorance, and what is domestic and public. In other words, it reintroduces the structural void, which for Claude Lefort—and many theorists he influenced including Rancière—defines democracy.

Aesthetic ignorance is capable of interrupting the police partitions of the sensible in a wide variety of settings from classrooms to protests. Drawing on Joseph Jacotot's pedagogical method, Rancière describes the figure of the ignorant schoolmaster. Without knowing Flemish, Jacotot instructs his Flemish-speaking students to learn French by relying on a French–Flemish translation of *Télémaque* (Rancière, 1991).[7] This schoolmaster disturbs the conflation of the teacher's position with knowledge and the student's position with ignorance. He does this when he presupposes equality, ignores that his position entitles him to explain material to the students, and his experience confirms that students are capable of learning the material—just as they learned their mother-tongue—without the schoolmaster's explanation. Jacotot's enactment of the democratic moment, the disidentification of mastery and knowledge, marks the refusal of the police order's ethical count that conflates the two forms of *savoir* into one. In this pedagogic form, aesthetic ignorance supplements the proper ethical count with the power of the ethically suppressed uncounted part—the power of the ignorant-schoolmaster that puts into question the naturalness of the knowing-schoolmaster and the ignorant-student pairs.

In a more strictly political setting, some protests rely on the refusal of the conflation of *ethos* and knowledge. This refusal characterizes enactment of democracy through aesthetic ignorance—that is, it blurs the distinctions between those who are qualified and unqualified to speak, see, and act. In so doing, enactment of democracy through aesthetic ignorance disrupts the police order's count of the parts that purports to leave no part uncounted. Rancière describes how in such an instance,

> when a small group of protesters takes to the streets under the banner We Are the People, as they did in Leipzig in 1989, they know that they are not the people. They create the open collective of those who are not the people that is incorporated in the state and located in its offices. They play the role of the uncountable collection of those who have no specific capacity to rule or to be ruled.
>
> *(Rancière, 2009a: 11)*

Without being granted the authority to do so, the protestors confirm their authority to speak in the act of speaking. Their presupposition and confirmation of equality delegitimizes preceding positive identification of the people and re-opens gaps in the police order by pointing to police order's miscount of the people—those who are qualified to speak and those who are not.

For Rancière, neither ignorance of *savoir* qua collection of knowledges, nor impersonal social processes is aligned with democratic logic. The refusal to teach creationism in a school where that was previously the norm—that is, the act of teaching evolutionary theory while completely ignoring creationist theory—is often lauded as progressive and emancipative. In contrast to the above examples, for Rancière, this particular shift and ignorance of one body of knowledge in favour of another would not disrupt ethical ignorance. This shift does not enact democracy given that just as before, the ignorant student is forced to learn a particular "correct" theory and the hierarchy between the student's and teacher's positions remains in place. Historically, Rancière's aversion to pinning democratic hopes on any accumulation of knowledge that leaves the hierarchical distribution of positions undisturbed has its roots in his reaction to the events of May 1968. In "On the Theory of Ideology" (1974) he explains that efforts to change the curriculum from what Marxists call ideology to Marxist "science" in the French academia leave intact the structure of authority and the distinction between those who can and cannot rule. Without disrupting the structure of authority and blurring the distinction between those who can and cannot rule, such efforts coincide with the police rather than democracy.

Impersonal social processes, such as industrialization, similarly fail at reframing the sensible, for they have no inherent democratic thrust and no reason not to reproduce the hierarchies and divisions of the police order. Contrary to conventional belief, according to Rancière, change in workers' condition must be won "*against* the development of great industry" (Rancière, 1975: 96; emphasis added). Towards this goal, he identifies three strategic targets that should be disturbed: the configuration of the very framing of work that supports the partition of time allotted for labour and leisure, the belief that work is work and should not be treated as a vocation, and the belief that one must be productive (Rancière, 1975: 89–90). Ignoring these expressions of conventional knowledge or ethical imperatives—whether this means using the night for artistic projects rather than resting for work during the day, making a vocation out of work, or being non-productive—undermines hierarchy with democracy.

Democracy, police . . . and transformation

The discussion above has focused on the practices of two dichotomous distributions: ethical ignorance and aesthetic ignorance. By re-addressing Rancière's conception of transformation, I want to raise the possibility of an additional form of ignorance associated with democracy—a form that works to disturb practices of ethical ignorance in the police order without presuming and confirming equality. Rancière describes transformation in terms of being an interruption, a disruption, a rupture, or even an overthrow of one partition of the sensible by another—of police logic by democratic logic. He fails, however, to develop the conception of the transformation to the same extent as the conceptions of what is transformed and what is transforming, or in epistemic terms ethical ignorance and aesthetic ignorance. Critics have raised a number of concerns with Ranciere's treatment of transformation, suggesting that he underestimates the effects of institutions (Sonderegger, 2012), that his thought is Manichean (Bosteels, 2009), and opens space for exegetic theories that, for example, highlight how literarity or "excess of words" is the condition of transformation (Chambers, 2013); and that acts of disidentification which he heralds actually involve identification (Norval, 2012). Of the theorists concerned with this issue, Étienne Balibar's intervention most effectively confronts the problem of the democratic *transformation* at the broadest level in Rancière's thought.

In *Politics and the Other Scene* (2002), Balibar suggests that Rancière's conception of politics is incomplete, reinforcing a mutually incomplete conception of transformation. Balibar makes a strong case that the conditions of transformation of the existing order are imminent to that order in both principle and practice. His insight sharpens the focus on the completeness of Rancière's aforementioned account of the protest. The Balibarian interpretation agrees with Rancière that in the protest the material *demos* on the street—democracy—confronts formal *demos* referenced in a constitution through participation in excess of authorized participation, in excess of formal representation (Balibar, 2010: 6–10).

By appealing to and acting on the principle of equality, the equal capacity to rule in particular, the material *demos* aesthetically ignores the ethical correspondence between *demos* and *ethos*, between the representation and the represented whose representation is the extent of their participation in ruling. Yet the democratic interruption involves more than *a jump* from police order's rigid coherence of *demos* and *ethos* to the democratic dissociation of the two. Balibar suggests that

> what is perhaps missing in this oscillation is a third meaning of the term *demos* which is neither material nor formal, but rather dynamic in the sense of pointing at the 'power' which imposes processes of democratization and keeps democratic institutions alive.
>
> *(Balibar, 2009a: 14)*

This third meaning of *demos* complementing the formal and the material, the transformed *demos* and the transforming *demos*, points at a particular form of what Balibar refers to more generally as transformation.

The dynamic *demos* made up of a "combination of 'movements', 'agencies' and 'struggles'" (Balibar, 2009a: 14) pushes the conflict between the formal meaning of the *demos* and the material meaning of the *demos* from inside the police logic rather than through an extrinsic confrontation with a democratic logic.[8] In other words, transformation in the form of the dynamic *demos* plays by police's rules, but sustains democratic institutions in the police order. This force thereby cultivates and expands the space for the enactment of democracy—for the "We Are the People" protest Rancière describes—without itself enacting democracy.[9]

Transformation also operates in Balibar's discourse on the idea of European citizenship and European language. It is here that I offer a brief glimpse at what I call "diversional ignorance" associated with democracy to distinguish it from aesthetic ignorance. While a national conception of citizenship is consistent with police logic and affirms that qualifications are necessary to rule, a new conception of equality presupposing citizenship dissociates it from *ethos*, and affirms equality of rights regardless of qualifications. National citizenship demands ethical ignorance so that citizens' senses exclusively correspond with their position, with the nation-state to which they belong (cf. Balibar, 2009b: 23–24). Aesthetic ignorance of this correspondence—allowing reconfiguration of the partition of the sensible and partition of positions—is an essential element of the national boundary blurring activity of equality presupposing transnational activists and the *sans-papier*. Their transnational actions between normatively separated places interrupt the rigid correspondence of citizenship qualifications and citizenship granting nation-states (Balibar, 2009b: 25).

In addition to the national and transnational forces bearing on citizenship, Balibar argues that the new citizens are

> also "ordinary" citizens who express their demands and expectations from a *European* point of view, unmediated by national and supra-national bureaucracies, or join efforts with foreigners (including refugees, legal and illegal aliens) to uphold basic human and civil rights.
> *(Balibar, 2009b: 25)*

The ordinary citizens who push the boundaries of citizenship within the police order neither maintain the existing police order nor presuppose equality. They build a different stage, a European stage, and their activity *invites* democracy by exposing the internal contradictions of the existing order without enacting democracy.[10]

Similar forces are at play in maintaining the existing configuration and facilitating reconfiguration of European languages. Formal equality of European languages enshrined in the European Constitution polices the distribution of languages. Each of the official language versions of the European Constitution is authoritative without recourse to any original version, and every piece of legislation must be translated into every official language. It is *as if* each language is a "closed totality" in Balibarian terms (cf. Balibar, 2009b: 18–22) or presupposing, to paraphrase Rancière, that European languages are tribal-idomatic rather than universal-global (1992). The formal equality presumes that each language is original and thereby maintains the correspondence between each national *ethos*, its linguistic totality and ethical ignorance in both its forms: ignorance of complexity of meaning appropriate to the tribal-idiomatic languages of other nation-states and ignorance of any distribution of languages other than the partition between tribal-idiomatic languages, which by nature cannot be global-universal.

This configuration is challenged by a democratic force that presupposes *as if*, and verifies that idiomatic language must not be tribal and global language must not be universal (Rancière, 1992: 60–63). The logic of this democratic force holds that idiomatic languages as part of cultures "have the same universal 'human' content, albeit expressed in different ways" (Balibar, 2006a: 6). In other words, the democratic force presupposes equality—that global language is no more qualified to be universal than idiomatic language. Being able to ignore the "necessity" of the tribal-idiomatic and global-universal pairings constitutes the sole practice of ignorance consistent with Rancière's democratic logic. The disidentification puts in question and allows for the reconfiguration of the existing distribution of languages and the parameters set by their idiomatic content. However, the existing partitioning of languages and the democratic force are not the only forces shaping the distribution of European languages.

The dynamic force immanent to the police order drives European language towards an impossible exterior European horizon and towards the interior one with all the ambiguity that the term Europe implies. The rise of English to become the *lingua franca* of the European Union applies pressure on the linguistic landscape and for Balibar marks a tendency towards a vertical organization of languages akin to being equally subsumed in or rather under English as a state (Balibar, 2009a: 15). However, English cannot become the European language because it is at the same time much more and much less than Europe (Balibar, 2004: 177–178).[11] The dynamic power proper to Europe for Balibar is *translation*, which he labels as the "language of Europe" and associates with a horizontal—reciprocatory—conception of citizenship (Balibar, 2004: 178; cf. 2009a: 9–16).[12] Translation neither has to subsume languages under an original language nor interrupt the police logic. Its displacement of the boundaries between nations imposes democratization in the affirmation of a European language, the language of translation.

Transformation, translation, and diversional ignorance

Complementing the existing linguistic order and the idiomatic-universal interruption, the dynamic democratizing force of translation involves diversional ignorance. More precisely, I locate this ignorance in the European context at the intersection of the problematics of translation and the Rancièrian formulation of the relation between the police partition and democracy. Doing so, I take the liberty to initially bypass some central concerns of translation studies including the possibility of translation in the face of the untranslatable, faithfulness to the original, and the implications of committing to a certain—hermeneutic, logical, or structuralist—theory of translation.

Within Rancière's framework, it is by now clear that the consistency of a translator's qualifications and her position are of central concern. Translation in the police order is the work exclusively of those qualified to translate, and this work is expected to reproduce rigid partitions without voids and remainders. Translators of European legislation, for example, must ethically ignore the exclusionary nature of the text-at-hand because they are not in the position of legislators, and because they are not in such a position, they must keep doing their work and remain ignorant of other possible partitions of positions. Yet necessarily failing at ethical ignorance, translators unavoidably push towards the displacement they are tasked with preventing. The failure of ethical ignorance constitutes the practice of diversional ignorance. Even presuming *as if* translation is an almost automatic mechanism for reproducing the exact meanings of texts from one idiomatic-tribal language into other idiomatic-tribal languages, it is bound to cultivate space for displacing the existing framing of *savoir*—to (over)produce sense and to exceed the translator's allotted position.

In one concrete example, the "same" European legislation regulating a particular tax in the French version puts emphasis on the liability of the supplier, the German version on "the place where the tax was due" and in Dutch on the "place where the supply was made" (Directorate General for Translation, 2012: 44–45).[13] I invoke this example not to interrogate what impact the legislation has, and how it affects implementation of law in different locales, but to point to the role of the problematics of translation and the associated diversional ignorance in compelling towards democracy; how a translator necessarily fails to remain in position by playing her role and encroaches on the position of the legislator without presuming equality.

Unlike Rancière's Jacotot, the translator does not aesthetically ignore and thereby divide into two the conjunction of knowledge and position. Unlike Rancière's joiner, she does not presume and verify equal capacity to do mundane work, and in addition judge beauty, thus multiplying one into two. Similar to ordinary European citizens' expression of a European point of view distinct from the activity of the *sans-papier* and transnational activists, a translator's translation—without presuming and enacting the idiomatic-universal—works against rigid meanings and thus sustains space for democracy. The translator's *ethos*-avoiding practice of diversional ignorance prevents settling on the exact meaning of texts. This in one sense invites translating again and again, and in another sense compels towards, but does not itself enact democracy.[14]

Conclusion

Thinking through the operation of diversional ignorance and its relation to democracy in European linguistic context entails asking, with Balibar, "where does the 'translation' process mostly take place, within or across the institutional borderlines?" (Balibar, 2006b: 15). Doing so demands a greater focus on the "dissolution of the markers of certainty" of linguistic, political and epistemic borders, while keeping both the rupture and transformational forces in view. I point to this trajectory for exploring diversional ignorance to complete the schematic sketch of the four practices of ignorance, their various relations to democracy and to each other.

As I have argued, Rancière's distinction between practices of ignorance associated with police logic and democratic logic obliges a move away from interpreting ignorance as an incapacitating condition. This complicates political theorization of epistemic qualifications for democratic participation—theorization that often neglects the operation of what he describes as aesthetic ignorance in the enactment of democracy. Drawing on Balibar's critique of Rancière's conception of the oscillation between police and democracy, I have suggested that an additional practice of ignorance—a practice I refer to as diversional ignorance—is critical for the enactment of democracy. This practice is critical in the sense that it compels towards democracy. By offering European translators as an example, I have raised the possibility of subjects who in their necessary failure at ethical ignorance, practice diversional ignorance and thereby cultivate space for democracy. This example leaves us with a trajectory towards two poles. One pole involves the complication of the Rancièrian partition between practices of ignorance aligned with democracy and police through the problematics of translation. The other pole involves resignification of the democratizing import of translation through conception of the operation of diversional ignorance and the part it takes vis-à-vis the other practices of ignorance. While these poles can be artificially separated for theoretical purposes, they are undeniably intertwined in thinking about such concerns as the meaning of European citizenship, European language policy, and the relation between European law and translation.

Notes

1 I am referring to Rancière's sense of epistemocracy as rule on the basis of knowledge (Rancière, 2010a: 51) and not Nassim Taleb's (2010) understanding of epistemocracy as a situation in which knowledge is approached with caution and humility.

2 The police logic accompanies the police order, which has to be distinguished from politics. As Samuel Chambers explains, "Rancière uses 'police,' 'policing,' and 'police order' to name any order of hierarchy. And thus he invokes this broader concept of "policing" to indicate both policymaking - as the term in English, though not in French, already connotes - as well as a wide array of economic and cultural arrangements" (2012: 42). Politics interrupts the police order. In Rancière words, "there is politics when there is a disagreement about what is politics, when the boundary separating the political from the social

or the public from the domestic is put into question. Politics is a way of re-partitioning the political from the non-political" (2011b: 4).

3 For his understanding of the meaning of democracy in terms of a "structural void", Rancière draws on the thought of Claude Lefort (Rancière, 2001: par. 15). For Lefort, democracy is instituted by "the dissolution of the markers of certainty" (Lefort, 1988: 19).

4 I call this Rancière's Plato because as Christina Tarnopolsky (2010) convincingly shows, Rancière at times confuses Plato's views with those of the characters in his dialogues.

5 The example of the worker in the palace I invoke is Rancière's example borrowed from Immanuel Kant.

6 In spite of Rancière's polemic against Bourdieu, his recent reflections on his own work draw him away from a position that shuns the role of institutions in bringing about democracy and closer to Bourdieu's valuation of institutions in reconfiguring the existing order. He clarifies that, against the Marxist opposition of real and formal democracy, I emphasized the part played by all the inscriptions of the democratic process in the texts of the constitutions, the institutions of the states, the apparatuses of public opinion, the mainstream forms of enunciation, etc. It is a point that clearly differentiates me from some radical political thinkers who want to tear the radicality of politics apart from any confusion with the play of state institutions (Rancière, 2011b: 5).

7 An examination of Jacotot's reasons for choosing the *Télémaque* and not another text complicates Rancière's view that "anyone is capable of making a translation" (Rancière, 1992: 58) regardless of whether the text is "*Télémaque* or any other" (Rancière, 1991: 38). As Javier Suso López (2003) reminds us, in the 19th century the *Télémaque* was lauded for its accessibility, elegance and simplicity of style, and beauty of language that made it—and perhaps not just any random text—central to Jacotot's pedagogical method.

8 As Balibar explains, this *demos* deconstructs sovereignty's "apparent unity: leaving on one side the idea of an "absolute" authority released from the control of laws (*legibus solutus*), and retaining on the other side the idea of a "revolutionary" collective agency which transforms social relations" (Balibar 2009a: 15). Balibar highlights how the dynamic *demos* points to the revolutionary force that drives the conditions for democratic enactment. In Politics and the Other Scene (2002), he follows a similar pattern in showing how for Marx and Foucault transformation involves internal movement of conditions undermining themselves.

9 This is not to say that the police order precedes the democratic moment, or that one logic precedes the other. Both Rancière and Balibar insist that the structuring absence gives meaning to the police order (Balibar 2002: 7; 2006b: 11; Rancière 2011b: 6). In other words, it is resistance that gives meaning to power and power that stipulates resistance.

10 Balibar invokes the European protests against the second Gulf War as an instance of ordinary citizens' expression of the European point of view that in effect puts in question others' attempts to speak for them and expands the space for democracy: "What makes the enormous importance of every form of trans-national mobilization of the rank and file – such as the anti-war protest in nearly all European capitals and big cities just before the beginning of the second Gulf War, but this is only a temporary and negative "Anti-American" type of mobilization – is precisely the fact that they *pluralize* the practice of politics, and peacefully *"destroy" the monopoly of representation* that the "political class" has acquired, with very ambiguous on the public spirit" (Balibar, 2009b: 25).

11 The problems with supporting English as the European language are thoroughly taken up by Phillipson (2008), MacKenzie (2009), and Van Parijs (2013) among others.

12 In identifying translation as the language of Europe, Balibar is following Umberto Eco whom he credits with the idea.

13 Other discrepancies in translation and their implications demand more attention than I can devote to them in this paper. Oliver Marchart's observation that "there is quite a variance" (Marchart, 2005: 85) in the wording of the translations of the European Constitution in particular raises questions about the relation between the role of translators, practices of ignorance, and the European distribution(s) of the sensible.

14 For an insightful discussion of the relation between translation, movement towards universality and production of political communities see Balibar's "*Sub specie universitatis*" (2006b: 11–15).

References

Balibar, E., 2002. *Politics and the Other Scene*. London: Verso.

Balibar, E., 2004. *We, the people of Europe? reflections on transnational citizenship*, Trans. J. Swenson. Princeton, N.J.: Princeton University Press.

Balibar, E., 2006a. *Strangers as enemies: Further reflections on the aporias of transnational citizenship*. Globalization WP 06/4, Institute on Globalization and the Human Condition, McMaster University, Hamilton, Ontario. http://globalization.mcmaster.ca/wps/balibar.pdf (accessed 28 February 2014).

Balibar, E., 2006b. Sub specie universitatis. *Topoi*, 25(1-2): 3–16.

Balibar, E., 2009a. Ideas of Europe: Civilization and Constitution. *Iris: European Journal of Philosophy & Public Debate*, 1(1): 3-17.

Balibar, E., 2009b. Europe as Borderland. *Environment and planning D: Society and space*, 27: 190–215.

Balibar, E., 2010. Antinomies of Citizenship. *Journal of Romance Studies*, 10(2): 1-20.

Best, J., 2014. *Governing Failure: Provisional Expertise and the Transformation of Global Development Finance*. Cambridge: Cambridge University Press.

Bosteels, B., 2009. Rancière's Leftism, or Politics and its Discontents. In: Rockhill, G., and Watts, P., eds. *Jacques Rancière: History, Politics, Aesthetics*. Duke University Press: 158–75.

Chambers, S.A., 2013. *The Lessons of Rancière*. New York: Oxford University Press.

Dalton, T.R., 1977. Citizen ignorance and political activity. *Public Choice*, 32(1): 85–99.

Dasgupta, S., 2008. "Art is going elsewhere. And politics has to catch it. An interview with Jacques Ranciere". *Krisis: Journal for contemporary philosophy*, 1: 70-77.

Davies, W. & McGoey, L., 2012. Rationalities of ignorance: on financial crisis and the ambivalence of neo-liberal epistemology. *Economy and Society*, 41(1): 64–83.

Delli Carpini, M.X. & Keeter, S., 1996. *What Americans Know about Politics and Why It Matters*. New Haven: Yale University Press.

Directorate General for Translation, E.U.E.C., 2012. *Quantifying Quality Costs and the Cost of Poor Quality in Translation: Quality Efforts and the Consequences of Poor Quality in European Commission's Directorate-General for Translation*, Publications Office of the European Union. http://www.poliglotti4.eu/docs/Publis/quality_cost_en.pdf (accessed: 28 February 2014).

Downs, A., 1957. *An Economic Theory of Democracy*. New York: Harper and Row.

Downs, A., 1960. Why The Government Budget Is Too Small in a Democracy. *World Politics*, 12(04): 541–563.

Friedman, J., 2005. Popper, Weber, and Hayek: The Epistemology and Politics of Ignorance. *Critical Review: A Journal of Politics and Society*, 17(1–2): i–lviii.

Hallward, P., 2005. Rancière and the Subversion of Mastery. In: Robson, M. ed., *Jacques Ranciere: aesthetics, politics, philosophy*. Edinburgh: Edinburgh University Press: 26–45.

Kirzner, I.M., 2006. Hayek and economic ignorance: Reply to Friedman, *Critical Review: A Journal of Politics and Society*, 18(4): 411–415.

Lefort, C., 1988. *Democracy and Political Theory*, Trans. Macey, D. Minneapolis: University of Minnesota Press.

Lopez, J.S., 2003. *Télémaque*, au coeur de la méthode Jacotot. *Documents pour l'histoire du français langue étrangère ou seconde*. http://dhfles.revues.org/1608 (accessed: 28 February 2014).

McGoey, L., 2009. Pharmaceutical Controversies and the Performative Value of Uncertainty. *Science as Culture*, 18(2): 151–164.

MacKenzie, I., 2009. Negotiating Europe's Lingua Franca. *European Journal of English Studies*, 13(2): 223–240.

Marchart, O., 2006. Distorted Universals. Europe, Translation, and the Universalism of the Other'. *Eurostudia: Transnational Journal for European Studies*, 2(10): 76–86. www.cceae.umontreal.ca/EUROSTUDIA-Transatlantic-Journal (accessed: 28 February 2014).

Murakami, M., 2008. Paradoxes of Democratic Accountability: Polarized Parties, Hard Decisions, And No Despot To Veto. *Critical Review: A Journal of Politics and Society*, 20(1–2): 91–113.

Norval, A.J., 2012. 'Writing a Name in the Sky': Rancière, Cavell, and the Possibility of Egalitarian Inscription. *American Political Science Review*, 106(04): 810–826.

Parijs, P. van., 2011. *Linguistic Justice for Europe and for the World*. Oxford; New York: Oxford University Press.

Pelletier, C., 2009. Emancipation, Equality and Education: Rancière's Critique of Bourdieu and the Question of Performativity. *Discourse: Studies in the Cultural Politics of Education*, 30(2): 137–150.

Phillipson, R., 2008. *Lingua Franca* or *Lingua Frankensteinia*? English in European Integration and Globalisation. *World Englishes*, 27: 250–267.

Rancière, J., 1974. On The Theory of Ideology (The Politics of Althusser). *Radical Philosophy*, 7 (Spring): 2–15.

Rancière, J., 1975. Utopistes, bourgeois et prolétaires. *L'Homme et la société*, 37–38: 87–98. http://www.persee.fr/web/revues/home/prescript/article/homso_0018-4306_1975_num_37_1_1600 (accessed 28 February 2014).

Rancière, J., 1991. *The Ignorant Schoolmaster: Five Lessons in Intellectual Emancipation*, trans. Ross. K. Stanford: Stanford University Press.

Rancière, J., 1992. Politics, Identification, and Subjectivization. *October* 61(Summer): 58–64.

Rancière, J., 2001. Ten Theses on Politics, trans. Bowlby, R., and Panagia, D. *Theory & Event*, 5(3).

Rancière, J., 2004a. *Disagreement: Politics and Philosophy*, Trans. Rose, J. Minneapolis: University of Minnesota Press.

Rancière, J., 2004b. *The Philosopher and His Poor*, Parker, A., ed. Parker, A., Oster, C., and Drury, J.D., trans. London: Duke University Press.

Rancière, J., 2006a. Democracy, Republic, Representation. *Constellations*, 13: 297–307.

Rancière, J., 2006b. Thinking between Disciplines: An Aesthetics of Knowledge, trans. Roffe, J., *Parrhesia*, 1(1): 1–12.

Rancière, J., 2007. Jacques Rancière: 'Il n'y a jamais eu besoin d'expliquer à un travailleur ce qu'est l'exploitation' Interview by Nicolas Truong. *Philosophie Magazine*, N. 10, June: 54–59. http://www.philomag.com/article,entretien,jacques-ranciere-il- n-y-a-jamais-eu-besoin-d-expliquer-a-un-travailleur-ce-qu-est-l- exploitation,375.php (accessed: 28 February 2014).

Rancière, J., 2008. The Misadventures of Universality. In: *Thinking Worlds: The Moscow Conference on Philosophy, Politics, and Art*, Berlin: 69–82.

Rancière, J., 2009a. The Aesthetic Dimension: Aesthetics, Politics, Knowledge. *Critical Inquiry*, 36(1): 1–19.

Rancière, J., 2009b. *Interview with Lawrence Liang*. Lodi Gardens. http://kafila.org/2009/02/12/interview-with-jacques-ranciere (accessed: 28 February 2014).

Rancière, J., 2009c. *Aesthetics and Its Discontents*, trans. Corcoran S. Cambridge: Polity Press.

Rancière, J., 2010a. *Dissensus: On Politics and Aesthetics*, trans. Corcoran, S. London: Continuum.

Rancière, J., 2010b. *Chronicles of Consensual Times*, trans. Corcoran, S. London: Continuum.

Rancière, J., 2011a. Against an Ebbing Tide: An Interview with Jacques Rancière. In: Bowman, P., and Stamp, R., eds. *Reading Ranciere*. New York: Continuum: 238–251.

Rancière, J., 2011b. The Thinking of Dissensus: Politics and Aesthetics. In: Bowman, P., and Stamp, R., eds. *Reading Ranciere*. New York: Continuum: 1–17.

Rancière, J., 2012. Work, Identity, Subject. In: Deranty, J.P., and Ross, A., eds. *Contemporary Scene: The Philosophy of Radical Equality*. New York: Continuum: 205–216.

Rayner, S., 2012. Uncomfortable Knowledge: The Social Construction of Ignorance in Science and Environmental Policy Discourses. *Economy and Society*, 41(1): 107–125.

Salam, R., 2003. Habermas vs. Weber on Democracy. *Critical Review: A Journal of Politics and Society*, 15(1-2): 59–86.

Somin, I., 1998. Voter Ignorance and The Democratic Ideal. *Critical Review: A Journal of Politics and Society*, 12(4): 413–458.

Somin, I., 2010. Deliberative Democracy and Political Ignorance. *Critical Review: A Journal of Politics and Society*, 22(2–3): 253–279.

Somin, I., 2013. *Democracy and Political Ignorance: Why Smaller Government is Smarter*. Stanford: Stanford University Press.

Sonderegger, R., 2012. Negative versus Affirmative Critique: on Pierre Bourdieu and Jacques Rancière. In: de Boer, K., and Sonderegger, R., eds. *Conceptions of Critique in Modern and Contemporary Philosophy*. Basingstoke: Palgrave Macmillan: 248–264.

Taleb, N.N., 2010. *The Black Swan: The Impact of the Highly Improbable Fragility*. New York: Random House LLC.

Talisse, R.B., 2004. Does Public Ignorance Defeat Deliberative Democracy? *Critical Review: A Journal of Politics and Society*, 16(4): 455–64.

Tarnopolsky, C., 2010. Plato's Politics of Disturbing and Disrupting the Sensible. *Theory and Event*, 13(4).

Wagner, W.E., 2004. Commons Ignorance: The Failure of Environmental Law to Produce Needed Information on Health and The Environment. *Duke law journal*, 53(6): 1619–1745.

Weinshall, M, 2003. Means, Ends, and Public Ignorance in Habermas's Theory of Democracy. *Critical Review: A Journal of Politics and Society*, 15(1–2): 23–58.

Part V

Ignorance in economic theory, risk management and security studies

31

Governing by ignoring

The production and the function of the under-reporting of farm-workers' pesticide poisoning in French and Californian regulations

François Dedieu, Jean-Noël Jouzel and Giovanni Prete

Introduction

Large areas of uncertainty still surround the relationship between environmental exposure to toxic materials, on the one hand, and human health, on the other. Several historical accounts have recently shown that this state of ignorance is not due only to the complex *nature* of the interactions between toxic agents and human bodies. Most of these accounts cast a light on the strategies set up by big corporations to hide the dangers of the toxic materials they use, sell or dispose of in the environment. The cases of tobacco smoke (Proctor 2012), global warming (Oreskes and Conway 2010), and toxic chemicals (Markowitz and Rosner 2003), provide evidence of these strategies contributing to the "social production of ignorance" over environmental health issues. Until now, these accounts have tended to focus on how industry draws on specific networks of scientists, politicians and experts in regulating agencies to produce doubts about the harmfulness of their products. These approaches tend to limit the role of governing bodies to that of organizations "captured" by private interests (McGarity and Wagner 2008). In so doing, they overlook the fact that for governing bodies, ignorance can have a value in itself. For instance, it helps contemporary states to reduce complex issues (Scott 1998) so as to make them "governable" (Foucault 2004). Recent environmental health studies support this thesis. The cases of indoor air pollution (Murphy 2006), of pesticides' effects on bees (Kleinman and Suryanarayanan 2013), and of the consequences of human exposure to chemicals in the soils of post-Katrina New Orleans (Frickel and Vincent 2007), show that ignorance is a useful resource for the control of toxic chemicals in the environment.

The aim of this chapter is to push further this idea by examining the ways in which public authorities legitimize and maintain ignorance over long periods of time in the field of environmental health. From an organizational and a comparative international perspective, based on the cases of France and California, this chapter highlights the usefulness of ignorance for the bodies which regulate pesticide occupational hazards. In those two agricultural regions, specific surveillance programs have been set up by regulatory agencies to monitor the impact of agricultural pesticides on the health of workers and/or residents. Yet, in spite of many suspicions expressed by scientists and advocacy groups, it is still difficult to know whether the daily use of pesticides causes serious illnesses among farm-workers or not. Part of this difficulty of "knowing" comes from the massive under-reporting encountered by these official surveillance programs. After justifying the need for international comparison to understand the mechanisms that produce ignorance, we suggest that the under-reporting of occupational pesticide poisoning is partly produced by the organizational characteristics of the surveillance programs that are supposed to monitor them. Thus, regulatory principles, risk assessment routines and the division of work between public agencies undermine the capacity of these programs to collect relevant data. Finally, we reflect on the function that this "organized" ignorance plays in the pesticide regulation systems, arguing that it is a means to solve some of the regulatory inconsistencies underpinning those systems. This functionalist view leads us to interpret ignorance as a mean to preserve a given social order, an insight inspired by Douglas's perspective on taboos (1966).

France and California: a similar gap in official data on pesticide-related occupational illnesses

Organization and ignorance

Pesticide poisoning among farm-workers is recognized to be largely under-reported both in France[1] and in California (Das et al. 2001). In both cases, official surveillance programs do exist, but have registered an average of only one or two hundred cases of occupational poisoning per year over the last decade.[2] This is a very low figure considering that about one million farm-workers are exposed to pesticides in France and in California. Drawing on the Californian case, Harrison (2011) and Cunningham-Parmeter (2004) stress that this under-reporting is largely due to the characteristics of the workers exposed to pesticides. Californian agriculture employs a large undocumented migrant workforce, and researchers generally link inadequate action on pesticides-related illnesses to the inability of this population deprived of many political rights to confront employers or make claims to the government. A comparison with the French situation encourages us, however, to widen the analysis beyond the focus on the dominated status of farm-workers. French agriculture relies much less on immigrant farm-workers than on farm owners themselves. French farms are organized as small businesses where farmers are their own employers and constitute the majority of the agricultural workforce. This workforce is highly heterogeneous, but it certainly cannot be reduced to a dominated population. It thus appears that the social characteristics of the workforce exposed to pesticides cannot suffice to explain the under-reporting of occupational pesticide poisoning.

International comparison between France and California encourages us to study the organizational design of the policy systems set up to regulate and monitor the use of pesticides. Rather than focusing on the differences between European and American "styles of regulation" (Vogel 1986) or "civic epistemologies" (Jasanoff 2004), we examine similarities in the risk regulation regimes in these two cases (Hood et al. 2001). Despite their regulatory differences, the French and Californian systems have very similar ways of assessing and controlling occupational pesticide poisoning. Considering that the two regulatory systems share many characteristics and face the same under-reporting issue, it is possible to draw the assumption that the source of under-reporting is – at least partly – located in the institutional design of policy tools used to identify and control pesticide poisoning among farm-workers.

Risk assessment and official monitoring programs

To understand how monitoring programs contribute to maintaining ignorance, it is necessary to briefly consider the regulatory system's main principles and rules for controlling chemical hazards in agriculture. The French and Californian systems both rely on a pre-market authorization based on an *ex ante* risk assessment procedure and on post-market surveillance programs to identify potential harmful effects of authorized substances on workers' health.

Firms that manufacture chemicals used to control "pests"[3] need to obtain an authorization issued by public authorities. This authorization is given on the basis of a risk assessment procedure. In California, the Department of Pesticide Regulation (DPR), which is in charge of pesticide regulation, performs the "first registration process" according to standards set up by the federal Environmental Protection Agency (EPA). In France, the "Agency for Food, Environmental and Occupational Health and Safety" (ANSES) is in charge of pesticide risk assessment, while the Ministry of Agriculture delivers the pre-market authorization. Based on this assessment, officials establish guidelines for "the safe use" of authorized pesticides, which have to appear on the label of each product sold.

Once the pesticide is on the market, public authorities implement programs to monitor its possible negative outcomes on health and the environment. Regarding occupational safety issues, France and California have set up surveillance programs to monitor pesticide-related illnesses and injuries among farm-workers. Both of these programs are "passive", insofar as they rely on different sources whose primary activity is not surveillance (physicians, poisoning center) to gather information about cases of poisoning and the symptoms. The report of a poisoning triggers an official investigation into the precise circumstances of the poisoning. The French pesticide poisoning monitoring network, called "Phyt'attitude", is governed by the "Mutualité sociale agricole" (MSA), the administrative body in charge of farmers' social security system. This surveillance program gives a key role to MSA occupational physicians. They are supposed to report any occupational pesticide poisoning they are aware of, with the victim's authorization, to a group of toxicologists. The toxicologists decide whether or not the reported symptoms can be attributed to an exposure to pesticides. In California, the state runs two surveillance programs. The main one, considering the number of cases reported, is the "Pesticide related illness surveillance program" (PISP). This program is set up by the DPR to ensure that all incidents related to pesticide exposure, involving either farmers or the population living nearby, are reported. The PISP data are collected through various sources (mainly physicians, hospitals and poisoning centers), and serve to launch an investigation process to determine the circumstances of the poisoning. This process is led by County Agricultural Commissioners (CAC), who are local officials appointed in each of the 58 counties of California by an elected supervisory board for 4 years, with the mission to ensure local agricultural law enforcement. The second surveillance program is the "Tracking pesticide related illnesses and injury" program set up by the occupational health branch of the California Department of Public Health. Its function is slightly different from that of the PISP, in the sense that it only looks for information on occupational health issues, with the goal of improving workers' health and safety provisions.

All these monitoring programs codify the pesticide-related incidents they record in databases, and are supposed to help public authorities to take measures to reinforce workers' safety and to make regulatory changes regarding the control of pesticides. For instance, observing a string of intoxications related to a same product over a short period of time could encourage authorities to restrict the use of this product. This could entail light regulatory change such as the modification of the "safe use" guidelines on the product's labels (e.g. recommending the use of gloves when manipulating the product) or more substantial change, such as the banning of the use of a pesticide on some or on all crops. Yet such restrictive measures are rarely taken, due to the small number of cases these programs are able to identify each year.

The official production of ignorance: the reductionism of organizational data

In this section we focus on two specific mechanisms that undermine the capacity of pesticide surveillance programs to collect data on the harmful effects of these substances on farm-workers' health. First, we show that the design of regulatory schemes aimed at controlling pesticides actually induces an implicit framing of occupational poisonings as the result of mistakes committed by farm-workers, and the farmers' consequent unwillingness to report them. Second, we suggest that the division of work between official agencies in charge of pesticide regulation compounds the difficulties of pesticide poisoning reporting.

Errors and violations: how pesticide poisonings become invisible

Policy tools often incorporate implicit views and assumptions on the objects they are supposed to govern. Such is the case for the pre-market and post-market tools used in France and in California to control the dangers of pesticides. They promote an implicit view of occupational pesticide poisonings as consequences of the errors made by the farm-workers and farmers themselves. This framing makes it very difficult for those actors to report on the problems they may encounter when using these substances in the fields.

In the French regulatory regime, the *ex ante* risk assessment procedure entails the calculation of the "acceptable operator exposure level" (AOEL based on *in vivo* tests on rodents) for each product, and the calculation of the predictable level of exposure for the farm-workers who will use the product. This level is calculated from models which take into account several parameters, such as quantity of product used per hectare, type of spraying, etc. If the predicted level of exposure is considered "unacceptable", the firm wishing to put the pesticide on the market can suggest protective gear (gloves, masks, coveralls) so as to reduce the level of exposure below an acceptable limit. The degree of protection of such gear is also pre-defined by the exposure assessment models. If the pesticide manufacturer convinces the risk assessment agency that exposure will not exceed the AOEL, the product may be authorized. It then has to be sold with a label describing all the conditions necessary for its "safe use", including protective gear.

This regulatory regime puts the onus of protection on the final user of the product, namely the farmer or agricultural worker, and implicitly promotes the view that "a product correctly used doesn't cause an accident".[4] Recent epidemiological and ergonomic studies (Garrigou et al. 2008) have underlined the limits of this regulatory approach, demonstrating the flaws and inappropriateness of the gear available to protect the workers against pesticides. Despite these studies, the "safe use" logic expresses the bottom line of French policies to prevent occupational diseases linked to pesticide use. When a pesticide poisoning case is reported through the Phyt'attitude program, agents of the Mutualité sociale agricole have to investigate so as to establish its causes. They mostly do so by trying to identify the errors the farmer made when using the pesticide. In particular, they investigate whether the farmer was wearing protective gear or not. Phyt'attitude reports insist that most of these accidents could have been avoided had the farm-workers worn the appropriate gear and paid more attention to the caution on the pesticide labels: "Among the contaminated farmers, 62% were not wearing gloves. Three circumstances of frequent intoxication: incident on the material, the preparation of the slurry and the work on the plot after treatment."[5] Like most of the agents involved in pre-market and post-market control of occupational pesticide poisoning, they tend to overlook the limits of protective gear and adopt an "error paradigm" perspective. This makes it very difficult for the farm-workers, whose responsibility is brought to the fore, to consult the MSA doctor in order to report an "incident" due to pesticide exposure. Their difficulty is compounded by the fact that the MSA physician needs to have complete details on the causes of the incident if this report is to be validated by the chief toxicologists.

In California, the "safe use" paradigm is also a central tenet of the regulatory system. The Californian DPR agents in charge of the surveillance program often argue that the "label is the law", suggesting that regulatory guidelines are enough to ensure workers' safety if they are followed. The extensive use of casual farm laborers has prompted the authorities to delineate the responsibilities of the employer growers. For instance, the federal Worker Protection Standard (WPS) requires growers to provide their employees with safety training and information on pesticide hazards.[6] Any poisoning involving pesticides is therefore likely to be considered as the result of a violation for which the grower might be deemed responsible. In the agricultural counties this puts high pressure on the County Agriculture Commissioners on whom the investigation of the pesticide-related incident relies. Appointed by local elected boards that are careful to protect the growers' interests, they must reconcile their state law enforcement mission with local political concerns, and take into account the agricultural industry's reliance on pesticides.[7] Reporting and investigating on pesticide poisonings can consequently be a sensitive task.

To reconcile these different components, the CACs report and investigate mostly those poisoning cases that might draw "negative publicity" both for themselves and for the growers concerned. Such "sensitive" cases generally involve a large number of victims, whether they are people living near the fields or large crews of poisoned workers, and are often the result of "drift" phenomena from pesticide spray, mist, fumes or odors carried from the target site by air. PISP reports illustrate the tendency of the surveillance program to focus on "drift" events and to interpret those events as accidents resulting from careless pesticide use:

> In 2010, pesticide drift was associated with 115 (83%) of 139 fieldworker illnesses in twelve separate episodes (. . .) Severe intoxications typically result from careless and often illegal use of pesticides. Using pesticides in excess of the specified application rate, besides being a violation of state and federal laws, greatly increases hazards to health without comparable improvement in efficacy.
>
> *(Summary of results from the "California pesticide illnesses program 2010". Available at: http://www.cdpr.ca.gov/docs/whs/pisp/sum_rpts/2010_sumdata.pdf)*

CACS have no choice but to report and investigate "sensitive cases", which can draw the attention of local media or other officials. They have to show that local authorities are dealing with the situation, and once the investigation has been launched they have to verify that the concerned growers complied with the regulations. It is therefore also in the growers' interests to report those "sensitive cases" quickly, as this is seen as a sign of good will and is likely to be taken into account in the decision concerning their fine.[8]

These "drift" cases are, moreover, often caused by exceptional weather conditions that are very difficult to foresee and avoid. This leaves room for the CAC to decide on the extent to which a violation has been committed by the grower, as the following case from the 2010 PISP report illustrates:

> Five hours after an application began, 32 fieldworkers arrived at a field to harvest strawberries about 1200 feet away from an ongoing insecticide treatment to a nearby field. Thirty-one of the workers reported that an odor from the neighboring application bothered them. The crew was moved away from the odor and finished the harvest from the previous day. As the fieldworkers continued to work, two workers' symptoms persisted. The farm manager, who was aware of the application and odor, told the 10 workers they could seek care if their symptoms persisted. In all, 22 fieldworkers reported symptoms and only the two who reported persistent symptoms were taken for care.The growers were cited for failure to take their employees for medical management. The records did not include the use of the pesticide involved, fenpyroximate. On interviews of the applicator, mixer/loader and supervisors, they said the insecticide applied was new to them. Weather station data showed wind was blowing between 3–7.7 mph southwest, towards the direction of the harvest crew.[9]

By investigating cases caused by exceptional circumstances, the CAC makes sure that he is fulfilling his law enforcement mission without interfering too much in the farm's business.The CAC can conclude that there has been a violation of the law, but such cases are rare, considering the small number of fines issued, as the report "Field of poison" written by Californian advocacy groups noted.[10] In short, the reporting of large pesticide drifts is the most politically acceptable form of pesticide poisoning reporting in California. In contrast, pesticide poisonings involving only one or two farm-workers have very little chance of making their way through the CAC agenda. This "blind spot" is worsened by the particular law enforcement focus: by referring to compliance with the guidelines given by the federal Worker Protection Standard (WPS), the CAC makes sure that the law is abided by at a collective level (the weather conditions required for pesticide spraying or fumigation, specific information and training regarding pesticide use and so forth). As we will see below, the other surveillance program set up by the California Department of Public Health (CDPH) records incidents related to individual handlers. However, the number of cases reported each year (approximately 150 per year during the 1998–2007 period)[11] through that program is even smaller than on the PISP. With such small numbers of cases, general trends regarding the individual poisoning of handlers cannot be identified.

A "structural" ignorance

The division of work is recognized as a source of "structural secrecy" (Vaughan 1996) within organizations, and has been put forward to explain mainly organizational failures. The specialization of tasks within organized systems, combined with organizational practices and social and geographical distances between agents, are clues to identify potential problems or warning signals. This can be applied to the under-reporting of pesticide-related poisoning both in France and in California.

In California, the specialization between two distinct agencies in charge of pesticide surveillance programs, the DPR and the CDPH, is an obstacle to adequate data collection. In spite of their similarities, the two programs differ in several respects. First, they rely on different sources of information. The CDPH's program relies mainly on the "doctor first reports", the medical files constituted for the workers' compensation system in case of an occupational injury. This source primarily concerns other kinds of accidents than pesticide poisoning. The 1998–2004 CDPH surveillance program report established that of the 1,605 known pesticide accidents, the majority stemmed from routine work (60.1 percent) and the application of pesticides (22 percent). The CDPH program also draws on the few post-accident investigations it is able to make after the reporting of an accident involving pesticides. Thus, whereas the DPR's PISP pays attention to cases involving numerous victims, the CDPH surveillance program spotlights individual workers handling pesticides.

A few years ago the CDPH and the DPR decided to share their data during monthly meetings so as to make their own analysis more accurate and robust. In fact, each department has access to specific information which could improve the surveillance activities of the other department. For instance, the DPR is keenly interested in the doctor first reports that the CDPH receives, which provide valuable information on the medical background of the victims. In turn, due to its limited human resources, the CDPH can investigate only superficially the cases of pesticide poisoning that it records, and may be interested in the *in situ* information contained in the CACs' investigation reports.

Yet, the different focus and target of the two agencies limit data sharing. As the CDPH targets individuals, it is unlikely to find the information it seeks, insofar as the CAC focuses on law enforcement at a collective level. For instance, the CDPH will want to know whether an injured handler was wearing his protective suit, whereas the DPR will verify whether the pesticide fumigation was authorized or whether the pesticide spray was used in the required weather conditions. In addition, the fear of losing control over a public policy field inhibits information sharing. According to CDPH agents, the DPR is sometimes not willing to provide information such as the name of the product involved in the poisoning. Likewise, the DPR does not let CDPH agents investigate on farms. As a CDPH physicians explains: "This is crazy, every time we try to investigate on a farm, we receive a phone call from DPR saying 'what the hell are you doing here?' I don't know, they must have spies all around."[12] Due to these challenges, information is shared with difficulty, and data gaps on pesticide poisonings remain numerous. These barriers explain why the PISP program remains the main source of information on pesticide-related illnesses. As a consequence and despite CDPH concerns, very little is known about the poisoning of the workers who handle pesticides on a day-to-day basis.

In France, the division of work between regulatory agencies worsens under-reporting in a different way, through a mechanism of responsibility fragmentation. Two agencies can officially be involved in post-market surveillance, the MSA and the ANSES. The MSA runs the Phyt'attitude program. Its officials are aware that their surveillance program largely under-reports pesticide poisoning of farmers. On many occasions they have stressed that this program cannot be the sole tool bearing the responsibility for ongoing post-market occupational health and safety surveillance. The ANSES, in charge of pre-market authorization, can also participate in improving surveillance by asking more systematically for complementary field studies of workers' exposure to the industry. However, the agency rarely makes such requests. In fact, ANSES experts generally hesitate to ask for more data once the pesticide is on the market because it would delay the first-registration processes handled by the agency, which are a priority. Instead, ANSES' experts, as well as firms manufacturing pesticides, argue that there is no need to provide such studies during the first registration. Both rely on the MSA Phyt'attitude surveillance program to substantiate their claim that there is no need for further data.[13] In short, the division of labor between the MSA and the ANSES allows both agencies to shift the burden of responsibility for the data gap onto each other. In other words, organizational specialization entails a fragmentation of responsibility that tends to legitimize under-reporting.

The function of ignorance: solving regulatory inconsistencies

So far we have underlined the fact that the under-reporting of occupational pesticide poisoning has various organizational and institutional sources in France and in California. We will now broaden our focus to show that, though it has different explanations, the under-reporting of pesticides' harmful effects is a means to ensure the stability and legitimacy of the risk regulatory regime framework that France and California share.

Uncomfortable knowledge for risk assessment

Risk assessment procedures rely heavily on toxicological knowledge and data to bring dangers into the realm of the knowable and measurable. They may nevertheless be at odds with certain forms of knowledge in which hazards are not readily translatable into assessable risks, and which tend instead to emphasize the uncertainty characterizing the risks. Social scientists who work on risk issues are familiar with this feeling that their knowledge is disregarded and considered to be bothersome by the institutions in charge of the assessment and management of those risks. Such "uncomfortable knowledge" (Rayner 2012) may also be produced by surveillance systems, as the case of pesticide risk assessment in France and in California illustrates. We suggest that really efficient surveillance programs in these two cases would bring to light data that would be too abrasive for the routines of pesticide risk assessment. Despite their current limitations, these programs already produce uncomfortable data. At the beginning of the last decade, for instance, the MSA Phyt'attitude program recorded several poisoning cases occurring during farm-workers "reentry" into treated fields. These data cast light on the gaps in the risk assessment procedure on that issue, and led to additional provisions regarding reentry intervals in the risk management process in 2006. Apple growers protested loudly against this regulatory change.

Apart from these immediate political costs, producing "too much" knowledge on farm-workers' pesticide poisoning could challenge the implicit assumptions on which policies to control those substances are based. Whereas these policies rely on the idea that occupational pesticide poisoning occurs as "discrete" (Nash 2004) and rather exceptional events, more accurate surveillance data might demonstrate that they are ubiquitous and barely preventable through guidelines and rules for safe use. They may also cast light on the limitations of the models used for risk assessment, by comparing them to other methods such as the ergonomic study of the actual daily tasks of exposed workers. Such data can appear through official surveillance programs but not exclusively. Physicians or other officials can also investigate on pesticide exposure and produce uncomfortable results that lead to significant regulatory changes. In France in 2001, an exposure study conducted by MSA agents showed that farmers were dangerously exposed to a particular form of sodium arsenite, a pesticide used in wine production to fight a mushroom attacking the grapevine. The study highlighted that farm-workers were contaminated by this carcinogenic pesticide even though they were wearing their protective equipment and following the "safe use" guidelines correctly. The results of this study, confirmed by Phyt'attitude data, led to the banning of this pesticide in 2001. Grape growers were furious about this decision because there was no alternative chemical to fight this plant disease. In California, in early 2010, two fruit quality inspectors sought care for similar symptoms after assessing Chilean grape imports. Upon arrival in the US, grapes are required to be treated with the fumigant methyl bromide (MeBr). The inspectors visited their physicians for neurological symptoms such as dizziness, memory disorders and difficulty walking. Medical evaluations confirmed they had MeBr poisoning. In response, Californian cold storage facilities installed methyl bromide monitoring devices and implemented various exposure control protocols such as ventilation, work hour restrictions and pre-purging of trailers before off-loading. Workers were educated on the situation through training and posting.[14] These results demonstrate the significant gap existing between "theoretical" risk assessment and the reality of exposure.

The "double" utility of under-reporting

Under-reporting can thus be considered as a resource for French and Californian authorities in charge of pesticide-related occupational hazards. It does not preclude agricultural business' strong reliance on chemicals, yet it maintains the illusion that the surveillance of pesticides is effective. With so few reported pesticide poisonings among farm-workers, changes in risk assessment and risk management procedures can only be incremental. Paradoxically, the inability of the regulatory system to produce effective surveillance data is a condition of its survival and legitimacy. Public authorities claim that surveillance programs play their role and can lead to regulatory changes. Thus, though exceptional, the rare examples of cases of regulatory change linked to surveillance data allow public authorities to believe in the usefulness of these monitoring programs. As Harrison (2011) notes, officials in charge of pesticide regulation have a contradictory discourse: whereas they acknowledge the fact that pesticide poisonings among farm-workers are underestimated by surveillance programs, they also point to the low figures of occupational injuries related to those products to reaffirm that they can be used safely. This ambiguity structures the institutional perspective through which public authorities notice and take into consideration the limitations of policies aimed at controlling pesticides in the workplace. These limitations are never considered as a symptom of political failure, but as the sign that there is still room for improvement within the regulatory system.

In short, the under-reporting of pesticide poisoning among farm-workers has a key function for the regulatory system: it helps to solve regulatory inconsistencies linked to the fact that experts and policymakers are confronted with two contradictory missions as far as pesticide control is concerned. On the one hand, they have to ensure effective pest control and protection of crops; on the other hand, they have to make sure that pesticides do not endanger farm-workers' health. Pushing knowledge production on occupational pesticide poisonings and their causes too far bears the risk of upsetting the tacit equilibrium between those two goals. Thus, it is necessary "not to know too much" about pesticide poisonings if those substances are to be governable. Ignorance can be viewed as a way to maintain a complex social compromise that supports intensive models of agricultural production.

Conclusion: ignorance and social order

This chapter has highlighted the relationship between ignorance and official regulation of environmental issues such as pesticides. The international comparison of regulatory risk regimes in agriculture shows that ignorance is both the outcome of a "machinery" of pesticide risk regulation (Kickert 1993; Rhodes 1997) and a means to ensure its legitimacy. As Moore and Tumin (1949) established, and prior to them Simmel with regard to secrecy (1906), ignorance has a social function. In Moore and Tumin's words, ignorance is not "an analytic element but rather a more or less hidden component of situations generally discussed in other terms . . . It may be viewed as an element or a condition of a circumscribed system" (1949: 795). In this instance it maintains a complex equilibrium between agricultural economic concerns and environmental and workers' protection, underpinning the principles and rules of risk regulation. Pushing this idea further, the social production of ignorance appears to be close to Douglas's insight on taboo. In *Purity and Danger* (1966), Douglas analyses pollution and taboo in relation to the whole social structure. She argues that these phenomena have not only an instrumental function (influencing one another's behavior), but also a fundamental symbolic function: the fear of sex and bodily pollution reflects hierarchies and boundaries, and helps maintain the social order.

In our case, the order is a political one. It concerns the way of regulating chemicals in agriculture, defined as "controlled use". This policy suggests that chemicals which are known to be dangerous for human health are safe as long as they are handled correctly. "Not knowing" about the heterogeneous and concrete ways in which pesticide poisoning occurs among farm-workers can therefore be interpreted as a means to maintain the agricultural "political order". The question of how this regulatory system is so well designed to maintain ignorance remains open. To what extent is it the unintended outcome of an institutional process of risk assessment framing? An historic perspective on these organizational regulatory systems should be able to provide answers to that question.

Notes

1 N. Bonnefoy (rapporteur) (2013). Pesticides, vers le risque 0. Mission commune d'information sur les pesticides et leur impact sur la santé. Rapport d'information pour le Senat n°42. ("Pesticides toward risk 0. Information mission on pesticides and their impact on health". Information mission for the Senate, Report n°42).
2 Average figure calculated from annual reports of the Pesticide Illness Surveillance Program of the Department of Pesticide Regulation (DPR) in California and the Phyt'attitude reports of the Mutualité sociale agricole in France.
3 Generic term given to insects and plant diseases that attack crops.
4 Interview with the General Director of UIPP in *20 minutes*, December 12, 2011.
5 http://www.msa.fr/lfr/phyt-attitude (free translation).
6 Such as the fields treated by pesticides, emergency medical facilities, etc.
7 This statement varies from county to county. Our data suggest that it depends of the sensibilities of each elected member of the board. Nevertheless, and to simplify our demonstration, we will base our analysis on the "rural" counties, those of the central Valley (Tulare, San Joaquin, Kern, etc.), in which agricultural business do play a key role.
8 The amount of the fine can be very high. It could reach 5,000 dollars per violation and/or per person intoxicated.
9 Ibid., p. 9.
10 In 2000, a majority of moderate fines (from $151 to $400) were issued by the CAC. In spite of the age of these data, they reflect the same political concerns by the CAC and growers. M. Reeves, A. Katten, and M. Guzman (2000), "Field of poison: Californian farm-workers and pesticides", one in a series of reports of Californian for Pesticides reforms, p. 6.
11 Occupational pesticide illnesses in California 1998–2007.
12 Interview with a CDPH agent, August 2013.
13 The new 2014 "modernization of agriculture" law will probably modify this organizational structure, as it transfers to the ANSES the responsibility to run a proper post-market surveillance program for pesticides.
14 California Environmental Protection Agency: summary of results from the California pesticide illness surveillance program, 2013.

References

Cunningham-Parmeter, K. (2004), A poisoned field: farmworkers, pesticide exposure, and tort recovery in an era of regulatory failure, *New York University Review of Law & Social Change*, 28, 431.

Das, R., Steege, A., Baron, S., Beckman, John, and Harrison, R. (2001), Pesticide-related illness among migrant farm workers in the United States, *International Journal of Environnemental Health*, 7, 303–312.

Douglas, M. (1966), *Purity and Danger: An Analysis of Concepts of Pollution and Taboo*, London and New York: Routledge.

Foucault, M. (2004), *Naissance de la biopolitique: cours au Collège de France (1978–1979)*, Paris: Gallimard.

Frickel, S., and Vincent, M. B. (2007), Hurricane Katrina, contamination, and the unintended organization of ignorance, *Technology in Society*, 29, 181–188.

Garrigou, A., Baldi, I., and Dubuc, P. (2008), Apports de l'ergotoxicologie à l'évaluation de l'efficacité réelle des EPI devant protéger du risque phytosanitaire: de l'analyse de la contamination au processus collectif d'alerte, *Pistes*, 10, 1 (online review).

Harrison, G. (2011), *Pesticide Drift and the Pursuit of Environmental Justice*, Cambridge, MA: MIT Press.

Hood, C., Rothstein, H., and Baldwin, R. (2001), *The Government of Risk: Understanding Risk Regulation Regime*, Oxford: Oxford University Press.

Jasanoff, S. (2004), *Designs on Nature: Science and Democracy in Europe and the United States*, Princeton, NJ: Princeton University Press.

Kickert, W. (1993), Complexity governance and dynamics: conceptual explorations of public network management, in J. Kooiman (ed.) *Modern Governance*, London: Sage, pp. 191–204.

Kleinman, D. L., and Suryanarayanan, S. (2013), Dying bees and the social production of ignorance, *Science, Technology and Human Values*, 38, 4: 492–517.

Markowitz, G., and Rosner, D. (2002), *Deceit and Denial: The Deadly Politics of Industrial Pollution*, Berkeley: University of California Press.

McGarity, T., and Wagner, W. E. (2008), *Bending Science: How Special Interests Corrupt Public Health Research*, Cambridge, MA: Harvard University Press.

Moore, W. E., and Tumin, M. M. (1949), Some social functions of ignorance, *American Journal of Sociology*, 14, 6, 787–795.

Rhodes, R. (1997), *Understanding Governance*, Buckingham, UK: Open University Press.

Murphy, M. (2006), *Sick Building Syndrome and the Problem of Uncertainty*, Durham, NC: Duke University Press.

Nash, L. (2004), The fruits of ill-health: pesticides and workers' bodies in post-World War II California, *Osiris*, 19, 203–219.

Oreskes, N., and Conway, E. (2010), *Merchants of Doubt: How a Handful of Scientists Obscured the Truth on Issues from Tobacco Smoke to Global Warming*, New York: Bloomsburry Press.

Proctor, R. N. (2012), *Golden Holocaust: Origins of the Cigarette Catastrophe and the Case for Abolition*, Berkeley: University of California Press.

Rayner, S. (2012), Uncomfortable knowledge: the social construction of ignorance in science and environmental policy discourses, *Economy and Society*, 40, 1, 107–127.

Scott, J. C. (1998), *Seeing like a State: How Certain Schemes to Improve the Human Condition Have Failed*, Yale, CT: Yale University Press.

Simmel, G. (1906), The sociology of secrecy and of secret societies, *American Journal of Sociology*, 11, 4: 441–498.

Vaughan, D. (1996), *The Challenger Launch Decision: Risky Technologies, Culture and Deviance at NASA*, Chicago: University of Chicago Press.

Vogel, D. (1986), *National Styles of Regulation: Environmental Policy in Great Britain and the United States*, Ithaca, NY: Cornell University Press.

32

To know or not to know?

A note on ignorance as a rhetorical resource in geoengineering debates

Steve Rayner

The stakes are simply too high for us to think that ignorance is a good policy.

(Caldeira & Keith 2010)

Introduction

Climate Geoengineering is defined by Britain's Royal Society as "the deliberate large-scale manipulation of the planet's environment to counteract climate change" (Shepherd et al. 2009). During the past half-decade the topic has been hotly debated among scientists, social scientists and a small but attentive community of NGOs and policy makers. Scientists and climate activists remain divided over the practicality and wisdom of such interventions. There are few gung-ho enthusiasts. Proponents are mostly cautious, even reluctant, while opponents are often appalled at the very idea.

The idea itself is not new. A 1965 report of the US President's Science Advisory Committee on the topic of climate change only considered what we would today call geoengineering approaches to the topic: climate adaptation and greenhouse gas mitigation measures are nowhere to be found within its covers. The idea of injecting aerosols into the stratosphere to manage solar radiation was explored in principle throughout the 1970s to 1990s (Budyko 1977, 1982; Marchetti 1977; U.S. National Academy of Sciences 1992).

Yet geoengineering has not yet progressed much further than the stage of an idea. As was the case for many years with climate adaptation, geoengineering has been a taboo topic. Hence, the concepts largely remain what social scientists term socio-technical "imaginaries" (Jasanoff & Kim 2009) embodying a wide range of conflicting assumptions about their physical and social characteristics, important aspects of which remain largely unexamined. While there are extant bits of "kit" that could potentially form part of one geoengineering system or another, none of the geoengineering concepts is even close to the stage where it could be deployed with any degree of confidence as to its efficacy in achieving desired results without unacceptable side effects or opportunity costs (Shepherd et al. 2009).

Geoengineering proposals are conventionally described as falling into two broad types: those that extract carbon dioxide from ambient air and sequester it, for example, in the ocean or under the ground, and those that reflect some of the sun's energy away from the earth. Following the terminology of the Royal Society, the first of these is referred to as carbon-dioxide removal or CDR and the second as solar radiation management, or SRM. There are interesting asymmetries between these two classes of technology. While CDR addresses the underlying problem of climate change – carbon dioxide emissions – SRM only treats one of the symptoms – temperature rise. CDR would take many decades to implement at sufficient scale to remove gigatons of carbon per annum, while SRM promises to be very fast acting. Most, although not all, CDR measures would not seem to raise any fundamentally new issues of governance or regulation, while the most widely discussed of the SRM proposals – stratospheric aerosols – raises the prospect of increasing international tensions unless implemented under some kind of international agreement.

Some CDR proposals, such as mechanical air capture of carbon (sometimes called artificial trees), are well-bounded, closed systems. Others involve releasing chemical agents into the ambient environment. Any geoengineering method involving the introduction of such deliberate "pollutants" into the oceans, the air, or on land is likely to prove controversial regardless of whether it is designed to reflect sunlight or remove carbon. For example, experiments designed to demonstrate CDR by adding iron to the ocean to encourage carbon-fixing plankton blooms have met with vociferous opposition (ETC 2010, 2012). Experimental geoengineering in the ocean is covered by the London Convention and Protocols which were originally designed to eliminate dumping waste at sea. (This is the common vernacular for the 1972 Convention on the Prevention of Marine Pollution by Dumping of Wastes and Other Matter, in force since 1975; in 1996, the "London Protocol" was established to further develop the Convention. Forty-four states are party to the Protocol; eighty-seven states to the London Convention.) However, there is no comparable international regime governing the atmosphere. Generally speaking the subset of SRM technologies that involve the introduction of sulphate aerosols into the stratosphere have attracted the most attention and been the principal focus of opposition.

Stratospheric aerosols have the potential to be relatively cheap, fast-acting, and are said to be close to being deployable. Therefore, it is argued that they merit serious consideration alongside conventional mitigation and adaptation as a tool to help deal with climate change (Keith 2013). Opponents fear that the same characteristics render stratospheric aerosols potentially catastrophic, inevitably inequitable, and ultimately ungovernable, so that even conducting research on them is, at best, a waste of resources or, at worst, the first step on a "slippery slope" towards an unacceptable outcome (Hulme 2014). Indeed, critics argue that even conducting research to explore the potential of solar geoengineering to deflect sunlight using stratospheric aerosols ought to be considered beyond the pale.

Both supporters and opponents of research agree that there are huge uncertainties and presently much that is simply unknown about the potential deployment of stratospheric aerosols. Under these conditions, the call for more research to understand the technologies, their intended and unintended consequences, and the conditions under which they might be deployed, if at all, may seem modest and rational. The Royal Society working group called for research expenditure of £10 million a year for 10 years to characterize the full range of geoengineering technologies. Caldeira and Keith (2010) suggested that the US should initiate a phased research programme at US$5 million, gradually increasing to $30 million. These hardly represent major opportunity costs relative to the overall size of the UK and US national research budgets or to current expenditures on alternative energy or climate adaptation. Yet even the idea of conducting research on the potential of stratospheric aerosols to cool the earth has been highly controversial, suggesting that concerns go much deeper than the issue of the opportunity costs of such research.

Various arguments are deployed on either side of the issue. For example, opponents of research worry about what insurers call "moral hazard". They fear that even doing research might send a signal to people and policy makers that they can let up on efforts to reduce their greenhouse gas emissions in the erroneous belief that solar geoengineering will save the day. Some advocates of research have expressed concern that a future "climatic emergency" (where there is a strong likelihood of reaching a disastrous tipping point or runaway climate change) might lead to the implementation of solar geoengineering without adequate understanding of its behavior: an argument that critics have described as "arming the future" (Gardiner 2010). However, one factor emerges strongly on both sides of the argument and is invoked both to justify and to oppose research into stratospheric aerosols. That factor is ignorance.

Both sides agree that humanity currently lacks the knowledge that would be necessary to deploy stratospheric aerosols on any scale. However, they are dramatically divided by their response to such ignorance. The arguments are well represented in two little books aimed at general audiences, which eloquently summarize the cases for and against respectively. The case for research is made by a North American engineer (Keith 2013) and that against is authored by a British geographer (Hulme 2014). Both have an extensive background and expertise in climate change policy issues.

Research advocates argue for improved computer modeling accompanied by complementary small-scale experiments gradually and cautiously scaled up over time. They see this as a pathway to deliver robust knowledge to inform decisions regarding full-scale implementation while avoiding any irreversible negative consequences (Caldeira & Keith 2010; Keith 2013).

However, opponents of such research argue that while computer models are reasonably good at predicting global temperature in relation to greenhouse gas concentrations, they remain poor in relation to other important climatic factors, such as precipitation. They argue that the complexity and uncertainties inherent in the climate and ecosystems responses are so massive that even if they were better understood they could not properly be represented in any conceivable computer modeling of stratospheric aerosol deployment in the foreseeable future (Hulme 2014). Attempts to model the impacts of the climate and ecosystems responses on human activity seem only to compound the uncertainties of the climate models.

A review of the modelling of geoengineering and its impacts (Hansson forthcoming) concludes that adding complexity to the models does not increase their accuracy. This echoes the earlier finding of Repetto and Austin (1997) that adding bells and whistles to integrated assessment models of climate change may make them appear more credible, but do not actually add to their accuracy or precision. Furthermore, including more complexity may make models more difficult for policy makers to interpret. While Smithson (1993: 148) has argued that "decision makers are better off with an accurate picture of how extensive their [the scientists] ignorance is than a false precise assessment", Bellamy et al. (2013) point out that revealing the complexities and uncertainties may make geoengineering science inscrutable to non-specialists.

It is also argued that science actually increases ignorance and uncertainty, or at least our awareness of them, by rendering unknown unknowns into known unknowns. Writing in the context of GMO controversies, Böschen et al. (2006: 294) argue that insights from science and technology studies show that "the sciences do not only generate knowledge but also increase ignorance concerning the possible side effects of scientific innovations and their technological application (Ravetz 1986; Funtowicz & Ravetz 2001; Wynne 1992; Nowotny et al. 2001)".

Writing specifically on geoengineering, Winter (2011) describes the current situation as one of "conscious ignorance" in which it is possible to know, even before research is conducted, that sufficient knowledge to justify the risk of using stratospheric aerosols can never be gained; that ignorance can be known in advance of research to be "irreducible".

Under these conditions, writes Mike Hulme:

> To embark on this course of action would indeed be to conduct a giant experiment, to take a leap in the dark. It is not possible to know what the consequences of such engineering would be. However much we are attracted to machinic metaphors to describe the natural world – picturing systems that can be re-tuned or re-engineered according to human desire or need – I do not believe the human mind has the ability to fathom the intricacies of how the planet functions. The simulation models upon which aerosol injection technology would rely are like calculative cartoons when it comes to making long-term predictions. There are limits to human knowledge; our species is a product of evolution, not its author or controller.
>
> *(2014: 112)*

Opponents of solar geoengineering sometimes also express concerns about the potential misuse of the technology as a weapon (e.g., Robock 2008). This seems to sit rather uneasily alongside the assertion of irreducible ignorance and consequent uncontrollability of solar geoengineering, in that successful weaponization would seem to imply a high degree of control to focus damage on an enemy.

Against the view of irreducible ignorance, it can be argued that the perfect should not be the enemy of the good. The only way that we can learn more about what ignorance is reducible and what is irreducible is to conduct research. In marked contrast to Hulme, David Keith writes:

> Our knowledge of the risks is not purely theoretical. Real-world experience gives confidence that those risks can be understood. To understand the risk of injecting a million tons of sulfur into the atmosphere, for example, we can study the 1991 eruption of Mt Pinatubo, which put eight million tons of sulfur into the stratosphere. And each year humans pump roughly fifty million tons of sulfur into the atmosphere as air pollution. This is not an argument that we should ignore the risk of putting one million tons of sulfur into the atmosphere for geoengineering, but it should give confidence that there is a strong empirical basis on which to assess these risks, and it is a reason to suppose that risks will be comparatively small.
>
> *(Keith 2013: 11–12)*

And

> [W]ere we faced with a one-time choice between making a total commitment to a geoengineering program to offset all warming and abandoning geoengineering forever, I would choose abandonment. But this is not the choice we face. Our choice is between the status quo – with almost no organized research on the subject – and commitment to a serious research program that will develop the capability to geoengineer, improve understanding of the technology's risks and benefits, and open up the research community to dilute the geo-clique. Given this choice, I choose research; and if the research supports geoengineering's early promises, I would then choose gradual deployment.
>
> *(ibid.: 12–13)*

For those of Keith's mind, not to do research is to remain ignorant of our ignorance. While research may not fully answer all of the questions that we would like, a well-designed programme of cautious research with clear stage gates and reviews is seen to have the potential to provide a better picture of the form and behavior of solar geoengineering technology. Perhaps such research would actually help to definitively clarify the case against deployment, taking the issue off the table once and for all.

How well does the sociology of ignorance help us to understand the conflict between supporters and opponents of solar geoengineering research, as exemplified in the arguments of Keith and Hulme? At least three concepts would seem to be relevant here: "undone science", "forbidden knowledge", and "post normal science".

There is a sense in which the situation appears to be an inversion of the idea of "undone science", defined by Frickel et al. (2010) as "areas of research that are left unfunded, incomplete, or generally ignored but that social movements or civil society organizations often identify as worthy of more research". Examples of such science include research into rare diseases and orphan drug development. But, the fit between the theory of undone science and the solar geoengineering case is only partial. Establishment organizations, such as the Royal Society, argue for, rather than against, research.

Frickel et al. recognize that "in some contrast to the role that social movement organizations and lay experts/citizen scientists play in exposing undone science and encouraging knowledge creation . . . the same actors can also play a powerful role in determining which knowledge is not produced" (ibid.: 463). They cite the case where supporters of the disease theory of alcoholism, as propounded by Alcoholics Anonymous, blocked NIH funding of research into controlled drinking therapies, which might call into question AA's core insistence on total abstinence. But in the case of geoengineering, the civil society organizations are divided. Environmental Defense actually co-sponsored with the Royal Society and Third World Academy of Science, a Solar Radiation Management Governance Initiative (SRMGI) to explore the conditions under which such research should proceed. On the other hand, the ETC group and Greenpeace have opposed such research, citing irreducible ignorance.

The concept of "undone science" seems to tell some of the story, but not all of it. It usefully highlights the fact that ignorance is mobilized as a resource in the institutional politics behind research funding, but Frickel et al. acknowledge that "more research is needed to understand the circumstances under which researchers decide to self-censor in response to pressure from outside groups" (ibid.: 463). Their account takes the starting positions in such cases for granted, implicitly rooting them in a fairly straightforward understanding of the self-interest of protagonists to control research funding or as a response to perceived professional or even personal threats. But self-interest of individuals or institutions does not seem to lie behind opposition to solar geoengineering which seems to be motivated primarily by concerns about physical and moral harm.

Kempner et al. (2005, 2011) also set out to explore decisions by scientists to self-censor their research through the idea of "forbidden knowledge" (Shattuck 1997), which they define as "a term that refers to knowledge considered too sensitive, dangerous, or taboo to produce" (Kempner et al. 2011: 476). Rather than focusing on the self-restraint of scientists responding to outside pressure, their focus is on the choices of scientists not to enter into certain kinds of inquiry because of ethical concerns about how the resulting knowledge might be misused or because the means of obtaining it would potentially cause harm. Forbidden knowledge is that which is prohibited by religious, moral or secular authority, such as human cloning; can only be obtained through unacceptable means, such as human experiments conducted by the Nazis; undermines social norms, such as certain types of research on substance abuse; or is believed to be unacceptably dangerous, such as biological or chemical weapons (Kempner et al. 2005).

Sometimes individual decisions to self-censor research find institutional expression. For example, this was the case with the moratorium on recombinant DNA research arising from the 1975 Asilomar Conference (Berg et al. 1975).

However, the demand for a moratorium, or even outright prohibition, of solar geoengineering research, doesn't quite fit this model either. It is not so much the exercise of self-restraint on the part of scientists, as it is polarized disagreement between those advocating research and other scientists, ethicists, and activists who oppose the very idea. Where issues are highly polarized, it is common for scientists and activists on both sides to call for more scientific research to resolve disputed or poorly understood facts, whether the issue is acid rain, mad cow disease or badger culling. It is unusual for one side to call for a ban on research altogether. Notwithstanding the concern in some quarters about weaponization of stratospheric aerosols, most opponents of research are not concerned that it might reveal knowledge that could maliciously be put to harmful use. Their concern seems to be that research is likely to fail to reveal potential inadvertent harms, perhaps leading to a sense of false security that the technology is safe enough to be implemented.

Research opponents offer a preemptive ethical argument against research and in favour of remaining ignorant of the potential technical capabilities of solar geoengineering even if it were possible to do so. For example, Hulme (2014: 92–93) writes, "Aerosol injection is not simply about stabilising or restoring the global climate. It is an intervention that has profound repercussions for what we think it is to be human. It would forever alter our sense of moral duty and ethical responsibility" and "I make my position clear: I do not wish to live in this brave new climate-controlled world" (ibid.: xii).

In summary, the rhetorical deployment of ignorance in the case *for* solar geonengineering seems quite straightforward: conducting some research is the only way to reduce ignorance about the technology. However, the case *against* solar geoengineering research seems to be two-fold. Ignorance is a binding constraint – "we simply cannot know" – and ignorance is a source of virtue – "it saves us from folly".

These two aspects of the argument are strongly redolent of the orthogonal dimensions of "ignorance and uncertainty" and "decision stakes" used by Funtowicz and Ravetz (1985) to introduce the idea of "post-normal science". Ignorance and uncertainty includes the elements of inexactness, uncertainty and ignorance surrounding the precision of estimates and measurements, adequacy of methods and appropriateness of concepts involved in technical studies. Decision stakes contains not only the technical assessments of benefits and costs but judgments about what is fair and even the societal determination of what is valued (Figure 32.1).

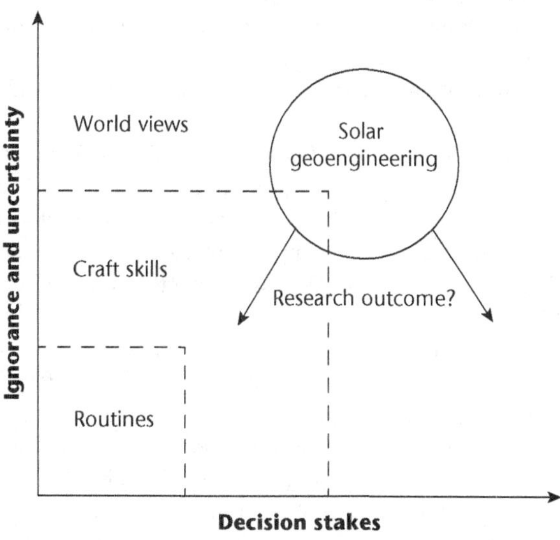

Figure 32.1 The implications of reduced ignorance are different for supporters (left arrow) and opponents (right arrow) of research

Where both ignorance and stakes are low, decision-making is characterized by routine procedures and applications of formal decision rules to well-known data. Where either ignorance or stakes rise, decision-making relies much more heavily on the interpretive and anticipatory craft skills of scientific and political practitioners. Where either dimension is high, decision-making is dominated by the competing worldviews of the people involved and is likely to be conducted in an adversarial mode that Funtowicz and Ravetz situate within the post-normal paradigm. Solar geoengineering is clearly high on both dimensions. The very absence of information about a technology that does not presently exist places it far from the origin on the dimension of ignorance. The competing rhetorics of "arming the future" versus "a brave new climate-controlled world" emphasize that the decision stakes in this discourse are not confined merely to concerns about possible side-effects of the technology, but embody fundamentally different world views about what it means to be human and our relationship with nature.

The explicit objective of research advocates is to move solar geoengineering down the ignorance scale. Their hope is that it will also clarify the decision stakes in terms of the potential impact on climate and any side effects. But, Funtowicz and Ravetz's framework suggests that merely increasing technical knowledge of the characteristics of solar geoengineering cannot attenuate the kinds of concerns expressed by Hulme and like-minded critics and may even exacerbate them. The decision stakes for research opponents include questions about the kind of world we want to live in that are broader than simply its climate. Those who see solar geoengineering as incompatible in principle with the values inherent in their worldviews are likely to continue to resist research precisely because ignorance in this case is a virtue that preserves us from folly. Contrary to the claim of Caldeira and Keith (2010: 62) that "The stakes are simply too high for us to think that ignorance is a good policy", for research opponents it is precisely because the stakes are so high that ignorance is seen as a good policy. To subvert the common aphorism, in this case, ignorance is power.

But while Funtwicz and Ravetz provide a useful map to describe the dynamics of the dispute, their framework does not explain why the various protagonists take such different views of the same "facts", or rather lack of them. To cast some light on this question, I turn to the related ideas of institutional and epistemic culture. The theory of institutional culture originated by Mary Douglas (1970, 1986) proposes that hierarchical, competitive and egalitarian ways of organizing each sustain, and are sustained by, characteristic argumentative frameworks, appeals to different sources of authoritative knowledge, and procedures for dealing with uncertainty and ignorance.

Hierarchical cultures tend to favour carefully designed, staged procedures with well-defined decision rules. As such they often attract the soubriquet "technocratic". Competitive cultures place a strong emphasis on individual expert judgements, craft skills and "the right stuff". Egalitarian cultures generally place a strong emphasis on extensive discussion and debate involving a wide cross-section of actors, often seeking to amplify the voices of the weak and powerless (Rayner 1992).

Applying this perspective to the Funtowicz and Ravetz framework, we expect that members of hierarchical cultures are likely to try and locate as much of a problem as close to the origin of the diagram as possible, and will view ignorance as susceptible to domestication, while egalitarian cultures will seek to frame the same issue far away from the origin, requiring extended discourse, and resistant to settlement by appeal to technical resolution.

The related concept of epistemic cultures specifically explores the operation of comparable epistemic "preferences" in the sciences with regard to how they generate both knowledge (Knorr-Cetina 1999) and non-knowledge (Böschen et al. 2006). In particular, Böschen et al. (2010: 790) identify a "control-oriented scientific culture of nonknowledge", characterized by an epistemic focus on the control of the experimental conditions and the avoidance of disruptive factors; a "single case-based experience . . . which shows a tendency to define non-knowledge as a problem of the individual expert"; and a "complexity-oriented culture . . . characterized by a high degree of openness toward unanticipated events as well as uncontrollable and context-sensitive settings".

The different approaches taken by Keith and Hulme seem to indicate clear epistemological preferences. Keith's arguments reflect the hierarchical and control-oriented cultures that might seem to characterize the engineering disciplines and what Rayner and Malone (1998) describe as the more quantitative "descriptive" style of social and policy science. Hulme's arguments display the characteristics of the egalitarian and complexity-oriented cultures that we might expect from what Rayner and Malone describe as the more qualitative "interpretive" social sciences. Rayner and Malone also note the propensity of the descriptive approach to lead to an essentially utilitarian approach to decision-making focused on maximizing the general welfare, while the interpretive approach leads practitioners towards a more deontological rights-, duty- or virtue-based position, again as reflected in the differences between Keith and Hulme, as well as other protagonists on both sides of the geoengineering research debate.

Concluding thoughts

If, as I suggest, the arguments for and against geoengineering research are significantly informed by fundamentally different epistemological cultures, then where does that leave us? Rayner and Malone argue that policy is strengthened when descriptive and interpretive epistemologies are used to complement each other. But geoengineering seems to provide a limited opportunity for this as the opponents of research have little ground for compromise. If they allow "just a little" research or research under clear constraints, then they have already conceded their position that the use of stratospheric aerosols should be unthinkable. This is the crux of Hulme's "slippery slope".

I do not have a definitive answer to "Where does this leave us?" I can only offer my own perspective as an actor the geoengineering field. In proposing the "Oxford Principles" for the governance of geoengineering research (Rayner et al. 2013), I have already accepted, in principle, Keith's argument for transparent research conducted explicitly in the public interest, although I reserve judgement on any eventual deployment. In contrast to Keith, passing a technical research stage gate should not automatically lead to an assumption of deployability, however gradual. This is because I find myself equally committed to Hulme's position that the disagreement over stratospheric aerosol research is not merely a technical debate about the safety or efficacy of the proposed technology but is, at heart, a debate over the kind of society we want to live in. In his earlier work "Why we disagree about climate change" Hulme argues that we should not merely ask "What can we do about climate change?" but also "What can climate change do for us?" In that same spirit I would ask "What can the geoengineering research discourse do for us by way of stimulating discussion of the kind of world we wish to inhabit?"

It may be that the geoengineering debate is at a point that is almost never recognized in other techno-science debates until after the moment is passed. At the time of writing, the value differences are clear, and there are no strong science claims to hide behind in articulating those values (Sarewitz 2004). Quite the contrary, everyone seems to acknowledge that we currently know very little. Once research gets under way (if it does), then the debates will likely change, and explicitly begin to focus on what's being learned by the research, and what it tells us. And once that happens, debates over the science will displace the debate over the values. While in principle this doesn't have to happen, it always does, as we know. So we have, now, a moment of clarity. Capturing that clarity and making sure that it does not get corroded, camouflaged, or otherwise elided in the form of competing knowledge claims seems to be a worthy governance or policy goal.

References

Bellamy, R., Chilvers, J., Vaughan, N. E., & Lenton, T. M. (2013). 'Opening up' geoengineering appraisal: Multi-Criteria Mapping of options for tackling climate change. *Global Environmental Change,* 23(5), 926–937.

Berg, P., Baltimore, D., Brenner, S., Roblin, R. O., & Singer, M. F. (1975). Summary statement of the Asilomar conference on recombinant DNA molecules. *Proceedings of the National Academy of Sciences of the United States of America,* 72(6), 1981.

Böschen, S., Kastenhofer, K., Rust, I., Soentgen, J., & Wehling, P. (2010). Scientific nonknowledge and its political dynamics: The cases of agri-biotechnology and mobile phoning. *Science, Technology & Human Values,* 35(6), 783–811.

Budyko, M. I. (1977). *Climatic Changes.* American Geophysical Union, Washington, DC.

Budyko, M. I. (1982). *The Earth's climate: Past and future.* Academic Press, New York.

Caldeira, K., & Keith, D. W. (2010). The need for climate engineering research. *Issues in Science and Technology,* 27(1), 57–62.

Douglas, M. (1970). *Natural symbols: Explorations in cosmology.* Barrie & Rockliffe, London.

Douglas, M. (1986). *How institutions think.* Syracuse University Press, Syracuse, New York.

ETC (2010) *Geopiracy: The case against geoengineering.* ETC Group, Ottawa, Canada.

ETC (2012) Informational Backgrounder on the 2012 Haida Gwaii Iron Dump. ETC Group, Ottawa, Canada. Available at: http://www.etcgroup.org/content/informational-backgrounder-2012-haida-gwaii-iron-dump.

Frickel, S., Gibbon, S., Howard, J., Kempner, J., Ottinger, G., & Hess, D. J. (2010). Undone science: charting social movement and civil society challenges to research agenda setting. *Science, Technology & Human Values,* 35(4), 444–473.

Funtowicz, S. O. & Ravetz, J. R. (1985). Three types of risk assessment: A methodological analysis. In C. Whipple & V. Covello (eds) *Risk analysis in the private sector.* Plenum Press, New York.

Funtowicz, S., & Ravetz, J. (2001). Post-normal science. Science and governance under conditions of complexity. In *Interdisciplinarity in Technology Assessment.* Springer, Berlin, Heidelberg, pp. 15–24.

Gardiner, Stephen M. (2010). Is 'arming the future' with geoengineering really the lesser evil? Some doubts about the ethics of intentionally manipulating the climate system. In Stephen M. Gardiner, Simon Caney, Dale Jamieson, & Henry Shue (eds) *Climate Ethics: Essential Readings,* Oxford University Press, New York, pp. 284–312.

Hansson, Anders (forthcoming) Ambivalence in calculating the future: The case of re-engineering the world. *Journal of Integrative Environmental Sciences.*

Hulme, M. (2014). *Can science fix climate change?* Polity Press, Cambridge.

Jasanoff, S., & Kim, S. H. (2009). Containing the atom: sociotechnical imaginaries and nuclear power in the United States and South Korea. *Minerva,* 47(2), 119–146.

Keith, D. (2013). *A case for climate engineering.* MIT Press, Cambridge, MA.

Kempner, J., Perlis, C. S., & Merz, J. F. (2005). Forbidden knowledge. *Science,* 307(5711), 854.

Kempner, J., Merz, J. F., & Bosk, C. L. (2011, September). Forbidden knowledge: Public controversy and the production of nonknowledge. *Sociological Forum,* 26(3), 475–500.

Knorr-Cetina, K. (1999). *Epistemic cultures: How the sciences make knowledge.* Harvard University Press, Cambridge, MA.

Marchetti, C. (1977). On geoengineering and the CO2 problem. *Climatic Change,* 1(1), 59–68.

Nowotny, H., Scott, P., & Gibbons, M. (2001). *Rethinking science.* Polity Press, London.

President's Science Advisory Committee (1965). *Restoring the quality of our environment.* White House. Washington, DC.

Ravetz, J. R. (1986). Usable knowledge, usable ignorance incomplete science with policy implications. In W. C. Clark and R. E. Munn (eds), *Sustainable development of the biosphere,* Cambridge University Press, Cambridge, pp. 415–32.

Rayner, S. (1992). Cultural theory and risk analysis. In S. Krimsky & D. Golding (eds), *Social theories of risk.* Praeger, Westport, CT, pp. 83–115.

Rayner, S. & Malone, E. L. (1998). The challenge of climate change to the social sciences. In S. Rayner & E. L. Malone (eds) *Human choice and climate change: An international assessment, Volume 4, what have we learned?* Battelle Press, Columbus, OH.

Rayner, S., Heyward, C., Kruger, T., Pidgeon, N., Redgwell, C. & Savulescu, J. (2013). The Oxford Principles. *Climatic Change*, 121(3), 499–512.

Repetto, R., & Austin, D. (1997). *The costs of climate protection: A guide for the perplexed.* World Resources Institute, Washington, DC.

Robock, A. (2008). 20 reasons why geoengineering may be a bad idea. *Bulletin of the Atomic Scientists*, 64(2), 14–18, 59.

Sarewitz, D. (2004). How science makes environmental controversies worse. *Environmental Science and Policy*, 7, 385–403.

Shattuck, R. (1997). *Forbidden knowledge: From Prometheus to pornography*. Harcourt Brace, Orlando, FL.

Shepherd, J., Caldeira, K., Cox, P., Keith, D., Launder, B., Mace, G., MacKerron, G., Pyle, J., Rayner, S., Redgwell, C., & Watson, A. (2009). *Geoengineering the climate: Science, governance and uncertainty*. The Royal Society, London.

Smithson, M. (1993). Ignorance and science dilemmas, perspectives, and prospects. *Science Communication*, 15(2), 133–156.

U.S. National Academy of Sciences (1992). *Policy implications of greenhouse warming: Mitigation, adaptation, and the science base.* Panel on Policy Implications of Greenhouse Warming, U.S. National Academy of Sciences, National Academy Press, Washington, DC.

Winter, G. (2011). Climate engineering and international law: Last resort or the end of humanity? *Review of European Community & International Environmental Law*, 20(3), 277–289.

Wynne, B. (1992). Uncertainty and environmental learning: Reconceiving science and policy in the preventive paradigm. *Global Environmental Change*, 2(2), 111–127.

33

Unfolding the map

Making knowledge and ignorance mobilization dynamics *visible* in science evaluation and policymaking

Joanne Gaudet

> [T]he generation of Experiments being like that of Discourse, where one thing introduceth an hundred more which otherwise would never have been thought of.
>
> *(Grew 1673: A6)*

> [S]ince the faculties of Plants do often lie more recluse; it is best therefore not wholly to acquiesce in such Conjectures as their tastes or other properties may suggest; but to subjoyn Experiment.
>
> *(Grew 1673: 41)*

The main goal in this chapter is to explore how a mapping of knowledge and ignorance mobilization dynamics in science (Gaudet 2013: 11) can play a role in science evaluation and policymaking. The standard science epistemic map – where only knowledge is valued – is thus unfolded, making knowledge *and* ignorance mobilization dynamics more visible. An emphasis on mapping is in keeping with practices by natural scientists who construct visualizations for natural scientific knowledge, making it more visible and thereby hopefully easier to communicate (Gross and Harmon 2014). The starting point for the chapter is not the proposed mapping, however; instead, it is in the seventeenth century with the above quotes from Nehemiah Grew in 1673.

The opening quotes capture the essence of epistemic dynamics in burgeoning scientific experiments[1] in the seventeenth century. The disproportionate (cf., 'one thing introduceth an hundred more') and dynamic interplay between knowledge and what remained unknown (cf., ignorance – 'the faculties of Plants do often lie more recluse', or nescience – 'would never have been thought of') were already evident for experimental natural philosophers (see Anstey 2005; Gaukroger 2006).

Natural philosophy (as the study of nature, Hannam 2010: 6) had then only recently split into speculative natural philosophy and experimental natural philosophy. Speculative natural philosophers did not systematically engage in observation or use experimentation to propose explanations for nature and its phenomena (Anstey 2005: 215). Moreover, the types of entities (ontological considerations) that were offered to support speculative natural philosophy explanations included 'inexplicable occult qualities, substantial forms, virtual extension, sympathies and antipathies' (2005: 221). In contrast, experimental natural philosophers delved into 'the collection and ordering of observations and experimental reports with a view to the development of explanations of natural phenomena based on these observations and experiments' (2005: 215).

What is more, as Johns suggests, is that the success of an experiment for experimental natural philosophers was at least in part tied to its ability to generate further experiments (1998: 470). Success viewed this way meant constructing and valuing new ignorance. Ignorance here refers to the limits and borders of knowing (see Gross 2010: 68). Moreover, ignorance is non-pejorative as what scientists know is not (yet) known in science (see Ivainer and Lenglet 1996; Logan 2009). For a seventeenth-century experimenter, valuable ignorance could thus fuel further experimentation. The *intentional* and *explicit* knowledge and ignorance dynamic practices that natural experimental philosophers engaged in persist in contemporary science in and out of the laboratory (see Bhaskar [1975] 2008: 58; Gross 2010: 30; Latour 2000; Overdevest et al. 2010).

The use of mapping is enlisted here to make scientific knowledge and ignorance dynamics – like those Grew (1673) and his fellow experimental natural philosophers engaged in over three hundred years ago – more visible (see mapping of ignorance typologies in Hess 2010: 5). In addition, mapping can make intentional and unintentional inclusion and exclusion of ignorance more visible. Thus, the underlying argument in the chapter is the following: Although science evaluation and policymaking typically focus on and value scientific knowledge – mapping of, and acknowledgement of – knowledge *and* ignorance mobilization dynamics is crucial to account for scientific practices of valuing ignorance (see Firestein 2012; Davies 2011; Roberts and Armitage 2008). The focus of the chapter is therefore intentionally on epistemic dynamics.

The chapter proceeds in two parts. First, I present mapping for knowledge and ignorance dynamics and their respective mobilization in science (Gaudet 2013: 11). It extends mapping of topologies for knowledge and ignorance developed by Gross (2010: 71). Second, harnessing mapping dynamics, I briefly explore two Canadian cases of science evaluation and policymaking. In the first case, I investigate the Council of Canadian Academies' consideration of expert opinion on knowledge gaps as a potential socio-economic impact indicator for science performance (Expert Panel on Science Performance and Research Funding 2012: 41). The case explicitly acknowledges the role of ignorance in science evaluation. In the second case, my attention turns to a decision by Health Canada, a federal department, to remove some calcitonin-containing drugs off the Canadian market following research on their potential cancer risk (Health Canada 2013b). The change highlights a need for evergreen[2] science policies that take knowledge and ignorance mobilization dynamics in science seriously. By evergreen science policy, I refer to policy that has emergent properties explicitly acknowledging potential new scientific knowledge or ignorance that can lead to a need for change in policy direction. Given that the focus in the chapter is on epistemic dynamics, I only briefly locate the second case within literatures on post-market surveillance and regulatory bodies (i.e., Carpenter 2006; Lexchin 2014). The chapter closes with reflections on the role of mapping in the sociology of scientific knowledge and ignorance.

Mapping knowledge and ignorance mobilization dynamics in science

In Figure 33.1, I present mapping for knowledge and ignorance mobilization dynamics in science (Gaudet 2013: 11) that was originally inspired from knowledge and ignorance topological mapping developed by Gross (2010: 71). Typically, only the top half of the map would retain the explicit attention of policymakers and science evaluators. In contrast, the unfolded mapping in Figure 33.1 attempts to convey scientific practices of dynamic and dialogical knowledge and ignorance construction and mobilization where new knowledge can lead to more ignorance, and ignorance itself can lead to more ignorance (see Smithson 2009: 24; Gross 2010: 173). Before looking at dynamics however, I tend to definitions.

Nescience here is understood as the complete absence of knowledge (Gross 2010: 68) and therefore lies outside of the mapping. Once constructed, however, and frequently in response to surprise, it can lead to ignorance and knowledge (Gross 2010). Surprise is used in the way Simmel (1922) proposed it where it can 'be freed from its psychological and sentimental meaning as a logical category for the relation between different contents' (quoted within Gross 2010: 38). Therefore, 'something is surprising when a pre-existing set of experiences and a horizon of expectation turn out to be inappropriate, since [a given] situation contradicts any anticipation' (2010: 37, my adaptation in brackets). Essentially, a contradiction in anticipation can motivate a researcher to construct new ignorance to account for surprise.

Moreover, in keeping with Gross (2010: 49), knowledge refers to a justified belief connected to purpose (or use), and two sub-types are existing and new knowledge (Gaudet 2013: 5). The broader category of ignorance for its part refers to the borders and the limits of knowing (see Gross 2010: 68). Two ignorance sub-types are active non-knowledge and latent non-knowledge. Active non-knowledge denotes 'the limits and the borders of knowing that are intentionally or unintentionally taken into account for immediate or future planning, theorizing and action' (Gaudet 2013: 5). In contrast, latent non-knowledge is *not* taken into account and therefore not mobilized by actors within or outside of science (examples in Frickel et al. 2010; Kempner et al. 2011). If it is eventually mobilized by actors, it exits latency to be constructed as new active non-knowledge. Finally, knowledge and ignorance mobilization, respectively, refer to the use of justified beliefs or the borders and the limits of knowing towards the achievement of goals (social, cultural, political, professional and economic) (Gaudet 2013: 7). These definitions already convey some relational dynamics, but a closer examination of Figure 33.1 renders their wider range.

Multiple actors including scientists, policymakers, stakeholders, brokers, and funders can engage in knowledge and ignorance mobilization (Gaudet 2013). A quick overview of Figure 33.1 starts with an understanding that linkages are conceptual and can sometimes depict causal relationships. Step numbering is solely for ease of reference to locate processes and dynamics at particular junctures in the model, for example, and do not refer to a sequential process. Existing knowledge, typically in written (print and electronic) cultural archives such as scientific journal articles and books, includes existing written ignorance (not displayed). Lastly, in spite of portraying a one-dimensional diagram, the model attempts to capture complexity and dynamic layers with recursive relationships that create new instances of ignorance or knowledge and their sub-types.

Starting on the left-hand side of Figure 33.1, the two overarching and related epistemic categories are knowledge and ignorance. Respective sub-types link within the overarching categories. As discussed above, for example, new ignorance can *not* be mobilized and therefore remain excluded (and at least temporarily not valued by scientific actors) as latent non-knowledge (step 1). Alternatively, ignorance *can* be mobilized and constructed as valuable active non-knowledge (step 2), active non-knowledge can lead to the construction of new active non-knowledge (step 3), and latent non-knowledge can eventually be constructed as active non-knowledge (step 4). Finally, new knowledge can join existing knowledge (step 6). Between the categories, knowledge can lead to the construction of more ignorance (step 7), active non-knowledge can lead to

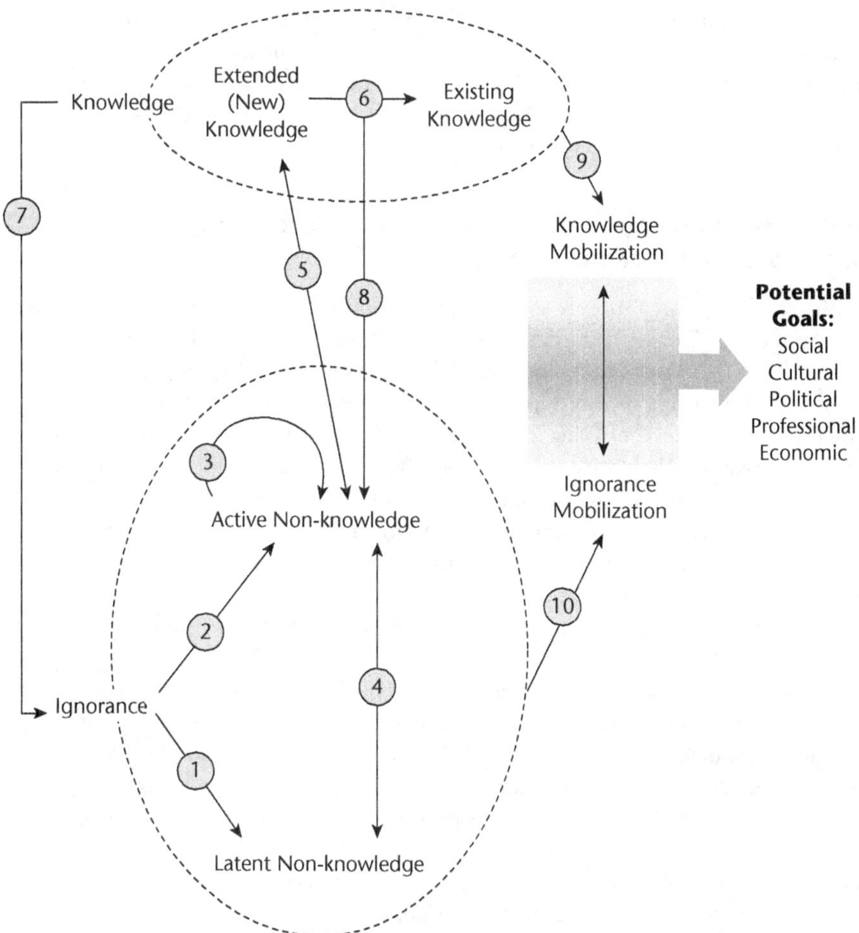

Figure 33.1 Model of knowledge and ignorance mobilization dynamics in science*

Source: Gaudet 2013: 11.

Note: *Numbering is for ease of reference and does not refer to a sequential process. Arrows are conceptual and sometimes depict causal relationships.

the construction of new knowledge (step 5), and judgements on manuscripts in journal editorial peer review (conceptualized between new and existing knowledge) can lead to the construction of new active non-knowledge (step 8).

Finally, the right-hand side of Figure 33.1 focuses on actors, mobilization, and goals. Actor knowledge (step 9) and ignorance (step 10) mobilization dynamics are distinct yet remain in tension and link with potential mobilization goals (i.e., social, cultural, political, professional, and economic). Here I highlight differential mobilization of knowledge and/or ignorance that actors can engage in. By this, I mean that actors can mobilize more or less knowledge and/or ignorance, thus differentially. An example is actors in a basic research laboratory who engaged in higher ignorance mobilization in comparison to lower knowledge mobilization in a biological sciences case study (Gaudet et al. 2012).

A last consideration is that my use of a model such as Figure 33.1 does not mean that I conceptualize knowledge and ignorance exclusively as property. Rather, I advance that competent actors engage in situated mobilization (see Wehling 2006: 87), be they scientists, policymakers, stakeholders, brokers, or funders. Lastly and in keeping with the main argument in the chapter, the overview of dynamics in Figure 33.1 renders scientific knowledge and ignorance dynamics visible and thus potentially useful for science evaluators and policymakers. I use the model to explore two cases, starting with a first case in science evaluation.

Expert opinion on knowledge gaps as a socio-economic impact indicator in science evaluation

The first case focuses on a specific socio-economic impact stemming from scientific activity – 'expert opinion on knowledge gaps' (Expert Panel on Science Performance and Research Funding 2012: 41) – framed in a 'Logic model for the selection of appropriate indicators'. The logic model was part of a project report entitled 'Informing Research Choices: Indicators and Judgment' by the Council of Canadian Academies (the Council). The board members for the Council who oversaw the project included representatives from the Royal Society of Canada, the Canadian Academy of Engineering, the Canadian Academy of Health Sciences, and the Canadian public (2012: ii). The logic model was presented as a 'common policy tool [that] can provide an instructive organizing structure for theoretical linkages between funding and the expected impacts and societal benefits from investing in discovery science' (2012: 40). Socio-economic impact here refers to an assessment of how results obtained from research are more broadly relevant (2012: 40).

The main element of interest in the case, 'expert opinion on knowledge gaps' (2012: 41), was framed as a potential indicator of scientific socio-economic impact in the context of Canada's science and technology strategy (2012: 41). Expert opinion on knowledge gaps is of interest because it explicitly acknowledges potential scientific impact beyond what is known in science.

Referring to Figure 33.1, 'knowledge gaps' can be understood as active non-knowledge or valued ignorance. Constructed as potential socio-economic impact, it is intentionally taken into account for possible future use in planning, theorizing, and action inside or outside of academia. Actors could therefore mobilize this active non-knowledge to construct new knowledge (step 5) or potentially further new active non-knowledge (step 3). Furthermore, 'expert opinion' implies a competent actor (cf., a scientist) to construct a knowledge gap as valuable active non-knowledge. Once constructed, other actors can mobilize the active non-knowledge. For example, a policy-maker can mobilize it to inform policy with political, social, and economic goals. Alternatively, a stakeholder or commercial actor could mobilize the active non-knowledge to construct a new research project or commercial venture, thereby meeting professional and economic goals.

For science evaluators, therefore, socio-economic impact in this case refers to emergent properties when it considers the limits and the borders of knowledge. To be sure, knowledge gaps are not a final impact 'product'. Impact instead rests in emergent relational potential for knowledge gaps as valuable active non-knowledge. Made visible in Figure 33.1, emergent relational potential can touch on several potential impact spheres including social, cultural, political, professional, and economic. From a focus on science evaluation in this first case, the second case shifts more specifically to scientific epistemic dynamics and science policy.

Knowledge and ignorance dynamics and evergreen science policies

The second case focuses on post-market surveillance by Health Canada that led to 'changes in the availability and recommended conditions of use of drugs containing calcitonin' (Health Canada 2013b). A Government of Canada federal department, Health Canada's mandate includes health-related policy, legislation, regulation, and activities such as drug approval, and post-market surveillance. The hormone in question, calcitonin, is naturally present in the human body and is known to increase calcium levels in the bones and lower these in the blood (European Medicines Agency 2012: 1). Commercial synthetic forms of the hormone are used in pharmaceutical products. In Canada, synthetic '[c]alcitonin is used as a nasal spray to treat osteoporosis (loss of calcium in bones) [. . .] and as an injection to treat Paget's disease (a chronic bone disorder) and hypercalcemia (high blood calcium)' (Health Canada 2013b).

Especially relevant in the chapter is that initial conditions of use for calcitonin containing products approved nearly 30 years ago by Health Canada (Health Canada 2013a: 4) did not anticipate that long-term use of the products could potentially lead to increased risk of various types of cancer. The unanticipated increased cancer risks are understood in this case as nescience or the complete absence of knowledge (outside of Figure 33.1). As Lexchin (2014) advanced, 'a prolonged period on the market is no guarantee of safety' (Lexchin, 2014: e18). Understood within an epistemic framework, length of market use does not equate with safety, rather knowledge and active non-knowledge remain on 'probation' with respect to potential new ignorance.

Prior to this construction of nescience, active non-knowledge for synthetic calcitonin containing drugs had generally revolved around these drugs' health impact on osteoporosis, Paget's disease, and hypercalcemia. An example is research on nasal calcitonin's ability to increase bone mass density and to lead to reductions in various types of fractures for individuals with osteoporosis. Newly constructed knowledge (step 5 in Figure 33.1) on the topic joined existing knowledge (step 6) (i.e., Tuck and Datta 2007: 530–531).

Once constructed, however, nescience led scientists to produce new active non-knowledge (step 2) on the link between calcitonin products and cancer. Further research helped construct new knowledge (step 5) that joined existing knowledge (step 6) such as a difference in increased risk of cancer for long-term use with higher doses and intranasal use in comparison to short-term use with minimal effective doses through injection and infusion (Health Canada 2013a: 2–3; European Medicines Agency 2012: 2). With this new active non-knowledge, the above active non-knowledge on the drugs' potential health impact for osteoporosis appeared to shift to latent non-knowledge (step 4).

In addition, active non-knowledge on the link between calcitonin products and cancer led to the construction of new active non-knowledge (step 3) pertaining to *how* calcitonin products could potentially lead to certain malignancies (cancers) (see limited scholarship of vitro research on human prostate cancer cell lines in Miacalcin team – Novartis 2013: 63–64). Not all types of cancer (or disease) with a potential link with calcitonin appear to have been considered for further research, however, and remain unstudied as examples of latent non-knowledge (step 1).

As the above dynamics illustrate, post-market surveillance performed by Health Canada and health regulatory agencies around the world (i.e., the European Medicines Agency and the Food and Drug Administration in the United States) at least *implicitly,* if not *explicitly,* acknowledges potential science knowledge and ignorance mobilization dynamics. Surveillance monitors unanticipated or surprising consequences with potential human health impact.

Post-market surveillance therefore constitutes an example of an 'evergreen science policy' process if it explicitly places active non-knowledge and knowledge on 'probation' with respect to potential new knowledge or ignorance. I define evergreen science policy as policies that have emergent properties explicitly acknowledging the potential construction of new epistemic relations as portrayed in Figure 33.1 (cf., new active non-knowledge, new ignorance, or new knowledge). Evergreen policy is therefore flexible and accommodates refinement, development (see Parliament of Canada Standing Committee on Environment and Sustainable Development 2008), or perhaps dissolution in response to the construction of emerging epistemic relations.

For policymakers, the challenge in creating evergreen policies is to convey the potential for change in scientific knowledge and ignorance without appearing to compromise the validity of scientific knowledge framing the policy. Figure 33.1 can support policymakers to perform this task in two ways. First, in Figure 33.1 scientific knowledge and ignorance are not understood in linear and finite relation, but rather explicitly in dynamic and potentially dialogical relations. Validity, therefore, does not rest in knowledge stability, instead it remains probationary to potential anticipated change. Second, policymakers can use Figure 33.1 as a tool to educate stakeholders, partners, funders, and the general public on scientific epistemic practices. By doing so, these actors can see and learn to expect and value change in scientific knowledge and ignorance.

Moreover, a focus on epistemic dynamics here might wrongly convey simplicity in post-market surveillance. Simplicity belies underlying complexity. As Jasanoff argued, regulatory science is complex given that it is performed 'at the margins of existing knowledge' (Jasanoff, 1990: 79) that not only entails knowledge production, but also prediction, involving numerous actors and accountabilities (1990: 77). Research shows that post-market surveillance is fraught with challenges including conflicting institutional relations of power over decision-making, problems with enforcement (Carpenter 2006; Light 2010), and potential increased exposure of users prior to the withdrawals of unsafe drugs (Lexchin 2014: e18). Where post-market surveillance actors can enter an epistemic framework is in how they mobilize, or do not mobilize, new ignorance or knowledge and for which (perhaps conflicting) goals they do so, or not (steps 9 and 10).

Finally, the model can help policymakers and non-scientific actors understand and learn how to engage in the relationship between latent non-knowledge and active non-knowledge (step 4) in science. For example, policymakers wishing to enlist a wider range of non-scientific actors to participate in shaping publicly-funded science and science policy can use the model to illustrate how health issues that matter to citizens, as latent non-knowledge, can eventually be constructed as active scientific non-knowledge. This final consideration is part of wider dynamics on the democratization of science and technology and citizen participation in science policy (i.e., Callon et al. 2001; Kelly 2003; Rask 2008; Selin and Hudson 2010).

Conclusion

I advanced in this chapter that a model of knowledge and ignorance mobilization dynamics in science could play a valuable role in science evaluation and policymaking. In essence, the model represents the unfolding of the typical map focussed on scientific knowledge. In the first case, active non-knowledge was explicitly acknowledged in science evaluation (cf., the Council report). Understood within a model of knowledge and ignorance mobilization dynamics (Figure 33.1), further potential epistemic relations (to new knowledge and/or active non-knowledge) and actor mobilization goals become more visible for science evaluators looking to account for impact as emergence.

In the second case, seeing post-market surveillance of a pharmaceutical product through a model of knowledge and ignorance mobilization dynamics (Figure 33.1) illustrated the multiplicity of new knowledge and ignorance mobilized, or not mobilized in the case of latent non-knowledge. It was also in the second case that I proposed the concept of evergreen policy with emergent properties explicitly acknowledging the potential construction of new epistemic relations. What is more, for policymakers, a model like that in Figure 33.1 could be a useful tool to account for validity in a context of expected change, and as a tool to educate and empower actors outside of science such as stakeholders, partners, funders, and the general public.

To conclude, I explore two implications from the use of a model of knowledge and ignorance mobilization dynamics in science evaluation and policymaking. First, such a model equips science evaluators and policymakers with concepts that reflect dynamic scientific epistemic practices. Second, there are at least two consequences of acknowledging such dynamics. First, scientific knowledge can no longer be conceived of as permanent – it retains potential changing relations with ignorance. Second, active and latent non-knowledge can no longer be conceived of as permanently regarded or disregarded by scientists. Rather, scientific knowledge and active and latent non-knowledge retain expected and ongoing shaped and reshaped relations with knowledge and ignorance and their sub-types. Ultimately, the model highlights relational mobilization dynamics with valuable scientific knowledge and ignorance as was the case for experimental natural philosophers in the seventeenth century. The unfolded map reflects a sociology of knowledge and ignorance.

Acknowledgements

I am grateful to the Principal Investigator of a PrioNet Canada research laboratory, Xavier Roucou, and his students and research assistants who inspired me to develop ignorance mobilization as complementary to knowledge mobilization and the mapping in Figure 33.1. The ideas, arguments, analysis, and remaining errors are solely mine, however, and do not necessarily reflect the views of individuals above. Funding was provided in part by a Joseph-Armand Bombardier Canada Graduate Scholarship from the Social Sciences and Humanities Research Council of Canada.

Notes

1 I focus on epistemic dynamics. This introductory discussion on experiments is not intended as a history of experimentation that investigates analytical, demonstrative, and synthesis functions in experimentation. An example of such analysis is Shapin and Schaffer's (1985) history of early scientific experimentation. Pickstone (2001), for his part, bemoans the lack of a typology for experimentation and proposes a history of experimentation that draws on biological and medical sciences (2001: Chapter Six).

2 I acknowledge Dr. Amanda MacFarlane, a researcher at Health Canada, for having introduced me to the concept of 'evergreen' science policies.

References

Anstey, P. R. (2005) 'Experimental versus Speculative Natural Philosophy', in P. R. Anstey and A. Schuster (eds) *The Science of Nature in the Seventeenth Century*, Dordrecht, The Netherlands: Springer.

Bhaskar, R. ([1975] 2008) *A Realist Theory of Science*, London: Verso.

Callon, M., P. Lascoumes, and Y. Barthe (2001) *Agir dans un monde incertain: essai sur la démocratie technique*, Paris: Seuil.

Carpenter, D. (2006) 'Reputation, Gatekeeping and the Politics of Post-Marketing Drug Regulation', *Virtual Monitor: Ethics Journal of the American Medical Association*, 8: 403–403.

Davies, W. (2011) 'Knowing the Unknowable: The Epistemological Authority of Innovation Policy Experts', *Social Epistemology*, 25: 401–421.

European Medicines Agency (2012) 'Questions and Answers on the Review of Calcitonin Containing Medicines: Outcome of a Procedure under Article 31 of Directive 2001/83/EC', London: European Medicines Agency.

Expert Panel on Science Performance and Research Funding (2012) 'Informing Research Choices: Indicators and Judgment: The Expert Panel on Science Performance and Research Funding', Ottawa: Council of Canadian Academies.

Firestein, S. (2012) *Ignorance: How It Drives Science*, New York: Oxford University Press.

Frickel, S., S. Gibbon, J. Howard, J. Kempner, G. Ottinger, and D. J. Hess (2010) 'Undone Science: Charting Social Movement and Civil Society Challenges to Research Agenda Setting', *Science, Technology, & Human Values,* 35: 444–473.

Gaudet, J. (2013) 'It Takes Two to Tango: Knowledge Mobilisation and Ignorance Mobilisation in Science Research', *Prometheus: Critical Studies in Innovation* 21 (3): 169–187.

Gaudet, J., N. Young, and M. Gross (2012) 'Ignorance Is Power: Science in Practice Epistemic Mobilization Dynamics', Presented at the Canadian Sociological Association (CSA) 2012 Conference in Kitchener-Waterloo, May 28–June 2, 2012.

Gaukroger, S. (2006) *The Emergence of a Scientific Culture: Science and the Shaping of Modernity 1210–1685,* Oxford: Clarendon Press.

Grew, N (1673) *An Idea of a Phytological History Propounded Together with a Continuation of the Anatomy of Vegetables, Particularly Prosecuted upon Roots,* London: printed by J.M. for R. Chiswell.

Gross, A. G. and J. E. Harmon (2014) *Science from Sight to Insight: How Scientists Illustrate Meaning,* Chicago: The University of Chicago Press.

Gross, M. (2010) *Ignorance and Surprise: Science, Society and Ecological Design,* Cambridge, MA: The MIT Press.

Hannam, J. (2010) *God's Philosophers: How the Medieval World Laid the Foundations of Modern Science,* London: Icon Books.

Health Canada (2013a) 'Media lines: Information Update on Drugs Containing Calcitonin', Ottawa: Health Canada. Obtained under the Access to Information Act, October 9, 2013.

——. (2013b) 'Press Release: Important Changes to the Availability and Conditions of Use for Drugs Containing Calcitonin', Ottawa: Government of Canada.

Hess, D. (2010) 'Social Movements, Publics, and Scientists', Invited Plenary Lecture, Japanese Society for Science and Technology Studies, Tokyo.

Ivainer, T. and R. Lenglet (1996) *Les ignorances des savants,* Paris: Maisonneuve & Larose.

Jasanoff, S. (1990) *The Fifth Branch: Science Advisers as Policymakers,* Cambridge, MA: Harvard University Press.

Johns, A. (1998) *The Nature of the Book: Print and Knowledge in the Making,* Chicago: The University of Chicago Press.

Kelly, S. E. (2003) 'Public Bioethics and Publics: Consensus, Boundaries, and Participation in Biomedical Science Policy', *Science, Technology & Human Values,* 28: 339–364.

Kempner, J., J. F. Merz, and C. L. Bosk (2011) 'Forbidden Knowledge: Public Controversy and the Production of Nonknowledge', *Sociological Forum,* 26: 475–500.

Latour, B. (2000) 'Du principe de précaution au principe du bon gouvernement', *Études,* 3934: 339–346.

Lexchin, J. (2014) 'How Safe Are New Drugs? Market Withdrawal of Drugs Approved in Canada between 1990 and 2009', *Open Medicine,* 8: e14–e19.

Light, D. W. (2010) 'Bearing the Risks of Prescription Drugs', in D. W. Light (ed.) *The Risks of Prescription Drugs,* New York: Columbia University Press.

Logan, D. C. (2009) 'Known Knowns, Known Unknowns, Unknown Unknowns and the Propagation of Scientific Enquiry', *Journal of Experimental Botany,* 60: 712–714.

Miacalcin team – Novartis (2013) 'Briefing Book: FDA Joint Reproductive Health Drugs and Drug Safety and Risk Management Advisory Committee Meeting on the Benefit/Risk of Salmon Calcitonin for the Treatment of Postmenopausal Osteoporosis'. Available at: http://www.fda.gov/downloads/AdvisoryCommittees/CommitteesMeetingMaterials/Drugs/ReproductiveHealthDrugsAdvisoryCommittee/UCM341781.pdf (accessed October 12, 2013).

Overdevest, C., A. Bleicher, and M. Gross (2010) 'The Experimental Turn in Environmental Sociology: Pragmatism and New Forms of Governance', in M. Gross and H. Heinrichs (eds) *Environmental Sociology: European Perspectives and Interdisciplinary Challenges,* New York: Springer.

Parliament of Canada Standing Committee on Environment and Sustainable Development (2008) 'Evidence'. Available at: http://www.parl.gc.ca/HousePublications/Publication.aspx?DocId=3445464&Mode=1&Language=E (accessed July 27, 2013).

Pickstone, J. V. (2001) *Ways of Knowing: A New History of Science, Technology, and Medicine,* Chicago: University of Chicago Press.

Rask, M. (2008) 'Foresight: Balancing between Increasing Variety and Productive Convergence', *Technological Forecasting & Social Change,* 75: 1157–1175.

Roberts, J. and J. Armitage (2008) 'The Ignorance Economy', *Prometheus,* 26: 335–354.
Selin, C. and R. Hudson (2010) 'Envisioning Nanotechnology: New Media and Future-Oriented Stakeholder Dialogue', *Technology in Society*, 32: 173–182.
Shapin, S. and S. Schaffer (1985) *Leviathan and the Air-Pump: Hobbes, Boyle, and the Experimental Life,* Princeton, NJ: Princeton University Press.
Smithson, M. (2009) 'The Many Faces and Masks of Uncertainty', in G. Bammer and M. Smithson (eds) *Uncertainty and Risk: Multidisciplinary Perspectives,* Sterling, VA: Earthscan.
Tuck, S. P. and H. K. Datta (2007) 'Osteoporosis in the Aging Male: Treatment Options', *Clinical Interventions in Aging*, 2: 521–536.
Wehling, P. (2006) 'The Situated Materiality of Scientific Practices: Postconstructivism – a New Theoretical Perspective in Science Studies?', *Science, Technology & Innovation Studies,* Special Issue 1: 81–100.

34

Ignorance is strength?

Intelligence, security and national secrets

Brian Rappert and Brian Balmer

Introduction

Ignorance pervades the areas of intelligence, security and national secrets. In their quest to know about the activities of others, defense and intelligence agencies must cope with gaps in their knowledge, outwardly project some sense of what they know, but also conceal precisely how much they know and do not know. Ignorance is both an obsession and forgotten, embraced and rejected, induced and deterred, milled and disregarded, as well as lived with and ever sought to be banished. The Janus-faced quality of ignorance – living with it while trying to eliminate it – not only pertains to such contrasts, but also the frequent suggestion, suspicion or paranoia that any claim to know (or not) proffered by those in the business of intelligence and national security might be an act of deliberate deception.

This chapter takes as its topic the challenge of knowing about what is often purposefully rendered difficult to know about matters of defense, intelligence and security. In the light of this challenge, it seeks to develop an appreciation of how commentators across varied disciplines characterize the relation between knowledge and ignorance in matters associated with intelligence, security and national secrecy. The first section of the chapter explores how ignorance can become a resource when dealing with defense and security matters. We then shift focus to explore how ignorance and collective identity relate to each other before, during and after acts of violence. Our final section is more reflexive, and considers methodological issues arising from the study of security and ignorance that have implications for the wider community of ignorance researchers. In covering this ground, it will be possible to extend issues addressed elsewhere in this Handbook: the practices for establishing doubt and certainty, ignorance as a resource, the relationality of knowledge and ignorance, the importance of both in the production of identity, and the methodological challenges of research into 'unknowing'.

Ignorance and intelligence: a fickle relation

This section develops an appreciation of the fickleness of whether ignorance is judged as asset or as threat by working through the inter-relations of knowledge and ignorance. To start, intelligence in matters of national security is conventionally conceived as the activity of providing information to policy makers so as to aid decision-making. With such rationalistic formulations, the analysis or assessment provided by agencies of the state reduces uncertainty and unknowns. The label 'intelligence' herein stands for the end-product analyses as well as the processes for deriving them. Both are presented as reducing ignorance – for instance about adversaries' capabilities or intentions – through the production of valid, timely and relevant knowledge. The classic 'cycle of intelligence', developed by NATO in the Cold War, embodies this outlook on intelligence: a sequential process starting with requirement setting (directing what is required by end users), leading to collection, then processing, dissemination and user feedback (Ormand 2010).

And yet the situation is routinely acknowledged by practitioners, scholars and others to be far more complicated than suggested in such classical conceptions. Recent ethnographic work within intelligence communities has demonstrated how the intelligence cycle, along with databases and other intelligence tools, all operate on the assumption that there is 'raw data' to feed into the intelligence process. Despite being an actors' category, 'raw data' is anything but raw – having been 'pre-cooked' through numerous pragmatic, political or organizational processes (Räsänen and Nyce 2013). To take an example of such processes from a different study, the sheer volume of short, daily briefings that intelligence analysts needed to write – at the expense of longer, more analytical pieces – made some in the community regard the work as being more like journalism than intelligence (Johnston 2005).

This gap between the idealistic and quotidian experience of doing intelligence occurs, not least, because the objects of investigation might be difficult to grasp and because others might well undertake counterintelligence to thwart such efforts. Before and after the 1991 Gulf War, for instance, Iraq had deployed measures to disguise and deceive other governments about its nuclear, biological and chemical weapons capabilities. For Goffman and others, intelligence and international diplomacy in relation to national security has served as a paradigmatic area for mapping the moves, countermoves and counter-countermoves whereby individuals and groups seek to influence each other's thinking (see, for instance, Goffman 2007; Barnes 1994). Concealment is a commonplace tactic in such deception gaming. So too can be openness. State censors have been adept in using the selective release of information as means of distraction and disguise (Hutchings 1987). An overall point is that concealment and openness exist in a dynamic and co-constitutive relationship. Each act of 'openness' provides the conditions for new attempts at concealment and vice-versa. As a result of the considerations above, many commentators have written about the importance of acknowledging the general incomplete and partial view provided by intelligence reports (Betts 2007).

These are not the only recognized limitations of conceiving of intelligence as information-aiding-decision-making. Many commentators have argued that pre-existing knowledge and expectations can result in a threatening ignorance (Dupont 2003). In relation to the 2003 Iraq War, for instance, in light of the past practices of deception and denial by Iraq, the lack of evidence about nuclear, chemical and biological capabilities in the build up to the 2003 invasion simply hardened the judgments of some that careful concealment was at work.[1] With the failure to find so-called 'weapons of mass destruction', many questions have been asked since whether Western intelligence agencies and political leaders misled others, were misled by others or misled themselves.[2] Conversely, from the perspective of preventing intelligence reaching the enemy, the UK Government in the 1960s went to great lengths to conceal what was absent: that they had no stockpile of chemical weapons (Balmer 2010). In such situations of uncertainty about opponent's capabilities, war can be conceptualized as one means of experimentally testing out assessment of the other (Weyer 1994).

Within the field of Intelligence Studies and Security Studies, explanations for the inaccuracy of threat assessments in Iraq and elsewhere often focus on the dangers of preconceptions (Jackson 2010; Boudeau 2007; Barron 2006; Leonard 2011). The manner in which new intelligence gets 'layered' on top of existing beliefs, the manner in which individuals project (or 'mirror') their rationalities on to others, and the manner in which intelligence can be turned to support political goals have long been identified as leading to unfounded certainty (Jervis 1985; Betts 2007). The concern with the pervasiveness of how intelligence gathering can be self-sealing and self-reinforcing calls in doubt rationalistic conceptions whereby information reduces uncertainty and unknowns. Intelligence can be dangerous when its secret status is taken as giving it an exaggerated importance.

Other academic analyses have sought to locate ignorance and its implications squarely within institutional practices. For instance, both Vogel (2013) (with regard to bioweapons threats) and Eden (2004) (with regard to damage from nuclear weapons) defined the organizational contexts and processes that result in some considerations not entering into national security assessments and the resultant deficiencies in policy-making. The process of self-sealing, self-reinforcing security is described in detail in Edwards' (1997) history of computing, *The Closed World*. He argues that the desire to use computers to control the battlefield was exemplified during the Vietnam War, where US Operation Igloo White attempted to track electronically all enemy movements along the Ho Chi Min Trail. Despite the ground sensors being easily circumvented and even duped, Operation Igloo White was not immediately abandoned because the computers continued to record 'successful' detection along the trail.

Additional concerns are routinely raised about how treatments of intelligence as information-aiding-decision-making can lead to situations very much otherwise. In a world of necessarily bounded capabilities, the attempt to find out about some matters invariably means foregoing others, a condition that can produce blind spots and strategic surprise (Vattimo 1992). More generally, the production of new understandings leads to new uncertainties and unknowns. This is perhaps particularly so in the case of matters of national security because it does not refer to some objective condition of safety. Rather, security is a perception wherein determinations of threats can expand as a nation's understanding of, and place in, world changes (Yergin 1977). In response to the multiple human and technical factors that limit apprehension, some have called for recognition of how ignorance characterizes intelligence-based decision-making. Herein, echoing Socrates, wisdom consists of appreciating the limits of what is understood.

In a wide ranging analysis of themes related to the many forms, types and implications of non-knowledge for matters of national security, Daase and Kessler (2007) argued that once knowledge and non-knowledge are both seen as constitutive for decision-making:

> non-knowledge cannot be reduced to some 'lack' of knowledge that could be solved by looking harder at the facts or processes of conjecture and refutation. [. . .] The 'fight against terrorism' is characterized by the interplay of rather distinct logics and forms of non-knowledge.
>
> *(Daase and Kessler 2007: 430)*

This condition also had reflexive implications for academic studies, fields such as international relations, which have to recognize the forms of non-knowledge, contingency and probability that pervade them.

By raising the question 'for whom?', this quote signals another set of considerations about ignorance. What counts as 'unfounded', 'failure' or 'certain' understanding often turns on who is taking part in making evaluations. Of course, governments not only routinely try to keep secrets from adversaries but also from the publics from which they derive their legitimacy. Shils (1956) distinguishes these two versions of secrecy using the terms functional (practically necessary) and symbolic (tending to maximum loyalty or even paranoid) secrecy. The latter also encompasses secrets that are kept merely to avoid embarrassment rather than enhance national security. Yet, especially in the areas of security and international relations, the openness of government has its limits and is often seen to have its limits (Gusterson 1996). So, another noteworthy feature of the 2003 Iraq War was the manner in which intelligence was brought into political debate.[3] Much of the controversy that followed the post-war failure to find nuclear, biological or chemical weapons centered on the dissection of assessments that have not been publicly available in past armed conflicts.

In matters of national security the relevance of information goes far beyond its role in (however adequately or inadequately) informing decisions and actions. Instead, its representations figure prominently in symbolic identity contests over legitimacy and credibility. Who is deemed an authoritative speaker often turns on perceptions of access to sequestered information. Claims to access what is not equally available set some apart from others. It is perhaps not surprising then that security organizations within and outside of government often limit access to seemingly inconsequential information. Doing so facilitates the imputation that much unspecifiable expertise and infrastructure stands behind policies and practices. Such evocations can then shore up the credibility of those speaking. It can also create – whether deliberately or otherwise – the unfounded impression that someone, somewhere, actually does know what is happening (Balmer 2006). Concealing the extent of knowledge or ignorance can further lead to what has been termed 'security theatre', where elaborate measures are taken (e.g. at airports) that provide an empty display in order to create an impression of security, without actually making anyone more secure (Schneier 2003).

Yet it should not be assumed from this that governments always try to represent themselves as the possessors of knowledge. This can shift depending on the situation. Within discussions of civilian deaths from war, for instance, at times and in relation to certain types of deaths, governments have sought to argue they do not and cannot reliably know the numbers of those killed in combat (Rappert 2012). Likewise, scientists advising on Cold War biological weapons policy could invoke their cultural authority as producers of certain knowledge to act as legitimated doubters, claiming not to know in situations when not everyone claiming ignorance was granted the same credibility (Balmer 2012). These claims of authoritatively not knowing underpinned the advisors' pleas to continue a program of biological weapons research.

Further aspects of how the role of information extends beyond decision-making can be identified. For instance, ignorance is part and parcel of the dynamic shaping the 'moral economies' of security-related organizations which enables those within them to undertake their work (Gusterson 1996; Gould and Folb 2002; Wright and Wallace 2002; Bussolini 2011). Compartmentalization during the Manhattan Project, for instance, closed off the potential for ethical debate (Thorpe 2004). And yet the strictures of secrecy should not be conceived of as simply negative or inhibitory. Practices of establishing and maintaining secrecy help constitute (and can be constituted by) lines of experimental and field practices. For example, when a civilian fishing trawler strayed into a Cold War field trial of biological warfare agents, rather than inform the trawler crew, the imperative to maintain secrecy turned the accident into a monitoring exercise akin to an 'experiment of opportunity' (Balmer 2004).

Ignorance in the formation of identity and memory

The previous section covered questions about 'who knows what' and the role of ignorance as more than just an absence of knowledge. We change direction in this section to ask about the role of ignorance in what might be called ontological (or identity) questions: What is the nature of war? What is the nature of the perpetrators and victims of aggression? As such, this section explores the role of ignorance in the development of individual and collective identity.

War, of course, involves killing; yet oddly enough, war cultivates a particular ignorance about killing. An important vehicle for this ignorance is the increasing impersonalization and bureaucratization of killing that characterized war in the twentieth and twenty-first centuries (Roland 2003). This has frequently rendered invisible the identity and humanity of the dead. With respect to nuclear warfare, for example, Nash (1980) – whose job was to select potential targets for nuclear strikes – describes how those targeted were reduced to figures and charts in what he terms 'the bureaucratization of homicide'. Cohn (1987), writing from a feminist perspective, analyses the 'neutral' language of nuclear strategy, which reduces mass casualties to 'collateral damage' or peace to 'strategic stability'.

Moving away from nuclear war, Bauman (1989) points to similar distancing strategies – animated by a means-end efficiency – that depersonalized the victims of the Holocaust. Ignorance about such acts of domination and violence can be structured and cultured by a variety of social processes (Einwohner 2009). This can result in acts – such as widespread rape during conflict – being both widely acknowledged but never explicitly mentioned (Mookherjee, 2006). This ignorance of what is known as a form of denial is discussed by Žižek (2004) in relation to Donald Rumsfeld's often cited assessment of the pre-2003 threat from Iraq. Besides the known knowns, known unknowns and unknown unknowns, Žižek adds a category of 'unknown knowns', matters which are denied even though they act as reference points for public values. Referring to the maltreatment of prisoners in Abu Ghraib, he argues:

> If Rumsfeld thinks that the main dangers in the confrontation with Iraq were the 'unknown unknowns', that is, the threats from Saddam whose nature we cannot even suspect, then the Abu Ghraib scandal shows . . . the main dangers lie in the 'unknown knowns' – the disavowed beliefs, suppositions and obscene practices we pretend not to know about.
>
> *(Žižek 2004)*

Another way in which war generates ignorance lies in attempts to count the dead. Once again, a task designed to reduce ignorance and uncertainty also generates uncertainty. It appears evident from the intense efforts by some nations and groups to establish the exact number of *their* troops killed and injured in conflict that such counts are treated as a meaningful. Numbers at least offer the possibility of signifying individual suffering, something often denied in the rhetorics of war (Scarry 1985). And yet, as bureaucratic tabulating exercises, casualty statistics provide a summation of abstractions that stifle comprehension as they enable it. Casualty numbers on their own cannot determine how those numbers should be understood – whether they are disproportionate, relatively small, a cost that needed to be paid, etc. At a more general level, Martin and Lynch (2009) have argued that counting is not simply an enumeration of what is 'out there', because decisions have to first be made about what and how to count (for example, there may be multiple ways to incorporate, ignore or exclude 'stray' people in counts of rioters, regardless of their putative claim that they just happened to be in the vicinity and were not protesting but were counted).

Along similar lines, the killing of non-combatants has been an issue throughout the written record of conflict (Rummel 1994). What can be said with some confidence about this long and checkered history is that the acceptability of non-combatant deaths has been subject to varying evaluation over time. Stone (2007) notes that in the wake of the 1991 Gulf War, the number of civilian casualties was a political and contested issue. Official counts differed markedly from those provided by methods that, by extrapolating from pre-war demographic trends to what the population would be if the war had not happened, incorporated measures of the wider effects wrought by the destruction of infrastructure. To take another example, as World War II approached 'total war', civilian deaths were commonplace. The saturation bombing of major cities in Europe and the Pacific sought to inflict unendurable suffering and terror for the people on the ground. While regarded as more or less regrettable among operations planners, there could be no doubt that people would die in substantial numbers as cities were reduced to smoking rubble (Schaffer 1985). Official estimates of the number killed were bound up with domestic and international politics. At times, deaths to enemy populations were inflated so as to bolster the lethality of force (Grayling 2006). Particularly after fighting ceased, though, concerns about whether victorious domestic populations might come to regret what had been done in their name led to a reluctance to know the effects of bombing (Garrett 1997; Knightley 2004).

Knowing ignorance

This section turns to methodological issues in the study of ignorance and security. The editors of this volume have noted that attempts to study what is missing, the case with all forms of non-knowledge, raise a number of challenges for empirical research. As they point out: 'After all, how can a researcher know what an individual or an observed group of actors themselves do not know?' (Gross and McGoey, this volume, Chapter 1). Likewise, how can a researcher have confidence in what can be known about matters that may well have been deliberately obscured from understanding? And further, how can investigators avoid succumbing to what the anthropologist Michael Taussig (2003) called 'the craving for certainty that secrecy inspires'?

The foregoing discussion in this chapter should make it apparent that the conceptual shift from ignorance as an absence, to more relational and graded views of ignorance assists a methodological shift. Many of the studies we have cited in this chapter seek to de-emphasize ignorance as, first, all or nothing (either knowledge is absence or presence), and second, as operating in a temporally or spatially sequential manner. Instead, in various ways, they replace this conceptualization with notions that invoke background-foreground, waxing-waning and similar metaphors. This enables research questions to be asked about what, how and why certain silences, unknowns and absences are produced while, often simultaneously, other matters are prominently talked about, are regarded as known, and fill a presence.

Take the historical archive. In relation to matters of security and intelligence, official archives of the state occupy a tension ridden position. Their documentation provides an indispensible – even one and only – resource in making sense of the knowns, unknowns, actions and inactions of statecraft. And yet, whatever the amount of materials made ready, archives are open for question regarding what is not in them and thereby what cannot be understood through them. Layered in meaning and highly crafted as resources, questions can be posed about what is made accessible in archives, what is incomprehensible, what remains outside of them, what is redacted within them, what should be taken as accurate, etc. Rather than such concerns simply taken as a forming a barrier to analysis, historians have sought ways of reading documentation in terms of its limitations. So, archival research on declassified documents needs to discount decisions taken at particular committee meetings as 'the decision', rather than as a marker in a flow of decision-making of which only a portion is in the written record. Another way to address limitations has entailed shifting the goal of research from detecting the hidden meanings of archival material, to appreciating the taken-for-granted presumption of officials that informed the production of 'officialdom' records of colonizers (Stoler 2009). In this sense, we need self-awareness that archive-dependent accounts of secrecy and ignorance construct their own transparency, because even a partial story purports to reveal something previously unknown.

Relatedly, when dealing with heavily redacted material of officialdom, another analytical move is to shift away from treating these documents as partial (and thereby flawed) historical texts to productive cultural images (Office of Experiments 2013; Nath 2014). As images that inspire public speculation about their meaning, the documents can inspire debate that can move far beyond the control or influence of the state; a debate open to social analysis and understanding.

Yet another strategy in the study of statecraft has been for social science accounts to explicitly note what is not included within them – through the active redacting of their own accounts or the explicit flagging of what is absent from them (Rappert 2014). A goal of such techniques has been to express and reproduce the conditions of knowledge production in matters of national security. By drawing readers into an explicit and active role of making sense of the types of information gaps that characterize national security discussions for both scholars and practitioners, the purpose is not simply to marshal pregnant blanks to fashion an engrossing story. Rather it is to cultivate an awareness of the sensitivities and skills useful in investigating secrets and ignorance.

Still others have taken the blacked out, redacted, pulled, etc. as the starting point for investigation. As Manguel (1995) has contended in relation to censorship, attempts to quash can have the paradoxical effects of drawing attention to that which is meant to be suppressed. Paglen (2009) has used this effect as a starting point for empirical inquiry into secret military establishments, which he terms the 'blank spots' on the map. Particularly in relation to geography and space, he has sought an appreciation of how those matters deliberately kept from being known can 'announce their own existence' through the traces left from hiding. Since buildings, personnel and technologies cannot be made immaterial, examining efforts to do so provides a basis for analysis. It is through the study of the ongoing spatial and temporal management of the contradictions of 'secret keeping' that it is possible to develop a sense of how tightly twined and mutually constitutive knowledge and ignorance can be in practice as well as how contradiction underpins state secrecy (Paglen 2010).

Another possible basis for inquiry is to find ways of testing notions of ignorance. For instance, governments have long and consistently argued their use of force is consistent with the principles of international law (Barak 2011). And yet the often lack of disclosure about the basis for such evaluations and the use of hypothetical scenarios to justify contested technologies has raised doubts for some. In such a circumstance, one way of probing understanding and promoting learning is to reverse the typical onus in place. The recent negotiation of an international ban of cluster munitions, for instance, started with a widely encompassing definition and then required governments to determine what exclusions should be made to a wide-ranging prohibition. In other words, exclusions to a prohibition had to be 'argued in', rather than 'argued out'. This shift provided a basis for analytical engagement with the ignorance of officials and how ignorance (and ignorance of ignorance) often underpins humanitarian debates about the rights and wrongs of conflict (Rappert 2012: Chapter 4).

Conclusion

In this chapter, through our discussion of intelligence and security, we have moved away from various polarized views of ignorance and knowledge. In particular, we have turned our back on the strong division between 'ignorance-as-absence' versus 'knowledge-as-presence', and between 'ignorance-as-asset' and 'ignorance-as-threat'. While ignorance is frequently characterized as something missing that needs restoring, our discussion cites many studies that clearly demonstrate how the production, feigning and claim to be authoritative possessors of ignorance can be made to work as a resource. We have also shown how ignorance can be deployed in attempts to remove, render 'neutral' or absent inconvenient atrocities from the routine business of killing. And, we have briefly discussed methodological possibilities for the social research community to take the study of ignorance forward. Despite our overall argument to view ignorance in these more nuanced terms, social actors themselves seem quite capable of portraying ignorance in either nuanced or stark terms. As such, it remains an open and intriguing question as to what is at stake for those we study when they employ ignorance in these various ways.

Notes

1 For a history of UN inspections in Iraq see Blix (2004).
2 See Dutch Committee of Inquiry on the War in Iraq (2010); US Senate (2004); Foreign Affairs Committee (2003); Intelligence and Security Committee (2003); WMD Commission (2005); Parliamentary Joint Committee on ASIO, ASIS and DSD (2004).
3 See Number 10 Downing Street (2002) and CIA (2002).

References

Balmer, B. (2004) 'How Does an Accident Become an Experiment? Secret Science and the Exposure of the Public to Biological Warfare Agents', *Science as Culture* 13, 2, pp. 197–228.

Balmer, B. (2006) 'A Secret Formula, A Rogue Patent and Public Knowledge about Nerve Gas: Secrecy as a Spatial-Epistemic Tool', *Social Studies of Science*, 35, 5, pp. 691–722.

Balmer, B. (2010) 'Keeping Nothing Secret: United Kingdom Chemical Weapons Policy in the 1960s', *Journal of Strategic Studies* 33, 6, pp. 871–893.

Balmer, B. (2012) *Secrecy and Science: A Historical Sociology of Biological and Chemical Warfare*. Farnham, UK: Ashgate.

Barak, E. (2011) *Deadly Metal Rain: The Legality of Flechette Weapons in International Law*. Leiden: Brill.

Barnes, J.A. (1994) *Pack of Lies*. Cambridge: Cambridge University Press.

Barron, P. (2006) 'Interview a Statesman, Design a Set', *BBC Newsnight*, 20 January. Available at: http://news.bbc.co.uk/1/hi/programmes/newsnight/4631408.stm. Date last accessed: 20 February 2011.

Bauman, Z. (1989) *Modernity and the Holocaust*. Ithaca, NY: Cornell University Press.

Betts, R. (2007) *The Enemies of Intelligence: Knowledge and Power in American National Security*. New York: Columbia Press.

Blix, H. (2004) *Disarming Iraq*. London: Pantheon.

Boudeau, C. (2007) 'Producing Threat Assessments: An Ethnomethodological Perspective on Intelligence on Iraq's Aluminium Tubes', in B. Rappert (ed.) *Technology and Security: Governing Threats in the New Millenium*. Basingtsoke, UK: Palgrave.

Bussolini, J. (2011) 'Los Alamos as Laboratory for Domestic Security Measures: Nuclear Age Battlefield Transformations and the Ongoing Permutations of Security', *Geopolitics* 16, 2, pp. 329–358.

CIA (2002) *The National Intelligence Estimate: Iraq's Continuing Programs for Weapons of Mass Destruction*. Langley, VA: CIA.

Cohn, C. (1987) 'Sex and Death in the Rational World of Defense Intellectuals', *Signs* 12, 4, pp. 687–718.

Daase, C. and Kessler, O. (2007) 'Knowns and Unknowns in the "War on Terror": Uncertainty and the Political Construction of Danger', *Security Dialogue* 38, 4, pp. 401–425.

Dupont, A. (2003) 'Intelligence for the 21st Century', *Intelligence and National Security* 18, 4, pp. 15–39.

Dutch Committee of Inquiry on the War in Iraq (2010) 'Report of the Dutch Committee of Inquiry on the War in Iraq', *Netherlands International Law Review* 57, pp. 81–137.

Eden, L. (2004) *Whole World on Fire: Organizations, Knowledge and Nuclear Weapons Devastation*. Ithaca, NY: Cornell University Press.

Edwards, P. (1997) *The Closed World: Computers and the Politics of Discourse in Cold War America*. Cambridge, MA: The MIT Press.

Einwohner, R. L. (2009) 'The Need to Know: Cultured Ignorance and Jewish Resistance in the Ghettos of Warsaw, Vilna, and Łódz', *The Sociological Quarterly* 50, 3, pp. 407–430.

Foreign Affairs Committee (2003) *The Decision to Go to War in Iraq*. London: HMSO.

Garrett, S. (1997) *Ethics and Airpower in World War II*. New York: St Martin's Press.

Goffman, E. (1970) *Strategic Interaction*. Oxford: Basil Blackwell.

Gould, C. and Folb, P. (2002) 'The Role of Professionals in the South African Chemical and Biological Warfare Programme', *Minerva* 40, 1, pp. 77–91.

Grayling, A. C. (2006) *Among the Dead Cities*. London: Bloomsbury.

Gusterson, H. (1996) *Nuclear Rites: A Weapons Laboratory at the End of the Cold War*. Berkeley: University of California Press.

Hutchings, R. (1987) *Soviet Secrecy and Non-Secrecy*. London: Macmillan.

Intelligence and Security Committee (2003) *Iraqi Weapons of Mass Destruction – Intelligence and Assessments*. London: HMSO.

Jackson, P. (2010) 'On Uncertainty and the Limits of Intelligence', in L. Johnson (ed.), *The Oxford Handbook of National Security Intelligence*. Oxford: Oxford University Press.

Jervis, R. (ed.) (1985) *Psychology and Deterrence*. London: Johns Hopkins University Press.

Johnston, R. (2005) *Analytical Culture in the US Intelligence Community: An Ethnographic Study*. Washington, DC: Center for the Study of Intelligence.

Knightley, P. (2004) *The First Casualty: The War Correspondent as Hero and Myth-maker from Crimea to Iraq*. Baltimore, MA: Johns Hopkins University Press.

Leonard, J. W. (2011) 'The Corrupting Influence of Secrecy on National Policy Decisions', in S. Maret (ed.), *Government Secrecy* (Research in Social Problems and Public Policy, Volume 19). London: Emerald.

Manguel, A. (1995) 'Daring to Speak One's Name', *Index on Censorship* 24, 1, pp. 16–29.

Martin, A. and Lynch, M. (2009) 'Counting Things and People: The Practices and Politics of Counting', *Social Problems* 56, 2, pp. 243–266.

Mookherjee, N. (2006) 'Remembering to Forget: Public Secrecy and Memory of Sexual Violence in the Bangladesh War of 1971', *Journal of the Royal Anthropological Institute* 12, pp. 433-450.

Nash, H. T. (1980) 'The Bureaucratization of Homicide', in E. P. Thompson (ed.), *Protest and Survive*. Harmondsworth, UK: Penguin.

Nath, A. (2014) 'Beyond the Public Eye: On FOIA Documents and the Visual Politics of Redaction', *Cultural Studies <=> Critical Methodologies* 14, 1, pp. 21–28.

Number 10 Downing Street (2002) *Iraq's Weapons of Mass Destruction: The Assessment of the British Government*, 24 September. London: Stationery Office.

Office of Experiments (2013) 'On Being Overt Secrecy and Covert Culture', in E. Fisher and R. Fortnum (eds) *On Not Knowing*. London: Kettle's Yard.

Ormand, D. (2010) *Securing the State*. London: Hurst & Company.

Paglen, T. (2009) *Blank Spots on the Map: The Dark Geography of the Pentagon's Secret World*. New York: Dutton.

Paglen, T. (2010) 'Goatsucker: Toward a Spatial Theory of State Secrecy', *Environment and Planning D* 28, pp. 759–771.

Parliamentary Joint Committee on ASIO, ASIS and DSD (2004) *Intelligence on Iraq's Weapons of Mass Destruction*, No. 47/2004. Canberra: Parliament of Australia.

Rappert, B. (2012) *How to Look Good in a War*. London: Pluto.

Rappert, B. (2014) 'Present Absences: Hauntings and Whirlwinds in "-graphy"' *Social Epistemology* 28, 1, pp. 41–55.

Räsänen, M. and Nyce, D. (2013) 'The Raw is Cooked: Data in Intelligence Practice', *Science, Technology, & Human Values* 38, 5, pp. 655–677.

Roland, A. (2003) 'Science, Technology and War', in M. Nye (ed.), *The Cambridge History of Science, Volume 5: The Modern Physical and Mathematical Sciences*. Cambridge: Cambridge University Press.

Rummel, R. (1994) *Death by Government*. New Brunswick, NJ: Transaction.

Scarry, E. (1985) *The Body in Pain: The Making and Unmaking of the World*. Oxford: Oxford University Press.

Schaffer, R. (1985) *Wings of Judgment*. Oxford: Oxford University Press.

Schneier, B. (2003) *Beyond Fear: Thinking Sensibly about Security in an Uncertain World*. Göttingen: Copernicus Books.

Shils, E. (1956) *The Torment of Secrecy: Background and Consequences of American Security Policies*. Lanham, MD: Ivan R Dee.

Stoler, A. L. (2009) *Along the Archival Grain*. Oxford: Princeton University Press.

Stone, J. (2007), 'Technology and the Problem of Civilian Casualties in War', in B. Rappert (ed.), *Technology and Security: Governing Threats in the New Millennium*. Basingstoke, UK: Palgrave.

Taussig, M. (2003) 'Viscerality, Faith, and Skepticism', in B. Meyer and P. Pels (eds.), *Magic and Modernity*. Stanford, CA: Stanford University Press.

Thorpe, C. (2004) 'Against Time: Scheduling, Momentum, and Moral Order at Wartime Los Alamos', *Journal of Historical Sociology* 17, 1, pp. 31–55.

US Senate (2004) *Report on the U.S. Intelligence Community's Pre-War Intelligence Assessments*, 7 July 2004. Washington, DC: US Senate.

Vattimo, G. (1992) *The Transparent Society*. Cambridge: Polity Press.

Vogel, K. (2013) *Phantom Menace or Looming Danger? A New Framework for Assessing Bioweapons Threats*. Baltimore, MD: Johns Hopkins University Press.

Weyer, J. (1994) 'Actor Networks and High Risk Technologies: The Case of the Gulf War', *Science & Public Policy* 21, 5, pp. 321–334.

WMD Commission (2005) *Final Report of the Commission on the Intelligence Capabilities of the United States Regarding Weapons of Mass Destruction*, 31 March. Washington, DC: The Commission on the Intelligence Capabilities of the United States Regarding Weapons of Mass Destruction.

Wright, S. and Wallace, D. (2002) 'Secrecy in the Biotechnology Industry: Implications for the Biological Weapons Convention', in S. Wright (ed.), *Biological Warfare and Disarmament: New Problems/New Perspectives*. Lanham, MD: Rowman & Littlefield.

Yergin, D. (1977) *Shattered Peace: The Origins of the Cold War*. London: Penguin.

Žižek, S. (2004) 'What Rumsfeld Doesn't Know That he Knows about Abu Ghraib', *In These Times* (http://www.lacan.com/zizekrumsfeld.htm) (accessed 8 May 2014).

35

Ignorance and the sociology of economics

Oliver Kessler

Introduction: a path not taken

The recent world economic crisis has led to a discussion on the 'crisis in economics', which flared up in 2008–2009. For many, the economic crisis has not only shown the folly of modern finance legitimized through heady concepts such as 'rationality', 'efficiency' and 'financial innovation', but it has also pointed to the blind spots of contemporary economics itself. The charge economics had to face was not just that it did not see the crisis coming (as always, there were unheard voices – but it is always easier to point to them *ex post* than to listen to them *ex ante*), but rather that it was actively involved in bringing about 'modern finance', including its instruments, models and 'ideology'. This 'actively bringing about' has at least two dimensions: the participation of academic economists and the 'inscription' of economic theory into the social fabric of modern finance itself.

In particular, the literatures of financialization and performativity, as different as they are, have already successfully detailed the extent to which economics and modern finance are 'productively intertwined'. The financialization literature has highlighted how 'financial innovation' was framed by analogy to technological innovation as something 'socially' beneficial. This frame carried much of the 'belief system' that legitimized the spread of new financial instruments and their 'light-touch' regulation (Engelen et al. 2011). Similarly, if the performativity debate has shown one thing, it is that it is impossible to separate clearly between the practices of financial markets on the one hand and a detached academic discipline 'economics' on the other (Callon 1998: 8; MacKenzie and Millo 2003: 107). From this perspective, the assumed objectivity of economic theory is a myth in need of demystification.

This 'demystification' is the task of the 'sociology of economics', which seeks to understand the external and internal social forces that shape both economics and its role and function within society.[1] The sociology of economics explores how the epistemic authority of economics is produced, how it evades critique, and how it limits the range of policy options.[2]

The last economic crisis provided such a moment, where change seemed possible and in which a debate flared up upon the limits of economic theory itself. This was one of the rare moments when economics tried to observe its own disciplinary boundaries. This momentary lapse of reasoning was best encapsulated by Alan Greenspan's insight that the crisis had led him to believe that there was a flaw in his 'ideology', that is, his belief in the rationality and self-correction [or today: resilience] of markets (Bloomsberg 2008). Yet as quickly as the debate was opened, it also calmed down. This raises the question of why this debate has not led to significant disciplinary discussion about the foundations of economics itself. I suspect that one of the reasons for the current silence is that this debate unluckily merged two distinct questions: the question of why economists did not see the crisis coming, that is, a case of collective myopia; and the question about the role of economics in bringing about modern finance, that is, its performative power. What has happened is that the debate essentially has focused on the first dimension (myopia) and not on the second. The first one can be answered by demanding 'better' theories and more 'empirical' data. The second question would have demanded a reflexivity turn; in other words, a rethinking of the foundations, boundaries and performative power of economics. This second dimension is silenced and actually – given the disciplinary confines in economics – needs to be silenced and ignored. It is beyond reach, in the realm of the unsayable.

In this chapter, I argue that this move of leaving the more challenging question unanswered is not due to just institutional and monetary interests (even though this certainly plays a role), but due to the disciplinary inability of economics to reflect upon its own boundaries. I argue that one of the performative consequences of the reign of formal reasoning in economics is its *incapacity* to reflect upon its own meta-theoretical presuppositions. Modern economics formed by excluding the very questions it now would need to reconsider. The consequences are twofold: first, the ignorance built into the disciplinary structures makes fundamental change difficult. This includes intra-disciplinary structures (like career paths, journal rankings, etc.) as well as the perceived position of economics vis-à-vis other (social) sciences. However, there is also a second – more practical consequence: with economics serving as the 'theoretical' backbone of financial practices, history is bound to repeat: expectations of some 'complex' change in global finance will be disappointed. A fundamental reform of global finance would also require a new theoretical backbone that could count as legitimate and authoritative knowledge. This would require a re-description of finance, the advent of different categories and semantic distinctions that could de-stabilize the current meanings. Such an alternative might be found in economic sociology and heterodox economics, but as these alternatives find themselves ignored by orthodox economics, their role will most likely remain marginal. The current system simply reproduces itself.

To pursue this argument, this chapter is structured in three parts. The first part briefly returns to the debate on the 'crisis of economics' in 2008–2009 and outlines the two dimensions of the debate. The second part reconstructs the changing constellation of economic thought. Given space limits, this part necessarily has to work with shortcuts and general statements that cannot do justice to the complexity of economics as a discipline. Yet I do hope to be able to show (a) how today's orthodoxy was produced and entrenched, and (b) why 'critique' and 'reflexivity' from a sociological point of view will not gain ground within orthodox economics. In other words, this part provides a narrative of why economics has become blind to its own construction and embedded epistemological assumptions. Hence, most critiques will be answered by the same arguments (or even silence) as before. The third part reconstructs some of the consequences outlined above before a conclusion summarises the argument.

From the economic crisis to the crisis of economics

That crises are subject to public debate is to be expected, especially when its epicenter is the US economic system. However, that a scientific discipline like economics finds itself on the cover of public magazines must be new to many members of that profession. Yet soon after the crisis broke out, it quickly became clear that more was at stake than the literature on government or market failure implied. Many of the beliefs and policies that led to the crisis where justified on the basis of economic theory. Whether it was the idea that freely operating markets are efficient and self-equilibrating, that regulations cannot work 'against the market' (note the collective singular), or that financial innovation leads to growth and benefits the entire economy, they all had their home basis in economic theory. In addition, it is now common knowledge that economic theory does not simply describe financial practices in a neutral and objective way. Rather, these practices are made possible through the practical employment of economic models.[3]

That economics attracts critique is, of course, not new and the history of critique on neoclassic models is long.[4] Yet this time things look differently: the debate was not led in books or academic journals, but economics itself suddenly faced uneasy publicity. Journals like *Newsweek* asked, 'what good are economists anyway?'[5] Or they wondered, 'what went wrong with Economics?'[6] This public debate was kindled by newspaper debates between economists who tended to place blame on other economists. Jadhish Bagwati, for example, accused economists of being 'capitalism's pretty detractors'[7] and Paul Krugman pointed out that other economists were ignorant of Keynes's logic,[8] while many heterodox economists accused economics for its irrelevant formalism.[9]

The debate gained a different publicity when Queen Elizabeth II, during a visit to the London School of Economics in November 2008, asked "Why did not anybody see the crisis coming?"[10] Her question challenged economics directly and demanded a response that could re-legitimate its scientific claims. The answer was provided in a letter by Tim Besley and Peter Hennessy (Besley and Hennessy 2009: 8): nobody saw the crisis coming as it was beyond the 'collective imagination' of economists. The difficulty was

> seeing the risk to the system as a whole rather than any specific financial instrument or loan. Risk calculations were most often confined to slices of financial activity, using some of the best mathematical minds in our country and abroad. But they frequently lost sight of the bigger picture.
>
> *(ibid.: 8)*

The problem with this answer is the equivocality of 'collective imagination'. On the one hand, it means that economists based their hopes on wrong models. The analysis of David Colander et al. (2008) moves to that direction. They confirm that

> [t]he implicit view behind standard models is that markets and economies are inherently stable and that they only temporarily get off track. The majority of economists thus failed to warn policy makers about the threatening system crisis and ignored the work of those who did. Ironically, as the crisis has unfolded, economists have had no choice but to abandon their standard models and to produce hand-waving, common-sense remedies. [. . . .] It is not enough to put the existing model to one side, observing that one needs 'exceptional measures for exceptional times'. What we need are models capable of envisaging such 'exceptional times'.
>
> *(Colander et al. 2008: 2)*

This direction demands the development of more 'realistic' models. For example, as Colander et al. argue, these models have to include the heterogeneity of agents as the recent turn to behavioural economics already explores. This would then allow economists to analyse coordination mechanisms between these heterogeneous actors and does not assume them away by assuming a 'representative' actor with rational expectations (ibid.: 10).[11]

On the other hand, 'collective imagination' refers to the limits of the discipline's imagination itself. This argument points to the limits that arise from formal reasoning and mathematical modelling (see also Morgan 2012). The use of mathematics itself makes economics systematically blind to certain problems (see Hodgson 2012).[12] This stream of argument identifies a deeper problem: the over-use of mathematics and the very biases inscribed into the practice of mathematical model building itself. This second meaning of 'collective imagination' calls for a debate about the performative consequences of economic theory. It calls for a reflexivity of economics not just in the sense of being aware of one's assumptions, but in being aware of how one's *mode of observation alters the world itself.*

The debate took seriously the first meaning but largely neglected to explore the second. What we can observe is that the call for more 'realistic' models dominates the debate and that behavioural modelling and 'empirical' experiments turn into the new mainstream. Yet this implies that the window of opportunity for a more substantive re-orientation of economics has already closed. As I will argue in the next section, this neglect of the second dimension is not accidental.

Sociology of economics and uncertainty

The last part discussed how the economic crisis has also led to a crisis within economic thought. This debate touched upon two dimensions: the active role of economic thought in bringing modern finance about, and its collective myopia and inability to predict the crisis. As the discussion on the concept of 'collective imagination' suggested, this debate subsequently called for better theories and abandoned the 'reflexivity' part. The silence and ignorance on reflexivity is the logical consequence of economics' development during the last 30 to 40 years. It is a failure of 'collective imagination' indeed, but slightly different from what the discussion suggests so far. I suggest that an analysis of the 'collective imagination' of economics, that is, an analysis of its ignorance, calls for a reframed sociology of economics (see McGoey 2012).

One way of proceeding to a sociology of economics is by means of discourse analysis. What economics can see and not see, what is taken for granted or seen as failure, success or valid argument depends on the vocabulary in which it 'speaks', reads and writes. The conceptual grid determines the horizon of visibility and delimits the range of possible arguments. Through an analysis of how economic concepts became fixed, a reconfigured sociology of economics can trace the performativity of economics and re-open the contingency of economic concepts.

In this section, I will take the example of the distinction of risk and uncertainty to show how this distinction provided a way to address meta-theoretical problems in the 1930s and 1940s. Today's orthodoxy was created through an exclusion of uncertainty as a distinct rationality. Thereby, meta-theoretical discussions about the limits of formal knowledge, the status of rationality and philosophy of science were foreclosed and the tight coupling of economics with formal reasoning manufactured.[13] This absence of uncertainty today is so natural that it is rarely even mentioned anymore. As a consequence, those approaches that separated uncertainty from risk and thus explored the limits of formalism, such as Post-Keynesianism, evolutionary institutionalism or Austrian economics, were moved to the margins of the discipline and broadly perceived as less scientific.[14]

To reconstruct how this change took place, it is useful to differentiate three periods in the history of economic thought. In the first period, from its advent as economics (as opposed to political economy) to the 1920, economics became a distinct discipline that separated itself from political science and sociology. In the second period, from the late 1920s to the early 1970s, a plurality of approaches co-existed with a dominance of the neo-classical synthesis and model-based argumentation. The period from the mid-1970s until today has seen the spread of rational expectation models in both microeconomics and macroeconomics that have transformed the outlook of economics completely. For the history of uncertainty in economics, the period from the 1930s to the late 1950s is of particular importance. In the 1930s, the notion of uncertainty was well established and has attracted considerable attention. By the late 1970s, it had disappeared.

To see how uncertainty is linked to meta-theoretical considerations in general and the limits of formalism in particular, let us look at two examples: John M. Keynes and Friedrich von Hayek. As a number of his celebrated quotes indicate, Keynes separated uncertainty from risk on epistemological grounds (Keynes 1936: 148). When probability relations are known, such as in roulette, we deal with risk and not uncertainty. Uncertainty relates to situations where probability relations are unknown, when we have no scientific basis to project necessary developments. Instead, in situations of uncertainty we simply do not know. This is what is meant when Keynes asserts that the 'very uncertain' is something different than the 'very improbable' (ibid.: 148).

Keynes's concept of uncertainty has meta-theoretical repercussions. Through its neglect of uncertainty, he accused Marshallian economics of engaging in false rationalization that was based on 'Benthamite calculus'. As he emphasizes: 'The hypothesis of a calculable future leads to a wrong interpretation of the principles of behaviour which the need for action compels us to adopt' (Keynes 1937: 222). Instead of 'cold calculation', uncertainty refers to the problem of practice and practical judgements where, in Keynes' words,

> human decisions affecting the future, whether personal or political or economic, cannot depend on strict mathematical expectation, since the basis for making such calculations does not exist; and that it is our innate urge to activity which makes the wheels go round, our rational selves choosing between the alternatives as best we are able, calculating where we can, but often falling back for our motive on whim or sentiment or chance.
>
> *(Keynes 1936: 162–3)*

In the end, knowledge cannot be framed in terms of theorems or probablitistic propositions. Rather, actors would make use of a different kind of knowledge – conventional judgements, animal spirit and spontaneous optimism – that all are beyond mathematical calculus. If economics strives for mathematical rigour, it will simply not understand the problem of practice.

Another tradition that takes uncertainty seriously is the Austrian School. Carl Menger in his *Principles of Economics* accuses Adam Smith of having provided a too materialist account for economic progress. He makes clear that antecedent to the division of labour there is a division of knowledge which has to be understood in its own terms. Even though the Austrian tradition is fragmented and proponents entertain different conceptions of the key problem, the knowledge problem is nevertheless its key characteristic. Where the Keynesian and the Austrian traditions differ is in their assessment of the scientific status of uncertainty. Keynes believed that uncertainty could be tamed scientifically. One could argue that the presence of uncertainty structures Keynes' views on the potential malfunctioning of markets, the inauguration of macro-economic methodology and the role of the interventionist state. Despite the salience of uncertainty, the primary purpose of economic theory is still *the rational reconstruction* of these variables to make them accessible to scientific scrutiny and finally 'manageable'. The Austrian tradition, in contrast, always argued that uncertainty requires a distinct approach that – today – is to be sought in sociology. Menger was adamant that the application of scientific standards and methods to 'economics' leads to wrong conclusions. In contrast to what was later called the unity of science position, Menger argued that every field of analysis requires its own standards and methods.

Hayek[15] emerged as the most famous representative of this line of thought. He showed that particularly in the analysis of complex phenomena where actors act according to their own pre-suppositions, history and expectations, science 'captures' only a small part of the relevant knowledge. As he describes it:

> Today it is almost heresy to suggest that scientific knowledge is not the sum of all knowledge. But a little reflection will show that there is beyond question a body of very important but unorganized knowledge which cannot possibly be called scientific in the sense of knowledge of general rules: The knowledge of the particular circumstances of time and place. It is with respect to this that practically every individual has some advantage over all others in that he possesses unique information of which beneficial use might be made.
>
> *(Hayek 1945: 521)*

Hayek extends the line of thought initiated by Menger: in contrast to the Keynesian treatment of uncertainty, Austrians challenge the 'scientific' approach, suggesting that 'scientific methods' cannot capture the dispersion, plurality and fragmented nature of knowledge.[16]

As common as uncertainty was as a point of reference in the second period, including the plurality of approaches and epistemologies, things began to change with the advent of the expected utility revolution. In 1951, Kenneth Arrow published an influential article which formulated a critique of the epistemology of uncertainty. According to him, the question of uncertainty would not arise under complete knowledge, so all concepts of uncertainty are somehow the same, regardless of what we call them. The question is rather how agents deal with uncertainty. For him, Bayes's induction provides the best answer here. New information and new experience could then be described by a change in probability assessment, that is, as a rational adjustment to new information on the basis of conditional probabilities.[17] On this basis, Harsanyi also argued for a concept of uncertainty that can be framed as risk, that is, in terms of probabilities (see Harsanyi 1967). Starting from an assumption of uncertainty and ignorance about the other's pay-off function or the action space, it is nevertheless possible to re-describe the situation in terms of condition probabilities, as long as the players draw their probabilities from an objective probability distribution of possible types of actors. As he confirms:

> This postulate follows from the Bayesian hypothesis, which implies that every player will use his *subjective* probabilities exactly in the same way as he would use known *objective* probabilities numerically equal to the former. The only difference is that in G the probabilities used by each player are subjective probabilities whereas in G* these probabilities are objective (conditional) probabilities. But by the Bayesian hypothesis this difference is immaterial.
>
> *(Harsanyi 1967: 174)*

This argument about the possible closure of the probability space, and hence the exclusion of uncertainty, came along not only with a praise for mathematical formalism for the study of economic practices, but also with the marginalization of those approaches that discussed uncertainty and challenged the move to formal reasoning in economics.[18] All these tendencies and movements eroded the emphasis on uncertainty and reoriented the core of the discipline towards a strong affinity to the natural sciences (see Fourcade 2009).

One of the consequences of this shift is that it expanded economics as a career option for mathematicians and physicists who, as it turned out, were even better equipped for the new economics than many 'traditional' economists. From this perspective, the institutional and disciplinary dimension of economics produce a 'lock in' effect in the way economics constantly reproduces itself through publications, degrees and careers (see again Fourcade, 2009 on this point).

At this point, it is now also visible how the social contingency unfolds and allows for incremental change: the closure of certain meta-theoretical considerations and debates structures the way economics can answer new challenges. It simply cannot de-stabilize the foundations of its own discipline, but rather calls for more 'empirically' informed modelling and embraces now behavioural finance. Hence, there is a revived discussion between 'rational' economics and psychology. Yet, when we look closer at the literature and its experiment-driven research design, the change is a change within the same philosophy of science that is based on given probability distributions and an assumed objective observer (who is still outside the models). This debate reinforces and does not change the dominant scientific standards, the role of formalism or models in economic theorizing, and it does not change the kind of expertise and authority valued within economics itself.

Performing economics in the crisis

The last part has outlined how uncertainty was effaced from economics and how this was irremediably linked to the advent and spread of formalism and modelling. It thereby showed how the vocabulary of risk and uncertainty determines what economists see and don't see, how their collective imagination is 'constructed' and how this relates to the way knowledge is produced (including how expertise is signalled), authority internally assigned (that is, the construction of 'stars' and 'elites') and the range of legitimate argumentation delimited. Economics hence is more than just a particular way of studying human behaviour, it is a way of life. Yet, as the last section has outlined, in the very way in which the boundaries of economics are drawn, there are political processes of inclusion and exclusion to be found. This all suggests that the use of a scientific vocabulary is never innocent or neutral, but always political.

One way in which the disciplinary 'imagination' translates into practice is the way economists frame problems and thereby already determine the range of possible solutions, possible arguments and possible critique. It is the economic vocabulary and not state preferences or pressure groups that determine the limits of the sayable. For example, a substantial reform of global finance was high on the agenda in 2008. Yet already in the G20 meetings in London and later in Seoul the debate shifted. In the Korea Communiqué, the G20 emphasized that: 'the recent events highlight the importance of sustainable public finances and the need for our countries to put in place credible, growth-friendly measures, to deliver fiscal sustainability, differentiated for and tailored to national circumstances' (G20 2010: 1).[19] What is re-introduced here is the idea of market-discipline and an acknowledgement of austerity politics on the basis of 'economic' ideas of stability and the role and limits of politics. What comes to an end is the 'need' to revise the financial architecture, including the discussion of global initiatives and grand reform proposals. This G20 meeting in Korea is the product of a longer and more subtle process that started in the aftermath of the G20 summit in London (G20 2009). Since then, one could sense that the overall discursive change and its practices do not translate into a comprehensive reform of financial markets. Since the meeting in London, deliberations were not directed to the creation of new structures, but *took place within existing structures.* A 2010 G20 meeting of finance ministers in Busan further established that the system would largely stay the same.

This does not mean that all reform proposals have come to a halt and nothing happens. Already a cursory look at the publications of the Financial Stability Board (FSB), the Bank of International Settlement (BIS), the International Monetary Fund (IMF) or the European Central

Bank (ECB), for that matter, reveal the magnitude and diversity of current initiatives under way. Yet these reforms are driven by functionalist hopes for technical solutions deprived of their political nature: Basel III, a regime to deal with compensations, and a couple of new standards and transparency requirements are functional solutions to functionalist problems. However, there will be nothing like a new 'Bretton Woods' or some other new set of constitutive rules or a renewed financial architecture that somehow could be seen as a new mode of regulation or institutionalization of this assumed new Keynesianism. What once seemed like a viable alternative now again belongs to the realm of utopia.

This raises the question of how this window of opportunity was closed. Why did the crisis not translate into a broader debate about the financial architecture? I think the answer is surprisingly quite prosaic: the G20 acts on the recommendation by the Financial Stability Board (FSB). When one reads the documents (including the documents by the IMF and the BIS), one can detect a discursive link between stability and efficiency, that is stable markets are assumed to be efficient and vice versa. A crisis can then only be understood as a market or government failure of otherwise stable markets. Via a discursive feedback loop with the idea of asymmetric information as the driving force of inefficiency and instability, the solution is then sought in increased transparency and improvement of 'existing' rules and regulation. This might have the advantage that the debate can focus on more technical questions concerning the basis of 'scientific' and empiricist methods, but it thereby fails to take issue with more constitutive questions of how finance is to be framed and understood.

Conclusion

When we turn back time for around 10 to 15 years and look at the tone and contours of academic debates, it is astonishing and disorienting to what extent economics and its formalism was praised as the 'Queen' of the social sciences. When we extend the perspective and take into consideration the period after WWII, then the dominance of economics vis á vis other social sciences is even more telling. The literature on economic imperialism highlights the extent to which economics not only transformed itself, but was able to shape and delimit other disciplines. In fields such as International Relations and Political Economy, in particular, many of economics' key concepts were implemented into their constitutive boundaries. This asymmetry holds true even today and shapes many scholarly practices outside economics itself, ranging from writing styles and journal evaluations up to the point of authoritative evaluators of research proposals on 'the economy'.

Things appeared to change with the North Atlantic crisis. The burst of the bubble in the real estate market that led to almost a complete implosion of global financial markets has opened a debate about the limits of economics as a discipline. Yet soon after the debate flared up, it was swiftly closed and silenced. This contribution took the current silence as a vantage point to inquire into the 'ignorance' of economics itself. I argued that the failure of the collective imagination, as some economists have pointed out, is as fascinating as it is vacuous. Next to the dimension of collective myopia, collective imagination also points to a reflexivity of economics. Naturally, this aspect was not taken any further by most economists themselves. Yet moving in that direction suggests that the collective imagination is linked to the very vocabulary in which the economy is written, read and performed.

This chapter has revisited the distinction between risk and uncertainty to show how the exclusion of uncertainty from economics today serves as the very 'other' of the current formalism and modelling in economic theory. It recognizes that exclusion opens the way for a sociology of economics that analyses how economic knowledge is constructed, how authority is assigned and how the boundaries of economics are reproduced. By using the financial crisis as an example, this contribution outlines the practical value of a new sociology of economics.

Notes

1 This also implies that the sociology of economics challenges economics on meta-theoretical, methodological and disciplinary grounds.
2 Even though it cannot be developed in this chapter, I think a large part of the story can be found in the way economics historically constructed its concepts. Concepts don't represent reality, but are the product of disciplinary struggles and disciplinary politics. The conceptual grid through which economics makes sense of its world and 'thinks' then also limits the range of the observable, the sayable and thus the communicative horizon of critique. A boundary that I tried to capture through the concept of 'social contingency'.
3 See references above on performativity, Callon (1998) and MacKenzie and Millo (2003). Also MacKenzie et al. (2008).
4 See Arjo Klamer and David Colander (1990) *The Making of an Economist* (Boulder, CO: Westview Press), Randall G. Holcombe (1989) *Economic Models and Methodology* (New York: Greenwood); Tony Lawson (2003) *Reorienting Economics* (London: Routledge), David Bell and Irving Kristol (eds) (1981) *The Crisis of Economic Theory* (New York: Basic Books), Joseph A. Schumpeter (1982) 'The "Crisis" of Economics – 50 Years Ago', *Journal of Economic Literature* 20 (September): 1049–59, Edward Fullbrook (2003) *The Crisis of Economics: Post-Austistic Movement – The First 600 Days* (London: Routledge). See also Ben Bernanke (2010) *The Implications of the Financial Crisis For Economics* (New York: Federal Reserve) http://www.federalreserve.gov/newsevents/speech/bernanke20100924a.pdf.
5 *Business Week* (16 April 2009).
6 *The Economist* (16 July 2009).
7 Jadish Bagwati (2009) 'Feeble Critiques: Capitalism's Petty Detractors', *World Affairs* 172(2): 36–45.
8 Paul Krugman (2009) 'How Did Economists Get It So Wrong?' *The New York Times* (2 September).
9 Tony Lawson (2009) 'The Current Economic Crisis: Its Nature and the Course of Academic Economics', *Cambridge Journal of Economics* 33(4): 759–77. See also Sheila C. Dow, Peter E. Earl, John Foster, Geoffrey C. Hartcourt, Geoffrey M. Hodgson, J. Stanley Metcalfe, Paul Ormerod, Bridget Rosewell, Malcom C. Sawyer and Andrew Tylecote (2009) 'Letter to the Question', 10 August, 1–3, and Geoffrey Hodgson (2011) 'Reforming Economics after the Financial Crisis', *Global Policy* 2(2): 190–5.
10 http://www.theguardian.com/uk/2009/jul/26/monarchy-credit-crunch (last accessed 30 September 2014).
11 As Colander noted on p. 7: Technically, rational expectation models are often framed as dynamic programming problems in macroeconomics. But, dynamic programming models have serious limitations. Specifically, to make them analytically tractable, researchers assume representative agents and rational expectations, which assume away any heterogeneity among economic actors. Such models presume that there is a single model of the economy, which is odd given that even economists are divided in their views about the correct model of the economy. While other currents of research do exist, economic policy advice, particularly in financial economics, has far too often been based (consciously or not) on a set of axioms and hypotheses derived ultimately from a highly limited dynamic control model, using the Robinson approach with 'rational expectations'.
12 See note 9 above.
13 For the 'risk as uncertainty' approach see in particular Kenneth Arrow (1953) 'The Role of Securities in the Optimal Allocation of Risk Bearing', *Review of Economic Studies* 31(1): 91–96, John Harsanyi (1967) 'Games with Incomplete Information Played by "Bayesian" Players I–III, Part I, The Basic Model', *Management Science* 14: 159–82, Jack Hirshleifer and John G. Riley (1992) *The Analytics of Uncertainty and Unformation* (Cambridge: Cambridge University Press). For references to the 'risk vs. uncertainty' approach see Wendt (2001), op. cit., and below.
14 Of course, economics is not one undefined mass and there are various traditions and streams in both orthodox and heterodox thought. It is beyond the scope of this chapter to discuss them all in detail (for example, this chapter will not deal with the American (old) institutional movement or evolutionary economics). Yet as this part focuses on the distinction of risk and uncertainty, I will only concentrate on four aspects: the classic rational choice, behavioural economics, Keynesian, and the Austrian tradition. This allows us to assess what is at stake in the risk/uncertainty debate.

15 See, in particular, "Economics and Knowledge" (1937) and "The Use of Knowledge within Society" (1945).
16 See also 'The Pretence of Knowledge', reprinted in Friedrich August von Hayek (1996) *Die Anmaßung von Wissen* (Tübingen, Germany: Mohr), 3–15.
17 See note 14 above.
18 This movement gained further momentum in the rational expectation revolution in the early 1960s, which cannot be discussed in detail at this point.
19 http://www.g20.org/Documents/201006_Communique_Busan.pdf (last accessed 15 June 2010).

References

Arrow, Kenneth (1953). 'The Role of Securities in the Optimal Allocation of Risk Bearing', *Review of Economic Studies* 31(1): 91–96.
Bagwati, Jadish (2009). 'Feeble Critiques: Capitalism's Petty Detractors', *World Affairs* 172(2): 36–45.
Bell, David and Kristol, Irving (eds) (1981). *The Crisis of Economic Theory*, New York: Basic Books.
Bernanke, Ben (2010). *The Implications of the Financial Crisis for Economics*, New York: Federal Reserve. http://www.federalreserve.gov/newsevents/speech/bernanke20100924a.pdf (last accessed February 25, 2014).
Besley, Timothy and Hennessy, Peter (2009). 'The Global Financial Crisis – Why Didn't Anybody Notice?' *British Academic Review* 14: 8–10.
Bloomsberg (23 Oct 2008). 'Greenspan Concedes to "Flaw" in His Market Ideology', http://www.bloomberg.com/apps/news?pid=newsarchive&sid=ah5qh9Up4rIg.
Callon, M. (ed.) (1998). *The Laws of the Market*, Oxford: Blackwell.
Colander, David, Foellmer, Hans, Haas, Armin, Kirman, Alan, Juselius, Katarina, Sloth, Brigitte, and Lux, Thomas (2008). 'The Financial Crisis and the Systemic Failure of Academic Economics', Kiel Working Paper 1489: 1–17.
Colander, David, Foellmer, Hans, Haas, Armin, Kirman, Alan, Juselius, Katarina, Sloth, Brigitte, and Lux, Thomas (2009). 'How Should the Collapse of the World Financial System Affect Economics?', *Real World Economics Review* 50: 118–21.
Dow, Sheila C., Earl, Peter E., Foster, John, Hartcourt, Geoffrey C., Hodgson, Geoffrey M., Metcalfe, J. Stanley, Ormerod, Paul, Rosewell, Bridget, Sawyer Malcom C., and Tylecote, Andrew (2009). 'Letter to the Question', 10 August, 1–3.
Engelen, E., Ertürk, I., Froud, J., Johal, S., Leaver, A., Moran, M., Nilsson, A. and Williams, K. (2011). *After the Great Complacence: Financial Crisis and the Politics of Reform*, Oxford: Oxford University Press.
Fourcade, Marion (2009). *Economists and Societies*, Princeton, NJ: Princeton University Press.
Fullbrook, Edward (2003). *The Crisis of Economics: Post-Austistic Movement – The First 600 Days*, London: Routledge.
Harsanyi, John (1967). 'Games with Incomplete Information Played by "Bayesian" Players I-III. Part I. The Basic Model', *Management Science* 14: 159–182.
Hayek, Friedrich August von (1937). 'Economics and Knowledge', *Economica* 4: 33–54.
Hayek, Friedrich August von (1945). 'The Use of Knowledge within Society', *American Economic Review* 35(4): 519–30.
Hayek, Friedrich August von (1996). *Die Anmaßung von Wissen*, Tübingen, Germany: Mohr.
Hirshleifer, Jack and Riley, John G. (1992). *The Analytics of Uncertainty and Information*, Cambridge: Cambridge University Press.
Hodgson, Geoffrey (ed.) (2012). *Mathematics and Modern Economics*, Cheltenham: Elgar. Holcombe, Randall G. (1989). *Economic Models and Methodology*, New York: Greenwood.
Keynes, John Maynard (1936). *The General Theory of Employment, Interest and Money*, London: Macmillan.
Keynes, John Maynard (1937). 'The General Theory of Employment', *Quarterly Journal of Economics* 51(2): 209–23.
Klamer, Arjo and Colander, David (1990). *The Making of an Economist*, Boulder, CO: Westview.
Krugman, Paul (2009). 'How Did Economists Get It So Wrong?' *The New York Times*, 2 September 2009.
Lawson, Tony (1985). 'Uncertainty and Economic Analysis', *The Economic Journal* 95: 909–27.
Lawson, Tony (2003). *Reorienting Economics*, London: Routledge.
MacKenzie, D. and Millo, Y. (2003). 'Constructing a Market, Performing Theory', *American Journal of Sociology* 109(1): 107–45.

MacKenzie, D., Beunza, D., and Hardie, I. (2008). 'A Price Is a Social Thing: Towards a Material Sociology of Arbitrage', in J. Beckert, R. Diaz-Bone, and H. Ganßmann (eds) *Material Markets: How Economic Agents Are Constructed*, Clarendon Lectures in Management Studies, Oxford: Oxford University Press, 85–109.

McGoey, Linsey (2012). 'The Logic of Strategic Ignorance', *British Journal of Sociology* 63(3): 553–76.

Morgan, Mary (2012). *The World in the Model: How Economics Works and Think,* Cambridge: Cambridge .University Press.

Schumpeter, Joseph A. (1982). 'The "Crisis" Of Economics – 50 years ago', *Journal of Economic Literature* 20 (September): 1049–59.

Wendt, A. (2001). 'Driving with the Rearview Mirror: On the Rational Science of Institutional Design', *International Organization* 55(4): 1019–49.

36

Decision-theoretic approaches to non-knowledge in economics

Ekaterina Svetlova and Henk van Elst

Introduction

The aim of this contribution is to provide an overview of conceptual approaches to incorporating a decision maker's non-knowledge into economic theory. We will focus here on the particular kind of non-knowledge which we consider to be one of the most important for economic discussions: non-knowledge of possible consequence-relevant uncertain events which a decision maker would have to take into account when selecting between different strategies.

It should be noted that – especially after the recent worldwide economic crisis – economics has been frequently blamed for neglecting this kind of non-knowledge. Allegedly it failed to incorporate unexpected events into its theoretical framework, which resulted in severe negative consequences for economies and societies. (For example, the subprime mortgage crisis or the Lehman Brothers bankruptcy of 2008 can be viewed as "Black Swan events" in the sense of Taleb (2007).) We argue, however, that such blatant accusations are not entirely justified. When one looks back at the long history of the debate on uncertainty and non-knowledge in economics, one will identify ongoing efforts to formalize these conceptually difficult issues by means of the mathematical language on the one hand, and tireless criticisms of this formal approach on the other. The first movement is often interpreted as essentially excluding non-knowledge from economic theory, while the second is considered as a heroic effort to re-establish this issue in the scientific discourse (Frydman and Goldberg 2007; Akerlof and Shiller 2009). However, we would like to stress and demonstrate that both developments are deeply interwoven and, rather, mutually support and complement each other.

In the course of the debate, the theoretical representations of non-knowledge have taken some specific technical forms. In this paper, we review the historical development of two basic approaches to formalizing non-knowledge in economic theory, in the context of static one-shot choice situations for decision makers. These are

1 representations of non-knowledge of a decision maker in terms of *probability measures, or related non-probabilistic measures*, over sets of mutually exclusive and exhaustive consequence-relevant (past, present or, in most applications, future) states of Nature;
2 modelling unawareness of a decision maker of potentially important events by means of sets of states that are *less complete* than the full set of consequence-relevant states of Nature.

As is well known, the most popular method to deal with non-knowledge in economic theory has been to formalize it by means of probability measures; this approach allowed quantifying the matter and, thus, to rationalize and to "cultivate" it (Smithson 1989: 43). Introduced into economic theory by Edgeworth, Jevons and Menger during the so called "marginal revolution" in the late 19th century, probability measures, especially frequentist probability measures as probabilities learned from the past, were celebrated as instruments that allowed quantifying and measuring manifestations of uncertainty (cf. Bernstein 1996: 190ff). However, the euphoria was halted by the critiques of Knight (1921), Keynes (1921, 1937), Shackle (1949, 1959) and Hayek (1945) who argued that application of frequentist probability measures precludes systematic analysis of the principal non-knowledge of some consequence-relevant events. They initiated the first line of discussion on non-knowledge in economics and decision-making theory; namely, they raised the question as to what extent non-knowledge can be represented by means of measurable or immeasurable probability concepts, or if other, non-probabilistic measures are necessary. Knight's (1921) solution, for example, was the famous distinction between *risk* as situations where probabilities of uncertain events can be unambiguously and objectively determined, and *uncertainty* as situations where they cannot be accurately measured and, therefore, should rather be treated as "estimates of the estimates," or subjective probabilities.

This critique gave rise to an axiomatic approach to the definition of subjective probability measures by Ramsey (1931) and de Finetti (1937) who demonstrated that such measures can always be derived from the observed betting behaviour of a decision maker (namely their willingness to bet), and that they can be powerfully used to formalize a decision maker's proclaimed utility maximization. Both authors helped to establish the concept of *probabilistic sophistication* which posits that – even if objective probability measures cannot be determined – the decision maker's behaviour can always be interpreted in a way *as if* they have a subjective probability measure which they employ in their personal calculations of expected utility. In this approach, *individual* imprecise knowledge on consequence-relevant events was conceptualized to form a basis for the introduction of an adequate probability measure to represent this status, and this method rendered the whole discussion about measurability and objectivity of probability measures obsolete for the coming years. Savage (1954) famously combined probabilistic sophistication with the expected utility theory as conceived originally by Bernoulli (1738) and von Neumann and Morgenstern (1944) to arrive at a subjective expected utility theory. Savage's axiomatization of decision-making under conditions of uncertainty thus led to the formalization of non-knowledge of the likelihood of uncertain events in terms of a *unique (finitely additive) Bayes–Laplace prior probability measure* over a complete space of consequence-relevant states of Nature. The latter is assumed to be known to a decision maker before committing to a certain action.

Yet, this theoretical move to "absorb" non-knowledge by means of probability distributions obviously precludes the consideration of "unknown unknowns" (e.g. Li 2009: 977), as, by assumption, this space of states of Nature is common knowledge for all decision makers. The prior probability measures employed just formalize non-knowledge of *which* uncertain event from a given list of possibilities will occur. The incorporation of *surprises* into a theoretical framework, however, necessitates a notion of incomplete sets of uncertain events on the decision maker's part. Surprising events, by definition, cannot be known at the instant of choice and, thus, cannot be part of the set of events possible known to a decision maker. However, many accounts which aspire to introduce true non-knowledge and uncertainty into economic theory primarily criticize the use of a unique and additive prior probability measure over a given set of states of Nature, but maintain the assumption that the latter set is finite and exhaustive, and that the states are mutually exclusive. These works thus pursue the first line of research mentioned above. In their attempt to formally deal with true uncertainty of some events, and so to re-establish this issue in economic theory, they replace the unique, additive prior probability measure by entire *sets* of additive prior probability measures (e.g. Gilboa and Schmeidler 1989, Bewley 1986, 2002), by non-additive prior probability measures (e.g. Schmeidler 1989, Mukerji 1997, Ghirardato 2001), or they introduce some alternative non-probabilistic concept such as fuzzy logic, possibility measures, and weights (Zadeh 1965, 1978; Dubois and Prade 2011; Kahneman and Tversky 1979).

We interpret all of these works as attempts to conceptualize Knightian uncertainty in mathematical terms. In all of these cases, non-knowledge is generally captured by an *unknown probability measure*. However, we would like to stress that theorizing about the principal non-knowledge of some events necessitates the aforementioned representation of *the incompleteness of a decision maker's subjective space of consequence-relevant states of Nature*, because only then the failure of probability theory to represent non-knowledge and surprises adequately can be overcome. This state of affairs motivates the discussion of the second line of research on non-knowledge in the list above. Here, we are dealing with attempts to formalize choice situations where decision makers are aware of the fact that they do *not* possess the full list of consequence-relevant states of Nature due to unforeseen contingencies. In our view, the development of this second line shifts emphasis from the issue of the importance of prior probability measures in dealing with non-knowledge to the more fundamental question as to what extent the full space of consequence-relevant states of Nature can actually be known to a decision maker in the first place.

In what follows, we first present in the next section the standard mathematical framework in terms of which discussions on the formal representation of non-knowledge and uncertainty in economic theory are usually conducted. Subsequently, we describe developments of the inclusion/exclusion movements of non-knowledge along the two lines mentioned above. In the third section we address the representation of non-knowledge based on the usage of (various kinds of) probability measures, while in the fourth section we discuss the representation of non-knowledge based on particular formal descriptions of the state space. Finally, we conclude with a discussion and provide a brief outlook.

The basic mathematical framework

In economic theory, non-knowledge of the likelihood of uncertain events at the initial decision stage of a static one-person, one-shot decision problem is the crucial feature. Formulated within the set-theoretic descriptive behavioural framework developed by Savage (1954) and Anscombe and Aumann (1963), a decision maker chooses from a set F of alternative acts. The set $\Delta(X)$ of consequences of their choice (i.e., von Neumann–Morgenstern (1944) lotteries over sets X of outcomes) depends on which relevant state of Nature out of an exclusive and exhaustive set Ω will occur following a decision (the state-contingency structure). In this framework, acts are perceived as mappings of states of Nature into consequences, $F = \{f\!: \Omega \rightarrow \Delta(X)\}$. An ordinal binary preference relation $\succsim$ is defined over the set F, which in turn induces an analogous preference relation on the set $\Delta(X)$ via the mapping. The actual state of Nature $\omega \in \Omega$ that *will* be realized is usually understood as a move by the exogenous world which resolves all uncertainty (Nature "chooses" the state of the world; Debreu 1959; Hirshleifer and Riley 1992: 7). The decision maker *does not know* which consequence-relevant state of Nature will occur, but (like the modeller) has complete knowledge of all possibilities. In the subjective expected utility context of Savage (1954) and Anscombe and Aumann (1963), this kind of non-knowledge is formalized by means of a unique finitely additive prior probability measure over the set of states of Nature, $\mu \in \Delta(\Omega)$, which expresses the decision maker's assessment of the likelihood of all uncertain events possible. Existence of such a prior probability measure (usually interpreted as representing a decision maker's beliefs) is ensured provided the preference relation $\succsim$ on F satisfies the five behavioural axioms of weak order, continuity, independence, monotonicity and non-triviality (see Anscombe and Aumann 1963: 203f; Gilboa 2009: 143f). As is well known, this axiomatization gives rise to a subjective expected utility representation of the preference relation $\succsim$ on F in terms of a real-valued preference function $V\colon F \to \mathbb{R}$, where for every act $f \in F$ one defines

$$V(f) = \int_{\Omega} (E_{f(\omega)} U) \mu\,(d\omega)$$

Here $U\colon X \to \mathbb{R}$ constitutes a decision maker's real-valued personal utility function of an outcome $x \in X$, and it is unique up to positive linear transformations; $E_{f(\omega)} U$ denotes the expectation value of U with respect to the von Neumann–Morgenstern lottery $f(\omega) \in \Delta(X)$. The decision maker weakly prefers an act $f \in F$ to an act $g \in F$, namely $f \succsim g$, whenever $V(f) \geq V(g)$. It is presupposed here that the prior probability measure is used to express the non-knowledge of the decision maker about exactly *which state (from the given exhaustive list) will occur.* Figure 36.1 outlines the structure of the decision matrix for a static one-person, one-shot choice problem in the subjective expected utility framework due to Savage (1954) and Anscombe and Aumann (1963). We remark in passing that the exposition by the latter two authors in particular provided the formal basis for more recent decision-theoretical developments by Schmeidler (1989), Gilboa and Schmeidler (1989) and Schipper (2013).

The decision matrix suggests that, besides coding uncertainty about the likelihood of events via a unique prior probability measure, there are at least two further ways to incorporate aspects of a decision maker's non-knowledge: *either* to suppose that the particular kind of prior probability measure is unknown (while the set of consequence-relevant states of Nature is complete), *or* to accept that the set of consequence-relevant states of Nature can be known only incompletely. In the second case, non-knowledge of events is directly captured by means of *non-knowledge of the full state space, allowing hereby for unexpected events.* In what follows, we will discuss these two general possibilities to formally deal with non-knowledge in more detail – the application of various probability measures on the one hand, and the representation of incomplete state spaces on the other.

First way of formalization: probabilistic and non-probabilistic approaches

As already mentioned, application of additive prior probability measures to capture non-knowledge about the likelihood of uncertain events has been the silver bullet of economic theory in dealing with this problem. In terms of elements of the decision matrix in Figure 36.1, *both* the modeller and the decision maker have complete knowledge of all consequence-relevant states of Nature, and of all possible outcomes/lotteries over outcomes contingent on these states. In

Prior probability measure $\mu \in \Delta(\Omega)$	$\mu(\omega_1)$	$\mu(\omega_2)$	...	$\mu(\omega_n)$	$n \in N$
acts *F*/states Ω	ω_1	ω_2	...	ω_n	
f_1	p_{11}	p_{12}	...	p_{1n}	*consequences* $p_{ij} \in \Delta(X)$
f_2	p_{21}	p_{22}	...	p_{2n}	(lotteries over outcomes *X*)
$\vdots$	$\vdots$	$\vdots$	$\ddots$	$\vdots$	

Figure 36.1 Decision matrix

this respect, both subjects need to be perceived as omniscient. However, throughout the entire history of applications of probability theory in various manifestations in the economic science, discussions have revolved around the question whether different kinds of definitions of probability measures are measurable at all in economic settings, and thus suitable to represent non-knowledge of some events. According to Knight (1921), the conceptual basis for such an operationalization is principally absent from economic life in most cases. Thus, mathematical and statistical probabilities are – though basically measureable – not applicable in an economic context.

The concerns as formulated in the works of Knight (1921), Keynes (1921), and also Shackle (1949), however, were played down for a while by the opposing movement of strong formalization and specific exclusion of non-knowledge of the probability measure from the theoretical economic framework: Ramsey (1931), de Finetti (1937) and Savage (1954) demonstrated that subjective probabilities can be measured in principle when taking a behavioural approach. Follow-up research, however, drew attention to cases in which *non-knowledge of the probability measure* is essential for decision-making. Especially after Ellsberg's (1961) paper, a new branch of research appeared that endeavoured to re-introduce absence of perfect knowledge of relevant probability measures into economic theory. Ellsberg (1961) had demonstrated empirically that many people tend to prefer situations with known probability measures over situations with unknown ones, thus violating Savage's (1954) behavioural "sure thing principle" axiom in particular. He explicitly referred to situations with unknown probability measures as "ambiguous" and named the phenomenon of avoiding such situations "ambiguity aversion" (this corresponds to the term "uncertainty aversion" coined by Knight 1921).

Subsequently, efforts to formalize *Knightian uncertainty* were resumed. Relevant work has been developing in two directions (cf. Mukerji 1997: 24). First, it was stressed that, in Savage's (1954) static choice framework, the decision maker 'mechanically' assigns probabilities without differentiating between those cases in which they have some knowledge and, thus, can reason about the likelihood of future events, and those cases in which they are completely ignorant about what might happen. Secondly, Savage's (1954) framework precludes from modelling the decision maker "... who doubts his own ability to imagine and think through an exhaustive list of possible states of the world" (Mukerji 1997: 24). Savage's (1954) axiomatization assumes that the decision maker is completely unaware of the limitations of their knowledge about the future. However, as surprises are a part of real life, this assumption is too strong and cuts back the power of the theory.

Both lines of research represent the efforts to include the limitations of a decision maker's knowledge into economic theory. In the remaining parts of this section, we briefly discuss the development of the first line of research mentioned in the introduction which employs alternative concepts of probability measures, and then, in the next section, we turn to review representations of non-knowledge by means of various formalizations of the state space.

Knight's (1921) work, and later Ellsberg's (1961) paradox, gave way to the intuition that there are differences in how people assign and treat probability measures, and that those differences are related to the quality of the decision maker's knowledge. Some probability measures are based on more or less reliable information (evidence, or knowledge), and some result from a default rule based on ignorance. For example, there should be a difference between probability as formed by an expert and by a layman. The intuition behind Schmeidler's (1989) *non-additive prior probability measures framework* is exactly this: the bets on a well tested and fair coin and on an absolutely unknown coin "feel different," though we assign 50–50 probabiltiy distributions in both cases (Gilboa et al. 2008: 179).

The failure of Savage's (1954) model to account for differences in the knowledge quality in both cases was called by Gilboa et al. (2008: 181) "an agnostic position." Ellsberg (1961) underlined this issue empirically and demonstrated that the preference of a decision maker for "known" probabilities violates the "sure thing principle" in Savage's axiomatization: people do not necessarily behave as though they were subjective expected utility maximizers. To model a decision maker's state of imperfect knowledge in such situations more accurately, there were suggestions to replace the unique prior probability measure with an entire *set of prior probability measures* (Gilboa and Schmeidler 1989; Bewley 1986, 2002): non-knowledge regarding the likelihood of uncertain states of Nature here is linked to the number of elements contained in a decision maker's set of prior probability measures used in calculations of expected utility of acts and consequences, and so is represented in a more comprehensive fashion than in Savage's (1954) framework. For example, to account for their ignorance, the decision maker assigns not a unique prior probability to an event but rather a certain *range* of values. In the case of the untested coin (when knowledge of the coin's properties is vague or non-existent) this range for head/tail could be "between 45 and 55 percent." We note that Epstein and Wang (1994) later extended Gilboa and Schmeidler's (1989) multiple-priors approach to intertemporal settings.

A different way to account for the limitations of a decision maker's knowledge of future contingencies was the development of *non-probabilistic concepts*, for example, fuzzy logic and possibility theory (Zadeh 1965, 1978; Dubois and Prade 2011). Interestingly, the economist Shackle (1961), whose work was ignored for decades, was one of the founders of this particular line of research. For Shackle, *possibility* in particular expresses the incompleteness of a decision maker's knowledge about the future, and hereby allows representing the "*degree of potential surprise*" of an event. Possibility as a measure of subjective non-knowledge is less precise ("fuzzier") than probability and is based either on a numerical (quantitative) or on a qualitative scaling of events from "totally possible" to "impossible." Those measures must not be additive. It means that two or more events can be simultaneously considered as absolutely possible (their possibility is equal to 1) or impossible, "surprising" (the possibility is equal to 0) on a totally ordered scale L. The modern formalized version of this idea allows for a mapping π from a finite set of states S to the scale L:

> The function π represents *the state of knowledge of an agent* (about the actual state of affairs) distinguishing what is plausible from what is less plausible, what is the normal course of things from what is not, what is surprising from what is expected.
>
> *(Dubois and Prade 2011: 3)*

Despite this seemingly radical innovation, and some promising applications in the economic science (e.g., Dow and Ghosh 2009), the possibility theory could not "revolutionize" decision theory. Zadeh (1978: 7), the founder of fuzzy logic, famously hinted that "our intuition concerning the behaviour of possibilities is not very reliable" and required the axiomatization of possibilities "in the spirit of axiomatic approaches to the definition of subjective probabilities," i.e., in line with Savage's (1954) axiomatization. To make the connection with decision theory, such a theoretical framework was successfully developed by Dubois et al. (2001). Also, more generally, various probability–possibility transformations were discussed, i.e., how to translate for example quantitative possibilities into probabilities and vice versa. In the end, as Halpern (2005: 40) states, "possibility measures are yet another approach to assigning numbers to sets," implying all benefits and limits of alternative probability theories.

Finally, – and this is very crucial for our discussion – note that the set of possible consequence-relevant states of Nature in all cases discussed in this section, i.e., in the case of a unique prior probability measure, in the case of a set of prior probability measures, for non-additive prior probability measures, and in the possibility framework, is assumed to be finite, so that a real surprise (a completely unexpected event) cannot be incorporated. However, to properly account for surprising events, this list should not be modelled as exhaustive. It is crucial to emphasise in this context that assigning subjective probability zero does not help to represent true unawareness of particular events because

> [s]tatements like 'I am assigning probability zero to the event *E* because I am unaware of it' are nonsensical, since the very statement implies that I think about the event *E*.
>
> *(Schipper 2013: 739; cf. also Dekel et al. 1998)*

By definition, a decision maker should be perfectly unaware of surprising events before committing to a specific action, and it lies in this very nature that this issue cannot be captured solely by means of more or less well-defined probability measures.

Second way of formalization: genuine non-knowledge of the state space and the possibility of true surprises

The second line of thought of incorporating non-knowledge on a decision maker's part into economic theory likewise has its history and tradition. It was recognized by a number of authors that in order to include true non-knowledge concerning future contingencies and surprising events into the framework of decision theory, it is necessary to shift research efforts from the issue of determination of adequate (prior) probability measures (i.e., risk and uncertainty in the modern economic parlance) to the issue of representation of a decision maker's *unawareness* with respect to possible states of Nature beyond their imagination which could also affect the consequences of their choice behaviour. This unawareness may be interpreted as a manifestation of a decision maker's natural bounded rationality. Their non-knowledge should not be limited to just a lack of knowledge as to which state from the exhaustive list of states of Nature will materialize ("uncertainty about the true state"), but rather non-knowledge about the full state space itself should be a part of decision theory. This challenge was met in the economics literature in particular by Kreps (1979), Fagin and Halpern (1988), Dekel et al. (1998, 2001), and Modica and Rustichini (1999). Their proposals presuppose a coarse (imperfect) subjective knowledge of all consequence-relevant states of Nature possible, and so criticize a central assumption in Savage's (1954) and Anscombe and Aumann's (1963) axiomatizations of a decision maker's choice behaviour, suggesting a radical departure from their frameworks. First of all, proving two famous impossibility results, Dekel et al. (1998) demonstrated that the standard partitional information structures of economic theory (i.e., the set-theoretic state space models discussed earlier in "The basic mathematical framework") preclude unawareness. Specifically, in such settings, only two very extreme situations can be captured: either a decision maker has *complete knowledge* of the full space of consequence-relevant states of Nature (as has the modeller), or they have *no knowledge* of this state space whatsoever. In addition, Dekel et al. (1998) made explicit crucial epistemic properties of true unawareness: e.g., that it is necessarily impossible for a decision maker to be aware of their own unawareness (technically termed AU introspection); cf. also Heifetz et al. (2006).

Following this discussion, new accounts were developed which suggested different ways to depart from the set-theoretic state space concepts of Savage (1954) and of Anscombe and Aumann (1963); foremost from their assumption on the existence of an exhaustive list of mutually exclusive consequence-relevant states of Nature which is available to both the modeller and the decision maker alike. These new accounts formalize a principally different kind of non-knowledge compared to the non-knowledge of (prior) probability measures over a complete state space: *unawareness* of potentially ensuing important events, or of additional future subjective contingencies. In terms of elements of the decision matrix in Figure 36.1, *only* the modeller now has complete knowledge of all consequence-relevant states of Nature, and of all possible outcomes/lotteries over outcomes contingent on these states. The decision maker has a restricted perception of matters depending on the awareness level they managed to attain.

Three ways to overcome Dekel et al.'s (1998) impossibility results concerning standard partitional information structures can be identified in the economics literature, two of which maintain the status of a (now enriched) state space concept as a *primitive* of the framework proposed. These are

1 the two-stage choice approach
2 the epistemic approach, and
3 the set-theoretic approach.

We now briefly review these in turn.

One solution is to formalize an endogenous subjective state space of a decision maker as a *derived concept*, as was initially suggested by Kreps (1979, 1992), and then further developed by Dekel et al. (2001) and Epstein et al. (2007). These researchers proposed a decision maker who is unaware of certain future subjective contingencies, and a modeller who can infer a decision maker's subjective state space regarding these contingencies from observing the decision maker's choice behaviour. (To a certain extent this strategy can be viewed as analogous to Savage's (1954) reconstruction of a decision maker's beliefs from their revealed preferences.) Kreps (1979) developed a *two-stage model* in which a decision maker first chooses from a set of finite action menus. Subsequently, a particular state of Nature is realized. The decision maker chooses a specific action from the selected menu only afterwards. The central idea is that although the decision maker does not know all the states that are possible, they know their subjective subset of possibilities, and this subset is not exogenous. The decision maker anticipates future scenarios which affect their expected later choices from the action menus and their ex ante utility evaluation of these menus. Thus, these scenarios (or the subjective state space) form the basis for ordinal binary preference relations with respect to the menus and can be revealed through observation of those preferences.

The more unaware a decision maker is regarding consequence-relevant states of Nature, the more flexibility they prefer by choosing the menus during the first phase. This intuition was more rigorously formalized by Dekel et al. (2001), who provided conditions required to determine the endogenous subjective state space uniquely. For example, they replaced the action menus by menus of lotteries over finite sets of actions, in the spirit of Anscombe and Aumann (1963). Epstein et al. (2007) proposed ways for the two-stage choice approach to account for a decision maker's manifested uncertainty aversion according to Ellsberg's (1961) empirical result. The pioneers of the unawareness concept depart from Savage's (1954) and Anscombe and Aumann's (1963) axiomatizations by replacing the state space in the list of primitives by a set of menus over actions which are the objects of choice. This theoretical move allows for dealing with unforeseen contingencies due to a decision maker's natural bounded rationality, the latter of which is manifested by their inability to list all the states of the exogenous world that could be relevant. For further details on this approach refer also to Svetlova and van Elst (2012).

In the *epistemic approach* to formalizing a decision maker's unawareness, initiated by Fagin and Halpern (1988), and subsequently pursued by Modica and Rustichini (1999), Heifetz et al. (2008), and Halpern and Rêgo (2008), a modal logic syntax is employed to elucidate the fine-structure of the (consequence-relevant) states of Nature. Such states are here perceived as maximally consistent sets of propositions which are constructed from a set of countably many primitive propositions, their binary truth values, and a set of related inference rules defined on the set of propositions. The propositional logic models so obtained extend the standard Kripke (1963) information structures of mathematics. The concrete awareness level attributed to a decision maker is associated with a specific subset of consistent propositions and their corresponding binary truth values; the awareness level varies with the number of elements in these subsets. Depending on the approach taken, the awareness level of a decision maker in a given state of Nature is expressed in terms of an explicit awareness modal operator defined over propositions (Fagin and Halpern 1988), or indirectly in terms of a knowledge modal operator (Modica and Rustichini 1999, and Heifetz et al. 2008).

While Fagin and Halpern (1988) in their multi-person awareness structure deal with a single state space and propose two kinds of knowledge (implicit and explicit) a decision maker may have depending in their awareness level, Modica and Rustichini (1999) in their one-person generalized partitional information structure distinguish between the full state space associated with the modeller on the one hand, and the (typically lower-dimensional) subjective state space of the decision maker on the other. A projection operator between these two kinds of spaces is defined. A consequence of this construction is that a 2-valued propositional logic obtains in the full state space, while a 3-valued propositional logic applies in the decision maker's subjective state space: a proposition of which they are not aware at a given state can be neither true nor false. Thus, unawareness of a decision maker of a particular event is given when this event cannot be described in terms of states in their subjective state space. According to Halpern and Rêgo (2008), an advantage of addressing the issue of the fine-structure of the states of Nature is that this offers a language of concepts for decision makers at a given state, as well as flexibility for covering different notions of awareness. Furthermore, these authors demonstrated that all of the propositional logic models of the epistemic approach to unawareness referred to above are largely equivalent. So far, propositional logic models have not been tied to any specific decision-theoretic framework.

The *set-theoretic approach*, finally, can be viewed as a less refined subcase of the propositional logic models of the epistemic approach in that it discards the fine-structure of the states of Nature, thus leading to a syntax-free formalization of unawareness. The key realization here is that in order to overcome Dekel et al.'s (1998) troubling impossibility results regarding a non-trivial representation of unawareness in standard partitional information structures, an entire hierarchy of disjoint state spaces of differing dimensionality should be introduced amongst the primitives of a decision-theoretic framework to describe decision makers that have attained different levels of awareness.

Heifetz et al. (2006) deal with this insight by devising in a multi-person context a finite lattice of disjoint finite state spaces which encode decision makers' different strengths of expressive power through the cardinality of these spaces. Hence, these state spaces share a natural partial rank order between them; every one of them is associated with a specific awareness level of a decision maker. The uppermost state space in the hierarchy of this unawareness structure corresponds to a full description of consequence-relevant states of Nature and may be identified either with an omniscient decision maker or with a modeller. The different state spaces are linked by projection operators from higher ranked spaces to lower ranked spaces. These projection operators are invertible and filter out knowledge existing at a higher level of awareness that cannot be expressed at a lower level. In this way, it is possible to formulate events at a given state of which a decision maker of a certain awareness level has no conception at all. A 3-valued logic applies in each state space, with the exception of the uppermost one where the standard 2-valued logic obtains. Unawareness respectively awareness of a decision maker of a particular event are formally defined indirectly in terms of a knowledge operator, which satisfies all the properties demanded of such an operator in standard partitional information structures; cf. Dekel et al. (1998): 164f. We remark that the Heifetz et al. (2006) proposal may have the potential to provide a framework for capturing Taleb's (2007) "Black Swan events" in a decision-theoretic context. For this purpose a scenario is required where no decision maker's awareness level corresponds to the uppermost state space in the hierarchy.

A related set-theoretic framework was suggested by Li (2009). In her "product model of unawareness," she distinguishes factual information on the (consequence-relevant) states of Nature from awareness information characterizing a decision maker, and so provides a formal basis for, again, differentiating between the full space of states of Nature and a decision maker's (generically lower-dimensional) subjective state space. With a projection operator between these two spaces defined, events of which a decision maker is unaware can be made explicit.

In contrast to the epistemic approach, direct contact with decision theory was recently established by Schipper (2013) for the set-theoretic unawareness structure of Heifetz et al. (2006). He puts forward an awareness-dependent subjective expected utility proposal in the tradition of Anscombe and Aumann (1963), where a set of awareness-dependent ordinal binary preference relations for a collection of decision makers is defined over a set of acts on the union of all state spaces in the lattice. Acts map consequence-relevant states of Nature in this union to von Neumann–Morgenstern (1944) lotteries over outcomes contingent on these states. That is, preferences for acts can now depend on the awareness-level of a decision maker, and thus may change upon receiving new consequence-relevant information. This is clearly a major conceptual step forward concerning representations of non-knowledge in economic theory, especially since it focuses on the important multi-person case. However, also Schipper's (2013) proposal is likely to suffer from Ellsberg's (1961) paradox, as decision makers' experimentally manifested uncertainty aversion has not been formally addressed in his framework. In this respect, one expects that Schipper's (2013) work could be combined with the multiple-priors methodology of Gilboa and Schmeidler (1989) in order to settle this matter, in analogy to Epstein et al.'s (2007) extension of the work by Dekel et al. (2001) in the context of the two-stage choice approach.

Discussion

Having reviewed the major approaches to non-knowledge in static decision-making frameworks, we would now like to address some open questions. We discussed concepts that investigated two key elements of the decision matrix in Figure 36.1: the space of consequence-relevant states of Nature, and prior probability measures over this space. Until recently, both approaches have been developed detached from one another: the respective papers have been concerned with *either* the determination of adequate probability measures, *or* with handling imperfect knowledge of the state space. However, the paper by Schipper (2013) makes an important attempt to connect both of these issues. In our view, further work should be done in this direction.

Moreover, other elements of the decision matrix, particularly *the set of available actions* and *the set of possible consequences*, have been widely excluded from the discussion about non-knowledge in economics to date. We suggest that more conceptual work should be done to clarify if it is justified to presuppose that actions and their consequences are perfectly known to decision makers, as has been the case in economic decision-making theory so far. Another important open question is how the elements of the decision matrix – probability measure, state space, actions and consequences – are related to each other. For example, recent research on performativity, reflexivity and non-linearity (cf. see the recent special issue on reflexivity and economics of the *Journal of Economic Methodology*) suggests that actions chosen could causally influence states of Nature; cf. also Gilboa (2009).

These considerations raise the issue of the very nature of, respectively, the states possible, the actions available, and their resultant consequences. It is important to properly understand what it means *to know* states, actions and consequences, *to be aware or unaware* of them. For example, obviously it makes a difference to conceive of possible states as "states of nature" or as "states of the world" (Schipper 2013: 741). Both types of states differ concerning the role of the decision maker. In a "states-of-nature" approach, the decision maker, i.e., their beliefs and actions, is irrelevant for the construction of the state space: only Nature plays against them. Thus, the elimination of non-knowledge *(of the future?)* would depend on the improvement of our understanding of the physical world. If, however, we conceive of the states as "states of the world," the decision maker's beliefs and actions are a part of the world description, with the necessity to consider the interrelation of all elements of the decision matrix, as well as the interconnections between the decision matrices of different decision makers as a consequence. For the conception of non-knowledge, our understanding of the social world would be as relevant as our views about the physical world. We think these insights, which relate to epistemic game theory, should be further developed, though the complexity of a resultant theoretical framework might become its own constraint.

Finally, we would like to ask if the assumption of omniscience on the part of the *modeller* in the unawareness concepts reviewed is justified. Is it warranted to presuppose that there is an institution that possesses a complete view of all states of Nature possible, while an ordinary *decision maker* has only imperfect knowledge of them? Heifetz et al. (2006: 90) stress that "unawareness . . . has to do with the lack of conception." For us, this conception includes knowledge of the interrelationships between all elements of the decision matrix. But who possesses this knowledge? And, given the complexity of those interrelations, *can* anybody possess this knowledge at all? To date, present-day economic modellers have not settled this issue.

Acknowledgement

We thank the editors of this volume and an unknown referee for useful comments on an earlier draft.

References

Akerlof G. A., and Shiller R. (2009) *Animal Spirits: How Human Psychology Drives the Economy, and Why it Matters for Global Capitalism* (Princeton, NJ: Princeton University Press).

Anscombe F. J., and Aumann R. J. (1963) A definition of subjective probability. *The Annals of Mathematical Statistics* 34: 199–205.

Bernoulli D. (1738) Specimen theoriae novae de mensura sortis. English translation: 1954. Exposition of a new theory on the measurement of risk. *Econometrica* 22: 23–36.

Bernstein P. L. (1996) *Against the Gods — The Remarkable Story of Risk* (New York: Wiley).

Bewley T. F (1986) Knightian decision theory: Part I *(Cowles Foundation: discussion paper).*

Bewley T. F. (2002) Knightian decision theory: Part I. *Decisions in Economics and Finance* 25: 79–110.

Debreu G. (1959) *Theory of Value: An Axiomatic Analysis of Economic Equilibrium* (New Haven, CT and London: Yale University Press).

Dekel E., Lipman B. L., and Rustichini A. (1998) Standard state-space models preclude unawareness. *Econometrica* 66: 159–173.

Dekel E., Lipman B. L., and Rustichini A. (2001) Representing preferences with a unique subjective state space. *Econometrica* 69: 891–934.

Dow S. C., and Ghosh D. (2009) Fuzzy logic and Keynes's speculative demand for money. *Journal for Economic Methodology* 16: 57–69.

Dubois D., and Prade H. (2011) Possibility Theory and its applications: where do we stand? IRIT Institut de Recherche en Informatique de Toulouse, http://www.irit.fr/~Didier.Dubois/Papers1208/possibility- EUSFLAT-Mag.pdf, accessed on June 23, 2014.

Dubois D., Prade H., and Sabbadin R. (2001) Decision-theoretic foundations of qualitative possibility theory. *European Journal of Operational Research* 128: 459–478.

Ellsberg D. (1961) Risk, ambiguity, and the Savage axioms. *The Quarterly Journal of Economics* 75: 643–669.

Epstein L. G., and Wang T. (1994) Intertemporal asset pricing under Knightian uncertainty. *Econometrica* 62: 283–322.

Epstein L. G., Marinacci M., and Seo K. (2007) Coarse contingencies and ambiguity. *Theoretical Economics* 2: 355–394.

Fagin R., and Halpern J. Y. (1988) Belief, awareness, and limited reasoning. *Artificial Intelligence* 34: 39–76.

de Finetti B. (1937) La prévision: ses lois logiques, ses sources subjectives. *Annales de l'Institut Henri Poincaré* 7: 1–68.

Frydman R., and Goldberg M. (2007) *Imperfect Knowledge Economics: Exchange Rates and Risk* (Princeton, NJ: Princeton University Press).

Ghirardato P. (2001) Coping with ignorance: unforeseen contingencies and non-additive uncertainty. *Economic Theory* 17: 247–276.

Gilboa I. (2009) *Theory of Decision under Uncertainty* (Cambridge: Cambridge University Press).

Gilboa I., and Schmeidler D. (1989) Maxmin expected utility with non-unique prior. *Journal of Mathematical Economics* 18: 141–153.

Gilboa I., Postlewaite A. W., and Schmeidler D. (2008) Probability and uncertainty in economic modelling. *Journal of Economic Perspectives* 22: 173–188.

Halpern J. Y. (2005) *Reasoning about Uncertainty* (Cambridge, MA: MIT Press).

Halpern J. Y., and Rêgo L. C. (2008) Interactive unawareness revisited. *Games and Economic Behavior* 62: 232–262.

Hayek F. A. (1945) The use of knowledge in society. *The American Economic Review* 35: 519–530.

Heifetz A., Meier M., and Schipper B. C. (2006) Interactive unawareness. *J. Econ. Theory* 130: 78–94.

Heifetz A., Meier M., and Schipper B. C. (2008) A canonical model for interactive unawareness. *Games and Economic Behavior* 62: 304–324.

Hirshleifer J., and Riley J. G. (1992) *The Analytics of Uncertainty and Information* (Cambridge: Cambridge University Press).

Kahneman D., and Tversky A. (1979) Prospect Theory: an analysis of decision under risk. *Econometrica* 47: 263–292.

Keynes J. M. (1921) *A Treatise on Probability* (London: Macmillan).

Keynes J. M. (1937) The general theory of employment. *The Quarterly Journal of Economics* 51: 209–233.

Knight F. H. (1921) *Risk, Uncertainty and Profit* (Boston, MA: Houghton Mifflin).

Kreps D. M. (1979) A representation theorem for "preference for flexibility". *Econometrica* 47: 565–577.

Kreps D. M. (1992) Static choice and unforeseen contingencies. *Economic Analysis of Markets and Games: Essays in Honor of Frank Hahn*, edited by P. Dasgupta, D. Gale, O. Hart and E. Maskin (Cambridge, MA: MIT Press): 259–281.

Kripke S. A. (1963) Semantical analysis of modal logic I. Normal modal propositional calculi. *Z. Math. Logik Grundl. Math.* 9: 67–96.

Li J. (2009) Information structures with unawareness. *J. Econ. Theory* 144: 977–993.

Modica S., and Rustichini A. (1999) Unawareness and partitional information structures. *Games and Economic Behavior* 27: 265–298.

Mukerji S. (1997) Understanding the nonadditive probability decision model. *Economic Theory* 9: 23–46.

von Neumann J., and Morgenstern O. (1944) *Theory of Games and Economic Behavior* (Princeton, NJ: Princeton University Press).

Ramsey F. P. (1931) Truth and probability. *The Foundations of Mathematics and Other Logical Essays* (London: Routledge and Kegan Paul): 156–198.

Savage L. J. (1954) *The Foundations of Statistics* (New York: Wiley).

Schipper B. C. (2013) Awareness-dependent subjective expected utility. *International Journal of Game Theory* 42: 725–753.

Schmeidler D. (1989) Subjective probability and expected utility without additivity. *Econometrica* 57: 571–587.

Shackle G. L. S. (1949) *Expectations in Economics* (Cambridge: Cambridge University Press).

Shackle G. L. S. (1959) Time and thought. *The British Journal for the Philosophy of Science* 9: 285–298.

Shackle G. L. S. (1961) *Decision, Order and Time in Human Affairs*, 2nd ed. (Cambridge: Cambridge University Press).

Smithson M. (1989) *Ignorance and Uncertainty: Emerging Paradigms* (New York: Springer).

Svetlova E., and van Elst H. (2012) How is non-knowledge represented in economic theory? In Birger Priddat and Alihan Kaballak (eds.) *Ungewissheit als Herausforderung für die ökonomische Theorie: Nichtwissen, Ambivalenz und Entscheidung* (Marburg: Metropolis): 41–72, arXiv:1209.2204v1[q-fin.GN].

Taleb N. N. (2007) *The Black Swan – The Impact of the Highly Improbable* (London: Penguin).

Zadeh L. A. (1965) Fuzzy sets *Information and Control* 8: 338–353.

Zadeh L. A. (1978) Fuzzy sets as a basis for a theory of possibility. *Fuzzy Sets and Systems* 1: 3–28.

37
Organizational ignorance

Joanne Roberts

Introduction

Although ignorance is an intrinsic element in social organizations (Moore and Tumin, 1949), it has attracted little interest from management scholars (Roberts, 2013). However, the importance of regaining ignorance through unlearning and forgetting in order to facilitate openness to new knowledge is increasingly recognized (Hedberg, 1981; Martin De Holan and Phillips, 2004; Tsang, 2008; Antonacopoulou, 2009). Nevertheless, studies of organizational ignorance are limited because they focus predominantly on its elimination through better knowledge management practices (Harvey et al., 2001; Zack, 1999), rather than on its strategic deployment (Roberts, 2013). Consequently, management scholars and practitioners need to develop a deeper appreciation of organizational ignorance.

To advance understandings of organizational ignorance this chapter provides a typology of organizational ignorance with the aim of promoting a managerial approach to the unknown. Before examining organizational ignorance, it is necessary to begin by considering the meaning of ignorance.

What is ignorance?

Ignorance is usually defined as a lack of knowledge or information (*OED*, 2003: 862). If knowledge is defined as 'justified true belief', ignorance can be viewed as the absence or distortion of justified true belief. One might then argue that ignorance is the absence of empirically valid knowledge. However, as Smithson (1989) notes, the adoption of this approach requires established criteria for absolute knowledge or truth, yet knowledge may be socially constructed, so truth, and the absence of truth, depends on a given perspective or system of belief. Hence, like knowledge, ignorance may be socially constructed.

Related to ignorance is the condition of being ignorant, that is, of lacking knowledge. To be ignorant is also associated with being rude, discourteous, or stupid. A person with no knowledge may be referred to as an ignoramus. Moreover, to ignore refers to a failure or refusal to notice something or someone.

Of course, any attempt to gain an appreciation of ignorance is dependent on knowledge of its existence. Ignorance may take the form of a *known unknown* or an *unknown unknown* (Gross,

2010; Proctor, 2008; Witte et al., 2008). Ignorance, as *known unknowns*, denotes knowledge of what is known about the limits of knowledge; there are certain things that we know that we do not know. Ignorance, as unknown unknowns, refers to a total absence of knowledge, such that we are not aware of our ignorance. *Unknown unknowns* are completely beyond anticipation, and, as Gross (2010) notes, the revelation of such ignorance can be a source of surprise. Even so, experience tells us that in the future some unknown unknowns will be revealed. Both known unknowns and unknown unknowns derive from an absence of knowledge.

Other types of ignorance also warrant consideration. Ignorance can, for example, result from ignorance about knowledge, which gives rise to *knowable known unknowns, unknown knowns* and *errors*. A *knowable known unknown*, which Congleton (2001) calls rational ignorance, differs from a known unknown in that it is knowable given sufficient motivation and resources to acquire it. *Unknown knowns* refer to things that we do not know that we know (Witte et al., 2008). They include the tacit knowledge that individuals are not always aware that they possess (Polanyi, 1967). Unknown knowns denote ignorance of existing knowledge rather than ignorance itself. Such ignorance does not prevent the use of the unknown knowledge. *Errors* arise from distortion, founded on confusion or inaccuracy, or incompleteness, based on uncertainty or absence (Smithson, 1989). Errors can occur because of the limited cognitive capacity of humans (Simon, 1955).

A further type of ignorance emerges from the refusal to recognize knowledge or its unconscious suppression; this includes *taboos* and *denials* (Witte et al., 2008). A *taboo* is socially constructed ignorance in the form of a social prohibition or a ban on certain knowledge, perhaps because it is viewed as dangerous or polluting. For instance, knowledge of cannibalism is taboo in most societies. *Denials* represent the ignoring or repressing of knowledge that is too painful to know or that does not fit with one's current understandings of the world. Knowledge that does not correspond with one's existing cognitive frameworks creates a degree of dissonance, which can challenge understanding. Tolerating such cognitive dissonance through denial is a common response and is sometimes referred to as wilful ignorance or wilful blindness (Berry, 2008; Heffernan, 2011). The loss of a loved one can initially evoke such ignorance.

Ignorance also arises from the conscious suppression of knowledge through *secrecy* either by individuals or by organizations (Proctor, 2008). Ignorance arises for individuals and organizations when they are subject to the secrecy of others. Certain types of secrets may be socially sanctioned, such as those arising from the individual's right to privacy. Hence, ignorance can also be identified with *privacy* - the ability of an individual or group of individuals to restrict access to, or information about, themselves. Unlike secrecy, privacy is multilateral in nature and it is enshrined in the laws of many countries and in the United Nations Universal Declaration of Human Rights. Existing and evolving social and cultural practices together with information and communication technologies also determine patterns of privacy. For instance, the disclosure of private information about celebrities by members of social media sites like *Twitter* and *Facebook* is currently testing the enforcement of privacy laws.

Organizational ignorance

The negative connotations that accompany the concept of ignorance together with the methodological challenges of investigating it go some way to accounting for its neglect in management research and practice. Yet, as March and Simon (1993: 2) note: '[o]rganizations are systems of coordinated action among individuals and groups whose preferences, information, interests, or knowledge differ.' These differences in knowledge indicate different patterns of ignorance between individuals within organizations.

Organizational ignorance takes a number of forms. First, it can be defined as the all pervasive ignorance of the organization's members or the relative ignorance between members across different parts of the organization. Second, organizational ignorance is relative to that of other organizations and external parties, including competitors, suppliers and customers. Third, organizational ignorance can arise from earlier organizational decisions, such as investment in the development of knowledge in a certain area relative to another. Finally, and perhaps surprisingly, organizational ignorance can include unknowns unique to individuals in the organization when such ignorance is actively sought and deployed by the organization.

In the sub-sections that follow, the forms of ignorance identified in the previous section are considered in an organizational context. In this way, the typology of organizational ignorance developed in my earlier work (Roberts, 2013) is briefly outlined. This typology is summarized in Figure 37.1.

Organizational unknown unknowns and known unknowns

In an organizational context, an *unknown unknown* refers to a state of ignorance at a specific point in time for all members of the organization. The existence of unknown unknowns in an abstract sense have been recognized for some time in organizations concerned with high risk Research and Development (R&D), like those in the field of aerospace engineering where the term has long been abbreviated to 'unk unks' (Longstaff, 2005). An organization may discover the existence of prior unknown unknowns through, for instance, the recruitment of staff with knowledge sets that are new to the organization, the acquisition of new equipment, R&D, the purchase of business services, interaction with customers and suppliers, and the actions of competitors. Recognizing that the organization is exposed to unknown unknowns can stimulate speculative thinking with the aim of transforming them into known unknowns. Techniques that can be used to surface such ignorance include scenario planning – also known as scenario thinking or scenario analysis, which involves combining the known and the unknown to produce a number of internally consistent scenarios of the future incorporating a wide range of possibilities (Shoemaker, 1995). Similarly, foresight studies, by anticipating the future, also seek to uncover existing unknowns (Loveridge, 2009).

Organizational *known unknowns* indicate an awareness that certain knowledge is beyond that known by the organization and its members. Although known unknowns may be overcome through learning, the recruitment of staff, R&D, the purchase of knowledge embedded in capital equipment, or the purchase of business services, like unknown unknowns, they may extend beyond the organization. As a result, there is no guarantee that investment in extending the organization's knowledge will remove this form of ignorance. Known unknowns give organizations choices in terms of where to focus strategic resources. For instance, an organization may withdraw from areas that expose it to known unknowns by refocusing on its core competencies (Prahalad and Hamel, 1990) and outsourcing exposure to such ignorance. In a sense, outsourcing of activity may indicate recognition of the limits of knowledge and its management within organizations.

Known unknowns drive innovation and creativity in all parts of the organization from R&D and design to customer relations, marketing and human resource management. Ignorance may not only stimulate the search for new knowledge, but surprisingly the lack of knowledge, unknown unknowns, can also be an important element in facilitating the creativity of groups within the organization. This is because the naivety and innocence of the

Source of Ignorance	*Type of ignorance*	*Example*
Absence of knowledge	Unknown unknowns	Ignorance that is beyond anticipation. Recognized in high risk sectors such as aerospace, where they are known as 'unk unks'.
	Known unknowns	A known incompleteness of knowledge, at various levels of the organization, which can lead to the outsourcing of exposure to such ignorance or can direct R&D efforts.
Ignorance about existing knowledge	Knowable known unknowns	Knowledge that is not central to the organization's core competencies. Access to such knowledge can be outsources to save on the organization's cognitive resources. For instance, many organizations outsource business services like advertising and legal service.
	Unknown knowns	Unrecognized tacit knowledge, such as that embedded in routines and practices. We often know more than we can articulate – such knowledge may be evident in intuition, instinct, and business hunches.
	Errors	Mistakes caused by human error or systems failures. For instance, one of the most common medical errors is the prescription of the wrong dose of medicine. In certain circumstances, this type of ignorance can be fatal.
Ignorance from suppressing knowledge	Taboos	Organizational cultures can enforce certain behaviours and knowledge to the detriment of others making some behaviours or knowledge taboo.
	Denials	The refusal to recognize major changes in the business context, which require the adoption of new business models. For instance, many retailers that denied the importance of online shopping in the early years of the Internet are now finding that their competitiveness is severely curtailed because of this earlier denial.
	Secrecy	Trade secrets, like the recipes for Coca-Cola or Kentucky Fried Chicken.
	Privacy	Confidentiality agreements with employees, customers and suppliers.

Figure 37.1 Typology of organizational ignorance

Source: Developed from Roberts (2013).

young or those inexperienced in a particular field of expertise can be important forces driving forwards the boundaries of knowledge. Such individuals are not inhibited by knowledge of the difficulties they face in pursuing a particular task. It is only at a later date that with hindsight they become aware of their earlier ignorance. Moreover, the development of new ideas and products often requires creators to 'think outside the box', hence ignorance of the box, in terms of existing knowledge in a particular field, can enhance creativity (Roberts and Armitage, 2008).

Orson Welles's directorial debut at the age of 25 is a useful illustration of how the ignorance of an individual can result in the development of new knowledge. Widely recognized as one of the world's most famous and highly rated films, Welles produced *Citizen Kane* (1941) with no previous filmmaking experience. Almost 20 years later Welles explained where he got the confidence to make the film (Wheldon, 1960 [2002]: 80): 'Ignorance, ignorance, sheer ignorance.' Knowing little about filmmaking, Welles thought that a camera could do anything the eye and the imagination could do. This ignorance allowed him to challenge the boundaries of existing knowledge in the field and to develop innovative cinematographic practices and narrative structures, which continue to influence filmmaking today. However, it is important to note that Welles achieved this through the combination of his own ignorance and the knowledge and experience of other members of the film's production team. Therefore, organizations may employ ignorance in the form of an ignoramus to identify new possibilities and act as a catalyst for creativity.

Newcomers to an organization are normally ignorant of many of its norms and practices. Although they may join an organization because of their specialist knowledge, they are also valuable because by combining this knowledge with their ignorance of the organization they are able to ask questions that would never occur to existing members. In this way, the ignorance of newcomers can help existing members to adopt a new perspective with potentially beneficial consequences for new knowledge creation. It is only through recognizing the potential of ignorance to stimulate creativity that it is possible to identify methods to harness its potential. Yet ignorance alone is unlikely to be productive, since it must be combined with existing organizational knowledge to facilitate constructive outcomes.

Organizational knowable known unknowns, unknown knowns and errors

An organizational *knowable known unknown* refers to ignorance that the organization is not motivated to overcome through the expenditure of the necessary resources. The choice regarding the acquisition of knowledge about knowable known unknowns will depend on the costs and benefits involved and the organization's strategy. Where a knowable known unknown becomes of significance to the organization's activities, an investment will be made in acquiring the appropriate knowledge whether through learning, staff recruitment, R&D or the purchase of knowledge embedded in capital equipment or business service. Such ignorance reflects the knowledge priorities of organizations. Within organizations, knowledge and ignorance will be unevenly distributed. Consequently, knowable known unknowns can be sustained within, or confined to, parts of the organization through the process of specialization and coordination. In this way, the organization is able to economize on cognitive resources, allowing for an uneven internal distribution of knowledge across the organization and within groups.

Organizational *unknown knowns* denote knowledge that is unrecognized in the organization. For example, they may be embedded in tacit routines (Nelson and Winter, 1982). Neither the workforce nor the management acknowledges such unknown knowns, and they are not reflected in the organization's formal structure. Ignorance in the form of unknown knowns may also underpin creativity. The importance of unarticulated knowledge in the form of intuition, for example, is a key element in the act of creation (Koestler, 1976). Thus, acknowledging and valuing unknown knowing in the form of instincts, intuition and insights unsubstantiated by evidence has a role in the management of this type of ignorance about knowledge.

Organizational *error* signifies ignorance arising from the bounded rationality of individual organizational actors and the limitations of managerial attention (Simon, 1955, 1973). Hence, limited cognitive capacity, combined with the nature of human cognition, creates scope for organizational error (Berry, 2008; Harvey et al., 2001). Rapidly and perpetually changing environments stretch the organization's cognitive resources, thereby increasing the capacity for organizational error. Organizational error can often be traced to the actions of individual organizational actors or a failure in organizational systems. For example, Kruger and Dunning (1999) provide evidence to show that individuals have difficulties assessing their own level of competence, which can lead to inflated self-assessments and therefore error. Although organization wide systems, including expert computer-based systems, can be introduced to minimize individual error, managers themselves and those that design the systems may also have inflated views of their own competence, with implications for the organization as a whole and the systems upon which it depends. As knowledge advances, problems becomes more complex and so too do efforts to control errors.

Organizational taboos, denials, secrecy and privacy

Ignorance is unambiguously socially constructed when its source is the suppression of knowledge. Organizational *taboos* refer to ignorance embedded in the social and cultural context of the organization and/or the context within which it is situated. Taboos may be actively cultivated in an organization to influence the behaviour of its members. The induction of new organizational members may involve the promotion of certain areas of knowledge and particular behaviours and working patterns to the exclusion of others. For instance, the behaviours, practices and methods of working in a top international accountancy firm like PricewaterhouseCoopers, which is working within a highly regulated field of professional practice, will be very different from those at the Internet giant Google, which seeks to challenge existing online services through continual innovation. While particular ways of working are promoted, others are neglected and may even be regarded as inappropriate or taboo. For example, playing computer games at work may be fine in a Google-type environment, but this would be taboo in an accountancy organization where every 15 minutes of an employee's time is billable.

Taboos may also derive from the external environment. Organizations may learn to exploit taboos by using them to promote certain products or services to customers or by using them in management strategies. However, at the same time, by supporting certain attitudes, taboos can act as a barrier to the introduction of new knowledge thereby potentially reducing the competitiveness of organizations operating in fast-changing environments.

Organizational *denials* occur when the values and norms embedded in the organization blind its members to knowledge that does not fit easily with the existing frameworks of understanding. Organizational denials can also result from what Janis (1972) calls 'groupthink'. In the search for unanimity, organizational members ignore evidence that contradicts the validity of a group's decision. Evidence of such denials can be found in the organizational debacles of Enron and Lehman Brothers (Swartz and Watkins, 2003; McDonald, 2009). In both cases, employees raised concerns about the functioning of the business. Yet, the management of these organizations failed to take on board the warnings, with the result that both organizations eventually filed for bankruptcy. Consequently, denial can prevent the implementation of new approaches to management in a timely fashion.

In addition, organizational denial can prevent creative and positive responses to rapid environmental change. This is evident in the film and music industry where digital technologies and the Internet are leading to ever-increasing amounts of digital piracy, which is making traditional business models that rely on outdated intellectual property regulation obsolete. Even so, many large entertainment conglomerates cling to their outmoded production and delivery approaches rather than find new ways to generate revenue in their sector (Knopper, 2009).

Organizational *secrecy* (Anand and Rosen, 2008) also holds relevance for understanding organizational ignorance. Secrets within organizations create deliberate areas of ignorance, which has consequences for the distribution of organizational power (Dufresne and Offstein, 2008). For instance, organizations may encourage the suppression of knowledge where its release might have a negative impact on performance; in many organizations levels of remuneration are confidential to avoid the divisiveness that salary differentials might stimulate among team members. Secrecy pervades creativity in the commercial sector despite the growing business interest and participation in open innovation (Chesbrough, 2003). Trade secrets represent the strategic employment of ignorance through the suppression of knowledge (Proctor, 2008). Many trade secrets are unknown and only come to light in retrospect, that is, when the secret is revealed. Other trade secrets, like the recipe for Coca-Cola, become known in the sense that there is knowledge of the secret but not of the exact details of the knowledge being suppressed. Such strategies purposely sustain ignorance among competitors, consumers and employees.

Organizational *privacy* refers to ignorance about employees, customers or suppliers or to the organization's commitment to maintaining the privacy of individuals whilst acquiring knowledge of significance to the organization's ability to undertake its activities. There may be a need for individual members to disclose certain knowledge to an organization, for example, concerning disability. Such information may be provided on the condition that it will be kept private and not widely circulated. In addition, the privacy of customers is often important, and, in sectors like medicine and law, providers are bound by professional codes of conduct that ensure confidentiality.

The recognition and protection of privacy supports the development of a relationship of trust between the organization and its members, customers and suppliers. Furthermore, placing trust in organizational members by allowing them high levels of autonomy and privacy over their working practices can be an important component in the construction of a satisfactory work environment. The elimination of privacy in the workplace through the introduction of mechanisms of surveillance can severely reduce trust and undermine working relations, leading to the loss of productive staff. For instance, Alge et al.'s (2006) research identified links between information privacy to empowerment and empowerment to creative performance and organizational citizenship behaviour. There are, then, cases in which management's ignorance of the activities of workers can have a positive impact on productivity. Moreover, from a managerial perspective, the maintenance of a degree of ignorance creates a position of vulnerability, a prerequisite for the development of a relationship of trust with employees, customers or suppliers.

Clearly, organizational ignorance is not as straightforward as simply an absence of knowledge. While it is very much related to organizational knowledge, it is independent from it because it can also be employed strategically within the organization and in the wider environment in relation to customers, suppliers, and competitors. Importantly, ignorance is often not absolute but relative between organizations and organizational actors. It can, therefore, be mobilized consciously for the benefit of individuals, groups, and organizations.

Conclusions

Ignorance warrants further consideration among management scholars and practitioners. Purposively incorporating ignorance into management strategies requires a new way of thinking about organization. For management scholars, a greater emphasis on challenging current knowledge, unlearning, forgetting and openness to the unknown is necessary. Managers need to adopt new perspectives involving a willingness to tolerate organizational ignorance where it offers possible benefits, and renewed efforts to consider it where it holds latent negative outcomes. In addition, a readiness to manage the benefits or costs of ignorance, which, although currently beyond comprehension, may be revealed at any time, is required. Managers need to develop strategies that explore and nurture their capacity to expect the unexpected. For, as Taleb (2007) suggests, we all need to be aware of our lack of knowledge as much as of our knowledge if we are to improve our ability to cope with the unexpected. Given the rapidly evolving technological, socio-cultural and political context, a readiness for the unexpected is an important source of competitiveness for organizations in the contemporary world.

Acknowledging the potential value of organizational ignorance paves the way for its active management. Knowing what is not known can be as important to organizational performance as knowing what is known. Different types and sources of ignorance require different management approaches that themselves offer scope for diverse outcomes. An awareness of the various types of ignorance provides the first step towards the development of techniques to manage the unknown.

References

Alge, B. J., Ballinger, G. A., Tangirala, S. and Oakley, J. L. (2006) 'Information Privacy in Organizations: Empowering Creative and Extra Role Performance', *Journal of Applied Psychology*, 91(1): 221–32.

Anand, V. and Rosen, C. C. (2008) 'The Ethics of Organizational Secrets', *Journal of Management Inquiry*, 17(2): 97–101.

Antonacopoulou, E. P. (2009) 'Knowledge Impact and Scholarship: Unlearning and Practising to Co-create Actionable', *Management Learning*, 40(1): 421–30.

Berry, W. (2008) 'The Way of Ignorance', in B. Vitek and W. Jackson (eds) *The Virtues of Ignorance: Complexity, Sustainability, and the Limits of Knowledge*, Lexington, KY: University of Kentucky Press, pp. 37–49.

Chesbrough, H. W. (2003) *Open Innovation: The New Imperative for Creativity and Profiting from Technology*, Boston: Harvard Business School Press.

Congleton, R. D. (2001) 'Rational Ignorance, Rational Voter Expectations, and Public Policy: a Discrete Informational Foundation for Fiscal Illusion', *Public Choice*, 107: 35–64.

Dufresne, R. L. and Offstein, E. H. (2008) 'On the Virtues of Secrecy in Organizations', *Journal of Management Inquiry*, 17(2): 102–6.

Gross, M. (2010) *Ignorance and Surprise: Science, Society, and Ecological Design*, Cambridge, MA: The MIT Press.

Harvey, G. M., Novicevic, M. M., Buckley, M. R. and Ferris, G. R. (2001) 'A Historical Perspective on Organizational Ignorance', *Journal of Managerial Psychology*, 16(6): 449–68.

Hedberg, B. (1981) 'How Organizations Learn and Unlearn', in P. C. Nystrom and W. H. Starbuck (eds) *Handbook of Organizational Design*, Volume 1, Oxford: Oxford University Press, pp. 3–27.

Heffernan, M. (2011) *Willful Blindness: Why We Ignore the Obvious at Our Peril*, New York: Walker & Company.

Janis, I. L. (1972) *Victims of Groupthink: A Psychological Study Of Foreign-Policy Decisions and Fiascoes*, Boston: Houghton, Mifflin.

Knopper, S. (2009) *Appetite for Self-Destruction: The Spectacular Crash of the Record Industry in the Digital Age*, New York: Free Press.

Koestler, A. (1976) *The Act of Creation*, London: Hutchinson.

Kruger, J. and Dunning, D. (1999) 'Unskilled and Unaware of It: How Difficulties of Recognizing One's Own Incompetence Lead to Inflated Self-assessments', *Journal of Personality and Social Psychology*, 77(6): 1121–34.

Longstaff, P. H. (2005) *Security, Resilience, and Communication in Unpredictable Environments Such as Terrorism, Natural Disasters, and Complex Technology*, November, Center for Information Policy Research, Harvard University. Available at: http://pirp.harvard.edu/pubs_pdf/longsta/longsta-p05-3.pdf (accessed 22 March 2014).

Loveridge, D. (2009), *Foresight: The Art of and Science if Anticipating the Future*, New York: Routledge.

March, J. and Simon, H. (1993) *Organization*, 2nd Edition, Oxford: Wiley-Blackwell.

Martin De Holan, P. and Phillips, N. (2004) 'Remembrance of Things Past? The Dynamics of Organizational Forgetting', *Management Science*, 50(11): 1603–13.

McDonald, L. with Robinson, P. (2009) *A Colossal Failure of Common Sense: The Incredible Story of The Collapse of Lehman Brothers*, London: Ebury Press.

Moore, W. E. and Tumin, M. M. (1949) 'Some Social Functions of Ignorance', *American Sociological Review,* 14(6): 787–95.

Nelson, R. R. and Winter, S. G. (1982) *An Evolutionary Theory of Economic Change*, Cambridge, MA: Belknap Press.

Oxford Dictionary of English (*OED*) (2003) Oxford: Oxford University Press.

Polanyi, M. (1967) *The Tacit Dimension*, London: Routledge.

Prahalad, C. K. and Hamel, G. (1990) 'The Core Competence of the Corporation', *Harvard Business Review,* 68(3): 79–91.

Proctor, R. N. (2008) 'Agnotology: A Missing Term to Describe the Cultural Production of Ignorance (and Its Study)', in R. N. Proctor and L. Schiebinger (eds) *Agnotolology: The Making and Unmaking of Ignorance*, Stanford, CA: Stanford University Press, pp. 1–33.

Roberts, J. (2013) 'Organizational Ignorance: Towards a Managerial Perspective on the Unknown?' *Management Learning*, 44 (3): 215–36.

Roberts, J. and Armitage, J. (2008) 'The Ignorance Economy', *Prometheus: Critical Studies in Innovation,* 26(4): 335–54.

Schoemaker, P. (1995) 'Scenario Planning: A Tool for Strategic Thinking', *Sloan Management Review,* 36(2): 25–40.

Simon, H. A. (1955) 'A Behavioural Model of Rational Choice', *Quarterly Journal of Economics*, 69: 99–118.

Simon, H. A. (1973) 'Applying Information Technology to Organizational Design', *Public Administration Review*, 33(3): 268–78.

Smithson, M. (1989) *Ignorance and Uncertainty: Emerging Paradigms*, New York: Springer.

Swartz, M. and Watkins, S. (2003) *Power Failure: The Rise and Fall of Enron*, London: Aurum Press.

Taleb, N. N. (2007) *The Black Swan: The Impact of the Highly Improbable*, London: Penguin Books.

Tsang, E. W. K. (2008) 'Transferring Knowledge to Acquisition Joint Ventures: An Organizational Unlearning Perspective', *Management Learning,* 39(1): 5–20.

Wheldon, H. ([1960] 2002) 'The BBC *Monitor* Interview. Broadcast by the BBC on 13th March 1960', in M. W. Estrin (ed.) *Orson Welles: Interviews*, Jackson, MS: University Press of Mississippi, pp.77–95.

Witte, M. H., Crown, P., Bernas, M. and Witte, C. L. (2008) 'Lessons Learned from Ignorance: The Curriculum on Medical (and Other) Ignorance', in B. Vitek and W. Jackson (eds) *The Virtues of Ignorance: Complexity, Sustainability, and the Limits of Knowledge*, Lexington, KY: The University Press of Kentucky, pp. 251–72.

Zack, M. H. (1999) 'Managing Organizational Ignorance', *Knowledge Directions,* 1, (Summer): 36–49. Available at: http://web.cba.neu.edu/~mzack/articles/orgig/orgig.htm (accessed 22 March 2014).

38

Managing with ignorance

The new ideal

Allison Stewart

Living in ignorance

The Emperor's New Clothes is a fable that describes a dystopian realm in which a narcissistic emperor is tricked by a pair of weavers into believing that they are able to weave a beautiful cloth. This cloth also has a practical purpose, in that it is invisible to anyone who is "unfit for his office or unforgivably stupid" (Andersen, 1837 [1983]: 77). Due to the rumour of this startling power, the weavers are able to make the emperor and his ministers believe that they are unfit for their roles, rather than admit that they are unable to see the cloth. After the emperor wears the robe of the invisible cloth in public, the fable ends with a child revealing to all that the emperor is not, in fact, wearing any clothes.

One of the messages conveyed in this fable is that any leader would be a fool to reveal that he or she is ignorant. Fables are usually cautionary tales, relayed to stitch together the fabric of societal expectations. Perhaps it is not surprising, then, that this message has uncomfortable parallels to examples of everyday behaviour in business. No manager wants to appear unknowledgeable to his or her supervisor, and admitting ignorance can be seen as a sign of weakness and incompetence. Rather, managers generally want to be seen to increase their knowledge, and in so doing, presumably decrease their ignorance. Such preferences contributed to the rise of the field of knowledge management in the 1990s, which was popularised as a "sustainable source of competitive advantage" (Nonaka, 1991) and initiated a series of initiatives focussed on greater knowledge transfer between and within businesses.

However, very little attention has been paid to why people might want to *not* increase their knowledge, or what could be termed the "incentive for ignorance," even though ample evidence exists that ignorance is a driver of behaviour. Successful managers, for example, are not those who micro-manage every decision; rather, they choose to be ignorant of some details in favour of viewing the bigger picture, trusting those working for them to inform them of pertinent details when needed. Alas, poor managers also engage in ignorance, either inadvertently because they are unaware of their lack of knowledge, or because they choose not to ask for or seek out information that might not be to their liking. The organisational objective should therefore not be to focus on apportioning blame for ignorance, but rather to seek to understand in which circumstances the outcomes of ignorance are likely to be productive, and in which they can be destructive.

It is somewhat understandable that the concept of ignorance has received little attention, as it is always more difficult to examine what is missing than what is present. Proctor (2008: 2), however, suggests that the lack of research about ignorance is "remarkable, given (a) how much ignorance there is, (b) how many kinds there are, and (c) how consequential ignorance is in our lives." Ignorance has a significant role to play in management, and both scholars and practitioners in the field must begin to address its absence. If not, both the productive and destructive outcomes of ignorance will continue to proliferate in business.

Ignorance as behaviour

Ignorance has been maligned through the ages, at least since Socrates' claim that there is "one only good, namely, knowledge; and one only evil, namely, ignorance" (see Plato c. 380 BCE, as cited in Laertius, 1853: 68). This juxtaposition of knowledge and ignorance is used in many comparisons; ignorance is often associated with a "lack" of knowledge, or with other antonyms that by nature make it a negative construct. Indeed, Mair, Kelly and High (2012) suggest that it is this very dichotomous characterisation of the relationship between knowledge and ignorance that is responsible for the association of knowledge with "good" and ignorance with "bad":

> Established ways of thinking about ignorance tend to take knowledge as their primary object and to see ignorance as a purely negative phenomenon, as the null state that obtains when the flow of knowledge is interrupted. In this view, ignorance can have no characteristics and no effects other than those that follow from the absence of whatever knowledge is lacking.
>
> *(Mair, Kelly and High, 2012: 3)*

Seen from this oppositional perspective, ignorance cannot be a driver of behaviour in its own right; it is only the absence of behaviour. However, scholars like Smithson (1989), Proctor (2008) and McGoey (2012) are starting to change the view of ignorance from the antithesis of knowledge to that of a dynamic and creative entity. McGoey (2012: 3) states that ignorance should be considered "a productive force in itself . . . the twin and not the opposite of knowledge," a perspective that allows ignorance to be perceived as unique and potent. While Proctor, in his work on agnotology (2008), primarily characterises ignorance in a negative frame, viewing ignorance as a tool for power struggles, he nevertheless attributes a motivation to ignorance that is frequently lacking in studies of knowledge. Framed in this way, ignorance moves from the background to the foreground of study, allowing an increased focus on how behaviour can be driven by such a force.

Through this shift in focus to ignorance as the subject of study, a number of other concepts can be drawn on to provide evidence. Groupthink, for example, is the situation in which a group collectively produces a decision that is the result of a reinforcement of common ideas, as well as a choice to be ignorant of alternative ideas (Janis, 1971). This wilful ignorance has the reward of social acceptance and reinforcement. In a similar vein, Zerubavel (2006) refers to "public secrets," which generate an expectation of societal ignorance:

> A conspiracy of silence, whereby a group of people tacitly agree to outwardly ignore something of which they are all personally aware . . . revolving around common knowledge that is practically never discussed in public, undiscussables and unmentionables that are "generally known but cannot be spoken."
>
> *(Zerubavel, 2006: 2–3)*

This again reinforces the ideal demonstrated in the example of *The Emperor's New Clothes* depicted above. In the world of business, some authors have suggested that both the global financial crisis and the collapse of Enron were caused by a number of intelligent people faced with a compelling reason to ignore the seemingly obvious consequences of their collective behaviour (Elkind and McLean, 2005). Given this incentive for ignorance, the question of intent is problematic; did these individuals intend to deceive, and to cause the impacts that ultimately resulted from their behaviour? There is evidence to suggest that some did, but that many others may have enacted a wilful blindness of the situation, choosing to forgo their concerns and prioritise other considerations. Heffernan's (2012) work on wilful blindness provides many other examples of similar situations in which both individuals and societies chose to avoid problematic information.

Prior research has also shown that ignorance can have positive or useful outcomes. Douglas's examination of the concepts of "structural amnesia" (1986) and "forgotten knowledge" (1995) illustrates that societal harmony often relies on "gaps in historical knowledge" (ibid.: 15) that allow new histories to be built which represent a coherent or preferable past. She illustrates this with the example of Evans-Pritchard's (1940) anthropological study of the African Nuer tribe, in which he found that cattle rights were allocated through a selective forgetting of the shared ancestry of different tribe members. As Douglas says, "it is not wrong to forget, it is not necessarily sad to forget, and we should not, cannot, strive strenuously to remember everything we ever knew" (1995: 15). Thus, ignorance can be both useful and necessary to the continuation of society, and can drive behaviour in much the same way as the quest for greater knowledge. In the management field, Anteby and Molnar (2012) also suggest that some things have to be forgotten in order for consistency to be preserved in organisations. In their study of a company's internal bulletins over a 50-year period, they find that:

> forgetting in a firm's ongoing rhetorical history—here, the bulletins' repeated omission of contradictory elements in the firm's past (i.e., structural omission) or attempts to neutralize them with valued identity cues (i.e., pre-emptive neutralization)—sustains its identity. Thus, knowing "who we are" might depend in part on repeatedly remembering to forget "who we were not."
>
> *(Anteby and Molnar, 2012: 515)*

In these examples, collective ignorance acts to avoid conflict, or to protect beliefs that would otherwise be untenable. Another positive example of ignorance in business is provided by management guru Peter Drucker, quoted in Cohen (2009) on the subject of "Liberty Ships," which were built by the United States (US) during World War II. Drucker claims that ignorance was responsible for the success of this building effort; since the US did not know how to build ships, they used manufacturing techniques from similar industries to reconceptualise the traditional methods of shipbuilding, with surprising results:

> Approaching this problem out of his ignorance, Kaiser [an American industrialist] built almost 1,500 ships at two-thirds of the time and at a quarter of the cost of other shipyards previously . . . Interestingly, despite the fact that they were not built to last, a couple are still around and in use.
>
> *(Cohen, 2009: 62)*

Thus, as a driver of behaviour, ignorance can also be seen to have a positive effect in business.

The examples illustrated above also highlight the difference between different motives for ignorance. However, they also illustrate the challenge of focussing on motivations; the difference between lack of awareness, useful forgetting, self-denial, public secret and strategic ignorance are not always clear.

Changing the perception of ignorance in management

A primary issue with the treatment of ignorance is the automatic negative value judgement with the party "engaged" in ignorance. The problem with this perspective is that it focuses on an error in attribution, for at the heart of any debate on ignorance is the problem that people cannot know the minds of others, and thus are forced to project supposition into the situation. When the focus of ignorance is shifted from personal attribution to the outcome of the ignorance, the discussion can equally be shifted from apportioning blame to determining solutions.

In most literature that deals with the topic of ignorance, the subject in question is how much the subject of the research "knew," as compared to the degree to which they were ignorant, or employed strategic ignorance. For example, McGoey's (2009) work on pharmaceutical company Merck & Co's actions in concealing the harmful side effects of the drug Vioxx seeks to explore what those in the company knew, and what they attempted to conceal from users in the interests of generating greater profit from an unsafe drug. While the evidence presented is compelling, the article also draws attention to the fact that the uncertainty surrounding the allegations led to the share price increasing during the time that the company was facing a significant number of lawsuits. McGoey calls this phenomenon the "performative value of uncertainty" (ibid.: 155), which could also be cast as an inability of observers to determine the extent of ignorance that could be fairly attributed to those involved. Because of this confusion, the detrimental effects of the ignorance are obfuscated, regardless of the blame that could be attributed to them.

These investigations into the motivations and psychological workings of ignorance are absolutely critical to understanding the concept and its ability to encourage behaviour. However, they require the researcher to engage in examinations of the minds of others. How much is one able to conceal from oneself? How does one know what information the mind turns away from, or refuses to acknowledge? How do we know that the subject "knew," and that they were not too busy to stop and consider the bigger picture that now seems to be obvious? These investigations also require, by their very nature, a value judgement on ignorance; was it unintentional, and therefore forgivable, or strategic, and therefore punishable?

For business leaders, this quandary leaves them in a difficult position. On the one hand, they cannot admit to ignorance because the term ignorance is perceived negatively in business contexts. However, they must admit that they did not know about problems, or they will be forced to confront the reasons for which they failed to act. Therefore, to more productively engage in a discussion on ignorance, we must focus not on the motivations for ignorance, but on the outcomes, and whether these were favourable or detrimental. In Drucker's example of the Liberty Ships, ignorance was useful, and promoted innovation; in the Vioxx example, ignorance was useful to avoid prosecution, but also detrimental to the company's reputation.

Beginning instead with the premise that ignorance is a driver of behaviour, outlawing the concept of ignorance to the realm of the unmentionable in management contexts does not lead to a higher ideal in management, but instead creates an opportunity for detrimental ignorance to rule. That ignorance exists is inalienable; what has been denied until now is the ability for it to be both a destructive *and* productive force in management contexts.

Ignorance in context: researching the Olympic Games

How, then, to research the outcomes of ignorance? Methodologically, this poses a simpler challenge than researching the motivations of ignorance, as the researcher need not infer the state of mind of those being studied. However, it is still more difficult to find evidence of ignorance than evidence of knowledge; it is akin to mapping the white space on a page rather than the text. Rayner's (2012) work on "uncomfortable knowledge" provides a useful suggestion in addressing this challenge. According to his research, information "lying on the boundaries of what is organizationally knowable and not knowable" (ibid.: 111) can be the origin of this uncomfortable knowledge, which by its very nature is un-acknowledgeable and un-discussable. As such, looking for evidence of ignorance along these boundaries can help to identify the gaps that are the subject of interest. The study of ignorance in management also faces the challenge of encouraging managers to discuss a subject that is implicitly not discussed in management. As Lee (1993) recommends in his methodological work on researching sensitive subjects, it is sometimes acceptable to conceal the objective of a study, as long as the subjects of the study are still able to engage in informed consent. Thus, in researching management, it may be necessary to characterise the subject of the research in a slightly different frame.

Taking this direction from the literature, I developed a study that examined the boundaries between several different organisations involved in developing the Olympic and Commonwealth Games, with a focus on the ways in which ignorance is productive and those in which it is destructive in planning. Following Lee's (1993) suggestion, I characterised the research in the context of the risk and uncertainty of "not sharing" information in the planning and management of the Games:

> The duration of these [Games] programmes, their substantial cost, and their profile and impact on a wide variety of stakeholders create an environment that can lead to sub-optimal outcomes if host cities are not provided with necessary information. When combined with the ongoing uncertainty over the planning horizon of the Games and the increasing complexity of their delivery, the need to manage the risk inherent in these events is intensifying.
>
> *(Stewart, 2012: 316)*

Thus, the characterisation of ignorance was concealed, but the ultimate objective of the research was communicated. For the purposes of the study, I investigated several boundaries: first, those between different sections, or functions, within the Organising Committees (OCs) of the Games; second, the boundaries between the OCs and external organisations like the International Olympic Committee (IOC) and government partners; and, third, the boundaries between the OCs of different Games, for example the Vancouver 2010 and Sochi 2014 Winter Olympics.

By gathering qualitative data through interviews and observation of interactions, and quantitative data through historical records, patterns of knowledge and ignorance were identified within each of these boundaries, with both favourable and detrimental outcomes. For example, ignorance of the enormity of the effort required to plan and execute an Olympic Games was found to be advantageous to OCs in early planning stages when they have a limited absorptive capacity, defined as "the ability of a firm to recognize the value of new, external information, assimilate it, and apply it" (Cohen and Levinthal, 1990: 128). On the other hand, ignorance of the challenges faced by other Games, for example in the consistency of cost overruns experienced by all Games (Flyvbjerg and Stewart, 2012), can be detrimental for the host city and country who have to fund the overruns when they occur.

More detail on these patterns can be found in Stewart (2012), as the intent is not to present the full results of this study here. On the contrary, the subject of interest here is the methodological approach to researching ignorance in management contexts. As mentioned above, the very association of research with the term "ignorance" can be enough to prevent managers from wanting to participate. However, the extent to which this was realised in this research was significantly greater than I had anticipated.

One of the organisations agreed to an arrangement in which I would undertake an unpaid part-time internship to conduct work on behalf of the organisation, while also using the material for the purposes of the research. The organisation required that I sign a confidentiality agreement before starting the work, which stipulated that I was permitted to use information collected through the interaction for research purposes, while the organisation would be permitted to review a final copy of any publications to ensure that no confidential information was released. The research progressed over the course of six months, and interviews were conducted with a number of individuals throughout the organisation. These interviews were recorded, and participants were informed that interviews were for the dual purposes of the organisational role and the research. The work required for the internship was completed.

One year after the completion of the internship, I submitted a draft of a paper for publication to the organisation. The first response was positive, with the recipient commenting, "it is an excellent piece of research, with some interesting outcomes"; however, it also noted a concern that "a few of the quotes . . . could impact the reputation of [the company]" (Email correspondence, 25 September 2012). In the second response, the organisation requested that all interviews collected with the organisation be removed from the research because "the general sense from [the company] is that the conclusions reached in the report are highly negative in nature and do not reflect the work that [the company] has delivered" (Email correspondence, 26 September 2012). In a series of discussions that followed, it was clear that the organisation had expected a positive "review" of their knowledge management practices, and was not interested in being associated with research that did not present this view, despite the terms of the initial agreement to which they had agreed.

The most interesting aspect of these exchanges is that they did not relate to the nature of the confidentiality agreement, but rather to the association of the company with the very concept of ignorance. These concerns were perpetuated even after the quotes in the paper were anonymised such that no individual, organisation, or even country could be determined from their content; over 100 people from six different organisations and five countries were engaged in the study. As such, their confidentiality was not in question; rather, it was the content itself that was problematic because the "highly negative" work had a potential "impact on reputation." Further, the focus on outcomes did not successfully overcome the bias of attributing motivation, at least from the perspective of the organisation studied.

The irony of this interaction is that the research proposed an acceptance of ignorance as a driver of behaviour, and suggested ways in which the organisation might seek to improve future performance through a better understanding of the opportunities for detrimental ignorance in their work, much as is represented in this chapter. Yet, the organisation studied went to great lengths over a period of several months to try to prevent the research from being shared, even requesting a permanent embargo on the contents of the paper ever being released. The feedback from this organisation demonstrates how difficult the study of ignorance will be for those researchers who attempt it. It also highlights how much work will be required to change the existing perception of ignorance in management, and move to a place where ignorance is an accepted, or even, in certain cases, a celebrated part of management.

Moving forward: managing with ignorance

No one said this was going to be easy. As evidenced by the example above, the predisposition to avoiding association with ignorance is a powerful driver of action, and many managers will resist association with the term in order to avoid accepting the negative value judgement that comes with it. Those who seek to call attention to ignorance in management will be received warily by their peers, who may even choose to distance themselves from any potential fallout.

Nevertheless, the benefits for managers who take this risk are considerable. By shifting the focus from the motivations of ignorance to the outcomes of ignorance, managers are freed from the yoke of knowledge, and can engage in productive discussions about what they do not know. Further, managers can benefit from understanding the detrimental role of ignorance in driving their behaviour, and that of their teams, and can attempt to determine how to minimise the effects of detrimental ignorance.

For academics considering exploring ignorance in management, there is an equal health warning; the research will not always be accepted positively, and will be fraught with challenges. However, the study of ignorance, or agnotology to use Proctor's (2008) term, is showing useful and productive outcomes. As a driver of behaviour, ignorance is an untamed landscape that can benefit significantly from further research. It is the hope of this researcher that the suggestions in this chapter can help to frame the way forward for the study of ignorance in management.

References

Andersen, H. C. (1837 [1983]) "The Emperor's New Clothes." In *Hans Christian Andersen: The Complete Fairy Tales and Stories*, translated by E. C. Haugaard. New York: Anchor Books.

Anteby, M. and V. Molnar (2012) "Collective Memory Meets Organizational Identity: Remembering to Forget in a Firm's Rhetorical History." *Academy of Management Journal*, 55(3): 515–540.

Cohen, W. A. (2009) *A Class with Drucker: The Lost Lessons of the World's Greatest Management Teacher.* New York: AMACOM.

Cohen, W. M. and D. A. Levinthal (1990) "Absorptive Capacity: A New Perspective on Learning and Innovation." *Administrative Science Quarterly*, 35(1): 128–152.

Douglas, M. (1986) *How Institutions Think.* Syracuse, NY: Syracuse University Press.

Douglas, M. (1995) "Forgotten Knowledge." In *Shifting Contexts: Transformations in Anthropological Knowledge*, by Marilyn Strathern. Association of Social Anthropologists of the Commonwealth, Conference, Oxford, England.

Elkind, P. and B. McLean (2005) *The Smartest Guys in the Room: The Amazing Rise and Scandalous Fall of Enron.* London: Penguin Books.

Evans-Pritchard, E. E. (1940) *The Nuer.* Oxford: Oxford University Press.

Flyvbjerg, B. and A. Stewart (2012) "Olympic Proportions: Cost and Cost Overrun at the Olympics 1960–2012." Saïd Business School working paper. Available at: http://papers.ssrn.com/sol3/papers.cfm?abstract_id=2238053.

Heffernan, M. (2012) *Willful Blindness: Why We Ignore the Obvious at Our Peril.* New York: Walker and Company.

Janis, I. L. (1971) "Groupthink." *Psychology Today*, November: 43–6, 74–6.

Lee, R. (1993) *Doing Research on Sensitive Topics.* London: Sage Publications.

Mair, J., A. Kelly and C. High (2012) "Introduction: Making Ignorance and Ethnographic Object." In C. High, A. Kelly and J. Mair, eds., *The Anthropology of Ignorance: An Ethnographic Approach*, pp. 1–32. New York: Palgrave Macmillan.

McGoey, L. (2009) "Pharmaceutical Controversies and the Performative Value of Uncertainty." *Science as Culture*, 18(2): 151–164.

McGoey, L. (2012) "The Logic of Strategic Ignorance." *British Journal of Sociology* 63(3): 553–576.

Nonaka, I. (1991) "The Knowledge-Creating Company." *Harvard Business Review*, 69: 96–104.

Plato (circa 380 BCE) *The Republic.* Cited in Laertius (1853), translated by B. Jowett. Available at: http://classics.mit.edu/Plato/republic.html.

Proctor, R. N. (2008) "Agnotology: A Missing Term." In R. N. Proctor and L. Schiebinger, eds., *Agnotology: The Making and Unmaking of Ignorance,* pp. 1–36. Stanford, CA: Stanford University Press.

Rayner, S. (2012) "Uncomfortable Knowledge: The Social Construction of Ignorance in Science and Environmental Policy Discourses." *Economy and Society*, 41(1): 107–125.

Smithson, M. (1989) *Ignorance and Uncertainty: Emerging Paradigms.* New York: Springer-Verlag Publishing.

Stewart, A. (2012) "Knowledge Games: The Achievement of Ignorance in Managing Olympic and Commonwealth Mega-Events." University of Oxford, Thesis. Available at the Bodleian Library, Oxford, UK.

Zerubavel, E. (2006) *The Elephant in The Room: Silence and Denial in Everyday Life.* Oxford: Oxford University Press.

39

Fictional reflections: Taking it personally

Medical ignorance

Ann Kerwin

Editors' note

Academically dealing with something that is not there (i.e. knowledge) certainly calls for new ways of presenting and registering of what is not there. Accordingly, this section concludes with a fictional thought-piece from Ann Kerwin, a narrative contemplation of how different individuals cope with new knowledge, from a patient suspecting but refusing to acknowledge that she may have cancer, to oncologists struggling to admit their own ignorance of treatment options.

Mary

The twenty-third day of November.
That was the day Mary first felt the lump in her lower right breast.
Something. Beneath the surface. A lump.

Mary was in the shower. Something. Something was there. Not small. Mary probed. Willing herself not to, she probed again. Still there. Not small. Slumping against the wet tile, Mary nearly vomited. *This cannot be happening. This is more than I can deal with. Please, let it not be*, she pleaded. Divorced for six years, chronically overworked, financially pressed, Mary had, on the recent occasion of her thirty-third birthday, dared to hope for a better year for herself and her eight-year-old daughter Morgan. But on the morning of the twenty-third day of November, stunned and shaking, Mary dried herself, dressed and left for work. For the first time in a decade, she was tempted to pray.

Days passed. Mary spent a good deal of time trying not to think about the lump.

Weeks passed. Mary recalled reading somewhere, perhaps in a woman's magazine, that not all breast lumps are cancerous. Hers might be something else. It might disappear. By turns panicked, distant, tortured, heartsick, Mary turned her mind to getting on with the necessities of life.

Months passed. It was still there. Like armed invaders, questions assaulted Mary. She repelled them. There was no space in Mary's life for what-ifs. She could not not work. She had no money to spare. She must take care of Morgan. Even before the twenty-third of November, Mary felt exhausted; at such moments slipping away held its charms. But Mary *had* to live - for Morgan. Morgan's father was not child-friendly. Abandoning them to reclaim his bachelor's freedom, Tom had long ceased to acknowledge his once-family. Her mother would be, at best, a grudging, unbalanced caretaker. Morgan was innocent, precious, trusting. Mary lived for Morgan.

Mary did not know for certain that she had cancer. She wanted to leave the matter there. But Mary could not languish in blissful ignorance: she knew enough to fear. Despite the adversity of recent years, Mary had always assumed that she and Morgan would make a better life together, that she would see Morgan through primary school, teenage years, through university, into a loving relationship, and beyond. Now she didn't know.

There was so much, just now, that Mary didn't know.

Claire

Claire was not good with people.

Claire knew that she was not good with people. Consequently, she took pains.

During her lunch hour, Claire reviewed the files of the four patients she would meet this afternoon. All would be expecting bad news. Most would be traumatized. Each had been referred to Claire, a senior oncologist at a busy university hospital where today she must confirm what each most likely feared: they have cancer. In her most reassuring manner, Claire would urge the stricken people before her not take the diagnosis as a death sentence. Slowly and gently, she would brief them on prognosis, treatment regimes, assistance and referrals. Yet, however softly Claire spoke, however carefully she chose her words, over the next four hours Claire must relay to four strangers dreadful, dreaded life changing news. She never felt adequate to the task.

Her one o'clock appointment would be with Mary, a thirty-three year old single parent with metastatic breast cancer. It had been Claire's first reaction: things did not look good for Mary. Ten days ago, she had consulted a doctor who ordered tests, then more tests. He referred Mary to the Cancer Center where, in less than an hour, Claire would put into words what the young woman had likely long feared – that she had breast cancer, that she would need surgery and prolonged treatment, that multiple organs were involved. If Mary were to continue as Claire's patient, Claire hoped that she would learn to sync with Mary's personality, to sense when and how to reach out, speak or stay silent, to intervene or let her be. But now, at this emotively charged juncture in her life, Mary - the person, not the cascade of diagnostic results and images before Claire – was a black box to Claire, a human mystery propelled by awful circumstance into this office and, most likely, into a painful odyssey of interventions by scalpel, chemicals and radiation. Before her day was over, Claire would meet four interpersonal question marks in parlous circumstances.

Claire sometimes wished that she were more like Carlos.

During their long Oncology residency, Claire and Carlos had bonded over shared dedication to patient care. Practicing in different countries now, they remained, courtesy of Skype, colleagues at a distance. Carlos felt that, whatever people might say when they were overwhelmed by cancer's predation and oncology's punishing protocols, deep down patients wanted to live. He premised his care and counsel on this injunction: *Face the unknown, maintain hope.* Frequently Carlos urged Claire to bear in mind the campaign to defeat AIDS.

Carlos

Early on, medicine had nothing effective to offer patients, Clarita. Confronted with their vast ignorance, biomedical communities roused themselves to ask new questions, challenge verities, and explore. In turns enormously promising and discouraging, disturbingly economic and political, the long quest for a cure has reshaped what we think and can think today, what we do and can do. AIDS has not been conquered, but it has been tamed. Funding permitting, patients who have made it to this day may live for decades. For cancer I cherish similar hope.

Biomedical understanding, tools, and technologies have advanced remarkably since we entered medical school. Oncology chapters in today's medical text books little resemble the established wisdom of our student days. Current options for diagnosis and treatment outstrip the meagre roster of our intern days. Vast online resources proliferate, flowing globally. But for all these inroads, I have no cure to offer patients and few treatments without suffering. To bolster my hope, I remind myself that each year we learn more. Scavenging resources from the once-unknown, we leverage them to ask new questions and interrogate old answers. We conjecture, weaving strands of surmise to span what we don't yet fathom. Sometimes, if we are open, humble or desperate enough, we revive or revisit neglected or discredited alternatives. Through it all, we unlearn prodigiously. But I detect no linear triumphalist progress, Clarita. Far from it. Stumbling into revelation and misdirection, clarity and confusion, continually surprised, often discouraged, fascinated and baffled, unsettled by what we must reject and uncertain how to reframe, the far flung community of investigators guesses, tests, errs, and tries again. I don't know enough, my friend, to have faith that we will find a cure. But I have hope.

I recall the two-faced deity *Janus Bifrons* whose giant statues graced Rome's public spaces. One of the god's opposed faces was said to herald openings and beginnings, the other endings. One countenance announced war, the other peace. I feel that I navigate between analogous faces of medical ignorance. One visage reminds me that I don't know what I need to know to save my patients. I depend on a vast web of other humans, most unknown to me, all imperfect, who research, invent, summarize, fund, and disseminate, in ways I neither know nor understand, somehow, mysteriously, producing the knowledge and tools I deploy. I take my place in nested layers of institutions, incomprehensible webs of interdependent professions, corporations and communities which, our friend Irina reminds, limit and potentiate me in ways I am too ignorant, enmeshed, manipulated and busy to probe, much less resist. Laboring in this murky mix, frustrated by medical ignorance, I confront it as an adversary; I feel it warring against me, impeding me, presiding over unwelcome endings - options, dreams, lives.

Medical ignorance *bifrons* obstructs. It also harbors hope. The face of new beginnings opens onto a vast domain of unknowns, a fertile *terra incognita* teeming with potential solutions. It is, perhaps, an opaque or dimly understood universe of things, or relationships we have yet to discover or fail to recognize, that we repress, suppress, misconstrue or misinterpret. To produce medical remedies, social practices and arrangements I don't now see but wish to, I fix my sights on this, my ally.

Ever the philosopher, you resist my naive dualisms. But I need a narrative, not a theory, to guide me, Clarita. Thus I situate myself in ancient epic odyssey tales - those grand, petty, tragic, comic, solemn, all too human sagas which begin *in media res*, in the middle of things. I too journey *in media res*. Of the many things I believe today, I don't know which, or how many, are false. I don't know how much of what I do daily is medical ignorance masking as medical knowledge. I don't know what I need to know to ask better questions. I don't know where to go to find better answers. I can't get far enough removed from my own mind, culture, era, and institutions, from my and our binds, blinds, biases and *epistemes* to reliably discern what I do daily that I oughtn't, what I think that I shouldn't, what I ignore, omit, overlook or deny to someone's cost. But I cannot wait for a more enlightened day to do my work. Despite my failings, I must do, decide, advise, prescribe, intervene in the imperfect here and now, *in media res*. Lacking requisite knowledge, I must have hope. I must offer it.

Claire

Carlos was a good man. In the wake of his buoyant hope, and despite their uncertainty and his, Carlos would sweep his patients and their loved ones through the grueling circuit of therapies their flawed profession had learned enough to provide. All would feel cared for, Claire knew. They were. Claire cared. But she lacked Carlos' uplifting optimism.

Carlos was right. They had witnessed astounding breakthroughs in recent decades. But Claire reckoned daily with this: even as she worked to ease her patients' suffering, she was a party to it. Biomedicine knew too little to counter cancer without inflicting, sometimes substantial, harm. In soft measured tones Claire would detail for patients the oncological interventions recommended to preserve their lives. But she could not help imagining how the treatments she described might ravage them. The aim was to deliver them from cancer entirely, or at least to buy enough time with loved ones to justify the pain. But there were no guarantees and, for some, Claire had misgivings. Carlos had one unifying narrative: *Cling to hope; journey on.* But where Carlos saw hope, Claire might see pain. Where Carlos felt possibility, she might feel devastation. When Carlos told patients that he did not know, he injected a beam of hope – *Anything might happen.* Claire felt medicine's impotence keenly.

Claire had earned first class honours and a Masters in Philosophy at Oxford. When they met as trainee doctors, Claire the Philosopher and Carlos the Classicist avidly theorized over coffee breaks on late night shifts. Carlos still did. Claire did not. Her attention was elsewhere. Claire had devoted years to the study of bodies and bodies of information. She was still learning to deal with embodied beings. Mostly she served by listening. She always listened to Carlos' evolving conjectures, neither critiquing nor concurring. Claire surmised that her friend needed to weave and re-weave his narratives of ignorance and hope because he was not a dispassionate physician. He cared deeply for his patients and their loved ones; he took their pains and losses personally; his musings and metaphors refueled him. Alone, waiting for her colleague, mentor, patient and dear friend Irina to drop by, Claire recalled that, in those long ago days, she and Carlos had not conceived of ignorance as a resource. Rather, they speculated that . . .

ignorance is part and parcel of the game of life. It is woven into the players, intrinsic to the cards we are dealt, a feature of every hand and gambit. For all our pomp, we humans labor under operational constraints. Confined to five senses, one brain, one body, one lifespan, a limited community of associates, and some tools of our own devising, what the best of us can sense, conceive and comprehend is only a minute part of what there is to be known. Finite beings dwarfed by what-is, we are destined to know and not know in unequal portions. Our ignorance may seem a rare lapse, void or faux pas in otherwise glitteringly knowledgeable lives. But lived experience belies this. Beneath the placid surface of taken-for-granted lives, unknowns roil. They riddle everything we think we know. They pervade every human endeavor. If knowledge is empowering, it is also fragile, contingent, and porous. As the ancient Stoics acknowledged, for human beings – headstrong, excruciatingly vulnerable creatures, torn between outsized dreams and restricted capacities, desperate to control – such battered wisdom seems bitter medicine indeed.

Even then Claire the Philosopher knew that Claire the Clinician must calibrate delicately how, how much, how often, to whom and when to communicate "I don't know" or "medicine does not know." Decades on, she had no philosophy left to spin. Just as Carlos needed to voice his evolving relationship with medical ignorance so did her patients in strife. They had, after all, ample reason to reflect on what she and her profession did not know. For them Claire's youthful musings and Carlos' latest grappling held little allure. Claire understood. Their conceptions might emerge in diatribes or lamentations but Claire listened respectfully, neither critiquing nor concurring.

Cancer has killed many.
It has its grip in me.

Absent essential medical knowledge, my life will be lost.

Your ignorance, medical ignorance, is the ally of a hostile invader.

Therefore, your ignorance, medical ignorance, is my enemy.

I need you to know enough to vanquish it.

I don't want to hear about how much ignorance there is.
I don't want to hear about the someday hope that somehow, by means you don't now know,
you will find in what you don't yet understand what I require to live.
I need you to know enough right here, right now, to cure me.

Please understand:
I am not the doctor. I am not well. I am desperate. I am vulnerable. I cannot play the long game.
I take your medical ignorance very personally.

Claire frowned. Irina was late.
Irina was rarely late. Claire frowned again.
Irina had late stage terminal cancer. She would not live long. Few knew it.

Born in the former Soviet Bloc, the slight soft-spoken, seventy-two year old nephrologist and medical sociologist had trained in her native land, and by a circuitous route, forged an iconoclastic hybrid career. Twelve years ago the medical school's Dean had astounded their community by creating for Irina a Professorship in Medical Ignorance. Dubbing herself Cynic-in-Residence, Irina had vigorously tackled her brief: to dis-illusion colleagues and students about biomedical institutions and power.

Irina could not remember not distrusting institutions.

She and her compatriots may have lacked American's vaunted "free speech," but many had cultivated exquisite sensitivities to what they were not supposed to know. From early days they were schooled to peep behind the curtains of Party puppet shows. Performances might be given in the Kremlin or Politburo, in medicine, media or the market, in academe, the arts or other arena. But many knew to ignore the story lines, scenery and costumes. They concentrated, rather, on detecting the hidden puppet masters, discerning their arts and artifice, and decoding scripted messages. Keenly they analyzed: Who and what had not been shown? What was the audience to have been enticed to accept, reject, deny, avoid or ignore? What had been omitted, suppressed or underplayed? What had been negated? What alleged facts, necessities or inevitabilities were not? Importantly: Who orchestrates? Who benefits? Who suffers? And how? It was an art form, a social practice, a way of knowing that ran so deep it became a way of being. Bravely, underground presses, covert meetings and performances disseminated what was not to be known, repudiating false knowledge, repopulating their ravaged reference points. Irina had been raised with the conviction that the very things of which people were to remain ignorant were their proper business. They might feel powerless. But they need not be clueless.

In the waning months of her life, Irina confided to Claire that in her dozen years she had accomplished little. Despite her best efforts, most of Irina's bright diligent students and colleagues remained astonishingly, frighteningly naive. She had gravely underestimated their resistance to unlearning. Intrigued, often enlightened by their Professor of Medical Ignorance, most happily left it to Irina to investigate what they seemed content not to know.

Irina knew that she would be missed. Her extraordinarily generous colleagues would mourn her. Irina's students would remember her. She would leave some behind to carry on her mission. But for the most part the dedicated people of this medical-industrial complex would not peer behind the curtains of its puppet shows. Busy with other things, they would perceive no need to learn what Irina had learned as a child. For all their kindness and dedication, most would remain as Irina had found them: culpably incurious about the critical, often covert, social forces which shape the enterprise upon which they lavish their energy, resources, talent and care – and on which countless vulnerable people depend. This is the reason to take the workings of power and institutions seriously, Irina felt: things to do with medicine affect people profoundly – vast numbers of people with much to gain, much to lose, and little power to choose.

Claire could still recall Irina's Inaugural Professorial Address. Irina began, "When I arrived at my first job in your country, the University website advertised its core business: *knowledge production, knowledge dissemination,* and *knowledge transmission. Knowledge production* was research, a lucrative, prestigious enterprise. *Knowledge dissemination* was publishing, a valued core subsidiary. *Knowledge transmission* was teaching and public outreach, low-level, often factory, labor. Fully occupied with their holy trinity, I could see that knowledge would not just happen. It would be made, constructed, shaped, molded, set in motion and directed by certain people for certain purposes, in a certain place and time. Little was said about ignorance except that the University's funding mandate was to decrease it through teaching and research.

Let us not leave ignorance at that.

For if knowledge can be produced, skillfully and deliberately, so can ignorance. If knowledge can be disseminated and transmitted, so can ignorance. If institutions can work mightily to promote the creation and maintenance of knowledge, they can vigorously engineer the creation and maintenance of ignorance. Like knowledge, ignorance can be made, constructed, shaped, molded, set in motion and directed by certain people for their purposes, in a place, at a time. Indeed, there are ignorance factories.

One word, "ignorance," shelters wildly various phenomena. Among them we find: Socratic ignorance (held to be a sophisticated form of knowing), stupidity, vacuity, secrecy, suppression, ineffability, bigotry, privacy, tact, discovery-in-waiting, disinformation, misinformation, apathy, and more. Hence I will sow confusion and poor communication (themselves alleged byproducts of ignorance) if I speak too generally about medical ignorance. Here is my focus. For many years I have been concerned, professionally, personally, and politically, with several pathogenic varieties of medical ignorance making. I have in mind practices which are intentionally, expertly constructed to actively bring it about that certain people will not know important things, to their harm or disadvantage, or those of others. By secrecy, omission, and misdirection, by suppressing or falsifying information, and other means, ignorance producers aim to strategically create and maintain a lack of knowledge of medically related matters of import to others. When successful, people do not know things that they have a legitimate interest or compelling need to know. They do not know that they do not know. They do not care that they do not know that they do not know. Thus they remain quiescent, even unthinkingly compliant, in matters they have every right to take personally.

Lest you suspect that your new Professor exhibits symptoms of paranoid personality disorder, and dismiss her ramblings, I will offer examples of malignant medical ignorance production, dissemination and transmission which adversely affect the care you provide for vulnerable people in this facility. All are your proper concern. But I speculate that you do not know enough to be concerned. I suspect that your medical ignorance on these matters has been successfully engineered."

Irina then relayed examples which remained the talk of the campus. Two years before, Corporation X had released Model Q patient monitor, despite protests from X's engineers over Q's occasional unreliability. Irina had their attention now. Their hospital used Model Q monitors exclusively. X's defecting engineers and administrators had fastidiously documented their concerns and executives' responses – to falsify results, sanitize company records, purge objectors, and repel external scrutiny. Presented with compelling evidence, several medical advocacy groups worked to call attention to Q's deficiencies pre-release. Administrators at their own hospital had been briefed, Irina revealed. "Had you known of this?"she asked. "Was it not your business to know?" Did they know that their hospital, now a for-profit, and X were owned by the same conglomerate? Irina presented more examples, more evidence, evincing more shock. Long ago Claire and Carlos had theorized that beneath the placid surface of taken-for-granted lives, unknowns roil. It was not what they had in mind – this malign, deliberate manufacture of medical ignorance – but it surely fit.

The painstaking investigative work required to expose the kinds of medical ignorance Irina deplored remained daunting. Cloaked in commercial secrecy in institutions with experienced public relations and aggressive legal departments, many practices Irina sought to reveal were easily secreted, suppressed, and "re-packaged;" key people might be deceived, discredited, intimidated or co-opted. To Irina's disappointment, few medical people took on the work. Claire knew – they were otherwise occupied. Fiercely determined, Irina had looked outward for harmful medical ignorance. More and more, Claire looked within. When she could, Claire volunteered for *Medecins Sans Frontieres* and served on professional committees on poverty, equity, and health care inclusiveness. Working outside her institution, and sometimes her country, Claire got mortified glimpses of her narrow world – and of some of her biases, prejudices, myopia, avoidances, negligence, habits, lapses, inadvertence and inattention. These too could harm. Humbled, Claire had cause to examine herself and her profession. Beyond molecules and MRI's was a world of sociopolitical medical ignorance, constructed and maintained, which Claire, at her late age, was just beginning to explore.

Claire looked at her watch. Two minutes to one o'clock. Claire frowned.

Despite being very ill now, Irina refused to leave her mobile on. Claire felt very concerned for her friend, but she would have to investigate later. Claire was about to meet four very vulnerable people and, very likely, some of their loved ones. These would be difficult hours for all of them. As Claire walked down the long corridor toward the small Oncology waiting room to call for her one o'clock appointment, Mary, she heard sobbing. Entering, Claire saw Irina on a leather settee with her arms around a young woman whose body shook with convulsive weeping.

Silently, Claire mouthed, "Mary?"

Irina nodded.

Very quietly Claire lowered herself onto the settee; placing her hand gently on the small of Mary's heaving back, in silence, unnoticed, Claire waited.

40

Afterword: Ignorance studies

Interdisciplinary, multidisciplinary, and transdisciplinary

Michael Smithson

Multiple views and orienting strategies

The study of ignorance does not land neatly in any one discipline. It splatters across disciplines without any respect for disciplinary boundaries. From astrophysics to zoology, most disciplines have perspectives for dealing with the unknown, employing methods from mathematics to discourse analysis. These perspectives have, understandably, their own specialized linguistic-conceptual frameworks and usually are disconnected from one another. There are no universal meanings even for technical terms such as "probability" or "risk." Each discipline perceives ignorance through its own lens. Ignorance can be viewed as an absence or neglect of information, a failure to understand information, a mental state, a moral condition, a public problem, an economic commodity, a manufactured product, or an aspect of a culture.

How, then, are we to attain an overview of ignorance that does not marginalize or misrepresent these various perspectives? After all, the feasibility of an over-arching framework for ignorance is an open question. Nevertheless, ignorance inevitably will be encountered in multidisciplinary, interdisciplinary, and transdisciplinary dialogues, scholarship, and research. This Handbook is a source of starting-points and benchmarks for such dialogues and collaborations. Its chapters provide both guidelines to and exemplars of key orienting strategies for understanding ignorance. We will review these strategies briefly, before continuing on to an overview of the Handbook and a survey of the possibilities opened up by its contributors.

A primary orienting strategy is to consider ignorance as socially constructed rather than as somehow imposed on humankind by a recalcitrant and complex universe. An attribution of ignorance entails a point of view for the attributor (including self-attribution), and other viewpoints may yield different accounts of who is ignorant of what. So, an effective starting-point for the study of ignorance is examining what people think or say it is, to whom they attribute it, how they respond to it, and what uses they put it to. Many of the chapters in this volume make use of this orienting strategy, including a linguistic treatment (the chapter by Janich and Simmerling), and investigations into the politicization of the unknown (e.g., chapters by Bogner, by Chua, and by Dedieu, Jouzel, and Prete).

A subsidiary orienting strategy in studying the social construction of ignorance focuses investigations on any of three kinds of "construction." First, there are constructed unknowns in the sense that any proposition that does not pass for legitimate, recognizable knowledge in a knowledge community may therefore be deemed non-knowledge of some kind, e.g., ignorance, falsehood, or fiction. For this to occur, the knowledge community must share, or at least be able to debate, criteria for establishing when something is known or not known. Rayner's chapter is a case in point, whereby both supporters and opponents of geoengineering research agree that there are great uncertainties about the potential consequences of deploying of stratospheric aerosols. There are also chapters in the Handbook that explore situations where the unknown is not agreed upon. The chapter by Frickel and Kinchy proposes that ignorance, as well as knowledge, can be geographically local so that some things are knowable in certain places but not in others. The chapter by Zimmermann is a case-study in almost mutually exclusive ignorances via his interactions with a Chinese musician colleague. And Friedman's chapter probes the extent to which fallibilism can provide a productive middle course between dogmatism and scepticism.

A second subsidiary approach is investigating deliberately generated, maintained, and/or imposed unknowns, whether in the course of ordinary social interaction, through state or corporate strategic manipulations, or multilateral arrangements such as privacy (Smithson 2008a, b). Again, a prerequisite for strategically constructed ignorance is that its purveyors and recipients must already share criteria for recognizing what "ignorance" is. McGoey (2007, 2012) has adopted this observation as a major theme in her work. There is also an earlier literature on what has been called the "manufacture of doubt" (e.g., Proctor 1995 and Michaels 2008). The chapter by Dedieu, Jouzel, and Prete advances a thesis that this kind of ignorance is useful for aspects of governance. Rappert and Balmer argue that the "production, feigning and claim to be authoritative possessors of ignorance can be made to work as a resource." Likewise, Thiel elaborates the uses of appeals to ignorance in denials of culpability for criminal acts.

Finally, there are unintended unknowns that are generated as a by-product of some social or psychological processes. Again, even post-hoc recognition in a knowledge community of the rise of new unknowns requires some prior consensus on the nature of ignorance. Examples include the identification of unanticipated risks generated by technological innovation, and new questions for research generated by prior research. One version of this theme is that the conversion of non-knowledge into knowledge also may generate new non-knowledge (e.g., Gross 2010, or Firestein's chapter). Gaudet's chapter pursues this theme to an interesting conclusion, namely advocating "evergreen science policies" as having emergent properties that explicitly acknowledge the potential construction of new epistemic relations and concomitant unknowns.

In a third orienting strategy, we can recognize that conceptualizations of the unknown and states of unknowing are grounded in how the human brain works, and yet also are culturally and historically specific. People think and act as though there are different kinds of ignorance, and as though those distinctions are important to them. This is partly due to the workings of the brain, and the chapter by Smithson and Pushkarskaya lays out our current understandings thereof. However, it also is a product of the society and culture of the times, and tracing the evolution of these concepts over time can enhance our understanding of how people think about unknowns and what they do with them. Hacking's (1975) study of the emergent modern meaning of the word "probability" is a pioneering example. Mills's chapter presents another instance, when he delineates the differences between older and newer forms of "white ignorance."

A fourth orienting strategy is counter-balancing the prevalent view of ignorance as negative and unwanted with a viewpoint recognizing that ignorance can be useful, fungible, or even liberating. This identifies a perennial blind-spot in Western culture (Smithson 2008a, b; McGoey 2012). We can begin removing this blind-spot by recognizing that unknowns play major productive and constitutive roles in human cognition, social interaction, culture, and politics. These roles are no less central than those played by knowledge, and are not simply opposites of the roles played by knowledge. People have vested interests in unknowns, and reasons for not knowing, not wanting to know, and/or not wanting others to know. People have uses for unknowns, and they trade them for other things. Knowledge may be power, but so is ignorance. Relevant chapters in this connection include those by Elliott, by Haas and Vogt, by Rappert and Balmer, by Stocking and Holstein, by Dedieu, Jouzel, Prete, by Thiel, and by Wehling.

A fifth orienting strategy focuses on the question of when and how ignorance gets unmade. Answers to this question typically hinge on the provenance of ignorance. We shall see that the crucial distinctions here are between conscious and unconscious forms of ignorance (e.g., as contrasted between chapters by Mills and Gilson, and chapters by Gaudet and by Haas and Vogt), and emic versus etic viewpoints regarding the provenance of ignorance. Of course, unmaking ignorance also requires capabilities, motivations, and interests sufficient for its undoing. Some of the chapters pose questions about what varieties of ignorance are "worthwhile" to undo, but also which should be maintained or instated. We will see that some perspectives have a space wherein they can transform ignorance into a sometime virtue.

Let us now turn to my overview of this Handbook. There probably is no "best" way to assemble an overview, but all of the chapters make substantial contributions to at least one of four fundamental issues: the varieties of ignorance, its construction, its uses, and its unmaking. The following survey therefore consists of sections on each of these. Afterward, we shall briefly examine the many paths that ignorance studies may travel in the future.

Varieties of ignorance

As studies of ignorance have accumulated, so have realizations that ignorance is multifarious. The past three decades have seen several typologies of ignorance (e.g., Smithson 1989; Faber and Proops 1998; Gross 2007), and the chapters in this Handbook also present numerous distinctions and typologies. The salient distinctions strongly depend on the starting point adopted by the taxonomist. For instance, Smithson's taxonomy turns on a grammatical distinction by separating the passive-voice "error" (being ignorant of something) from the active-voice "irrelevance" (ignoring something), and proceeds to further sub-classifications within each of those voices. Gross's typology, on the other hand, utilizes meta-cognitive distinctions. "Nescience" (an unawareness of unknowns) is a kind of precursor to conscious ignorance, which in turn is divided into reducible and irreducible unknowns. Thus, "nonknowledge" is ignorance that is sufficiently specified that, at least in principle, we could eradicate it or overcome it. "Negative knowledge," on the other hand, is Karin Knorr Cetina's (1999) term for knowledge about what we cannot know or do not want to know. Janich and Simmerling add a temporal dimension to our understanding of how ignorance is referred to in natural languages.

There are many alternative criteria on which such typologies may be founded. The chapter by Smithson and Pushkarskaya lists six "evidentiary" criteria: neurobiological, consequentialist, doxastic, correlational, functional, and cultural. Böschen et al. (2010) propose three "dimensions": awareness of unknowns, intentionality in the construction of unknowns, and temporal stability of unknowns. Elliott's chapter introduces "selective ignorance," when people produce or disseminate specific sorts of information about a topic or phenomenon while failing to produce or disseminate other information about it. Marder and Somin both bring in "rational ignorance," whereby a person elects to remain ignorant of something because they deem it not worth the time and effort to gain knowledge about it. And Mills and Gilson elaborate varieties of what Tuana (2006) terms "wilful ignorance," a type of meta-ignorance combined with an unwillingness to address it. Which criteria are helpful will depend in good part on the questions about ignorance that are under investigation and the epistemological positions adopted by the investigators.

Perhaps the most important insight into such criteria is that many of them are "silent" about the others. As Smithson and Pushkarskaya point out, it seems unlikely that findings regarding, say, consequentialist criteria for distinguishing among types of ignorance would imply anything about what distinctions the brain makes among varieties of ignorance. Even criteria that appear to be related to one another provide no hard-and-fast restrictions. The absence in a culture of a word equivalent to our modern meaning of "probability" does not imply that members of that culture do not understand games of chance. The commonplace moral distinction people draw between lies (a type of distortion) and omissions (a type of absence) in polite conversation may or may not involve Böschen et al.'s intentionality in their construction and deployment. The prospect that one theoretical or discipline-based view of ignorance may not have much to say about another need not be discouraging, but it does impel ignorance scholars to take due care in describing the basis of their particular view and avoiding hubristic claims to either holism or reductionism.

When we discuss terms representing ignorance, we are in the realm of language. In their chapter, Janich and Simmerling bring linguistics to the study of ignorance. That discipline has much to contribute, but to date has been largely silent on this topic. They point out that studying ignorance via linguistics requires multiple methods, and outline an ambitious research program accordingly. They observe that terms for varieties of ignorance are highly context-dependent and vary in meaning and nuance across cultures. They also introduce temporal aspects in references to unknowns, highlighting the ways in which particular terms invoke the future and/or past.

Work by scholars such as Mills and Hacking also underscores the importance of tracing the evolution of terms for unknowns and the meanings of those terms. The compilation of numerous corpuses of text data in recent times offers new and exciting possibilities for research on this topic. What follows next is a brief illustration of these possibilities.

Google's Ngram comprises a database of millions of books and/or excerpts from books. As Figure 40.1 illustrates, entering the terms for not knowing such as "ignorance," "ignorant," "uncertain," "unknown," and "falsehood" into the Ngram corpus of English-language books yields an interesting and consistent trend, namely a decline in the relative frequency of these terms from the 19th to the end of the 20th centuries, with a recent upturn in their occurrence (the ordinate in the graph is the logit transformation of the relative frequency, i.e., $\log(p/(1\text{-}p))$, where p is the proportion of the corpus in which a term is mentioned in a given year. Technical details are in Smithson 2015).

The trends in relative frequency over time are driven by the decline in certain kinds of religious discourse and, later on, the rise of specific kinds of secular philosophical and scientific discourses. For example, the correlation between the relative frequencies of the terms "ignorance" and "God" over this period is .90, and even when first-order autocorrelation is removed from both series (i.e., de-trending the series), the correlation remains moderately positive at .31. Briefly, most of the earlier occurrences are (largely Christian) religious discourses chiefly concerning the culpability of sinners who are ignorant of their sins, of those who are involuntarily ignorant of specific Christian doctrines, and of God's judgment on those who have never been exposed to the teachings of the Bible. The more recent secular discourses turn to epistemological questions regarding the nature of ignorance and whether there are unresolvable unknowns, but they also carry debates about the morality of (in)voluntary ignorance into the secular realm (see Smithson 2015 for further elaboration of these findings). Over nearly two centuries, this

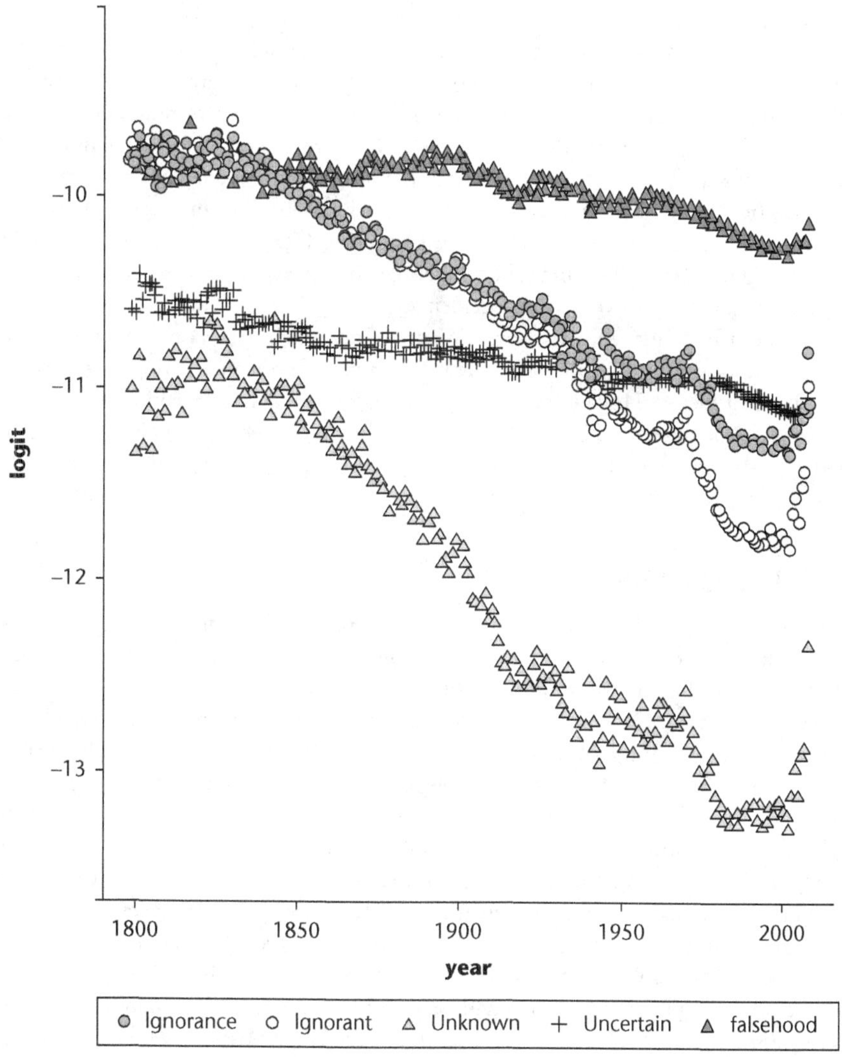

Figure 40.1 Trends in Google Ngram results for terms of not knowing in literature (1800–2000)

corpus of books reflects both the relativization and secularization of ignorance as a concept and, implicitly, the gradual disappearance of an all-knowing deity and eventual realization of one of the most profound implications of the Enlightenment: That there may be matters unknown to and unknowable by any being in the universe, i.e., universal irreducible ignorance.

Finally, a considerable wealth of information on the evolution of representations of ignorance may be found by studying how the treatment of unknowns has developed in specific disciplines or professional domains, including those disciplines utilizing formal logical or mathematical representations of unknowns. Svetlova's chapter on formalisms for representing unknowns in economics is an excellent case in point. Hers is a counter-argument to Ravetz's claim that economists have been in denial about ignorance (also see Quiggin 2008).

Svetlova takes as her main concern "non-knowledge of possible consequence-relevant uncertain events which a decision-maker would have to take into account." This is state space ignorance, where we do not know what all of the possible outcomes are (see also its treatment in Smithson and Pushkarskaya's chapter). She traces the emergence in economics of the realization that restricting the representation of unknowns to first-order probability distributions will not suffice to handle state space ignorance or Knightian uncertainty. After reviewing mathematical frameworks for dealing with indeterminate (Knightian) probability measures, she then covers proposals for doing the same with state space ignorance. Her account could be extended still further by including generalized probability theories that do allow for state space ignorance and enable incorporating new events from evidence (Walley 1996; Coolen and Augustin 2009). Links also could be made with the experimental psychological literature demonstrating that humans underestimate the likelihood of heretofore unseen events occurring (e.g., Fischhoff et al. 1978) and that they can be misled by being primed to an incorrect partition of the state space (e.g., Fox and Rottenstreich 2003). This is one of the cutting edges of behavioral economics, that part of economics where, at last, the model of the omniscient and rational decision-maker is losing its grip.

Constructing ignorance

There are numerous motivational and functional accounts of how and why ignorance is constructed. Many of these refer to the intentional generation, imposition, and maintenance of ignorance, for oneself and others. Some of the chapters in this Handbook focus on this kind of ignorance construction. However, there also are unintended, inadvertent ways in which ignorance gets constructed. Some of these operate simply through the exercise of individual preferences, and others are by-products of social and political processes.

To begin, some social norms involve generating or maintaining nonknowledge. A benign example of a social norm for temporarily withholding information is creating pleasant surprises. Receiving birthday gifts, watching movies, and reading novels are activities that can be ruined if their hidden contents are revealed prematurely. Thus, there is a tacit agreement between the knower and the ignoramus. Moral injunctions and norms regarding selective ignorance abound in childrearing. Responsible parents routinely deal with the question of what their children should and should not know. Norms and practices in politeness also encompass injunctions and conventions about what cannot or must not be said (the classic work here is Brown and Levinson 1987, but also see Franke's chapter on "negative theology"). Such practices include indirect or deliberately ambiguous references to the unsayable as well as its outright omission.

Likewise, there are contexts where lying is normatively appropriate and expected. The most obvious cases of virtuous lying are in competitive games, warfare, and other strongly competitive settings. Bluffing in poker, body-faking in ball-games, and spreading disinformation among the enemy in a war are all cases where lying is viewed as legitimate. Robinson (1996) observes that the more competitive the situation and the higher the stakes, the more likely that deception will be expected or even required.

And then, of course, there are many examples of deliberate efforts to create and harness ignorance for political and/or economic ends, whether through propaganda, suppression, neglect, or secrecy. As Chua points out, a potential consequence of such efforts are secondary reconstructions of ignorance by the targets of these efforts. Chua's example is the aftermath of socialist rule in Mongolia which involved the destruction and suppression of Buddhist traditions, giving rise to a sense of loss within the populace that "is today played out in discourses of ignorance, absence and uncertainty."

Several chapters bring up ignorance constructions that exemplify what could be called the social control of curiosity. A key driver is that first-hand reality testing and knowledge seeking may be perceived as dangerous or as violating sacrosanct values. Elliot's chapter on "selective ignorance" is prototypical in this regard. Taking a cue from Proctor (2008), he traces the varieties of decisions to study a topic in some ways but not others, or to attend to some pieces of information while ignoring others. The motivations behind these decisions range from obvious economic and political interests to more subtle implicit biases and conventions that can mould scientific inquiry. There is a natural link between the social control of curiosity and debates over "dual use dilemmas" (Rappert and Selgelid 2013), where fears about proposed experiments or technological developments concern the potential misuse of potentially beneficial research or technology. Present-day examples include biotechnology and nanotechnology, such as the genetic sequencing of the 1918 influenza A (H1N1) virus (a.k.a. the "Spanish flu") and also its resurrection using reverse genetic techniques.

Another theme in the literature on selective ignorance concerns the ways in which stereotypes and prejudice can generate ignorance. Kourany's chapter begins with the notion that science produces ignorance while also producing knowledge, but hers is a different take on this from writers such as Firestein. She is squarely in the agnotology camp, pointing out how decisions to pursue one particular line of research may close off or preclude pursuing others (echoing the "undone science" themes presented by Rayner and Hess). Her chief example is the ways in which science has focused on men and ignored women, and the deleterious consequences for women.

On the other hand, ignorance (or at least, doubt) also can be an unintended by-product of debate or balanced coverage of an issue. Journalists have been taken to task recently for giving "equal" time to global warming disbelievers, on grounds that the scientific consensus is so strong that lending credibility to disbelievers does the public a disservice. Stocking and Holstein's findings suggest that the equal-coverage rule also may function as a let-out for journalists who are ignorant about the science concerned. In a study of American media, Boykoff and Boykoff (2004) found that more than half of all stories on global warming from 1988 through 2002 gave equal time to climate denialists, with another 35 percent giving time to them while recognizing the consensus view. These journalists' uncertainties were then transmitted, wittingly or not, to their audiences.

One of the greatest engines of inadvertent ignorance production is specialization and the division of labor. Specialization can be viewed as an ignorance arrangement. Obviously, specialization relieves specialists and the lay public of trying to absorb amounts of information that are beyond their capabilities and time. But there is a second, often overlooked function that makes specialization attractive. In a network of cooperative specialists, specialization spreads the risk of being ignorant about the wrong thing at the wrong time, by diversifying ignorance (Smithson 2008b). As the American comedian Will Rogers observed, everyone is ignorant, but on different topics. In a large population of specialists who are networked and trust one another, it is very likely that for any exigency someone will know how to deal with it. In this connection, Stewart's chapter seeks to challenge the heuristic of ignorance as solely negative in management contexts, proposing instead that organizations must accept ignorance as an inherent driver of both necessary and problematic behavior if the latter's effects are to be avoided.

There are also the ways in which our own preferences and social inclinations inadvertently combine with those of the others around us to generate shared, implicit, collective ignorance and meta-ignorance. This type of implicit ignorance construction proceeds in two steps. First, our preferences generate habits that constrain our experiences and therefore the span of our knowledge. Second, we tend to associate with other people whose preferences, habits, and experiences are similar to our own, so our friends, workmates, and family are unlikely to fundamentally transform our knowledge-base. And so we, along with our associates and families, become locked into a self-reinforcing cell of shared ignorance.

Greater freedom of choice really helps us to be even more ensnared by our love of the familiar, and sophisticated marketing and advertising are strengthening this trap. Thanks to the Internet, we can find and join groups who share our most arcane interests. A fan of, say, 1950s electronic music can find far-distant fellow fans on the Internet. We now are able to identify and connect with people who are as similar to ourselves as we please. Likewise, following the personalized recommendations provided by Amazon, Pandora radio, eHarmony, and so on, helps one become even more firmly entrenched in one's habits.

Using ignorance

Some of the most productive research on ignorance has focused on the uses people have for it and its consequences. Most, although not all, of the work on this topic attends to strategic uses of ignorance in the service of short-term interests, but there are also quasi-functionalist accounts of how ignorance arrangements are woven into social practices and even institutions. In some contexts, certain kinds of ignorance are even viewed as virtuous. The principal breakthrough in this line of work has been the growing realization that ignorance is not always something that people want to eliminate, because it is useful to them.

Proctor (1995) documented the influences of professional, economic, and political interest groups on American governmental priorities and funding of cancer research. One of his primary findings was that the American government collaborated with private enterprise in generating doubt about the environmental and industrial causes of cancer. Michaels' 2008 book on the manufacture of doubt followed Proctor's lead. He identified three primary messages orchestrated by the tobacco industry to challenge the scientific consensus linking smoking with lung cancer. More recently, Oreskes and Conway's 2010 book on similar themes appeared, updated to include accounts of how doubts concerning climate change and global warming were manufactured in particular by organizations employing tactics inspired by the tobacco industry's example.

McGoey (2012) highlights four strategic uses of ignorance in the controversy over the licensing of Ketek, an antibiotic drug that was found to be toxic to the liver. First, the manufacturer, Sanofi-Aventis, employed risk-detection systems that actually obscured warning signs. Second, they, along with American Food and Drug Administration regulators, selectively withheld information from the FDA independent advisory committee. Third, they directed regulatory staff to remain silent about concerns over drug safety. Fourth, they ignored the implications of known limitations of methods for detecting drug risks. To her list we can add one more: One of the Sanofi researchers involved in the Ketek trials was indicted for fraudulent research practices.

In their 1949 paper, Moore and Tumin described five functions of ignorance: preserving privilege; reinforcing traditional values; preserving fairness in competition; maintaining stereotypes; and motivating effort in the face of unknown outcomes. Moore and Tumin's analysis may seem as though ignorance mainly serves conservative values and causes. However, ignorance has its functions regardless of one's political orientation.

For instance, uncertainty can serve both sides of a political and scientific controversy simultaneously. Smithson (1980) presents an account of how both environmentalists and industrialists used initial uncertainties about the effects of chlorofluorocarbons on the ozone layer to bolster their agendas. Each side had seized on one of the two most common responses to profound uncertainty. The environmentalists' position was a precursor of the precautionary principle: Ban chlorofluorocarbons until it can be proven that they are not harmful. The industrialists' argument reflected a well-known status-quo bias: Allow chlorofluorocarbon production and marketing to continue until they are proven harmful. Each camp had clear uses for ignorance in aiding their cause.

Rayner's chapter on geoengineering points to a similar bifurcation in the uses of scientific ignorance. One group of engineering experts favors research into the prospect of using stratospheric aerosols to mitigate the effects of global warming. Another group of experts opposes this research. Both sides agree that we currently lack the knowledge necessary to deploy stratospheric aerosols effectively or safely. Research advocates claim that improved computer modeling along with small-scale experiments can be cautiously scaled up in such a way as to avoid any irreversible negative effects and eventually produce the knowledge needed. Opponents argue that the extensive complexity and uncertainties in climate and ecosystems responses preclude adequate modeling of stratospheric aerosol deployment, and that experimentation is bound to result in catastrophe. So, the main issue in dispute is whether ignorance about these matters is reducible or not, in other words whether this is a case of resolvable ignorance or negative knowledge.

The geoengineering example also demonstrates the utility of being able to dictate what can and cannot be known. Expert status often depends as much on maintaining a monopoly over what is difficult or impossible to know as it does on a monopoly over specialist knowledge. So, specific kinds of ignorance have different functions and uses. In this case, reducible ignorance serves the interests of the pro-research experts whereas irreducible ignorance serves the interests of the anti-research experts.

Ignorance underpins some forms of "social capital" (Smithson 2008b). Privacy amounts to a multilateral ignorance arrangement, whereby we agree that certain kinds of information about ourselves will not be available to others without our consent. As Roberts observes in her chapter on organizational ignorance, privacy is enshrined in law in many countries and in the regulatory regimes of organizations. Wehling's chapter investigates a special kind of privacy, the right not to know one's own genetic make-up (and therefore for no-one else to know it either). Although this right is legally recognized in some countries, it also is widely contested, especially in connection with risks of inherited diseases or disorders.

Respecting others' privacy is virtuous behavior, thus, virtuous ignorance. People who violate privacy norms pose a threat to the person(s) about whom they have obtained private information. A right to privacy amounts to a right to at least some control over who knows what about you. In fact, privacy is a close cousin to censorship, especially when censorship is agreed to by those in power and the public on whom it is imposed.

Social relations based on trust and friendship operate in a similar manner. Trust relationships require observance of an interesting kind of privacy. If one person is monitoring another or insisting that they fully account for their actions, the person under surveillance will conclude that the monitor does not trust them. In his chapter, Ogien's treatment of trust points to this requirement of ignorance for trust to work (as does Smithson 2008b), when he proposes trust as a possible antidote to laypeople's doubts about science. Trust, therefore, is both an example of a social relation that requires tolerance of undesired uncertainty (the risk of being exploited) in favor of desired uncertainty (freedom to seize opportunities for new relations) and, of course, virtuous behavior.

And so, we have arrived at examples of virtuous ignorance that are socially mandated and underpin some important forms of social capital: privacy, trust, and friendship. We can add politeness and civility to this list. Moreover, an organizational culture favouring creativity, initiative, and entrepreneurship requires the toleration of at least some ignorance, as implied in Stewart's chapter. Roberts also remarks that organizations may stimulate creativity and the identification of new possibilities by hiring an ignoramus.

A proposal for an interesting type of virtuous ignorance may be found in Kourany's chapter. She chooses sides in the debate about whether research on male–female cognitive differences should cease: "In short, Rose, Marks, and other scientists are advocating ignorance regarding cognitive differences between men and women, and they are doing this in order to help bring about a more adequate picture of women." This is an example of undone science as virtuous ignorance, and her closing remarks make this claim. There are links to be forged between discourses about virtuous ignorance of this kind and the discourses around dual use dilemmas.

Unmaking ignorance

How does ignorance get destroyed or unmade? Accounts of this process differ according to whose viewpoint provides the account and whether ignorance is believed to be available to conscious inspection. We may employ the long-standing emic–etic distinction from cultural anthropology (see, e.g., Kottak 2006, p. 47) to distinguish the attributor's (etic) viewpoint from the ignoramus' (emic) viewpoint. In the etic viewpoint, conscious ignorance is unmade by the attributor (or a third party) unmasking the truth so that the ignoramus is able to comprehend it and correct her or his understanding. Unconscious ignorance, on the other hand, requires more than unmasking; heretofore unconscious issues must be brought to conscious awareness. In the emic viewpoint, the ignoramus remedies conscious ignorance by deliberate inquiry or learning that converts non-knowledge into knowledge. Rectification of unconscious ignorance cannot be undertaken deliberately, but may be achieved by serendipitous revelations. Table 40.1 displays the resulting typology of unmaking ignorance.

Some chapters in the Handbook discuss the question of when an emic or etic viewpoint is appropriate or productive. For instance, Chua raises the question of how anthropologists are to deal with actions in which the actors do not have an interpretation or explanation to offer. Likewise, Michael's chapter turns the study of ignorance on the social sciences, pointing to "behaviors that participants engage in that are not necessarily so easily grasped by the researcher—they are, in one way or another, systemically ignored—Othered—in the processes of conducting research and producing analysis."

There are four well-established varieties of etic accounts. The "manufacture of doubt" camp includes theories and studies of how ignorance is imposed on the public by powerful actors such as governments and corporations. Exemplars are Proctor's (1995) careful documentation of tobacco corporations' and lobbyists' systematic attempts to raise doubts about the causal link between smoking and lung cancer, and more recent writings on interest-group campaigns to discredit climate scientists' predictions and accounts of global climate change (e.g., Michaels 2008 and Oreskes and Conway 2010). Chapters in this volume with direct connections to the manufacture-of-doubt literature include those by Elliott, by Rappert and Balmer, and by Stocking and Holstein. Ogien addresses the questions of whether doubt about science produces ignorance, and whether dispelling such doubts requires scientific expertise. He distinguishes the

Table 40.1 Typology of ignorance unmade

		Ignoramus Awareness	
		Conscious	*Unconscious*
Attributor	Etic	Unmasking	Consciousness-Raising
Perspective	Emic	Knowledge-Gaining	Serendipitous Revelation

"practice" of doubt from a "strategy" of doubt, that latter of which is taken to represent "doubt-mongering" as in climate change deniers.

A second etic account is exemplified by Ungar's (2008) article on ignorance as a "public problem." He asks why, in the age of "knowledge" or "information," ignorance not only persists but seems to have increased and intensified. He is neither the only commentator, nor the first, to have observed this trend. Clearly, along with an information explosion, we also have had an ignorance explosion, perhaps its most obvious manifestation being the vast multiplication of publicized risks. As Ungar points out, one of the symptoms of ignorance as a public problem is that despite the common-sense notion that there is a common stock of knowledge that all healthy, normally-functioning members of society should know, in reality it is extremely difficult to produce a stable consensus on what this common stock should include. Marder's chapter identifies this problem, and Firestein's contribution also does so but from a different angle. Firestein begins with the observation that science raises more questions than it answers, and that public ignorance of this propensity generates misunderstanding and distrust of science and scientists.

The third etic camp covers ignorance attributed primarily to human "heuristics and biases," mental shortcuts and dispositions that depart from a "rational agent" benchmark. The burgeoning literature in this camp derives mainly from the psychology of judgment and decision-making under uncertainty (e.g., Kahneman, Slovic, and Tversky 1982) and behavioral economics (e.g., Ariely 2008). Examples include the fundamental attribution error, confirmation bias, and hindsight bias. Handbook chapters drawing on this literature include those by Smithson and Pushskarskaya, and by Roy and Zeckhauser. Friedman's chapter on Popper and fallibilism also lands in this camp. She asks whether Popper was overly optimistic in asserting that science progressively undoes ignorance, despite its fallibility. She also questions whether fallibilism itself, a middle course between dogmatism and scepticism, can deliver any more conclusive guides toward truth.

The fourth etic account is exemplified through the chapters in this Handbook by Mills and by Gilson. This is the kind of ignorance that Tuana (2006) names "wilful" ignorance, despite being a largely unconscious product of socialization and social position. The most widely discussed versions of this kind are Mills's "white ignorance" and various feminist theorists' versions of what could be called "male ignorance." To permit some generalizability, we could think of this as "social-stereotype" ignorance.

These four etic accounts of ignorance raise different issues regarding how to undo ignorance. The manufacture-of-doubt and public problem camps are the most straightforward of the four, because ignorance seems eradicable simply by education, or removing the blinders or distortive lenses imposed by powerful agents. The onus is on the educators and blinder-removers to persuade the blind that in so doing they are granting them true vision (e.g., that smoking really causes lung cancer, or that global warming is real and anthropogenic).

However, at least two traps await the unreflective educator or blinder-remover. The first is the problem raised by Ungar, of agreeing on what the public truly needs to know. Does everyone need to be numerate, or even literate? The second is a common dilemma confronting educators, arising from the fact that most citizens lack the free time and motivation to learn about things that authorities think they should know. Smithson (2008a) refers to it as the "persuasion-versus-information-glut dilemma." Communicators with an educational or persuasive interest will want to impose their messages on the public. However, while information is a multiplier resource, attention is zero-sum. A surfeit of messages in an unregulated forum can drive the public to tune out altogether. The scarce resource being threatened with depletion is not information or knowledge, but attention.

The cognitive-illusion and social-stereotype kinds of ignorance present even greater difficulties for would-be removalists. Both kinds are said to arise from subconscious processes. If so, then conscious reflection on one's mental processes is not likely to be capable of rooting them out. Attempts at "consciousness raising" or "debiasing" may backfire, in fact. As McNerney (2013) observes, readers of articles or books on biases and heuristics may erroneously convince themselves that they no longer suffer from biases, simply because they are now aware that these exist. However, biases are largely unconscious, so when they introspect on their own thinking they miss the processes that produce the errors, thereby self-confirming that their thought processes are free of bias.

The social-stereotype kind of ignorance presents a third barrier to unmaking: motivation. The broad claim is twofold. First, people in privileged positions are motivated to view their position as legitimate or even inevitable (e.g., believing that Caucasians are a "master race" or that men are innately superior to women). Second, the same people are not motivated to critically inquire into or test the veracity of such views. It is very difficult to unmake ignorance that is neither accessible to conscious inspection nor desired to undo.

Turning now to emic accounts, the Handbook includes examples of three kinds. The "knowledge plus serendipity" account is represented in the chapter by Gaudet, who elaborates the ways in which scientific experimentation produces ignorance valued by scientists (as in Firestein's chapter, and Roberts and Armitage 2008). Likewise, the chapter by Haas and Vogt advances the thesis that ignorance plus inquiry can improve ignorance, even when it does not yield further knowledge.

The chapter by Kuhlicke links ignorance to vulnerability as well as surprise (or serendipity). This link hinges on the concept of vulnerability as openness to possibilities, whether potentially harmful or beneficial. In his framework, wilful ignorance may underpin a type of denial that renders individuals or groups vulnerable to surprises.

A second emic account involves "rational ignorance," as elaborated in the chapters by Somin and by Marder. While neither of them provides an explicit account of how rational ignorance is unmade, its basis in judgments by the ignoramus about what to ignore because it is irrelevant implies that if the ignoramus revises her or his view about irrelevance then the newly relevant matters no longer may be ignored. Marder and Somin both draw attention to the issue of voter ignorance in democratic countries, whereby voters neglect political issues on grounds of personal irrelevance or unimportance. Marder observes that there is a contradiction between the democratic ideal (everyone participates and is treated equally) and the widely held idea that democracy can succeed only if the populace is sufficiently knowledgeable.

The third kind of emic account hinges on "undoing censorship or taboo." Relevant Handbook chapters include those by Rappert and Balmer, by Hess, by Kempner, by Rayner, and by Franke. Rappert and Balmer argue that, in the context of military secrecy and intelligence, concealment and openness exist in a dynamic and co-constitutive relationship. Each act of "openness" provides the conditions for new attempts at concealment and vice-versa. Rayner's and Hess's chapters deal in "undone science," such as the debates about geoengineering, where the very idea of conducting research is controversial. Although they do not mention it, this territory includes dual-use dilemmas (Rappert and Selgelid 2013). Hess makes the point that sometimes politicization of science can open the way for undone science to become done after all.

The "censorship-taboo" account includes aspects of self-regulation. Kempner takes us into the realm of self-censorship, whereby scientists avoid taking on a research topic that is taboo or politically fraught. Franke explicates the concept of "negative theology," wherein it is deemed permissible to say what God is not, but not to make claims about what God is. A part of Chua's chapter focuses on the self-cultivation of ignorance as a way of breaking with the past (by refusing to know about it).

Kessler's chapter deals with the "unsayable" in the discipline and practice of economics. He argues that the heavy reliance of orthodox economics on formal reasoning and mathematics forces economists into ignoring fundamental meta-theoretical considerations. He revisits the Keynesian and Knightian distinction between risk and uncertainty, arguing that uncertainty has largely been excluded from economics, and the global financial crisis of 2008 was unforeseen by economists for that reason.

Finally, can we overcome ignorance of ignorance or, in my coinage (Smithson 1989), "meta-ignorance"? Ravetz is among the early contributors to a literature on this topic (Ravetz 1993). His chapter begins by tracing the development of the Enlightenment view of positive knowledge that abhorred ignorance and dismissed the Socratic ideal of attaining complete awareness of one's ignorance. There is no room for inconclusiveness in the Cartesian version of science. Ravetz expresses hope for a return to the Socratic ideal, stopping short of proposing ways by which this return could be effected but hinting that it somehow might emerge from the democratization of knowledge via the Internet and its new forms of collaboration.

But perhaps the key lies in a more traditional realm. Two chapters focus on literature as a means to undoing meta-ignorance. Bennett summarizes three traditional viewpoints regarding the question of whether poetry has anything to convey about knowledge and/or ignorance: The ancient view that poets are ignorant and poetry is in some senses a source of ignorance, a more modern view that poetry is concerned neither with knowledge nor with ignorance, and finally a perspective claiming that poetry actually does convey knowledge of a defensible kind. Bennett introduces a fourth viewpoint, "that literature embraces, explores, celebrates the condition by which we are all beset, that it confronts us with the human condition of not knowing." He points out that even the narrator of a story can (and does) reveal that they don't know what they're narrating. For him, therefore, literature performs a Socratic function in making us aware that we do not know what we think we know.

Roy and Zeckhauser turn to literature to provide two training grounds on ignorance: anticipation and contemplation. They combine insights from literary concepts with those from the literature on cognitive biases to craft strategies and prescriptions for understanding and dealing with ignorance. Here, they share with Bennett a crucial insight, namely the power of fiction to undo meta-ignorance by presenting digestible possibilities that may be indigestible as actualities.

The next ignorance explosion

This Handbook announces the arrival of ignorance as a topic for serious study in a wide variety of disciplines. Many of its chapters chart paths for deep and productive journeys into the terrain of ignorance. I will conclude this review by highlighting just three areas where there already are ample resources for near-term developments and transformations. This is not meant to be an exhaustive list, but merely what I hope is a tempting glimpse into a very broad terra incognita.

As Janich and Simmerling aptly declare, "speaking (and writing) about uncertainty and ignorance . . . is a linguistic issue through and through." Linguistic research and theory are sorely needed here, including everything in this from computational linguistics to discourse analysis. Both recent advances in theory and methods in linguistics and the capacity to access "big data" via the Internet render the linguistic study of ignorance completely ready for undertaking.

Several chapters feature accounts of the ways in which particular disciplines or professions deal with ignorance, e.g., anthropology (Chua), economics (Svetlova), geoengineering (Rayner), music (Zimmerman), and theology (Franke). I mentioned earlier that systematic studies of the treatment of unknowns in specific disciplines or professional domains will be of value. The anthology by Bammer and Smithson (2008) is a preliminary attempt at this enterprise and while much remains to be done, the tools are at hand to do so. An early benchmark for this kind of work is Kline's (1980) definitive account of the loss of certainty in mathematics early in the twentieth century.

The only chapter not mentioned thus far in my review is Kerwin's fictitious piece. While hers is not an academic essay, it raises many of the issues dealt with more formally in other chapters, all in one place. The affordances of a story give her the freedom to juxtapose and pit various views of ignorance against one another; for example, ignorance as a resource and a liability, or ignorance as an ally and an enemy. Kerwin's chapter also brings us face to face with a neglected topic worthy of research: The emotions linked with the experience of ignorance. Kerwin observes that ignorance can be a source of fear and despair, and yet also of hope. At first glance, one might concur with Gudykunst and Nishida's (2001) proposition that anxiety is the emotional equivalent of uncertainty. Kerwin's thought-experiment debunks it. Several positive psychological states with affective elements, such as hope, aspiration, curiosity, suspense, and thrill, actually require ignorance for their existence. Little is known about this relationship between ignorance and emotion, despite the recent surge of interest, since Damasio's (1994) pioneering work, in the role of emotions in risk perception and decision-making. There is scope here for contributions across the humanities and human sciences.

Much has changed since I began writing about ignorance in near-isolation during the 1980s, and certainly since Moore and Tumin's 1949 paper. Ignorance has been largely rehabilitated as a respectable topic for scholarship and research. The literature on ignorance has dramatically increased in many areas including anthropology, behavioral economics, communications, health and medicine, literature and cultural studies, management science, philosophy, political science, psychology, and sociology. Many of the Handbook chapters will stimulate the acceleration of this increase. This could be the next ignorance explosion: a vast expansion of theoretical developments, empirical work, new methods, and applications in ignorance studies.

References

Ariely, D. (2008) *Predictably Irrational*, New York, NY: HarperCollins.

Bammer, G. and Smithson, M. (Eds.) (2008) *Uncertainty and Risk: Multidisciplinary Perspectives*, London: Earthscan.

Böschen, S., Kastenhofer, K., Rust, I., Soentgen, J., and Wehling, P. (2010) "Scientific nonknowledge and its political dynamics: The cases of agri-biotechnology and mobile phoning," *Science, Technology, and Human Values*, 35: 783–811.

Boykoff, M. T. and Boykoff, J. M. (2004), "Balance as bias: Global warming and the U.S. prestige press," *Global Environmental Change*, 14: 125–136.

Brown, P. and Levinson, S. C. (1987) *Universals in Language Usage: Politeness Phenomena*, Cambridge, UK: Cambridge University Press.

Coolen, F. P. and Augustin, T. (2009) "A nonparametric predictive alternative to the imprecise Dirichlet model: The case of a known number of categories," *International Journal of Approximate Reasoning*, 50: 217–230.

Damasio, A. R. (1994) *Descartes' Error: Emotion, Reason and the Human Brain*, New York, NY: Putnam.

Faber, M. and Proops, J. L. R. (1998) *Evolution, Time, Production and the Environment*, Berlin: Springer.

Fischhoff, B., Slovic, P., Lichtenstein, S., Read, S., and Combs, B. (1978) "How safe is safe enough? A psychometric study of attitudes towards technological risks and benefits," *Policy Sciences*, 9(2): 127–152.

Fox, C. R. and Rottenstreich, Y. (2003) "Partition priming in judgement under uncertainty," *Psychological Science*, 14(3): 195–200.

Gross, M. (2007) "The unknown in process: Dynamic connections of ignorance, non-knowledge and related concepts," *Current Sociology*, 55: 742–759.

Gross, M. (2010) *Ignorance and Surprise: Science, Society, and Ecological Design*, Cambridge, MA: MIT Press.
Gudykunst, W. B. and Nishida, T. (2001) "Anxiety, uncertainty, and perceived effectiveness of communication across relationships and cultures," *International Journal of Intercultural Relations*, 25: 55–71.
Hacking, I. (1975) *The Emergence of Probability: A Philosophical Study of Early Ideas about Probability, Induction and Statistical Inference*, Cambridge, UK: Cambridge University Press.
Kahneman, D., Slovic, P., and Tversky, A. (Eds.) (1982) *Judgment under Uncertainty: Heuristics and Biases*, New York: Cambridge University Press.
Kline, M. (1980) *Mathematics: The Loss of Certainty*, Oxford: Oxford University Press.
Knorr Cetina, K. (1999) *Epistemic Cultures: How the Sciences Make Knowledge*, Cambridge, MA: Harvard University Press.
Kottak, C. (2006) *Mirror for Humanity*, New York, NY: McGraw-Hill.
McGoey, L. (2007) "On the will to ignorance in bureaucracy," *Economy and Society*, 36: 212–235.
McGoey, L. (2012) "Strategic unknowns: Towards a sociology of ignorance," *Economy and Society*, 41: 1–16.
McNerney, S. (2013) "The bias within the bias," *Mind Guest Blog, Scientific American*, May 2013, http://blogs.scientificamerican.com/mind-guest-blog/2013/05/15/the-bias-within-the-bias/.
Michaels, D. (2008) *Doubt Is Their Product: How Industry's Assault on Science Threatens Your Health*, Oxford: Oxford University Press.
Moore, W. E. and Tumin, M. M. (1949) "Some social functions of ignorance," *American Sociological Review*, 14: 787–795.
Oreskes, N. and Conway, E. (2010) *Merchants of Doubt: How a Handful of Scientists Obscured the Truth on Issues from Tobacco Smoke to Global Warming*, New York, NY: Bloomsbury Press.
Proctor, R. N. (1995) *Cancer Wars: How Politics Shapes What We Know and Don't Know about Cancer*, New York, NY: Basic Books.
Proctor, R. N. (2008) "Agnotology: A missing term to describe the cultural production of ignorance (and its study)," in R. Proctor and L. Schiebinger (Eds.), *Agnotology: The Making and Unmaking of Ignorance*, Stanford, CA: Stanford University Press, 1–35.
Quiggin, J. (2008) "Economists and uncertainty," in G. Bammer and M. Smithson (Eds.) *Uncertainty and Risk: Multidisciplinary Perspectives*, London: Earthscan, 195–203.
Rappert, B. and Selgelid, M. (Eds.) (2013) *On the Dual Uses of Science and Ethics: Principles, Practices, and Prospects*, Canberra, Australia: ANU E-Press.
Ravetz, J. (1993) "The sin of science: Ignorance of ignorance," *Knowledge: Creation, Diffusion, Utilization*, 15: 157–165.
Roberts, J. and Armitage, J. (2008) "The ignorance economy," *Prometheus*, 26: 335–354.
Robinson, W. P. (1996) *Deceit, Delusion and Detection*, Thousand Oaks, CA: Sage.
Smithson, M. (1980) "Interests and the growth of uncertainty," *Journal for the Theory of Social Behavior*, 10: 157–168.
Smithson, M. (1989) *Ignorance and Uncertainty: Emerging Paradigms*, New York, NY: Springer-Verlag.
Smithson, M. (2008a) "The many faces and masks of uncertainty," in G. Bammer and M. Smithson (Eds.) *Uncertainty and Risk: Multidisciplinary Perspectives*, London: Earthscan, 13–26.
Smithson, M. (2008b) "Social theories of ignorance," in R. Proctor and L. Schiebinger (Eds.), *Agnotology: The Making and Unmaking of Ignorance*, Stanford, CA: Stanford University Press, 209–229.
Smithson, M. (2015) *The Deployment of Ignorance and Related Terms in English-Language Books: Ngram Analyses*. Unpublished manuscript, The National Australian University, Canberra, Australia.
Tuana, N. (2006) "The Speculum of Ignorance: The Women's health movement and epistemologies of ignorance," *Hypatia*, 21: 1–19.
Ungar, S. (2008) "Ignorance as an underidentified social problem," *British Journal of Sociology*, 59: 301–326.
Walley, P. (1996) "Inferences from multinomial data: Learning about a bag of marbles (with discussion)," *Journal of the Royal Statistical Society, Series B*, 558: 3–57.

Index